URBAN ECONOMICS
READINGS AND ANALYSIS

URBAN ECONOMICS
READINGS AND ANALYSIS

Edited by Ronald E. Grieson

Queens College and the Graduate Center, City University

LITTLE, BROWN AND COMPANY   BOSTON

PREFACE

The recent focus upon problems of our cities has stimulated a large and diverse body of literature to be produced in urban economics. The most important contributions to this literature are presented in this book, with an analytically unifying discussion of the main issues. This combination of readings and text makes the book sufficiently self-contained to be used as a single source for a range of courses in the academic curriculum. Supplemental readings are suggested, however, to offer greater flexibility in meeting a variety of student and teacher interests. The theoretical rigor of the text makes it suitable for more advanced courses, though its careful statement in verbal rather than mathematical form is designed for the students of the introductory course.

All areas of urban economics are broadly presented in this volume. The list of topics reveals the diversity of the field: marginal and benefit-cost analysis, with emphasis on externalities and the social rate of discount; the growth and stability of incomes earned in urban activities; the location, use, and value of land in metropolitan areas; transportation; housing, zoning, urban renewal, and new towns; pollution and congestion; poverty and discrimination; public finance, including revenue sharing and property taxes; the administration and political subdivision of urban areas. Poverty and discrimination, housing and transportation receive the most comprehensive treatment.

In addition to the full range of topical coverage, there is a fairly complete representation of economists' points of view for each topic. The readings are almost always presented in their entirety so that the reader can experience the unedited ideas of the authors.

The introductions to each chapter present an overall view of economics and policy alternatives for each area along with an explanation of the relevant economic mechanisms. The methodological appendix contains a particularly concentrated discussion of analytic tools. For the introductory course, light coverage of this appendix is recommended. For the advanced course having a microeconomics prerequisite, the appendix should be expanded into a thorough review of value theory and welfare economics. The treatment of this appendix should determine the economic sophistication of the course. My own experience has been that it is best taken up just before the section on transportation.

I have tried where possible to indicate the relation between economic mechanisms and two other critical dimensions of urban life: social and political circumstances, and humane and aesthetic improvement. These issues are for the most part beyond the scope both of this volume and of the commonly defined professional competence of economists. Since my belief about the relation between economic and noneconomic aspects of social systems has undoubtedly influenced my own contribution to this book, I would like to make it explicit. I believe there are no irreconcilable differences between people of different wealth, income, or race, and that the goals of both equity and efficiency can be met simultaneously, improving all of society.

Ralph Beals, Walter Carter, and Richard Caves deserve special thanks for their comments on the introductions.

CONTENTS

Chapter 4

TRANSPORTATION

Chapter 5

ZONING, HOUSING MARKETS, AND URBAN RENEWAL

Chapter 6

POLLUTION

Chapter 7

POVERTY

Chapter 8

DISCRIMINATION

Chapter 9

METROPOLITANISM

Chapter 10

URBAN PUBLIC FINANCE

Chapter 11

METHODOLOGICAL APPENDIX: MARGINAL ANALYSIS, BENEFIT-COST, AND THE SOCIAL RATE OF DISCOUNT

Chapter 1

THE ALLOCATION OF RESOURCES IN CENTRAL CITIES

The crisis faced by present-day cities can be attributed to three causes: the misallocation of physical and human resources within the central city; the need for income transfers to poor residents and to the institutions of these cities; and racial discrimination, which has had many of its major impacts in the central city.

Let us first look at the allocation of physical resources. What could cause the city's public facilities and capital to be misused (misallocated) and misdirected (improperly invested)? Inadequate criteria to determine proper use of existing social capital can bring about the over- or underuse of facilities. If a good that costs a positive amount in economic or social terms is given away free, it will be overused. Too many resources will be allocated to its production, and potential revenue to the city will be lost. Similarly, overpricing or overtaxing a good whose costs (social and economic) to the city are below the price or tax will bring about underinvestment in and underuse of the good. Prices that are too high and prices that are too low are both undesirable.

The problem of misallocation of resources within the central city includes investment and pricing decisions in transportation, zoning, land use, housing, and pollution. As Wilbur Thompson so dramatically points out, many of the central cities' problems result from underpricing valuable, scarce resources. Improper pricing distorts both investment decisions and the use of existing public facilities, which in turn create misallocations in the private sector. In the area of transportation, central cities have underpriced expensive road and parking facilities. Indeed, these facilities are usually given away free, inviting too much use and producing congestion. Road use would surely be reduced if commuters were made to pay the full costs, which are substantial. The commuter not only imposes upon the city the costs of building, maintaining, and policing roadways,

1

but also causes delays for other commuters and creates pollution, noise, dirt, and tension for other drivers, pedestrians, and residents of the city.

If the road user were compelled to pay the costs of the harmful side effects he inflicts upon others, he would be deterred from excessive use of underoccupied rush hour automobiles. This would improve the allocation of resources, increase the amenities of urban life, and redistribute income from wealthy suburban commuters to poorer city dwellers.

Overinvestment in roads and parking lots is closely related to inadequate charges for road use. Because roads are crowded, more seem to be needed. More are built. Tolls on overcrowded roads would reduce congestion, however, and divert some drivers to public transportation, others to car pools. Increased usage of mass transportation would help stimulate needed investment in mass transportation facilities, which seems to allow cost savings as scale grows, to have fewer negative externalities, and probably to have more equally shared benefits.

Decisions on zoning and land use have also involved misallocations of resources and in many cases made income distribution more unequal. Local communities frequently use zoning to keep out poorer residents, because the commuters fear that poorer residents consume more in public services than they pay in taxes. Large minimum lot-size and minimum house-size requirements are the zoning tools that exclude the poor, raise housing costs, and lower the housing supply for the entire metropolitan area. Restrictive building codes and union membership restriction have similarly raised construction costs and reduced the housing stock. These practices have hurt the poor, who cannot afford adequate housing and are denied access to high-paying construction jobs, but have been beneficial to the owners of older housing and to construction union members.

Excessive property taxes on renter-occupied housing have contributed to resource misallocation. Property taxes reduce the quantity and quality of housing by raising its price to the consumer and its cost to the developer. These taxes are undesirable since housing investment ordinarily generates no harmful neighborhood effects. In fact, quality housing generates benefits for the community which would actually justify a subsidy. We have heavily taxed beneficial, quality housing, but lightly taxed expensive, harmful auto use. In some cities, annual property taxes exceed $1,000 per apartment (one-third of their rent), but automobile commuters make no financial contribution to the operation of the city, in spite of the costs they impose on it.

Polluters have been allowed to discharge waste products into our limited supplies of clean air, water, and land without consideration for the aesthetic, material, and health hazards that such misuse imposes upon others. If polluters were required to pay the social cost of the damage, they would restrict the amount of discharges they emit and increase investment in antipollution devices.

The administration of urban areas has been unsatisfactory because central cities are often not the optimal agencies to perform efficiently and comprehensively the functions for which they have responsibility. They are too small to coordinate metropolitan transportation, pollution control, and income redistribution; they are too large to administer education, garbage collection, local street maintenance, and community improvement. The city is thus an ambiguous halfway house between metropolitan and local government.

Poverty is a special problem of cities. A high percentage of the city population is poor, but the city lacks funds with which to provide services for them. The consequent underinvestment in health and educational resources devoted to the poor is both an effect and a cause of urban poverty. Cities have worked hard in attempting to provide health, education, and welfare for their many underprivileged who are often excluded from suburbs. We have thus been left with many poor central city residents and governments.

The solution to central city problems, both physical and financial, lies not only in more efficiently allocated social and private facilities and better use of them, but in more broadly based social participation in financing those health, education, and welfare services that are worthwhile and desirable. A much greater portion of the financing of these income-redistributive social services ought to be borne by the metropolitan area, state, and nation, since the unbearably high property taxes that would have to be levied in political jurisdictions with a high concentration of the poor would lead to the deterioration and destruction of such communities.

All the city's problems are related. Failure to price goods and services at full cost not only leads to overuse, but also deprives the city of much-needed revenue. The need for adequate revenues leads to excessive property tax rates which often still do not provide sufficient funds with which to finance public services and assistance to the poor. Property taxes reduce investment in quality housing, which is desirable for upgrading the city's deteriorating housing stock.

High taxes plus inadequate public services in the city help induce the middle class to relocate in the suburbs, further diminishing the city's tax base. The same suburbs exclude the poor and minority families by inefficient, unfair overzoning. Suburban overzoning both lessens the metropolitan area's housing stock and concentrates the poor in the central city. The poor then occupy central city housing at greater than optimal densities, hastening its deterioration and placing greater demands on strained central city finances.

Proper pricing and allocation of resources in the city will reduce the problems of poverty and discrimination, as will federal anti-discrimination programs help reduce all the city's other problems. Unfortunately, the city has the authority to initiate only some of the measures needed to improve the quality of its environment.

In the rest of the book we will deal with these central city functions and problems. Whatever your interest in the city, a complete understanding of it requires knowledge of all relevant city functions and problems.

THE CITY AS A DISTORTED PRICE SYSTEM

Wilbur Thompson

We treat the scarcest thing in our cities — street space at the rush hour — as if it were free goods. We offer "free" such public facilities as museums, marinas, golf courses. We insist on equal pay for teachers everywhere throughout the urban area. All of these are instances of bad economics, the result of public failure to understand the city as a price system. And small wonder, since the complex set of prices that shape the city are largely subtle, hidden prices, a subterranean maze of rewards and penalties. It is doubtful that the local public managers of any city in the country can even roughly describe, much less defend, the network of "prices" that push and pull at the fabric of the city and so hamper them at every turn.

The failure to use price — as an *explicit* system — in the public sector of the metropolis is at the root of many, it not most, of our urban problems.

Wilbur Thompson is Professor of Economics, Wayne State University.
Reprinted from Psychology Today Magazine, August, 1968. Copyright © Communications/Research/Machines, Inc.

Price, serving its historic functions, might be used to ration the use of existing facilities, to signal the desired directions of new public investment, to guide the distribution of income, to enlarge the range of public choice and to change tastes and behavior. Price performs such functions in the private marketplace, but it has been virtually eliminated from the public sector. We say "virtually eliminated" because it does exist but in an implicit, subtle, distorted sense that is rarely seen or acknowledged by even close students of the city, much less by public managers. Not surprisingly, this implicit price system results in bad economics.

We think of the property tax as a source of public revenue, but it can be re-interpreted as a price. Most often, the property tax is rationalized on "ability-to-pay" grounds with real property serving as a proxy for income. When the correlation between income and real property is challenged, the apologist for the property tax shifts ground and rationalizes it as a "benefit" tax. The tax then becomes a "price" which the property owner pays for benefits received — fire protection, for example. But this implicit "price" for fire services is hardly a model of either efficiency or equity. Put in a new furnace and fireproof your building (reduce the likelihood of having a fire) and your property tax (fire service premium) goes up; let your property deteriorate and become a firetrap and your fire protection premium goes down! One bright note is New York City's one-year tax abatement on new pollution-control equipment; a timid step but in the right direction.

Often "urban sprawl" is little more than a color word which reflects (betrays?) the speaker's bias in favor of high population density and heavy interpersonal interaction — his "urbanity." Still, typically, the price of using urban fringe space has been set too low — well below the full costs of running pipes, wires, police cars and fire engines farther than would be necessary if building lots were smaller. Residential developers are, moreover, seldom discouraged (penalized by price) from "leap frogging" over the contiguous, expensive vacant land to build on the remote, cheaper parcels. Ordinarily, a flat price is charged for extending water or sewers to a new household regardless of whether the house is placed near to or far from existing pumping stations.

Again, the motorist is subject to the same license fees and tolls, if any, for the extremely expensive system of streets, bridges, tunnels and traffic controls he enjoys, regardless of whether he chooses to drive downtown at the rush hour and thereby pushes against peak capacity or at off-peak times when it costs little or nothing to serve him. To compound this distortion of prices, we usually set the toll at zero. And when we do charge tolls, we quite perversely cut the commuter (rush-hour) rate below the off-peak rate.

It is not enough to point out that the motorist supports road-building through the gasoline tax. The social costs of noise, air pollution, traffic control and general loss of urban amenities are borne by the general taxpayer.

In addition, drivers during off-peak hours overpay and subsidize rush-hour drivers. Four lanes of expressway or bridge capacity are needed in the morning and evening rush hours where two lanes would have served if movements had been random in time and direction; that is, near constant in average volume. The peak-hour motorists probably should share the cost of the first two lanes and bear the full cost of the other two that they alone require. It is best to begin by carefully distinguishing where market tests are possible and where they are not. Otherwise, the case for applying the principles of price is misunderstood; either the too-ardent advocate overstates his case or the potential convert projects too much. In either case, a "disenchantment" sets in that is hard to reverse.

Much of the economics of the city is "public economics," and the pricing of urban public services poses some very difficult and even insurmountable problems. Economists have, in fact, erected a very elegant rationalization of the public economy almost wholly on the *non*-marketability of public goods and services. While economists have perhaps oversold the inapplicability of price in the public sector, let us begin with what we are *not* talking about.

The public economy supplies "collectively consumed" goods, those produced and consumed in one big indivisible lump. Everyone has to be counted in the system, there is no choice of *in* or *out*. We cannot identify individual benefits, therefore we cannot exact a *quid pro quo*. We can not exclude those who would not pay voluntarily; therefore we must turn to compulsory payments: taxes. Justice and air-pollution control are good examples of collectively consumed public services.

A second function of the public economy is to supply "merit goods." Sometimes the majority of us become a little paternalistic and decide that we know what is best for all of us. We believe some goods are especially meritorious, like education, and we fear that others might not fully appreciate this truth. Therefore, we produce these merit goods, at considerable cost, but offer them at a zero price. Unlike the first case of collectively consumed goods, we could sell these merit goods. A schoolroom's doors can be closed to those who do not pay, *quite unlike justice*. But we choose to open the doors wide to ensure that no one will turn away from the service because of its cost, and then we finance the service with compulsory payments. Merit goods are a case of the majority playing God, and "coercing" the minority by the use of bribes to change their behavior.

A third classic function of government is the redistribution of income. Here we wish to perform a service for one group and charge another group the cost of that service. Welfare payments are a clear case. Again, any kind of a private market or pricing mechanism is totally inappropriate: we obviously do not expect welfare recipients to return their payments. Again, we turn to compulsory payments: taxes. In sum, the private market may not be able to process certain goods and services (pure "public goods"), or it may give the "wrong" prices ("merit goods"), or we simply do not want the consumer to pay (income-redistributive services).

But the virtual elimination of price from the public sector is an extreme and highly simplistic response to the special requirements of the public sector. Merit goods may be subsidized without going all of the way to zero prices. Few would argue for full-cost admission prices to museums, but a good case can be made for moderate prices that cover, say, their daily operating costs (*e.g.,* salaries of guards and janitors, heat and light).

Unfortunately, as we have given local government more to do, we have almost unthinkingly extended the tradition of "free" public services to every new undertaking, despite the clear trend in local government toward the assumption of more and more functions that do not fit the neat schema above. The provision of free public facilities for automobile movement in the crowded cores of our urban areas can hardly be defended on the grounds that: (a) motorists could not be excluded from the expressways if they refused to pay the toll, or (b) the privately operated motor vehicle is an especially meritorious way to move through densely populated areas, or (c) the motorists cannot afford to pay their own way and that the general (property) taxpayers should subsidize them. And all this applies with a vengeance to municipal marinas and golf courses.

PRICES TO RATION THE USE OF EXISTING FACILITIES

We need to understand better the rationing function of price as it manifests itself in the urban public sector: how the demand for a temporarily (or permanently) fixed stock of a public good or service can be adjusted to the supply. At any given time the supply of street, bridge and parking space is fixed; "congestion" on the streets and a "shortage" of parking space express demand greater than supply at a zero price, a not too surprising phenomenon. Applying the market solution, the shortage of street space at peak hours ("congestion") could have been temporarily relieved (rationalized) by introducing a short-run rationing price to divert some motorists to other hours of movement, some to other modes of transportation, and some to other activities.

Public goods last a long time and therefore current additions to the stock are too small to relieve shortages quickly and easily. *The rationing function of price is probably more important in the public sector where it is customarily ignored than in the private sector where it is faithfully expressed.*

Rationing need not always be achieved with money, as when a motorist circles the block over and over looking for a place to park. The motorist who is not willing to "spend time" waiting and drives away forfeits the scarce space to one who will spend time (luck averaging out). The parking "problem" may be re-interpreted as an implicit decision to keep the money price artificially low (zero or a nickel an hour in a meter) and supplement it with a waiting cost or time price. The problem is that we did not clearly understand and explicitly agree to do just that.

The central role of price is to allocate — across the board — scarce resources among competing ends to the point where the value of another unit of any good or service is equal to the incremental cost of producing that unit. Expressed loosely, in the long run we turn from using prices to dampen demand to fit a fixed supply to adjusting the supply to fit the quantity demanded, at a price which reflects the production costs.

Prices which ration also serve to signal desired new directions in which to reallocate resources. If the rationing price exceeds those costs of production which the user is expected to bear directly, more resources should ordinarily be allocated to that activity. And symmetrically a rationing price below the relevant costs indicates an *uneconomic* provision of that service in the current amounts. Rationing prices reveal the intensity of the users' demands. How much is it really worth to drive into the heart of town at rush hour or launch a boat? In the long run, motorists and boaters should be free to choose, in rough measure, the amount of street and dock space they want and for which they are willing to pay. But, as in the private sector of our economy, free choice would carry with it full (financial) responsibility for that choice.

We need also to extend our price strategy to "factor prices"; we need a sophisticated wage policy for local public employees. Perhaps the key decision in urban development pertains to the recruiting and assignment of elementary- and secondary-school teachers. The more able and experienced teachers have the greater range of choice in post and quite naturally they choose the newer schools in the better neighborhoods, after serving the required apprenticeship in the older schools in the poorer neighborhoods. Such a pattern of migration certainly cannot implement a policy of equality of opportunity.

This author argued six years ago that

> Egalitarianism in the public school system has been overdone; even the army recognizes the role of price when it awards extra "jump pay" to paratroopers, only a slightly more hazardous occupation than teaching behind the lines. Besides, it is male teachers whom we need to attract to slum schools, both to serve as father figures where there are few males at home and to serve quite literally as disciplinarians. It is bad economics to insist on equal pay for teachers everywhere throughout the urban area when males have a higher productivity in some areas

and when males have better employment opportunities outside teaching — higher "opportunity costs" that raise their supply price. It is downright silly to argue that "equal pay for equal work" is achieved by paying the same money wage in the slums as in the suburbs.

About a year ago, on being offered premium salaries for service in ghetto schools, the teachers rejected, by name and with obvious distaste, any form of "jump pay." One facile argument offered was that they must protect the slum child from the stigma of being harder to teach, a nicety surely lost on the parents and outside observers. One suspects that the real reason for avoiding salary differentials between the "slums and suburbs" is that the teachers seek to escape the hard choice between the higher pay and the better working conditions. *But that is precisely what the price system is supposed to do: equalize sacrifice.*

PRICES TO GUIDE THE DISTRIBUTION OF INCOME

A much wider application of tolls, fees, fines and other "prices" would also confer greater control over the distribution of income for two distinct reasons. First, the taxes currently used to finance a given public service create *implicit* and *unplanned* redistribution of income. Second, this drain on our limited supply of tax money prevents local government from undertaking other programs with more *explicit* and *planned* redistributional effects.

More specifically, if upper-middle- and upper-income motorists, golfers and boaters use subsidized public streets, golf links and marinas more than in proportion to their share of local tax payments from which the subsidy is paid, then these public activities redistribute income toward greater inequality. Even if these "semiproprietary" public activities were found to be neutral with respect to the distribution of income, public provision of these discretionary services comes at the expense of a roughly equivalent expenditure on the more classic public services: protection, education, public health and welfare.

Self-supporting public golf courses are so common and marinas are such an easy extension of the same principle that it is much more instructive to test the faith by considering the much harder case of the public museum: "Culture." Again, we must recall that it is the middle- and upper-income classes who typically visit museums, so that free admission becomes, in effect, redistribution toward greater inequality, to the extent that the lower-income nonusers pay local taxes (*e.g.,* property taxes directly or indirectly through rent, local sales taxes). The low prices contemplated are not, moreover, likely to discourage attendance significantly and the resolution of special cases (*e.g.,* student passes) seems well within our competence.

Unfortunately, it is not obvious that "free" public marinas and tennis courts pose foregone alternatives — "opportunity costs." If we had to discharge a teacher or policeman every time we built another boat dock or tennis court, we would see the real cost of these public services. But in a growing economy, we need only not hire another teacher or policeman and that is not so obvious. In general, then, given a binding local budget constraint — scarce tax money — to undertake a local public service that is unequalizing or even neutral in income redistribution is to deny funds to programs that have the desired distributional effect, and is to lose control over equity.

Typically, in oral presentations at question time, it is necessary to reinforce this point by rejoining: "No, I would not put turnstiles in the playgrounds in poor neighborhoods, rather it is only because we do put turnstiles at the entrance to the playgrounds for the middle- and upper-income groups that we will be able to 'afford' playgrounds for the poor."

PRICES TO ENLARGE THE RANGE OF CHOICE

But there is more at stake in the contemporary chaos of hidden and unplanned prices than "merely" efficiency and equity. *There is no urban goal on which consensus is more easily gained than the pursuit of great variety and choice — "pluralism."* The great rural to urban migration was prompted as much by the search for variety as by the decline of agriculture and rise of manufacturing. Wide choice is seen as the saving grace of bigness by even the sharpest critics of the metropolis. Why, then, do we tolerate far less variety in our big cities than we could have? We have lapsed into a state of tyranny by the majority, in matters of both taste and choice.

In urban transportation the issue is not, in the final analysis, whether users of core-area street space at peak hours should or should not be required to pay their own way in full. The problem is, rather, that by not forcing a direct *quid pro quo* in money, we implicitly substitute a new means of payment — time — in the transportation services "market." The peak-hour motorist does pay in full, through congestion and time delay. But *implicit choices* blur issues and confuse decision-making.

Say we were carefully to establish how many more dollars would have to be paid in for the additional capacity needed to save a given number of hours spent commuting. The *majority* of urban motorists perhaps would still choose the present combination of "under-investment" in highway, bridge and parking facilities, with a compensatory heavy investment of time in slow movement over these crowded facilities. Even so, a substantial minority of motorists do prefer a different combination of money and time cost. A more affluent, long-distance commuter could well see the current level of traffic congestion as a real problem and much prefer to spend more money to save time. If economies of scale are so substantial that only one motorway to town can be supported, or if some naturally scarce factor (*e.g.,* bridge or tunnel sites) prevents parallel transportation facilities of different quality and price, then the preferences of the minority must be sacrificed to the majority interest and we do have a real "problem." But, ordinarily, in large urban areas there are a number of near parallel routes to town, and an unsatisfied minority group large enough to justify significant differentiation of one or more of these streets and its diversion to their use. Greater choice through greater scale is, in fact, what bigness is all about.

The simple act of imposing a toll, at peak hours, on one of these routes would reduce its use, assuming that nearby routes are still available without user charges, thereby speeding movement of the motorists who remain and pay. The toll could be raised only to the point where some combination of moderately rapid movement and high physical output were jointly optimized. Otherwise the outcry might be raised that the public transportation authority was so elitist as to gratify the desire of a few very wealthy motorists for very rapid movement, heavily overloading the "free" routes. It is, moreover, quite possible, even probable, that the newly converted, rapid-flow, toll route would handle as many vehicles as it did previously as a congested street and not therefore spin off any extra load on the free routes.

Our cities cater, at best, to the taste patterns of the middle-income class, as well they should, *but not so exclusively.* This group has chosen, indirectly through clumsy and insensitive tax-and-expenditure decisions and ambiguous political processes, to move about town flexibly and cheaply, but slowly, in private vehicles. Often, and almost invariably in the larger urban areas, we would not have to encroach much on this choice to accommodate also those who would prefer to spend more money and less time, in urban movement. In general, we should permit urban residents to pay in their most readily available "currency" — time or money.

Majority rule by the middle class in urban transportation has not only disenfranchised the affluent commuter, but more seriously it has debilitated the low-fare, mass transit system on which the poor depend. The effect of widespread automobile ownership and use on the mass transportation system is an oft-told tale: falling bus and rail patronage leads to less frequent service and higher overhead costs per trip and often higher fares which further reduce demand and service schedules. Perhaps two-thirds or more of the urban residents will tolerate and may even prefer slow, cheap automobile movement. But the poor are left without access to many places of work — the suburbanizing factories in particular — and they face much reduced opportunities for comparative shopping, and highly constrained participation in the community life in general. A truly wide range of choice in urban transportation would allow the rich to pay for fast movement with money, the middle-income class to pay for the privacy and convenience of the automobile with time, and the poor to economize by giving up (paying with) privacy.

A more sophisticated price policy would expand choice in other directions. Opinions differ as to the gravity of the water-pollution problem near large urban areas. The minimum level of dissolved oxygen in the water that is needed to meet the standards of different users differs greatly, as does the incremental cost that must be incurred to bring the dissolved oxygen levels up to successively higher standards. The boater accepts a relatively low level of "cleanliness" acquired at relatively little cost. Swimmers have higher standards attained only at much higher cost. Fish and fisherman can thrive only with very high levels of dissolved oxygen acquired only at the highest cost. Finally, one can imagine an elderly convalescent or an impoverished slum dweller or a confirmed landlubber who is not at all interested in the nearby river. What, then, constitutes "clean?"

A majority rule decision, whether borne by the citizen directly in higher taxes or levied on the industrial polluters and then shifted on to the consumer in higher product prices, is sure to create a "problem." If the pollution program is a compromise — a halfway measure — the fisherman will be disappointed because the river is still not clean enough for his purposes and the landlubbers will be disgruntled because the program is for "special interests" and he can think of better uses for his limited income. Surely, we can assemble the managerial skills in the local public sector needed to devise and administer a structure of user charges that would extend choice in outdoor recreation, consistent with financial responsibility, with lower charges for boat licenses and higher charges for fishing licenses.

Perhaps the most fundamental error we have committed in the development of our large cities is that we have too often subjected the more affluent residents to petty irritations which serve no great social purpose, then turned right around and permitted this same group to avoid responsibilities which have the most critical and pervasive social ramifications. It is a travesty and a social tragedy that we have prevented the rich from buying their way out of annoying traffic congestion — or at least not helped those who are long on money and short on time arrange such an accommodation. Rather, we have permitted them, through political fragmentation and flight to tax havens, to evade their financial and leadership responsibilities for the poor of the central cities. That easily struck goal, "pluralism and choice," will require much more managerial sophistication in the local public sector than we have shown to date.

PRICING TO CHANGE TASTES AND BEHAVIOR

Urban managerial economics will probably also come to deal especially with "developmental pricing" analogous to "promotional pricing" in business. Prices below cost may be used for a limited period to create a market for a presumed "merit good." The hope would be that the artificially low price would stimulate consumption and that an altered *expenditure pattern* (practice) would lead in time to an altered *taste pattern* (preference), as experience with the new service led to a fuller appreciation of it. Ultimately, the subsidy would be withdrawn, whether or not tastes changed sufficiently to make the new service self-supporting — provided, of course, that no permanent redistribution of income was intended.

For example, our national parks had to be subsidized in the beginning and this subsidy could be continued indefinitely on the grounds that these are "merit goods" that serve a broad social interest. But long experience with outdoor recreation has so shifted tastes that a large part of the costs of these parks could now be paid for by a much higher set of park fees.

It is difficult, moreover, to argue that poor people show up at the gates of Yellowstone Park, or even the much nearer metropolitan area regional parks, in significant number, so that a subsidy is needed to continue provision of this service for the poor. A careful study of the users and the incidence of the taxes raised to finance our parks may even show a slight redistribution of income toward greater inequality.

Clearly, this is not the place for an economist to pontificate on the psychology of prices but a number of very interesting phenomena that seem to fall under this general heading deserve brief mention. A few simple examples of how charging a price changes behavior are offered, but left for others to classify.

In a recent study of depressed areas, the case was cited of a community-industrial-development commission that extended its fund-raising efforts from large business contributors to the general public in a supplementary "nickel and dime" campaign. They hoped to enlist the active support of the community at large, more for reasons of public policy than for finance. But even a trivial financial stake was seen as a means to create broad and strong public identification with the local industrial development programs and to gain their political support.

Again, social-work agencies have found that even a nominal charge for what was previously a free service enhances both the self-respect of the recipient and his respect for the usefulness of the service. Paradoxically, we might experiment with higher public assistance payments coupled to *nominal* prices for selected public health and family services, personal counseling and surplus foods.

To bring a lot of this together now in a programmatic way, we can imagine a very sophisticated urban public management beginning with below-cost prices on, say, the new rapid mass transit facility during the promotional period of luring motorists from their automobiles and of "educating" them on the advantages of a carefree journey to work. Later, if and when the new facility becomes crowded during rush hours and after a taste for this new transportation mode has become well established, the "city economist" might devise a three-price structure of fares: the lowest fare for regular off-peak use, the middle fare for regular peak use (tickets for commuters) and the highest fare for the occasional peak-time user. Such a schedule would reflect each class's contribution to the cost of having to carry standby capacity.

If the venture more than covered its costs of operation, the construction of additional facilities would begin. Added social benefits in the form of a cleaner, quieter city or reduced social costs of traffic control and accidents could be included in the cost accounting ("cost-benefit analysis") underlying the fare structure. But below-cost fares, taking care to count social as well as private costs, would not be continued indefinitely except for merit goods or when a clear income-redistribution end is in mind. And, even then, not without careful comparison of the relative efficiency of using the subsidy money in alternative redistributive programs. We need, it would seem, not only a knowledge of the economy of the city, but some very knowledgeable city economists as well.

FURTHER READINGS

Hoover, Edgar M., and Vernon, Raymond. *Anatomy of a Metropolis.* Cambridge: Harvard University Press, 1959.

Jacobs, Jane. *Death and Life of Great American Cities.* New York: Random House, 1961.

Thompson, Wilbur R. *A Preface to Urban Economics.* Baltimore: Johns Hopkins Press, for Resources for the Future, Inc. 1965.

Vernon, Raymond. *Metropolis 1985.* Cambridge: Harvard University Press, 1960.

Chapter 2

GROWTH, INCOME, AND ECONOMIC STABILITY

In this section we examine the phenomena that cause cities to develop and grow, analyze the benefits and costs of added growth — thus permitting the estimation of the optimal size of a city — and develop a methodology for the prediction of city size, growth, and income.

The long-run explanation of why cities exist rests initially upon the competitive ability to produce certain goods — comparative advantages of different locations in the production and transportation of different goods and services. These goods form the city's export base. Once a city is established, its size creates economies of agglomeration that induce further growth. Economies of agglomeration occur when output per capita increases with larger contiguous populations. Diseconomies may also accrue to higher-density populations within metropolitan areas, although the economies of agglomeration in total population size can compensate for them.

There are two economies of agglomeration: those in production and those in consumption. In production, activities that are intensive in communications, information, and personal contacts have the greatest economies of agglomeration. Witness the concentration of law, advertising, merchandising, insurance, art, newsgathering, publishing, corporate administration, fashion, entertainment, wholesaling, banking, and finance in New York City. Other activities having economies of agglomeration in production are those that rely upon large, diversified, highly skilled labor forces, such as small firms engaged in electronics, consulting, architecture, research, and development of new products.

What economies of agglomeration in consumption would be found in a large city? A large population would permit, in addition to large-scale and more competitive merchandising, a greater proliferation of small specialty shops, services, and public facilities whose clientele is a small percentage of the population. Only a large population will have sufficient demand to support a diversity of such amenities as fine restaurants, boutiques, art galleries, antique shops, museums, theaters, and symphonies.

Look now at the circumstances that have encouraged cities to develop at specific locations. These include access to inexpensive transportation (water, rail and recently road and air), nearness to natural resources, favorable climate, harbor quality, natural beauty, the diversity of the local population, and historical tradition.

An excellent harbor on the North Atlantic would give a city a comparative advantage in import-export trade and would later lead to the development of finance and insurance, whereas location on a navigable river near iron and coal deposits would give that city an advantage in the production of iron and steel.

Given the long-run forces that underlie the creation and evolution of cities, can a city predict and optimize its growth? First, the city must decide if it can and should encourage expansions of population and industry. Then it must find ways to predict its growth so as to plan for its future public service and investment needs.

In deciding the optimal amount of population and industry for a city, economists must look at the costs and benefits of increased size. Costs of growth include those of providing transportation, education, sanitation, roads, and police protection for the expanded industry and population. In addition, the city's population may incur heightened social costs of pollution and congestion. The benefits of growth most often cited are those of greater employment, incomes, and public services for the city's residents along with some proliferation of consumer products and services not previously available.

How can a city estimate the increase in city income that will occur because of natural or induced growth? To calculate the rise in income generated by introducing new industry into a community economists sometimes use the community economic base study. The study is used to predict the effect of changes in export demand on city income and population, so that planners can anticipate the increased demand for public services and investment. As outlined in our reading by Charles Tiebout, the economic base study is a Keynesian multiplier model applied to a locality. The model considers increased sales of goods by the city to areas outside the city as exogenous demand, or increased export base, and assumes that the income of the city will go up by a predictable multiple of the gain in exports. The increase in city income divided by the increase in the city's exports is defined as the base multiplier (the predicted change in city income is equal to the change in city exports times the base multiplier). The multiplier is estimated from past data on changes in city income and exports.

How accurate is this method and how large a multiplier can we expect? Cities are small and highly variable units whose multipliers are likely to be lower and more unstable than the Keynesian multiplier for the nation as a whole. Localities spend a large proportion of their increased income on imports, which vary with changing consumer tastes. The multipliers customarily do not exceed one and one-half and can be approximately one for a city experiencing full employment, inflation, or a very high propensity of import. Low multipliers and conversely high import propensities can be attributed to one or more of several circumstances, such as small city size, nearly complete specialization in the production of one good, or diseconomies of increased size. Larger cities have a lower ratio of exports to total output than smaller cities, because a relatively larger proportion of their output is for local consumption. Input-output studies showing the amounts of various resources used by the city's economic activities can be used to analyze the labor requirements and industry composition that specialization or growth will bring about. Undertaking an economic base study may engender a valuable familiarity with a city, but is not likely to lead to precise predictions.

Another problem to consider is the effect upon a city specializing in the production of one export to achieve growth, and perhaps higher per capita incomes, rather than producing a variety of goods. The result of specialization can be a city lacking flexibility, diversity, and stability over the business cycle. The opportunity cost of producing other goods is driven up as the resources that would go into other sectors are bid away by the export goods production. Benjamin Chinitz presents a case study comparing a diversified with a specialized city, which illustrates how specialization can lead to such undesirable results.

Just how large should a city be? Economic analysis of this problem yields the conclusion that there is no one best size for all cities, but that the optimal size for any city depends on its productive capabilities in combination with the demand for its output. The optimum size for each city can be achieved by pricing all goods and services, both public and private, at their full incremental (marginal) social (public and private) cost.

Analysis of the cost of production for cities' services shows that there are increasing returns to scale in providing many public and private goods. That is, the unit cost of producing a good or service falls as the quantity demanded rises. A small town needs one fire truck. The ratio of fire trucks to citizens lessens as population rises, hence there are economies of scale or decreasing costs in providing fire protection. Economies of scale in fire departments exist as departments serve larger populations of up to 300,000. Eventually as population grows decreasing returns or increasing costs in the provision of some goods and service are experienced. These diseconomies can be seen in the rising cost of providing additional housing or highway capacity in large cities — the cost to build one more housing unit or stretch of highway is greater than the cost of building the first units. Some goods, like mass transit, have persistent economies of scale.

Some have interpreted decreasing returns to mean that our largest metropolitan areas are too populous. This need not be true if there are increasing costs in the provision of most public goods. Economies of scale or agglomeration in the production and consumption of other private and public goods could still outweigh the diseconomies. William Alonso has collected data on per capita land values in metropolitan areas which suggest that per capita output increases or at least remains constant as population increases. Possibly the elimination of externalities such as pollution and traffic congestion might result in a not undesirable expansion of our larger metropolitan areas. The existence of economies of scale and agglomeration to expanded population in small towns is likely to mean we have too many of them and would benefit from some consolidation. Similarly, new towns that are not planned suburbs or nearby satellites of larger cities may have only limited economic potential.

In conclusion, individual cities can probably have little effect upon their growth. They would achieve optimal size by adopting pricing policies that account for all costs and benefits of each activity (internalizing negative and positive externalities, i.e., pollution, congestion, building quality) and by investing only in resources whose benefits exceed costs.

A METHOD OF DETERMINING INCOMES AND THEIR VARIATION IN SMALL REGIONS [1]

Charles M. Tiebout

I

INTRODUCTION

This paper is concerned with the determinants of income of a small region (community). The approach will be through modified national (regional) income accounts, especially the international sector. The analysis is cast largely in terms of aggregative national income analysis, but in some cases differs by more than a matter of degree. What is sought is the classification and theoretical analysis of the major exogenous and endogenous variables of a community. Finally, the results of some empirical research in the area will be noted.

ALTERNATIVE APPROACHES

This framework is presented in contrast to two other approaches to community economic research: the more general approach and input-output studies.[2]

Until recent years many studies in community economics tended to be of a descriptive character. Research undertaken by city planners and chambers of commerce tended to be of this nature. Some interesting work of this broader type may be familiar.[3] Often these studies did not deal with any

Charles M. Tiebout was formerly Professor of Economics, University of Washington.

Reprinted with permission from Charles M. Tiebout, "A Method of Determining Incomes and Their Variations in Small Regions," *Papers and Proceedings of the Regional Science Association* (1955), pp. F1–F12.

[1] The author is indebted to W. F. Stolper and F. G. Adams of the University of Michigan for their help and suggestions.

[2] An example of the former: Homer Hoyt. "Homer Hoyt on the Economic Base," *Land Economics.* Vol. XXX, No. 2 (May 1954), pp. 183–91. (Note especially the bibliography.) For an example of input-output see: W. Isard, R. Kavesh, and R. Kuenne. "The Economic Base and Structure of the Urban-Metropolitan Region," *American Sociological Review.* Vol. XVIII, No. 3 (June 1953), pp. 117–21.

[3] One of the classics of this type is: Robert Haig. *Major Economic Factors in Metropolitan Growth and Arrangement. Vol. I of Regional Survey of New York and Its Environs.* N.Y.C., 1928.

specific question, but merely tried to shed some light on the structure of the region.

In recent years input-output matrices have become a popular tool of regional research. The limitations of input-output have been noted by Dorfman and Isard[4] and, perhaps, a more serious limitation by Vail.[5] Nevertheless, the input-output technique is still a fascinating tool for regional research. There is no desire to quibble over whether or not the approach presented below is a supplement to or alternative for input-output analysis.

REGIONAL SIZE

This paper deals with the incomes of small regions; for the sake of a number say under 200,000 population. As used here "size" is taken as a composite of population and space. A region is considered small if, and only if, it has neither a large population nor is geographically large. Of course, if regions are too small the usefulness of aggregation is nil. The income determinants of one tank town are not very interesting even to an alcoholic.

It is necessary to note this size feature since the determinants of income are themselves a function of regional size. Illustrative of this point is the case of exports. For example, if the region under consideration is the whole world, then by definition exports could not be a determinant of income levels. On the other hand, in an exchange setting, a region defined as one person in space has its whole income determined by exports. Obviously, for the regions between these extremes, the importance of exports tends to be inversely correlated to the size of the region considered.

Here it is assumed that the region for study is small enough in relation to the overall space of which it is a part that there is no foreign trade multiplier feedback. This means shocks are a one-way affair. For example, a decrease in demand for Argus cameras would lower the income of Ann Arbor, Michigan, and consequently, the Ann Arbor demand for imports. As usually formulated the foreign trade multiplier tells us the reaction would proceed by lowering the income of the rest of the nation due to the fall in Ann Arbor demand. This is explicitly ruled out by assumption. In international trade this is the small nation case quits analogous to the situation of the competitive wheat farmer.

[4] Robert Dorfman. "The Nature and Significance of Input-Output," *The Review of Economics and Statistics*. Vol. XXXVI, No. 2 (May 1954), pp. 121–33, and Walter Isard. "Regional Commodity Balances and Interregional Commodity Flows," *American Economic Review*. Vol. XLIII, No. 2 (May 1953), pp. 167–80.

[5] Stefan Valavanis-Vail. "Leontief's Scarce Factor Paradox," *Journal of Political Economy*. Vol. XII, No. 6 (Dec. 1954), pp. 523–28.

II

ANALYTICAL FRAMEWORK

The problem now becomes to construct a framework in which the exogenous elements of the community income can be isolated. Since, by definition, these activities are assumed to generate the community's income, let us go along with the term "basic activities." Those variables of the community income which are considered as endogenous are termed "non-basic activities." Hence, the income of the community has two sectors: the basic corresponding to the exogenous sector and the non-basic or endogenous sector. No doubt this may be familiar to some of the readers, since the concept of the "economic base" has recently come up in the literature.[6] Since this analysis draws on this sort of approach, it is worth a moment's look.

Quoting from a summary article on this subject:

> ". . . the economic base of a city is by definition made up of export activities of the community. These activities involve the export of goods, services, and capital to purchasers who are outside the community or come from the outside."[7]

Those industries which serve only local needs are called non-basic.[8] Retail trade is, for the most part, considered non-basic. Here the discussion generally stops except for the details of measurement, definition, and the like.

BASIC ACTIVITIES OF THE COMMUNITY

Let's leave this basic activity approach for a moment and consider the community in an interregional setting. Traditional analysis of the foreign trade multiplier, somewhat simplified, tells us that the level of exports and domestic investment are the exogenous variables in setting the nation's

[6] See among others: John Alexander. "The Basic–Non-basic Concept of Urban Economic Functions," *Economic Geography*. Vol. XXX, No. 3 (July 1954), pp. 246–61. R. B. Andrews. "Mechanics of the Urban Economic Base," *Land Economics*. Vols. XXIX–XXXI (May 1953 and continuing). Isard, Kavesh, and Kuenne, *op. cit.* Homer Hoyt, *op. cit.*

[7] Richard B. Andrews. "Mechanics of the Urban Economic Base: Problems of Base Area Delimitation," *Land Economics*. Vol. XXX, No. 4 (Nov. 1954), p. 309.

[8] It appears that the term "economic base" as used by Isard, Kavesh, and Kuenne, *op. cit.* differs from the above. In their case to the total exports of a new steel mill is added the exports of agglomerating industries as well. Along with this is added the local expansion of activities including households who "also behave like industries" (p. 118). If this interpretation is correct, it would appear that in a town that arose because a steel mill was erected in a desert, *all* economic activity is basic.

income. With these known and the propensities to consume and import given, the system is solved for the income.[9]

In like manner for the community, those activities whose level is set either by non-economic forces for by forces beyond the control of the community are the ones classed as basic or exogenous. These need not be the same as those termed basic in the literature. The reason they are called basic here is that *given their level, the system is determinate.* Before contrasting these with the non-basic activities it would be well to see what sectors fall under this basic classification.

Gross exports, for the most part, constitute the main element in determining regional income.[10] One would expect the "value added by export" sector to be the major item in the "community income arising out of basic activity" account. Also included in this account would be the income arising in "export linked" activities. Using the example of Argus Camera in Ann Arbor, a local firm supplying them with buffing wheels would be considered as exporting even though its sales are to a local firm, i.e., Argus. Conceptually, the way to find the linked firms is to drop the exports to zero while holding other demands (consumer, housing, etc.) constant. Those firms which fall out are export linked.

But merely to list export activities as basic as is done in the literature misses the point. Exports are important as a determinant of income. In this connection one important case should not be overlooked. This is the case of exports to the contiguous area. Even though it is over 200,000 population New York City will illustrate this point. New York exports to the suburban area in the form of retail sales. These are exports as much as any manufacturing sales as most base studies point out. But the point here is that the level of retail sales to the suburbs is itself tied to the level of New York income via the commuters. A drop in New York income will drop suburban income and in turn will cut retail exports to the suburbs. Hence, the level of retail exports is not necessarily an exogenous variable. On the other hand, retail sales may be exogenous if the demand is not determined by the city itself. A different example will illustrate this point. It may be that the export demand for retail sales in the city of Peoria, Illinois, is largely derived from sales to farmers. Unlike the commuters the income of the farmer does not depend on the income of Peoria itself, but on the demand for farm products. In this case the account "value added by retail sales to non-residents" is exogenous. In the New York example it is not. The point is that one needs to know something about the market in the con-

9 See the classic article: Lloyd Metzler. "Underemployment Equilibrium in International Trade," *Econometrica.* Vol. X, No. 2 (April 1942), pp. 97–113.

10 See: W. F. Stolper. "The Volume of Foreign Trade and the Level of Income," *Quarterly Journal of Economics.* Vol. LXI, No. 2 (Feb. 1947), pp. 285–310; J. J. Polak. "The Foreign Trade Multiplier," *American Economic Review.* Vol. XXXVII, No. 5 (Dec. 1947), pp. 889–97.

tiguous area before activities can be classed as basic or non-basic. It involves a question of the overlap of the labor market area with the shopping area.[11]

NON-BASIC ACTIVITIES: ENDOGENOUS VARIABLES

The usefulness of this analysis depends on the validity of the assumption that one group of the communities' activities are in fact endogenous. This implies that given the level of income generated by basic activities, i.e., "income arising out of basic activities," one is theoretically able to predict total community income. Its usefulness would be enhanced if it could be further demonstrated that the proportion of the non-basic activities, measured in dollars, is the same for similar communities. Put another way, two communities with the same "value added by basic activities" accounts would be expected to have the same "value added by non-basic activities" account.[12] Two conditions are necessary for this conclusion about the similarity of non-basic activities: (1) that consumption habits do not vary among communities and (2) the production actually undertaken is similar. It is worth considering each of these conditions in a bit more detail.

The chief activities in the "income arising from non-basic activities" sector are retail and service trades. By making some assumptions about the nature of two communities the position of these non-basic activities will become clear. Suppose two communities have the following in common: (1) per capita income in basic activities is the same, (2) both cities are located in approximately the same position in a Lösch spatial system, and (3) as (2) implies both communities are of approximately equal size. *In these communities one would expect the level and distribution of the spendings on non-basic activities to be the same.* In communities where the above conditions are not fulfilled, but the differences are known, the level and distribution of non-basic activities spendings can still be predicted. Looked at another way it merely states that how much, on what, and where people spend their incomes does not vary from community to community.[13] Empirical evidence on this point will be noted later.

The second assumption that the production actually undertaken is similar is more critical. In effect what is said is that if the level of exogenous variables is set and the "income arising in basic activities" is given, the level and structure of non-basic activities will follow. Alternatively, for every

---

[11] Let: W = wages paid foreigners; R_f = retail purchases abroad by residents; and R_e = retail export to foreigners. Then a shopping center might be defined as satisfying the following conditions: $W_f' + aR_f \ aR_e$ where a = 1/propensity to consume retail goods.

[12] The above remark should be qualified by noting that a community located in the proximity of a large city would be expected to have a smaller part of its income created by non-basic activities, since shopping would be done in the city.

[13] Obviously less is spent on heat in California than in Minnesota, but this can be accounted for.

dollar of basic activity income there will be created two cents worth of barbering. The fact that this is largely the case is due to the low entry costs of these activities. The cost of entering the trades and services is low both in terms of capital requirements and managerial know-how. Experience in communities points up this feature. The number of automobile dealers, barbers, shoe stores and the like varies with the size of the community. One community will not experience a shortage of shoe stores while another has too many. If there is a shortage, in all probability, it will be a temporary affair. This need not be the case in basic activities. The closing of a manufacturing plant and the consequent drop in community income do not necessarily produce a reaction to fill the void. No young entrepreneur or branch plant comes in to offset the drop. In many cases the solution is a migration of population and a reduction of the community size to fit its new and lower "income arising from basic activity" account.[14] In some cases the community, although more likely the economic system, induces new firms into the area. The point is that this may not happen.

SUMMARY

In summary, the argument has been that for any community there exists a fairly sharp division of the community's national income. Part of this income, "income arising out of basic activities," is exogenous in that its size is determined either by non-economic forces or by forces outside the community. It was pointed out the export demand need not be exogenous with respect to exports to the contiguous area even though one assumes no foreign trade multiplier feedback for distant spaces. Finally, it was shown that as opposed to basic activities one may define a sector, "income arising from non-basic activity." Non-basic activities are characterized by high mobility and with common consumption habits known, appear in a predictable array given the basic activities.

III

EMPIRICAL EVIDENCE

Although statistical work in this area is limited, some support of this thesis is noted. That exports do act as a determinant of income is shown by a

---

[14] This is the sort of problem that comes up in communities whose solution to a recession is to try and open more barber shops. If successful through a shop-at-home campaign, it raises the ratio of non-basic to basic activities. This raises the communities' multiplier by reducing the propensity to import and makes it all the more sensitive to a future given dollar drop in basic activity levels.

variety of international trade studies. Simpson's interesting study of the Pacific Northwest points up the role of exports in regional analysis.[15]

Studies concerning the basic–non-basic premise have had varied results. Hildebrand and Mace, in a study of Los Angeles, found a high correlation over time between the basic–non-basic ratio.[16] In a study of the Wichita multiplier the Federal Reserve Bank of Kansas City was less successful in relating the basic to non-basic ratio in Wichita.[17] In part, this failure reflects the big production changes in the bomber plant. One interesting series of studies of this sort has been carried on by John Alexander.[18] Here, unlike the above studies, the non-basic and basic activities were determined by survey methods. The similarity in structures of the non-basic activities in the two communities studied is striking.

Two further sources of statistical verification are in process. One is looking at the survey of the Bureau of Labor Statistics, *Family Income, Expenditures, and Savings in 1950,* to test the hypothesis that consumption patterns are predictably similar in various communities. The other concerns some work we are finishing up on the Ann Arbor Balance of Payments. Here, via surveys, as well as the usual statistical sources, the dollar values of the national income accounts, especially the foreign sector, have been estimated. When this study is completed and extended back a few years, we hope to be able to add something to basic activity analysis as an approach to the determinants of community income.

[15] Paul B. Simpson. *Regional Aspects of Business Cycles* and a *Special Study of the Pacific Northwest.* Study prepared for the Bonneville Administration, and supported by the University of Oregon, and the Social Science Research Council, 1953.

[16] G. H. Hildebrand and Arthur Mace. "The Employment Multiplier in an Expanding Industrial Market: Los Angeles County, 1940–47," *Review of Economics and Statistics.* Vol. XXXII, No. 3 (Aug. 1950), pp. 241–49.

[17] . . . "The Employment Multiplier in Wichita." *Monthly Review.* Federal Reserve Bank of Kansas City. Vol. XXXVII, No. 9 (Sept. 1952), pp. 1–7.

[18] Alexander, *op. cit.*

CONTRASTS IN AGGLOMERATION: NEW YORK AND PITTSBURGH

Benjamin Chinitz

The natural inclination of a scientist when confronted with a new problem is to try to solve it with old tools. When he is finally convinced that the old tools will not do the job, he retreats to his shop to fashion some new tools. The burden of my argument in this paper is that we have reached the stage in regional economics when we must begin to fashion some new analytical tools.

When I say regional economics I have in mind specifically the analysis of the growth and structure of the economy of geographic subdivisions within a national economy. This type of analysis is now being carried on in at least a dozen metropolitan areas throughout the country and in numerous other types of subdivisions, large and small. I have been associated with two such studies: the New York Metropolitan Region Study . . . and the Pittsburgh Economic Study, which is at its halfway mark, having been initiated in June, 1959, and being scheduled for completion in June, 1962. My observations, as the title of my paper suggests, are drawn from these two immersions in regional economics.

The basic-nonbasic approach to the analysis of a region has been under severe attack from many quarters in recent years. But I think it is fair to say that alternative approaches have differed in degree of refinement more than in kind. Fundamentally, we still go about our business in the same way. We try to identify the autonomous influences operating on the region and chart a network of interdependence between sectors within the region. I have no quarrel with this approach. I find it difficult to frame the problem otherwise. My quarrel is with the limitations of the maps of interdependence which are typically drawn.

I will surely be doing some of my colleagues an injustice with the following generalization but, begging their pardon, I state it anyway: our efforts so far have been almost exclusively devoted to the demand dimension of interdependence. The supply side has been virtually ignored. Let me elaborate.

Benjamin Chinitz is Professor of Economics, Brown University.
Reprinted from Benjamin Chinity, "Contrasts in Agglomeration: New York and Pittsburgh," *American Economic Review* 51 (May 1961), pp. 279–289.

The basic-nonbasic model is a way of coming to grips with the demand side of interdependence in one fell swoop. The links in the output-income-consumption chain, the links in the output-capital-formation chain, the links in the output-tax revenues-government spending chain, and the links in the output-materials purchased-output (i.e., input-output) chain, are all subsumed under one grand link between the exogenous and the endogenous elements of the system. Sometimes we can get away with this leap over a lot of treacherous ground just as in football a seventy-yard pass from the thirty-yard line occasionally results in a touchdown. To maintain the metaphor, most of us prefer to gain more yardage on the ground before passing into the end zone.

So we move in small steps. We try to chart the flows between our sectors in greater detail. A dollar of output of industry A, we observe, generates a demand for the output of industry C which is not equal to the demand generated for the output of industry C by a dollar of output of industry B. We observe, further, that a dollar of output of industry A generates more or less personal income than a dollar of output of industry B. If we are really keen observers, we might even discover that a dollar paid out to workers in industry A generates demands for consumer goods, housing construction, and government services which are different from the demands generated by a dollar paid out to workers in industry B.

My point is that in the main we improve upon the crude basic-nonbasic approach by a process of flow disaggregation — a process which hopefully will reduce our margin of error. I characterize this activity as the application of old tools to new problems for the obvious reason that input-output relationships, consumption functions, investment functions, and the like are old tools which were fashioned to solve the problems of a national economy. Furthermore, all those tools are used to come to grips with the demand side of the interdependence between sectors in a regional economy.

When I say that the supply side has been ignored, I mean simply that we have not come to grips with the following question: How does the level of activity in industry A in a given region influence the factor supply curves confronting industry B in the same region? Let me hasten to exclude one kind of effort from my indictment. We certainly have tried to incorporate the influence on industry B of the availability of the output of industry A as an input to industry B. Probably the best example of this kind of work is the Isard-Kuenne study of the impact of the Fairless Works. But this is only one of a number of supply relationships which need to be explored and, as far as I can tell, they have not received adequate attention from regional economists.

My former colleagues on the New York Metropolitan Region Study staff could certainly register a strong objection at this point. After all, another term for supply interdependence is external economies and diseconomies, and there is certainly a lot of discussion about them in a number of volumes of the New York study.

But this discussion is limited to two problems: one has to do with intra-industry external economies and diseconomies; the other has to do with the influence of the aggregate size of the region on the costs of individual firms. The first problem is too narrowly defined and the second too broadly defined from my point of view.

Nevertheless, I believe, regional economics owes a great debt to the New York Metropolitan Region Study for highlighting these external relationships. It was only after we were confronted with the problem of understanding certain features of the Pittsburgh economy that we at the Pittsburgh Study felt compelled to probe more deeply into the nature of these inter-industry effects.

Pittsburgh, as a metropolitan economy, stands in sharp contrast to New York with respect to these three summary variables: size, industrial structure, and rate of growth in recent decades. New York is between six and seven times the size of Pittsburgh. New York has a much more diversified industrial structure. And, while New York has grown at just a bit less than the national rate for the last thirty years, Pittsburgh has grown at less than half the national rate in the same period.

Superficially, all these contrasts fit a familiar pattern. Large areas are more diversified than small areas. Diversified areas exhibit more stability in their growth because their fortunes are not tied to the fortunes of a few industries. In these terms, Pittsburgh's story seems easy to tell.

Unfortunately the matter cannot rest there. Pittsburgh is much more specialized than any large SMA with the exception of Detroit, including many which are no larger than Pittsburgh and many which are considerably smaller. The question, why is it not diversified, therefore, remains largely unanswered. Of course, if we could accept the lack of diversification as inevitable, we might not have to try to understand it. For it is difficult to quarrel with the proposition that the future of such as area can be safely projected once we project the future for its one or two dominant industries. But here we may be caught on the horns of a dilemma. Suppose we project a sharp decline in the dominant industries along with a modest decline in the region's minor industries. True, the dominant industries will retard the growth of the region but in the process they will also decline in relative importance. The region will then become more diversified in its old age, so to speak. What then? Do we correct for the increased diversification? Does it open up new opportunities to the region?

The need to understand the whys and wherefores of diversification should therefore be quite apparent. This has led us to consider the question which I posed earlier: How does the growth of one industry in an area affect the area's suitability as a location for other industries?

But we are not yet ready to assert that the latter question has to be answered. We might avoid it if we could show that different degrees of diversification in areas of comparable size are due simply to the fact that some areas have a variety of locational advantages which makes them attractive to a variety of industries while other areas offer advantages only to a small number of industries. Observe for example the figures in Table 1 for Cleveland and Pittsburgh.

Pittsburgh is way ahead in glass and primary metals and leads also in food and electrical machinery. Cleveland, on the other hand, is ahead in textiles, printing, chemicals, fabricated metals, nonelectrical machinery, and transportation equipment. On the whole, Cleveland is a much more diversified manufacturing center. But maybe this is just the outcome of the process by which individual industries gravitate to those areas which are best for them. If Cleveland had attracted the 154,215 employees in primary metals, it might still look more like itself than like Pittsburgh in the rest of its manufacturing profile.

I cannot assert positively that this is an unsatisfactory way of approaching the matter, but I can suggest a number of reasons why I find it necessary to go beyond it. For one thing, this approach implies that location of industry is heavily determined by transportation factors or, as we say in our jargon, transport oriented. By this we mean that the location of markets and materials and the transport network determine the geographic distribu-

TABLE 1.   EMPLOYMENT IN SELECTED MANUFACTURING
INDUSTRIES, 1957

	Cleveland	Pittsburgh
Food	14,532	20,459
Textiles and apparel	14,130	3,550
Printing and publishing	14,618	10,042
Chemicals and products	17,959	6,823
Stone, clay and glass	3,260	21,372
Primary metals	46,894	154,215
Fabricated metals	38,378	31,298
Machinery, nonelectrical	52,552	23,534
Electrical machinery	20,746	27,652
Transportation equipment	55,570	11,047
Total	311,471	358,239

Source: Bureau of the Census, Annual Survey of Manufactures, 1957.

tion of industries. If a lot of industries end up in one place, presto, you have a diversified regional economy.

Nobody believes that the logic of location runs in these terms for the majority of manufacturing industries. My former colleague, Robert Lichtenberg, of the New York Study, after a painstaking review of factors influencing industrial location classified 50 per cent of American manufacturing as nontransport oriented. P. Sargent Florence has repeatedly emphasized in his writings that transport orientation is a minor influence in location. There is also a fairly general consensus that the proportion of industry which is transport oriented is diminishing as time goes on.

Once we recognize that variations in production costs are important determinants of location, we cannot avoid the consideration of interindustry factor cost relationships. Production costs are not given by nature, except that nature may influence the cost of energy and the cost of plant. These are trivial determinants alongside the influence exerted by the way in which a region's natural advantages are exploited. If we ask why are wage rates higher in one area than another, it is only in rare cases that nature will provide the answer. In most cases the explanation will run in historical terms; that is, in terms of the heritage of each region as it bears on labor supply.

For many purposes it is sufficient to recognize the difference in wage rates, and there is no compulsion to explain why it exists. A firm which is seeking a maximum profit location for a new plant might very well take the wage-rate differential as given — a type of behavior which fits so well the textbook model of a competitive firm. Even so, a conscientious consultant might very well post a warning signal. After all, a plant represents a twenty-year commitment. What is the wage differential likely to be twenty years hence? Be that as it may, it is certainly inappropriate to take wage-rate differentials as given in a twenty-year projection for a region. A static atomistic approach will not do for a problem in aggregate dynamics.

I also find the multiple-locational-advantages theory of diversification unsatisfactory for another reason. It permits us to assess an area's potential for growth only with reference to industries with known locational requirements. But in a projection, it is difficult enough to anticipate the bill of goods, let alone to project the locational needs of the industries which will be producing them. This may suggest that we ought to give up the ghost. Those who have this alternative are blessed. The rest of us have to seek ways to mitigate the curse. One is to develop the concept of a region's capacity for attracting new industries with considerable freedom of location from a transport point of view. If we are to develop such a concept, we need to probe into the region itself more deeply than we do when we locate industries one by one.

I have said enough — perhaps too much — about my reasons for raising these questions. I will now proceed to the main business of this paper, which is to offer some hypotheses about interindustry influences on factor costs. To begin with, I think that the net has to be spread a lot wider than most people assume. I propose to consider all the traditional categories: entrepreneurship, capital, labor, and land, in that order.

ENTREPRENEURSHIP

This is a production factor which, to my knowledge, no one has tried to price out at different locations. The implicit assumption, I suppose, is that the supply schedule of entrepreneurship is identical at all locations. Our colleagues studying international differences in growth reject this assumption explicitly. I am convinced that we need to reconsider its validity in regional economics.

When you tell a location analyst that a firm is where it is because its founders prefer to live there, he throws up his hands. Such cases, he claims, are outside his domain. Our own experience suggests that for many industries cost is almost invariant with location — or at least there is no "min min" location. Yet we are reluctant to treat such cases as random phenomena because we feel there are significant variations in the cost of entrepreneurship. Moreover, these differences may be large enough to offset other cost differences.

I came to this notion by reflecting on the differences between New York and Pittsburgh, but I hasten to say that area size is only one variable. For a given size of area, the entrepreneurial supply curve is also a function of certain traditions and elements of the social structure which are heavily influenced by the character of the area's historic specializations.

The proposition I offer is this: An industry which is competitively organized — in the neoclassical sense of the term "competition" — has more entrepreneurs per dollar of output than an industry which is organized along oligopolistic lines. The average establishment in the apparel industry, for example, has one-sixth as many employees as the average establishment in primary metals. Furthermore, multi-unit firms account for 82 per cent of the employment in primary metals, while they account for only 28 per cent of employment in apparel. Now you may have as much management per dollar of output in primary metals as you have in apparel, but you certainly do not have as many managers who are also risk-takers and this is my definition of an entrepreneur.

What is the consequence of this? My feeling is that you do not breed as many entrepreneurs per capita in families allied with steel as you do in families allied with apparel, using these two industries for illustrative purposes only. The son of a salaried executive is less likely to be sensitive to opportunities wholly unrelated to his father's field than the son of an independent entrepreneur. True, the entrepreneur's son is more likely to think of taking over his father's business. My guess is, however, that the tradition of risk-bearing is, on the whole, a more potent influence in broadening one's perspective.

I think I have formulated a proposition which can at least theoretically be tested, although I confess that I have not tested it yet. For all I know, this may already be a well-established proposition in entrepreneurial history.

But if an oligopolistic environment has a lower entrepreneurial birth rate, there remains the question of how receptive it is to the in-migration of entrepreneurs. Here, too, I would argue that the competitively organized area has an edge. Receptivity as measured by factor costs we shall discuss under separate headings later on. What I have in mind now is receptivity as it relates to the entrepreneur's "utility function." There is an aura of second-class citizenship attached to the small businessman in an environment dominated by big business. It manifests itself in many small ways, such as the kinds of social clubs he can belong to, the residential areas he will comfortably fit into, the business organizations he can join, and so forth. The ease of entry, to borrow a concept from industrial organization, is considerably greater in an environment dominated — not dominated, to be more exact — by small firm industries. I am not sure that we can satisfactorily test this notion, but I am hopeful.

CAPITAL

Many of the same observations are relevant to regional differences in the availability of capital. Here, too, we are dealing with a factor whose cost is typically assumed to be invariant with respect to location. This is surely not so. It is true that capital is almost perfectly mobile, provided the probability distribution of returns is approximately known. G.M. and U.S. Steel can raise capital almost anywhere with equal ease. But a small firm embarking on a new enterprise will find a much more receptive ear over the home counter than it will over-the-counter in "foreign" places. The cost of transferring confidence may be high enough to give us a capital-supply function which has distance as an important independent variable.

Once we admit of such immobility, it becomes relevant to inquire into differences in local capital supply among areas. Again the industrial organization of the dominant industries strikes me as an important variable. A major source of capital to new firms in general is the undistributed profit and unexpended depreciation allowance of old firms. Now, the surplus capital which accumulates inside large multiplant companies, I would argue, is more mobile interregionally within the company than intraregionally outside the company. A large corporation is more likely to respond to investment opportunities in its traditional activity at other locations than to investment opportunities at home in unrelated industries. The small firm, by contrast, is more likely to make its surplus capital available to other local enterprise in another industry than to a distant enterprise in the same industry. (Actually, I have overstated the case to avoid a complex formulation. All I need to argue is that the marginal rate of substitution between local and foreign outlets is greater [smaller] for the large multiplant firm [small firm]. Given an equivalent array of investment opportunities at home, the surplus capital of the multiplant industry is more likely to "leak" out to other areas.)

The commercial banks, of course, also play a vital role in the initial financing of new business. Are banks in one area more receptive than banks in another area to the demands of new business and, if so, are these differences in attitude shaped by the industrial traditions of the area? I say yes, on both counts. My conviction on this point is based less on deductive than on inductive reasoning. I have been told that this is the case. Having been told, I can think of some fairly good reasons why this might be the case. When banks cater to a competitively organized industry, they are more likely to accept the insurance principle of making money, not on each customer, but on the average customer. If you have U.S. Steel and Westinghouse on your rolls, you do not have to learn to make money on the insurance principle.

In the present state of my knowledge, I am not too optimistic about being able to test these hypotheses empirically. However, I am not prepared to pronounce them as untestable. This is an altogether too easy way out. I believe if we think hard enough, we can spell out some corollaries which, if we dig hard enough, we can subject to empirical test.

LABOR

Now we come to what most will assume and I am prepared to concede is the cost factor, which is most sensitive to interindustry influence. Yet, even here, I suspect I will be spreading my net farther than most people would.

First, the wage level. My colleague on the Pittsburgh Study, Mel Bers, is exploring this question in great detail. The presumption that the wage level in the dominant industry influences the wage level in other industries is one which no one can seriously question. I am confident that Bers's research will throw more light on the network of interdependence than anything that has been done so far. Bers is also immersed in the study of the influence of labor organization in the dominant industry on the structure of wages in the region. These two issues are inseparable in his framework.

But there are other influences relating to labor cost and supply which are not generally recognized. Bers found, for example, that the rate of participation of married women in the labor force in the Pittsburgh region is far below the average for metropolitan areas. When standardized for industry mix, however, it turns out that the rate is as high as you would expect it to be. The question arises, therefore, do these women represent a potential supply or not? Why are not female-labor-using industries attracted by the surplus? Wages aside, there are at least two other factors relating to the character of the dominant industries which influence the outcome.

The first is the dispersion within the region of the plants of our dominant industries. The ratio of central city employment to SMA [Standard Metropolitan Statistical Area] employment in manufacturing is much lower in Pittsburgh than in any of the large SMA's. Outside the Central City, the gradient in Pittsburgh is also flatter. The reasons are obvious. Our industries could not be piled up one on top of another as in the garment district even if our land were flat. The topography encourages still greater dispersion. But the importance of this for our purposes is that the early dispersion of manufacturing (plus the dispersion of mining) led to a dispersal of population which is also unmatched among our large SMA's. To the extent that pools of female labor are relevant to industrial location, Pittsburgh is at a disadvantage because a greater radius is required to form a pool of a given size. One must bear in mind that the areas in which the plants of the dominant industries operate are not exactly the most desirable as sites for other kinds of industry. (We shall return to this point later on.)

The second point has to do with the work schedule of the man in the family. Steel is a three-shift industry. The typical worker is not assigned to a particular shift for an indefinite period. Instead he works from 8:00 to 4:00 for some time, then 4:00 to 12:00 for some time, then 12:00 to 8:00 for some time. He also has to put in his share of weekends. It is reasonable to suppose that under these conditions the housewife is somewhat less willing to work than under ordinary conditions. Taken together, these factors tend to dissipate some of the labor force advantages we normally attribute to SMA's. And they are consequences of characteristics of the dominant industries.

LAND

We normally assume that an SMA is large enough in area to nullify any considerations of site availability as a location factor except for industries with very special requirements like steel and chemicals. In general, I think this is a sensible approach. Nevertheless, I feel compelled to attach some importance to the impact of an industry's operations on the quality of the air and water in the surrounding area. Pittsburgh, as you all know, was notorious until recent years for its smoke and dust. There were three causes for this condition. The principal one was the use of soft coal as fuel in households and industry. A second was the steel industry. And a third was the railroads with their steam engines. All this has changed now and I do not mind using this forum as an opportunity to plug the radical improvement in the quality of Pittsburgh's air. A white shirt will now stay white in Pittsburgh for as long as it will in any city in the country. But it will take some time to work off our reputation. And furthermore, at a time when the reputation was founded in fact, it was bound to exercise a restraining influence on the growth of subsidiary industries in the region.

INTERMEDIATE GOODS AND SERVICES

So much for the primary factors of production. I said earlier that location analysts have paid attention to a dominant industry's impact on the location of other industries which are oriented to the supply of the product of the dominant industry. But agglomeration is nourished more by the availability of a wide range of goods and services created in the first instance by the growth of the dominant industries. Transportation is the classic illustration of this phenomena. One industry attracts the service, and a second industry coming in finds that the service is available at costs which are lower than they would be in virgin territory. The second industry also finds already in existence a whole community of suppliers of business services such as legal, accounting, duplicating, etc.

The question I raise is whether the emergence of these services and their availability to other industries depends on the character of these industries which trigger development in the first instance. I think much depends on the internal organization of these industries. Large firms incorporate many of these services within their own operations because they can achieve scale economies within the firm. They are much more fully integrated and therefore depend less on outside suppliers. On the one hand, this means that, dollar for dollar, their business is less of a stimulus to the creation of a community of independent suppliers. On the other hand, the new entrant is not likely to find that the company is anxious to spread its fixed costs by making its services available to outsiders.

Again, consider the classic example of external economies: transport services. A firm which operates its own truck fleet on an exempt basis is specifically forbidden by the ICC to transport freight as a common carrier. Imagine then that you have two communities of equal size. In one of these, all the firms rely on common carriage. Hence service to and from a wide variety of places is available to all comers. In the other community, every firm has its private truck fleet. True, the roads are built and this helps a lot. But there is no service available to the new firm coming in unless it starts big.

We do know that Pittsburgh is not up to par in employment in ancillary services. This is indicated by a calculation of location quotients based on the 1950 Census of Population. The Duncans in their recent book, *Metropolis and Region,* also found that Pittsburgh had less than the national average per capita employment in service industries broadly defined. Only Detroit among the SMA's of 1,000,000 population or more shared this characteristic with Pittsburgh. It goes without saying, that much of my reasoning is applicable to Detroit as well.

SUMMARY AND CONCLUSIONS

It should be apparent by now that what I am reaching for is the specification of a function which relates external economies and diseconomies to industry structure, size being held constant. My feeling is that we have been too prone to associate external economies and diseconomies with size. We have been disturbed at not being able to derive a satisfactory correlation between the two. What I have tried to do is explore some of the residual variation around the size function. I recognize the difficulties of adequately formulating and testing these notions. But I do not think we can afford to ignore them because they are difficult if, as I maintain, they are relevant to an understanding of the dynamics of area development.

To come back to my first point: I think we are not using the optimal combination of tools in regional analysis. We know we can do a lot more to refine the methods we use to trap what I have called the demand side of interdependence. We need bigger and better regional input-output tables, regional capital coefficients, regional consumption functions. But we are not equating marginal returns in all directions if we do not, at the same time, push vigorously on the supply side of the problem.

I said we need new tools in regional analysis. I am prepared to modify that statement in favor of this one. We need to make better use of some old tools which we have not yet applied very extensively to regional analysis. We need to work out the regional implications of market organization.

FURTHER READINGS

Chinitz, Benjamin. *City and Suburb: The Economics of Metropolitan Growth.* Englewood Cliffs, N.J.: Prentice-Hall, 1965.

Due, John F. "Studies of State-Local Tax Influences on Location of Industry." *National Tax Journal* 14 (June 1961).

Engerman, Stanley. "Regional Aspects of Stabilization Policy." In *Essays in Fiscal Federalism,* edited by Richard A. Musgrave. Washington, D.C.: The Brookings Institution, 1965.

Hirsch, Werner Z., ed. *Regional Accounts for Policy Decisions.* Baltimore: Johns Hopkins University Press, for Resources for the Future, Inc., 1966.

Isard, Walter, et al. *Methods of Regional Analysis, An Introduction to Regional Science.* Massachusetts Institute of Technology and John Wiley and Sons, Inc., 1960.

Meyer, John R. "Regional Economics: A Survey." *American Economic Review* 53 (1963).

Tiebout, Charles M. "The Community Economic Base Study." Supplementary paper no. 16. New York: Committee for Economic Development, December 1962.

Chapter 3

LOCATION AND LAND USE

When an individual decides to live in an urban area, how does he choose the particular metropolitan area and his residential site? Many factors influence his choice: the availability of employment and business opportunities; the availability of housing; the level of public services; the diversity of consumer opportunities; the existence of climatic, recreational, natural, and cultural amenities; the location of friends and relatives; the social attitudes of the area.

How do these different factors in residential site choice translate themselves into a location for a city and a pattern of land use within it? An individual's interest in economic opportunity depends upon where such opportunities lie. What features make one site a more productive location for a city than another site? An important but declining factor in the productivity of a locality is its nearness to major transportation facilities.

In earliest day, cities were located on rivers and harbors because the least expensive way of shipping most goods and the only way of importing goods from other countries was by water. As railroads developed, a city located at a major railroad terminal could enjoy inexpensive transportation. A location nearer markets or raw materials reduces transportation costs, making a locality more productive and providing employment and business opportunities.

Land is valuable as a location for a city relative to the costs of transporting raw materials, intermediate goods, final products, and people. Within a city, land values and land use are also related to travel and transportation. In the suggested reading by Leon Moses and Harold Williamson, there is a discussion of the city's location at a rail terminal as an important factor in determining its early growth. They also consider the influence of the truck and the automobile on the patterns of land use within metropolitan areas. The reading by Edwin Mills adds cultural and climatic amenities to important resources for a city. In the future the availability of amenities to cities will undoubtedly grow in importance. 39

Several factors determine the demand for urban land and the pattern of land values and uses thereby generated. What determines the value of land within a metropolitan area? Assuming that city land is not to be used for agriculture and that all city land is alike except for location (hence abstracting ourselves from differences in elevation, foliage, view, water availability), all land would be equally productive or fertile for office, home, or manufacturing use if transportation was costless. A more productive location reduces the cost and time of travel and communications for its occupant. A site that lowers or minimizes travel costs increases the desirability or profitability of residences and firms on that site. Users are therefore willing to pay more for homes, factories, and offices at the preferred location. The difference in rents for otherwise equal offices or residences is equal to the differences in locational advantage (transportation costs) associated with the site. Considering the whole population of a city, it is not unreasonable to view individual travel as random from point to point within the city. To the extent that this is so, the geographic center of the metropolis will be the point of minimum cost of such travel. Consequently, tenants and owners are willing to pay the highest rents or purchase prices for central city structures. Core-centered mass transit facilities further strengthen the central city's locational advantage.

At any location, structures are built until the rising cost of greater density or height is equal to the rent. Since central city structures command the highest rents, they will be built to the greatest density (height) in the metropolis. Because well-located structures command the highest rent and are built at greater density, larger economic profits or producer's surplus is earned on them. Consequently, developers are willing to pay more for a site (land) the more advantageous its location. In competition, developers will bid up the value of better-located sites until the value of all sites reflects their locational advantage, which is equal to the surplus accruing to the land. Central city land thereby becomes the most valuable in the metropolitan area. Simultaneously, the high value of central city land causes its use to be economized by high-density occupation — high-rise offices, commercial, and residential structures. (For a more detailed discussion of this mechanism see my "Economics of Property Taxes and Land Values" [Cambridge, Mass., 1971].)

Location away from the core raises the cost and time involved in travel to and communications with the core, and hence the entire metropolis. Correspondingly, land values fall continuously as distance from the central city increases. Land values diminish as one moves further from the central city. This change is called the *land price gradient*.

Faced with a declining land price gradient (as analyzed here and in William Alonso's article) but with rising travel and communication costs at greater distances from the core, firms and individuals compare their relative preference for more land versus less travel and locate at a distance from the city where their relative preferences are proportional to the lessening price of land. Activities located away from the core include single-story, mass-production manufacturing facilities along with local retailing, professional, and service enterprises. All these activities can take advantage of the large quantities of inexpensive land found as one moves away from the city's center. (The quantity of land available at any distance from the core increases in proportion to the square of the distance from the center.) If we regard land and location as separate factors of production, these suburban activities use relatively much land and relatively little location (transportation and communications). Firms that use very little land, such as communications, finance, and central administrations remain in the central city. These organizations are location (transportation and communication) rather than land intensive.

John Meyer, John Kain, and Martin Wohl explain that development of the motor vehicle has lowered the cost of travel and therefore the economies of agglomeration in the central city, raising the value of suburban land and diminishing the steepness of the land value or price gradient. Many families and firms desiring larger quantities of land have taken advantage of the inexpensive motor-vehicle transportation and have left the central city. Their departures have brought about lower central-city densities. The interstate highway system has further increased the attractiveness of the suburbs to mass-production manufacturing.

In spite of high central city land values, it is often rational for low-income dwellers to reside in the city (although institutional and social restrictions have certainly exaggerated this tendency). Since many low-income families find commutation from the suburbs by private automobiles or commuter railroads relatively expensive, they choose the central city with its inexpensive mass transit. Low-income families thereby have incentive to outbid higher-income residents for urban land and older residential structures, then occupy them at higher densities. This pattern of lower-income families outbidding higher-income ones for urban land as higher-income families move further and further from the central city has continued since the 1800's. Some upper-income families have always remained in the most prestigious central city locations, contrary to the general pattern.

Suburbanization has not continued totally uninterrupted. Upper-income families have been returning to our cities, because their preference for leisure and urban culture has risen over their preference for land. The return of upper-income groups has sometimes created a land-use conflict between upper- and lower-income groups. The low-income groups experience great difficulty in moving to suburbs, partly because of discrimination, and find themselves being outbid for the urban land they previously held. In the future, as low-income groups (black and white) find increased housing opportunities in suburbs and a greater portion of our population locates in the lower-density cities of the southeast and the southwest, the conflict will probably be alleviated.

TRANSPORTATION AND PATTERNS OF URBAN DEVELOPMENT

AN AGGREGATIVE MODEL OF RESOURCE ALLOCATION IN A METROPOLITAN AREA[1]

Edwin S. Mills

INTRODUCTION

The purpose of this paper is to put forth a simplified, aggregative model that will help to explain the sizes and structures of urban areas. The viewpoint taken is that the basic characteristics of cities are to be understood as market responses to opportunities for production and income. Properties of production functions are at the heart of the explanation of city size and structure in the model developed here, in much the way that properties of production functions are at the heart of modern neoclassical growth theory.

The general ideas that motivate the selection of the model developed below are commonplace in the voluminous recent literature on urban economics and geography. It has frequently been observed that the large size and rapid recent growth of urban areas are responses to income and em-

Edwin S. Mills is Professor of Economics, Johns Hopkins University.

Reprinted with permission from Edwin S. Mills, "Transportation and Patterns of Urban Development: An Aggregative Model of Resource Allocation in a Metropolitan Area," *American Economic Review* (May 1967), pp. 197–200.

[1] The research reported in this paper was supported by a grant from Resources for the Future. Part of the work was done while the author was in residence at the Rand Corporation. I have benefited greatly from an unpublished manuscript by Richard Muth [2].

ployment opportunities provided there. It is but a small step from this observation to the assumption that the conditions of production differ in crucial respects as between urban and non-urban areas and as between urban areas of different size. Likewise, it is a common observation on the structure of cities that the nature and intensity of land use vary greatly from city to city and from one part of a city to another. Again, it is but a small step to recognize that a major element of factor substitution is involved in this phenomenon and to analyze models whose production functions will explain the observed factor substitution. Indeed, factor substitution is the most dramatic characteristic of urban structure. For example, the relative price of housing varies somewhat from one part of a city to another, but such variation is small compared with the variation in the relative prices of factors used to produce housing — principally land and structures. It is not unusual for land values to vary by a factor of from ten to one hundred within a distance of ten or twenty miles in a large metropolitan area. And the tremendous variation in capital-land ratios — from skyscrapers and high-rise apartments downtown to single story factories and single family homes on two-acre lots in the suburbs — is the market's response to these dramatic variations in relative factor prices.

The model developed below is intended to shed light on these and other factors. To keep the mathematics within manageable proportions, it is necessary to make significant compromises with reality. In the work that follows, two major areas of compromise can be identified. First, the demand side has been slighted almost to the point of exclusion. This has been necessary in order to focus attention on what seem to me to be the crucial factors; namely, input substitution and technology. Second, the degree of aggregation is uncomfortably high. Even with these two areas of compromise, the model is quite cumbersome. Its solution is pragmatic and inelegant.

A WORLD WITHOUT CITIES

It is clear that the existence, size, and structure of cities are closely related to transportation costs. The avoidance of transportation costs is not, however, a sufficient reason for the existence of cities. Indeed, it may help in focusing ideas to state explicitly a set of assumptions — each of which finds a respectable place in important economic models — which imply that there would be no cities.

Consider a general equilibrium model in which an arbitrary number of goods is produced either as inputs or for final consumption. The only non-produced goods are land and labor, each of which is assumed to be homogeneous. Assume that each production function has constant returns to scale and that all input and output markets are competitive. Utility functions have the usual properties and have as arguments amounts of inputs supplied and products consumed. Under these circumstances, consumers would spread themselves over the land at a uniform density to avoid bidding up the price of land above that of land available elsewhere. Adjacent to each consumer would be all the industries necessary — directly or indirectly — to satisfy the demands of that customer. Constant returns assures us that production could take place at an arbitrarily small scale without loss of efficiency. In this way, all transportation costs could be avoided without any need to agglomerate economic activity.

AN ABSTRACT DESCRIPTION OF A CITY

The two assumptions in the previous section most in conflict with reality are that land is homogeneous and that production functions all have constant returns to scale. Relaxation of either is sufficient to justify the existence of cities. Reasons for relaxing them and for the alternatives to them that are employed below are discussed in the next two paragraphs.

If some land is more productive than other land, it will pay to concentrate production on the better land, thus producing a city. The location of almost all U.S. cities can be understood in terms of land heterogeneity, most having been located near cheap water transportation. There are two ways to represent this heterogeneity in formal models. One is to assume that several variables related to land enter the production functions — natural resources, topography, climate, etc. — and that these variables are available in different amounts at different sites. Another is to assume just one land input, but to assume that different sites have associated with them different efficiency parameters in production functions. For a variety of reasons, the latter representation is chosen in this paper. With this convention, I would say that Baltimore's location results from the fact that some goods — especially transportation services — can be produced more efficiently there than further inland. The limited availability of desirable land will show up as decreasing returns as the amount of land used increases, forcing resort to less and less productive land. I will summarize this assumption by saying that efficiency parameters require locational indexes.

Location theorists have identified a variety of factors that lead to "agglomeration economies." The most important and best articulated of these factors is increasing returns to scale. This leads to agglomeration, not only of the activity in question, but also of other activities vertically related to it. Among other sources of agglomeration economies, most can probably be represented approximately as scale economies, at least in an aggregative model. Provided that the notion of scale economies is interpreted broadly, so as to include indivisibilities, it is undoubtedly important in determining city sizes. There are large numbers of specialized business and consumer services for which the per business or per capita demand is so small that a large city is needed to support even a few suppliers.

It is obvious that either locational effects on efficiency parameters or increasing returns will justify the existence of a city. Furthermore, conditions of production impose a finite limit on the efficient size of the city. Suppose we consider the possibility of doubling the population of a city by doubling the height of every building. If this were feasible and if twice as many people now traveled between each pair of points as before, then it would lead to just twice the demand for transportation as before. But if transportation requires land as an input, it must use more land after the doubling of population than before. Thus, some land previously used for buildings must now be used for transportation, thus requiring new buildings at the edge of the city. But the edge of the city has now moved out, and some people must make longer trips than before, requiring more transportation inputs. Thus, a doubling of the city's population requires more than doubling transportation inputs. For a city of sufficient size, this "diseconomy" in transportation will more than balance any economy of size resulting from increasing returns in production. Another factor that entails the same result is the fact that, as the city's population grows, efficient production of goods requires the use of somewhat more land as well as of somewhat higher structures. At least this is true of any production function that has diminishing returns to factor proportions. Consequently, as a city grows, it moves out as well as up, and this entails diseconomy in transportation resources.

It was suggested above that the exhaustion of favorable land may show up as decreasing returns to scale in production. On the other hand, it was also stated that increasing returns in production is the most important agglomeration economy. It is thus important to formulate a model that is consistent with either increasing or decreasing returns to scale and to let the data tell us which assumption is appropriate.

A THEORY OF THE URBAN LAND MARKET

William Alonso

The early theory of rent and location concerned itself primarily with agricultural land. This was quite natural, for Ricardo and Malthus lived in an agricultural society. The foundations of the formal spatial analysis of agri-

William Alonso is Professor of Regional Planning, University of California, Berkeley.

Reprinted with permission from William Alonso, "A Theory of the Urban Land Market," *Papers and Proceedings of the Regional Science Association* 6 (1960), pp. 149–159.

cultural rent and location are found in the work of J. von Thunen, who said, without going into detail, that the urban land market operated under the same principles.[1] As cities grew in importance, relatively little attention was paid to the theory of urban rents. Even the great Marshall provided interesting but only random insights, and no explicit theory of the urban land market and urban locations was developed.

Since the beginning of the twentieth century there has been considerable interest in the urban land market in America. R. M. Hurd[2] in 1903 and R. Haig[3] in the twenties tried to create a theory of urban land by following von Thunen. However, their approach copied the form rather than the logic of agricultural theory, and the resulting theory can be shown to be insufficient on its own premises. In particular, the theory failed to consider residences, which constitute the preponderant land use in urban areas.

Yet there are interesting problems that a theory of urban land must consider. There is, for instance, a paradox in American cities: the poor live near the center, on expensive land, and the rich on the periphery, on cheap land. On the logical side, there are also aspects of great interest, but which increase the difficulty of the analysis. When a purchaser acquires land, he acquires two goods (land and location) in only one transaction, and only one payment is made for the combination. He could buy the same quantity of land at another location, or he could buy more, or less land at the same location. In the analysis, one encounters, as well, a negative good (distance) with positive costs (commuting costs); or, conversely, a positive good (accessibility) with negative costs (savings in commuting). In comparison with agriculture, the urban case presents another difficulty. In agriculture, the location is extensive: many square miles may be devoted to one crop. In the urban case the site tends to be much smaller, and the location may be regarded as a dimensionless point rather than an area. Yet the thousands or millions of dimensionless points which constitute the city, when taken together, cover extensive areas. How can these dimensionless points be aggregated into two-dimensional space?

Here I will present a non-mathematical over-view, without trying to give it full precision, of the long and rather complex mathematical analysis which constitutes a formal theory of the urban land market.[4] It is a static model

---

[1] Johan von Thunen, *Der Isolierte Staat in Beziehung auf Landwirtschaft und Nationalekonomie*, 1st vol., 1826, 3d vol. and new edition, 1863.

[2] Richard M. Hurd, *Principles of City Land Values*, N.Y.: The Record and Guide, 1903.

[3] Robert M. Haig, "Toward an Understanding of the Metropolis," *Quarterly Journal of Economics*, 40: 3, May 1926; and *Regional Survey of New York and Its Environs*, N. Y.: New York City Plan Commission, 1927.

[4] A full development of the theory is presented in my doctoral dissertation, *A Model of the Urban Land Market: Locations and Densities of Dwellings and Businesses*, University of Pennsylvania, 1960.

in which change is introduced by comparative statics. And it is an economic model: it speaks of economic men, and it goes without saying that real men and social groups have needs, emotions, and desires which are not considered here. This analysis uses concepts which fit with agricultural rent theory in such a way that urban and rural land uses may be considered at the same time, in terms of a single theory. Therefore, we must examine first a very simplified model of the agricultural land market.

AGRICULTURAL MODEL

In this model, the farmers are grouped around a single market, where they sell their products. If the product is wheat, and the produce of one acre of wheat sells for $100 at the market while the costs of production are $50 per acre, a farmer growing wheat at the market would make a profit of $50 per acre. But if he is producing at some distance — say, 5 miles — and it costs him $5 per mile to ship an acre's product, his transport costs will be $25 per acre. His profits will be equal to value minus production costs minus shipping charges: $100 - 50 - 25 = \$25$. This relation may be shown diagrammatically (see Figure 1). At the market, the farmer's profits are $50, and 5 miles out, $25; at intermediate distance, he will receive intermediate profits. Finally, at a distance of 10 miles from the market, his production costs plus shipping charges will just equal the value of his produce at the market. At distances greater than 10 miles, the farmer would operate at a loss.

In this model, the profits derived by the farmers are tied directly to their location. If the functions of farmer and landowner are viewed as separate, farmers will bid rents for land according to the profitability of the location. The profits of the farmer will therefore be shared with the landowner through rent payments. As farmers bid against each other for the more profitable locations, until farmers' profits are everywhere the same ("normal" profits), what we have called profits becomes rent. Thus, the curve in Figure 1, which we derived as a farmers' profit curve, once we distinguish between the roles of the farmer and the landowner, becomes a bid rent function, representing the price or rent per acre that farmers will be willing to pay for land at the different locations.

We have shown that the slope of the rent curve will be fixed by the transport costs on the produce. The level of the curve will be set by the price of the produce at the market. Examine Figure 2. The lower curve is that of Figure 1, where the price of wheat is $100 at the market, and production costs are $50. If demand increases, and the price of wheat at the market rises to $125 (while production and transport costs remain constant), profits or bid rent at the market will be $75; at 5 miles, $50; $25 at 10

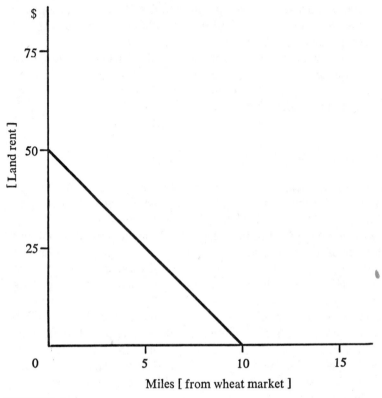

FIGURE 1

[Figure 1 assumes that all land will be used at the same intensity, thereby causing the cost of producing wheat to be the same at all locations. Realistically and theoretically, land near the market will be used more intensively (more labor and fertilizer per acre) until the marginal cost of the last bushel of wheat grown per acre is equal to wheat's value at the location. The bushels grown per acre will be one at ten miles from the market and will increase toward the center. The profits from growing wheat at the center will be the producer's surplus (the difference between the value and cost of wheat produced per unit land at the location) from producing wheat at the center. Not only will the producer's surplus per bushel of wheat (and its value) be higher at the market than at any other location, but the number of bushels per acre will also be highest. Therefore, the producer's surplus will not only be higher but will accrue to a larger output. At ten miles from the market, one hundred bushels of wheat per acre would be produced at a cost of $50.00 and have a value of $50.00, setting the value of land at zero. At five miles from the market, 150 bushels of wheat per acre would be produced at a cost of $80.00 and have a value of $112.50, leaving a surplus of $32.50 to be capitalized into the value of land. Finally, at the market 200 bushels of wheat per acre might be produced at a cost of $125.00 and have a value of $200.00, yielding a value of land per acre of $15,000. The value of land (or rent or price of a square foot of structure) would rise faster than the value of a bushel of wheat and produce a steeper (nonlinear) land value gradient than the wheat price gradient. For a further explanation, see Ronald E. Grieson, *The Economics of Property Taxes and Land Value.* — Ed.]

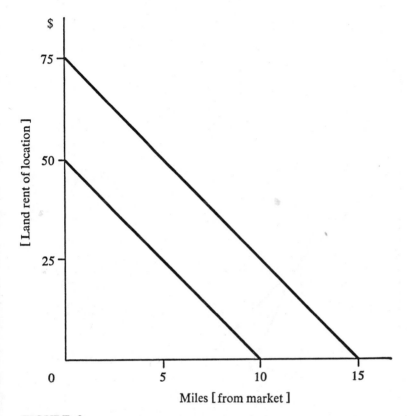

FIGURE 2

[Figure 2 is based upon the assumption of a fixed density of structure (or crop growth) per unit land. If density and the cost functions for different land uses (structures or crops) are allowed to vary, different structures renting at different prices per square foot (crops selling at different prices) could exist simultaneously in the same neighborhood. — Ed.]

miles, and zero at 15 miles. Thus, each bid rent curve is a function of rent vs. distance, but there is a family of such curves, the level of any one determined by the price of the produce at the market, higher prices setting higher curves.

Consider now the production of peas. Assume that the price at the market of one acre's production of peas is $150, the costs of production are $75, and the transport costs per mile are $10. These conditions will yield curve *MN* in Figure 3, where bid rent by pea farmers at the market is $75 per acre, 5 miles from the market $25, and zero at 7.5 miles. Curve *RS* represents bid rents by wheat farmers, at a price of $100 for wheat. It will be seen that pea farmers can bid higher rents in the range of 0 to 5 miles from

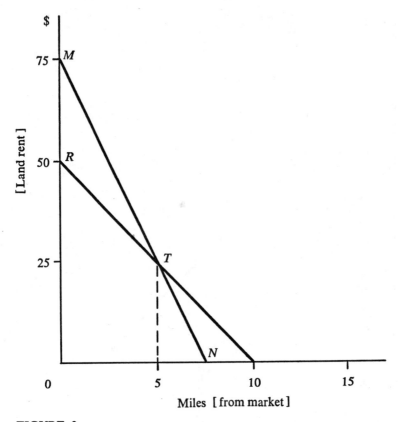

FIGURE 3

the market; farther out, wheat farmers can bid higher rents. Therefore, pea farming will take place in the ring from 0 to 5 miles from the market, and wheat farming in the ring from 5 to 10 miles. Segments *MT* of the bid rent curve of pea farming and *TS* of wheat farming will be the effective rents, while segments *RT* and *TN* represent unsuccessful bids.

The price of the product is determined by the supply-demand relations at the market. If the region between zero and 5 miles produces too many peas, the price of the product will drop, and a lower bid rent curve for pea farming will come into effect, so that pea farming will be practiced to some distance less than 5 miles.

Abstracting this view of the agricultural land market, we have that:

(1) land uses determine land values, through competitive bidding among farmers;

(2) land values distribute land uses, according to their ability to pay;

(3) the steeper curves capture the central locations. (This point is a simplified one for simple, well-behaved curves.

Abstracting the process now *from* agriculture, we have:

(1) for each user of land (e.g., wheat farmer) a family of bid rent functions is derived, such that the user is indifferent as to his location along any *one* of these functions (because the farmer, who is the decision-maker in this case, finds that profits are everywhere the same, i.e., normal, as long as he remains on one curve);

(2) the equilibrium rent at any location is found by comparing the bids of the various potential users and choosing the highest;

(3) equilibrium quantities of land are found by selecting the proper bid rent curve for each user (in the agricultural case, the curve which equates supply and demand for the produce).

BUSINESS

We shall now consider the urban businessman, who, we shall assume, makes his decisions so as to maximize profits. A bid rent curve for the business-man, then, will be one along which profits are everywhere the same: the decision-maker will be indifferent as to his location along such a curve.

Profit may be defined as the remainder from the volume of business after operating costs and land costs have been deducted. Since in most cases the volume of business of a firm as well as its operating costs will vary with its location, the rate of change of the bid rent curve will bear no simple relation to transport costs (as it did in agriculture). The rate of change of the total bid rent for a firm, where profits are constant by definition, will be equal to the rate of change in the volume of business minus the rate of change in operating costs. Therefore the slope of the bid rent curve, the values of which are in terms of dollars per unit of land, will be equal to the rate of change in the volume of business minus the rate of change in operating costs, divided by the area occupied by the establishment.

A different level of profits would yield a different bid rent curve. The higher the bid rent curve, the lower the profits, since land is more expen-sive. There will be a highest curve, where profits will be zero. At higher land rents the firm could only operate at a loss.

Thus we have, as in the case of the farmer, a family of bid rent curves, along the path of any one of which the decision-maker — in this case, the businessman — is indifferent. Whereas in the case of the farmer the level of the curve is determined by the price of the produce, while profits are in all cases "normal," i.e., the same, in the case of the urban firm, the level of the curve is determined by the level of the profits, and the price of its prod-ucts may be regarded for our purposes as constant.

RESIDENTIAL

The household differs from the farmer and the urban firm in that satisfaction rather than profits is the relevant criterion of optional location. A consumer, given his income and his pattern of tastes, will seek to balance the costs and bother of commuting against the advantages of cheaper land with increasing distance from the center of the city and the satisfaction of more space for living. When the individual consumer faces a given pattern of land costs, his equilibrium location and the size of his site will be in terms of the marginal changes of these variables.

The bid rent curves of the individual will be such that, for any given curve, the individual will be equally satisfied at every location at the price set by the curve. Along any bid rent curve, the price the individual will bid for land will decrease with distance from the center at a rate just sufficient to produce an income effect which will balance to his satisfaction the increased costs of commuting and the bother of a long trip. This slope may be expressed quite precisely in mathematical terms, but it is a complex expression, the exact interpretation of which is beyond the scope of this paper.

Just as different prices of the produce set different levels for the bid rent curves of the farmer, and different levels of profit for the urban firm, different levels of satisfaction correspond to the various levels of the family of bid rent curves of the individual household. The higher curves obviously yield less satisfaction because a higher price is implied, so that, at any given location, the individual will be able to afford less land and other goods.

INDIVIDUAL EQUILIBRIUM

It is obvious that families of bid rent curves are in many respects similar to indifference curve mappings. However, they differ in some important ways. Indifference curves map a path of indifference (equal satisfaction) between combinations of quantities of two goods. Bid rent functions map an indifference path between the price of one good (land) and quantities of another and strange type of good, distance from the center of the city. Whereas indifference curves refer only to tastes and not to budget, in the case of households, bid rent functions are derived both from budget and taste considerations. In the case of the urban firm, they might be termed isoprofit curves. A more superficial difference is that, whereas the higher indifference curves are the preferred ones, it is the lower bid rent curves that yield greater profits or satisfaction. However, bid rent curves may be used in a manner analogous to that of indifference curves to find the equilibrium location and land price for the resident or the urban firm.

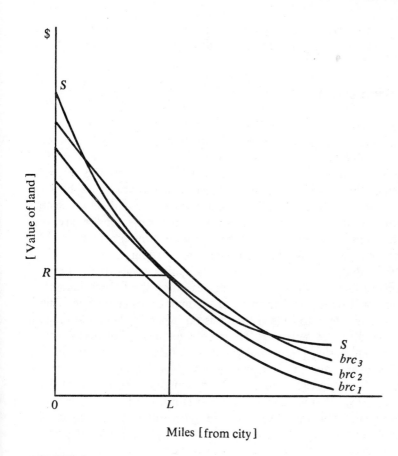

FIGURE 4

Assume you have been given a bid rent mapping of a land use, whether business or residential (curves $brc_{1, 2, 3,}$ etc., in Figure 4). Superimpose on the same diagram the actual structure of land prices in the city (curve SS). The decision-maker will wish to reach the lowest possible bid rent curve. Therefore, he will choose that point at which the curve of actual prices (SS) will be tangent to the lowest of the bid rent curves with which it comes in contact (brc_2). At this point will be the equilibrium location (L) and the equilibrium land rent (R) for this user of land. If he is a businessman, he will have maximized profits; if he is a resident, he will have maximized satisfaction.

Note that to the left of this point of equilibrium (toward the center of the city) the curve of actual prices is steeper than the bid rent curve; to the right of this point (away from the center) it is less steep. This is another aspect of the rule we noted in the agricultural model: the land uses with steeper bid rent curves capture the central locations.

MARKET EQUILIBRIUM

We now have, conceptually, families of bid rent curves for all three types of land uses. We also know that the steeper curves will occupy the more central locations. Therefore, if the curves of the various users are ranked by steepness, they will also be ranked in terms of their accessibility from the center of the city in the final solution. Thus, if the curves of the business firm are steeper than those of residences, and the residential curves steeper than the agricultural, there will be business at the center of the city, surrounded by residences, and these will be surrounded by agriculture.

This reasoning applies as well within land use groupings. For instance, it can be shown that, given two individuals of similar tastes, both of whom prefer living at low densities, if their incomes differ, the bid rent curves of the wealthier will be flatter than those of the man of lower income. Therefore, the poor will tend to central locations on expensive land and the rich to cheaper land on the periphery. The reason for this is not that the poor have greater purchasing power, but rather that they have steeper bid rent curves. This stems from the fact that, at any given location, the poor can buy less land than the rich, and since only a small quantity of land is involved, changes in its price are not as important for the poor as the costs and inconvenience of commuting. The rich, on the other hand, buy greater quantities of land, and are consequently affected by changes in its price to a greater degree. In other words, because of variations in density among different levels of income, accessibility behaves as an inferior good.

Thus far, through ranking the bid rent curves by steepness, we have found the relative rankings of prices and locations, but not the actual prices, locations, or densities. It will be remembered that in the agricultural case equilibrium levels were brought about by changes in the price of the products, until the amount of land devoted to each crop was in agreement with the demand for that crop.

For urban land this process is more complex. The determination of densities (or their inverse, lot size) and locations must be found simultaneously with the resulting price structure. Very briefly, the method consists of assuming a price of land at the center of the city, and determining the prices at all other locations by the competitive bidding of the potential users of land in relation to this price. The highest bid captures each location, and each bid is related to a most preferred alternative through the use of bid rent curves. This most preferred alternative is the marginal combination of price and location for that particular land use. The quantities of land occupied by the land users are determined by these prices. The locations are determined by assigning to each successive user of land the location available nearest the center of the city after the assignment of land quantities to the higher and more central bidders.

Since initially the price at the center of the city was assumed, the resulting set of prices, locations, and densities may be in error. A series of iterations will yield the correct solution. In some cases, the solution may be found by a set of simultaneous equations rather than by the chain of steps which has just been outlined.

The model presented in this paper corresponds to the simplest case: a single-center city, on a featureless plain, with transportation in all directions. However, the reasoning can be extended to cities with several centers (shopping, office, manufacturing, etc.), with structured road patterns, and other realistic complications. The theory can also be made to shed light on the effects of economic development, changes in income structure, zoning regulations, taxation policies, and other. At this stage, the model is purely theoretical; however, it is hoped that it may provide a logical structure for econometric models which may be useful for prediction.

ECONOMIC CHANGE AND THE CITY:
A QUALITATIVE EVALUATION AND SOME HYPOTHESES

John R. Meyer
John F. Kain
Martin Wohl

Information, particularly qualitative information, is by no means lacking on the basic processes that shape and condition urban growth and determine the dimensions of the urban transportation problem.[1] As is often true in re-

John R. Meyer is Professor of Economics, Yale University; John F. Kain is Professor of Political Economics, Harvard University; Martin Wohl is Director of Transportation Studies, The Urban Institute, Washington, D.C.

Reprinted by permission of the publishers, from John R. Meyer, John F. Kain, and Martin Wohl, *The Urban Transportation Problem,* Cambridge, Mass.: Harvard University Press, Copyright, 1965, by The Rand Corporation.

[1] The hypotheses and impressions presented have been gathered from several sources. The following are among the more important and suggestive: Benjamin Chinitz, *Freight and the Metropolis* (Harvard University Press, Cambridge, Mass.,

search, demand has created its own supply and there has been a proliferation of studies on the problems and characteristics of the modern American city. Unfortunately, the results have seldom been collated or evaluated for common elements and tendencies; but certain basic patterns are discernible and widely recognized. These, in turn, are the obvious bases upon which

1960); William L. Garrison, et al. (*Studies of Highway Development and Geographic Change,* published in cooperation with the Bureau of Public Roads of the Department of Commerce and the Washington State Highway Commission [part of the University of Washington Highway Economic Series], University of Washington Press, Seattle, 1959); Harlan W. Gilmore, *Transportation and the Growth of Cities* (The Free Press, Glencoe, Ill., 1963); Charles M. Haar, *Land-Use Planning* (Little, Brown & Co., Boston, 1959); Edgar M. Hoover, *The Location of Economic Activity,* Economic Handbook Series, Seymour E. Harris, ed., McGraw-Hill, New York, 1948); Edgar M. Hoover and Raymond Vernon, *Anatomy of a Metropolis* ([part of the New York Metropolitan Region Study, Raymond Vernon, Director, Max Hall, Editorial Director], Harvard University Press, Cambridge, Mass., 1959); Edgar M. Horwood, *et al., Studies of the Central Business District and Urban Freeway Development* ([part of the University of Washington Highway Economic Studies], University of Washington Press, Seattle, 1959); Homer Hoyt, *One Hundred Years of Land Values in Chicago* (University of Chicago Press, Chicago, 1933); Walter Isard, *Location and Space-Economy* (published jointly by The Technology Press of MIT and John Wiley & Sons, New York, 1956); Richard L. Meier, *Science and Economic Development: New Patterns of Living* (published jointly by the Technology Press of MIT and John Wiley & Sons, New York, 1956); John Meyer, *et al., Economics of Competition in the Transportation Industry* (Harvard University Press, Cambridge, Mass., 1959); Robert B. Mitchell, and Chester Rapkin, *Urban Traffic: A Function of Land Use* (Columbia University Press, New York, 1954); Wilfred Owen, *Cities in the Motor Age* (The Viking Press, New York, 1959); Wilfred Owen, *The Metropolitan Transportation Problem* (The Brookings Institution, Washington, D.C., 1956); Harvey S. Perloff, ed., *Planning and the Urban Community, Essays on Urbanism and City Planning Presented before a Seminar Sponsored by the Joint Committee on Planning and Urban Development of Carnegie Institute of Technology and University of Pittsburgh* (University of Pittsburgh Press, Pittsburgh, Pa., 1961); Princeton University Conference, *Urban Development and Urban Transportation* ([Conference held April 30 and May 1, 1957], Princeton University Press, Princeton, N.J., 1957); Chester Rapkin and William G. Grigsby, *Residential Renewal in the Urban Core,* Institute for Urban Studies (University of Pennsylvania, University of Pennsylvania Press, Philadelphia, Pa., 1960); Richard U. Ratcliff, *Urban Land Economics* (McGraw-Hill, New York, 1949); Lloyd Rodwin, *The Future Metropolis* (George Braziller, New York, 1961); Martin Segal, *Wages in the Metropolis: Their Influence on the Location of Industries in the New York Region* (vol. 4 of the New York Metropolitan Region Study, Harvard University Press, Cambridge, Mass., 1960); Ezra Solomon and Zarka Bibija, *Metropolitan Chicago: An Economic Analysis* (Graduate School of Business, University of Chicago, The Free Press, Glencoe, Ill., 1959); Raymond Vernon, *The Changing Economic Function of the Central City* (Area Development Committee of Committee for Economic Development, New York, January 1959); Raymond Vernon, *Metropolis 1985: An Interpretation of the Findings of the New York Metropolitan Region Study* (vol. 9 of the New York Metropolitan Region Study, Harvard University Press, Cambridge, Mass., 1960); and Robert C. Wood (with V. V. Almendinger), *1400 Governments: The Political Economy of the New York Metropolitan Region* (vol. 8 of the New York Metropolitan Region Study, Harvard University Press, Cambridge, Mass., 1961).

to erect a set of working hypotheses about urban growth and transportation requirements.

Before these hypotheses are discussed, however, certain premises must be established. To begin, it is a virtual certainty that the spatial pattern of a city in a free-enterprise society is the collective result of a large number of separate business and household location decisions and transportation choices. These decisions are made in a context of and are influenced by economic, sociological, and technological circumstances, usually beyond the immediate control of the decision-maker. They are also constrained, and to some extent directed by, public policies — zoning ordinances, building codes, transportation policies, and the like. On this premise, the kind, the extent, and the importance of these different determining influences must be known if city structure and changes in it are to be understood.

QUALITATIVE ASPECTS OF RECENT TRENDS IN URBAN GROWTH

Probably the most commonly noted tendency in U.S. urban growth is the decline in the relative (and often absolute) importance of the central parts of most urban areas. As noted previously, attempts to arrest this tendency account for much of the public's concern and many specific policy proposals to aid cities. The relative decline of CBD's (central business districts) and central cities [2] is attributable to several important technological and economic changes that make decentralization a more possible, more economic, or more desirable choice for an increasing number of household and business decision-makers.

Specifically, both recent and historical developments in transportation and communication technology have had two major impacts on city structure. First, these developments have made different parcels of land increasingly homogeneous for most manufacturing, retailing, wholesaling, residential, and other uses. Second, and in contrast to the first, recent improvements in transportation and communications have simultaneously made it increasingly possible to centralize *control* of management functions at one point in space. The first of these two effects, greater homogeneity of land, works toward decentralization *within* cities while the second, ability to centralize control activities, tends toward greater concentration in particular cities. Specifically, the first effect tends to increase the attractiveness of the outer ring of a metropolitan area as opposed to the core, while the sec-

---

[2] CBD's are usually defined as the high-density commercial and business cores of cities. Central cities are the areas within the incorporated limits of the major cities of metropolitan areas.

ond makes major cities, particularly major commercial, financial, and office centers, more attractive than lesser cities.

To the extent that there are compelling reasons for locating central offices or control activities in downtown areas, the new ability to centralize control functions may partially or even fully offset the effects of decentralizing influences within the city. However, as will be documented more fully in subsequent chapters, with the possible exception of the nation's commercial capital, New York, and Los Angeles, Houston, San Francisco and perhaps one or two other major regional centers, the forces creating growth in CBD's seem slight in comparison with the forces operating toward decentralization.

Increasing homogeneity of land by itself, of course, would generate *absolute* decline of the CBD only if land at the outskirts of a city were both cheaper and at the same time as good a site for activities previously located at the city core. *Relative* decentralization of cities will occur, though, even without actual relocation of existing activities, to the extent that new individuals or businesses find the outskirts technologically as good a location and cheaper than the CBD in terms of land cost (construing these broadly to include adjustment for differences in public and other services). For reasons that will be shortly elaborated, there are also important and compelling reasons why the open land at the edges of a city may be positively advantageous for many activities — and even if land costs per unit were more than at the center of the city. In general, activities that require large blocks of land almost totally free of constraints on noise or fume levels or, more importantly, a need to conform to the block pattern layout of city streets, will find peripheral locations attractive. Urban renewal can often offset these advantages of peripheral land partially, but seldom fully.

The most common cited cause of decentralization, however, has been the combined economic and technological revolution in consumption patterns since the development of the internal combusion engine. The automobile has made it technically feasible for people to live in dispersed residential locations, while rising personal incomes and mass production have made such a development economically possible. The desire, apparent particularly among younger Americans, for single-family dwellings with attached play-yards and lawns historically seems to have been both overwhelming and undeniable, at least as long as per capita incomes continued to rise. The consequence has been what some observers have called "urban sprawl," and the automobile has become one of the villains of modern city planning. In economic parlance, automobiles and suburban living space appear to be complementary superior goods (that is, consumption of one increases with increases in the consumption of the other and consumption of both goes up when per capita income increases).

The rise of suburban living has had an impact, in turn, on the location of retailing and service activities (and accompanying job opportunities) that have traditionally followed their markets. The symbol — sometimes an emotionally charged symbol — of the locational change in these activities is the suburban shopping center surrounded by parking lots for automobiles. Of course, it is really enhanced total purchasing power at the outskirts combined with mobility and flexibility afforded by private automobiles, rather than simple expansion of population, that makes development of satellite shopping areas economically feasible. Accordingly, increasing per capita incomes in suburban areas, as well as the automobile, have contributed to the relative decentralization of some retail activities. As a matter of perspective, it is well to recall that central shopping facilities have always accounted for a smaller proportion of the retailing activity in large American cities than in small ones, the implication being that commercial decentralization is an accompaniment of urban growth *per se*.

The rise of the suburban shopping center also reflects forces other than simple growth in population, auto ownership, and personal income. For one thing, it is a function of changing and improving merchandising techniques. The economies to be gained from grouping the retailing of many products at one location have long been recognized, whether the grouping is done by putting independent stores together in an arcade, or by having single ownership in the form of a supermarket or department store. Even more pertinently from the standpoint of urban transport analysis, starting anew in a suburban location often makes it possible to design retailing areas that are more compatible with modern transportation, warehousing, and distribution technologies than is possible in older downtown sectors. Technological changes of particular importance in this regard have been the replacement of horses and buggies by automobiles; of horsedrawn drays by panel, pick-up, and other small trucks; of stairs by elevators and escalators; of hired delivery by do-it-yourself; and of human labor by fork-lift trucks. Their impact on city design has been to make separation of vehicular and pedestrian traffic much more desirable, if not mandatory, than it was in an age of low vehicular speeds; to reduce the need for wide, horizontal access strips for moving local freight and, in general, the space required for local drayage; to make vertical movement of small freight packages considerably more efficient than in the past; and to decrease the need for large on-site inventories or for warehouses attached directly to the retail store. These factors, taken together with the increased use of private passenger vehicles and their accompanying need for parking space, dictate that an efficient physical layout for retailing will approximate that of a modern suburban shopping center. Indeed, it can be argued with considerable validity (but at the expense of some oversimplification) that the most serious problem of existing CBD's is that they were designed for an outdated set of technological conditions, the most serious single problem being an inadequate separation of truck, private vehicular, and pedestrian traffic.

As implied by earlier remarks about land homogenization, central-city troubles do not start and end with the relocation of residential and retailing sites. Other forces have also been at work eroding the so-called economic base of the city by reducing CBD employment in industrial and other activities. Some of the more important of these technological changes are concerned with the virtual revolution in the intercity transportation of both persons and freight.

Changes in the intercity movement of passengers have been sharply dramatized by the current economic agonies of rail passenger travel. Many who previously traveled by taking a short trip to the downtown area of their city and catching a train, now find it more convenient simply to "hop in" the family automobile and drive directly to their destinations. If they pass through the central area at all, they do so quickly and consume only the services of a downtown traffic policeman or of an urban freeway. For long trips (for example, over 500 miles), particularly business trips, the choice has increasingly been to go by air. For a number of obvious geographic, cost, and land-requirement reasons, intercity airline transportation always has tended to have its transfer point from local to intercity vehicle — the airport — located outside of and at some distance from older CBD's.

These technological developments in passenger transportation have also reduced the relative concentration of hotel, restaurant, and allied services at central-city locations. The need for hotel and restaurant services has by no means disappeared in downtown areas, but the relative proportions of such activities in central and suburban locations have been altered significantly. The growth of both auto and air travel has contributed, of course, to this decentralization of restaurants and the proliferation of motel accommodations.

The rail freight business also has been profoundly affected by recent technological changes, particularly by the development of piggyback and container shipment, whose full effects are yet to be felt. Simply described, containerization is an effort to obtain the line-haul economies of rail or water transport while retaining the flexibility and economies of truck origination and termination of shipments. The use of containers and trucks for origination and termination avoids or significantly reduces classification costs, product damage, and time losses incurred in the railway yards and on docks.

Container shipment also acts as a force for decentralization by extending the range of industries which can afford to be away from rail sidings and can depend exclusively on highway transportation for origin and termination of shipments. Industries such as steel mills and thermoelectric plants, which consume large amounts of bulky, nonsoluble raw materials, continue to be more strongly rail-oriented, though the development of bulk movement of solids in pipelines could alter even this factor in the future.

The shift to container shipment of high-value manufactured goods may be faster, moreover, than the inherent economies would dictate, as a result of price discrimination in rail rate structures. At present, carload rates normally are quoted according to "value of service," with much larger mark-ups on the actual transportation costs attached to shipments of high-value goods than of bulk commodities. Container rates, however, are independent of the nature of the goods in the containers, and have usually been set at a level just below the line-haul cost of truck shipment. In time, as the apparent change to container shipment develops, cities can expect new land-use demands for highway-oriented warehouse and shipping facilities and some reduction in those geared to rail sidings.

Other technological and economic reasons for relocating industry at non-central points derive from the fact that high labor costs and advancing technology have jointly contrived to make it increasingly desirable for more and more manufacturing operations to be placed on a continuous process or automatic material-handling basis. It is almost always cheaper to employ these techniques in a one-story than in a multistory plant. In fact, it is often prohibitively expensive if not almost technologically impossible to employ them in older, multistory buildings.

A one-story plant, however, requires more land per square foot of workspace than does a multistory building. Accordingly, if everything else is equal (for example, there are no compelling reasons relating to transportation or recruitment of work force for remaining in a downtown location), the introduction of these new technologies suggests a simultaneous switch to outlying areas of lower real estate values, particularly large unencumbered tracts which offer room for expansion as well.

Similarly, electronic data processing is a technological change with important implications for the location of what might be called "the bookkeeping industries," an outstanding example being an insurance company, with its need to maintain extensive files and records. Another is the check and deposit servicing performed by commercial banks. Similarly, billing and collecting give rise to a large proportion of the direct labor charges of many public utility operations. Finally, many governmental activities are large-scale record and bookkeeping activities.

The main locational impact of electronic data processing has stemmed from the reduced need of these bookkeeping industries to recruit large forces of semiskilled female clerks. In the past, central locations for these industries were often dictated by the fact that women usually had neither the income nor the incentive to justify owning automobiles; rather, they relied on public transportation. For large insurance firms, in particular, this historically has been a major reason for remaining in a downtown location. Accordingly, once electronic data processing freed insurance firms from so heavy a reliance on unskilled female labor, and the expansion of automobile ownership made it easier to recruit all types of labor at noncentral locations, many firms moved out of the central core of the city. Usually the new site has been either an area of relatively low land value just beyond the city core (what is sometimes called the "frame" of the CBD) or, more commonly, a suburban location with even lower land value and more convenient to the suburban residences of the executive, managerial, and technical personnel employed by insurance firms.

A similar but not so widespread movement to the suburbs by the bookkeeping activities of public utility and banking firms is visible. These firms have generally lagged behind the insurance companies in adapting electronic data processing to their bookkeeping needs, largely because they usually find the adaptation much more complicated. Recent technological developments, however, seem to be rapidly eliminating the remaining obstacles. A consideration still tending to retard the removal of bookkeeping activities to suburban areas has been the large investments many banking, insurance, and public utility firms have long maintained in downtown property.

Still another important technological revolution greatly influencing land uses and values in urban areas is the communications revolution now under way. Clearly, the full effects of this revolution are yet to be felt. Indeed, it is difficult at the moment even to perceive what the over-all effects might be. At least to some extent, new developments in communication technology will be offsetting — centralizing some activities and decentralizing others. Before us, though, are such intriguing and unexplored innovations as closed-circuit television, phonovision, and facsimile transmission.

At least one major impact of these innovations does seem obvious, however; a reduced need for locating all the functional activities of a given industrial firm or type of business in close proximity. Rather, it is becoming increasingly feasible to locate different functions about the city at points of maximum locational advantage. For example, such industries as women's apparel, clothing accessories, costume jewelry, and others producing specialized high-fashion goods seem to have a very real need to locate their showrooms and selling activities in reasonably central locations, thus minimizing the need for visiting buyers to travel to see the various wares. In essence, sellers in these industries strongly desire to be located in a central market so as to ensure the maximum possibility of wares being seen by important buyers. Once the marketing pattern is set, strong reasons thus exist for staying close to the central group.

Traditionally, at least in New York, these industries have also tended to perform their manufacturing functions very close to their showrooms; but with improved communications and transportation there may no longer be any great advantage in doing so. If not, showrooms may stay where they are while the manufacturing operations relocate over time at the periphery of the city or other locations with cost advantages. It also seems possible that the market place itself may move to a less central location. When most business travel is by airplane, a cluster of showrooms close to the airport would seem to be as logical as one near the rail terminal. Indeed, the recent growth of hotel and exposition facilities near big-city airports suggests that this development is already well under way.

New developments in communication technology have also exerted a decentralizing influence on other urban activities. The most dramatic example is television, which in a very real sense brings many of the entertainment — and even cultural — amenities of the central city directly into the private home. It is easy to understand why a young married couple with children hesitates to spend money for a baby sitter, parking fees, show tickets, or expenses for a trip into town to see a nightclub performance, or movie, or concert, when they can see it in their own home. To a lesser extent, television has also brought live theatre into the home. Similarly, pay television may create very large markets for even such highly specialized activities as operas, concerts, and new theatrical productions; if so, these activities would no longer require locations in the central city in order to generate enough demand to be justified economically. Such a development would be, moreover, only a continuation of well-established trends in the entertainment and theatrical field. At the turn of the century, music halls and other popular forms of entertainment could only be sustained at downtown or central theatrical locations. This was even more true for the legitimate theater. The moving picture and, more recently, television have obviously altered these circumstances. Television has created such a massive single-point-of-time market for music hall, vaudeville, and other popular entertainment that sponsors can actually be found to present such theater on a free basis (so long as they are allowed time for commercials). In short, recent developments in communication techniques have eliminated the necessity for a downtown site to produce and present theatrical entertainment. The presentation can now be made in the home or neighborhood motion picture theater, while actual production is performed at an industrial site which (because of land requirements and few transportation needs) usually is best located on a city's periphery.

A somewhat different and less predictable influence on city structure is exerted by public policy. For example, it is often argued that stricter zoning ordinances and building codes ordinarily originate at central locations, and spread slowly to suburbs and rural areas. To the extent this argument is correct, and to the extent that stricter zoning ordinances and building codes increase the cost of locating certain activities at a particular site, there is an obvious incentive for locating away from the center of the city.

Real doubts might be entertained, however, on how important this factor actually is, particularly as an influence on business location decisions. Many business organizations seem to find that conventional building codes and, to a lesser extent, zoning ordinances tend to impose standards well below the minimum that they would desire or adhere to on other grounds. Furthermore, there is some evidence that if a business finds a zoning ordinance really onerous it can often obtain an exemption from the political authorities, who usually desire to attract or keep job opportunities in their localities. On the other hand, there is a possibility that residential building, especially of a speculative or "tract" type, has been attracted to outlying areas by the prospect of more flexible zoning and building code requirements. Even in such cases, however, there are often important offsetting influences. For example, suburban areas usually have higher minimum-lot requirements than do central areas.

Another distinctly different influence possibly working toward decentralization of urban areas is commonly cited by businessmen actually making location decisions. Simply put, some of their decisions seem to have been influenced by the fact that moving to a less central location also tends to reduce or eliminate labor troubles. Built-up central locations usually have well-established unions, while suburban or rural locations may not; accordingly, a company with a serious labor union problem may find escape by moving. Also, less turnover and higher quality labor may be experienced at suburban locations.[3] How important these considerations might be is, however, difficult to assess.

As noted previously, the strongest argument favoring increased growth of central cities seems to be an argument applicable to strengthening the position of certain very large cities at the expense of lesser cities, rather than to centralization within a given urban area. Specifically, recent advances in communication, the rapidity of air travel, and the growth of electronic data processing appear to make district offices less necessary relative to regional offices, and regional offices less necessary relative to central or national offices. In short, technological progress has made greater centralization both possible and desirable in office and managerial control functions. These developments were first observed in the railroad industry as early as the 1930's, and since World War II they have become pronounced in certain other industries having geographically dispersed manufacturing and sales functions. As a result, medium-size and, particularly, large-size metropolitan areas may be adding central office functions at the expense of smaller ones. Another trend, reinforcing the development of more office activity in CBD's, is the increasing proportion of the manufacturing work force com-

---

[3] A. J. Bone and M. Wohl, "Massachusetts Route 128 Impact Study," *Highway Research Board Bulletin 227*, 1959, pp. 34–38.

prised of skilled, college-trained engineers and managers. That is, the central office function itself seems to be gaining at the expense of line operations, with very highly skilled manpower and new capital equipment being substituted for unskilled labor.

Another development potentially favoring central cities, but probably not too extensive in importance, can be found in the retailing field. As per capita income has risen, certain highly specialized (and sometimes highly expensive) consumer wants have become more prevalent. As a rule, serving these wants is economically feasible only if a fairly large market area is served. In fact, some of these markets (for example, those for expensive European *haute couture* and works of art) are feasible only at a few locations even in a market as extensive as the total American market. Development of such markets, therefore, should benefit large cities in particular, though recent experiments with closed-circuit television marketing may somewhat offset these effects.

SOME IMPLICATIONS AND PREDICTIONS

Good hypotheses should yield some testable predictions, of course. In the present context this criterion may be applied by posing the following fundamental question: What will the city of the future resemble if the technological and economic influences just described are in fact the actual determinants of city structure?

To begin, it is necessary to define the implications for the location and design of basic intercity freight transportation operations. Historically, the development and the geographic structure of cities have been heavily influenced or dominated by such considerations as the location of seaports, inland waterways, railroad terminals, and other freight-handling facilities. A major implication of the preceding analysis, however, is that there will be less and less reason in the city of the future for manufacturing and other business activities to be located near such transportation facilities. Furthermore, the facilities themselves will not be as near the centers of the cities. Indeed, there seem to be compelling reasons for the withdrawal of both transportation and manufacturing activities to lower-cost, less-encumbered sites at the edges of the cities, particularly if withdrawal would facilitate the introduction of new production techniques and the integration of rail and truck operations.

The most advantageous sites for the relocation of freight transportation activities appear to be at points of intersection between rail lines and circumferential highways already in place or planned for most major urban centers. (Without a circumferential highway, relocation would take place at sites where existing rail facilities and new urban expressways or freeways are conveniently juxtaposed, and the comments that follow would not be materially changed.) A circumferential highway, placed in the first large band of uninhabited land just beyond the city limits or built-up suburban residential area, provides an almost ideal site for the performance of truck-to-rail transfers, particularly at the point of intersection with rail facilities. Large parking lots for storing and moving containers for truck trailers, and rail sidings required to create piggyback or containerized trains, are conveniently located there.

Manufacturing and other businesses requiring transportation inputs can be expected to locate reasonably close to these new transportation facilities. *Ceteris paribus,* if the market for land rentals and leases works with reasonable efficiency, the firms locating closest to the new transportation terminals would be the ones with the largest transport requirements. Indeed, industries with very large transportation input requirements — for bulky raw materials, for example — might still be expected to require rail and water sidings. Therefore such industries may have an understandable reluctance to leave central or other locations where rail marshalling yards and industrial siding facilities are already well established. Two such industries would appear to be steel manufacturing and thermoelectric plants.

Experience and logic also suggest that locations along circumferential highways, particularly at lower-rental points some distance from rail-highway intersections, would offer excellent advantages for the bookkeeping industries. At such points, for example, the recruitment of a labor force and the maintenance of harmonious labor relations may sometimes be simpler than at more central locations. Also, a certain amount of prestige and advertising value apparently attaches to a building that is visible from the highway and placed in a well-landscaped industrial park. These industries, particularly insurance, also generate a workday traffic of agents traveling to the office from neighboring cities or towns, so that a suburban highway location can be a useful and economical compromise among disparate workday travel demands.

Some wholesaling activities, by contrast, may not move quickly to peripheral industrial areas, because wholesaling is often inextricably intertwined with the selling function. Face-to-face consultation with purchasers and others using the wholesaler's services is often required. Furthermore, the fact that some retailing will remain in the downtown area in and of itself should hold some wholesaling nearby. In general, many wholesale and warehousing functions probably will continue, as in the past, to occupy lower-value areas with rail facilities just beyond the central core; however, the railroad facilities obviously will become less important if, as expected, containerized shipping of high-value goods is increasingly emphasized.

Certain wholesale and warehousing functions oriented to servicing manufacturing industries, on the other hand, might be expected to relocate to the periphery simply to be closer to their customers. In general, such relocation should be a somewhat slower process and follow after adjustments in transportation and manufacturing.

Local consumer industries, such as bakeries, candy factories, and breweries, might also be expected to follow a mixed pattern. They will be tempted, of course, to follow their customers and retail outlets to suburban locations; and such moves will often reduce total distribution costs by eliminating the necessity to originate all shipments in congested downtown areas. On the other hand, the total trip length from factory to consumers is likely to increase with decentralization, and the face-to-face contacts needed for much of the selling in these industries will be somewhat difficult or the travel required will be more burdensome at less central locations. Accordingly, some of these industries will probably relocate into the frame of the urban core while others will move all the way out to the periphery.

The ultimate effect of these developments will be to create, in very rough approximation, a new band or perhaps many bands of manufacturing and commercial activity circumscribing the city just beyond presently built-up environs. It suggests what is often described as a "tree" or "ring" theory of city growth. In these new peripheral bands, the city of the future should have most of its light and medium manufacturing and a great deal of its transportation and bookkeeping operations. Almost by definition, the bands would usually be close to existing outlets for intercity air and auto travel. It would not be surprising, moreover, if the railroads and bus companies began relocating their passenger terminals (for whatever passenger business they retain) at points near the intersections of railroads and circumferential highways. In fact, one possible way to save something of the intercity rail passenger business might be to rationalize the operation by eliminating high-cost, highly taxed downtown rail passenger terminals. Private automobiles, parking lots, and buses might be an obvious part of a plan for connecting new suburban rail terminals to central and other city locations.

It is unlikely, however, that all railway tracks will be eliminated from the center of the city. Some will be needed to serve heavy raw-material-consuming industries, such as iron and steel, and those warehousing activities that may not move for some time to come. In many cases, moreover, it might be too difficult for the railroads to establish belt lines or circumferential rail lines to avoid the city; a simple 1- or 2-track right-of-way would then have to be maintained through the city, particularly where such natural obstacles as rivers or ravines are already bridged near the city center. Some downtown tracks will also be needed in cities where seaport or other special facilities must be served.

On balance, however, railroads should require far less downtown real estate in the future because of their reduced need for passenge terminals, passenger yards, and marshalling yards at central locations. There should be an even greater proportional reduction in transportation employment opportunities, since labor intensive yard and record-keeping activities should be more efficient at new suburban locations. Similarly, the trend toward containerized shipment should reduce the demand for longshoremen in downtown areas of seaports.

These movements toward the periphery will radically alter, of course, the central core of the city. An obvious question is, what will be left? Basically, it would seem that the city's future will depend on "control activities" requiring immediate, face-to-face communication. In particular, the city may be uniquely suited for what has been called the "central office function." This means, above all, that the city is advantageous as the site for the executive offices of business managers. These, in turn, attract legal, advertising, and financial services that cater to central office functionaries and usually are not uniquely tied to any one firm or industry. For example, one might expect a commercial bank to retain a central location for its loan, trust, and other offices requiring immediate face-to-face contact with business management, even if the more routine banking functions move outward. As a corollary, some restaurants and hotels should remain, since central offices are one of their prime sources of demand.

Many government activities, involved with bookkeeping and record-keeping, seem to be logical candidates for movement to the suburbs, but political and other considerations may keep them near central locations. (Boston is an interesting case in point, whereby the recent location plans for a new Federal office building were shifted from a noncentral to a central location on this basis. This is, of course, in contrast to some of the larger new Federal establishment locations in Washington, D.C. — such as the CIA and the National Bureau of Standards.) Furthermore, many government activities, particularly those dealing with tax collection and government-business relationships, often involve the face-to-face contact characteristics of central office operations. Most other government functions, many with very high employment potentials, such as police and fire departments, schools, and post offices, must follow population in much the same way that retailing does. Therefore, even government employment could decentralize.

As already noted, some retailing functions can be expected to remain in the central core; further, since the relative proportion of higher-income employment may increase in the core area, downtown retailing may become increasingly specialized and oriented to higher-income tastes, particularly since high-volume mass merchandising probably will continue to migrate to the suburbs. While secretaries and clerks may sustain a reasonably large popular demand for general retailing, downtown retailing will probably decline in relative if not absolute importance.

The remaining market for live entertainment also might be expected to concentrate in the central core. There may be exceptions; athletic enterprises that consume a good deal of land, for example, may be strongly motivated to move either to the suburbs or to the frame of the CBD. But live theatre and other cultural activities will probably remain in the central core. Even the need for parking space should not impede this pattern, since the demand for downtown parking space is ordinarily much lower in the evenings than in the daytime.

Stockbroking and related types of financial sales functions might also be expected to remain in central areas. Again, these are activities in which face-to-face consultation and rapid communication are usually very helpful. Accordingly, the stockbroker will tend to locate near his customers; and since higher-income groups do most of the investing, the core with its central offices is likely to remain the best location for stockbrokerage firms. On the other hand, closed-circuit television and phonovision could change these expectations.

Obviously, if these hypotheses about the future location of business and office activities are correct, a very extensive relative, if not aggregate redirection of activity is implied. Basically, relatively fewer blue-collar and lower-grade clerical employees will find work in the central core, while both the aggregate and relative proportions of higher-grade technical and managerial personnel may increase, especially in regional and national headquarter cities.

Shifts in employment opportunities for different income groups at different points in the city also can be expected to have important implications for residential location choices. Paradoxically, even slum areas around the cores of central cities may become attractive residential sites for the higher-income groups who will be increasingly employed nearby; and this attraction is likely to be greater as the city grows and commuting distances lengthen between the suburbs and core. On the other hand, the dispersion of lower-income manufacturing, transportation, and clerical workers to suburbia should continue, perhaps at an accelerated pace. These people will tend to settle near the plants in which they work. Finally, following the traditional pattern, a few very-high-income people will doubtless continue to live at or beyond the very periphery of the metropolitan area. They will include that unusually hardy breed of commuters who can stand the long daily trip into the central city, as well as the managers and technicians employed in the manufacturing, insurance, and banking service activities located around the city's periphery.

A special problem of residential site location is posed by the choice constraints usually imposed on certain minority groups. If there were no large minority groups in a city, it seems highly likely that the future residential pattern would be one of very-high-value (and probably high-rise) residences close to the city center, and a gradual tapering off in values with distance from the city center, stabilizing eventually at the point where the general mass of lower-income housing begins. This neat pattern may be made impossible, however, by the entrapment of new immigrant and minority groups in areas of high residential density just beyond redeveloped higher-income residences near the core.

The creation (or continuation) of centrally located segregated or slum areas would very likely retard higher-income residential redevelopment near the core. In particular, higher-income people with families may elect to join the long-haul commuters from the periphery, in part because of the "necessity" to rely on suburban rather than central city schools. Indeed, one might speculate that the "hardy commuter breed" is very much comprised of family-man executive types. Minority group clustering is also likely to influence the residential location decisions of secretarial and other skilled but lower-paid workers employed in the core area, generally forcing them farther out than they might otherwise choose to live.

SUMMARY

Both early and recent improvements in transportation and communication technology have tended to create distinctly larger areas of homogeneous land use in urban areas. Superimposed on this "leveling influence," which has tended to reduce the relative attractiveness of the central city, is the further tendency of some recent technological changes, particularly in passenger transportation and those influencing the physical layout of manufacturing production, to make unencumbered open spaces, usually found only at the outskirts of a city or beyond, advantageous for certain activities. Indeed, without much question, the overwhelming impact of technological changes, recent and remote, on urban locations or structure has been to reduce densities and decentralize or disperse functions. Containerization, the jet age, telecommunications, mechanized methods of materials handling, continuous processing, do-it-yourself deliveries, automation — all these connote recent technological changes that have had a decentralizing influence on the location of urban job opportunities. The ability of Americans to afford decentralized residential locations, private yards, and automobiles as their incomes have risen has of course strengthened the trend toward urban dispersal. These decentralizing influences have been only slightly counterbalanced by other developments, particularly in the performance of managerial control functions. These underlying forces for decentralization almost surely would have been set in motion, moreover, with or without the assistance or hindrance of public policy, since they stem from fundamental changes in technology, income levels, family status, and consumer tastes.

These technological and economic developments have clear implications for the structure and organization of American cities. For example, as urban employment opportunities and residences become still more dispersed, the city center should become increasingly more specialized in office, white-collar, and service activities and less and less a locale for manufacturing, transportation, and other blue-collar jobs. The pattern will be complicated at almost every turn, though, by the very special difficulties and problems created by the often-encountered clustering of minority groups' housing possibilities. Furthermore, the rate of adjustment of urban location decisions to new technological conditions, if not the absolute character of these decisions, will always be influenced and sometimes obfuscated by the inertia of existing circumstances and commitments. Urban change, in short, tends to proceed in a slow, evolutionary fashion. The net effect is to create a complex set of urban problems in which it is sometimes difficult to identify the basic trends, let alone solutions. Still, a cogent, well-defined set of hypotheses about urban change is discernible and their testing against available data is essential to the design of better transportation policies for urban areas.

FURTHER READINGS

Alonso, William. *Location and Land Use*. Cambridge, Mass.: Harvard University Press, 1964.

Borts, George H. "Returns Equalization and Regional Growth." *American Economic Review* 50 (1960).

Grieson, Ronald E. "The Economics of Property Taxes and Land Values." Working paper no. 72. Cambridge, Mass.: Massachusetts Institute of Technology, 1971.

Harris, R. N. S.; Tolley, G. S.; and Harrell, C. "The Residence Site Choice." *The Review of Economics and Statistics* 50 (1968), pp. 241–247.

Hoover, Edgar M. *The Location of Economic Activity*. New York: McGraw-Hill, 1963.

Isard, Walter. *Location and Space Economy*. Cambridge, Mass.: M.I.T. Press, 1960.

Moses, Leon, and Williamson, Harold F. "The Location of Economic Activity in Cities." *American Economic Review* (May 1967), pp. 211–222.

Neutze, George M. "Major Determinants of Location Patterns." *Land Economics* (1967), pp. 227–232.

Sjaastad, Larry A. "The Costs and Returns of Human Migration." *Journal of Political Economy* (October 1962), part 2.

Wingo, Lowdon, Jr. *Transportation and Urban Land*. Baltimore: Johns Hopkins Press, for Resources for the Future, Inc., 1961.

Chapter 4

TRANSPORTATION

The urban transportation problem consists largely of too many vehicles and perhaps too many persons attempting to enter and leave central cities during the morning and evening rush hours, resulting in overcrowded and congested transportation systems. Sharp peaks in travel demand reduce the productivity of transportation facilities, increase travel time and cost for the commuter, and produce pollution, discomfort, and noise for the commuter and resident. It is difficult to find the optimal mix, quantity, and use (or rationing) of a city's transportation facilities.

Decisions about investment in transportation projects should be made by comparing the benefits (defined to include aesthetic, social, income distributional, and aesthetic components) with the costs (similarly defined) of the project. The optimal amount of investment in any mass transit or highway system would be the amount that equates long-run marginal social benefit with cost. Once this optimal system is built or adapted, it is desirable that the individual users pay the short-run marginal social cost of using it, so that the user makes demands on the system only if the benefits he will derive exceed the social cost (his private cost plus the external cost).

Fundamentally, differences between private and social costs cause congestion. An additional driver during rush hour may see a trip as desirable when he compares his private benefits and costs, but the social cost of the trip, the driver's private cost plus the external costs of further delay, pollution, and noise he will impose upon society may exceed his private benefit from the trip. Many lower-priority rush hour trips would be canceled and the allocational efficiency of society's resources increased if the driver considered the full social cost of the trip when making his decision. John Meyer, John Kain, and Martin Wohl have calculated the   73 private costs and benefits of using various forms of commuting. They conclude that an individual would choose the private passenger vehicle as the most economical and convenient means of travel, except in extremely crowded situations. But Lyle Fitch and William Vickrey show that the private passenger automobile is often not the socially optimal choice when the costs of pollution-congestion and highways are added to the private costs of automobile use.

Drivers might be made to take into account the true marginal social cost of making a trip during periods of high road demand if scarce rush hour capacity could be rationed through congestion tolls set equal to the external cost of a trip. Congestion tolls could be levied on bridges, tunnels, and highways except where the geography of a city (too many access roads) makes them impractical. Highway tolls that are higher at rush hours than at other times would reduce peak-load congestion, and would encourage more people to use car pools and mass transit. Special charges for parking and de-parking at peak hours would be an alternative solution.

In setting the price for a mass transit system that already exists, fares should be equal to the short-run marginal social cost of an additional user. The social marginal cost varies with the time of day. During off-peak hours there is no congestion and few trains are required. The marginal cost of additional passengers is very low as they fill empty seats in infrequently scheduled trains. As demand rises to its peak, additional trains, personnel, and power must be brought into operation to accommodate the crowding. Many of the railroad cars and much of the labor used during peak hours sit completely idle in off-peak hours, so we can see that both costs and the number of passengers rise during peak hours. Many costs incurred by transit systems would not arise if it were not for peak hours.

By the criterion of economic efficiency, prices should be high during rush hours and low at other times, because there is an increasing short-run marginal cost of providing mass transit capacity during peak hours. Calculations have shown that optimal fares might be double their present level during peak hours and one-half their present level during off-peak hours. This pricing system would have important indirect benefits. The elderly and the unemployed would automatically get low transit fares during the off-peak hours in which they usually ride. If the optimal transportation system is not yet in operation, short-run marginal cost pricing of the existing network is still the efficient policy, although prices will change when the optimal long-run system is built.

Marginal social cost pricing during peak and nonpeak usage

leads to a deficit in financing a facility if its provision is subject to increasing returns to scale and a surplus in the case of decreasing returns (see the suggested reading by Herbert Mohring). Congested urban highways are likely to be subject to decreasing returns and urban mass transit facilities to increasing returns, in which case correctly priced urban roads would generate a profit that could be used to subsidize mass transit.

Urban trains are subject to economies of scale and not undesirable deficits because once the cost of railroad rights-of-way and tracks has been incurred, the increase in cost required to expand passenger capacity (the marginal cost) is much smaller than the average cost. If mass transit systems are then priced at marginal cost for efficiency, average cost will not be covered and the systems will run in deficit.

Urban highways, on the other hand, cannot easily accommodate increases in ridership and are subject to diseconomies of scale. They become overcrowded and congested during peak hours. The congestion slows the flow of traffic. Use of urban highways involves more time, cost, and pollution. As more urban roads are built, they use progressively more valuable land and in addition require greater expenditures on site clearance, relocation of displaced firms and individuals, and intricate construction. These increasing costs, or decreasing returns, cause marginal to exceed average cost. In these circumstances, marginal cost pricing yields a profit, or surplus.

William Vickrey and Robert Solow have shown that the financial price of using land for additional central city roads represents less than one-quarter of the social cost, attesting to the likelihood that we underestimate the true cost of urban highways when we make investment decisions. When individuals relocate from the urban center to the fringe of the metropolitan area, they will increase total travel. Therefore if the same quality of road transport service is maintained, the city will need expanded highway facilities, incurring more congestion and pollution.

Another institutional roadblock to efficient urban transportation systems restricts the number of licensed taxis allowed to operate within a city. Restrictive licensing was instituted during the Depression to protect taxi owners' incomes and has resulted in an inadequately small number of taxis charging excessively high fares — fares that bring about inefficiency and inequity because they are set at a level above cost and thereby yield above-normal (monopolistic) profits to taxi owners. (Licenses often sell for amounts exceeding $30,000 in Boston and New York, reflecting above-cost fares.)

Taxis provide door-to-door service for people between the commuter railroad and home or office. This eliminates the need to use an automobile for an entire travel cycle and reduces peak-hour congestion and parking problems. Taxis also provide connections for air, ship, and bus travelers, along with transportation for occupational and recreational needs. The poor and elderly, who are financially or physically unable to operate automobiles, ride taxis and jitneys to distant suburban employment and for personal needs. Mass transit would not be able to meet the special demands created by locational isolation or disability. Thus, low-income people in the cities are the most greatly handicapped because of restrictive taxi licensing. The success in Washington, D.C., of allowing free entry and employing zone fares ought to encourage other cities to lessen restrictions.

Having discussed the pricing of resources used in transportation systems, we can examine future transportation investments that are desirable in urban areas. Few additional central city highways seem justified, whereas congestion tolls to improve allocation and investments to increase highway quality are desirable. There are decreasing returns from constructing additional highways into the city, where street and parking capacity is limited and where the cost of increasing the capacity is high and rising. In his article on financing government services (see the suggested readings), Vickrey finds that automobile user charges do not cover the variable costs of maintenance, repair, sanitation, and policing of urban roads and highways and pay only about one-third of the capital cost, leaving a considerable deficit to be financed by the cities. Another example of the high and rising cost of urban highways is the estimated $23,000 cost of providing constant quality road and parking facilities for every additional automobile commuting to Washington, D.C., at rush hour.

The funds collected by the Federal Highway Trust Fund through gasoline taxes, which are now legally required to be expended on highway construction, could be distributed to local governments to meet local transportation needs and with substantial portion of the funds could go to urban areas. Reductions in the rate of the federal gasoline tax may also be desirable, when combined with congestion tolls and more careful highway construction programs.

We must consider the desirability of further investment in mass transit facilities with and without the institution of congestion tolls. Without the existence of congestion tolls, research both by Leon Moses and Harold Williamson and by Thomas Domencich and Gerald Kraft has demonstrated that even the provision of free mass transit would not significantly diminish rush-hour highway congestion. The subsidy needed to deter highway use was found to be at least two to three times the present mass transit fares. Even free transit would not significantly effect highway congestion, although it would attract many new riders whose benefit would be below the cost of providing the service and in some cases it would provide high cost mass transit facilities for a minimal increase in suburban ridership at the expense of urban residents.

The demand for mass transit is quite responsive to amenities (frequency of service, cleanliness, safety, and comfort), so that providing higher-quality facilities and instituting peak-hour pricing would improve community welfare. If these improvements are made and automobile congestion tolls are levied to encourage more efficient use of highways and off-peak commuting, highway congestion would decrease and mass transit ridership would increase. Then it would be financially worthwhile to improve and expand mass transit in high-density cities.

Where does the commuter railroad appear on the urban scene? Efficient management, increased quality of service, and a decrease in restrictive union rules could substantially lower the cost of commuter railroads. Reduced cost would permit lower prices and attract more riders, taking advantage of the economies of scale inherent in rail transportation. The trains would probably run a deficit when priced at marginal cost, or slightly above, because of declining costs — economies of scale — to increasing ridership. The subsidization of the deficit by the public would be justified because train use is likely to be desirable and have a favorable benefit-cost ratio. Congestion tolls on highways would help to increase the demand for commuter railroads.

Compare two extreme types of transportation systems at work in two kinds of cities. One would be a high-density, centralized city made up of high-rise office and apartment buildings, limited street and parking capacity, with a rail rapid transit system similar to New York, Boston, Philadelphia, and San Francisco. Another would be a decentralized, low-density city with large amounts of valuable land used to provide street and parking capacity similar to Los Angeles, Dallas, and Miami. Washington, D.C., and Chicago lie between these two alternatives. The first city would have made a large investment in rapid transit and now finds high congestion and parking tolls necessary to meet mounting congestion perhaps caused by overcentralization. The second city would have made a large investment in highways and now finds that mass transit is inapplicable although rush-hour congestion remains as the city decentralizes further and devotes more valuable land to roads and parking facilities.

Whether one picked the high- or low-density model would depend on a comparison of the value put upon low-density industrial and residential sites with the economies of agglomeration of high-density land use. There is still considerable controversy over which city is more desirable and efficient. Meyer feels that Los Angeles is probably more efficient given our technology and that BART (Bay Area Rapid Transit) is probably unjustified for San Francisco; Vickrey feels New York is more efficient and the BART system justified.

TRANSPORT: KEY TO THE FUTURE OF CITIES

Wilfred Owen

The greater mobility afforded by improved transport is highly valued by today's urban resident. Transport has made city dwellers the beneficiaries of more time, more space, and more opportunity for a fuller life. It may be called a resource-enriching (as well as a resource-using) element in urban life.

The radius of the city has now been extended to embrace new suburban development where the choice of a different kind of urbanism is offered to those who seek more room for living or for the location of industries. New circumferential expressways speed the motor vehicle from one side of the city to the other without passing through the center, and an entirely new urban geography has been introduced by the closer association of outlying communities.

Urban dwellers have greatly enlarged their job opportunities and social contacts as a result of the shorter travel times now possible, and the shopping center has introduced new methods of retail business and of housekeeping. Mobility for the city dweller has also meant more variety of recreation, more vacations, and more weekends away; and for many it has made possible both a house in the city and one in the country or at the beach.

The air age has introduced still further opportunities for those who live in cities, for the airplane has made it possible for businessmen to maintain

Wilfred Owen is Senior Fellow, The Brookings Institution.

Reprinted with permission from Wilfred Owen, "Transport: Key to the Future of Cities," in Harvey S. Perloff, ed., *The Quality of the Urban Environment* (Washington: Resources for the Future, Inc., 1969), pp. 205–213.

contact with customers and associates throughout the country, and for professionals of all kinds to co-operate with one another to a degree that was impossible when intercity travel was confined to surface methods. Equally important, for millions of urbanites the airplane has opened the doors to the rest of the world, with resulting international exchanges on a scale hardly conceived of a few years ago.

These are some of the "new resources" and opportunities that transport technology has made available to an urban society. But there are obstacles to realizing their full advantage. The lowest income groups have not been able to afford automobiles or airline tickets, so that for them no new doors have been opened. For millions too poor to own a car or otherwise barred from driving, the trends have actually meant greater limitations on the degree to which urban life can be fully enjoyed. For these people the new patterns of urban development are not well served by public transport or by travel on foot, so that jobs, schools, entertainment, and recreation may all be inaccessible. Even those with the money to pay for mobility often find that the conflict between the space requirements of motorization and the constraints of urbanization result in congestion, loss of time and temper, and new kinds of transport problems. In addition, the provision of transport facilities has often been accomplished without regard for community values, resulting in a progressive deterioration of the urban environment for all residents of the city, rich and poor alike.

The changes brought about by the combination of increased motorization and urbanization have had other unfortunate effects. Those who own automobiles have used them to flee from the problems of the city, leaving the poor and the disadvantaged behind in the slums. Their flight has not only destroyed the true function of the city center but has led to an exploitation of suburban land that produces monotony and conformity in housing and in some cases a new kind of low-density slum. Travel routes from city to suburb have at the same time created roadsides that have polluted the land, in much the same way that urban traffic and industry have polluted the air. Thus a combination of affluence and poverty, of mobility and immobility, and of urban investments without comprehensive development planning has resulted in a strange mixture of run-down cities, disorderly suburbs, blighted landscapes, and in many cases, a poor quality of urban living.

The question, then, is how to reap the advantages of modern transport in order to enhance urban life and at the same time to minimize the deleterious side effects. To achieve these objectives will involve new designs for urban settlement, the appropriate selection of transport technologies, a desirable balance between public and private transport, and the use of transport facilities as a means of building better communities. What can be done will depend partly on the basic economic and social conditions governing urban living in future years, including the success of measures to eradicate poverty and to cope with racial injustice. But the future course of urbanization will also depend on how well we grasp the opportunities for innovations in urban living that modern technology makes possible, and especially the opportunities afforded by the technological revolution in transport.

UNDERLYING CAUSES OF CONGESTION

History tells us that transport problems have been a major part of the problems of cities for many years, regardless of the kind of transport technology. American cities undertook to relieve traffic congestion by constructing elevated railways and subway facilities before the motor vehicle appeared on the scene. Surface transit vehicles were usurping so much street space in Boston sixty years ago that a subway was constructed to clear the way for the horses and electric cars using the streets.[1] Traffic at rush hours was described back in 1905 as the number one problem of large cities in the United States, and pictures of urban traffic jams in the days of the horse and carriage testify that congestion was bad long before the motor vehicle made it worse. As early as 1902 it was suggested that solutions could best be found "by starting on a bold plan on comparatively virgin soil" rather than attempting "to adapt our old cities to our newer and higher needs." [2]

Contemporary geography provides us with additional evidence that transport problems cannot stem entirely from transport methods, and that they obviously have more deep-seated cause. Traffic congestion in cities has become acute all over the world. Tokyo, with its extensive commuter railways and rapid transit, is as overwhelmed by traffic as Los Angeles, with its automobiles and freeways. Delhi, with its bullock carts and teeming masses of people, is no less inundated by rush hour traffic than Bangkok, with its buses and bicycles. Istanbul is by no means a motorized city, but its traffic jams are no less exasperating than the more spectacular ones of Rome or Paris.

History and geography both tell us, then, that no matter how people move in big cities, there is almost always an uncomfortable degree of congestion and frustration. Often it seems that the more affluent a nation becomes, and the more advanced its technology, the less successful it is in coping with its traffic problems.

Why have cities allowed themselves to be the victims rather than the beneficiaries of the new mobility? Part of the answer lies in the failure to recognize that there are two aspects to the transport problem: the supply of transport capacity, and the demand created by the various activities

[1] Edward Dana, "Reflections on Urban Transit" (an address before the Canadian Club, Montreal, April 21, 1947).
[2] Ebenezer Howard, *Garden Cities of Tomorrow* (1902), p. 134.

taking place in the city. The only times we take both sides of the problem clearly into account is when a pipeline is laid or an elevator installed in a building. In both these cases the capacity of the transport facility is specifically related to the traffic that is to be generated, either by an oil refinery or by the predetermined use of a building.

Designing transport for a whole city is a much more complex task, of course, but the same conditions and solutions obtain. The basic cause of congestion lies in the failure to strike a balance between transport demand and supply. Failure to take the demand aspects into account will continue to make chronic congestion in big cities inevitable. "The time has already come when we are wasting our substance by attempting to squeeze more cars, goods, and people into smaller and smaller areas. The simple geometry of the plan will surely defeat us no matter how long we postpone the day by ingenious engineering." [3]

In the central areas of large cities today, restoration and rebuilding is taking place on a scale that has not been equaled for many years. But the efficiency of this new urban investment will be seriously impaired if the resulting densities and arrangements of urban structures are not accommodated by appropriate measures to facilitate the movement of people and goods. Either transport plans will have to be designed to cope with the congestion being created by urban building programs or the rebuilding itself will have to be tailored to what the transport system can accommodate. Tackling half the problem leads to no solution.

The key question is: What density of development and what systems of activity and land use are to be sought for urban areas under various circumstances in order to assure a satisfying urban environment in which people can move around? There are many reasons favoring a reduction of the congested living typical of most close-in areas of large cities, but it is also questionable whether today's typical suburb and disorderly sprawl are acceptable alternatives. Should urban size and density be reduced, as is often argued, in the interests of physical and mental health, civic order, recreation, scenic beauty, and convenience? Proposals have been made to restrict the size of cities on the grounds that "effective planning of a metropolis is impossible unless a limit is placed on its maximum size and population." [4] But too low a density denies the purposes of the city and has serious economic disadvantages as well. What size and shape and design of cities will be most satisfactory under various circumstances? Is not the answer to be sought first in asking what cities are for, how they came to develop as they

---

[3] G. Holmes Perkins, "The Regional City," in Coleman Woodbury (ed.), *The Future of Cities and Urban Redevelopment* (University of Chicago Press, 1953), p. 39.

[4] William A. Robson (ed.), *Great Cities of the World: Their Government, Politics, and Planning* (Macmillan, 1954), p. 103.

did, why they have continued to grow, and what technological and economic factors appear to be altering some of the age-old concepts of what the city of the future should be like?

Originally men came together in cities because by closer association they were able to accomplish far more than would have been possible had the co-operation and interaction permitted by close urban living been denied. Every kind of goal — from walled protection to industrial production and the pursuit of science and the arts — has been achieved through the interaction of human beings in a community.

This community development in older times was possible only where nature provided the transport capabilities necessary to enable cities to feed themselves. The great cities of the world were originally dependent on water transport. Later, with the development of steam power, they also flourished at the junction of rail lines. Today, in an age of road and air transport — and telecommunications — it is possible for cities to grow at locations where neither water nor rail facilities are uniquely inviting. Yet the older cities continue to grow in total population and in geographic area, as if no basic changes in technology had taken place.

Large cities continue to expand both because of natural growth and because they are able to accept more and more people from the outside without noticeable strain. Growth by accretion has occurred because of individual decisions to take advantage of the urban infrastructure, its markets, and all of the external economies available in a settled community. But these decisions are made without appropriate actions to compensate for the resulting social costs. For instance, a new plant coming to New York benefits from existing markets and infrastructure, and from the great variety of service industries already there to meet its requirements and reduce its risks. The fact that this newly arrived enterprise may increase the congestion and costs of urban living for everyone does not influence the location decision. The city continues to grow because newcomers can still benefit, even if their arrival is detrimental to those already there. The transport situation deteriorates, like everything else, and extensive new public investments can often do no more than maintain standards of service at levels that are barely tolerable.

New technology now makes it likely, however, that some other pattern of urban settlement would make more economic and social sense. For if the original purpose of cities was to enable men to be in closer proximity, and thus communication, with one another, have we not reached the point where the very size of urban agglomerations makes human interaction increasingly difficult and costly? And does not technology make it possible to achieve these interactions through more extensive transport and communications rather than simply through togetherness and more intensive crowding? The time has arrived for a new kind of urbanization that avoids the dense-packed continuous buildup, yet gives more freedom of communications than ever before.

URBAN DEVELOPMENT AND TRANSPORT TECHNOLOGY

We are now on the threshold of very great advances in the art of transport and communications, and in the capacity of man to enjoy this new order of mobility. Looking first at intercity transport, we see that very soon the airplane will evolve into a vehicle of giant dimensions capable of carrying many hundreds of people at low cost, and many tons of freight at rates competitive with surface transport. These developments could have enormous influence on the spatial distribution of industry.

Two opposite trends in the speed of transport will also influence the design and location of cities. One is the acceleration of aircraft movement to supersonic speeds, which will bring people all over the world within very short travel time of each other. The other is deceleration of aircraft movement to zero miles an hour by new techniques of hovering. The latter will bring air travel to large numbers of cities that previously were too small to support scheduled service.

Along with these potentials are the possibilities of high-speed intercity ground transport. One is the air cushion vehicle, which may attain speeds of up to 250 miles per hour. Another is the automated highway to permit high-speed motor traffic through electric propulsion and electronic guidance. These methods of movement, combined with low-cost transmission of voice and picture by satellite communication systems, could make possible geographically extensive regional cities and close association among widely dispersed centers of population. It may prove easier to maintain contacts through high-speed transport serving large numbers of moderate-sized communities than to journey through the continuous built-up areas of a small number of super-cities. High-speed intercity transport may offer an antidote to low-speed city transport.

This, in fact, is what has been happening to date in the air age. People complain about how much time it takes to get to and from the airport, and that more time is spent going short distances on the ground than long distances in the air. They conclude from this that speeding up the airplane is not going to be much help; that what we need to do is to speed up ground transport.

From another viewpoint, however, speeding up the airplane can help to compensate for the fact that transport on the ground is so bad. And it is far easier and cheaper to improve performance in the air. For improving conditions on the ground involves not simply improving transport but rebuilding the whole urban community. The point here is not that ground transport improvements should be neglected, but that high-speed intercity travel can be and often is a desirable economic trade-off. The trip to the airport in many cities is annoying, but the fact that jet-propulsion has cut flying time in half often makes it seem worthwhile.

But new transport technology also offers the possibility of improving local circulation, either on the ground or in the air, and this could help to make high densities more feasible. Automated highways, for example, will permit many times the number of vehicles presently accommodated by a lane of ordinary highway. Parking may also be automated in great storage areas. Electric vehicles can overcome the problems of noise and fumes, and new techniques of tunnel construction, such as the laser beam, may help to develop lower-cost underground transport systems. Urban transit will also be able to take advantage of the air cushion principle to provide quiet and vibrationless movement without wheels, and computer control of bus routing may permit surface pickup and delivery of passengers at costs as low as one-fourth to one-tenth of taxi costs. Local air bus service with vertical take-off and landing capabilities also offers hope for metropolitan area transport.

In the movement of freight, equally promising methods may ease the burden on city streets. One is the substitution of non-transport solutions for what once were transport problems. Already the use of gas and electricity has appreciably reduced urban traffic in fuel. Now solid wastes are being either incinerated or ground and moved by pipe. Other transport-saving devices may be developed through food processing, nuclear power, and the shift from petroleum to electricity for automobile propulsion. Freight movement may also be facilitated by underground belt conveyors, the movement of solids by pipeline, and the extension of container transport systems. Higher buildings and the use of high-speed elevators introduce further possibilities of making supercities manageable.

Vertical development has become increasingly attractive as the cost of building high structures has declined. Tall buildings offer the advantage of conserving ground space and making it economically feasible to maintain large surrounding areas of open land. The skyscraper can also be used for a variety of purposes, including work places as well as living space, schools, recreation, and services. Transportation among these activities by elevator provides low-cost automatic service that is designed from the start to meet the demand. This vertical system of urban-living-with-a-view accomplishes many of the goals of urban design that have been frustratingly difficult to achieve on a horizontal plane.

It seems fair to say, therefore, that the new transport techniques and other technical innovations at our disposal offer a wide set of options, from greater dispersal to still greater concentration. But other factors need to be taken into account, and in particular the anticipated changes in population and in economic and social conditions.

THE IMPLICATIONS OF ECONOMIC GROWTH

Economic trends will combine with technology to change the character of urban settlement. First of all, we confront a very sizable expansion of the urban economy. Between 1966 and 1985 the population of the United States is expected to increase by 50 million. Gross national product in two decades may be double what it is today, so that within less than a decade, the average family income in the United States may rise to $10,000 per year. Together these two factors mean that a great deal of new urban development will be taking place which potentially can be of much higher quality than the cities of the past. In about a decade and a half we will be building the equivalent of 1,000 new cities, each with a population of 50,000.[5]

What is in question is the extent to which we will in fact be building new communities to meet the new demand, focusing growth in existing large metropolitan areas, or expanding exurbia beyond the limits of today's urban boundaries.

One of the most significant influences will be the effect of affluence on the expansion of private transport. Automobile ownership will continue to increase more rapidly than population in the next two decades as a general increase in economic activity is accompanied by a more equitable distribution of income. As families move up the income ladder, increased expenditure for transportation always follows. For example, in 1966 only 28 per cent of families with annual incomes of between $1,000 and $2,000 owned an automobile, but 93 per cent of families with incomes of $7,500 to $10,000 were car owners, and 30 per cent of them owned two cars or more.[6] In the low income brackets, less than 6 per cent of consumer expenditure went for transport; in the highest brackets, expenditure was between 12 and 15 per cent.[7]

How much of an increase in automobile registrations is likely can be judged to some extent by past relations between car ownership and population. There was one car for every 2.4 persons in the United States in 1965,

[5] Robert C. Weaver, "The Significance of Public Service in American Society" (Address to the 50th Anniversary Celebration, Institute of Public Administration, University of Michigan, May 25, 1964), p. 5.

[6] Automobile Manufacturers Association, *Automobile Facts and Figures* (Detroit: AMA, 1967), p. 39.

[7] *Household Income and Expenditure Statistics No. 1, 1950–1964* (Geneva: International Labour Office, 1967), p. 247.

compared to 4.8 persons per car in 1948. Over the next two decades better cars and better roads, along with economic growth, may be expected to produce a still greater density of automobile ownership. The upward trend in motoring has been closely comparable to trends in gross national product, which, together with the further growth of the suburbs, will mean an increasing number of multiple-car families. The possibility of one car for every two people appears to be a conservative expectation and would mean a total of some 130 million cars by 1985. The probable addition of 20 million trucks would raise total 1985 registrations to the 150 million mark.

The outlook for more motorization makes the prospects for high-density living less inviting, for, granted the other factors that might make good circulation more feasible in large urban agglomerations, the presence of great numbers of additional private vehicles will certainly favor a more open type of urban design. Other forces may be expected to press in the same direction. They include the demand for more urban space per person, both at home and at work, as well as additional space requirements for the new machines and processes of automated offices and industries. Space requirements per person may also be expected to increase with the decline in working hours, for leisure time will expand the requirements for recreation.

Along with the deconcentration that will be encouraged by these trends, industrial location decisions will be made with less concern for transport and more concern for climate and recreational opportunities. This will mean a continuing decentralization of activities throughout the country. For good transport and communications are making it possible for economic activities to be situated over wide areas of the country recently considered inaccessible.

Within this general framework of deconcentration and decentralization, we can expect to find that very different kinds of urban patterns will emerge. The giant city will be encouraged to grow still bigger by the increasing ability of transport to feed and supply large urban populations, by the growth of vertical structures and vertical transport by elevator, and by the low-cost exploitation of underground space. At the same time, there will be the opportunity to accommodate new urban growth in more moderate-sized cities, which either are entirely new or have been created through the expansion of existing towns. These settlements might offer most of the advantages of the larger cities, and some additional advantages as well. They would introduce an urban pattern that might be called the new regional city — a whole region of urban development that includes countryside as well as more densely built-up urban areas. As Lewis Mumford has envisioned, the farmer and the city man, separated through all history, could be brought together in the regional city, where rural residents could enjoy the same benefits of education, medicine, and cultural activities as the urban dweller, and where the apartment dweller could enjoy the advantages of the open country.

Such new towns could be designed and built from the start to incorporate a balance between transport supply and the traffic-generating activities of the community. The new towns could also serve as a necessary supplement to renewal of the old; for the satisfactory deconcentration of existing cities will require alternative sites for industry and housing outside the old built-up areas.

Still another direction for the coming urbanization will be much wider extensions of exurbia, so that people can live in the country yet lead a life that is essentially urban and urban-related. Transport and communications, together with innovations in power, will permit dispersal of urban living over the entire countryside.

All of the alternatives for the urban future appear to meet a need, and to reflect what, in fact, is already taking place. Yet each of these solutions, if it was the only one offered, might be quite unsatisfactory. The supercity, for example, may reach a practical limit at which increasing marginal social costs cannot be sustained. The opposite course of unrestrained dispersal may also prove too costly — especially in the sense of restricting human interaction, and of devouring open space. The concept of the regional city, on the other hand, may make allowance for both concentration and dispersal, and for the old cities as well as the new towns associated with them.

What seems to be called for is both many kinds of urban settlements and further experimentation with new forms, in order to offer a variety of options that will suit a variety of tastes. And the selection of how and where one lives will necessarily dictate the choices of transport that can be made available. Cities need to be very different places for different kinds of people who are doing different kinds of things.

Transport needs will vary accordingly. Maximum fulfillment for an individual may mean different things. For instance, for a painter, it may mean living in the largest city and communicating with other painters locally but also on a world-wide basis through works displayed in museums. For another individual engaged in scientific research, and participating perhaps with people similarly engaged in other countries, the concept of city is global, and his work calls for intercity and intercontinental mobility. Urban location and transport needs also vary with different age groups, different family sizes, and different levels of income. Some have reasons to be close to the city center, and others to stay farther out. The degree of dependence on one form of transport or another will be contingent on these conditions, and on a large number of other variables that will make the choice different for different occasions.

What we are concerned with is accommodating variety and making options available for those who live in cities, whether the setting is supercity, small city, suburbia, or exurbia. To meet these requirements we will need to develop a strategy for urban settlement that encompasses the whole nation. We need a national policy for urbanization that permits us to have supercities that can be lived in and moved in; dispersal that does not preempt the growing requirements for open space and recreation; suburbs that provide a more open type of development, yet avoid isolation; new towns that profit from the lessons of old towns; and groups of urban places in regional associations linked together by modern transport and communications. But if one option is not to interfere with the realization of another, there must be broad standards and policies for the whole.

URBAN TRANSPORTATION

John R. Meyer

DEFINITION

Urban transportation can be viewed from many perspectives. For the city planner, urban transportation is a tool for shaping or creating a city with certain desired characteristics. For local businessmen and property owners, urban transportation is a force that creates or modifies real estate values and business potentials. For the engineer, urban transportation is a challenge to design facilities to meet the needs of the community while remaining within budgetary constraints. For the economist, it is a bit of all of these things plus a problem in public finance.

To the consumer, however, urban transportation is something rather different. Users, naturally enough, are interested in getting to and from work or school, to and from shopping, to and from homes of friends and family, and to and from the locations of recreational activities — as economically and expeditiously as possible. To the consumer, moreover, satisfactory transportation implies not only economy and speed, but also such factors as comfort, privacy, protection from bad weather, schedule frequency and flexibility, and a host of other considerations. In short, urban transportation is a consumer good and, like others, is purchased because of intangible as

John R. Meyer is Professor of Economics, Yale University.

Reprinted from John R. Meyer, "Urban Transportation," in James Q. Wilson, ed., *The Metropolitan Enigma* (Washington: Chamber of Commerce, 1967), pp. 34–55.

well as tangible considerations. One of the least understood aspects of urban transportation is exactly what value consumers place on each of these considerations in making their choices.[1]

Clearly, then, many different objectives might be served by urban transportation plans or, at least, many people *think* that different urban transportation plans might serve a variety of objectives. From the standpoint of analyzing urban transportation problems objectively this creates certain difficulties — specifically, that of discerning which goals (or which compromise between different objectives) are to be served.

In this report, we shall take the consumer point of view and accept as given present governmental arrangements. This is not to say that this point of view or these arrangements are necessarily optimal.[2] Rather, it is simply an assertion that there seems to be no clearly obvious and feasible alternative. As a corollary, this acceptance of present institutional arrangements also means a heavy emphasis upon quantifiably measuring what current behavioral choices actually are.

THE SETTING AND TRENDS [3]

One of the more striking facts about urban transportation in the United States today is the extent to which it is dominated by the highway. It is reasonably clear that, like it or not, the automobile is here to stay, at least for a while. According to the 1960 Census of Population, about 64 per cent

[1] Among the better of the few studies available are W. Y. Oi and P. W. Shuldiner, *An Analysis of Urban Travel Demands* (Northwestern University Press, Evanston, Ill., 1962); S. L. Warner, *Stochastic Choice of Mode in Urban Travel: A Study in Binary Choice* (Northwestern University Press, Evanston, Ill., 1962); and L. N. Moses and H. F. Williamson, Jr., "Value of Time, Choice of Mode, and the Subsidy Issue in Urban Transportation," *Journal of Political Economy,* 71:247–264 (June 1963). Other sources of detailed information are area transportation studies performed for specific cities or municipalities, e.g., Chicago, Pittsburgh, and Philadelphia. For some suggestive questionnaire information on public attitudes toward different transport modes see the Editors of *Fortune, The Exploding Metropolis* (Doubleday & Company, Inc., Garden City, N.Y., 1958); and John B. Lansing, *Residential Location and Urban Mobility: The Second Wave of Interviews* (Survey Research Center, University of Michigan, Jan. 1966), as well as two earlier reports in the same series involving the same author.

[2] As Senator Claiborne Pell has aptly put it (in *Megalopolis Unbound: The Supercity and the Transportation of Tomorrow,* New York, 1966, p. 88): "We must debate our intentions and preferences and, within the limits of our constitutional, democratic system, devise at least a philosophical plan for a future growth on a regional national basis. Only then will the specific local plans for municipal development have coherence and integrity."

[3] Documentation and more detailed presentation of the materials presented in this section can be found in J. Meyer, J. Kain, and M. Wohl, *The Urban Transportation Problem* (Harvard University Press, Cambridge, Mass., 1965), Chapters III, IV, and V.

of all work trips in United States urban areas were made by auto. Only about 20 per cent of all urban area work trips are made by public transit; if one looks only at the central city portions of these urban areas, the public transit figure increases, but only to 26 per cent. Indeed, almost half as many people walk to work as use public transit in urban areas.

Of course, the level of public transit usage for work trips varies widely among urban areas. It is less than 2 per cent in some of our smaller cities (e.g., Eugene, Oregon, or Bay City, Michigan), well over half in New York City (61 per cent), and between one-third and one-half in several other cities (e.g., Chicago, Boston, Washington, New Orleans, and Philadelphia). Clearly, transit is here to stay, at least in our largest cities.

More significantly, approximately 70 per cent of all public transit work trips in the U.S. are made entirely on local streets or highways (mainly using buses but also involving some streetcars). In addition, a third or so of those using rail transit on reserved rights-of-way also use bus or other local street transit for some portion of their work trips. It would appear that well over 70 per cent of all public transit used for getting to and from work occurs on urban streets or highways and an even higher portion of public transit usage for all purposes is probably on such facilities (since rail transit is more highly specialized in serving work trips than other transit modes). And rail transit is not only a small fraction of all public transit, it is concentrated in a few areas. About one-half of all rail commuting is done in New York City.

The obvious implication of all this is that popular discussion that assumes that the fundamental urban transportation problem is one of choosing between private auto or rail rapid transit is badly misdirected, especially for cities other than New York City and, possibly, Chicago. At a minimum, such an assumption diverts attention from ways of improving the performance of those modes that account for the vast majority of all transit.

Nor is there any reason to believe that rail transit will become much more widely used in the near future. In large measure the attractiveness of rail as compared to other modes of transit depends on the number of persons demanding transit service in a particular urban corridor during the rush hours; this, in turn, depends on where people work and how densely populated are their residential neighborhoods. As illustrated by the comparative costs shown in Figures 1 and 2, the greater the demand volume and urban density, the lower the cost per passenger trip of transit. Even so, only where there are high-density residential areas (Figure 2) is the cost of rail transit lower than other forms; where densities are medium (Figure 1), buses are cheaper. These costs are also dependent on the means employed to get rail commuters to and from their homes and whether subways are used in central business areas. Rail transit improves if subways are used but is disadvantaged if people must drive and park their own cars at the

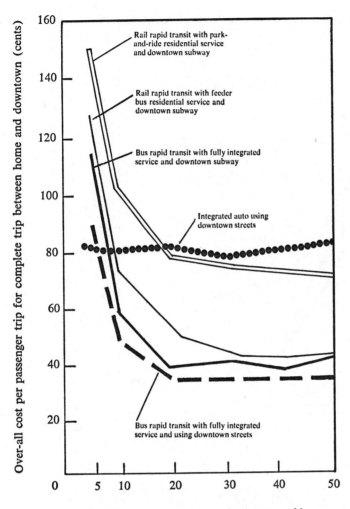

One-way hourly passenger volume per corridor
at maximum load point (thousands)

FIGURE 1. *Over-all home-downtown passenger-trip costs for medium residential density along corridor (e.g., as in Pittsburgh), hourly downtown passenger-trip originations of ten per block at the home end, 10-mile line-haul facility, and 2-mile downtown distribution system route length. Park-and-ride denotes use of a private auto for the trip from home to the railroad station, with the car parked at the station during the day.* Integrated service *indicates that the same vehicle is used for residential or downtown service as for the line haul between residential areas and downtown. (Reprinted by permission of the publishers from Meyer, Kain, and Wohl,* The Urban Transportation Problem, *Cambridge, Mass.: Harvard University Press, 1965. Copyright 1965 by the Rand Corporation.)*

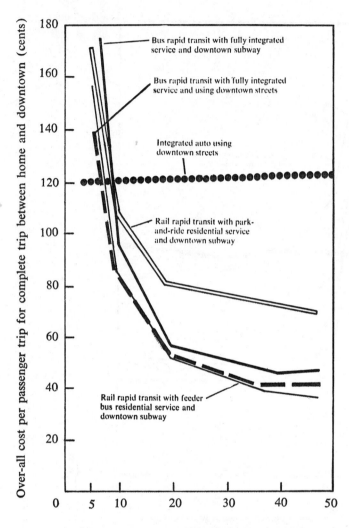

One-way hourly passenger volume per corridor
at maximum load point (thousands)

FIGURE 2.   *Over-all home-downtown passenger-trip costs for high residential
density along corridor (e.g., as in Chicago), hourly downtown passenger-trip
originations of ten per block at the home end, 10-mile line-haul facility, and
2-mile downtown distribution system route length. (Reprinted by permission of
the publishers from Meyer, Kain, and Wohl,* The Urban Transportation Problem, *Cambridge, Mass.: Harvard University Press, 1965. Copyright 1965 by the
Rand Corporation.)*

rail station. The conditions necessary to make rail transit economical — i.e., maximum hourly passenger transit volumes per corridor in excess of 40,000 — are found in the U.S. today only in New York City; indeed, only Chicago and New York have corridor flows exceeding 25,000 per hour. Very few urban corridors in the U.S. have hourly transit maximums in excess of 10,000 or 15,000 and those generally have rail transit service already.

It is significant that there has been a slow but steady decline in the demands placed upon urban transport systems. These downward trends have been created by a slow decline in employment opportunities in central business districts. . . . Specifically, the number of people requiring service into and out of major central business districts during the morning and (even more important) evening rush hours has for the most part been declining or, at least, remaining steady. The peak demand placed upon the urban transportation system by rush hour entry and egress from central business districts is crucially important, since it roughly determines the maximum capacity needs of the urban transportation system; these, in turn, are fundamentally important in determining the costs of different urban transport modes.

While rush hour demands have been declining or staying the same, the transport capacity available for meeting these peak demands to and from central business districts has been increasing. For the most part this increase in capacity has been the result of highway construction, particularly of high performance highways with limited access. There has also been a small increase in transit route mileage, though this is often coupled with a reduction in schedule frequencies. Schedule frequency reductions, however, have been mainly in off-peak periods. Since public transit systems have continued to be primarily oriented to serving central business districts, the public transit capacity available for meeting peak hour central business district requirements has tended to remain constant or, in a few cases, to have increased somewhat.

Given this combination of a slowly declining or steady level of peak hour demands plus an increase in available capacity, some slow improvement in the over-all performance of urban transportation systems has taken place. Contrary to popular impression, it does *not* take the average commuter longer to travel the same distance in the city today as formerly. On the contrary, the point to point travel times required between various centrally located workplaces and residential sites has, on the whole, been reduced in most U.S. cities in the last ten or fifteen years. During the rush hours, though, these improvements have been relatively small. A typical urban commuter trip that might have taken 25 minutes ten or fifteen years ago probably takes some 20 minutes or so today. The improvement, moreover, is likely to be shared by public transit systems as well as by private automobiles. Better expressways, for example, usually mean that fewer cars use local streets on which the buses operate, so that the buses (as well as the cars that remain on the local streets) usually experience a 3 to 7 mile per hour improvement in speed whenever a parallel urban expressway is completed nearby. Similarly, any reduction in demands on a rail transit system (caused, say, by the greater attractiveness of private automobiles on improved highways) usually means that the rail transit system is somewhat less congested during rush hours and can therefore reduce waiting times at major downtown stations and thereby marginally improve its performance speed.

Needless to say, faster rush hour speeds resulting from major improvements in the highway system are only a fraction of the higher speeds now possible during off-peak or non-rush hours. Average speeds of 50 or 60 miles an hour or more are not uncommon experiences on urban expressways during off-peak periods today. These are to be contrasted with speeds rarely in excess of 35 or 40 miles an hour during rush periods today, which, while an improvement on the 30 mile or less speeds of a decade or so ago, are still not fast by modern standards.

Perhaps an even more relevant measure of performance for an urban transportation system is the time required to "decongest" or evacuate central business districts in the evening rush hours. (The evening rush seems more pertinent than the morning since a higher level of demand is placed upon the system in the evening, apparently because of the addition of shoppers and other travellers to normal commuter demands.) A major problem with this measure is that it is somewhat difficult to define objectively. Roughly speaking, however, it can be represented as the time period during which the capacity of the central portion of the urban transportation system is more or less fully utilized because of outgoing commuters and other travellers. To an approximation, it seems that in most major U.S. cities this period has shortened by about 30 to 40 per cent in recent years, say, from approximately an hour or so in the late 1940's to approximately 40 minutes today. (These numbers will vary, of course, from city to city.)

Evacuation times for central business districts also make evident another important aspect of urban transportation. It is simply quite unrealistic to speak about the "elimination of congestion" as a major goal for urban transportation planning, at least so long as most businesses choose to close shop at approximately the same hour of the day. To speak of eliminating most congestion in or around major central business districts during the evening rush hour under such circumstances is very much like speaking of eliminating congestion in or around a major football stadium just after the final whistle. To do so would require an inordinately large transport capacity — inordinately large in the sense that the cost of completely eliminating congestion under such circumstances probably would be considered outrageous by most consumers.

THE PROBLEM

If there has been a slow but steady improvement in the performance of urban transportation systems, why do we hear so much discussion of a so-called urban transportation "crisis"? The answer lies in a complex set of considerations of which probably the most important is what might be termed "a failure of anticipations."

This failure of anticipations is in great part a consequence of the uneven rates of improvement in off-peak and peak performances of urban transport systems. Travelling across congested urban areas at 50 or 60 miles an hour on a high-performance highway during an off-peak period seems to be an exhilarating experience, and urban commuters, quite humanly, would like to duplicate the experience during the rush hours. The difficulty, of course, is that too many of them wish to do so at one time and thus it becomes impossible without a vast increase in capacity. Whether or not they would be willing to pay the high price is open to debate. There is considerable evidence, though, that if we had a free market in the provision of urban highway commuter facilities, some considerable expansion of such facilities would probably take place.

To put it another way, in our modern affluent society an improvement from 25 to 30 or 35 miles an hour or so in the average performance speed of private transport systems during the rush hours has not satisfied some commuters. This is particularly true since many of them have chosen to give up the improved transport time by living further away from their workplaces. Thus, the average time required to commute from home to workplace and return has remained more or less constant. People have apparently been willing to incur higher transportation costs in order to achieve a lower cost for a certain quality of housing or yard space. . . . Possibly, too, as one social psychologist has hypothesized, the typical male wage earner considers the time it takes to get between work and home as the only time that is truly his own, without interruption by foreman or wife. It is possible (no one knows) that some commuters are reluctant to reduce this time.

At any rate, more and better public transit seems to have a considerable attraction for many commuters, *not* because they want to use the transit themselves, but because they hope that it will attract *other* auto drivers off the roads. Those remaining could then realize faster speeds and less congestion on the highways. The alternative of trying to provide sufficient highway capacity so that they can commute at 50 miles an hour or so even during the rush hours is likely to be expensive both in terms of direct dollar outlays and in terms of property displacement. Indeed, if we were to go down this "road," some of the wilder claims about paving over our urban areas might actually be realized!

Another sense in which anticipations may have been frustrated is because of different rates of increase in urban real estate prices between central and peripheral locations. While it is difficult to find good evidence, the common belief is that central business district property values have not grown at as high a rate as suburban commercial properties. To the extent such differential property value increases have occurred, it is apparently due to a complex set of influences that can best be summarized as a reduction in the demand for the services of central city property. Changes in manufacturing, transportation, communication, and bookkeeping technologies seem to have made many businesses more independent of central locations. In short, there are not as many good reasons today for businesses to put up with the congestion and other high costs of central locations. . . .

Historically, the creation of high property values in downtown areas has occurred because such sites are at the point where major transport networks, both inter-city and intra-city, converge. Many owners of central business properties therefore have looked on expansion of the transport system — in particular, increasing the extent to which the transit network is centered on their properties — as a means of producing an increase, or a greater increase, in property values. This is especially true if the cost of providing such transport improvements does not fall upon the owners of central properties. Then they can hardly lose. Such owners naturally become strong advocates of government subsidies to improve downtown transportation facilities, particularly when the tax base used to supply such subsidies is statewide or nationwide. However, if urban property values today are less dependent on public transit service than they were under more primitive technological conditions, then it is not clear that improved transit access will confer major benefits upon centrally located properties.

In general, there is little evidence that the provision of public transit greatly modifies locational choices, at least in the aggregate. This raises questions about the feasibility of using urban transport policy as a tool for achieving a particular urban physical form. Specifically, the number of people desiring to live at higher residential densities (i.e., in apartment houses or multiple dwelling units seems to be mainly dependent upon age composition of the population, the number of families with two or more wage earners, per capita income levels, and the relative costs of single family dwellings and apartments. Similarly, a businessman's choice of site will depend as much upon his need for land (say, to achieve an economical one-story layout of his production line) or the extent to which he is dependent or not dependent upon heavy rail or water transport as upon accessibility to urban public transit. In particular, as buses and private automobiles have become available, the need to be near an urban rail rapid transit facility has been considerably reduced for virtually all classes of employers, even those heavily reliant upon female secretarial or clerical work forces (e.g., insurance companies). As a consequence of these and related trends, the patterns of decentralization or industrial relocation being experienced by American cities are no different for those with well-developed or highly utilized public transit systems as for those without such a "public transit tradition."

However, while public transit is apparently not sufficient to create any gross increase in urban residential or work place densities, the availability of high-performance public transit along a particular corridor may concentrate whatever demand for high-density living or work locations may exist in the community. Stated another way, the availability of high-performance public transit may relocate or concentrate dense activities but there is no evidence that it creates a new demand for such density. As a corollary, to justify extensive expenditure on high-performance public transit because it creates higher land values and property taxes on adjacent properties is a rather dubious procedure. Whatever increase occurs may only be the result of a transfer of values from one place to another rather than an increase in the total property tax base of the community. Of course, to the extent future high density residential development is concentrated along a new public transit facility, its basic economic prospects will be improved.

Another source of much of the public talk about an "urban transportation crisis" may result from a confusion of other urban problems with transport problems. For a variety of reasons (see the paper by Dick Netzer, "Financing Urban Government," in this volume) our major cities have faced increasing financial difficulties throughout the postwar period. The creation of express highways in central urban areas often seems, at least superficially, to accentuate these financial problems. Expressway construction removes property from the tax rolls; highway competition reduces the demand for public transit and thereby increases the transit deficits normally borne by city governments; expressways make it easier for middle-class people employed in central business districts to live in suburban residential locations, so that they can more easily "escape" their fiscal responsibilities in the city. There are at least partial answers to each of these arguments: without improved highway access urban properties generally might be reduced in value (e.g., by a more rapid exodus of manufacturing and other employment to suburban locations); improved urban highways should reduce the operating costs of urban bus transit (because of reduced congestion and improved operating times); without the expressways, the middle classes might remove their places of employment as well as their places of residence from central urban areas. Exactly what the net result is of these opposing considerations is difficult to determine.

Furthermore, the argument may be more or less beside the point. The financial problems of city governments are almost certainly more attributable to over-reliance on property taxes, and, at least in some states, to inadequate urban representation in state legislatures than to urban transportation choices. Similarly, making the central city a more attractive place for the middle classes almost surely depends on solving the problems of urban Negro ghettos as much as it does on transport policy. An interesting question is this: How many more middle-class whites employed in central business districts would choose to live closer to their places of work, rather than in remote suburbs, if the price of urban residences near central business districts were not in some cases artificially inflated or otherwise made less attractive by the existence of a captive Negro market for central locations?

Another source of confusion is the complex interdependency that exists between transport choices and the physical adequacy of our older central business districts. Manufacturing lofts, narrow streets and sidewalks, and other physical characteristics of older central business districts were determined by and suitable for a different set of technologies than seems optimal today. The creation of improved highway access to the fringes of these older business districts without taking compensating action in the physical design and layout of the districts themselves can lead to very difficult congestion and other transport problems. Under the circumstances, it is obviously quite tempting to seek at least a short run solution or amelioration of the problem by attempting to reduce the pace of modernization in transport technologies.

A better longer-term solution may lie, however, in adjusting the physical layouts of these older business areas to modern technological circumstances, at least to the extent that doing so is not prohibitively expensive. The major public policy for facilitating such changes has been, of course, urban renewal. Whether or not one agrees with the methods or objectives of that program, it is reasonably clear that renewal does make a major contribution toward adjusting the physical characteristics of central urban areas so as to make them more compatible with modern transport and other technologies. Rarely have urban renewal planners gone as far or been as imaginative as they might in making these accommodations. For example, many urban renewal plans have not separated different classes of vehicular and pedestrian traffic.

POLICY ALTERNATIVES

When discussing urban transportation policies it is necessary to distinguish sharply between the situation in our very largest cities, particularly those that are older, and that in our newer or smaller cities. From the economic and engineering viewpoint, these distinctions are important if for no other reason than that residential and workplace densities are crucial in determining the relative cost of different modes of urban transportation. As noted, the greater the density of residences and workplaces, the easier it is to design a reasonably inexpensive and relatively high quality public transit service. Similarly, the layout and width of existing streets in central areas can have an important impact on the relative costs of different urban transportation modes. Older cities with crooked or narrow streets almost certainly will have greater difficulty accommodating automobile traffic than newer cities with wide avenues and gridiron street layouts. Furthermore, the desirability of exploring the "third dimension" for expansion of urban transportation facilities — be it either tunneling or the use of elevated structures — is likely to be greater when streets are narrow and crooked. The greatest single advantage of rail transport over other forms of urban transportation is its lower cost for accommodating large volumes of traffic in tunnels or on elevated structures.

Under the circumstances, therefore, the older and larger cities that already haxe extensive rail rapid transit systems are almost certainly well advised to keep these facilities operational. Furthermore, on the grounds that investments in right-of-way and many other facilities used in rail transit are sunk (i.e., have low salvage or alternative opportunity value) and therefore are best ignored, rail transit when already in place can be an exceedingly inexpensive means of serving high density urban corridors. In some cases, moreover, further investment in central portions of these systems, so as to improve their service characteristics or reduce costs, might be quite attractive on economic marketing grounds.

Somewhat the same propositions apply to railroad commuter services, but *only* to the extent that these commuter services also serve reasonably large volumes — as in New York or Chicago. Even with right-of-way and roadbed maintenance costs ignored, suburban commuter rail lines serving less than a thousand or two commuters per day are likely to be exceedingly expensive. (In Boston, for example, about $500 per year per passenger is required in public subsidy to maintain existing suburban rail commuter services.)

Lengthy extensions of existing rail rapid transit systems into low-density residential areas face many of the same economic difficulties as small-scale suburban rail commuter operations. The additional revenues will usually be less than the additional costs. And, of course, the capital costs are likely to be high; such costs are not sunk and are quite certainly avoidable. The only major exception to this rule will occur when the extension represents a revival of a previous rail transit type of service and therefore can be made at relatively low costs (as in the case of the Skokie shuttle in Chicago).

The provision of parking lots near suburban rail stations is not likely to improve matters in any large measure. Parking lots, even in suburban locations, do involve some expense (though this fact may be disguised by an implicit subsidy). Even more important, by the time the suburban resident has driven his car to the railroad station he has incurred a substantial proportion of the total costs involved in using his automobile as a commuter vehicle. Specifically, the additional cost of continuing in the car to work location will not be very large unless the workplace is in a very dense central business district. Obviously, too, completing the commuter trip in the automobile has the additional advantage of eliminating a transfer with all that may imply about loss of time and exposure to bad weather.

For the smaller and newer cities the major policy problem is likely to be how to increase highway capacity effectively without a major restructuring of the existing urban areas. The newer and smaller cities not only have lower residential and workplace densities (making highway transport, either by private auto or bus, less costly and better able to render integrated no-transfer service than rail) but they also have fewer opportunities for perpetuating or converting existing rail facilities into public transit.

Most of these newer and smaller cities already have or shortly will have extensive limited-access, high-performance highway systems coming to the very edge or even penetrating their central business districts. This capacity is likely to be quite sufficient to meet all demands placed upon it except during the rush hours. On the presumption that expansion of capacity to a level sufficient to accommodate rush hour traffic with only limited congestion is too expensive, the solution for these cities is one of achieving better utilization of high-performance highways during peak periods. Special tolls or license fees for use of centrally located highways during rush hours would be one means of achieving such discipline. Another would be to apply more physical controls by, for example, improving traffic signals, restricting access to high-performance facilities (so as to avoid extreme congestion that chokes highways and actually reduces peak hour capacity), or reserving lanes or otherwise giving priority to public transit buses during the rush hours. The physical control of access to high-performance urban expressways may provide a particularly simple means of creating inexpensive high-performance transit. Specifically, if access to the expressways is limited so as to maintain high performance capability (e.g., 50 miles an hour or so) and if buses are given priority access to these facilities during the rush hours, it should be possible to design high-performance express bus services between central workplaces and suburban residential locations at relatively low cost. Ultimately, better utilization of urban highways might also be achieved by automation which would permit closer spacing of vehicles on expressways (as well as improving safety).

To determine which of these solutions should be preferred involves several difficult evaluations. Special tolls or license fees normally encounter a number of political objections: they seem to give the "rich" preferential access to what is commonly considered to be a public good. A more serious objection from the economic standpoint is the fact that implementing a useful toll system on urban highways is likely to be quite expensive, especially on a per mile basis, since urban trips are rather short. Furthermore, unless implemented on a fairly wide scale and with sophisticated differentiation between different classes of facilities, the application of the pricing techniques may do as much harm as good.[4] Specifically, selective application of tolls to only a few urban facilities during the rush hours can have adverse repercussions on other facilities because of the high degree of substitutability between different portions of the system; for example, the gain through reducing congestion on the highway to which the tolls are applied may be more than offset by displacement of vehicles to untolled facilities, thereby creating congestion and accompanying losses on these facilities.[5]

Physical controls (as, for example, by restricting access to high-speed highways) usually are less expensive to implement (though still far from free). They will not differentiate as well as a good pricing or toll system, however, between different classes of users and the intensity of different groups' desires to use urban highways. Physical controls, incidentally, may create spillover effects on other facilities in much the same fashion as price rationing. The congestion created or added to facilities receiving diverted traffic may offset the improvement achieved by imposition of the controls on a high performance facility. In general, physical controls represent a somewhat more gross approach to achieving the same ends as price rationing. There is superficial evidence, though, that physical controls are somewhat more politically acceptable than tolls or special license fees.

The major disadvantage of automation as a means of increasing urban highway capacity during peak periods is that it is likely to be quite expensive. While the technology is relatively simple conceptually, the costs could run as high as $500 or $600 per vehicle. In addition, some investment would be required in electronic devices as part of the highway, but these should be relatively inexpensive, at least compared with the costs of automating the vehicle itself. Automation also requires close cooperation between public highway authorities and the vehicle manufacturers, something which has not been easy to achieve in the past.

Still another policy alternative for improving the performance of urban transport systems is, as implied previously, to restructure older central business districts to better suit them to modern technologies. In this connection, one can imagine elevated sidewalks, malls or plazas for exclusive

[4] H. Mohring, "Urban Highway Investments," *Measuring Benefits of Government Investments* (R. Dorfman, ed.), The Brookings Institution, Washington, D.C., 1965.
[5] M. Wohl, "The Short-Run Congestion Cost and Pricing Dilemma," *Traffic Quarterly*, January 1966.

pedestrian use, better facilities for loading freight vehicles so as to remove such operations from major arterials or streets, and so forth. These measures, quite obviously, can be expensive. However, if incorporated into an urban renewal project, undertaken for other reasons as well, the costs may not be prohibitive.

EVALUATION

The best urban transportation policy for any particular city quite obviously will depend on its physical characteristics, political inclinations, history, and traditions. As a corollary, policies based solely on such simple slogans as "achieving balanced transportation" are quite likely to be deficient. There is no reason to believe that every mode of urban transportation has to be developed in every city and that every urbanite must be given a choice between several different modes. To pursue such a policy is almost certain to be prohibitively expensive. Given the many demands placed upon the limited financial resources of city governments, it would seem wise to pursue somewhat less extravagant or ambitious programs.

To the extent that there is some truth in the notion of balance in urban transportation programs it would seem, rather, to lie in the fact that the different policy alternatives outlined in the previous section are not mutually exclusive. Restructuring older central business districts to better suit modern transport technologies is likely to be a reasonably wise policy whether a community continues, say, to place heavy reliance on rail rapid transit or becomes increasingly oriented to highway modes. Similarly, disciplining the use of central urban highway facilities during rush hours is likely to be productive whether or not public or private transportation is emphasized. Finally, even if a high-performance rail rapid transit system is to be continued, development of better express bus services between various parts of the city may still be attractive.

In general, four basically different transportation systems seem to be emerging in most of our metropolitan areas. The demands placed upon these four systems are, in turn, very much a function of the changing industrial and residential location patterns discussed earlier.

The first of these systems might be described as *traditional public transit*. This system serves people employed in central business districts who also reside reasonably close by. In smaller and less dense cities this system's functions are customarily performed by buses, while in our larger, denser, and older cities they may be performed by rail transit. Costs per trip on these systems are customarily quite low. The typical trip is relatively short and takes approximately 15 or 20 minutes to complete. The clientele will be secretaries and other clerical workers employed in banks, offices, stores, and similar activities as well as service workers, very often from minority groups, with jobs in hotels, restaurants, and related activities.

The second system is *long distance commutation*. Its main function is to move people from relatively distant suburban residential locations to work-places at the heart of the central business district. The typical trip is a good deal longer than that performed by traditional public transit. The clientele usually has a much higher average income and comes from management or the professions. These systems tend to have very high performance charac-teristics, so that even though the typical trip is considerably longer, the travel time required does not rise proportionally. The costs per trip for these systems also tend to be high, commonly being over one dollar per trip and sometimes as high as three dollars per trip or more. (It should be emphasized that these costs are very often *not* fully paid by the users in the form of assessed charges.) Rail commutation is a very common mode for these trips, especially in our larger and older cities. Operation of a pri-vate automobile over high speed urban expressways is another popular choice for these trips. Occasionally, high speed express buses may be used.

The third system pertains to *cross-commutation,* designed for commuters who find both their employment and residences in suburban areas. An almost complete cross-section of urban America — blue-collar, clerical, managerial, and professional — are likely to be involved. For the most part these trips are made today by private automobile, although occasionally the bus is used. (Better marketing and design of bus transit might well in-crease the percentage using public transit for these trips, but the poor finances and, possibly, the traditional conservatism of transit management have tended to prohibit experimentation with new transit services aimed at capturing more of this market.) An important feature of this type of com-muter trip is that the demand for it is growing very rapidly and there is every reason to expect that it will continue to grow.

The fourth type of basic urban transportation system might be described as an *inside-out system*. It serves worktrips made by people living in rela-tively central locations and working in the suburbs. The Negro female domestic working in a suburban home and living in a centrally located ghetto is the archetype; today, however, she is probably increasingly joined by male Negroes as employment opportunities in manufacturing, inter-city transportation, and even wholesaling and retailing are increasingly found at suburban locations while housing opportunities remain restricted to the central ghetto. Furthermore, many white families with two or more workers, at least one of whom is employed in the central business district and one in a suburban workplace, have often found central city residential locations convenient.

The usual technical description of these outbound commuter trips is "reverse commutation," but this suggests that the central city systems described above can adequately serve these outbound commuter trips on their "empty backhauls." This, however, is an oversimplification because the origination and destination patterns required for these inside-out trips is often very different from that of downtown-oriented transit. For example, it is unlikely that a Negro male employed in a suburban industry will be adequately served by a simple reversal of a downtown system. The chances of these systems serving the outbound white commuter well are also remote since he normally does not live as close to the central business district as the minority groups.

The fact that conventional public transit or commuter systems have not served these inside-out trips well has been documented recently by Negro complaints about difficulties in reaching certain employment opportunities. Such complaints were recognized in the McCone report on the Watts riots. These inside-out trips are very often performed by private automobiles, with the cost of the trips being reduced by car-pooling. Some recent public transit experiments financed by the Department of Housing and Urban Development (as in Watts, for example) may eventually reduce this reliance upon private automobile.

It should be quite clear that since the groups served by these four different basic urban transportation systems are rather different, the incidence of benefits derived from improvements in these systems will vary considerably. For example, improvement of the long-distance, high-performance suburb-to-downtown systems will tend primarily to benefit higher income groups. To the extent that development of these systems is subsidized from public funds the implicit income transfer probably would be regressive. By contrast, expenditures aimed at improving conventional short-haul central city transit will almost certainly benefit mostly low- to middle-income groups.

It is also clear that future demands placed upon these different systems may vary widely. The need for cross-haul services between suburban residences and workplaces seems to be growing most rapidly while the demand for conventional public transit seems to be declining. Demands for long-distance commutation seem to be more or less constant or slowly increasing, depending upon the extent to which a particular downtown area houses office and related service activities. Finally, as long as housing opportunities for minority groups are primarily limited to centrally located ghettos, the demand for "inside-out" commutation is likely to grow.

Thus, in light of anticipated future needs, public policy might well focus attention on the development of cross-haul and inside-out systems. Any such emphasis would depart, of course, from that implicit in the development or subsidization of long-distance rail commuter lines, an all too characteristic emphasis in recent urban transportation planning.

The most neglected aspect of urban transportation planning would seem to be devising means to meet cross-haul or reverse commuter trips better via public transit. The need is for experimentation with new and more flexible forms of public transit and the establishment of more public transit routes that traverse *only* suburban and non-central locations. In particular, many cross-haul and reverse commuter trips are almost certainly better served by public transit that does *not* become involved in downtown congestion with all that implies in time losses and increased operating costs. More intensive analysis of basic urban commuter markets and a concomitant improvement in marketing strategies employed by public transit managements would greatly facilitate these developments.[6]

In summary, it must be recognized that cities are constantly undergoing change. There are many reasons for believing that the changes in workplace and residential location being induced by ever-changing manufacturing, bookkeeping, transportation, and communication technologies may result in radically different urban transportation patterns in the near future. Indeed, one of the major failures of many urban public transit systems has been their failure to serve new workplaces in suburban or metropolitan ring locations. If present trends in residential and workplace locations continue, the major unmet urban transportation needs ten or twenty years from now may well be between, within, and across the outer portions of our large metropolitan areas rather than to-and-from the core.

That future, however, is still some time away. The most urgent policy question seems to be whether cities will choose to solve any short-run transportation problems they face by using rather blunt and unsophisticated methods (in the form of heavy capital investments in immobile and inflexible rail transit used on a standby or part-time basis for a few hours a day) or whether the self-discipline can be mustered to organize the extensive urban street and highway capacity already in place to better serve today's needs. Remembering that over 70 per cent of public transit is now performed on highways, the possibilities for immediate gain from such discipline would appear quite promising. Perhaps the money saved might be better spent on educational, recreational, and rehabilitation programs more directly related to making the central city a better place to live.

[6] Lewis M. Schneider, *Marketing Urban Mass Transit: A Comparative Study of Management Strategies* (Boston, 1965), presents several interesting ideas on how these improvements might be implemented.

PRICING IN URBAN AND SUBURBAN TRANSPORT

William S. Vickrey

I will begin with the proposition that in no other major area are pricing practices so irrational, so out of date, and so conducive to waste as in urban transportation. Two aspects are particularly deficient: the absence of adequate peak-off differentials and the gross underpricing of some modes relative to others.

In nearly all other operations characterized by peak load problems, at least some attempt is made to differentiate between the rates charged for peak and for off-peak service. Where competition exists, this pattern is enforced by competition: resort hotels have off-season rates; theaters charge more on weekends and less for matinees. Telephone calls are cheaper at night, though I suspect not sufficiently so to promote a fully efficient utilization of the plant. Power rates are varied to a considerable extent according to the measured or the imputed load factor of the consumer, and in some cases, usually for special-purpose uses such as water heating, according to the time of use. In France, this practice is carried out logically by charging according to season and time of day for all consumption but that of the smallest domestic consumers; rate changes at the consumers' meters are triggered by a special frequency signal actuating a tuned relay which connects or disconnects auxiliary registers. But in transportation, such differentiation as exists is usually perverse. Off-peak concessions are virtually unknown in transit. Such concessions as are made in suburban service for "shoppers' tickets" and the like are usually relatively small, indeed are often no greater than those available in multitrip tickets not restricted to off-peak riding, and usually result in fares still far above those enjoyed by regular commuters who are predominantly peak-hour passengers.

In the case of suburban railroad fares, the existing pattern is even contrary to what would be most profitable in terms of the relative elasticities of demand. Both on a priori grounds and on the basis of the analysis of the historical experience recently made by Elbert Segelhorat in a . . . Columbia dissertation, it is clear that the price elasticity of the off-peak traffic, at current fare levels at least, is substantially higher than that of peak-hour traffic. If, for example, the average suburban family spends $300 per year for commuting and peak-hour trips and $50 per year for occasional off-

William S. Vickrey is McVickar Professor of Economics, Columbia University.

Reprinted with permission from William S. Vickrey, "Pricing in Urban and Suburban Transport," *American Economic Review* 53 (May 1963), pp. 452–465.

peak trips and the commutation fares were increased by 5 per cent, causing a 1 per cent drop in this traffic, while off-peak fares were reduced 40 per cent, with a 30 per cent increase in traffic, gross revenues per commuting family would go up from $350.00 to $350.85, with operating costs if anything reduced slightly, since nearly all costs are determined by the peak traffic level. The riding public would on the average be substantially better off: the above typical family, if it maintained the same pattern of usage, would pay only $315 + $30 = $345 instead of $350 as formerly, and any adaptation that it chose to make to the new rates would represent a further benefit, since the alternative of no change would still be open to it if it preferred. Things may not work out quite this neatly in practice, but the potential for substantial gains from even more drastic revisions in the rate structure is certainly there.

Fare collection procedures are sometimes urged as an excuse for not going to a more rational fare structure, but here there has been a deplorable lag behind what a little ingenuity or modern technology makes possible. There would be relatively little difficulty in devising apparatus for collecting subway fares on as elaborate an origin, destination, and time basis as might be desired, simply by dispensing a coded check at the entrance turnstile against the deposit of an interim fare, this check being deposited in an exit turnstile which will then either refund any excess or release only on the deposit of the remainder of the fare. Bus fares represent a problem that has yet to be satisfactorily solved, but considering the vast waste of the time of operators and passengers through delays caused by present fare collection methods, a concerted attack on this problem should yield high dividends. For commuter railroads, the possibility exists of issuing machine-readable subscriber's cards, with passengers making a record of their trips by inserting the card in a register at the origin and destination stations and being billed according to the time, origin, and destination of the trips actually made by the subscriber, his family, and guests. Something like this seems to be in the offing for the new San Francisco system, which in many respects is more of a commuter service than an urban transit system. Actually, it is not even necessary to enclose the stations in order to use such a system: proper registering at the stations can be enforced by dispensing a dated seat check to be displayed during the trip and deposited in registering out at the destination.

Even short of such mechanization, existing ticketing arrangements are needlessly clumsy, involving in many cases a duplication of effort between station agent and conductor and fairly elaborate accounting and auditing procedures. The New York Central has recently taken a step forward in this respect by arranging to mail monthly commutation tickets to patrons and receive payment by mail. Gross delinquency appears to be running appreciably less than the saving in ticket agents' time, and the net credit loss is undoubtedly much less than this, since many who fail to return or pay for their tickets in fact do not use them, as when they die or move away. Another wrinkle worth trying would be the use of a universal form of multiride ticket, to be sold by ticket agents or conductors at a flat price of $5.00 or $10.00, validated for bearer and those accompanying him, with a liberal time limit, for a number of rides or trip units depending on the stations between which it is designated to be used by appropriate punches at time of sale. An off-peak differential could be provided in conjunction with this type of ticket by providing that two units would be charged for an off-peak ride as against three units for a peak-hour ride. The ticket itself, for a typical suburban route, need be no larger than an ordinary playing card. Accounting would be greatly simplified, conductor's cash fare transactions would be both simplified and greatly reduced in number, and the use of the service would become much more convenient for passengers. Such a ticket would provide a more effective off-peak differential than the shoppers' type of ticket, since those who are either going or returning during the peak or are returning at a later date cannot usually avail themselves of such tickets.

But while suburban and transit fare structures are seriously deficient, the pricing of the use of urban streets is all but nonexistent. Superficially, it is often thought that since reported highway expenditures by the state and federal government are roughly balanced by highway tax and license revenues, the motorist is on the whole paying his way. But what is true on the average is far from true of users of the more congested urban streets. Much of the expenditure on such streets is borne by city budgets supported slightly if at all by explicit contributions from highway sources, in most states. More important, much of the real economic cost of providing the space for city streets and highways does not appear in the accounts at all, being concealed by the fact that this space has usually been "dedicated" to the public use at some time in the past. It is extremely difficult to make close evaluations from the scanty and scattered data available, but very roughly it appears to me that if we take the burden of all the gasoline and other vehicular taxes borne by motorists by reason of their use of city streets, this amounts to only about a third of the real economic cost of the facilities they use. In current terms, the high marginal cost of increased street space becomes painfully apparent whenever a street widening scheme is evaluated. Even in terms of long-range planning, urban expressways cost many times as much as expressways in rural areas built to comparable specifications, and while the flow of traffic may be greater, this is not enough to come anywhere near amortizing the cost out of the taxes paid by the traffic flowing over the urban expressways. Even when tolls are charged in conjunction with special features such as bridges or tunnels, these seldom cover the cost of the connecting expressways and city streets. And except where the street layout is exceptionally favorable, such tolls usually have an unfavorable effect on the routing of traffic.

The perversity of present pricing practices is at its height, perhaps, for the East River crossings to Long Island and Brooklyn. Here the peculiar political logic is that the older bridges are in some sense "paid for," and hence must be free, while tolls must be charged on the newer facilities. The result is that considerable traffic is diverted from the newer facilities that have relatively adequate and less congested approaches to the older bridges such as the Manhattan and the Queensboro bridges, which dump their traffic right in the middle of some of the worst congestion in New York. The construction of the proposed expressway across lower Manhattan from the Holland Tunnel to the Manhattan and Williamsburgh bridges would be at least less urgent, if not actually unwarranted, in view of its enormous cost, if, as would seem possible, traffic could be diverted from the Manhattan Bridge to the Brooklyn-Battery tunnel by imposing tolls on the Manhattan and other East River bridges and reducing or removing the toll on the tunnel.* The delusion still persists that the primary role of pricing should always be that of financing the service rather than that of promoting economy in its use. In practice there are many alternative ways of financing; but no device can function quite as effectively and smoothly as a properly designed price structure in controlling use and providing a guide to the efficient deployment of capital.

The underpricing of highway services is even more strongly pronounced during peak hours. Even if urban motorists on the average paid the full cost of the urban facilities, rush hour use would still be seriously underpriced; moreover, this underpricing would be relatively more severe than for transit or commutation service. This is because off-peak traffic on the highways and streets is a much larger percentage of the total than is the case for either transit or commutation traffic; and therefore in the process of averaging out the costs, much more of the costs properly attributable to the peak can be shifted to the shoulders of the off-peak traffic than can be thus shifted in the case of transit or commutation service. The effect of this is that while the commutation fare problem is chiefly one of the overpricing of off-peak travel, and to a minor extent if at all one of underpricing of peak travel, the problem of the pricing of automobile travel is chiefly that of remedying the underpricing of peak travel, and to a relatively minor extent if at all of the overpricing of off-peak travel. These two relationships combine to give the result that even if motor traffic and commuter train traffic each on the whole fully paid their way on the basis of a uniform charge per trip, the proportion by which the peak-hour motorist would be

---

* New York City appears to have abandoned the Lower Manhattan Expressway, but still does not impose congestion tolls. — Ed.

subsidized by the off-peak motorists would be far greater than the proportion by which the peak-hour commuter is subsidized by the off-peak commuter.

A quantitative indication of the seriousness of the problem of peak-hour automobile traffic is derivable from some projections made for Washington, D.C. Two alternative programs were developed for taking care of traffic predicted under two alternative conditions, differing chiefly as to the extent to which express transit service would be provided. The additional traffic lanes required for the larger of the two volumes of traffic would be needed almost solely to provide for this added rush hour traffic, the less extensive road system being adequate for the off-peak traffic even at the higher overall traffic level. Dividing the extra cost by the extra rush hour traffic, it turned out that for each additional car making a daily trip that contributes to the dominant flow, during the peak hour, an additional investment of $23,000 was projected. In other words, a man who bought a $3,000 car for the purpose of driving downtown to work every day would be asking the community, in effect, to match his $3,000 investment with $23,000 from general highway funds. Or if the wage earners in a development were all to drive downtown to work, the investment in highways that this development would require would be of the same order of magnitude as the entire investment in a moderate-sized house for each family. It may be that the affluent society will be able to shoulder such a cost, but even if it could there would seem to be many much more profitable and urgent uses to which sums of this magnitude could be put. And even if we assume that staggering of working hours could spread the peak traffic more or less evenly over three hours, this would still mean $8,000 per daily trip, even though achievement of such staggering would represent an achievement second only to the highway construction itself. At 250 round trips per year, allowing 10 per cent as the gross return which a comparable investment in the private sector would have to earn to cover interest, amortization, and property and corporate income taxes, this amounts to over $3.00 per round trip, or, on a one-hour peak basis, to $9.00 per round trip, if staggering is ruled out. This is over and above costs of maintenance or of provision for parking. When costs threaten to reach such levels, it is high time to think seriously about controlling the use through pricing.

It is sometimes thought that pricing of roadway use would apply chiefly to arterial streets and highways and that it would have no application to streets used mainly for access, which should allegedly be paid for by property taxes on the abutting property to which access is given. But the relevant criterion is not the function performed, but the degree of congestion that would obtain in the absence of pricing. To be sure, there would be little point in levying a specific charge for the use of suburban residential side streets or lightly traveled rural roads, since the congestion added by an increment in traffic is virtually nil in such circumstances and the wear and tear usually negligible. In effect, at these levels of traffic the economies of scale are such that marginal cost is only a small fraction of the average cost. But this does not hold for roadways used for access at the center of a city. A truck making a delivery on a narrow side street may cause as much congestion and delay to others as it would in many miles of running on an arterial highway. Even in the case of a cul-de-sac that is used exclusively for access and carries no through traffic, a firm with frequent deliveries will make access more difficult for his neighbors; only by specific pricing of such use can the firm requiring much access be differentiated from firms requiring relatively little, and encouraged to locate where its activities will be less burdensome to the remainder of the community; or to receive and ship goods at times when less congestion is generated. Some of the worst traffic congestion in New York occurs as a result of the way access is had to firms in the garment district; restrictions on truck size and exhortations have produced only minor improvement. It seems likely that a suitable charge for such use of road space would be more acceptable than an arbitrary and drastic ban, and that with a definite financial incentive methods might be found to avoid the creation of congestion.

But talk of direct and specific charges for roadway use conjures up visions of a clutter of toll booths, an army of toll collectors, and traffic endlessly tangled up in queues. Conventional methods of toll collection are, to be sure, costly in manpower, space, and interference with the smooth flow of traffic. Furthermore, unless the street configuration is exceptionally favorable, tolls often contribute to congestion over parallel routes. However, with a little ingenuity, it is possible to devise methods of charging for the use of the city streets that are relatively inexpensive, produce no interference with the free flow of traffic, and are capable of adjusting the charge in close conformity with variations in costs and traffic conditions. My own fairly elaborate scheme involves equipping all cars with an electronic identifier which hopefully can be produced on a large-scale basis for about $20 each. These blocks would be scanned by roadside equipment at a fairly dense network of cordon points, making a record of the identity of the car; these records would then be taken to a central processing plant once a month and the records assembled on electronic digital computers and bills sent out. Preliminary estimates indicate a total cost of the equipment on a moderately large scale of about $35 per vehicle, including the identifier; the operating cost would be approximately that involved in sending out telephone bills. Bills could be itemized to whatever extent is desired to furnish the owner with a record that would guide him in the further use of his car. In addition, roadside signals could be installed to indicate the current level of charge and enable drivers to shift to less costly routes where these are available.

Other methods have been devised in England, where the country can less well afford the vast outlays demanded by our rubber-tired sacred cow, and where street layouts are such as to make provision for large volumes of vehicular traffic both more costly and more destructive of civic amenities. One scheme suggested for use in a pilot scheme for the town of Cambridge involves the use of identifiers to actuate a tallying register, the rate of tallying being governed by impulses the frequency of which would vary according to the degree of traffic congestion existing in the zone in which the car is reported to be. Another extremely simple and low-cost but less automatic device would consist of a meter installed in each car so as to be visible from outside, which could be wound up by the insertion of a token sold at an appropriate price — the token being subject to inspection through a window and being destroyed when the subsequent token is brought into place. The driver can control the rate at which the meter runs down by a lever or switch which simultaneously displays a signal which will indicate to outside observers the rate currently being charged. The driver is then required to keep this signal set to correspond with the rate in effect in the zone in which he is driving as indicated by appropriate wayside signals. Extremely simple methods of varying the rate at which the meter runs down have been devised in England, which for the time being I must treat as confidential. The rate can appropriately be a time rate rather than a distance rate, since the greater the congestion the greater is the appropriate charge, so that no connection to the wheels is needed and the whole meter can be extremely compact, rugged, and cheap. The chief difficulty with this method is the likelihood that drivers will "forget" to turn the rate of the meter up promptly on entering a higher rate zone, but given a reasonable amount of policing this difficulty might be overcome after an initial period of habituation.

A slightly more elaborate version of this method would call for the changes in the meter rate to be actuated automatically in response to signals emitted from wayside equipment at the boundaries of the various zones. This would probably raise the cost to something above the level of the response block method. On the other hand, both this and the previous method are somewhat better adapted to serving to assess charges for parking as well as for moving about within an area, so that the cost of servicing and installing parking meters could be properly credited against the cost of the new system.

Another version would call for the meter to be run down by pulses emitted from cables laid along the roadway, with the pulse rate varied according to traffic density and other factors. Alternatively, the cables could be arranged to emit continuously and located across the roadway — the number of cables turned on at any one time being varied according to traffic conditions. Reliability of operation can be assured by using two alternative frequencies in alternate cables successively. The cables need not be spaced evenly, but for economy in operation may be placed in groups so that they can be energized from a single source. With either of these methods, any failure of the meter to operate could be checked by requiring the meter to be placed in plain view and arranging for a visible signal to be changed cyclically as the meter is actuated.

Adequate methods for enforcement of each of the schemes seem available which are reasonably simple, with the possible exception of the manual system, where minor negligence might be difficult to check and lead to major negligence. With identifier methods, the registering of the proper vehicle number could be checked by having a few of the detector stations equipped with apparatus to display the number being registered, which could be compared with the license plate by observers. Errors due to malfunction, as well as most fraudulent tampering, would show up as a matter of course during the processing of the records, as each record showing a car entering a zone must match the immediately succeeding record for that car leaving that zone. Cameras can also be arranged at some locations to take pictures of cars not producing a valid response signal. With meters, arrangements can be made to hold used and mutilated tokens in a sealed box; these could be inspected and their number compared with a non-resettable counter with a capacity not likely to be exceeded during the life of the car, as a part of an annual safety inspection program.

Ultimately, one would expect that all cars in an entire country would be equipped with meters or electronic identifiers. Initially, however, it would be necessary to make some provision for cars from other areas. Cars in transit or making infrequent visits to the congested area could be given the freedom of the city in a spirit of hospitality. Cars making a longer stay or more frequent visits would be required to equip themselves — say at cordon points established along the major arteries entering the controlled area. Unequipped cars would be prohibited from using the minor streets crossing the boundary of the controlled area. Such provisions would be particularly easy to enforce with electronic identifier methods: unequipped cars passing major control points would set off a camera; unequipped cars using routes prohibited to them would set off an alarm signal, facilitating their apprehension. With a meter system, checking on unequipped cars would have to be largely a manual operation and would probably be considerably less rigorous. Actually a similar problem occurs at present in enforcing provisions against the use of out-of-state license plates in a given state for longer than a limited period.

Such charging for street use could have a far-reaching impact on the pattern of urban transportation and even on the patterns of land use, by promoting a more economical distribution of traffic between various modes, the various modes being used in accordance with their suitability for the particular trip in the light of the costs involved, instead of, as at present, being chosen to suit the preferences and whims of the individual regardless of the impact on others. Motorists will no longer be maneuvered into the position of being forced to pay for a luxury that they can ill-afford. Mass transportation will have an opportunity to develop in line with its inherent characteristics, eventually developing a quality and frequency of service that will in many cases be preferred even to the spuriously low-priced private car transportation that might be provided in the absence of a system of specific charges. Traffic-generating activities will tend to be located more rationally in relation to real transportation costs. For example, appropriate transportation charges might have been sufficient to have inhibited the construction of the Pan-American subway-jammer over Grand Central. Rapid vehicular transportation within congested areas, not now available at any price, will be generally available for meeting emergency and high priority needs where the cost is justified. Traffic will be routed more efficiently, so as to provide a smoother functioning of the roadway system as a whole. The levels of charge required to balance marginal cost and marginal benefit in the short run will provide a much more definite and reliable guide than is now available as to where and to what extent the provision of additional facilities can be justified. One can cite, for example, the extra half hour that the airlines have to allow during rush hours for the trip from East 38th Street to Idlewild [Kennedy], in spite of the fact that this route is almost entirely over grade-separated expressways.

One effect of such charging would be to change the relative attractiveness of different forms of mass transportation. Under present conditions, buses are involved in the same traffic tangle as the private car and are often further handicapped by their inferior maneuverability. It is then difficult to make a bus service sufficiently attractive relative to use of a private car to attract a sufficient volume of traffic to make the frequency of service satisfactory. In order to give the transit facility a chance to compete with the private automobile, it becomes necessary to provide some sort of reserved right of way. With buses this in theory takes the form of a lane reserved for them, but in practice this faces formidable problems in dealing with intersections and pickup points, and at best means that the lanes thus provided are likely to be underutilized, since it is seldom desirable to schedule just enough bus service to fully utilize a whole lane of capacity. These difficulties provide a strong argument for going to the very substantial expense of a rail rapid transit system.

With street use controlled by pricing, however, it is possible to insure that the level of congestion is kept down to the point at which buses will provide a satisfactory level of service, and rail rapid transit systems will be required only where a volume of traffic arises that will warrant their high cost on the basis of superior service and operating economies.

But while the most dramatic impact of street use pricing would be to permit the economical allocation of traffic among the various modes, it would be of great importance even in cases where intermodal substitution is not a factor. Even in a community entirely without mass-transit service, street pricing could have an important function to perform. For example, traffic between opposite sides of town often has the choice of going right through the center of town or taking a more circuitous route. Left to itself, this traffic is likely to choose the direct route through the center, unless indeed the center becomes so congested as to make it quicker to go the longer way around. In the absence of pricing, one may be faced with the alternatives of either tolerating the congestion in the center of town, or if it is considered mandatory to provide congestion-free access to the center of town, of providing relatively costly facilities in the center of town adequate to accommodate through traffic as well. With pricing it becomes possible to restrict the use of the center streets to those having no ready alternative and provide for the through traffic on peripheral roadways at much lower cost. Without pricing, bypass routes, though beneficial, often attract only part of the traffic that they should carry for the greatest over-all economy of transport.

Pricing of street use can in the long run have significant effects on the whole pattern of development of urban communities and on property values. While on general principles one can hardly imagine this impact to be other than beneficial, it is a little difficult to discern the net direction in which it would tend — for example, whether the concentration of activity at the center would increase or decrease. In order to gain insight into this problem I have been toying with a model which attempts to incorporate the essential element of choice of route, but in spite of drastically simplified structure and assumptions this model has so far resisted an analytical solution and will probably have to be worked out by simulation and successive approximations on a large electronic computer.

The model is as follows: Consider a community with a system of streets laid out in a circular and radial pattern; for simplicity, assume that the mesh of this network is small enough to be negligible; that is, that we can travel from any point in a radial and in a circumferential direction, but not at an angle. Thus any trip must be made up of radial segments and circular arcs. In effect, we assume perfect divisibility of road space, or that the capacity of a street is directly proportional to its width. In the neighborhood of any given point at a radius r from the center, a proportion of $w(r)$ of the area is devoted to streets, the remainder being devoted to business activities that generate one unit of traffic for each unit of net area; i.e., one unit of gross area originates and terminates $[1 - w(r)]$ units of traffic. The traffic originating at any one point has destinations distributed at random over the remainder of the business area; i.e., any tendency of related businesses to group themselves close together is neglected. The average cost of transportation per ton-mile (or passenger-mile) is given by some functional relation in which the density of traffic per unit roadway width is an argument. For example, we may put $x = A + B \, (t/w)^k$, where t is the volume of traffic in tons per hour and w is the width of the roadway in feet, A, B, and k being constants. A may be thought of as the operating cost of the vehicle, where the volume of traffic is negligible, the second term being the additional costs experienced due to delays resulting from congestion; k is the elasticity of this congestion cost, which can be thought of as being proportional to the number of added minutes required to cover a given distance as compared to the time required in the absence of conflicting traffic. A relation of this form was found to fit data from the Lincoln tunnel extremely well up to close to the point where a queue begins to accumulate, with a value of k of about 4.5, so that the marginal congestion cost is some $k + 1 = 5.5$ times the average congestion cost per vehicle. In other words, according to this data, an individual who has to take ten minutes longer to make a given trip than he would if there were no interference from other traffic causes 45 vehicle minutes of delay in the aggregate to other vehicles with whose movements he interferes. Unfortunately, comparable data for the more interesting case of travel over a network of city streets could not be found, but something of this order of magnitude is generally to be expected.

It can readily be shown that optimum allocation of the street space in a given small area between radial traffic and circular traffic calls for the space to be allocated in proportion to the traffic so that the average and marginal costs are the same in both directions. We can thus combine the circular traffic and the radial traffic and speak of the relation of costs to traffic in terms of aggregate ton-miles of traffic in both directions per acre of street area. Thus the cost per ton-mile can be taken to be $x = A + B \, (t/w)^k$, with x in cents per ton-mile, t in ton-miles per gross acre of land, and w the fraction of the land devoted to streets, in the particular neighborhood.

Given the density of traffic as a function of r, it is possible to determine the least-cost route for any given trip on an average cost basis in which the shipper bears only the delay costs experienced by him, and alternatively on a marginal cost basis where he must pay in addition a toll corresponding to the delay his trip imposes on others. By imposing the condition that the traffic distribution thus generated shall be one which produces the cost structure leading to the traffic distribution, one gets a differential equation which in principle can be solved to give equilibrium traffic patterns. The cost of this equilibrium traffic pattern can then be integrated over the entire area to give the total cost of transportation, and this can be done both for the marginal cost case and the average cost case to get the total saving in transportation cost over a given street network brought about by the pricing of street use.

Unfortunately, the differential equation that results is of the second order and third degree, and I suspect does not admit of an analytical solution in terms of well-known functions. The next step is recourse to solution of specific cases by successive approximations.

As a by-product of this calculation, one could then also derive the equilibrium rentals that would be paid by businesses at various distances from the center, on the assumption that rental differentials would correspond to the differentials in the costs of transportation borne by the business; because of the symmetry of origins and destinations, it would make no essential difference whether shipping costs were borne entirely by shipper, entirely by consignee, or shared between them.

A further step in the analysis would be to take total cost as determined by the distribution $w(r)$ of land between business and transportation uses at various distances from the center and treat this as a calculus of variations problem of choosing the function $w(r)$ so as to minimize the total cost of transportation. In this way one could compare the pattern of land allocation that would be optimal without pricing to that which would be optimal with pricing. Considering the complexity of the problem, I hesitate to make any guesses as to the nature of this difference, except to speculate that it is likely to be somewhat surprising to many of us.

I will wind up by laying before you one final piece of unfinished business, which is the problem of developing criteria for determining how much of the area in a particular neighborhood should be devoted to transportation, given the pattern of rents in the area. Conventional cost benefit analysis, if employed here at all, would tend to take the form of comparing the rent which private business would pay for the space with the reduction in transportation cost which would result from increasing the area used for transportation and decreasing the effective density of traffic. But in connection with the present model, this rule fails to yield optimal results. Let us imagine, to make things a little more explicit, that a Comprehensive Transportation Authority stood ready to rent or lease land, to be converted from or to transportation use, to or from private business, at a price reflecting the marginal productivity of land area in a particular location in reducing the total cost of carrying out a given number of ton-miles of traffic within a given neighborhood. In terms of our cost formula, the rental would be given by the partial derivative of total cost per unit area xt, with respect to changes in the proportion of total area devoted to transportation, w, the density of traffic t remaining unchanged. Thus:

$$-\frac{\partial(xt)}{\partial W} = -\frac{\partial}{\partial w}(At + Bt^{k+1}w^{-k}) = +kBt^{k+1}w^{-k-1}.$$

A business will then move to a higher rent location only if the saving in transportation costs borne by the particular business is greater than the difference in rent. However, since transportation costs are in this model borne in part by the firms with which a given firm deals, only half of the change in the transportation costs of the goods he receives and ships resulting from his change in location will be felt directly by the firm making the change, so that on the whole a firm will fail to move unless the saving in the costs of the shipments to and from the firm is twice as great as the net increment in the costs of transportation resulting from the reapportionment of the space devoted to transportation. In other words, the conventional cost-benefit analysis in terms of going rents has a strong tendency to leave business uneconomically dispersed and to result in too much space in the center of the city being devoted to transportation.

This conclusion is derived from an admittedly highly simplified model, which neglects such factors as the clustering of interrelated firms, the wide variations in the ratio of land to transportation requirements of various activities, and the possibilities for creating additional space by construction of multistory buildings, or for that matter, multilevel highways. But the model can plead not guilty to the charge of having ignored the journey to work and other passenger transportation, for, input-output analysis style, we can regard labor as the product of the household sector, and, Clayton Act to the contrary notwithstanding, as an article of commerce with a peculiarly high transport cost. The essential difference between this model and classical space economics models such as those of Von Thunen is that the latter imply a well-defined shadow price for each commodity at each point in the space, with transport taking place only between points where the price differential balances the transportation cost, whereas the present model allows for crosshauling and a certain amount of particularism in the relations between economic units. The real world presumably lies somewhere in between these two extremes. Study of journey-to-work patterns seems generally to reveal a situation a fairly long way from the Von Thunen extreme, with a great deal of crosshauling of labor of roughly comparable skill. According to this, a cost benefit analysis can justify devoting land to transportation only when the savings in transportation costs yield a return considerably greater than the gross rentals, including taxes, that private business would be willing to pay for the space. This in turn means that an even greater preference should be given to space economizing modes of transport than would be indicated by rent and tax levels. And our rubber-shod sacred cow is a ravenously space-hungry, shall I say, monster?

CONGESTION THEORY AND
TRANSPORT INVESTMENT

William S. Vickrey

"DEEPENING" AND "WIDENING" OF TRANSPORT INVESTMENT

Investment in transport facilities necessarily begins by being largely investment in the provision of new routes or new services under conditions of substantial indivisibilities and increasing returns to scale. Under these conditions the usual profitability tests for determining the desirability of specific investments lead generally to under- rather than to over-investment in transportation facilities. At this stage, cost-benefit analysis needs to include substantial elements of consumers' surplus on the benefit side in order to arrive at correct evaluations.

As investment proceeds, however, larger and larger proportions of transportation investment are made primarily, or at least in large measure, to relieve congestion on existing routes and to expand overall capacity. In such instances criteria based on apparent profitability may be seriously misleading in the opposite direction, and when notions of consumers' surplus are narrowly applied without regard to the overall situation, the errors may be compounded. This is especially likely to be the case where charges levied for the use of the existing and prospective competing facilities are far wide of the mark of representing marginal cost, as they often tend to be. It is this latter type of investment, designed to relieve congestion, with which this paper is concerned.

TYPES OF CONGESTION

For purposes of economic analysis it is useful to distinguish at least six types of congested situations, though they are in fact often encountered in various combinations. These can be designated simple interaction, multiple interaction, bottleneck, triggerneck, network and control, and general density.

Single interaction occurs whenever two transportation units approach each other closely enough so that one or the other must be delayed in order to reduce the likelihood of a collision, no other units being sufficiently close

William S. Vickrey is McVickar Professor of Economics, Columbia University. Reprinted with permission from William S. Vickrey, "Congestion Theory and Transport Investment," *American Economic Review* (May 1969), pp. 251–260.

to be immediately affected. This is the chief form of congestion encountered in light traffic. Total congestion delay tends to vary as the square of the volume of traffic; thus a motorist deciding on a trip under light traffic conditions will thereby inflict on others an amount of additional delay roughly equal to that which he himself will experience. (To be sure, for some types of vehicles the effect may not be symmetrical: slow-moving vehicles may tend to be relatively little delayed and fast-moving vehicles relatively more. The above relationship holds for an average vehicle.)

Multiple interaction tends to take place at higher levels of traffic density, short of capacity flows, where one can expect the average speed s to be a function of the flow of traffic $x : s = f(x)$. For traffic volumes ranging from about 0.5 to 0.9 of capacity, one can often fit a function of the form

$$(1) \qquad z = t - t_o = \frac{1}{s} - \frac{1}{s_o} = ax^k$$

where t is the time required to go a unit distance under actual conditions, t_o is the time required under very light traffic conditions, z is the average delay per vehicle, and a and k are constant parameters. For a relationship of this form, the total increment of delay given by

$$(2) \qquad \frac{d(zx)}{dx} = z + x\frac{dz}{dx} = ax^k + xak\,x^{k-1} = (1+k)z$$

that results from a unit increment of traffic thus works out to $k+1$ times the delay experienced by the vehicle itself. That is, for every minute of delay directly experienced by the added vehicle, k minutes of delay are inflicted on the remaining traffic. For situations where considerable congestion exists, k is likely to be in the range of from 3 to 5 or even higher. The previous case is essentially that where $k = 1$.

The pure bottleneck situation, which is the one that will chiefly concern us here, is one where a relatively short route segment has a fixed capacity substantially smaller relative to traffic demand than that of preceding or succeeding segments. There is thus relatively little delay as long as traffic remains below the capacity of the bottleneck, though small amounts of delay may occur as a result of stochastic variations in the level of traffic flow when the average flow is just below capacity. The important delays will occur when desired traffic flow continuously exceeds the capacity of the bottleneck for substantial periods. We then find that queues accumulate until either a period is reached when traffic demand is below capacity, or the prospect of waiting in the queue reduces the traffic demand by diverting it to another time or route or by suppressing the trip entirely.

A triggerneck situation develops from a bottleneck situation whenever the queue backed up from the bottleneck interferes with the flow of traffic not itself intending to use the bottleneck facility. The onset of incremental congestion may be quite sharp, and indeed in extreme circumstances a circular chain of triggerneck situations may bring traffic to a complete standstill, requiring that at least some of the vehicles involved actually back up before a forward movement can be resumed.

Network and control congestion results whenever the levels of traffic during the peak are reached requiring the application of additional control measures, whether in the form of regulations, stop signs, routing limitations, traffic lights, train controls, flight patterns and rules, or otherwise. Aside from the cost of these measures in themselves and even assuming that they are invoked only when the circumstances without them would be demonstrably worse, either from the standpoint of safety or delays, it is generally true that they cannot be applied with complete selectivity as to time and place, so that in most cases control measures required to take care of the most severe conditions will result in more delay under less severe conditions than would occur in the absence of controls, or with less restrictive controls adapted to the less severe conditions. Thus some of the delay experienced by off-peak traffic is in a medium-long-run sense caused by the increase in the peak traffic that made the controls necessary.

Finally there is a sense in which congestion costs in the long run are a function of the overall density of transportation flows in a given area for all modes combined and over all routes, even though some modes may contribute less to the total overall congestion relative to its traffic volume than other modes. Even if route separations are such that traffic on one mode has no immediate impact on traffic on the other modes, the construction of facilities to accommodate additional traffic on the one mode or route will not only encounter increased construction costs by reason of other existing facilities that cross its path, but such construction will at the same time be increasing the cost of constructing any other transportation facilities across its path in the future. In highly congested areas there is a very real sense in which long-run increasing costs may be encountered. It is very rarely that any account is taken, in the estimating of the cost of constructing facilities for a given transportation route and mode, of the increased costs of such future crossings by other links, even though good technical planning may sometimes make provision for such future crossings in the design.

ACCIDENTS AS A COST OF CONGESTION

In addition to the cost of delays, the cost of accidents constitute an often overlooked element in the costs of congestion. While the incidence of traffic accidents does not arise with traffic density quite as rapidly as do time delays, one does expect, a priori, that as vehicle interactions per vehicle-mile increase, accidents per vehicle-mile will also increase. There is, indeed, a certain amount of empirical evidence that in a significantly wide range of situations this increase in accident rates with increasing traffic densities does in fact occur: for grade-separated limited access highways in California, it was found that the marginal increment in the number of accidents associated with an increment of traffic on a given type of highway was approximately 1.5 times the average accident incidence per vehicle-mile.[1] Thus whatever may be the effect on accidents of shifting traffic from other highways to grade-separated expressways, there is in addition a favorable effect on accidents of building roads of the same type to more ample dimensions and greater capacity, and an adverse effect on the accident rate per vehicle-mile of increasing the flow of traffic on a given roadway.

Before taking full credit for this benefit, however, it is necessary to examine the net safety effects of increasing total traffic flow overall, and of attracting traffic from other safer modes, such as rail transit. Doing too much in the name of safety considered in a narrow context can actually increase the overall death rate.

CONSTRUCTION TO EASE BOTTLENECKS

Although the pure bottleneck situation is not typical of the general congestion picture, it is an important element in many cases of severe congestion and its relatively simple analysis does provide some valuable insights into the nature of the overall congestion problem.

Assume a situation in which $N = 7200$ commuters want to make a daily trip via a given bottleneck, and that in the absence of congestion their times of passing the bottleneck point would be distributed evenly over a period between $t_a = 8:00$ A.M. and $t_b = 9:00$ A.M., thus permitting each commuter to arrive at his downtown destination at a desired time. If the capacity of the bottleneck were to be enlarged to

$$v_m = \frac{N}{t_b - t_a} = 120 \text{ cars per minute,}$$

then of course the capacity would just meet the requirements and no queue other than that due to stochastic variation would occur.

If the capacity is kept smaller than this, i.e., $v < v_m$, then it becomes impossible for all the commuters to arrive at their destinations just at the desired times. Some, at least, will have to arrive either late or early. In the absence of tolls the steady state that results will involve varying degrees of queuing, with those arriving at their offices closest to their desired times

---

[1] See William Vickrey, "Automobile Accidents, Tort Law, Externalities, and Insurance," *Law and Contemporary Problems,* Summer, 1968, pp. 467–68.

generally having to spend relatively more time in the queue than those who choose to push their arrival time further away from the desired time.

To keep the model simple, let us suppose that all commuters uniformly value time spent at home at $w_h = 2$ cents per minute, and time spent at the office at w_o, which for time prior to the desired starting time we suppose is $w_o = w_p = 1$ cent per minute, and for time after the desired starting time is $w_o = w_j = 4$ cents per minute. Time spent in the queue has a value of $w_q = 0$. It is readily seen that if an individual is to be maximizing the overall value of his time, he must be leaving the bottleneck point, subsequent to any queuing he may have had to endure, at a time such that

$$\frac{d_q}{d_t} = \frac{w_h - w_o}{w_h - w_q}$$

(3)

$$= \begin{cases} 0.5 & \text{for } w_o = w_p = 1 \text{ cent/min} \\ -1.0 & \text{for } w_o = w_j = 4 \text{ cents/min} \end{cases}$$

where $q(t)$ is the amount of waiting in the queue required in order to leave the bottleneck point at time t. A fraction

(4) $$r = \frac{w_j - w_h}{w_j - w_p} = \frac{2}{3}$$

of the commuters will pass the bottleneck during the period of queue buildup and arrive at work at or before the desired starting time, the remaining fraction $1 - r = 1/3$ of the commuters will leave the bottleneck after 8:40 A.M. during the working off of the queue and arrive at or after the desired time. The total time required for the commuters to pass the bottleneck will be $N/v = 7200/v$, which will also be the length of time that a queue will persist, as long as $v < v_m$.

The length of the queue will build up linearly from zero at time

$$t_i = t_a - r\,[(N/v) - (t_b - t_a)]$$

(5)

$$= 8{:}40 - 4800/v$$

to a maximum wait in the queue of

(6) $$q_p = \frac{N}{v}(r)\frac{w_h - w_p}{w_h - w_q} = \frac{2400}{v}$$

for cars leaving the bottleneck at

(7) $$t_p = t_a + r(t_b - t_a) = 8{:}40 \text{ A.M.}$$

after which it will again decline linearly to zero at

$$t_j = t_b + (1 - r)[(N/v) - (t_b - t_a)]$$

(8)

$$= 8{:}40 + \frac{2400}{v}.$$

There will be a sharp discontinuity in the amount of delay experienced as the capacity of the facility is expanded past the point where $v = v_m = 120$ cars/minute. Below v_m, delay is inversely proportional to the capacity v, while at and above v_m the delay from queuing is zero. To be sure, matters will not usually work out as sharply as this, for there will usually be some variation in the desired rates of traffic flow near the peak rather than a peak that has an absolutely flat top, as has been assumed here for the sake of simplicity. Moreover, there will usually be some elasticity of traffic demand with respect to queuing time such as to suppress some traffic entirely rather than merely to shift its timing. Nevertheless, sharp discontinuities such as this emphasize the need for careful analysis of practical situations.

In practice, too, we are usually dealing with a dynamic situation in which traffic levels are generally growing at a substantial rate, while construction of additional facilities takes time and usually involves substantial lumps of additional capacity. In the face of such substantial penalties for either over- or underinvestment, substantial waste is likely unless some form of control over the use of the facilities is applied, such as is available through pricing, and which does not involve the wastes of queuing. Unlike the construction of additional capacity, prices can be adjusted upward or downward, as proves to be desirable, on relatively short notice and by relatively small increments.

Indeed, in the above situation one can readily compute the price structure that would just eliminate the queue and lead to efficient use, at least in the short run, of whatever facilities are actually in place. This will consist of a toll rising linearly from 0 at t_i to

$$(9) \qquad\qquad p_p = \frac{N_r}{v}\,(w_h - w_p) = \frac{4800}{v},$$

at t_p and then declining linearly to zero at t_j. With this pattern of tolls, each commuter will find that he can do no better for himself than to set out in time to pass the bottleneck at the same time that he would have left it after waiting in the queue in the zero (or constant) price situation. If traffic should fail to adjust its movement in such a fashion as to eliminate the queue, those finding themselves in the queue would have a motive to shift their travel time in such a way that the queue would be eliminated.

In the short run, the commuters are just as well off paying the variable toll and having no queue as they were before with no toll but with an equivalent queue; moreover there is no change in the pattern of arrivals at the city center. The revenue derived from the charges thus represents clear gain. We thus have an example of tax revenue that not only has no excess burden, it has no burden at all! To the extent that any of the revenue from the variable toll is used to reduce a preexisting flat toll, the motorists will be better off.

Obviously this does not mean that expansion of the capacity of the facility is never justified, but it does mean that the justification for such investment must be considered in an entirely different light if congestion charges are a possibility than if they are not. In the absence of congestion charges, a decision to expand facilities may have to be taken on an all or nothing basis. Expansion inadequate to take care of the entire traffic demand may result in a relatively slight improvement in conditions and may turn out to be hardly worthwhile, while a just slightly larger expansion might clear conditions up rather dramatically. Unfortunately, in a dynamically changing situation it is difficult to predict just what size of an improvement will in fact get over this threshold and for how long. It is easy to think of cases where an expansion of capacity felt to be quite ample when planned has turned out to serve merely to attract additional traffic until conditions are almost as bad as they were originally.

If, under conditions similar to the above, the levying of congestion charges is either an actuality or an alternative under consideration, benefits from the expansion of capacity are likely to be both smaller and less capricious in their behavior than if no pricing is contemplated. The net gain from the expansion of the bottleneck, assuming the adjustment of charges both before and after so as to just eliminate queuing, consists not of any reduction in queuing time (since there isn't any queuing) nor still less of the reduction in tolls, since this is merely a transfer from the government or operating agency to the users (and may entail substantial costs involved in securing an equivalent revenue from other sources), but simply in the fact that users will be traveling at times closer to the preferred times. The value of this shift in time may be measured by the difference in the value they place on their time at the two ends of the journey, i.e., $w_h - w_p$ = 1 cent/minute for reductions in the amount by which commuters travel in advance of the preferred time, and $w_j - w_h = 2$ cents/minute for reductions in lateness. The total value of this delay, under optimum charging and no queue, is given by

$$Nr(t_a - t_{[a]})(w_h - w_p)/2$$
$$+ N(1 - r)(t_\beta - t_b)(w_j - w_h)/2$$

(10)
$$= N^2 r \frac{1-r}{2}(w_j - w_p)\left[\frac{1}{v} - \frac{1}{v_w}\right]$$

$$= \$1440 \frac{120 - v}{v}.$$

Where queuing results from the absence of tolls, the average queuing time is half the maximum, or $q_p(\frac{1}{2}) = 1200/v$, which when evaluated for 7,200 cars per day at w_h 2 cents/minute amounts to $\$172,800/v$.

TABLE 1

Capacity (cars per minute)	Equivalent number of lanes	Duration of queue or toll (minutes)	Maximum wait in queue (minutes)	Average toll rate (cents)	Congestion cost ($/day)		
					Displaced arrival	Waiting in queue (= toll rev.)	Total without pricing
50	1.67	144.00	48.00	48.00	2016	3456	5472
60	2.00	120.00	40.00	40.0	1440	2880	4320
70	2.33	102.9	34.29	34.3	1029	2469	3498
80	2.67	90.0	30.00	30.0	720	2160	2880
90	3.00	80.0	26.67	26.7	480	1920	2400
100	3.33	72.0	24.00	24.0	288	1728	2016
110	3.67	65.6	21.91	21.9	131	1571	1708
115	3.83	62.6	20.87	20.9	63	1503	1566
118	3.93	61.0	20.33	20.3	24	1464	1488
119	3.97	60.5	20.17	20.2	12	1452	1464
119.999	4.00−	60.0	20.00	20.0	0.12	1440	1440
120.001	4.00+	0	0	0	0	0	0

The results, for various values of v, are summarized in Table 1.

Imposition of the optimal variable toll in each case eliminates queuing and results in toll revenues equal to the cost of the eliminated queuing. The displaced arrival cost will be the same whether or not the optimal toll is imposed, as this depends only on the capacity of the facility.

If we now suppose that initially we have a 2-lane bottleneck with $v = 60$ cars per minute, then without the control provided by the variation in the toll rate congestion costs will total $4,320 per day. Without help from toll adjustments, opening up a third lane at a cost of $2,000 per day would reduce congestion costs by only $1,920 and so would not be worthwhile, although opening up two new lanes at a cost of $4,000 would eliminate the entire $4,320 worth of congestion and yield a net gain of $320. On the other hand, the institution of variable tolls according to an appropriate pattern would cut congestion costs of the 2-lane bottleneck by ⅔ to $1,440 and result in a budget inflow of $2,880 instead of a budget outflow of $4,000 if the additional two lanes were built. If the overhead costs of obtaining public funds from other sources were as much as 10 percent — a not unreasonable figure if all of the unfavorable results of increased tax rates are allowed for — this budgetary shift would constitute a further gain of $688, for a total gain of $2,880 + $688 = $3,568, a substantially better result than any that can be obtained without toll variation, and much better, in particular, than the $320 gain from the 2-lane expansion.

If, on the other hand, the cost of expanding the bottleneck is relatively low, say $20 per day for each vehicle per minute of increase in capacity, so that some addition to capacity will be worthwhile in any event, variable tolls can still play a role in reaching the optimal result. In the absence of any tolls the best available alternative would again be to expand capacity to slightly above $v = 120$ cars per minute, so as to eliminate congestion entirely. If toll controls are available, however, it would not pay to carry the expansion much beyond $v = 90$, since expanding from $v = 90$ to $v = 100$ would reduce losses from displaced arrival by only $192, as compared with the cost of $200 for this expansion. In addition, such an increase might entail an increase in budgetary problems by the difference in revenues of $392.

The use of congestion tolls as an element in developing an efficient transportation system is thus not only a means of providing optimal adjustment in the short run but is likely to remain an important element even in the long run. It is only if the increment to capacity is provided in a manner that incidentally provides a substantially new and different route or a shorter origin to destination time for a substantial amount of traffic, or possibly where incremental costs of adding facilities for the collection of congestion charges *de novo* bulk large, that it would be possible to omit such charges from an optimally efficient scheme.

In practice, of course, most bottleneck situations are not as simple or as clear cut as the above case. The desired times of passing the bottleneck are not usually uniformly distributed, individuals vary in the values they assign to time spent in various places at various times, and to some extent the total number of trips made through the bottleneck would be affected by the tolls or the congestion conditions, probably in different ways for different users. These complications tend to lessen the sharpness with which critical capacity is determined, but in other ways they may enhance the effectiveness of appropriately graduated tolls and charges improving the efficiency of whatever facilities are constructed.

EXPANSION OF ROUTES IN THE PRESENCE OF ALTERNATIVE ROUTES

One situation that makes appropriately graduated charges even more essential is where a significant part of the traffic has closely competing alternative routes available to it. The classical paradigm of this situation is one where the alternative to the bottleneck route is, for a substantial portion of the traffic, a more circuitous or slower route of ample capacity. In the absence of any charges, the traffic will divide between the two routes so as to equalize total travel costs per vehicle, including travel time and also the queuing time on the bottleneck route. An enlargement of the bottleneck under these conditions will, if it falls short of being able to accommodate all of the traffic, simply result in enough traffic being diverted from the circuitous route to the enlarged bottleneck route to maintain the queue at the former level. The enlargement may thus produce no improvement in travel times at all, at least during periods of peak traffic. In a sense, such a costly enlargement proves worthless precisely because it is free.

In a more general vein, traffic often behaves like population. It has been said that if nothing stops the growth of population but misery and starvation, then the population will grow until it is miserable and starves. Similarly, if the use of private automobiles for access to the cores of large metropolitan areas is so attractive, under uncongested toll-free conditions, relative to other modes, that in effect nothing stops the growth of such traffic but congestion and delay, then such traffic will grow until sufficient congestion and delay are generated to constitute a deterrent, or until the core begins to suffer from gangrene, at which point a cumulative decline may set in that may be difficult to reverse, even with a belated introduction of appropriate toll graduation.

In practice a situation not too far from the classical paradigm often presents itself where attempts are being made to improve access to the core of a metropolitan area. In the absence of pricing, the alternatives may consist of (1) the *status quo,* (2) building an access facility sufficient for the traffic bound for the center, but which will immediately become so clogged with through traffic as to provide only moderate improvement in the speed and convenience of access to the center for a substantial part of the day, and (3) building a huge artery sufficient to take care not only of all local traffic but of any through traffic for which circumferential routes cannot be made sufficiently attractive to divert traffic from the central artery under uncongested conditions, and at the same time trying to bring the circumferentials close enough in and of such high grade as to divert as much of this traffic as possible. This third alternative is likely to prove astronomically expensive as well as disruptive of community amenities; the second alternative may in the end yield a very low return on the investment cost in terms of improvement of traffic conditions. Thus on balance the prospects of a net gain over the *status quo* may be rather dim whatever is done.

The availability of pricing opens up a new alternative of constructing central access facilities scaled to the requirements of traffic actually requiring to go to or from the center, with through traffic during the peak period being fairly thoroughly diverted to the circumferential routes by the charges imposed for the use of the central route. In some instances circumferentials that might not be worth their cost in the face of the difficulty of locating them so as to attract a sufficient volume of traffic in the absence of toll controls will become more worthwhile if pricing is available to help in the optimum distribution of traffic. With pricing such circumferentials may also be more readily located where construction is cheaper and less disruptive of amenities, and possibly also better suited for that part of their traffic that is not in any case tempted to use the central route, without fear that impairing their competitive relation to the central route would lead to undue congestion on the latter.

VARIATIONS IN THE VALUE OF TIME

An important but not essential element in the strategic importance of pricing as a factor influencing investment decisions is the existence of variations in the value of time, not only for different persons at the same time, but for the same individual at different times. In the absence of pricing, expansion of capacity must provide indifferently for individuals for whom the improvement will be worth relatively little as well as for those for whom it may be worth a good deal more. Pricing makes it possible to exclude the low-value uses and base the magnitude of the improvement primarily on the uses that are valued sufficiently highly so that they warrant the marginal cost of the final increment to the magnitude of the improvement. The selective effect of pricing on the costs of congestion would be to reduce still further the figures near the bottom of the "Displaced arrival" cost column of Table 1, enhancing the gains from the earlier increments to capacity and reducing the potential gains from the final increments. Potential improvements in efficiency and savings in construction costs are thus increased significantly over the amounts calculated on the basis of a uniform value for time.

There is, to be sure, likely to be an outcry at this point that pricing discriminates against the poor by forcing them off the congested highways. Actually the number of really poor individuals who are under any strong compulsion to drive cars with any regularity on the congested highways at peak hours appears to be quite negligible. The poorest among those significantly affected by a program of congestion charges are likely to be still somewhat above the poverty line. To the extent that this level of incomes is considered to be in need of a subsidy, there are surely better ways of determining needs than the amount of congested driving done.

A somewhat parallel outcry against the use of appropriately graduated landing fees as a means of controlling congestion at busy airports is even more difficult to justify. It is bad enough when a facility used primarily by the well-to-do is subsidized from tax revenues derived at the margin in large part from taxpayers of lower incomes; at uncongested airports this has at least the virtue of promoting better utilization. But when landing fees geared to congestion costs would substantially improve utilization while costing relatively little to assess and collect, even this excuse is lacking. In the airport case, moreover, those who would be charged the highest tolls, on a per capita basis, would be primarily general aviation planes operated in many cases for company executives and the like or private planes used for recreational and other purposes. Such users would in general be far better able to find acceptable alternatives, such as use of some of the smaller airports, if they are unwilling to pay the appropriate charges, than the patrons of the scheduled airlines. Landing fees reflecting congestion costs at various times could bring about a coordination of use that might well defer for a considerable time the need for resort to costly additional construction, often at less convenient locations. This can come about in part through the diversion of general aviation flights to other airports, through adjustment of airline schedules to reduce the concentration at the peak hours, by the use of larger planes and by scheduling for increased load factors, even without adjustment in the fare structure. If in addition some of the congestion charges can be shifted forward to passengers through the fare structure, some diversion of travel to less congested times and via less congested interchange airports may also aid in alleviating congestion. Such fare adjustments may also be essential if the best allocation of traffic between short-haul air travel and ground transportation, high-speed or otherwise, is to be achieved. A rush to construct additional airports to take care of threatened congestion may prove particularly costly at the present juncture in that improved navigational and flight control methods seem to be on the verge of substantially increasing the capacity of present airports.

EVALUATION OF INVESTMENT IN CONGESTION RELIEF

Finally, the information provided by a system of congestion control through pricing has an essential role to play in the evaluation of investments designed to afford relief from congestion. In the absence of congestion pricing, very little solid data exists on the value of varying degrees of congestion alleviation, and much of what exists is subject to considerable bias in the direction of overestimating the value of such improvements. For example, a recent study of changes in street use and traffic patterns in central London over the period from 1960 to 1966 came to the conclusion that what was widely touted as a significant improvement in traffic flow was actually no net improvement and possibly a deterioration from the standpoint of origin-to-destination volumes and times.[2] Many of the "improvements" during this period consisted of conversion to one-way traffic and the prohibition of certain turns involving crossing other traffic flows. Although average speeds and flow volumes of vehicles passing given points may have increased, these increases appear to have been used up in traversing more circuitous routes between given origins and destinations. In a similar way, higher speeds and volumes of traffic recorded on turnpikes and expressways often significantly overstate the increase in the transportation service accomplished as a result of their construction in terms of delivery from a specific origin to a specific destination. This is because distances, especially for shorter trips, are often longer via the new routes than via the old, though perhaps not as much as in the London example just cited.

[2] J. M. Thomson, "The Value of Traffic Management," *J. of Transp. Econ. and Policy,* Jan. 1968, pp. 3–32.

If, indeed, all routes were subject to appropriate congestion tolls, the level of these tolls would then be a good initial approximation to the value of the congestion relief afforded by investment in increased capacity, at least for small increments. For larger increments one could also then rely, to some extent, on estimates of consumers' surplus under each demand curve separately. But where charges for the use of alternative routes fail to reflect congestion costs at the margin, the problem becomes much more complicated. Not only must allowance be made for the indirect effects on competing routes but consideration must be given to the possibilities for improving efficiency through introduction of appropriate patterns of user charges. In the absence of the information that would be provided by the charging of appropriate tolls, planning of investment in expanded transportation facilities is half blind, and resort is sometimes had to arbitrary rules of thumb, such as that of providing capacity adequate to handle the traffic during the thirtieth heaviest hour of traffic out of the year. The capriciousness of such a rule should be fairly obvious.

Appropriate patterns of congestion tolls are thus essential, not only to the efficient utilization of existing facilities, but to the planning of future facilities.

FURTHER READINGS

Domencich, Thomas A., and Kraft, Gerald. *Free Transit: A Charles River Associates Study.* Lexington, Mass.: Heath Lexington Books, 1970.

Meyer, John R.; Kain, John F.; and Wohl, Martin. *The Urban Transportation Problem.* Cambridge, Mass.: Harvard University Press, 1966.

Mohring, Herbert. "Land Values and the Measurement of Highway Benefits." *Journal of Political Economy* 69 (1961).

Mohring, Herbert. "Optimization and Scale Economies in Urban Bus Transportation," *American Economic Review* 62 (September 1972), pp. 591–604.

Mohring, Herbert. "The Peak Load Problem with Increasing Returns and Pricing Constraints." *American Economic Review* (September 1970), pp. 693–705.

Moses, Leon N., and Williamson, Harold F. "Value of Time, Choice of Mode and the Subsidy Issue in Urban Transportation," *Journal of Political Economy* (June 1963), pp. 247–264.

Oi, Walter, and Shuldiner, P. W. *An Analysis of Urban Transportation Demands.* Evanston, Ill.: Northwestern University Press, 1962.

Owen, Wilfred. *The Metropolitan Transportation Problem.* Washington, D.C.: The Brookings Institution, 1966.

Steiner, P. O. "Peak Loads and Efficient Pricing." *Quarterly Journal of Economics* (November 1957), pp. 585–610.

Vickrey, William S. "Congestion Theory and Transport Investment." *American Economic Review* (May 1969), pp. 251–260.

Vickrey, William S. "Transportation Facilities," in "General and Specific Financing of Urban Services." In *Public Expenditure Decisions in the Urban Community,* edited by H. G. Schaller, pp. 70–81. Washington, D.C.: Resources for the Future, Inc. 1963.

Walters, Alan A. "The Theory of Measurement of Private and Social Cost of Highway Congestion." *Econometrica* (October 1961).

Williamson, O. E. "Peak Load Pricing and Optimal Capacity." *American Economic Review* (September 1966), pp. 810–827.

Chapter 5

ZONING, HOUSING MARKETS, AND URBAN RENEWAL

The demand for and supply of housing provide the setting for the discussion of three closely related questions of land-resource use: zoning, housing (including new towns), and urban renewal.

To understand the economics of these three phenomena we need to understand present policies and how they may differ from policies that might be considered optimal — that is, policies that would bring about a fair and efficient allocation of housing and land. This analysis will enable us to see what the effects of changes in current practices would be upon the quantity, quality, and price of housing, upon land use patterns and prices, and upon the distribution of income.

In many ways housing is the central issue in urban economics and the major determinant of the quality of urban life. For one thing, there may be a shortage of adequate housing or, if not an overall shortage, an undesirable distribution. Second, adequate housing is generally considered to be a socially desirable good. Finally, housing and land use patterns have great influence over the social, economic, and racial patterns of a metropolitan area. As has been previously stressed, location and the policies that affect it are probably the key factor in understanding urban economics. In our examination of these questions, we will define housing shortages (distortion in housing markets) and discuss the most effective policies for ending these shortages.

Our inquiry into zoning begins with an examination of its justification and necessity, along with its uses and abuses. The justification for zoning rests in the prevention of land uses that create uncompensated and unjustified harm to neighboring or adjoining land uses. Its legal basis rests upon the restriction in English common law against the imposition of nuisances upon neighbors, and upon the police power of the state to prevent acts harmful to health, safety, and welfare.

Economists would say that zoning exists to prevent individuals from creating harmful neighborhood effects (negative externalities) likely to bring about unfair income losses and inefficient land use. One may find it profitable to build a gasoline station in a residential neighborhood, ignoring the costs of the dirt, noise, and ugliness it will inflict on the surrounding community. Not only would the owners of the gasoline station be unlikely to compensate the harmed neighbors, but the compensation required might be large enough to make the site unprofitable for a gasoline station. This would indicate that the station probably should not be built, since it might well reduce the community's total welfare (defined to include the welfare of the potential gas station owner).

Without zoning, private individuals could and would have incentive to gain from actions that harm the community as a whole. Individuals could do uncompensated harm to their neighbors, and since these neighbors constitute only a small percentage of their clientele, there would be no real check on such undesirable activity unless legal remedies could be used to obtain compensation. Externalities in housing are akin to those involved in pollution and congestion — individuals have little reason to inhibit activities that harm others if they find them individually profitable.

Conversely, it might be argued that zoning regulations are not necessary since existing nuisance laws would enable the neighbors of the gas station to receive compensation or, if the gas station can be shown to do irreparable damage, to have an injunction issued preventing its location at the particular site. However, if individuals could initiate such legal action, the potential costs of litigations with uncertain outcomes would be likely to prevent investment in real estate and land development, especially since structures are expensive and are built on the basis of usefulness over many years. Without zoning, the quantity and quality of structures (for example, housing units) available may be insufficient. Zoning, on the other hand, can reduce the risks and costs of future litigation for both the proponents and the opponents of a particular land use. The avoidance of such costs increases the amount of resources available to all parties for other, more productive uses. Zoning usually consists of rules and regulations about the activities for which land may be used in an area, the density of land use, and the quality of structures. As Professor Davis' article explains, governments often use blanket zoning — the restriction of land use in a district to one or two categories — on the assumption that like uses generate mutually beneficial neighborhood effects (positive externalities) or are least bothered by each other's similar negative externalities. Private housing creates a neighborhood most conducive to other private housing, and smoky factories are the neighbors who find other smoky factories least objectionable. Often blanket zoning, which is thought to be both equitable and efficient by zoning authorities, ranks uses according to the desirability (level of positive externality) of each use. Single-family dwellings head the list, followed by multiple-family dwellings, apartment houses, retail commerce, light manufacturing, and heavy industry. There are also many subcategories and restrictions within each category of use. Zoning restrictions usually specify the lowest-ranking use allowed in an area, but often do not restrict higher uses from entry.

An activity that generates a negative externality might still be desirable for the community if its benefits outweigh the cost of its negative externalities. Going back to the example of the gas station, we see that although a gas station may create noise and dirt for its immediate neighbors, it can also provide convenient automobile servicing for residents of the community. The value of the convenience might be greater than the value of the harmful externalities. Spot zoning — granting a variance in the blanket zoning rule — would allow the gas station to be built.

One way to decide if the benefits of the gas station outweigh its costs to the community would be to require the gas station owner to compensate his neighbors for expected nuisance losses. The compensation could take the form of cash payment, services, or devices designed to minimize the harm done by the gas station. Requiring compensation for losses suffered would prevent undesirable gas stations from being built, but it might occasionally exclude desirable stations, part of whose benefits accrue to users and therefore are excluded from the station's future profits. Hence, the greatest compensation the gas station could afford would be below the value of its benefits to the community and might also be less than the compensation due the station's neighbors.

Such a case calls for a study of the benefits and costs of the station for the community. In theory, if the station were judged to have benefits greater than costs, it would be built, and neighborhoods being harmed would be compensated by the station owners, the entire community, or both. In practice, neighbors are often not compensated. Thus when a zoning exception (variance) is granted for a station having net costs, neighbors who are not compensated are unfairly deprived. On the other hand, if a variance is not granted for a station having net benefits, the opportunity is lost for compensating the small loss to immediate neighbors in order to bring a larger gain to the community. Adopting the principle of compensation would alleviate much of the friction, frustration, and inefficiency of our present zoning policies.

Considering several important examples of improper zoning can further understanding of the proper uses of zoning. There are two kinds of unoptimal zoning: inadequate or underzoning (allowing land uses whose benefits do not outweigh their negative externality costs), and overzoning, which consists of codes for an area that provide a higher level of land use than that which would maximize social benefit. Underzoning is often caused by failure to realize the importance of negative externalities that some land uses create. Too many highways, billboards, neon signs, and improper maintenance and destruction of historical and natural beauty have often been permitted. These excesses prevent cities from providing for human well-being to the extent they are capable of. Ex post facto under-zoning — introducing lower level uses into an area where people have already taken up residence — hurts existing owners who have built structures at a higher-quality level, although it benefits the owners of unused land and perhaps new residents. Underzoning reduces the total social benefit derivable from the community land, and simultaneously reduces the total value of land in the community.

Conversely, zoning an area for two-acre lots when half-acre lots would actually maximize the value of social welfare (and land) in the community is an example of overzoning. Why overzone? Who gains? Overzoning helps those in the community who have already built structures at below the new standard. Those who have houses on half-acre lots gain when the minimum lot size becomes one acre, because the potential number of houses in the community is lowered, thus raising the value of existing houses and diminishing the value of unused land. Besides the owners of unused land, those who cannot live in the community because of the new zoning ordinance are also hurt by overzoning.

If owners of existing housing want to exclude poor and minority groups while increasing the amount of property tax assessed on each new structure, they may overzone. Increasing the minimum plot or quality of housing required would raise the cost of living in the community. Wealthy communities may rule out multiple-family housing because of their desire to exclude the poor and disadvantaged, in part because the property taxes collected per resident of multifamily dwellings will be below that of the rest of the community. We can see that zoning left completely in the hands of localities has provided communities with the ability to overzone to the disbenefit of the metropolis. The financing of redistributive services like welfare and education through means of local property taxes has also given communities an incentive to overzone in order to keep property tax rates low. Both over- and underzoning reduce the total value of welfare that can be derived from the use of the community's natural and structural resources and are thus undesirable.

It seems likely that most overzoning has occurred in the suburbs. Suburban property owners have often overzoned in order to increase the financial value and social exclusiveness of their communities. Conversely, cities have been subjected to many pressures for underzoning from special interest groups (including the suburbanites desiring highways who have benefited at the expense of the city). The city's population is likely to be too large, transient, and uninterested to oppose such pressure groups.

It must be noted that the existence of a community of high-quality housing is not a priori evidence of overzoning, just as a community of lower-quality housing is not prima facie evidence of underzoning. Both communities can be optimally over- or underzoned. Optimal zoning only says that individuals should be forced, through payments and subsidies, to take into account the neighborhood effects (externalities) resulting from their actions. Even high-quality historic communities can experience too little maintenance, excessive commercial exploitation, and the destruction of historic charm.

It has been estimated that communities with less than 3 to 5 percent of total land area zoned for commercial use could actually increase residential property values by increasing the acreage allotted to commercial use. Since not all of the benefits of reducing overzoning would necessarily accrue to residential land values, even 3 to 5 percent is an underestimate of the minimum amount of land that ought to be zoned as commercial in a community and indicates that many exclusive communities may be too exclusive for their own good.

Is there any group who can be expected to vote for optimal zoning? Otto Davis suggests that renters will not vote for over- or underzoning of properly zoned areas, since, given their budget, they have freely chosen the price, quantity, and quality of housing best suited to them. They would have no desire to unoptimally alter the zoning pattern. But this argument is true only if renters have free and varied choice of housing — which may not be the case for disadvantaged groups — and if the community is already properly zoned. Thus, rather than saying renters will vote for optimal zoning, it is probably more accurate to say they will vote to preserve the status quo in zoning (whether it is optimal or not), since they probably prefer the community they reside in to remain as it is. Renters will only oppose unoptimal changes in zoning regulations if the zoning is already optimal.

If Davis's argument about renters having ease of mobility is true, then they will suffer only small losses if they must move from an area which becomes over- or underzoned. In contrast with property owners, who incur large capital gains and losses from zoning changes, renters would probably not have significant incentives to oppose changes in the status quo for better or worse. They can at best be expected to exert a mild influence in favor of retaining the existing zoning rules. They may even favor overzoning knowing that it will raise rents in the long run but improve the neighborhood in the short run, which is their primary interest.

How can optimal zoning be achieved? Zoning has two objectives: to protect the existing residents of a community from underzoning; and to protect potential residents (and the metropolitan area) from overzoning. The latter has often been neglected by small residential communities whose zoning boards consider only the gains to current residents from overzoning. Metropolitan-area representatives on their zoning boards might improve the situation. Local initiative plus areawide review and approval could be another answer to the zoning dilemma.

Our discussion of zoning has already started to answer the housing shortage question, defining a shortage to be less housing than would be achieved by an optimally functioning competitive housing market. The quantity of housing is a sophisticated concept, the technical definition of which is the total value of the housing stock when evaluated at the housing prices that would exist in an efficient market. This definition would value housing produced by a community which is overzoned at the lower prices the housing would sell for in efficient competitive markets (when all externalities are internalized). If in optimal competition ten units of housing would sell at $10,000 each, yielding a $100,000 housing stock, we would evaluate such housing at $10,000 per unit no matter what price it had in an overzoned community. If overzoning reduced the supply of housing in the area to eight units selling for $15,000 each, we would value the 8 units supplied by the overzoned community at $10,000 each, for a total of $80,000 rather than $120,000. The community decreased the housing stock by 20 percent by our definition, even though they raised its market price 20 percent. Therefore, any form of monopolistic practice or other inefficiency reduces the supply of housing below the optimal level and creates a shortage.

Are over- and underzoning the only phenomena that promote an unoptimally small housing stock? Closely related to zoning regulations are inadequate maintenance standards and upgrading requirements for older units, usually exempted from all changes in building codes and enforcement in general. Inadequate maintenance standards are likely to directly and indirectly bring about the deterioration of the housing stock to below optimal. Suboptimal maintenance of a piece of property indirectly reduces the housing stock by creating negative externalities for the rest of the neighborhood. As Davis explained with his prisoner's dilemma example, each owner individually chooses to undermaintain because he knows the rental and sale value of his unit depends more on the average level of maintenance in the community than upon his own maintenance and upgrading. Each resident thus has incentive to undermaintain, which reduces the value of the total community and increases the tendency of neighbors to undermaintain and depreciate their properties. Hence, it will not be profitable for any particular individual to maintain properly unless everyone else agrees to and does maintain properly.

Construction unions may also have caused the housing stock to be smaller than optimal. Individual craft unions have used their strength against many small contractors to obtain very large salary increases, running far ahead of wages in other sectors, even when unemployment and the wage rate in construction are high. Restrictive work rules which prevent the use of cost-saving technology (plastic water pipes, flexible heating and watering ducts and prefabricated constructions) have also elevated construction costs. Rules limiting union membership, often to relatives and individuals of the same ethnic group, have created a scarcity of skilled labor.

Such policies have all served to reduce the housing stock, make it more expensive and limit the opportunities of the poor to receive on-the-job training and advancement in construction trades. Mobile homes and prefabricated construction, which will be discussed later, have become popular in part because they circumvent craft union wages and work rules. Most intense in cities, these labor practices are often supported by the owners of older housing, as are overzoning and restrictive building codes. They want to avoid the increased competition of an increased supply of new housing.

Perhaps the most important inefficiency in the housing market has been the property tax on renter-occupied structures. This tax may exceed 5 percent of the value of housing and land per year in some urban communities. A property tax of 5 percent can constitute as much as 40 percent of the annual rent of an apartment and thus be equivalent to a 60 percent sales tax on renter-occupied residential structures. Why do we only say renter-occupied? The owners of owner-occupied homes are allowed to deduct their mortgage interest, return on equity, and local property taxes on their homes from their gross personal income in computing federal taxable income. This deductibility is allowed without the requirement that the rental values of the home be added to income, thus creating a subsidy to owner-occupied housing that is often greater than the property taxes paid. For example, if the mortgage rate is 6½ percent and property taxes are 2½ percent of the value of the home, then there will be an annual 9 percent cost of housing capital. If the homeowner is in the 28 percent federal income tax bracket he is able to avoid paying taxes on 9 percent of the capital value of the housing he occupies. He therefore saves 28 percent of 9 percent or 2.5 percent of the capital costs of his housing — an amount exactly equal to the property tax in this case.

The effect of property taxes on renter-occupied housing has been to raise the cost of such housing while reducing the quantity and quality of it. The property tax reduces the housing stock by diminishing both original investment and later upgrading. The only arguments that could possibly be made to defend the tax on property would be that it allows a fair measure of local autonomy and is easy to administer. These arguments do not carry much weight in comparison to the unfairness and misallocation created by the tax, however. Besides the owner-occupied versus renter-occupied distortion, the property tax assessments of similar houses in different communities often vary widely and the tax will be highest, creating its greatest distortions in allocation and income distribution, in communities where many poor renters live. These communities must fund very high public services from a very small tax base and their rental residents cannot take advantage of federal tax deduction offsets.

Adam Smith originally justified the property tax on the basis that it financed government services that protected property — police, fire, and the courts. But today local government services funded by property taxes include health, welfare, and education, which have no relation to property and whose benefits do not enhance structural values. It is absurd to try to finance welfare in poor communities by means of taxes on property. The same is true of education. With two-thirds of our national wealth in human capital and with much of the rest in nonproperty capital, the only equitable and efficient modes of taxation to finance these redistributive services are income and sales taxes at the federal, state, and local levels.

It is true that some public services, such as mass transit, do increase land values and thus could be paid for out of the gains (in fact, the resulting rise in land values is a measure of part of the benefit of mass transit extensions). The taxation of capital gains to land would be quite equitable since otherwise, owners of land near new subways would receive windfall gains. Land taxes are efficient since they create almost no distortion when placed on unimproved, unpromoted land values. Thus taxing land values for improvements in mass transit, streets, lighting, and other services that increase the value of land is usually considered fair and creates no distortion in resource allocation.

Land taxes involve little distortion because the quantity of land available at any location is fixed — supplied totally inelastically. Thus, most rent received for land is what economists define as pure rent — a payment that only allocates use efficiently and supplies the owner with revenue, but has no effect on allocation. Land taxes thereby will reduce the income and wealth of landowners but will not raise the rental land receives, being paid for fully by the owners of the land.

Public services like fire protection could efficiently and fairly be financed by the use of charges or taxes on property holders who have fire-prone dwellings. The fire tax would be a function of the expected cost to the fire department of servicing a particular structure. There could be similar taxes for unhealthy, unsafe, undermaintained buildings that harm inhabitants and neighborhoods.

We might perhaps use property taxes of 1 percent or so of the property value to finance some local administration and government services. This could be justified on the grounds of ease of administration and the argument that some public services augment the value of property, but remember even a 1 percent tax on rental property values is the equivalent of more than a 10 percent tax on rents.

How much of the property tax is borne by consumers and how much by landowners depends upon the elasticity of supply and demand for a particular type of structure. Richard Muth's article on housing calculates the elasticity of supply of housing to be 5 to 14 (that means a 1 percent increase in the price of housing will bring about a 5 to 14 percent increase in the quantity supplied), but this calculation considers housing built further from the center of the city to be of the same value as housing closer in, ignoring the additional costs of transportation with greater distance as a part of the price of the housing. My own method for calculating the elasticity of supply of housing on a fixed amount of land or in a given community yields the result that the long-run elasticities of supply range from 2 to 5, 5 being the elasticity of supply of high-rise apartments. Assuming a unitary elastic demand for housing, Muth's calculations indicate that 85 to 95 percent of the cost of property taxes is paid by the user in the long run (but offset through federal income tax deductions for owner-occupiers), whereas my calculation would indicate that 65 to 85 percent of the tax is paid by renters or users.

In the case of urban rental property, for which the model is especially suited, a 5 percent property tax could push the long-run supply of rental housing as much as 60 percent below what it would be in the absence of a property tax (this number is an upper limit based on the assumption of a 6 percent real interest rate, an elasticity of supply of residential construction of 5 and an elasticity of demand of 2). Conversely, eliminating such a property tax would increase the housing stock by 150 percent. Although this example is extreme, a 5 percent property tax could easily reduce the supply of structures by one-fourth to one-third in the long run. Eliminating the tax could increase the supply of housing by one-third to one-half (this example assumes a 6 percent interest rate and elasticities of demand and supply of −2 and 1 respectively). Incidentally, the renter would pay two-thirds of the total property tax, which is roughly equivalent to an 80 percent sales tax on rents in this example. Even under this very moderate assumption about the elasticity of supply, high property taxes have a very significant long-run effect on the quantity, quality, and price of rental housing. Eliminating or reducing property taxes would perhaps be the most significant action possible in ending the housing shortage.

If undermaintenance, high property taxes, and rent control continue long enough they can lead to a process of cumulative undermaintenance and excessive depreciation (underinvestment in upgrading) that causes buildings to become unusable and to be abandoned, creating the worst possible neighborhood effects and perhaps leading to deterioration beyond rehabilitation. After abandonment and ensuing vandalism, buildings cannot be repaired and the condition of the neighborhood discourages new construction. The only solution may then lie in one developer consolidating the entire neighborhood and upgrading or destroying all the existing structures. We will further discuss this process when we examine urban renewal.

Rent control, rent supplements, leased housing, public housing, urban renewal, new towns, and mobile homes are other solutions suggested to increase the supply and reduce the price of housing, while aiding the poor. Rent control sets the price at which housing can be rented below the price that would prevail in the market. But while price can be controlled, the quantity and quality of housing available cannot. Controlled rents below the market price (and therefore cost) of housing will lead to the deterioration and depreciation of the housing stock. The elasticities of supply of housing that would be calculated by Muth's and my models are large enough to demonstrate that the quantity of housing available is very sensitive to price. Because of this sensitivity, it is not unlikely that under rent control many buildings will be depreciated and abandoned in a period of a decade or so, as has happened in New York City. (Muth has shown that since World War II the number of standard units has increased and the number of substandard units has declined markedly in all cities except New York, which has had the only sustained rent control program in the nation.)

Rent control has other undesirable features. It causes the demand for housing to exceed the supply at the controlled, below-equilibrium price. People then engage in wasteful searches and resort to bribery aimed at finding rent-controlled units. Housing units are then allocated not by tastes and income but instead by bribery, chance, and whim. Old persons, whose children have matured and left the family, often occupy three and four bedroom units because they are inexpensive and because it would be difficult to find a smaller rent-controlled unit. Meanwhile, large families are occupying small units. Rent control can thus lead to some people finding no housing at all, whereas without controls the rent would rise in the short run, causing everyone (rich and poor) to consume less housing, providing something for everyone, and encouraging the construction of more units. Rent control also raises the costs of decontrolled units by restricting the area in which new units can be built and raising the density and hence cost at which they must be built. By decreasing the quantity and value to the city's housing stock, rent control also reduces the city's tax base. Most important, it can cause housing to be depreciated and undermaintained to the point of abandonment.

Public housing and rent subsidies are advocated as the solutions to the housing shortage. Irving Welfeld's essay and William Grigsby's readings demonstrate that public housing often costs much more than similar private housing. Public housing has often been built in poor and minority ghettos, creating a concentration of poor and minorities and more rather than less economic, social, and racial segregation. Because public housing is built for the poor, it has been restricted in quality to prevent it from being of obviously superior quality to that occupied by low- to moderate-income groups. The product of this restriction has been dehumanized, unaesthetic structures, which sometimes go unoccupied even in the face of a large subsidy.

High costs and intentionally excessive low quality have resulted in an unsuccessful program that provides little housing of an undesirable nature for few people. As Mr. Welfeld suggests, the notion of providing new housing for the poor is not too sensible when we look at the high cost of new housing in comparison to the much lower cost at which older housing can be taken over or upgraded by the poor, aided by income supplements or reduced property taxes. Most Americans, both rich and poor, live in old, not new, housing. There seems to be little point in advocating a radically different, more expensive housing mix for the poor. Jerome Rothenberg has recently completed a study of housing markets showing that not only is most housing old (90 percent of all Americans live in housing five or more years old), but that much of the present housing stock results from up- and downgrading of existing housing.

Professor Rothenberg found all housing markets to be very sensitive to changes in other housing markets, so much so that the construction of public housing for the poor may prevent downgrading of superior housing and upgrading of inferior housing for their use, thereby actually reducing the quantity of housing available to the poor. These points indicate that public housing is not a feasible effective policy for improving housing for the poor.

Welfeld's suggestion of subsidies for middle-income housing combined with increased income subsidies for poor families would be effective according to Rothenberg's model, but one wonders if the relationships and inefficiencies in housing markets do not call for an even broader policy. Since housing markets are related, increasing the supply of housing in one market will cause people (income groups) from markets in which there is an inadequate supply of housing to spill over into the expanded market. A housing policy is needed that would bring about adequate housing in all markets.

Such a policy would consist of a combination of actions: increased income transfers to the poor; reduced property taxes, particularly for renter-occupied housing; the elimination of over- and underzoning; the use of taxes and charges for fire-prone, unsafe, unsanitary, or undermaintained units; and the revision of overly restrictive building codes, union work rules, and union entry requirements. These recommendations would remove the many inefficiencies and inequities that plague housing markets.

When undermaintained housing leads to abandonment, and a neighborhood so overwhelmed by negative externalities that individual action is useless, sometimes only simultaneous upgrading or destruction and replacement of an entire area can remove the decay. But the difficulties in administering simultaneous upgrading or the difficulties in assembling large tracts for destruction are frequently claimed to be so great as to require government intervention and the use of condemnation. Private developers say that holdouts in an area who speculate on capturing all the gain of redevelopment so hamper and extend the time period needed for land assembly that the redevelopment becomes unprofitable without government aid. In government-aided urban renewal, the locality condemns the existing land and structures, and purchases them at a price largely set by the government authority. Then the locality sells the land to a developer with an approved design at one-fifth to one-third of the cost of purchasing and clearing the site. The federal government generally provides the subsidy, which is supposed to be required for positive neighborhood effects (externalities) to be generated by the project.

Urban renewal has been subjected to many apparently valid criticisms. It is said that urban renewal destroys more housing than it creates, is often poorly designed, is not worth the high cost, evicts property owners and renters (residential and commercial) without proper compensation, and has been used to further racial separation. It is perhaps to be expected that governments would use urban renewal to exclude the poor and attract the upper-middle class, since that would increase their property tax base and reduce their social service costs. The property tax and locally financed social services again become stimuli for antisocial policies. It is understandable that a community given the power of condemnation and desirous of obtaining a project which it will benefit from might well be overzealous and underestimate the value of homes, but it certainly does point out the need for stronger checks and balances against agencies' condemnation rights. Otherwise, urban renewal will often continue to be at the expense of, rather than for the benefit of, the poor. With so significant a set of challenges it would be desirable to establish a set of criteria for evaluating the benefits and costs of urban renewal projects.

As Davis, Whinston, and Rothenberg indicate, an urban renewal project is worthwhile if the benefits (the value of the new or renewed structures and land, plus positive externalities generated by them) exceed the costs (the value of the land and structures taken plus the cost of the project itself, which includes the cost of clearing the land, reallocating and compensating the previous tenants, building the new structures, and the cost of any negative externalities created by the new structure). Professor Rothenberg has estimated the benefit-cost ratios for urban renewal ranging from one-fourth to over one, though too frequently being less than one. These findings are not surprising when one considers that cities have often had severe time limits in competing for funds — funds going to those who apply for and submit projects most quickly. First-come-first-served allocation of federal funds does not lead to careful project selection, especially when a city can gain from any projects having a benefit-cost ratio of over one-fifth to one-third because the federal government is paying 67 to 80 percent of the cost. Unless there are externalities from urban renewal which extend beyond the city's borders, it might be best to simply give the cities lump-sum federal grants (or revenue sharing) that they could spend as they see fit.

Urban renewal has not and probably will not do much to increase the supply of housing available to the poor. Being realistic, however, one may recognize that even though urban renewal cannot provide housing for the poor, it might still provide a better urban environment. It might be desirable to continue urban renewal at a cautious pace, awarding projects that are thoughtfully designed, planned, and evaluated, while fully compensating those displaced by the project.

New towns are similar in concept to urban renewal in that a new community is built from scratch. The difference is that they are generally intended for previously uninhabited land at the edge of, or beyond the limits of, existing metropolitan areas. William Alonso's essay ably presents the case for and the case against new towns. They can be useful and interesting as experimental projects when they develop principles that may aid in the design and improvement of existing and future cities and suburbs, but are of very limited value in providing a significant amount of housing in the next thirty or forty years. New towns not of the generally applicable experimental type but intended as a general solution to the housing crisis would really just become more sophisticated upper-middle-class suburbs (of which we already have plenty). New towns do not answer demonstrated needs because they are detached from existing cities and living patterns. Moreover, they are generally expensive and built without interaction with their residents, thus necessarily being removed from the needs and wants of the future community. To design a new town, the designer must extrapolate an almost infinite amount of needs, wants, and desires of its residents (which are often not achieved in old communities with a great deal of designing, planning, time, effort, and resources devoted to them). These requirements make building a new town one of the most difficult architectural problems conceivable. Rigid monotony can often be the result.

New towns must not cause us to ignore the huge existing housing stock while searching for a technological panacea for our social ills, as we have often done in the past. If integration and adequate housing are to await new towns, society may neglect much of the existing trillion-dollar housing stock for a policy that would take generations to produce uncertain results. Realistic housing policies must meet the needs in existing metropolitan areas where people now are and where we have a huge human and physical investment. If we do not find solutions for them, the problems of cities will come as easily to new towns as they have come to suburbs.

The last solution to the housing crisis which we will take up in this section is mobile homes. While they do not seem applicable to the problem of central city housing, they may be a solution to the problem of inexpensive housing in rural areas and the fringe of metropolitan areas. Mobile homes have come to constitute 25 percent of all newly constructed housing and 90 percent of new housing costing under $13,000, achieving their greatest success in the Southwest.

Some of their popularity undoubtedly stems from the fact that little or no property taxes are assessed on them and that they can often be used and constructed without being subject to local zoning ordinances, building codes, union work rules and wages. These factors, which may artificially (they would not exist in an optimally functioning competitive housing market) contribute to the desirability of mobile homes, also cause localities to oppose large scale mobile home settlements. The effects have been greatest in the Northeast where property taxes, zoning, building codes, and unions are strongest.

The desirability of mobile compared to fixed structures in the absence of undesirable taxes and restrictions is still somewhat unclear. The building industry points out that mobile homes depreciate rapidly and are associated with undesirable neighborhoods, though rapid financial depreciation is not a conclusive condemnation of them by any means. The depreciation may in large part be due to several factors: their classification as consumer durables; rapid technological development of newer, better, and cheaper models; and risk in financing due to their mobility. The FHA has recently started financing mobile homes, which should help con-siderably. If mobiles last as long as most consumer durables they should be usable for 10 to 20 years, which is short compared to 30 or 40 years for fixed structures and which may make them look like an uneconomic choice. We must remember, however, that fixed structures come unfurnished and probably require far more home and garden maintenance than mobile homes. In addition, mobile homes use little land, are mobile, come equipped with most con-sumer durables and are priced between three and fifteen thousand dollars, bringing them within the reach of virtually all income groups. The undesirable neighborhoods they are supposed to create may be a myth based upon their previously transient nature.

It has been argued that mobile homes would lose their attractive-ness in the presence of less restricted and equally taxed fixed con-structions. This argument is only partially convincing when we realize that the highest ratio of mobile homes to fixed constructions is found in the Southwest and in rural areas where property taxes are low and building codes, zoning ordinances, and unions are all weak. Mobile homes thus appear to be a reasonable solution to the need for low and moderate income homes on the fringe of suburbs near growing mass-production employment.

ECONOMIC ELEMENTS IN
MUNICIPAL ZONING DECISIONS [1]

Otto A. Davis

Surprisingly enough, the phenomenon of municipal zoning affords a rich and challenging area for both the application of economic theory and for the "economic approach" to political theory. Zoning is of interest to the

Otto A. Davis is Professor of Political Economy, School of Urban and Public Affairs, Carnegie-Mellon University.

Reprinted with permission from Otto A. Davis, "Economic Elements in Municipal Zoning Decisions," *Land Economics* 39 (1963), pp. 375–386. Copyright 1963 *The Regents of the University of Wisconsin (Land Economics Magazine)*.

[1] The author is indebted to Professor James M. Buchanan of the University of Virginia for inspiration and encouragement during the development of the ideas ex-pressed in this manuscript. Of course, sole responsibility for errors remains with the author.

economic theorist because of its relation to certain peculiarities of the urban property market. These peculiarities, external economies and diseconomies, have never been completely understood, although it is generally agreed that the presence of such uncompensated externalities means that the unrestricted market cannot function in such a manner as to achieve Pareto optimality.

On the other hand, it has long been recognized that the political process determines at least some of the rules under which any market mechanism is allowed to operate. These politically determined rules may or may not be viewed as "good" in some broad social welfare sense of the term; but it is seldom indeed that the economist has worried about the method of selecting constraints and has turned his attention to an analysis of the types of rules which the democratic process might tend to impose upon the market mechanism.

This paper represents a modest effort to theorize about the nature of the constraints which a democratic political process will tend to impose upon the operation of the market mechanism in urban property. In order to accomplish this we must make a brief analysis of the operation of the price system in the urban property market.

ECONOMIC ANALYSIS

Despite various statements on the subject it should be abundantly clear at least to economists that the desire for zoning restrictions arises because of the presence of external effects in the urban property market. In other words, if one happened to own a house in an exclusive residential district, the possible location of a glue factory, beer joint, or even a gasoline service station on the adjacent lot would no doubt be upsetting since possible odors, noises, congestion, etc., might act to lower the value of the residence. In fact, all zoning restrictions — use, height, area, and density regulations — can be viewed as an effort to eliminate possible external diseconomies which the construction of "undesirable" property features might impose upon other properties in any given district. Thus this section will discuss briefly the effects of externalities in the urban property market.

An obvious effect of externalities is the following: An external economy will increase the capital value of affected properties and an external diseconomy will decrease the value. The value of properties not directly affected by an externality may or may not change but this point need not concern us here. Without considering uses which produce externalities we may say that, as far as investment and urban growth are concerned, external diseconomies or even the danger of this phenomenon tend to reduce the psychological or monetary return from urban property. Thus capital outlays are lower in their presence than would be the case in their absence and "marginally productive" lots may remain undeveloped if the danger of external diseconomies is present. External economies, of course, have the opposite effect upon urban investment.

Having stated briefly some of the effects of externalities in the urban property market, the question naturally arises whether or not externalities can be expected to occur; or, in other words, whether the price mechanism will function so as automatically to adjust for and eliminate externalities. This question can be answered, at least in part, by considering the effect of externalities upon location decisions.[2]

Any given property feature may create an external economy, an external diseconomy, or be neutral in its effects upon other property. Considering only two properties at a time there are six relevant combinations to be discussed. If properties mutually create external economies upon each other, the profit or utility maximization criterion would indicate that they will be attracted to each other. As an example, witness the development of shopping centers or clusters of retail stores so that customers may "spill over" from one shop into another. By similar reasoning it may be concluded that properties which mutually create external diseconomies upon each other jointly repel and will not be motivated to locate on adjacent lots. If properties are neutral in their effects upon each other then neither attraction nor repulsion exists between them.

If property A creates an external economy for property B but B is neutral in its effect upon A, then granted a locational decision by A, B is motivated to locate nearby. The opposite is not true. A locational decision by B does not affect the decision of A. An example here might be a restaurant and a university.

Two possibilities remain. If A creates an external economy for B, but B creates an external diseconomy upon A, then granted a locational decision by A, B has motivation to locate upon an adjacent site. Such a choice by B would, of course, impose a capital loss upon A. On the other hand, granted a locational decision by B, A would not be motivated by externality considerations to locate nearby. Many examples of this particular combination exist, with "expensive" and "inexpensive" residential dwellings being very obvious.

Finally, if A is neutral upon B but B creates an external diseconomy upon A, then B might decide to locate near A if internal considerations

---

[2] If the externalities happen to be of a non-separable variety, then equilibrium may be impossible to achieve. This possibility is ignored here because it would take us far beyond the scope of this paper. For a reference on this problem, see a paper by Andrew B. Whinston and myself, "Externalities, Welfare and the Theory of Games," *Journal of Political Economy*, June 1962, pp. 241–262.

warranted such a decision. An obvious example of this category is a single-family residence and a gasoline service station.

Of all these possibilities, zoning seems to be concerned only with the final two. Let us examine then how zoning tries to handle these two cases where external diseconomies might occur.

A BENEFICENT DICTATOR AND THE ZONING METHOD

In order to make sharp the distinction between the set of zoning constraints which are theoretically possible and the set of constraints which will be selected under our model of political action, let us assume that the city planner is a wise and beneficent dictator who has the authority to impose zoning ordinances without regard for the democratic process. How then would this wise and beneficent planner go about his task?

It would be necessary, of course, that the planner identify causes of external diseconomies. This is no simple task since the relevant external diseconomies seem to be caused by taste agreements among certain subsets of persons who happen to dominate the market for specific types of property. The planner must determine when these taste agreements are so significant as to cause an external diseconomy. Perhaps some examples will make this point clear. Consider first an exclusive, single-family, residential district. The planner might observe that the "representative purchaser" in the market for this particular type of residence preferred the quiet and the green open spaces associated with relatively large lawns and yards. Less expensive residences with smaller lots and yards would create an external diseconomy here since a person's enjoyment of his residence also has as a source the neighborhood. Similarly, apartment houses and businesses are considered not desirable in exclusive residential districts. This list could, of course, be extended but this does not seem necessary here. The main point is that the planner would have to classify various types of property and determine what property features might impose external diseconomies upon each type.

Having determined those property features which impose externalities upon each classification of property the planner then has to decide district boundary lines for each classification. This task is somewhat simplified by observing what exists. The planner would then write the ordinance forbidding or "segregating out" those properties and property features which might impose external diseconomies upon the property in each classification. Supposedly, since this "segregation process" would be aimed only at the elimination of external diseconomies, this beneficent planner would set up a "base" district(s) of exclusive, single-family residences. This base district would have the most stringent restrictions in the form of minimum yard and lot requirements, allowable uses and maximum building heights, etc. The remaining residential districts and the various business districts could be ordered as minimum yard and lot sizes decreased, maximum building heights increased, and allowable uses increased.

It is easily seen that this beneficent planner would face a difficult task which would be complicated by dynamic considerations of transition. However, aside from these dynamic complications, he would never be able to eliminate altogether the probability of occurrence of external diseconomies due to the fact that specific district boundary lines cannot exclude completely those effects which might happen "near" the line. Yet, one might suspect that this beneficent planner would be able to reduce the probable occurrence of external diseconomies, and that insofar as he was able to accomplish this reduction, persons might enjoy increased "security" and the urban property market would be moved "toward" Pareto Optimality. In fact, this simple segregation method alone cannot be said to accomplish this feat. The reason is that for certain uses "internal" profit considerations may be such that compensation theoretically could be paid for those external diseconomies which might be created. For example, it might be theoretically possible for a gasoline service station to locate in an exclusive residential district, pay compensation to those who suffer losses from the external diseconomies, and still make a profit.

On the other hand, if compensation were allowed or required, then this wise and beneficent planner might be able to make some appropriate adjustments in the rules although he would face difficult information problems since individuals affected by the external diseconomies might stand to gain by overstating their preferences. Yet, even without compensation, the zoning constraints which a truly wise and beneficent dictator would impose under the simple segregation method might be considered desirable since the probability of the occurrence of external diseconomies could be reduced.

CRUCIAL ASSUMPTIONS OF THE POLITICAL MODEL

Under modern zoning methods, either the planner or citizens may make proposals concerning a zoning ordinance. However, only the legislative body — the city council — has decision-making power. Legislative bodies, of course, consist of men who must make judgments based on practical politics in order to remain in power. Thus our present concern is to construct a model which might show how these matters of practical politics can alter the decisions from those which a wise and beneficent dictator might make.

Since political processes are complex and confusing, it is necessary that simplifying assumptions be made. Therefore, let us assume that every individual is able to perceive what is in his own self-interest and what is not and that he favors not those policies which might be considered "good" for the social entity but those policies which are in his own self-interest. Second, it is assumed that politicians act so as to be elected or re-elected; that is to say, they act so as to "maximize" the number of votes they can obtain in any election by "giving the people what they want." Finally, it is assumed that all councilmen are elected by the vote of all qualified voters in the city. This last assumption is made in order to avoid complicatory questions of legislative majorities under district representation. All these assumptions taken together mean that we may limit our attention to those policies which will be favored by simple majorities of the voters.

A LOOK AT THE PARTS

Suppose that the zoning ordinance of some given metropolis is undergoing revision, that the planner has submitted his proposal to the city council, and that the politicians are contemplating changes and alterations which might please the body politic. In order to avoid complications it is assumed that some ordinance will be adopted and that the only question is what restrictions are to be imposed. The method of analysis will be to examine first given individual districts under differing conditions in an effort to determine the type of restrictions which a simple majority in the district would prefer. It will then be argued that the fact that the politician tries to maximize votes in the entire municipality instead of the individual districts does not change the results of the analysis.

As the first case, let us suppose that an entrepreneur is proposing a new subdivision at the time of the zoning revision. Assume that the subdivision is large enough to constitute a district. Now note that, if he is constrained to follow the simple segregation principle, profit maximization implies that he subdivide in such a manner that no external diseconomies are created. He would, of course, desire that the regulations fit his particular situation and, if there were no problems of external diseconomies extending across his boundary lines, the wise politician would be willing to grant the entrepreneur's wishes in order to obtain his vote and support. On the other hand, if the general zoning regulations allowed him also to obtain initial variances for the construction of those properties which might create external diseconomies but whose "internal" considerations made it still profitable, then his overall profit position might be improved by this departure from the simple segregation principle. This case may seem to be uninteresting but it will turn out to be very important for policy purposes.

As a second case, consider a partially developed district. Suppose that the developer has constructed and sold residences on, say, one half the available land in the district. For the purpose of segregating out an entirely different problem let us make the unrealistic assumption that the boundary line cannot be changed. Now both the entrepreneur, who is assumed to own the undeveloped half, and the residents, who own and reside in the developed half, will wish to prohibit those property features and uses which might create external diseconomies. However, the resident property owners, as opposed to the developer, will desire to go one step further. If they are able to have the area "up-graded" or "over-zoned" (to get restrictions stricter than those which their property could meet) then any remaining construction in the area will have to be of a "higher" quality — more expensive, larger yards, etc. Since the value of any residential property depends upon the neighborhood in which it is located, then this higher quality construction will create external economies for the resident property owners and the value of their property will increase. There are several limiting factors here. The developer might refuse either to sell or allow further construction if he thought the ordinance might change in the future although the taste for the quiet of a semideveloped area on the part of the residents might make this alternative improbable. On the other hand, if no "favorable" change in the ordinance is forseen, then the best that the developer can do is to continue construction or sell lots since site values will bear the full effect of the ordinance-created external diseconomies.

In the above situation the wise politician, desiring to gain the support of as many voters as possible, would tend to favor the resident property owners with the result that the area might be "overzoned." [3] Note that the results of the above examples are not limited to the case of a subdivision. Assuming no renters to complicate the problem, "over-zoning" may occur in any type district if the number of resident property owners who consider their property as "developed" (meaning that they do not intend to invest in the development of alternative property in the given area at the time) outnumber those who do intend to develop additional property in the area if the politicians act so as to maximize votes and if the resident property owners do not choose to forego the possibility of a capital gain. The opposite does not hold true. If the developers outnumber the "statics," and if a change in the nature of the district — say, from residential to business — is not anticipated, then it can be expected that the area will be zoned "properly." Neither external economies nor diseconomies will be created.

Let us examine the more complicated case where renters are present. In order to avoid unnecessary complications, it is assumed that rents and values adjust "instantaneously" to externalities. Consider the subdivision example. Suppose that the developer has constructed and sold multifamily dwellings on lots comprising half the area of the district. Assume that the owners reside in the residences and have rented the several remaining apart-

---

[3] It should be noted that the term "over-zoning" is given a different meaning here from that which it usually has in the planning literature. The planner often uses the term to refer to a situation where "too much" land has been placed in some particular category.

ments in each building to other families. Once again, both the resident property owners and the developer will desire to prohibit those uses and features which might create external diseconomies. Also once again, the resident owners will desire to have the area "over-zoned." The crucial element here is the renters. Supposedly, the renters know that, if the area is "under-zoned," uses and features which create external diseconomies may be constructed and rents may fall. On the other hand, if the area is "over-zoned" then their neighborhood may become nicer but rents may rise. Finally, if the area is "correctly" zoned, then the present situation will continue.

In order to determine which set of restrictions the renters will favor, it is necessary to examine the alternatives which they faced when deciding to choose apartments in this particular area. Supposedly, the renters might have chosen apartments in a less attractive neighborhood at a lower rent or they might have chosen apartments in a more attractive neighborhood at a higher rent. However, these particular apartments in this particular area were chosen at given level of rents. There is no reason to suspect a change of tastes. The renters must be assumed to favor the "correct" zoning restrictions. Since in this example the renters plus the developer outnumber the resident property owners, the wise politician would favor the "correct" restrictions and the area would be properly zoned.

Once again this result can be extended. As long as the renters plus the developers outnumber those property owners who anticipate making no additional investment in property in the area, one can expect the "correct" restrictions to be imposed. If the situation is reversed, of course, then "over-zoning" can be expected to occur.

One word of caution is warranted here. It may be that in the real world residential renters are "transitory," meaning that they seldom expect to remain in the same location for a very long period of time. If, for example, they hold a lease which specifies the rent for the expected period of stay, they may be completely apathetic, not caring what restrictions are adopted. In such a case they would simply be left out of the counting process.[4]

Fortunately or unfortunately, the choice of zoning restrictions is not a "once and for all" phenomenon. Metropolitan growth and expansion imply that areas once suitable for one type of uses may, granted the passage of time, become more suitable for other types of uses. This possibility means, of course, that the zoning ordinance may need to be changed. Accordingly, let us now examine the political problem of district transition.

Assume a single-family residential district near the center of the city. Suppose that at some time in the past when the ordinance was enacted, single-family residences were the most productive uses for the area. Assume

---

[4] Of course, even if renters are not transitory, the possibility that rents would not adjust instantaneously could alter our conclusion.

that the residences are still owner-occupied. However, let us suppose that a portion of the property owners have decided that, granted the time which has lapsed, the most productive use of their land is business; that is to say, a portion of property owners desire to demolish their residences and construct department stores, grocery stores, etc. These property owners will desire a change in the ordinance. However, the desired uses may create external diseconomies for those property owners who still consider the most productive use to be residential housing. A conflict of interest arises and there are two possibilities which might result.

First, if all the property owners who desire to re-zone are located in one area, then a new district might be created for that area and the remainder of the old district remain residential. This result is sometimes accomplished in the case of shopping centers. Second, if the property owners who desire to re-zone are scattered over the district, then the result depends upon which group is in the numerical majority. Since the wise politician is assumed to maximize votes by doing what the majority prefers, then if we depart slightly from one original assumption and business investments have really become the most productive for the area but a majority of the residents do not realize this fact, investment will be delayed until a majority become aware of this possibility. This assumes, of course, that variances are not granted.

Do renters make any difference in the transition case? Assume a situation similar to the previous example except that the residences are apartment buildings, and suppose that all property owners have decided that the most productive uses are no longer apartment houses but business uses. Thus property owners desire that the area be re-zoned from residential to business in order that apartment buildings may be demolished and business structures erected.

If the renters are not apathetic, their attitudes can be crucial. It must be assumed, of course, that given their incomes they have chosen the "type" of structures and "type" of neighborhood which they prefer. The most extreme assumption which can be made is that equally desirable alternatives existed elsewhere for each individual at the time of his decision and that these alternatives still exist. However, granted the fact of having chosen to rent and having moved into the area and assuming no change in tastes, then the other alternatives can no longer be equally desirable since, if individuals are forced to rent elsewhere, they incur the expense of moving itself. Thus it would seem that if the renters outnumber the owners the district would not be re-zoned.

It might be argued that this conclusion is invalid since property owners can always evict their tenants. However, unless property owners agreed to act as monopolists and evict their tenants either by direct action, by collusively raising the level of rents above the competitive rates, or by agreeing purposely to allow their property to deteriorate, individual profit maximization, granted the zoning restrictions, might require that none of the above takes place with the result that tenants might remain "happy." It should be noted, however, that this situation gives rise to incentive for some individual to purchase all the property in the district so that tenants can be evicted and the area re-zoned.

Almost all of the above discussion assumed that district boundary lines were given and fixed. Of course, this is never the case. Whenever in any given district a group favors a set of restrictions not desired by the remainder of the individuals having "interests" in the area, then, if the members of this group are located in geographical proximity to each other, the possibilities exist that, if the sub-area in which this group is located is of a sufficient size and if the group is in a numerical majority in the sub-area, a special district may be created; or that, if the group is located near a boundary line of the given district, the boundary line simply may be changed. In either instance, granted the boundary line adjustments which a wise politician would make, the previous discussion still applies.

One important problem remains. It was earlier noted that the strict application of the segregation principle might result in the exclusion of uses which, although they might create external diseconomies upon other uses in the area, might be so profitable that, if it were possible to pay compensation, location in the area might still be warranted. However, in the absence of a mechanism with which the change in market values of the adjoining properties could be measured and in the lack of any type of compensation scheme, both property owners and renters would favor keeping such a use out of the district since the ordinance itself applies uniformly to all uses and the enactment of a zoning change for one use would allow other such uses to enter the area. The only possibility would be a variance which, under present rules, does not allow compensation.

THE TOTAL VIEW

The "methodology" up to this point has been that of examining a single district and, assuming that the politician was considering only the given district, trying to determine whether or not a majority of self-seeking and non-apathetic persons would favor restrictions which would eliminate external diseconomies. Although this procedure may be appropriate for "minor" ordinance revisions, it might be suggested that for "major" revisions where the politician simultaneously must consider many districts or even the entire municipality the previous results do not hold. It will be argued here that, aside from adjustments that might be necessary because of multiple counting of property owners and others, the results of the previous analysis do apply.

Two arguments seem worthy of our examination. First, it might be suggested that "over-zoning" could cause investment which might have gone to develop sites within the city to be used to develop sites outside the jurisdiction of the municipality. Thus it might be held that the city, whose major source of revenue is the property tax, would be faced with a loss of revenue which it otherwise could have gained, that such an event would result in taxpayers having to bear a "greater burden," and that recognition of this fact would tend to mitigate the demands for "over-zoning."

Several points are relevant here. First, since returns from "over-zoning" are direct and any possible burden would be indirect, one might suspect that individuals would tend to weigh direct returns more heavily. Second, insofar as expenditures are related to density as opposed to simple area, then a burden need not be created. Finally, and this is the important point, "over-zoning" need not discourage investment since, if owners of empty lots desire to see their property developed at all, site values will fall by an amount sufficient to compensate for at least a part of the ordinance-created externality.

Another argument why the previous political model might not be applicable to the case of a major zoning revision is that external diseconomies imposed upon properties in one area might not be neutral in their indirect effects upon property in other areas. If this were true, then it might be argued that, granted "adequate" zoning protection for his own property, any self-interest motivated property owner would favor either "under-zoning" or "no-zoning" for the remainder of the metropolitan area. Thus it might be stated that the direct result of our assumptions would be a zoning ordinance which left forty-nine percent of the property owners unprotected.

Fortunately, the above argument does not follow from the assumptions of the analysis. Assume any rental property which is "adequately" protected. The individuals who rent this property will desire to see all other areas zoned since any indirect external effects which caused a rise in the capital value of the protected property would also carry the implication of increased rents. Thus, as long as there are a significant number of renters, no wise politician would favor a policy which would result in zoning a part but not the whole. The previous analysis holds.

RATIONAL ENACTMENT

The previous analysis has suggested that zoning restrictions adopted through the democratic process need not be of an "ideal" type under which external diseconomies are simply eliminated. The possibility exists that an area may be "over-zoned" or that the ordinance may prevent transition. Thus the question arises as to whether or not it is "rational" for a metropolis to adopt a zoning ordinance at all. Let us briefly consider this question.

For any given metropolitan area individuals will know that the situation will not remain static, that the locational pattern will change, but the future development pattern will be unknown. Persons may have, of course, some expectations about future developments, but uncertainty will exist. Granted this situation, each individual, who is assumed to possess relevant knowledge, will compare the zoning with the non-zoning situation in an effort to determine expected gains or losses from the introduction of the ordinance.

Let us examine first the non-zoning situation. Any individual property owner will consider the following: First, he may gain in the municipal growth process either through development or re-development of his property, but, unlike the situation with zoning, he is always assured of being able to develop or re-develop in the manner which he considers most profitable. Second, if an external diseconomy is forced upon his competitors but not his own property, the result might be some gain in the form of an indirect pecuniary external economy. Third, an external diseconomy may be imposed upon his property with the result of a capital loss.

For the renter the non-zoning situation implies the following: First, if an external diseconomy is forced upon properties other than the one in which he is located, the result can possibly be a rise in his rent. Second, if an external diseconomy is forced upon the property in which he is located, he might or might not lose since the level of rents on property affected by the external diseconomy eventually must fall to a level where the "representative" renter is indifferent between that property and some alternative, but he could expect to be identical with the representative renter only by coincidence.

Let us now examine the situation with zoning. First, any property owner will know that he can gain from the development or re-development of his property but with zoning he is not assured of being able to do so in the manner which he might consider the most profitable. Second, if he owns property which is already developed, he may gain from "over-zoning." Third, if he owns property which is undeveloped, he may lose from "over-zoning."

For the renter the zoning situation carries the following implications: First, if he happened to be located in a structure in a "semi-developed" area, he could conceivably lose since, if over-zoning occurred, the level of rents might rise. However, in all probability this possibility will be judged as unimportant since rental structures are usually grouped together and not interspersed with owner-occupied structures. Thus the renter might expect that the combination of renters and owners of undeveloped property would "out vote" the owners of developed property. Second, the renter might stand to gain in the transition case by so zoning that redevelopment is not allowed.

Persons are assumed to favor zoning if they stand to gain from the enactment of the ordinance. Examination of the above list suggests that renters would stand to gain and thus would favor zoning. Those property owners who would favor zoning since they might stand to gain but never to lose would be: (1) those who consider their property fully developed, and (2) those who consider the possibility of a loss from the imposition of an external diseconomy upon their property greater than the possibility of a gain in the form of an indirect pecuniary external economy caused by external diseconomies being forced upon others. Three groups of property owners might favor no zoning. These are: (1) those whose expectations are the reverse of those in (2) above. However, this group will probably be unimportant since losses are direct and gains indirect, and since it can be shown that aggregate losses are almost always greater than aggregate gains. Group (2) is composed of those property owners who feel that they might be prevented from developing their property in the manner which they consider most profitable and group (3) is composed of owners of undeveloped sites who feel that they might lose from "over-zoning."

If this breakdown of the body politic is relevant, it seems reasonable to suppose that those who favor zoning will almost always outnumber those who oppose it in any metropolitan area. However, the existence of those who would oppose zoning or the assured lack of unanimity among the populace suggests that zoning cannot be said to move a municipality toward the Pareto optimality frontier in urban property.

CONCLUSIONS AND PROPOSALS

Insofar as the previous analysis is relevant to the real world it has suggested that the democratic process may not always impose those constraints which simply result in the elimination of external diseconomies in the pricing system in urban property. Instead, a democratic political process sometimes may impose regulations which result in over-zoning and non-transition. Yet it has been argued that a rational electorate will almost always choose an ordinance. Since few of us would recommend turning the enactment of zoning ordinances over to dictators, beneficent or otherwise — it seems important that ways be found to improve the institution. Since the analysis which has been used in this paper has not been checked against the "facts," the following specific proposals are speculative, suggestive, and provisional. They are not positive recommendations for immediate adoption.

Let us consider the expansion of the metropolis. Any metropolitan area generally expands through the process of subdivision. It has been noted that, if the subdivider-developer is constrained by the segregation principle, it will be in his interest to so subdivide and develop his property that external diseconomies are eliminated. On the other hand, if he is able to initially depart from the simple segregation principle, it may be possible for him to improve his profit position by constructing, as variances or non-conforming uses, those properties which are warranted by "internal" considerations even though they might reduce the value of adjacent lots. It is to be emphasized that, if the subdivider-developer operates in a competitive market, his maximum profit position is also optimal for society if "boundary line" externalities are ignored. The creation of external diseconomies becomes a "danger" only after the developed properties have been sold to various individuals.

In view of the above, it is proposed that the subdivider be required to draw up the ordinance for his subdivision subject to some constraints for boundary line externalities and that no change in the zoning restrictions for that area be allowed for a period of, say, ten years. The subdivider must be required, of course, to inform each prospective buyer of the restrictions and any possible non-conforming uses which he plans.

There are several arguments in favor of this method of initially adopting zoning restrictions. First, if the subdivider made a mistake in judging what constituted an external diseconomy, he would harm only himself since any prospective purchaser would know what the restrictions and plans for development were before buying and would be able to discount any allowable external diseconomies in deciding what he would be willing to pay for the property. Second, the danger of "over-zoning" would not immediately exist if the development of the subdivision were completed within the specified number of years.

In districts that are already zoned, the possibility exists that, if it were possible to measure objectively the effects of external diseconomies upon capital values and if a use were required to compensate for losses it imposed upon others, "internal" factors of cost and demand might still warrant locating in the area even though the strict application of the segregation principle would have forbidden it. The following is a brief outline of an attempt to construct a workable compensation scheme.

Suppose that the board of appeals were stripped of its power to grant use variances. Then suppose that the individual who desired such a variance was required to make detailed plans and was required to hold to these plans if a variance was granted. The variance could be granted only by a direct vote of property owners within the district. The rule for granting the variance might be, say, the unanimous consent of adjoining property owners and the consent of ninety percent of the remaining property owners in the area. Bribes would be legal, and compensation would be paid via bribes in order to obtain the vote of the required property owners.

This scheme is not, of course, perfect. It introduces a game element into the process of trying to obtain variances. It also overlooks possible effects upon renters. Its only virtue is that it does attempt to provide some sort of an approximation to a measure of the effects of external diseconomies and it does require compensation. Neither of these two proposals is concerned with the two problems, transition and "over-zoning," which might occur in the already "developed" portion of the metropolis. Accordingly, let us discuss briefly these two problems.

Once an area is partially developed, either through "original" development or re-development, in the absence of "over-zoning" which will push "empty" site values down to a point where the effects of external diseconomies is at least partially offset, uses upon which existing property in the area create external diseconomies will have extra incentive to stay away. Thus it seems unlikely that an area should ever be zoned "upward" within its own class unless urban renewal or complete re-development is to take place. Except for these events, it might be considered desirable to prohibit "up-grading" within given classes of property (residential, etc.). Property owners would have the choice of "down-grading" or changing classes, and the urban growth process can make the most profitable uses change in either of these two directions.

It was earlier suggested that one "danger" in transition is that renters prevent re-zoning. However, if the transition problem were divorced from the usual political process, this danger might not exist. Thus it is proposed that for the purpose of transition only the question be decided by a vote of the property owners in the district.

It should be emphasized again that these proposals are tentative. They are not intended to be a panacea. Not only were they based on an untested model, but even considering only the model the proposals are incomplete. The problem of restrictions upon properties which may impose external diseconomies upon properties in other districts, for example, was not discussed here.

THE ECONOMICS OF URBAN RENEWAL[1]

Otto A. Davis
Andrew B. Whinston

INTRODUCTION

In light of two implications of urban renewal, it is not at all surprising that this phenomenon provides an excellent area for the application of welfare economics. These implications are: First, that the market mechanism has not functioned "properly" in urban property; and second, that positive action can "improve" the situation. The propositions of welfare economics provide some tools for judging public policy measures such as urban renewal. But since these propositions themselves are based upon ethical postulates, it seems desirable that we begin our discussion of urban renewal by stating explicitly what we consider the role of the economist to be in this situation.

WELFARE ECONOMICS AND URBAN RENEWAL

Welfare economics itself provides one criterion, the Pareto condition, for judging public policy measures. The Pareto condition states that a social policy measure can be judged "desirable" if it results in either (1) everyone being made better off, or (2) someone being made better off without anyone being made worse off. This rule is, of course, an ethical proposition, but it requires a minimum of premises and should command wide assent.

On the other hand, the economist need not be limited solely to the Pareto condition in giving policy advice. This becomes especially true when the objective ambiguity of the terms "better off" and "worse off" is considered. Indeed, the role of the economist in the formation of social policy may be

Otto A. Davis is Professor of Political Economy, School of Urban and Public Affairs, Carnegie-Mellon University; Andrew B. Whinston is Associate Professor of Economics, University of Virginia.

Reprinted with permission from a symposium, Urban Renewal, appearing in *Law and Contemporary Problems* (Vol. 26, No. 1, Win. 1961), published by the Duke University School of Law, Durham, North Carolina, copyright, 1961, by Duke University.

[1] The authors would like to express their appreciation to Professors Donald A. Fink and Merton Miller, both of Carnegie Institute of Technology, and to Edgar M. Hoover and Melvin K. Bers, both of the Pittsburgh Regional Planning Association, for reading and criticizing the manuscript. Conversations with Professor W. W. Cooper, of the Carnegie Institute of Technology, were also beneficial.

compared to that of the consultant to an industrial firm. The consultant to a firm serves two functions. First, given the goals of the firm, he tries to find the best or most efficient means of achieving these goals. The second function of the consultant is equally important; he must try to clarify vague goals by pointing out possible inconsistencies and determining implications in order that re-evaluations and explicit statements can be made.

We conceive of the role of the economist as quite similar to that outlined for the consultant. First, the economist may try to clarify social goals by pointing out inconsistencies and determining implications of possible social rules. Second, if a goal happens to be given and agreed upon — *i.e.,* if a social welfare function is defined — then the economist might try to advise the body politic by proposing politics for the attainment of the defined goals.

It is in the above spirit that we consider the problem of urban renewal. Granted the individualistic basis of western civilization, it seems reasonable to assume that any action which satisfies the Pareto condition would improve social welfare and, therefore, should be desired by society. On the other hand, society might desire, granted the institutional form of political decision-making, certain actions which violate the narrowly conceived Pareto condition.[2] Certainly income redistribution would fit this category. And so may urban renewal.

Specifically, the social welfare function which we use has the following properties: If the sum of the benefits, measured by changes in capital values, exceeds the sum of the costs, then the action is termed desirable. While this welfare criterion may not seem clear at this point, it is appropriate to note here that a major portion of the remainder of the paper will be devoted to determining how benefits and costs are to be measured. What is important here is to make clear the basis upon which our judgments will be made.

Several characteristics of this welfare criterion should be noted here. First, any action which satisfies the narrowly conceived Pareto condition will satisfy this criterion. On the other hand, any action which satisfies the welfare criterion need not meet the Pareto condition unless compensation is required. Second, our criterion is concerned with the efficient allocation of resources. The question of the ethically desirable distribution of income will not be considered here, although some might hold that urban renewal is concerned with income redistribution. We merely point out that income redistribution can be more efficiently achieved through other means than urban renewal.

---

[2] It is worthy of note that it can be argued very convincingly, if the individualistic ethic is adopted, that any social welfare function must satisfy a broadly conceived Pareto condition — that is, a Pareto condition defined by political consensus. See, *e.g.,* Buchanan, *Positive Economics, Welfare Economics, and Political Economy,* 2 J. LAW & ECONOMICS 124 (1959).

THE PRICE MECHANISM AND URBAN BLIGHT

Having stated the position from which we shall make policy judgments, we now must examine the question of why urban renewal is necessary. In other words, why do "blighted" areas develop and persist? Why do individuals fail to keep their properties in "acceptable" states of repair?

Several arguments may be advanced as answers to the above questions. For example, it has been asserted that property owners have exaggerated notions of the extent and timing of municipal expansion. Hence they may neglect possible improvements of existing structures in anticipation of the arrival of more intensive uses which might bring capital gains.[3] Note that even if this argument is accepted as plausible — and the reason why property owners might have exaggerated notions about municipal expansion is by no means evident — it does not constitute an argument for urban renewal. Instead, one might infer that, given sufficient time, a transition to intensive and profitable uses would take place.[4] Then too, it can be argued that there is no reason to expect governmental authorities to have better judgment than individual entrepreneurs.

Aside from the previous "mistaken judgments" arguments, it might seem plausible at first glance to believe on the basis of price theory and the profit maximization assumption that urban blight could not occur. After all, would not profit-maximizing individuals find it to their advantage to keep their property in a state of repair? Certainly it seems reasonable to suppose that if individual benefits from repair or redevelopment exceed individual costs, then individual action could be expected and no social action would be necessary. We shall now attempt to demonstrate why rational individual action might allow property to deteriorate and blight to occur.

First of all, the fact that the value of any one property depends in part upon the neighborhood in which it is located seems so obvious as hardly to merit discussion. Yet, since this simple fact is the villain of the piece, further elaboration is warranted. Pure introspective evidence seems sufficient to indicate that persons consider the neighborhood when deciding to buy or rent some piece of urban property.[5] If this is the case, then it means that exter-

---

[3] Fisher, *Economic Aspects of Zoning, Blighted Areas, and Rehabilitation Laws,* 3 AM. ECON. REV. 334 (1942).

[4] Indeed, it can even be argued that this line of reasoning considered alone leads to the conclusion that urban renewal expenditures are wasteful. See, *e.g.,* Davis, *A Pure Theory of Urban Renewal,* 36 LAND ECONOMICS 221 (1960).

[5] This interdependence of urban property values has, of course, long been recognized. See, for example, the discussion in Alfred Marshall, *Principles of Economics* bk. 5, ch. 11 (8th ed. 1920). The following quote is especially interesting in this regard. "But the general rule holds that the amount and character of the building put upon each plot of land is, in the main (subject to the local building bylaws), that from which the most profitable results are anticipated, with little or no reference to its reaction on the situation value of the neighborhood. In other words, the site value of the plot is governed by causes which are mostly beyond the control of him who determines what buildings shall be put on it." *Id.* at 445.

nalities are present in utility functions; that is to say, the subjective utility or enjoyment derived from a property depends not only upon the design, state of repairs, and so on of that property, but also upon the characteristics of nearby properties. This fact will, of course, be reflected in both capital and rental values. This is the same as saying that it is also reflected in the return on investment.

In order to explain how interdependence can cause urban blight, it seems appropriate to introduce a simple example from the theory of games. This example, which has been developed in an entirely different context and is commonly known as "The Prisoner's Dilemma," appears to contain the important points at issue here.[6] For the sake of simplicity, let us consider only two adjacent properties. More general situations do not alter the result but do complicate the reasoning. Let us use the labels Owner I and Owner II. Suppose that each owner has made an initial investment in his property from which he is reaping a return, and is now trying to determine whether to make the additional investment for redevelopment. The additional investment will, of course, alter the return which he receives, and so will the decision of the other owner.

The situation which they might face can be summarized in the following game matrix:

		Owner II	
		Invest	Not Invest
Owner I	Invest	(.07, .07)	(.03, .10)
	Not Invest	(.10, .03)	(.04, .04)

The matrix game is given the following interpretation: Each property owner has made an initial investment and has an additional sum which is invested in, say, corporate bonds. At present, the average return on both these investments, the property and the corporate bonds considered together, is four per cent. Thus if neither owner makes the decision to sell his corporate bonds and makes a new investment in the redevelopment of his

---

[6] For an explanation of the "game theoretic" points of interest in the Prisoner's Dilemma example, see R. Duncan Luce & Howard Raiffa, *Games and Decisions*, 94–102 (1957). The reason for the intriguing title of this type of game theory analysis is interesting in itself. The name is derived from a popular interpretation. The district attorney takes two suspects into custody and keeps them separated. He is sure they are guilty of a specific crime but does not have adequate evidence for a conviction. He talks to each separately and tells them that they can confess or not confess. If neither confesses, then he will book them on some minor charge and both will receive minor punishment. If both confess, then they will be prosecuted but he will recommend less than the most severe sentence. If either one confesses and the other does not, then the confessor will receive lenient treatment for turning state's evidence, whereas the latter will get "the book" slapped at him. The Prisoner's Dilemma is that without collusion between them, the individually rational action for each is to confess.

property, each will continue to get the four per cent average return. This situation is represented by the entries within brackets in the lower right of the matrix where each individual has made the decision "Not Invest." The left hand figure in the brackets always refers to the average return which Owner I receives, and the right hand figure reflects the return of Owner II. Thus for the "Not Invest, Not Invest" decisions, the matrix entry reflects the fact that both owners continue to get a four per cent return.

On the other hand, if both individuals made the decision to sell their bonds and invest the proceeds in redevelopment of their property, it is assumed that each would obtain an average return of seven per cent on his total investment. Therefore, the entry in the upper left of the matrix, the entry for the "Invest, Invest" decisions, has a seven per cent return for each owner.

The other two entries in the matrix, which represent the situation when one owner invests and the other does not, are a little more complicated. We assumed, as was mentioned earlier, that externalities, both external economies and diseconomies, are present. These interdependencies are reflected in the returns from investment. For example, consider the entries in the brackets in the lower left corner of the matrix. In this situation, Owner I would have decided to "Not Invest" and Owner II would have decided to "Invest."

Owner I is assumed to obtain some of the benefits from Owner II's investment, the redevelopment contributing something to a "better neighborhood." For example, if the two properties under consideration happened to be apartment buildings, the decision of Owner II to invest might mean that he would demolish his "outdated" apartment building and construct a new one complete with off-street parking and other amenities. But this would mean that the tenants of Owner I would now have an easier time finding parking spaces on the streets, their children might have the opportunity of associating with the children of the "higher class" people who might be attracted to the modern apartment building, and so forth. All this means that (as soon as leases allow) Owner I can edge up his rents. Thus his return is increased without having to make an additional investment. We assume that his return becomes ten per cent in this case, and this figure is appropriately centered in the matrix. Owner II, on the other hand, would find that, since his renters also consider the "neighborhood" (which includes the ill effects of Owner I's "outdated" structure), his level of rents would have to be less than would be the case if his apartment building were in an alternative location. Thus we assume that the return on his total investment (the investment in the now-demolished structure plus the investment in the new structure) falls to three per cent. This figure is also appropriately entered in the matrix. For simplicity, the reverse situation, where Owner I decided to invest and Owner II decides not to invest, is taken to be similar. Thus the reverse entries are made in the upper right corner of the matrix.[7]

Having described the possible situations which the two owners face, consider now the decision-making process. Both owners are assumed to be aware of the returns which are available to themselves in the hypothesized situations. Owner I will be considered first. Owner I must decide whether to invest or not invest. Remember that the left hand entries in the brackets represent the possible returns for Owner I. Two possible actions of Owner II are relevant for Owner I in his effort to make his own decision. Therefore, Owner I might use the following decision process: Assume, first, that Owner II decides to invest. Then what decision would be the most advantageous? A decision to invest means only a seven per cent return on Owner I's capital, whereas the decision not to invest would yield an average return of ten per cent of the total relevant amount of capital. Therefore, if Owner II were to decide to invest, it would certainly be individually advantageous to Owner I not to invest. But suppose that Owner II decided not to invest. Then what would be the most advantageous decision for Owner I? Once again the results can be seen from the matrix. For Owner I the decision to invest now means that he will receive only a three per cent return on his capital, whereas the decision not to invest means that he can continue to receive the four per cent average return. Therefore, if Owner II were to decide not to invest, it would still be individually advantageous to Owner I not to invest.

The situation for Owner II is similar. If Owner I is assumed to invest, then Owner II can gain a ten per cent average return on his capital by not investing and only a seven per cent return by investing. If Owner I is assumed not to invest, then Owner II can gain only a three per cent return by investing, but a four per cent average return by not investing. Therefore, the individually rational action for Owner II is also not to invest.

The situation described above means, of course, that neither Owner I nor Owner II will decide to invest in redevelopment. Therefore, we might conclude that the interdependencies summarized in the Prisoner's Dilemma ex-

---

[7] Economists might think that we have used inappropriate and sleight-of-hand methods by lumping together old and new investments, and also by considering the average rate of return instead of marginal rates. Actually these methods are completely appropriate here due to the way we have simplified the problem to make the exposition of the game theory easier. The old investment does not represent a sunk cost, since it is yielding a return and thus has economic value. Both owners are assumed to have precisely the amount of money in bonds that is required for the redevelopment of their property. The rate of return on the bonds can be assumed to be the "social rate of return" and the best alternative available to the two individuals. Since the owners are interested in maximizing the total income from their capital, the above assumptions allow us to lump together and to use average rates.

ample can explain why blighted areas can develop[8] and persist. Before concluding the analysis, however, we might try to answer some questions which may at this point be forthcoming.

First of all, it might be suggested that we have imposed an unrealistic condition by not allowing the two owners to coordinate their decisions.[9] After all, does it not seem likely that the two owners would get together and mutually agree to invest in the redevelopment of their properties? Not only would such action be socially desirable, but it would seem to be individually advantageous. Note that while it might be easy for the two property owners in our simple example to communicate and coordinate their decisions,[10] this would not appear to be the case as the number of individuals increased. If any single owner were to decide not to invest while all other owners decided to redevelop, then the former would stand to gain by such action. The mere presence of many owners would seem to make coordination more difficult and thus make our assumption more realistic. Yet, this is precisely the point; it is the objective of social policy to encourage individuals in such situations to coordinate their decisions so that interdependencies will not prevent the achievement of a Pareto welfare point. In this regard, it is worthwhile to note that, if coordination and redevelopment do take place voluntarily, then no problem exists, and urban renewal is not needed.

Second it might be observed that, if coordinated action does not take place, incentive exists for either Owner I, Owner II, or some third party to purchase the properties and develop both of them in order that the seven per cent return can be obtained. And certainly, it cannot be denied that this often occurs in reality. However, it is necessary to point out here that, because of the institutional peculiarities of urban property, there is no assurance that such a result will always take place. Consider, for example, an area composed of many holdings. Suppose that renewal or redevelopment

---

[8] It is to be emphasized that these results depend upon the interdependencies or neighborhood effects being "sufficiently strong" to get a combination of returns similar to those which we used in the example. It is unlikely that this condition would be satisfied for all urban property. Our point is that similar combinations seem possible, and if they do occur, then they can explain one peculiar phenomenon of urban property. The explanation is presented later in the paper.

[9] It is worthy of note that experimental data concerning the prisoner's dilemma in other contexts tend to indicate that, if communication does not take place, players continually choose individually rational strategies. For the results of these laboratory experiments, see Scodel, Minas, Ratoosh & Lipetz, *Some Descriptive Aspects of Two-Person Non-Zero-Sum Games,* 3 J. CONFLICT RESOLUTION 114 (1959).

[10] It will be recalled that we made the example overly simple only for the purpose of exposition. While the consideration of many individuals would make the example more realistic, it would only make the game theory more complicated and not alter the result as far as this case is concerned.

would be feasible if coordination could be achieved, but that individual action alone will not result in such investment due to the interdependencies. In other words, the situation is assumed to be similar to the previous example except that many owners are present. Incentive exists for some entrepreneur to attempt to purchase the entire area and invest in redevelopment or renewal.

Now suppose that one or more of the owners of the small plots in the area became aware of the entrepreneur's intentions. If the small plots were so located as to be important for a successful project, then the small holders might realize that it would be possible to gain by either (1) using their position to expropriate part of the entrepreneur's expected profits by demanding a very high price for their properties, or (2) refusing to sell in order to enjoy the external economies generated by the redevelopment. If several of the small holders become aware of the entrepreneur's intentions, then it is entirely possible, with no communication or collusion between these small holders, for a situation to result where each tries to expropriate as much of the entrepreneur's profit as possible by either of the above methods. This competition can result in a Prisoner's Dilemma type of situation for the small holders. Individually rational action on their part may result in the cancellation of the project by the entrepreneur. Indeed, anyone familiar with the functioning of the urban property market must be aware of such difficulties and of the care that must be taken to prevent price-gouging when an effort is made to assemble some tract of land.[11]

If the above analysis is correct, then it is clear that situations may exist where individually rational action may not allow for socially desirable investment in the redevelopment of urban properties. Now such situations need not — indeed, in general will not — exist in all urban properties. The results of the analysis not only required special assumptions about the nature of investment returns caused by interdependencies, but it was also shown that, due to the special institutional character of tract assembly, the presence of numerous small holdings can block entrepreneurial action for redevelopment. These two conditions may or may not be filled for any given tract of land. However, we now may use the above results to *define* urban blight.[12] Blight is said to exist whenever (1) strictly individual action

[11] For example, Raymond Vernon states, "As the city developed, most of its land was cut up in small parcels and covered with durable structures of one kind or another. The problem of assembling these sites, in the absence of some type of condemnation power, required a planning horizon of many years and a willingness to risk the possibility of price gouging by the last holdout." Raymond Vernon, *The Changing Economic Function of the Central City* 53 (1959). [Reprinted in Chapter 1 of this volume. — Ed.]

[12] It is to be pointed out and emphasized that our definition of the term "blight" does not seem to be what is meant by the term in common usage where it has a connotation of absolute obsolescence. Our definition refers to the misuse of land in general and carries no such connotation. The difference in meanings is unfortunate, but we could not find a more appropriate term.

does not result in redevelopment, (2) the coordination of decision-making via some means would result in redevelopment, and (3) the sum of benefits from renewal could exceed the sum of costs. These conditions must be filled. We shall devote a major portion of the latter part of the paper to making this definition operational; but, for the moment, let it suffice for us to point out two factors. First, it is a problem of social policy to develop methods whereby blighted areas can be recognized and positive action can be taken to facilitate either redevelopment or renewal. Second, and this point may be controversial, blight is not necessarily associated with the outward appearance of properties in any area.

Since this second point may be subtle and seem contrary to intuitive ideas about blight, further discussion may be warranted. Note that we have defined blight strictly in relation to the allocation of resources. The fact that the properties in an area have a "poor" appearance may or may not be an indication of blight and the malallocation of resources. For several factors, aside from tastes, help to determine the appearance of properties. The situation which we have described, where individually rational action may lead to no investment and deterioration, is only one type of case. Another may be based on the distribution of incomes. Poor classes can hardly be expected to afford the spacious and comfortable quarters of the well-to-do. Indeed, given the existence of low income households, a slum area *may* represent an efficient use of resources. If the existence of slums per se violates one's ethical standards, then, as economists, we can only point out that for elimination of slums the main economic concern must be with the distribution of income, and urban renewal is not sufficient to solve that problem. Indeed, unless some action is taken to alter the distribution of income, the renewal of slum areas is likely to lead to the creation of slum areas elsewhere.[13] It is to be emphasized that slums may or may not satisfy the definition of a blighted area. On the other hand, the mere fact that the properties in some given area appear "nice" to the eye is not sufficient evidence to indicate that blight (by our definition) is absent.

One additional remark of clarification seems warranted. It is obvious that not all individuals are free to purchase or rent property in all areas of the metropolis. Discrimination — *e.g.,* by race — may create two or more

---

[13] It is a curious fact that renewal seems to be regarded as a "cure" for slum areas. For, granted the distribution of income and the fact that the poor classes simply cannot afford to pay high enough rents to warrant the more spacious and comfortable quarters, the renewal of all slum areas, unless accompanied by an income-subsidy program, would only be self-defeating and lead to social waste. Renewal of all slum areas could cause rents for the "nicer" quarters to fall temporarily within the possible range of the poor classes, but the rents would not be sufficiently high to warrant expenditures by the landlord to maintain the structure. New slums would appear, calling for more renewal activity. This process would simply continue. On the other hand, efficient slum-removal programs are possible, and one will be presented at a later point in this paper.

"separate" markets, and there seems to be no reason to suspect short-run equilibrium in the sense of investment return *between* markets. We simply note here that, granted the discrimination, this fact does not affect our definition of blight, nor does it alter the proposals which we shall present.

A BRIEF CRITIQUE OF PRESENT PRACTICES

Having seen that, due to externalities or interdependencies and the difficulty of tract assembly, individually rational action may allow blight to develop, we now turn our attention to questions of public policy. It bears repeating that wherever our definition of blight is satisfied, then resources are misallocated in the sense that some institutional arrangement — some means — exists under which redevelopment or renewal could profitably be carried out. The problem is to discover that institutional arrangement. We begin our search by examining briefly the relevant aspects of the present practices.

Title I of the Housing Act of 1949 [14] seems to have set the general pattern for urban renewal practices. While the Act of 1954 [15] broadened the concept, the general formula for urban redevelopment remains essentially unchanged. Both federal loans and capital grants are provided for the projects. Loans are generally for the purpose of providing working capital. The capital grants may cover up to two-thirds of the net cost of the project, with the remainder of the funds being provided by either state or local sources.[16]

The striking fact about the present program, and also about many of the proposals for extending that program, is the utter lack of a relevant criterion for expenditures. How much should be invested in urban renewal? How does one determine whether projects are really worthwhile? Does the present program attempt to "correct" the allocation of resources or does it simply result in further misallocation? There seems to have been little or no serious effort to find answers to these questions. In fact, it is widely admitted that there is a lack of adequate criteria even to determine what projects should be undertaken.[17]

[14] 63 Stat. 413, 42 U.S.C. §§ 1441–60 (1958).

[15] 68 Stat. 622, as amended, 42 U.S.C. §§ 1450–62 (1958); 68 Stat. 596, as amended, 12 U.S.C. §§ 1715*k*, 1715*l* (1958).

[16] There are, of course, conditions which must be satisfied before a community can be eligible for federal funds. See, *e.g.*, Comm'n on Intergovernmental Relations, Twenty-five Federal Grant-in-Aid Programs (1955).

[17] A remark by Morton J. Schussheim, Deputy Director of the Area Development Division of the Committee for Economic Development, is interesting in this respect. Mr. Schussheim writes, "It is true . . . that local officials responsible for urban renewal programs do not have adequate criteria for determining what projects to undertake and on what scale." "A Pure Theory of Urban Renewal: A Comment," 34 *Land Economics* 395 (1960).

It seems evident from the statements of mayors and others who propose expansions of the present program that the need approach to governmental expenditures underlies their suggestions. That is to say, a certain project "needs" to be carried out; and, granted this requirement, money is sought for the project. It should be evident that this approach to governmental expenditures may not result in the correct allocation of resources. The need approach obscures budgetary considerations and makes comparison of alternatives difficult, since a need is simply assumed without reference to other possible areas of expenditure. The need approach is arbitrary and overlooks the return on investment, an extremely important consideration for the problem of a rational allocation of resources.[18]

REDISTRIBUTION, THE COST-BENEFIT CRITERION, AND URBAN RENEWAL

Having pointed out that the existing institutional arrangements concerning urban renewal contain no explicit criterion for determining either the amount of such expenditure or when a project is desirable, we now propose the previously introduced benefits-cost criterion and will discuss later the institutional arrangements under which it could be applied. First, however, let us detail more fully our use of this criterion and the reasons for its selection.

We assume that income and utility are positively correlated. This means that if potential benefits, appropriately defined, exceed costs, then the conditions for Pareto optimality, in the absence of corrective measures, are not filled. It is possible for some action to be taken which will make one or more persons better off without making anyone worse off.[19] In this context, the action will take the form of investment in urban renewal.

It is to be emphasized again that the benefits-cost criterion refers only to the problem of efficiency — i.e., to the allocation of resources on the basis of a given distribution of income. However, it is possible to design programs which do redistribute income but which still are completely compatible with the benefit-cost criterion. The point is that the two problems — distribution and allocation — must be kept conceptually separate.

[18] It may be commonplace to point out that there exists for any given social action a social welfare function which is maximal for that action, and by definition this resource allocation is optimal. Our point is simply that it seems dubious that a type of need approach to forming criteria is reasonable, given that urban problems are not unique as a social problem.

[19] It is easy to see the exact relation between benefits-costs and the Pareto condition. If the sum of benefits exceeds the sum of costs for some particular action, then although some individual might be made worse off by the action, it is theoretically possible to pay compensation to that individual so that the Pareto condition will be satisfied.

Given the fact that interdependencies are a cause of blight, two kinds of actions are possible — preventive and reconstructive. We consider first preventive action.

As was pointed out earlier, the problem in preventing the development of blight consists essentially in finding methods of coordinating the decisions about investment in repair and upkeep so that the socially and individually desirable choices are equated. One step in this direction can be made through the development and use of a special type of building code which bears a superficial resemblance to municipal zoning.[20] It can be seen from the Prisoner's Dilemma example discussed earlier that it is individually desirable to invest *if there is assurance that all individuals will be constrained to make a similar decision.* The special building code specifying minimum levels of repair and upkeep can provide a rough approximation toward optimal levels of coordination.

A brief outline of the scheme follows: Since it is intuitively obvious that different types of property require different kinds of repair and types of upkeep, it would seem desirable that these building codes differ according to the type property under consideration. The role of the planner would be to try to determine the proper restrictions for each type of property. He could try to gather information on interaction effects through the use of statistical sampling techniques and questionnaires. He then could draw up districts and try to estimate the proper level of the building code for each district. A crude approximation to the benefit-cost criterion is easily supplied. It is advantageous to property owners mutually to constrain themselves to make "appropriate" repair expenditures, for this coordinates decisions. Therefore, the planner can simply submit the proposed code for each district to the property owners of that district; if the planner has proposed an appropriate code, then mutual consent should be forthcoming. If mutual consent is not obtained, then it would seem suitable to assume that the proper code for the district has not been proposed and that a new proposal would be necessary.[21]

[20] It is to be emphasized that the building code envisioned here bears only a superficial resemblance to zoning. The two tools are aimed at different problems. Municipal zoning tries to prevent the establishment of "undesirable" properties in specified neighborhoods. These special building codes would be aimed at the elimination of interdependencies affecting repair and upkeep decisions. For an elaboration on the complexities involved in municipal zoning, see Davis & Whinston, *The Economics of Complex Systems: The Case of Municipal Zoning* (O.N.R. Research Memorandum, Graduate School of Industrial Administration, Carnegie Institute of Technology, 1961).

[21] Our use of the term "mutual consent" may represent something of a subterfuge. In actuality, it may not be desirable to insist on unanimity nor would it seem desirable to use a simple majority. Something on the order of eighty to ninety per cent may be reasonable. For a discussion of the problems involved in voting and the difficulties associated with the selection of political decision rules, see James M. Buchanan & Gordon Tullock, *The Calculus of Consent* (1962).

While codes adopted via the above scheme should be helpful in preventing blight, it must be noted that implementation of this plan would require the selection of an appropriate institutional and legal framework. As economists, we do not pretend to know the legal difficulties which might be involved; but a joint effort by the two professions to set up the framework for such a scheme seems to us to be desirable.

Let us now turn our attention to the policy problem when blight is already in existence. Present practices provide something of a framework here; what is missing is a relevant criterion. Of course, it should be noted that it may sometimes be possible to obtain redevelopment through individual effort via the previously stated special-building-code method. In other instances, the optimal property uses may have changed from what they formerly were. The area may be composed of lots too small to obtain an orderly transition of property uses by means of the building code. It may be desirable to replan streets, or other reasons may be advanced for the usual type of urban renewal effort. Therefore, let us try to determine the appropriate comparison of costs and benefits when the usual type renewal activity takes place.

Let us assume that the city government has marked some blighted area for redevelopment. Taking the property tax rate as given, suppose that the city has raised funds for the project by selling bonds. With the money thus raised, the city has purchased the blighted area, using the right of eminent domain wherever needed. Suppose that the city has demolished the outdated structures, made adequate provision for public services, and then, having finished its part of the operation, sold lots to entrepreneurs who have agreed in advance to build, say, modern apartment buildings.

Note what city action has accomplished. It has removed the obstacles to private renewal. The right of eminent domain has removed the possibility of price-gouging and stubborn property owners acting so as to prevent the assembly of a large enough tract. Each entrepreneur who buys the lots from the city is assured that adjoining lots will also be suitably developed, so that interaction difficulties are eliminated.

One fact needs great emphasis here. *The elimination of externalities or interaction effects causes social and private products to be equated.* Therefore, if possible redistribution is left aside; and if for the moment problems are waived which arise from public projects where the market mechanism does not serve as an adequate guide, then it can be stated that revenues and expenditures can be made identical to costs and benefits. Therefore, renewal projects are warranted if, and only if, revenues exceed expenditures. And, even where problems associated with redistribution and public projects are not waived, it is still possible to make the revenue-expenditure criterion approximate the benefit-cost criterion, although some administrative difficulties are involved.

What are the appropriate comparisons of costs and benefits? Consider first the case without the complications. The costs of the local government include the acquisition of land, demolition and improvements, aiding the relocation of displaced families, and interest expenses.[22] The measurement of revenues is slightly more complicated. The primary item, of course, would be receipts from the sale of lots. Since we are dealing with local government, however, a tax on real property will exist. Since the discounted value of the tax is likely to be shifted onto the immobile resource — land — it is necessary to account for this factor. If the project is successful, the new structures should have a higher value than the old; so there should be a net addition to tax revenues. This net addition should be discounted to a present value and counted as a receipt from the project. Thus, a comparison of revenues and expenses is possible, and the project is warranted only if revenues exceed expenses.

We now consider the second case with the additional complications. Note that the previous discussion still applies here, with the following qualifications upon the administrative rules involved. If public projects such as parks, playgrounds, public buildings, and so forth, are planned in conjunction with the renewal effort, then estimates of the social benefit to be derived from these projects must be made by the governmental unit or units which ordinarily pay for them.[23] These estimated benefits are to be considered as revenues from the renewal effort, and the appropriate governmental units are to be required to contribute these amounts to the authority which administers the renewal activity. Thus the revenue-expenditure criterion should very closely approximate the benefits-cost criterion, depending, of course, upon how well the governmental units estimate the social benefits derived from the special public projects.

If there happens to exist some agreed-upon ethical distribution of income, then we point out first that urban renewal is not an efficient method of achieving redistribution. Possible benefits might accrue to special groups instead of the low-income classes. Other methods for simple redistribution exist which should be preferred to urban renewal. However, if the ethical distribution is connected with some arbitrary housing standard below which conditions are viewed as inadequate for "decent living," the cost-benefit criterion need not be rendered useless. Conditional subsidies could be granted to the low-income households living in substandard housing. These

[22] Peculiarly enough, the present-day requirement that individuals be paid for their property and the administrative rule of aiding individuals who may be dislocated to find new quarters affords a method of approximate compensation so that the Pareto condition can be satisfied.

[23] We assume that the units which ordinarily pay for this type of public projects are identical to the units which derive the benefits from these projects. If this is not the case, then further administrative adjustments have to be made, but these adjustments should be made anyway and should not be dependent upon possible urban renewal projects.

subsidies would make it possible for the cost-benefit criterion to work effectively for renewal purposes.

Several corollaries to the cost-benefit criterion should be pointed out. If problems of ethical income distribution are waived, then from the standpoint of a rational allocation of resources, no federal or state subsidies are needed for urban renewal purposes per se. Of course, the adjustments made for the second case may have to be accomplished, but note that in reality these are based upon considerations not directly dependent upon urban renewal. Renewal projects should not lose money. Indeed, they should result in a profit. On the other hand, granted the fact that constitutional and/ or statutory debt limits have often been imposed upon local governments, these should be waived for borrowing for urban renewal purposes. Finally, the local governments should be granted the power of eminent domain for urban renewal purposes.

CONCLUSION

In arriving at these indications for the use of the cost-benefit criterion in urban renewal, we started with the Pareto condition. However, it was suggested that other social welfare functions, which allow for income redistribution or even minimum condition housing, need not affect the usefulness of this criterion as long as the rational allocation of resources is viewed as a *conceptually separate* problem. It is to be emphasized that for the purpose of urban renewal, conceptual separation of the two problems can be achieved through the methods outlined above.

URBAN RESIDENTIAL LAND AND HOUSING MARKETS

Richard F. Muth

Economics is concerned primarily with the study of markets. Prices established on these markets play a crucial role in the allocation of resources to different uses and in determining the resulting level of the national income.

Richard F. Muth is Professor of Economics, Stanford University.

Reprinted from Richard F. Muth, "Urban Residential Land and Housing Markets," in H. Perloff and G. Wingo, eds., *Issues in Urban Economics* (Washington: Resources for the Future, Inc., 1968), pp. 285–288, 297–317. Copyright Johns Hopkins Press.

The markets for residential land and for housing are among the quantitatively most important of all urban markets. According to one estimate, about three-fourths of privately developed land is devoted to residential use in urban areas,[1] and consumers typically spend around one-fifth of their disposable incomes on housing. Most urban problems are related in one way or another to the operation of urban land and housing markets, and many — such as urban decentralization, poor-quality housing, and the residential segregation of Negroes — are more intimately related to them than to any other markets. Despite their importance, however, until lately urban residential land and housing markets have received little attention from professional economists. Because of the insistent claims of other problems, relating to depression, inflation, and economic growth, economists have tended to concentrate on these. With the increasing intensification of urban problems over the past ten or fifteen years, however, economists have devoted more and more attention to the study of urban residential land and housing markets.

In this paper I summarize some recent work on this subject. The first section is concerned principally with the aggregate demand and supply relations for residential land and housing in the urban area as a whole. . . . I shall consider the interrelations among the residential land and housing markets which exist in different parts of an urban area. [One section] is concerned with the reasons for the existence of separate markets for white and Negro housing and their interdependence, while [another] examines the market for slum versus good-quality housing. The final section examines the increasing decentralization of urban areas over time, especially during the decade of the fifties.

THE AGGREGATE DEMAND FOR AND SUPPLY OF URBAN HOUSING AND LAND

The supply of urban housing depends upon both production possibilities and the supply of productive factors, including land, to the housing industry.[2] Similarly, the demand for all urban or for urban residential land

---

[1] Harland Bartholomew, *Land Uses in American Cities* (Harvard University Press, 1955), especially p. 121.

[2] As the above statement suggests, by housing I mean that bundle of services produced both by structures and the land they occupy. The consumer demands for structures and for land are almost certainly closely interrelated, and treating land and structures as inputs into the production of a commodity called housing is a convenient way of handling their interrelationships. In addition, treating residential land as an input into production for final demand rather than as an item of final demand is more in accord with the usual treatment of other classes of land (for example, agricultural).

may be viewed as derived from the demand for the commodity it helps to produce, production possibilities, and the supply of other productive factors. As an alternative to estimating the structural equations of an econometric model embodying the above-noted relationships (data for which would be quite difficult to obtain), a great deal can be said about the probable magnitudes of housing supply and land demand elasticities based upon theoretical knowledge and bits and pieces of empirical evidence. In this section, then, I will first summarize the best information known to me about housing demand elasticities, production possibilities, and conditions of factor supply. I will then consider the implications of this informaton for the supply elasticities of housing and demand elasticities for urban land.

The demand for housing services, as distinguished from the asset or stock demand, in any area depends primarily upon total population, per capita or per family disposable income, and, to a lesser extent, the relative price of housing services. Apart from any changes in average family sizes or other demographic characteristics, one would, of course, expect housing demand to vary proportionally with population. Traditionally, it has been believed that, as a "necessity," housing demand is inelastic with respect to income. Many statistical investigations would seem to support this belief. However, the recent work of Reid [3] and myself [4] suggests that the income elasticity of housing demand is at least $+1$ and may be as large as $+2$. My comparisons of the rate of new residential construction over time and certain other comparisons in the work cited above suggest that the real-income–constant price elasticity of housing demand is about -1, though it too may be even larger numerically. I have since made other comparisons of the variation of housing expenditures among different parts of a city and among various cities. In the former case, the price of housing services varies because of variations in transport costs; in the latter, the price varies with variations in construction costs. The comparisons also suggest that the relative price elasticity of housing demand is about unity.[5] Since interest costs are about one-half of the costs of housing services, a unit price elasticity would imply an interest rate elasticity of demand for housing services of approximately -0.5.

Information on production possibilities can be summarized by relative factor shares, i.e., total payments to a factor divided by the total value of output, and the elasticity of substitution in production of one factor for others (at least if one is willing to assume constant returns to scale in the production of housing). From 1946 to 1960, the proportion of site to total

[3] Margaret G. Reid, *Housing and Income* (University of Chicago Press, 1962).

[4] Richard F. Muth, "The Demand for Non-Farm Housing," in Arnold C. Harberger (ed.), *The Demand for Durable Goods* (University of Chicago Press, 1960).

[5] These are discussed in detail in a monograph I am now preparing, entitled "The Spatial Pattern of Residential Land Use in Cities.". . .

property value for new FHA-insured houses rose from 11.5 to 16.6 per cent.[6] Since the costs of improvements to land may easily equal or exceed raw land costs, and interest costs plus property taxes are about three-fourths of the total costs of providing housing services, land costs are probably of the order of 5 per cent of the costs of housing services. Based upon weights typically used in residential construction cost indexes, labor and materials each account for approximately 45 per cent of the cost of structures or not quite 43 per cent of the cost of housing services. The rise in the share of land in the cost of providing housing in the postwar period, along with increasing land rentals, suggests a less than unit elasticity of substitution of land for structures in housing production. Indeed, the FHA reports that from 1946 to 1960, land costs increased by 180 per cent or more,[7] while during the same period construction costs rose by around 77 per cent.[8] Elsewhere, I have shown that the above-noted price changes and land shares imply an elasticity of substitution of about 0.75.[9]

Even for the nation as a whole, it appears that the long-run supply schedule for structures is highly elastic. In my study of changes in the rate of residential construction in the period between the two world wars, I found little or no tendency for building material prices or wage rates paid construction labor to vary with the rate of new residential construction.[10] The evidence I was able to examine suggests there is a high rate of mobility of firms into and out of the housebuilding industry, and there was little apparent tendency for fluctuations in the incomes of construction firms to be associated with significant fluctuations in housing prices. Maisel has found that large-tract builders in the postwar period have approximately 10 per cent lower costs than do the smallest housebuilders.[11] But so long as other builders exist in significant numbers, his findings merely imply that the large-tract builders will earn a rent attributable to their special advantages. I would expect the supply of structures to be even more elastic for any given urban area than for the nation as a whole, because, in the long run, building materials and probably construction workers and firms would shift among urban areas in response to differential changes in their prices

[6] U.S. Housing and Home Finance Agency, *Fourteenth Annual Report* (U.S. Government Printing Office, 1961), Table III–35, p. 110.

[7] *Ibid.*, p. 109.

[8] As measured by the U.S. Department of Commerce implicit residential non-farm deflator.

[9] Richard F. Muth, "The Derived Demand Curve for a Productive Factor and the Industry Supply Curve for a Productive Factor and the Industry Supply Curve," *Oxford Economic Papers*, Vol. 16 (July 1964), especially pp. 229 ff.

[10] Muth, "The Demand for Non-Farm Housing," pp. 42–46.

[11] Sherman J. Maisel, *Housebuilding in Transition* (University of California Press, 1953), pp. 189 ff.

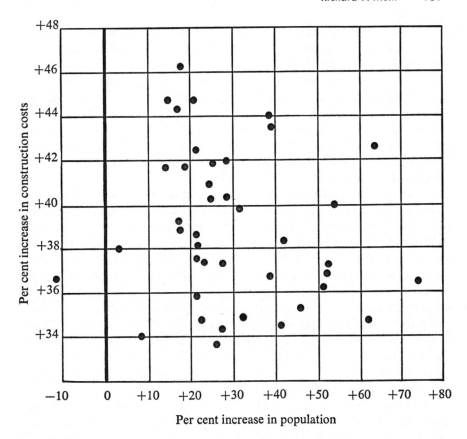

FIGURE 1. *Relation of change in population and change in construction costs, by city, 1950–60.*

or earnings. In this regard, the comparison of the change in urbanized area population and in construction costs for forty-one U.S. cities during the fifties, shown in Figure 1, indicates little if any association between them.[12] . . .

The greater responsiveness of housing output at greater distances from the CBD has another important implication. With an increase in housing demand, whether from increased population, disposable income per family, or, perhaps, subsidies to housing, the price per unit of housing services will

[12] The population data are from U.S. Bureau of the Census, *U.S. Census of Population: 1960,* Final Report PC(1)-1A (1961), Table 22. The measure of construction costs used is the (unpublished) Boeckh residential brick structures index, 1926 U.S. average = 100, for cities.

tend to increase everywhere. With a unit price elasticity of housing demand, the increase in price per unit will leave expenditures per household unchanged, so by the second form of equation (4) housing prices will rise by the same relative amount everywhere. But the value of housing produced is more responsive to price changes at greater distances from the CBD. It can be shown that, using the parameter values already described, the elasticity of the value of housing produced per unit of land would vary from about 7.5 to 22.5 over a ten-mile range. Thus, with an increase in housing demand, the output of housing and population would tend to grow more rapidly at greater distances from the CBD.

Since the total amount of land at any location within a city is fixed, the supply of land to the housing industry is again this fixed total less the non-residential demand for land. To the extent that the transportation system is radial (streets or highways, say), a given width with a given capacity would require a larger fraction of the available total land area closer to the CBD, and the required capacity for the intracity transportation system would be greater closer to the CBD.[13] Furthermore, if private, non-residential users find locations next to railroads or major highways especially desirable, the fraction of total land they use would decline with distance from the CBD. For these reasons one might expect the fraction of total land area which is used for residential purposes to increase with distance from the CBD. Since this fraction is bounded from above, however, it would have to increase at a decreasing relative rate after some point.

With the growth of the city and, thus, housing demand, changes in the fraction of land area use for residential purposes depend partly on the elasticity of supply of land to the housing industry. The latter, of course, is the negative of the elasticity of demand for land on the part of non-residential users. Since firms for whom the relative importance of land is small have a comparative advantage in locating where land rentals are high, one would expect the relative share of land for non-residential firms to increase with distance from the city center. As can readily be seen from equation (3), however, the latter will cause the non-residential demand elasticity to increase numerically with distance only if the elasticity of final product demand is numerically larger than the elasticity of substitution. To the extent that firms in a given local industry sell only a small part of the output coming into some nationwide — or even worldwide — market, the local industry's demand elasticity would be high and the above-noted condition would hold. If, on the other hand, a local industry is the sole supplier of a regional — or even citywide — market, its demand elasticity for land might grow numerically smaller with distance from the CBD.

---

[13] Cf. Edwin S. Mills, "An Aggregative Model of Resource Allocation in a Metropolitan Area," *American Economic Review,* Vol. 57 (May 1967), pp. 197 ff.

Systematic differences in demand elasticities for non-residential land might also arise because of differences in final product demand elasticities. Firms whose market area is the whole of the city tend to locate near the center in order to maximize accessibility to their market. Because there are fewer substitutes for their products than for the products of firms in the outer part of the city, the final product demand elasticities for firms near the center would tend to be numerically smaller. Both for this reason and the increasing relative importance of land noted in the preceding paragraph, there is a weak presumption that the non-residential demand elasticity for land increases numerically with distance from the CBD. If so, with an increase in population and housing demand, one might expect the fraction of urban land in residential use to grow more rapidly in the outer parts of cities. Of course, the fraction of land used for residential purposes is also affected by shifts in the demand for non-residential land. If, as an urban area grows, population tends to grow more rapidly in outer parts of cities, so would the demand for many types of retail and service outputs produced at widely scattered points throughout the city. In addition, the land used for transportation would tend to grow more rapidly at greater distances from the CBD. Such changes would tend to increase the non-residential demand for land relatively more in the outer parts of cities and to offset the previously noted tendency for the fraction of urban land used for housing to grow more rapidly there.

I shall now summarize the analysis of this section by considering its implications for the pattern of population densities in urban areas. Since population per unit of land used for residential purposes, or net population density, D, is

(1) $$D = \frac{P}{L} = \frac{\left(\frac{pQ}{L}\right) \times \frac{P}{H}}{(pq)}, \text{ where}$$

$P =$ population,

$H =$ number of households, and

$q =$ quantity of housing services consumed per household,

(2) $$\frac{d\ln D}{dk} = \frac{d\ln}{dk}\left(\frac{pQ}{L}\right) + \frac{d\ln}{dk}\left(\frac{P}{H}\right) - \frac{d\ln(pq)}{dk}.$$

It is frequently argued that larger families, especially those with young children, tend to locate in the outer parts of cities. While I have found a tendency for the average size of family to increase with distance from the CBD, the average change per mile — about 1 to 3 per cent — is quite small compared to the average change in population density — about 30 per cent per mile.[14] As noted earlier in this section, apart from the association with age of dwellings, there is little or no tendency for the average income level of an area to increase with k. Furthermore, a unit elastic demand for housing would suggest that expenditures on housing per household would be unaffected by variations in housing prices, so purely on locational grounds the third term of the right member of (2) is also small.

Apart from the effects of the age of dwellings on the location of households by income, then, the tendency for net population densities to decline with distance from the CBD would result almost wholly from the decline in the value of housing produced per square mile with distance. It might be argued, of course, that the decline in (pQ/L) also reflects the effects of age of dwellings, but [other data suggest] that this is not the case. (I shall comment further on this point in the following section.) Furthermore, it was suggested earlier that there are two effects upon the size of $(d\ln/dk)/(pQ/L)$ and, hence, the relative change in net population density at different distances that tend roughly to offset each other. First, stability of locational equilibrium for any individual household requires that the price gradient decline with distance. Secondly, though, the decline in land's relative share with distance means that the value of housing produced per square mile of residential land becomes more responsive to any given price change. Thus, net population densities tend to decline at a roughly constant relative rate with distance from the CBD.

Gross population density, or population per unit of total land area, depends upon the fraction of total land area used for urban purposes as well as upon net population density. If, as I suggested above, the fraction of land that is residential increases at a declining relative rate, gross population densities would decline at a smaller relative rate than net densities and the relative rate of decline would become numerically greater at greater distances from the CBD.[15] In my examination of data for south Chicago in 1960, however, I fail to find any appreciable variation in the fraction of land that is residential with distance from the CBD or with any other measure of accessibility; gross and net population densities respond in very much the same way to variations in these accessibility measures.[16] In addition, in my examination of the pattern of gross population densities in forty-six U.S. cities for 1950, I fail to find any significant tendency for gross population densities to decline at numerically increasing relative rates.[17]

---

[14] Muth, "The Spatial Pattern . . . ," Chap. 8.

[15] This follows easily from the fact that the log of gross population density is the sum of the logs of net population density and the fraction of total land that is residential.

[16] Muth, "The Variation of Population Density . . . ," pp. 178–179.

[17] Muth, "The Spatial Structure of the Housing Market," pp. 213–14. Of course, one might find gross population densities declining at a roughly constant relative rate if net density declined at a numerically decreasing relative rate and the fraction of land that is residential increased at a declining relative rate.

Thus, it appears to me that a negative exponential pattern of gross population densities in relation to distance is as good an approximation to actual patterns as any other.

OTHER FACTORS INFLUENCING THE CONSUMPTION AND PRODUCTION OF HOUSING IN DIFFERENT PARTS OF A CITY

Until quite recently, most writings on urban residential land and housing tended to neglect accessibility. They emphasized instead the dynamic effects of a city's past development upon current conditions, and preferences of different households for housing in different locations, especially as they are influenced by income. In this section I want to discuss some of the a priori reasons why population densities might be directly related to the age of dwellings and inversely related to the income of the inhabitants of an area. I also want to point out some of the empirical findings bearing on these relationships, which are described more fully in the Appendix. Finally, I will consider some of the reasons for the residential segregation of Negroes and whether Negroes pay higher prices for housing of given quality.

Because the marginal costs of transport to workers commuting to the CBD were almost certainly greater prior to the automobile and expenditures on housing per household were smaller (since incomes were lower), it would be anticipated . . . that the housing price gradient was larger. Thus, everything else being the same, housing prices would have been higher in areas close to the city center and lower in those parts of it near the edges. For this reason the output of housing per square mile was probably greater than its equilibrium for the auto era near the city center, while the converse was true in its outer parts. Hoover and Vernon have argued that, once an area has been initially developed, "neighborhood density patterns . . . have been rather stubbornly resistant to change." [18] They also note that zoning restrictions typically place an upper limit on population densities, and that these restrictions have grown up only after about 1920.[19] For these reasons one might expect that population densities and the output of housing per square mile would tend to be greater than they would otherwise be in those parts of the city developed prior to 1920.

When one examines population density and measures of the output of housing per unit of land in relation to distance from the CBD, the proportion of dwellings built prior to 1920, and the median income of a census tract, one does find some confirmation of this hypothesis. While adding age and income somewhat weakens the partial correlation between gross population density and distance, these correlations remain significantly negative.

[18] Edgar M. Hoover and Raymond Vernon, *Anatomy of a Metropolis* (Harvard University Press, 1959), p. 132.
[19] *Ibid.*, p. 133.

Surprisingly, though, while the partial correlation between population density and age . . . is positive in four of the six cities examined for the year 1950, it is significantly positive at the 0.10 level in only two of the cities. As measured by the proportion of dwellings which are in single-family structures, there appears to be a strong tendency for the physical output of housing per square mile to be above average the higher the proportion built prior to 1920. But in only one of the six cities does one find a significantly greater value of housing produced per square mile in older parts of the city. I suspect that the reason for the apparent contradiction is the lower prices per unit of housing service in older areas.

Population densities might also vary between older and newer areas because of differences in per capita expenditures on housing. With a unit elasticity housing demand, lower housing prices in older areas would not affect expenditures for housing. As was noted in the previous section, however, there is a strong tendency for higher-income households to inhabit newer housing. The best explanation for this tendency, I believe, is that older housing is more cheaply converted to occupancy by lower-income households, though it amounts to very much the same thing to say instead that higher-income households have stronger preferences for newer housing than have lower-income ones. In any event, because of the negative association between age and income one would expect to find a smaller average expenditure on housing per household in the older areas. In addition, . . . one notes a negative partial association between age and the per-family expenditure on housing when income is held constant. The latter might result from the fact that households with weaker preferences for housing tend to locate in older areas where the quantity of housing per dwelling is smaller.

There are several reasons why higher-income households might seek out locations in the outer parts of cities. One of the most obvious possibilities is that higher-income households have stronger preferences for space and privacy relative to structural features of housing. As Hoover and Vernon put it, "higher income people use their superior purchasing power to buy lower density," and "rising incomes and leisure are the basis for a demand for newer houses as such, and in general for more spaciously sited homes." [20] Also, the fraction who are homeowners typically increases with income, and, for a variety of reasons, most homeowners live in single-family, detached houses. The latter, of course, tend to be cheaper in the outer parts of cities, where land rentals are lower relative to construction costs. Finally, federal mortgage programs and the federal income tax advantage of home ownership [21] tend to reduce the relative price of housing

---

[20] *Ibid.*, pp. 169, 222.

[21] For a discussion of this subsidy, see Richard Goode, "Imputed Rent of Owner-Occupied Dwellings under the Income Tax," *Journal of Finance*, Vol. 15 (December 1960), pp. 504–30.

to homeowners and increase their expenditures on housing inclusive of the subsidy. Because they consume more housing, higher income households have a greater incentive to take advantage of these subsidies. . . . [T]he increased expenditures on housing lead the families affected by these subsidies to locate greater distances from the CBD where the price gradient is smaller. For these reasons one might expect population densities to be lower in census tracts where the average income level is higher. One might also expect part of the decline in population density with distance from the CBD to be due to the association between density and income.

Quite surprisingly, however . . . one finds little partial relationship between population density and income. While the partial correlation coefficient is negative for four of the six cities examined, it is significant at the 1-tail 10 per cent level only for one. In view of the strong positive relationship between income and expenditures on housing per household, this can be the case only if the value of housing output per square mile tends to increase with income. The latter relationship is indeed found . . . where the partial correlation coefficient is positive in all cities, rather strongly so in four of them. Even more puzzling, . . . one finds little partial correlation between income and the proportion of dwellings in single-family structures, which I interpret as varying inversely with the physical output of housing per square mile of land. To me, the best explanation for this apparent contradiction is as follows: because of favorable neighborhood effects, the price per unit of housing, and thus land rentals, tends to be greater in higher income areas, offsetting any tendency for higher-income households to live at lower population densities but producing a higher value of housing output per unit of land.

The residential segregation of Negroes has become one of the most important political and social issues of the day. There are several possible reasons for this segregation, or residential separation. Because Negroes tend to have lower incomes and different occupations than whites, one might suspect their segregation would result from these factors rather than from race itself. However, Taeuber has shown that little of the Negro segregation vis-à-vis the white population can be attributed to income and occupational differences.[22] Similar conclusions were reached by Pascal.[23] In the popular mind, the residential segregation of Negroes is felt to be due to a unique

[22] Karl E. Taeuber, "Negro Residential Segregation, 1940–1960: Changing Trends in the Large Cities of the United States" (Paper read at the annual meetings of the American Sociological Association, 1962); see also Karl E. Taeuber and Alma F. Taeuber, *Negroes in Cities, Residential Segregation and Neighborhood Change* (Aldine Publishing Co.: 1965).

[23] Anthony H. Pascal, "The Economics of Housing Segregation," *Abstracts of Papers Presented at the December 1965 Meetings* (New York: Econometric Society), p. 2.

aversion — not shared by the rest of the community — on the part of land-lords and real estate agents for dealing with Negroes. Such a hypothesis cannot account for many other forms of segregation, such as segregation in churches and fraternal organizations or the residential segregation of many other groups without apparent coercion. More importantly, if landlords, say, fail to rent to Negroes because of their own aversion, they will have a higher average level of vacancies and lower incomes than others. It would then be in their interests to sell out to others who do not possess the same aversions.

A much more satisfying explanation for racial segregation in housing is Becker's, namely that whites have a greater aversion to living among Ne-groes than have other Negroes.[24] Thus, the two groups would tend to in-habit disjoint residential areas, since some white households would be willing to offer more for the occupancy rights to a dwelling in an area oc-cupied largely by other white households than would a Negro resident. Not only is Becker's explanation consistent with most other forms of segrega-tion, but it readily explains the failure of landlords or real estate agents to deal with Negroes. By so doing the landlords would be faced with either decreased rentals from white tenants or a higher vacancy rate, the real estate agents with a loss of future business from some white residents of an area.

As Becker points out, residential segregation need not imply discrimina-tion, or higher housing prices relative to marginal costs of housing for Negroes.[25] Rather, the level of housing prices in the interior [26] of the Negro area relative to the white area depends upon the relative rate of growth of housing demand in the two areas as compared with the rate of change in their size. Indeed, Bailey has demonstrated that, under the conditions postu-lated by Becker, the only possible long-run equilibrium position under di-verse ownership of properties is one in which prices in the interior of the Negro area are lower than in the interior of the white area.[27] The latter is the case because, given equality of prices in the interiors of the two areas, prices will be lower on the white side of the boundary separating the two areas than on the Negro side. For this reason, owners of occupancy rights on the white side of the boundary will have the incentive to sell them to Negroes, and with the expansion of the Negro area relative to the white area housing prices will fall in the former and rise in the latter. Of course, if

---

[24] Gary S. Becker, *The Economics of Discrimination* (University of Chicago Press, 1957), p. 59.

[25] *Ibid.*

[26] That is, far enough from the boundary separating Negro and white residential areas so that prices are not affected by the presence of the other group.

[27] Martin J. Bailey, "Note on the Economics of Residential Zoning and Urban Renewal," *Land Economics*, Vol. 35 (August 1959), pp. 288–90.

Negro, relative to white, housing demand were growing fast enough for a long enough period relative to the growth of the Negro area, housing prices in the interior of the Negro area could rise above those in the interior of the white area.[28]

Census data on housing expenditures indicate that at a given money income level expenditures for housing by non-whites are as much as a third or more greater than expenditures by whites.[29] Such comparisons are frequently interpreted as demonstrating that Negroes pay higher prices per unit for housing. However, census data on contract rent include, in addition to space rent, expenditures for any furnishings and utilities included in the rental payment agreed upon, and a higher proportion of non-whites than whites inhabit rental housing. For a variety of possible reasons, the costs of supplying housing to Negroes may be higher. Most important, though, with a unit or elastic housing demand with respect to price, higher prices per unit would leave unchanged or reduce expenditures for housing, not increase them. If, however, one examines physical indicators that one would expect to reflect price variations, such as population densities, crowding, and the proportion of dwellings that are in single-family structures, the differences between Negro and white areas are small.[30] Furthermore, in a recently published study of the sales prices of single-family houses in the Hyde Park area of Chicago, Bailey actually finds lower prices in Negro areas.[31] Thus, it is far from clear that the residential segregation does in fact lead to higher housing prices for equivalent quality for Negroes.

FACTORS AFFECTING THE CONDITION OF URBAN HOUSING

Two of the most important urban problems of today are those popularly described as urban blight and suburban sprawl. The former, of course, refers to the poor, and perhaps deteriorating, condition of the central city housing stock, the latter to the striking tendency in recent years for population to grow at more rapid rates in the suburban parts of urban areas than in their older, more centrally located parts. It is widely believed that the two phenomena are intimately related, indeed, that urban blight is to a very great extent responsible for suburban sprawl. In this section I shall discuss various factors affecting the quality of a city's housing stock and some em-

---

[28] Becker, *op. cit.*, appears to have believed that housing prices in Negro areas were in fact higher than those in white areas, and offered essentially this explanation for the differential.

[29] For example, see Muth, "The Variation of Population Density . . . ," p. 176.

[30] *Ibid.*, p. 182.

[31] Martin J. Bailey, "Effects of Race and Other Demographic Factors on the Values of Single-Family Houses," *Land Economics*, Vol. 42 (May 1966), pp. 215–20.

pirical evidence which sheds light on their relative importance. The next and final section considers the question of urban decentralization.

Most explanations for the growth of slum or poor-quality housing in recent years are based upon factors that influence its supply schedule. In many, the increase in the supply of poor-quality housing results from a decline in the demand for good-quality housing. A variety of reasons, such as the development of automobile transportation, physical obsolescence, poor initial planning, and failure of local governments to supply a proper level of municipal services, have been suggested for the initial decline in the demand for good-quality housing. Whatever the reason for it, though, the decline in demand would lead to a fall in housing prices in the affected areas and thus to the returns to investment in residential real estate. For this reason landlords have reduced their expenditures for maintenance and allowed their properties to deteriorate in quality.

Another group of forces which might tend to increase the supply of poor-quality housing might be lumped under the heading of market imperfections and external economies. It is frequently asserted that capital market imperfections prevent property owners from undertaking expenditures on existing residential real estate in the older parts of cities that would otherwise be privately profitable or socially desirable. If such were the case, however, I would expect that, say, insurance companies would find it profitable to buy, rehabilitate, and resell large parcels of residential real estate in cities. Their failure to do so might be explained by imperfections in the market for existing dwellings, especially by the costs of assembling large tracts now under diverse ownership where any individual owner might try to hold out for a higher price than he might otherwise obtain if he suspects the assembler's intentions. Several features of our tax system are also said to increase the supply of slums. The accelerated depreciation provisions of the federal income tax laws keep older structures in use longer than they might be otherwise. To the extent that age of structure itself tends to reduce housing quality, these tax provisions would increase the proportion of the housing stock that is of poor quality. Property taxation may tend to reduce improvements to sites and their existing structures. In addition, if poor-quality units are taxed at lower effective rates than others, perhaps because assessments are based upon factors other than the income the property produced, the supply of slums will be increased.[32]

There are several kinds of external effects which might lead to too much poor-quality housing relative to the demand for it. Planners and others have long felt that non-residential land uses tend to reduce the values of sur-

---

[32] The forces noted in this paragraph are stressed by Jerome Rothenberg, "Urban Renewal Programs," in Robert Dorfman (ed.), *Measuring Benefits of Government Investments* (The Brookings Institution, 1965), pp. 303–4.

rounding residential properties. Such effects would, of course, provide a rationale for zoning regulations which limit the uses to which land may be put in different areas of a city. Davis and Whinston have recently argued that a single property owner's expenditure for improvement of a structure tends to make the immediately surrounding properties more desirable. Thus, owners of surrounding properties benefit, too, and are discouraged from making improvements in their own properties. In this way, from the social viewpoint, too little has been spent on improvement.[33] While such effects might be expected in all areas of the city, by limiting expenditures on existing dwellings they would tend to lower the average quality of the existing housing stock and increase the proportion below any given quality level. The Davis-Whinston effect provides a rationale for various building and occupancy codes which set minimum standards for different features of what we call housing, though not necessarily for codes which, in effect, attempt to impose middle-class standards on lower-income housing.

The same facts that bring about segregation of Negro and white residential areas hold true for lower-income and higher-income residential areas.[34] Thus, similarly, where the price per unit of housing is the same in the interior of the two areas, at the boundary separating them, prices per unit will be higher on the poor-quality side. Unlike the case of racial segregation, however, costs of conversion from good-quality to poor-quality use are likely to be of significant practical importance. These may take the form of expenditure in converting existing dwelling units to smaller ones or from the delay in recovering one's invested capital through deferral of maintenance and repair expenditures. In long-run equilibrium the price per unit of housing services in the interior of the poor-quality area, because of conversion costs, may be greater than in the interior of the good-quality area. But the boundary price differential implies that in long-run equilibrium, too large a portion of the existing stock of dwellings will be devoted to producing poor-quality housing. The Bailey boundary effect provides a rationale for zoning to prevent the poor-quality residential area from expanding too far, or, if it already has, for renewal of the area.

The expansion of the area occupied by poor-quality housing might also result from increases in the demand for such housing. The condition of dwellings inhabited, as well as the amount of space per person and other features, may be viewed as inputs into the production of a commodity called housing. Hence, anything which reduces the quantity of housing demanded, such as a fall in income per family, or a rise in the relative price of housing

[33] Otto A. Davis and Andrew B. Whinston, "The Economics of Urban Renewal," *Law and Contemporary Problems,* Vol. 26 (Winter 1961), pp. 105–17; also Rothenberg, *op. cit.,* pp. 299–301.

[34] See Bailey, "Note on the Economics of Residential Zoning and Urban Renewal," *op cit.*

services, might be expected to reduce the derived demands for housing quality and for space. As a consequence, one would expect that dwellings would decline in quality and that more persons would occupy a given floor space or number of rooms. Along these same lines, if Negroes paid higher prices per unit of housing, one would expect their consumption of housing to be smaller. A higher proportion of Negro households at a given income level would thus occupy poor-quality units, and the fraction of Negro households with more than, say, one person per room would be higher than for whites.[35]

It is not difficult to account for an increase in the demand for poor-quality housing in the central cities of urban areas on the hypothesis that it is but one aspect of a low consumption of housing per household. During the first half of this century the per capita stock of non-farm housing showed relatively little increase in the United States, mostly, I believe, because the relative price of housing rose greatly.[36] Low-income migrants to the United States have tended to congregate in cities, and large-scale migration of lower-income persons from the rural South to cities has occurred, especially during the forties. Also, the lower-income population has had a higher rate of natural increase than the higher-income population. Because of the Bailey effect described earlier, whatever the reason for their initial establishment in the older parts of the urban area, one would expect poor-quality housing areas to grow outward from their edges rather than for new concentrations to be established. It is quite likely, then, that the consumption of housing per household in the central cities of our metropolitan areas actually declined prior to 1950, and with it the demand for poor-quality housing increased. Now, if existing structures differ in their cost of conversion from good-quality to poor-quality housing — in particular, one might expect older dwellings and dwellings in multi-unit structures to be more cheaply converted than others — one would expect the relative price of poor-quality housing to rise as the demand for poor-quality housing increases. At the same time, the increase in demand would increase the returns to previously existing poor-quality dwellings.

In my opinion, there is strong evidence that differences in the fraction of the housing stock which is substandard[37] can best be accounted for by variations in the demand for poor-quality housing.[38] . . . [I]n five of the six

---

[35] Closely related to the above are the arguments that residential segregation restricts Negroes to areas of the poorest housing quality or that, through ignorance, recent immigrant and racial minority groups, especially Negroes, tend to inhabit poorer housing than do others. On the latter point, see Rothenberg, *op. cit.*, p. 302.

[36] For a fuller discussion, see Muth, "The Demand for Non-Farm Housing," pp. 73–74.

[37] That is, dilapidated and/or without private bath.

[38] I summarized this evidence and presented the more important empirical results in "Slums and Poverty" (paper read at the International Economics Association Conference on the Economic Problems of Housing, 1965). A more detailed empirical investigation is described in Muth, "The Spatial Pattern. . . ."

cities examined there is a strongly negative partial correlation between the proportion of substandard and median-income dwellings. . . . [S]imilar results are found when crowding [39] is compared with income. The income elasticities of the proportion that is substandard and of crowding . . . are quite similar, as would be expected if quality and space per person were inputs into the production of housing. These elasticities average about −2.5. In comparisons made among census tracts in south Chicago for 1950 and 1960, and in comparisons among various U.S. cities in 1950, I likewise find that the proportion that is substandard is strongly and negatively related to income. In these latter comparisons, in which many more variables are included . . . the elasticity of the proportion of dwellings that are substandard with respect to income was about −3.5. Furthermore, when separate partial repression coefficients of the proportion substandard on income are fitted for the lower and upper halves of the south Chicago tracts by median income, the differences are negligible. If ignorance of housing opportunities operated with greater force among the lowest-income groups, I would expect the response of housing quality to income differences to be greater in the lower half of the income distribution.

In view of the great variation of median family income among the census tracts of most cities, an elasticity of the magnitude noted above can account for great variations in the proportion substandard. In south Chicago in 1960, for example, median tract incomes range from a low of about $3,000 per family to a high of around $10,000; according to my estimates the proportion substandard would be only 0.5 per cent as great in the highest-income tracts as in the lowest. In addition, in my intercity comparison I find an elasticity of the proportion of dwellings that are substandard with respect to construction costs that is about the same numerically as the income elasticity. This would be expected, of course, if poor housing quality were symptomatic of a low consumption of housing per household, since the estimates noted in Section I suggest that the price and income elasticities of housing demand are about the same order of magnitude.

While there is strong evidence that variations in the proportion of substandard dwellings reflect variations in demand, there is little evidence that this proportion is affected by variations in supply. The comparisons . . . give little evidence of a negative partial correlation of the substandard proportion and distance from the CBD, as would be anticipated if an automobile-induced decline in demand had led to quality deterioration. My more detailed examination of data for south Chicago leads to the same conclusion. [Earlier data] show a marked tendency for a higher proportion of dwellings to be substandard in areas of older housing as do my south Chicago comparisons for 1950. In 1960, however, no such tendency is ap-

---

[39] The proportion of dwellings with more than one person per room.

parent in the south Chicago data. The south Chicago data also show a strong tendency for a higher substandard proportion in census tracts with an above-average rate of population turnover in 1950 but not in 1960. I am inclined to attribute the effects observed for 1950 to the lingering effects of rent control.[40]

My south Chicago and intercity comparisons gave little evidence that crowding leads to a deterioration of housing quality, while the proportion substandard was actually lower the higher the rate of population growth. The latter finding is directly contrary to the belief that diseconomies associated with rapid population growth lead to slum formation. Nor do I generally find a higher proportion of substandard dwellings in the areas adjacent to manufacturing or retail centers as would be expected from external diseconomies associated with surrounding uses of land. In this last connection, another recent study finds little or no tendency for housing values to vary inversely with the presence of non-residential land uses.[41] In my south Chicago comparisons, there is likewise no apparent tendency for a higher proportion of substandard dwellings in Negro tracts when this is evaluated separately from such factors as income differences. The last is contrary to what would be expected if residential segregation resulted in higher housing prices to Negroes or restricted them to areas of the worst housing quality.

Most important of all, perhaps, for appraising the increase-in-the-supply-of-slums hypothesis, is the suggestion in the south Chicago data that the effect of dwelling unit condition upon income is quite small. I estimated the elasticity of median tract income with respect to dwelling unit condition to be -0.07 in 1950, and -0.04 or even less for 1960. If dwelling unit condition has a negligible effect upon the location of households by income, or on the incomes of given households through the disabilities which result from inhabiting poor-quality housing, then the increased supply hypotheses cannot account for the negative association between housing quality and income.

One of the most striking pieces of evidence bearing on the reasons for the expansion of slums is the great decline in the proportion of dwellings substandard in the fifties. Estimates made by Duncan and Hauser indicate that, of the six Standard Metropolitan Statistical Areas (SMSA's) they studied, only in New York did the number of substandard dwellings in-

[40] Since rent controls reduce the profitability of investment in structures whose rentals are controlled, landlords reduced their expenditures for maintenance and repair. Such a reduction could well lead to a more rapid rate of deterioration in older structures. This is particularly true in areas of rapid population turnover.

[41] John P. Crecine, Otto A. Davis, and John E. Jackson, "Externalities in Urban Property Markets: Some Empirical Results and Their Implications for the Phenomenon of Municipal Zoning" (paper read at the annual meetings of the Southern Economics Association, 1966).

crease during the period 1950–56.[42] And here, rent controls are still in existence. In the five other SMSA's and in the cities of Chicago and Philadelphia the number of substandard dwellings declined by one-third in six years. Furthermore, around 90 per cent of this decline was due to the improved quality of given units. Now, none of the increased-supply theories can account for such an improvement, and on many one would anticipate a further decline in quality. Quality improvement is quite readily explainable on the demand hypothesis, however. Unlike the first half of the century, a substantial increase in housing consumption appears to have taken place during this period. Goldsmith's estimate of the value of the stock of private non-farm housekeeping units (including land) in 1947–49 prices, for example, increased by 23 per cent from the end of 1949 to the end of 1955,[43] while population increased only 12 per cent. While the absolute size of the low-income population of urban areas and the land area they occupy has continued to increase, and some dwellings have deteriorated as a result, increased consumption of housing per family implies a decline in the demand for housing below any given quality level. In fact, the rate of quality improvement noted by Duncan and Hauser is quite consistent with the income and price elasticities of the substandard proportion I have estimated from cross-section data. During the fifties, median family income in real terms grew at a rate of about 3 per cent per year and real construction costs by 1 percent per year. Given elasticities numerically equal to 3.5, such changes would imply a reduction in the substandard proportion of about 7 per cent per year or just slightly over one-third in six years' time.

Evidence on the price per unit of housing services is relevant both for appraising alternative theories of the spread of slums, and for judging whether, from the social viewpoint, too much poor-quality housing is being produced relative to the low-income demand for it. Direct data about the price of housing in slum versus other areas are quite difficult to obtain. Martin Bailey's study of the sales prices of single-family houses in the Hyde Park area of Chicago suggests that prices are lower in slum areas than in otherwise comparable good-quality housing areas.[44] In my study of south Chicago data for 1960, however, I found that net population density, the value of housing output per square mile of residential land, and crowding all tended to be significantly higher in areas where the proportion of substandard dwellings was higher, while the proportion of dwellings in one-unit

[42] Beverly Duncan and Philip M. Hauser, *Housing a Metropolis — Chicago* (The Free Press, 1960), pp. 56–58. The data used were from the 1950 Census of Housing and the 1956 National Housing Inventory, which employed identical definitions of housing condition.

[43] Raymond W. Goldsmith, *The National Wealth of the United States in the Postwar Period* (Princeton University Press, 1962), Table B-12, p. 253.

[44] Bailey, "Effects of Race and Other Demographic Factors on the Values of Single-Family Houses," *op cit.*

structures was lower.[45] These findings suggest that the price per unit of housing service is higher in slum than in other areas. Even more striking, perhaps, is the fact that in urban renewal projects site acquisition costs typically exceed the resale value of the cleared land. From data developed by Anderson, it would appear that through the end of 1962 site acquisition costs cumulated to slightly more than $2 billion, while expected proceeds from the sale of cleared land amounted to just under $1 billion.[46] If slum housing were less expensive per unit than better housing, such a difference could arise only if renewal has been premature, or poorly planned and executed.

It is clear, therefore, that the principal reason for slum housing is the low income of its inhabitants. Demolition, as in urban renewal, or programs such as stricter code enforcement, that raise the cost of producing poor-quality as contrasted with good-quality housing, do virtually nothing to attack the basic cause of slums. While these programs reduce the fraction of poor-quality housing, they also raise the price of housing for lower-income households. It appears that not only has the private market not produced too much poor-quality housing relative to the demand for it, but also that the private market has clearly responded to rising incomes by upgrading the average quality of the existing housing stock. Thus, it seems to me that measures taken to raise the incomes of lower-income groups offer the best prospect of solving the problem of poor-quality housing.

FACTORS AFFECTING THE SPREAD OF URBAN AREAS AND SUBURBANIZATION

Since the end of World War II, the suburban parts of an area have tended to grow more rapidly than the central city and, indeed, in many cases the population of the latter has actually declined. In popular discussion, this decentralization of urban populations is often viewed as a "flight from blight," an attempt to escape the undesirable physical and social conditions of central cities. This section will discuss the various reasons for decentralization in some detail, and present empirical evidence relevant for appraising them.

The preceding section discussed the growth of the poor-quality housing area in the central city. Even though this growth is more likely to have stemmed from an increase in low-income population than from the physical factors which lead directly to a decline in good-quality housing demand, it

---

[45] Muth, "The Variation of Population Density . . . ," p. 183.
[46] Martin Anderson, *The Federal Bulldozer* (The M.I.T. Press, 1964), Table 2.1, p. 21, and Table A.1, p. 231.

might still be responsible for an increase in good-quality housing demand in the outer parts of the urbanized area. Similar effects might result from the expansion of the Negro population of the central city.

Least obvious, perhaps, is the stimulus to suburbanization provided by current municipal fiscal arrangements. In our society some of the most significant redistribution of income and wealth is probably that provided by municipal governments through the provision of public education, health services and hospitals, and many welfare programs. Historically, municipal governments have been dependent primarily upon taxes levied within their own boundaries for funds to finance expenditures for these purposes. Even if middle- and upper-income households had no aversion to living among lower-income or minority groups, a growth in the lower-income population of the central city would probably tend to increase expenditures for municipal services relative to tax collections at previously existing rates. As a result, the tax burden on higher-income households and business firms in the central city would tend to increase. Since the resulting increase in taxes could not be escaped merely by moving to the other part of the central city, higher-income households and business firms would have an incentive to move beyond the boundaries of the central city.

Then, too, the distribution of population between the central city and its suburbs could be influenced by many of the forces affecting population density gradients. . . . One of the most obvious of these is improvements in transportation, which . . . would reduce the price gradient. As a result, the price of housing in the central part of the urban area would decline, while in the outer part it would rise. The latter would, in turn, increase the rental value of residential land in the outer parts of cities and lead to a conversion of land from agricultural to urban residential use. At the same time the output per unit of residential land would rise in the outer parts of cities . . . and population would be redistributed from the central to the outer parts of the area. Indirectly, the greater population growth in the outer part of the urban area might stimulate a higher proportion of business firms to locate in the outer part of the area to be nearer either their customers or workers. Directly, improvements in intracity transportation might reduce the relative costs of central city versus suburban locations for many non-residential land users.

Either population or income growth per family would lead to an increase in the demand for housing and for the products of most other users of land as well. In consequence, I would expect land to be converted to urban uses and the total land area of the urbanized area would increase. . . . I [have] argued that, because land's relative share is lower in the production of housing and probably other urban commodities as well, the value of housing produced is more responsive to price increases in the outer parts of urban areas. Hence, as the demand and therefore the price for housing services increases, both the value of the housing produced and the growth of population increase relatively more rapidly in the outer part of the urban area. The effect of this differential growth would, of course, be especially strong in the suburbs. . . . I also suggested several other reasons why, with rising incomes, the demand for housing in the outer parts of the urbanized area will grow relatively. . . . I argued that, if anything, the income elasticity of housing demand is likely to exceed that of the marginal costs of transport, so that with an increase in income the housing price gradient would decline. Secondly, if rising incomes increase the demand for newer structures, population would tend to grow relatively more rapidly in the outer parts of the urban area, which typically are newer. Finally, similar effects would result if higher-income households showed stronger preferences for space relative to structural features of housing, or for home ownership as such. The desire to take advantage of federal income tax advantages to home ownership and the federal mortgage programs available as their incomes increase also positively affect the demand for newer housing.

The urban decentralization of recent years is sometimes attributed to land speculation. Regardless of the reason, if land within the borders of an urban area is held vacant or in less-developed use than current conditions alone might justify, then the boundary of the urban area will tend to be further from the CBD than would otherwise be the case. It should be noted, though, that the failure to develop land currently is perfectly rational and need not be wasteful if the additional returns from doing so are less than the increased future conversion costs. In its vulgar form, the land speculation hypothesis claims that because the future rate of growth of an urban area, and especially its outer zones, is overestimated, or because individuals mistakenly believe that anticipated development will be concentrated in a particular direction, too much land is held for future development.

A more sensible reason that too much land might be withheld from its best use, based upon current conditions alone, is provided by the capital gains provisions of federal income taxation. The fact that the return from holding land for future use is taxed as a capital gain encourages more land to be held for future conversion than would otherwise be the case. If this were the only factor at work, one would expect the returns from landholding to be about equal to those from common stocks, which from recent work would appear to be of the order of 9 to 12 per cent. However, the holding of land for future development is a very risky undertaking, and the Friedman-Savage expected utility hypothesis[47] suggests persons may be willing to accept a lower average return for the small chance of a large gain. If so, the appropriate rates of return with which to compare the re-

[47] Milton Friedman and L. J. Savage, "The Utility Analysis of Choices Involving Risk," in *Journal of Political Economy*, Vol. 56 (August 1948).

turns to holding land would be those on highly risky investments, perhaps uranium stocks.

In another paper I have empirically examined the determinants of the spread of population within urban areas, especially its distribution between the central city and its suburbs, and the amount of land used for urban purposes.[48] Based on these results I would argue that increases in population and improvements in automobile transportation, as reflected in car registrations per capita, are sufficient to account for most of the suburbanization of population and change in land area which occurred during the fifties. During this period urbanized area population increased by about 30 per cent, and such an increase would, according to my estimates, cause the central city density gradient to decline by 15 per cent, or from 0.30 to just over 0.25. The growth in urbanized area population would also have caused its land area to increase by around 30 per cent and the central city population by 27 per cent. The effects of increased car registrations per capita, from 0.26 to 0.35 — almost a 35 per cent increase — are much more dramatic. By itself, this factor would cause the central city density gradient to fall from 0.30 to about 0.13, central city population to fall by about 14 per cent, and land area to increase by 47 per cent. The decline in the fraction of SMSA manufacturing employment inside the central city from 0.71 to 0.62 would reduce the density gradient by about 7 per cent and the central city population by slightly less than 4 per cent, but it would have a negligible effect upon land area. The increase in income over the decade would have reduced the density gradient by about 20 per cent. But the average central city and suburban incomes grew by about equal amounts, and changes in them have a roughly equal but opposite effect on central city population and urbanized area land.

There appears to be little evidence that urban decentralization has been a flight from blight. With one exception, none of the physical characteristics of the central city appeared to have any appreciable effect upon the distribution of an urbanized area's population. There is some evidence that a high proportion of either substandard dwellings or Negro population leads to a greater relative demand for housing in the outer part of a central city relative to its inner zones. But my comparisons give little reason to believe that these factors have had much impact upon the suburbanization of population or on the total land area used for urban purposes. Indeed, for the forty-six cities I studied, the proportion of substandard dwellings fell from 0.20 to 0.11 during the fifties, so a deterioration of the central city housing stock during the period could hardly have led to further decentralization in

[48] Richard F. Muth, "The Distribution of Population within Urban Areas" in Universities — National Bureau of Economic Research, *Determinants of Investment Behavior* (National Bureau of Economic Research, 1967). These results for the year 1950, plus additional ones for 1960, are included in Muth, "The Spatial Structure. . . ."

any case. It does appear to me, though, that where the income level of the central city is low relative to that of the whole urban area, there is a higher degree of suburbanization of population and more urban land than I would otherwise expect. This finding may reflect the municipal fiscal problem described earlier.

On the whole, it does not appear to me that urban decentralization has been carried too far. During the fifties, for the areas I studied, the increase in central city population averaged about 9 per cent and land area 81 per cent. In total, the effects discussed two paragraphs above imply increases of 9 per cent and 77 per cent respectively. For both 1950 and 1960, the fraction of the population living in the suburban parts of urban areas tended to be somewhat smaller and to respond much less to changes in urban area population and to factors affecting the central city density gradient than would be expected if population distribution in the suburbs were simply an extension of that in the central city. Finally, the preliminary findings of the only study I know of dealing with this matter show the returns from holding land subsequently put to residential or commercial use in the Philadelphia area to be about the same as the average for all common stocks.[49] There would not seem, then, to be any rationale for those governmental programs which seek to halt or reverse the decentralization of urban areas.

TOWARD A NEW FEDERAL HOUSING POLICY [1]

Irving Welfeld

For some time now, it has been generally accepted that the federal government has a duty to ensure adequate housing for all its citizens. Accordingly, Congress has enacted a long series of housing subsidized programs, based

[49] F. Gerard Adams, Grace Milgram, Edward W. Green, and Christine Mansfield, "The Time Path of Undeveloped Land Prices During Urbanization: A Micro-Empirical Study," Discussion Paper No. 24, Department of Economics, University of Pennsylvania (processed, July 1966).

Irving Welfeld is an attorney for the Office of General Counsel, Department of Housing and Urban Development.

Reprinted with permission from Irving Welfeld, "Toward a New Federal Housing Policy," *The Public Interest* 19 (Spring 1970), pp. 31–43. Copyright National Affairs, Inc., 1970.

[1] The point of view of this article does not necessarily represent the official view or policy of the Department of Housing and Urban Development.

on various forms of public-private partnership and using many sophisticated financial devices. Yet despite all these efforts extending over several decades, the results have been meager. The Douglas Commission put the matter this way:

> Over the years, accomplishments in subsidized housing are extremely inadequate. *The Nation in 30 years of public housing built fewer units than Congress, back in 1949, said were needed in the immediate next 6 years.* . . . One might suppose after years of talk and controversy . . . that by now the Nation would have managed to produce a sizable quantity of housing units for low-income families. The record is to the contrary.

Why have we done so badly? The fault lies with the basic approach we have taken. The key components of the present subsidy system — public housing, below market rate interest, rent supplement and the interest subsidy programs — all aim at solving the problem by providing new dwelling units for the poor. Because there is a shortage of standard units and many of the poor live in substandard units, the production of new units for the poor has the virtue of conceptual simplicity and goodness of intention. Unfortunately, the strategy does not work.

HIGH COST LOW RENT HOUSING

As a matter of elementary logic the strategy of providing new housing for our poorest citizens is an expensive way of approaching volume production. Let us assume that the total amount of government assistance and the cost per housing unit are constant. It follows that the number of units that can be subsidized varies inversely with the rental paid by the occupant of the average unit. And as the income of the potential occupant declines, the amount of the necessary per-unit subsidy increases — and the total number of units that can be subsidized declines. *Thus, by choosing to provide new housing for our poorest citizens, the federal government has adopted a most expensive strategy for increasing the nation's housing supply.*

What we mean by expensive can be seen by briefly examining the subsidy needed for public housing. The development of projects is financed through the sale by local housing authorities of bonds to private investors. The federal government guarantees the full cost of the principal and interest on the bonds. In recent years the actual payment has equalled 95 per cent of the debt service. The estimated total development cost of a unit of public housing in early 1969 was $17,250. Assuming a 40 year amortization and an interest rate of 5.55 per cent, the annual federal payment for each new unit of public housing comes out to $1,018.

Moreover, interest on these bonds is exempt from federal taxes. The resulting revenues loss to the federal government is estimated to be 40 per cent of the interest rate. For a $17,250 unit, this comes to another $283 per year.

These two amounts, which total over $1,300 annually, may be considered the minimum federal subsidy for a unit of public housing. But there are additional subsidies as well. A federal contribution of $120 per unit per year is available for housing units occupied by an elderly family, a large family, a family of unusually low income, or a family displaced by urban renewal or a low rent housing project. If the public housing development is located on an urban renewal site, there usually is a substantial write-down on land costs, a large fraction of which is paid for by the federal government.

Nor is the federal government the only source of subsidies. The exemption of the bonds from local income taxation results in a revenue loss at the local level. Moreover, the projects are exempt from local real estate taxation. It is true that the Local Housing Authority makes "payment in lieu of taxes," but such payment rarely exceeds 10 per cent of the shelter rents of the projects and is considerably smaller than expected tax revenues from new commercial, industrial, or residential development.

In light of these many subsidies, a conservative estimate of the total subsidy for a unit of public housing would be $1,500. This is a rather startling figure especially if compared to the market cost of decent housing in a suitable living environment. The most recent government statistics on standards of living tell us that a five-room unit in sound condition — with complete private bath, fully equipped kitchen, hot and cold running water, electricity, central or other installed heating, in a neighborhood free of hazards and nuisances, and with access to public transportation, schools, grocery stores, and play space for the children — could be obtained in metropolitan areas for approximately $1,400.

Assuming a rent-to-income ratio of 20 per cent, such a unit costs approximately $800 more than a family with an annual income of $3000 can afford. But the public housing subsidy is approximately double that amount! When that subsidy is added to the rent paid by such a family, the *total cost of the new public housing unit would be about $2,000, or approximately 150 per cent of the amount that a decent second-hand unit rents for on the open market.*

TRICKLE DOWN, TURN OVER

The question mentally poses itself: is the building of new housing the only viable means of achieving large-scale improvements for low income families now living in inadequate environments? What if assistance to the poor took the form of making available to them *existing* housing units? Would these existing units be old and obsolete by the time they became available to the poor? In other words, would reliance on some variant of the trickle-down approach be as unworkable as many now assume?

If one imagines the distribution of income in the United States as a pyramid, with a narrow group of high income households at the top which alone can afford newly constructed housing, then the answer to all these questions is "yes." But while this may once have been a realistic view, it no longer is. As the following statistics show, income distribution in present day America is more accurately represented in the shape of a diamond:

Income level	*Percentage of households*	
(In constant 1963 dollars)	*1929*	*1963*
Under 2,000	30	11
2,000 to 3,999	38	18
4,000 to 5,999	16	20
6,000 to 7,999	7	18
8,000 to 9,999	3	12
10,000 and up	6	21

Over the past two decades, this change in income distribution has significantly affected the housing of lower-income groups and has affected it for the better. In 1950, new housing needs for the nation as a whole were estimated at 20.5 million units, or 44 per cent of total housing supply; in 1960, this figure fell to 15.4 million units, or 26 per cent; and its projected 1970 level is 10.8 million units, or 16 per cent of the nation's housing supply. These gains held true even for housing in the central city and were primarily attributable to the output and productivity of private enterprise. The reason for this dramatic improvement is that, as a result of rising affluence, there has been a remarkable shift in the ratio of housing starts to household formation. During the 60 years preceding 1950, this ratio remained close to 1. But in the 1950's, the ratio stood at 1.5; and in the first 7 years of the 1960's, it rose to a level of 1.7.

In the wake of this increased volume of new construction, there ensued a redistribution of existing units that has vastly improved the housing of the poor. In a study of housing in New York City, Frank Kristof found that *construction of 64 new units gave rise to a "chain of turnover" that extended to a total of 90 additional units.* At the end of this process of turnover, all of the families involved enjoyed higher quality housing. It is true that their rent bills also rose as a result of this upward movement, but due to income increases, the new median rent remained equal to approximately one-fifth of family income. This process of turnover is not quite the same as "filtering" or "trickle down" — these concepts assume that the turnover that results from new construction will be accompanied by decreasing rents. But even without such cost reductions, *the turnover process does make sound housing available to income groups which cannot afford new construction*. It is this process that is largely responsible for the fact that, in 1960, a majority of families at the lowest income levels were living in standard housing.

Although there has been progress, it does not follow that such progress has been fast enough, or that further progress is inevitable, or that we can trust the market to eliminate slums entirely. But it would be equally erroneous to conclude that, because the turnover system does not work perfectly, we must completely disregard the system. To move from the fact of imperfection to the concept of original sin, one must rely not on logic but on theology.

POLITICAL UNPALATABILITY

The slow pace of present programs is explained not only by the economic inefficiency of the approach, but also by its political unpalatability. There is a basic inequity built into the "new housing for low income families" approach. A policy of taxing Peter to provide housing for Paul, who would otherwise live in squalor, has a simple appeal to human generosity. But a policy of taxing Peter to provide better housing than his own for Paul requires an almost saintly degree of altruism.

Congress in order to avoid the charge that the program will build "penthouses for the poor" has attempted to resolve the problem by limiting the amenities (both structural and environmental) of the new unit, thereby avoiding both the need for large subsidies and the possibility that those who don't have it will nevertheless be able to flaunt it. Accordingly, every housing subsidy program requires that the unit not be of "elaborate or extravagant design." In the rent supplement program, this dictum has been taken to mean that no unit may contain more than one bathroom — which, in turn, means that any new three-or-more bedroom apartment starts out as an undesirable unit. Air-conditioning was also forbidden, although in certain sections of the country any new unit without it is automatically substandard.

Other ways of limiting expenses have had equally unfortunate consequences. For instance, Congress has set various upper limits on permissible per-unit rents, construction costs, and mortgage amounts which have made it impossible to build new units in the major cities and suburbs of the north and west.

Attempts have also been made to channel the location of the housing so as to limit environmental amenity. A building, even of superior quality, to house the poor may not offend one's sense of equity if it is placed in an inferior neighborhood. If Peter has to pay for Paul's housing, he need not be forced to live next to Paul. The sentiment was translated into federal housing policy via the "workable program" requirement that had been imposed on most of the major housing programs and the need for cooperation from local governments to build and operate public housing. This has resulted in a local veto over sites. Suburban communities have often exercised the veto, if only to exclude modestly designed housing that does not bear an equal share of the property tax burden. As a result of this opposition, housing programs have been forced to build in the high-cost central city, where statutory cost limitations often make construction impossible. Even if housing can be built within those limits, it must often be located in a less than suitable neighborhood environment.

As a result of these pressures, public housing has been transformed in many major cities into a program for the elderly. Not only are the elderly likely to be better neighbors, thereby making site selection easier; but also the higher cost allowances and the additional federal subsidy make housing for the elderly economically and politically attractive. Thus, 62 per cent of the public housing units started in 1966, and 57 per cent of those started in 1967, were designed for the elderly. And there is reason to believe that these statistics understate the trend.

The present federal housing approach is impaled on the horns of interlocking political and economic dilemmas. New housing for the poor must be of sufficient quality to serve a market for at least the life of the mortgage (usually 40 years). It must, therefore, if it is not to be functionally obsolete many years prior to its attaining physical obsolescence, include certain facilities which were yesterday's and (possibly today's) luxuries. The dangers of false economy go beyond the structure itself. If the model tenements of the 19th and early 20th centuries are the building blocks of today's slums, the overly modest projects of today may be the cornerstones of the slums of tomorrow. Yet plain political reality makes it improvident to ignore the taxpayer argument that the necessity to provide decent housing for all is no reason to provide better housing than the unit in which he, the taxpayer, lives.

In spite of good intentions, the direct approach of providing new housing for the poor does not create a suitable framework in which to resolve these conflicting claims. To date, relatively little housing has been constructed; so little, in fact, that public action has destroyed more units of housing than all federally aided programs have managed to build. And, in spite of the distortions caused by directing programs toward the poor, federal housing policy ends by giving virtually no assistance to the very poorest. Like the original food stamp program, the operation of federal housing programs gives a lot to those who have a little, but nothing to those who have very little. For under all these programs, a tenant must contribute a certain portion of the shelter cost. In rent supplements, the portion must be 30 per cent of the approved rent; in public housing, the sum of the occupants' contributions must cover the operating expenses of the project.

A typical family in Detroit would need an income of $5,805 in order to enable a newly built public housing project to operate on a solvent basis on the assumption that the family would pay only 20 per cent of their income. During recent years many housing authorities have ignored these economic parameters. As a result almost every major public housing authority is presently facing a fiscal crisis. Attempts to raise rents have pushed tenant rent ratios in many cases far in excess of 25 per cent and have brought a wave of rent strikes. Congress reacting to this crisis in 1969 raised the public housing subsidy. For new projects it will be in the range of $2,000 per unit per year; thereby further restricting the expected volume, and moving the program from the category of expensive to that of absurd.

The obvious question at this juncture is why has federal housing policy continued to receive support in Congress. Part of the answer is to be found in a law of political physics — that a program in being tends to stay in being. But there is an additional explanation that has to do with the peculiar dynamics of liberal and conservative opinion in Congress. Faced with the need to do *something* about poor housing, liberals seem willing to accept a policy that produces only tiny numbers of housing units in the hope that, some day, the American people will rise up *en masse* and remove the constraints that vitiate that policy. Meantime, these liberals are content to wage a slow and ineffective struggle that aims at the merest marginal improvements. The conservatives also acknowledge the need for more housing but are deeply uneasy about the political principles implicit in the subsidy program. Yet as long as only a token number of units are built — usually in someone else's district — they are willing to go along with existing policy.

Federal housing policy is thus a classic instance of the art of muddling through. Neither conservatives nor liberals are satisfied with the results of that policy, but both groups continue to accept it because there are seemingly no alternatives. Given that failure to perceive alternatives, the most remarkable thing about federal housing programs is not that they are hampered by limitations, but rather that they exist at all.

SOME POPULAR ALTERNATIVES

INCOME DISTRIBUTION

If poverty is the primary cause of the housing problem, then the answer would seem to be to provide the poor with income. There are many variations to this redistributive strategy, such as increased welfare allowances, the negative income tax, or a guaranteed annual wage. What these approaches have in common — and what is perhaps their most attractive feature, given the present ineffectual state of federal housing policy — is that they promise to get the government out of the housing business.

Unfortunately, there is only the slightest chance that any of these programs would succeed in improving the housing of the poor. For even if a relatively generous redistributive program were enacted, the problem of "housing poverty" would almost certainly remain. Anthony Downs has explained the reason for such "housing poverty" as follows:

> The income which any household must attain to rent or buy adequate-quality housing without spending too high a proportion of its total income on housing is significantly higher than the "official poverty level" as defined by the Social Security Administration. This level is calculated by determining what the minimal adequate diet for a given sized household costs, and then multiplying by three. In 1967, this food-based approach resulted in a "poverty level" of $3,335 for a four-person household. An alternative method of defining poverty using housing as the base would be calculating the cost of renting adequate housing for a given-sized household, and then multiplying by four. Using this approach, and assuming that an "adequate" house was a newly built apartment unit constructed to meet federally-defined quality standards, the "housing poverty level" income for a four-person household in 1967 was $8,640. *But over 60 per cent of all U.S. households had income below this level in 1967. Thus it appears that a majority of Americans were "housing poor" in relation to new units.* [Italics added.]

In short, new housing is just too expensive for even a fairly drastic redistribution of income to help the very poor unless one wishes to favor them over those with average incomes, which is politically impossible.

USED HOUSING SUBSIDIES

If housing subsidies are needed, then perhaps they should be limited to *existing* units. Certainly this is a logical extension of the previous analysis. One virtue of this strategy is that the required federal payment per unit would be smaller. The cost of the previously used second hand three bedroom unit on the private market was approximately $1,400 per year. Even assuming no contribution by the tenant, this is $100 less than the minimum subsidy for an average unit of new public housing. Given the same total amount of subsidy, the smaller unit subsidies would increase the number of families which could benefit from a housing subsidy program.

Such an approach is also attractive on political grounds. The provision of standard used housing is a response that seems more nearly commensurate with the problem. Given the fact that the commandment only requires that we love our neighbors as ourselves, but not more so, it is far more likely that American voters, 98 per cent of whom are living in existing units, will find such a program a more palatable way of moving towards the Golden Rule.

There are two basic ways to provide a subsidy which bridges the gap between the rent the poor can afford and the rent the market demands for existing units. The government could subsidize a particular dwelling unit, thereby reducing the required rent, or it could subsidize a particular individual, thereby increasing the amount he has available for housing. In the former approach, the occupant loses the subsidy if he moves; in the latter approach, the subsidy moves with the occupant. Both these approaches are now used on a small scale.

MISSING INGREDIENT

In the past few years the latter housing allowance approach has acquired a considerable popularity among liberals. The Kaiser Committee, for example, recently praised such proposals on the grounds that they provide an efficient means for adjusting the supply of housing to the desires of consumers, that they will increase demand for standard units, and that they permit the consumer more freedom to choose a location and housing style that he likes. The irony in all this is that, just 20 years ago, a man like Charles Abrams could write of housing allowances:

> Subsidies paid directly to the tenant are advocated by real estate groups. Among the many objections to this plan, one is that it would make the tenant a permanent recipient of public charity. There is a vast spiritual difference between paying the required rent on a government-owned building and being on a permanent dole.

There was more to Abrams' criticism than a simple distaste for the real estate lobby. For his criticism was informed by the sad experience with housing allowances during the 1930's:

> During the depression in the 1930's New York City's emergency relief bureau spent $30,000,000 annually for rent — a sum, which, if paid annually, would have been sufficient to subsidize modern, low-rent housing for more than half of the City's slum dwellers. Yet not a single family got a decent home. If standards were raised adequately, the landlords would not have complied and the tenants would not have gotten homes. The dumb-bell flats that were 30 per cent empty simply filled up with the undoubling of families encouraged by rent relief and slum values zoomed. The plan would produce no new housing for slum dwellers and would extend the life of old ones.

The fact is that, even if programs restrict use of the subsidy to standard units, a used housing subsidy is of value only in areas in which there are vacancies in standard units — but that is not the typical situation we face today.

Thus even the housing allowance program shares many of the weaknesses of the project subsidy system and has some of its own as well. Unless one envisions that rental allowances will be raised to the level of public housing subsidies, or that the subsidy will be extended to those who are not poor, the expectation of upgrading slum properties or stimulating new construction through the housing allowance program is nothing more than a pipe dream. Indeed, as even the Kaiser Committee conceded, the most likely result of such a program would be, not the production of new housing, but the raising of rents on existing units. As long as it is directed exclusively at the low income segment of the housing market, a housing allowance program is no more effective an alternative to the current system of federal policy than Tweedledum was to Tweedledee.

A CONSTRUCTIVE ALTERNATIVE

It is clear that there are direct linkages between the production of new housing and the improvement of the lot of those who are housing poor. But if we are to achieve our national housing goal, *the question of housing production must be divorced from the question of housing assistance to low income families*. It *seems* reasonable to join these objectives because many of the poor are ill-housed. But the history of federal housing policy demonstrates that the result of this connection is more like a short circuit than a short cut.

There *is* an alternative. If we must simultaneously achieve large volume production and provide the poor with decent housing, there is no reason why we have to follow a single path to achieve these two objectives. And my suggestion is that the federal government should actually begin to follow a double path. It should pursue the objective of increasing housing supply *by subsidizing middle income households;* and it should alleviate the housing problem of the poor *by subsidizing low income families*. The effect, hopefully, would be to increase housing turnover and thereby free a sizeable portion of the existing housing stock for (subsidized) poor families.

Such a strategy would do away with the need for building further public housing projects; it will not, however, negate the need for providing housing assistance to low income families in order that they may afford to move into vacated housing. For this purpose either a variant of an existing used housing program or a new housing allowance program seems to be a perfectly adequate device.

What is required, above all, then, is a new program that will stimulate the construction of new housing for those who are not poor, and especially for those in the middle ranges of the income spectrum.

OUTLINE OF PROPOSAL[2]

1. Eligible tenants
   a. No income limits.
   b. Tenants receiving subsidy must pay at least 18 per cent of their income for shelter costs.
   c. Tenants chosen by random selection.
2. Amount of subsidy
   a. Difference between the greater — 18 per cent of income or 8 per cent of net assets and shelter costs.
   b. Not to exceed $800 except during periods of high interest rates.
3. Eligible project
   a. New or rehabilitated housing financed by a mortgage loan insured under a new section of the National Housing Act.
   b. Housing must be of high enough quality so as to be marketable and a sound investment for the life of the mortgage.
4. Location of unit
   a. Must be in a housing market in which there is a shortage of decent housing.
5. Eligible mortgagor
   a. Any private investor willing to limit his return to 8 per cent of his equity.
   b. Amortization period — 40 years.
   c. Interest rate — variable.
   d. Maximum amount — not to exceed 90 per cent of the lesser of (1) the cost of construction or (2) the debt service limitation (assuming that gross rent is calculated by assuming that units will be occupied by households that have incomes at the median for the community and that mortgagor receives the maximum annual subsidy per unit.

RENT RATIOS

The purpose of the program is to produce a large volume of housing units within the middle range of the market. In order to accomplish this, tenants that are adequately housed must be provided (in Louis Winnick's phrase) with "orchestra seats at balcony prices." The assumption is that, given a bargain, such tenants will seek better housing. Unlike the present housing programs, which have a captive audience, the new program cannot exact as the price of admission a high rent-to-income ratio. Nor is there any need to

[2] A more detailed explanation of the proposal is contained in my article "A New Framework For Federal Housing Aids" in the December 1969 issue of the *Columbia Law Review*.

use the rent-to-income ratio as a test of deservingness or as a guarantee that money saved on housing will not be spent for frivolous purposes.

Setting the rent-to-income ratio involves a trade-off between two competing values. The smaller the ratio, the greater the payment and the greater the incentive — but also the smaller the number of units that can receive a subsidy. Although 18 per cent is to some extent an arbitrary figure, it is low enough that it will not cause undue hardship, yet high enough to assure that the recipients are at least interested in theater.

INCOME LIMITS

The need for a subsidy will be determined by the relationship between the occupant's income and shelter costs in the local area. Unlike some present housing subsidy programs, in which the amount of the subsidy is not calibrated to the income of the occupant, the subsidy payments under the new program will be keyed to individual housing needs and would cease when they become unnecessary. This would occur when the tenant's income is equal to 5.55 times his rent. He would, however, continue to have the right to occupy the unit even if his income should become quite high.

A low income household will in effect be barred from the project because the subsidy is insufficient to enable him to afford the unit.

LOTTERY SELECTION

Just as in the selective service system there is no "just" way of choosing those who must serve, so too in the selective subsidy system there is no perfectly just way to select the beneficiary. A lottery, however, is at least a fair method of selection.

This lottery can be on a project-by-project basis. If a family wishes to live at a particular location, it registers with the developer or with the local FHA insuring office. When the project nears completion, a drawing is held and the winners are given the right to occupy by paying 18 per cent of their income. If a person wins but desires a unit which is not available, he is placed on a waiting list. If a person wins but cannot afford the unit, he is placed at the top of a list for a housing allowance or for an existing subsidized unit. If a person loses, he can try again at another project or when vacancies occur.

The draft lottery has been criticized on the ground that it is not a "reform but a random distribution of inequity." There are a number of important distinctions between the draft lottery and this proposed housing lottery. While the former imposes a "penalty," the latter selects the recipient of a gift. Nor is the subsidee the only winner. As a result of the turnover process, the entire community is indirectly the beneficiary. A lottery also provides useful marketing information. The number of registrants for a given lottery and their addresses assists in measuring the depth of the market at different locations and gives early warning of changes in older areas. But perhaps the greatest advantage of a lottery is that it provides a random distribution of minority families within new developments and within middle income neighborhoods.

THE SUBSIDY

The subsidy would be a payment equal to the difference between 18 per cent of the tenant's income and the approved FHA rental for the unit up to a maximum subsidy of $800 per unit per year. Because we are dealing with an economically mobile group, the average subsidy will be considerably less than the maximum. Assuming an average annual payment of $500 per unit, $500 million per year would support a million units a year. *This is a far greater amount of housing-per-dollar than is achieved under any existing program.*

QUALITY AND QUANTITY

The aim of the program is the production of additional units, therefore the primary emphasis will be on new construction. The housing must be attractive to families that have a moderate amount of choice. Therefore, the unit must be of a fairly high quality.

By not aiming at the low end of the income spectrum the new program will be able to achieve the twin objectives of quality and quantity. There are unlikely to be any objections to building these developments in outlying areas, since they will bear their "fair share" of the property tax burden and be as attractive as any other new developments both in physical appearance and in the class of the tenant. The new program, therefore, will avoid the locational limitations of present programs. This too will produce economic dividends because it is cheaper to build low-rise garden apartments on moderately priced land than high-rise elevator apartments on high-priced land. The only limitation on location will be that the units must be built in areas in which there is a housing shortage. If standard vacancies in an area rise above an acceptable minimum, new commitments will be halted.

As a matter of economic good sense the project will be designed to reach as broad a market of income eligibles as possible. This, of course, will usually involve something of a trade-off between high quality and quantity. However, the prospect of a more rapid availability of units to lower income families will, at least during the early years of the program, put priority on the latter goal. Therefore, the mortgage will be limited by a debt service limitation which assumes the units will be occupied by families with incomes at the median for the locality. In most instances this will accord with the best interest of the developer. Building a more expensive project will very likely constrict his market because all potential occupants with incomes below the median will have to pay in excess of 18 per cent of their incomes (the amount of the subsidy being fixed).

VICIOUS CYCLE, VIRTUOUS CIRCLE

By attempting too much, each of our present housing programs produces too little. By attempting in one fell swoop to produce large numbers of new housing units for the poor, each program has managed to antagonize a substantial part of the population. In order to redress their grievances, Congress has imposed restrictions that cripple the program's capacity either to produce very many units or to help very many of the poor. This in turn dashes the expectations of the poor and raises the need for new legislation, which starts the vicious cycle in motion again.

The alternative approach set forth here dissolves the bond between the production problem and the poverty problem. The new framework separates subsidies to facilitate new housing production from subsidies to alleviate the housing problems of the poor. Through these means it is possible to create a harmony of political interests and an economically efficient system. It might even be deemed a virtuous circle. Serving the needs of middle income families has obvious appeal in a predominantly middle class society. It also provides substantial benefits to poor families by allowing existing standard units to "flow down" to lower income families. This in turn makes the more politically acceptable forms of assistance to the poor economically viable, thereby resulting in the achievement of both goals — the elimination of poor housing and of housing poverty.

THE MIRAGE OF NEW TOWNS

William Alonso

Calling for "new towns" has long been a favorite activity of architects and architectural critics, but in recent years just about everyone seems to have taken up the cry. The list of such advocates now includes giant corporations,

William Alonso is Professor of Regional Planning, University of California, Berkeley.

Reprinted with permission from William Alonso, "The Mirage of New Towns," *The Public Interest* 19 (Spring 1970), pp. 3–17. Copyright National Affairs, Inc., 1970.

real estate developers, the American Institute of Planners, the mass media, the former President, the Urban Affairs Council of the current President, several state legislatures, various cabinet members, congressmen, senators, governors, the National Association of Counties, the National League of Cities, the United States Conference of Mayors, and Urban America.

The reasons for this surge of interest in new towns are elusive. Some of the advocacy is probably self-serving, as in the cases of congressmen or federal bureaucrats seeking to maintain diminishing constituencies, self-aggrandizing professional groups, and of business firms in pursuit of new markets. For many, glimmering images of simpler, future Camelots combine the American nostalgia for the small town with a desire to escape from the biting reality of our complex urban problems. But mostly the idea of new towns has some magic that fires the imagination, stirring some Promethean impulse to create a better place and way of life, a calm and healthy community of crystalline completeness.

These romantic associations make it difficult to analyze the new towns strategy as a rational policy. When a cabinet member speaks of "avoiding chaos," "organic balance," "creative possibilities," "building poems," "communities of tomorrow," and the like, he has adopted the vague rhetoric of architectural and utopian writers. This rhetoric abounds in code words. For instance, one of the most frequently stated reasons for new towns is that they will be *planned* (a term in urban matters that is acceptable to both the political right and left). But in itself, the fact that something is to be planned is of interest only to the professionals who get the work and to later chroniclers. To most people, such planning is merely an input, and the important question is one of output: what does such planning do to what the new town will do? Some other code words are *balanced, exciting, variety, living environment, choice, human scale.* To make sense of the new towns concept,[1] it is necessary to translate its advocates' rhetoric into clear language, and this in turn requires one to distinguish between purely instrumental objectives and their intended ultimate purposes.

---

[1] A comment on nomenclature may be helpful. Some have tried to draw a distinction between *new town* and *new community*, but today the terms are used almost interchangeably. *New community* has a slightly wider meaning and is often applied to subdivisions which would not be called *new towns* by anyone. On the other hand, some rebuilding within existing cities is being called "new towns in town." I shall reserve the terms *new towns* and *new community* to developments that are built at some distance from existing urban areas.

New towns may be either *independent* if they provide for the employment of their residents, or *satellite* if there is to be substantial commuting to existing centers. Most of the well-known new towns in this decade (Reston and Columbia) and of the recent past (Radburn or Forest Hills) have been satellites; but, historically, independent new towns have been quite numerous. In a sense, of course, almost every American city was an independent new town at the time of its founding. But the 19th century saw the intentional creation of a great many company towns (Lawrence, Lowell, Pull-

The discussion that follows will focus on proposed policies of directing to new towns only a substantial portion of our future urban growth rather than all. There are two reasons for this. The first is that, with the exceptions of some journalists, nobody seriously proposes to channel *all* further growth to new towns. Second, it is inconceivable that such a policy would work. The British experience is instructive here. As of December 1967, after 20 years of sustained effort, the population of new towns had grown by only 554,373, or only 1 per cent of the national population. During 1967, the population of the new towns grew by 34,577, which is less than 10 per cent of the yearly British population growth.

What are new towns for? I have discovered about two dozen principal objectives, some with several variants, and in the pages that follow, I will examine critically the main purposes new towns advocates have in mind. But let me here summarize briefly my principal conclusions. First, there is little force to the arguments of those who urge a major national commitment of effort and resources to a program for directing a substantial portion of our urbanization into new towns. On the other hand, there may be some sense in the limited use of new towns for the testing and development of technological, physical, and institutional innovations which might be applicable to the expansion and rebuilding of existing cities.

"WHERE SHALL THEY LIVE?"

It is common to argue that present urban areas cannot cope with the expected growth of urban population. A recent statement of this type was made by the National Committee on Urban Growth Policy. It predicted that from now until the year 2000 United States urban population will grow by 100 million, and recommended that to help accommodate this growth, we build 100 new towns of at least 100,000 population, and 10

---

man), utopian and religious new settlements, and towns developed by the railroads as they spanned the continent. Present day independent new towns are most frequently resort or retirement towns, although there are occasional instances of cities created to provide housing for workers in large isolated projects (Boulder City and the atomic energy towns of Oak Ridge and Los Alamos are examples). My discussion will include both types.

Finally, there are major differences between the new town and the concept of growth center. First, new town proposals are for newly built settlements, while growth centers are usually existing settlements which are to be expanded to the point of self-sustaining growth. Second, new town proposals often stress self-containment as a labor market, while growth center proposals often stress the role of providing jobs for those living in the surrounding region. Third and most important, new towns proposals are based on the idea of steering growth away from urban areas which are regarded as too big, while growth centers are viewed as steering growth toward under-employed populations or some unexploited resources. Although the two ideas somewhat complement each other, I shall concern myself with only new towns.

new cities of at least 1 million population. The very roundness of these figures suggests their tentativeness and leads one to wonder how the proposals might have differed if men had six fingers on each hand. Nonetheless, even accepting these targets, *the year 2000 would see only 7 per cent of the 300 million population residing in these new settlements,* with 80 per cent of the foreseen growth taking place in existing areas. If the hoped-for replacement of one-third of the existing dwellings is achieved, *almost 90 per cent of new housing would be produced in existing urban areas.* Thus, as radical as the National Committee's proposal seems, it would affect only a small part of our population and an even smaller part of our housing production. A program that marginal in its effect cannot stand very high on the list of national priorities.

Further, given the uncertain state of our knowledge, we cannot say that existing urban centers can absorb 80 million persons but cannot absorb 100 million. *If each of our smallest 200 metropolitan areas took in a half million persons, we could hold the 100 million without any of these areas exceeding 2½ million.* The National Committee's argument is further weakened when we examine the growth assumption: our national rate of population growth has declined steadily for the past 15 years and now stands at 1 per cent. At this rate, by the year 2000 the increase will be only 75 million — or 5 million less than the growth that the Commission allocates *existing* areas.

THE ARGUMENT FROM EFFICIENCY

Less crude than the lack-of-room arguments are those holding that further growth of large urban areas is inefficient. In brief, such arguments state that urban costs per capita rise with increasing urban size, or that marginal costs increase with population. According to this line of reasoning, urban areas grow beyond their "least cost" point because arriving people or firms are not discriminated against but are rather placed on the same footing as everyone else. They pay *average costs* (in taxes, etc.) and these are lower than the *marginal* costs that their arrival imposes. A considerable literature addresses itself to the shape of this cost curve and the location of its bottom, but the question has not been settled of whether costs rise disproportionately to population for a given level of services.

Whether they do or not, when the city is compared to a firm, and the concept of "efficiency" is introduced, an analysis based only on costs is incomplete. The objective of any unit of population is to make money, not to save it. In the case of a city, the point of minimum costs is relevant only if we assume constant product per inhabitant. It appears, however, that product and income per inhabitant rise with increasing population faster than costs, even taking into account differences in cost of living. *Efficiency arguments for diverting growth away from existing urban areas depend upon the assumption that new towns will enjoy a greater difference between marginal product and marginal cost, than is to be found in our cities. In fact, the opposite seems to be the case if we judge by existing cities that are comparable in size to proposed new towns.*

MIGRATORY WAY-STATIONS

It is often suggested that the new towns would intercept migrants from the rural areas on their way to large cities and would thereby give our large metropolitan areas time to absorb their earlier migrants. This image of a flood of rural immigrants, however, is quite out of date. Migration of farm population to metropolitan areas has dropped to an insignificant trickle, largely because there are so few farmers left; and migration of any sort plays a decreasing part in overall metropolitan growth. Of the 10.9 per cent growth of metropolitan areas during the 1960–66 period, only 22.6 per cent came from immigration as compared to 35 per cent during the 1950–60 period. Moreover, most of the domestic migration came from smaller urban places rather than from farms. Beyond this, the picture is confused. For example, compare the yearly rate of 492,000 migration into metropolitan areas with the rate of 138,000 migration out of nonmetropolitan areas and the rate of 377,000 civilian immigration *into this country* during the 1960–66 period. These figures suggest that nearly *three-fourths of the migratory increase into metropolitan areas is international in origin, and that only 6 per cent of metropolitan growth comes from domestic migratory flows.*

Many metropolitan areas, in fact, are losing population through out-migration. The fastest growing metropolitan areas, and the strongest magnets to migrants in proportion to their size, are those between 200,000 and 2 million, while those over 2 million were attracting only 0.2 migrants per hundred population per year, and those under 200,000 had net out-migration. Nine areas accounted for 81 per cent of all net in-migration, leaving an average of fewer than 500 migrants per year entering each of the others. To put it another way, *28 metropolitan areas in the south, southwest, mountain states, and Pacific coast accounted for 99 per cent of the net in-migration.* Please note: neither New York, nor Philadelphia, nor Chicago is among these twenty-eight.

Black migration to metropolitan areas during the 1960–66 period averaged 145,000 yearly — about 30 per cent of all net migration — down from a 172,000 yearly rate from 1950–60. From 1960–66, such migration accounted for some 34 per cent of the growth of black metropolitan population — *but only 31 per cent of these black migrants were from farms.* The black population is already far more urbanized than the white, and the shifting proportions of blacks among urban areas of diverse sizes indicates that, on the whole, they are moving not from farm to city but upward along the urban-size hierarchy.

Is this flow of migrants so large that we should reorganize our urban system to gain a breathing spell? It would appear not. If we exclude the 28 metropolitan areas in the developing and urbanizing crescent from the south to the Pacific states — and in these areas there is far less talk of an "urban crisis" than elsewhere — the other metropolises are trading either already urban migrants with each other or are swapping earlier migrants for new immigrants. New black migration from the farms is relatively small and declining, and the other black migration is primarily from small urban places to larger, urbanized areas.

Second, if new towns were developed, would they attract these migrants? Again, it would appear not. New towns or even new cities would of necessity be small, at least in the beginning, and the pattern of migration, especially for blacks, is away from smaller urban places toward bigger ones. Of course it might be that new towns of extraordinary amenity, offering strong inducements, and having a credible guarantee of future size might succeed in attracting people but there is no assurance that these arrivals would be the same migrants that were supposed to be intercepted. Further it may be that the cost of the inducements to effect such a geographic shift might be better used directly for the welfare and acculturation of the intended populations.

Third, if the new towns can attract population, would they do so in time? From the present state of vague discussions and the experience of such programs as urban renewal, one may estimate that ten years from now there may be some small beginnings on the ground, and that it would be another decade before the new towns would involve enough people to affect significantly the migration flows to metropolitan areas. Of course, a determined federal government could act much faster, breaking ground within a year and promoting fast growth by hothouse techniques. But this would make extremely unlikely those elements of amenity, detailed programming, technical and institutional innovation, private-public cooperation, and so forth, that are integral to most new town proposals. The dilemma is that quickly developed towns would be new but not innovative, and would be a poor magnet for migrants if we are to judge by existing cities of comparable size. On the other hand, innovative new towns would have a long gestation.

A variant of the objective of intercepting migrants for the relief of urbanized areas is the notion that industrial new towns, if established in rural or other areas of declining employment in primary production, could provide enough good jobs to ensure people a permanent alternative to out-migration.

This idea was advanced by the Department of Agriculture during the Johnson years under the label "urban-rural balance." The proposals included new towns, "growth centers" based on existing communities, and "new communities" that would encompass several counties in ways which were not clear. Although these proposals were not very specific, they apparently called for new towns that would be quite small, just large enough to absorb the district's surplus population.

It is true that standardized process manufacturing has been leaving the larger metropolitan areas and moving to smaller metropolitan areas, but it is doubtful that enough plants would locate in rural surroundings or in small towns for such a policy to be effective. Also, because the size of a plant typically increases with decreasing urban size, this suggested pattern would lead to a very large number of one company new towns under absentee ownership. Do we want this?

More important, it appears that the rate of out-migration does not vary with local hardship. Migrants leave at a steady rate regardless of local conditions, although such local conditions do affect the rate of *in*-migration. These facts have important policy implications. They suggest that population maintenance and jobs-to-people programs, if successful, may bring new people to depressed areas (which usually have a labor surplus) rather than retain the original residents who are leaving. It is well known that those who leave these areas are younger and better educated than those who stay behind, so that their departure weakens the local economy out of proportion to their number. Unfortunately, it appears that migrants entering depressed areas are more like the stayers than the movers (older, less educated, and less skilled), so that the newcomers do not replace the qualities lost through out-migration.

PRESERVING THE COUNTRYSIDE

It is sometimes suggested that new towns are needed to preserve agricultural land. This argument originated in Britain. But in this country, where historically *we have been abandoning agricultural land,* the argument lacks force. To accommodate 100 million people at suburban densities (with homes, factories, and so forth) would take about 14 million acres. This makes up less than 1 per cent of the United States mainland territory, less than 2 per cent of the present area in forests, and less than 5 per cent of the area now in crops. It is also only about one-half *the decrease* in planted crop acreage that occurred during the 1959–64 period. The territory to be occupied by urban growth, in short, is relatively small.

Beyond this one must question whether new towns would take up less space. It is hard to believe that they would. Densities are likely to be low, as the American preference for large lots meets low land prices, and most descriptions of new towns stress the land-consuming amenities that will be found there (such as parks, playing fields and artificial lakes). Some designers advocate very high density towns but it is doubtful that these would prove attractive. Some point out that growth at the margin of existing urban areas overruns some of the most valuable and productive agricultural land; but the value and productivity of this land derives not from its intrinsic fertility but from the more intensive use of capital, labor, and other inputs on land valued for its adjacency to urban markets. Growth of existing areas would merely slide these rings outward.

Another conservation-of-land argument is based on the sprawl of marginal urban growth. Sprawl is an ill-defined word, referring to a condition characterized by very large lots, or by a ribbon development along major highways, or by the leap-frogging of clustered development that results from speculation. Thus, by thin development or by leaving gaps, sprawl covers more land than continuous compact development. I am unaware of studies showing the extent to which bypassed land is withdrawn from agricultural production; the one study I know of that attempts an economic analysis of how sprawl functions concludes that it may be an effective way of withholding land from premature development at low densities.[2] This depends, of course, on whether growth eventually backtracks to fill in the gaps at higher densities when demand has ripened. My impression is that this does occur. But even if sprawl is dysfunctional it would seem that the effects of redirecting a fraction of urban growth to new towns would be correspondingly small.

A frequent argument for new towns is that sprawl is expensive because of additional utility and street costs. Although the proposition is plausible, studies show these costs to be quite insensitive to alternative forms of development. Even if these costs did vary, they are so small that their marginal changes with urban form would not justify much of anything. For instance, the 1966 per capita expenditures of local governments were $31 for utilities (including debt maintenance and transit) and $22 for streets.

SOME ECONOMIC ARGUMENTS

It is often suggested that new towns will stimulate the economy, presumably by their contribution to demand. Such an argument is often advanced by the same people who promise that new towns will be cheaper to develop and to run than the corresponding extension of existing urban areas. Such incon-

[2] R. O. Harvey and W. A. V. Clark, "The Nature and Economics of Urban Sprawl," *Land Economics* (February, 1965). See also, J. Lessinger, "The Case for Scatteration," *Journal of the American Institute of Planners* (August, 1962).

sistency aside, if new towns are to be used to stimulate the economy during recessions, their rate of development must conversely be slowed when the economy is working at full capacity. But new towns could not very well be used as a balance wheel for the cyclical control of the economy. Their lead times for decisions and action are far too long, and the success of various aspects of their development depends upon keeping to a time schedule. The heavy front-end investment reassured by new towns presents critical cash flow problems for the private developer, and a slowdown would be disastrous for him. From the public point of view, a slowdown would be extremely costly in terms of the opportunity costs of idle capital.

Most new town proposals stress that they will be as self-contained as possible, providing housing, jobs, schools, and shops for their residents, even if the proposals are for new towns on the edge of existing cities or in central city redevelopment projects. The purpose of this closure, often called "balance," is not altogether clear. It seems to stem in part from a desire to produce a sense of community that combats alienation — this will be discussed later — and in part from the intention of reducing commuting costs and congestion by reducing the distances involved. Two questions may be raised in this respect: (1) Does this make economic sense? and (2) Would it work?

As mentioned earlier, the cost-minimizing strategy makes sense only if productivity is fixed; in fact, income and most other measures of material welfare rise strongly with urban size. This is not the place to present a lengthy discussion of the reasons for this rise. They have to do with adaptability and innovative power and, in general, with the advantages of high *connectivity* for actual and potential interaction within a large system. In these terms, seeking closure at a small scale may economize on certain inputs (such as those of commuting) but result in lower per capita production (and lower disposable income after accounting for commuting costs) as well as the risks of instability and low adaptability which affect small cities. In small cities, a declining firm can be a local disaster, new firms are less likely to develop because of the sparseness of *linkages,* a dismissed worker has fewer chances for reemployment, a boy has fewer career opportunities, a woman fewer choices for shopping, and so on. In short, trying to save on transport costs may be penny wise and pound foolish.

But could such self-contained new towns be achieved? It seems to be quite hard. Several much admired European new towns, such as Tapiola, have about as many jobs as they have workers; but, in fact, residents work outside and outsiders commute to work inside. The British experience demonstrates how difficult it is to ensure labor market closure. British authorities have had extraordinary power since, in the face of a crushing housing shortage, they made the award of housing in new towns conditional on local employment and vice versa. The British new towns still show about the same number of jobs as workers but, after some years, 7.3 workers enter and leave the town in their daily trip to work for every 10 who live and work in the same new town.

People seem generally unwilling to constrain themselves to a localized and therefore small range of choices; and when feasible, they avail themselves of outside opportunities. It is extremely doubtful that new towns that are near metropolitan or other urban areas could maintain self-contained labor markets, with their residents making only occasional trips to the larger cities for specific services and facilities. Yet, if the new towns are not independent or self-contained, the space that intervenes between them and other opportunities can only lengthen travel and make it more costly. Thus a new town pattern of development might have an effect opposite from that intended, lengthening travel — except for those new towns in remote areas which are free from temptation. Yet virtually all our national territory, with the exception of some of our great deserts, is within commuting range of some existing urban center.

HEALTH, JUSTICE, OPPORTUNITY

One of the most persistently advanced purposes of the new towns might be classified under mental health. According to this view, big cities impose role-segmented contacts on people and keep them from knowing each other as whole persons. Due to the scale and impersonality of the city, people cannot understand the forces that affect their destinies and consequently experience alienation and *anomie*. New towns, by contrast, will be smaller and simpler; they will provide a single locus for home, school, job, shops, recreation, and civic activities; and thus they will afford deep and enduring relationships as well as a comprehensible environment in which the individual may participate and which he may, to a degree, control.

Millions of words by thousands of writers dispute this dismal picture of life in the big city and the correlative idealization of the small town. Jane Jacobs' picture of ethnic life in the big city makes even the most glowing description of new towns reminiscent of the atmosphere among strangers in an English train compartment. Studies by Gans, Young and Willmott, Fried, White, and others differ considerably from the traditional equation of the big city with alienation. On the other side, a far less flattering picture of life in the small city is drawn by Sinclair Lewis, Thomas Wolfe, John O'Hara, Warner, Kornhauser, the Lynds, and others. In sum, the traditional dichotomy between the alienating metropolis and the cohesive small city is a gross oversimplification, and it would appear that people can lead alienated or full lives in either place.

New towns present a particular difficulty to those who stress the importance of participation in their planning. The great problem with such participation is that several years of planning and development must take place before a new town has any residents. Except in rare cases where a specific group of families is to be transplanted to a new town, there appears to be no feasible mode of participation that would amount to more than a consumer survey. In this respect, new towns are rather like space ships. There must be a detailed plan for the vehicle and its course before the launching; and once under way, travelers can make only small choices of their own. This accounts for some of the tensions that commonly occur between residents and developers in some of the new towns now under way. The developers struggle to keep control of the nature and timing of the development according to their physical and financial plans, while the residents struggle to achieve the measure of local autonomy which is normal for a city or town.

Some writers associate physical and mental health directly with physical density of population rather than with life style. This argument is based on concepts of territoriality and personal space and derives from studies of the unfortunate effects of high density on rats, fish, lemmings, and large ungulates. But there has been no finding of comparable effects in the case of human beings. Further, this concern about the noxious effects of high densities is inconsistent with the concern about low densities created by sprawl.

It is sometimes suggested that new towns will be healthier in other ways. Walking or bicycling to work is salutary, the more so since there would be less automobile exhaust in the air. (One enthusiastic author includes the reduction of cancer among his new towns objectives.) Further, the small scale of new towns and their relative isolation would ease the dispersion of pollution and wastes. However, a new town policy would affect pollution levels for the vast majority only by the marginal amount accounted for by the population diverted from metropolitan areas, where any solution would continue to require some form of control over pollution sources. It is far simpler to take pollution from the people than to take the people away from pollution.

"Social balance" is a traditional objective of new town theorists, who argue that new towns should contain substantial social, economic, and ethnic diversity. In many cases it is proposed that such integration take place within districts of the town as well as in the town as a whole. The prospects for such a policy are not encouraging. Indeed, many early new towns made quite purposeful exclusions on economic and ethnic grounds. And some recent studies suggest that many people are attracted to new towns in part precisely by promises of "planned growth" and high levels of amenity which they interpret as code words for social exclusion. At the extreme, some of the "new communities" in major cities are advertising guards, fences, gate check points, and other security measures. Recent studies of the British new towns, which were supposed to mix social classes, indicate that wealthier classes have tended to leave the towns and that residential areas are now differentiating by class.

There is also an economic barrier to such social balance. At present we cannot produce new housing for people below middle class income levels without heavy subsidies. In existing cities, the less affluent live in housing made cheap by age and the filtering process of the market. If new towns lack a stock of older housing, "social balance" would require enormous subsidies. They are not likely to be forthcoming because the urban majority will see no reason why new towns, as against old cities, should get them.

One argument for new ones which is now in great favor is that they will increase the range of choice of living environments. It is far from clear, however, in what ways new towns would differ from existing cities of equivalent size. Architectural and other physical features seem to be the principal probable differences, but there are also suggestions for such diverse sorts of new towns as a black town (Soul City, proposed by Floyd McKissick), a technological utopia (the Minnesota Experimental City), hippie communes, maximum security developments, and resort towns. Although those who want to live in such special settlements should be able to do so, the provision of such exotic residential opportunities for various minorities does not appear to constitute an adequate basis for a large scale national new towns program. It makes no economic sense, and it is a political absurdity.

Considerations of land use are often adduced in behalf of new towns. One of these is the difficulty of assembling large tracts of land on the edge of metropolitan areas because of their fractioned ownership and the game-like complexities of speculation. Large tracts may permit economies of scale in construction and allow certain interesting design features. Hence, urbanization should be easier where large pieces of land can be put together, presumably at some distance from existing settlements. But if there are such great advantages to large development tracts, much could be done to make land available at the margin of existing cities through institutional instruments such as land banks, property and capital gains taxes, and public intervention through policy powers and eminent domain. Choosing distant locations for the sake of land assembly is a rather roundabout way of getting the job done. True, it isn't easy to assemble large tracts. But it isn't easy to build new towns, either.

The companion argument is based on land prices. Suburban land prices have risen sharply for many years, and it is suggested that development on cheap, distant land would both provide land at less cost to new town residents and discourage speculators at the edges of existing cities. The lower price for new town residents would certainly facilitate the development of new towns. But would it justify? The price of urban land is based primarily on the value of its location by reason of its accessibility. Cheap land will probably be inconvenient land, and might prove to be very expensive land by the time you get through providing transportation, utilities, etc.

FINDING ALTERNATIVE ENVIRONMENTS

Perhaps the most deep-seated reason for wanting new towns lies in images of their physical form. The new towns literature usually offers photographs of European new towns where the sun always shines. Nevertheless, the specifics of the alternative environments provided by new towns are elusive. There is no dominant school of thought: some plans feature cluster housing and grade separation of different types of traffic; others are based on mixing various types of buildings and land uses which are usually separated; still others emphasize outdoor facilities; and a few plans envision towns of medieval densities, or domes covering the entire town for climate control.

Yet the technological alternatives foreseen for new towns are generally minor or undeveloped. What is persuasive is the notion that new towns would be more beautiful and sensually satisfying than most of our cities and suburbs. No one can avoid being struck by the aesthetic poverty of most of our urban environments. Other places and other times, with only a fraction of our resources, have produced districts and whole cities whose extraordinary beauty and efficiency contribute greatly to the pleasure of their inhabitants.

Two causes for the ugliness of urban America suggest themselves. The first is that we lack feasible models of superior physical environments. Most of the physical design ideas proposed for new towns *could* apply to residential and commercial land uses and *could* be incorporated into the extension and rebuilding of existing urban areas. Here and there, this is actually occurring. But there is little doubt that new towns might have a powerful demonstration effect and assist greatly in the diffusion of design innovation.

The second reason for environmental drabness is that urban beauty is a public good and, as such, is difficult to produce through a market economy. Production of beauty may conflict with other uses of the urban plant. Moreover, beauty is not only not measurable but also highly problematic: what is beautiful to some is ugly to others. To a large extent, new towns would substitute developers' control for the market, and permit expert opinion to determine what is beautiful and how much to pay for it. In this respect, alas, they would not be likely to help existing cities frame institutional mechanisms to produce urban beauty. Our cities are not governed by appointed experts but by elected politicians and the forces of the market.

One of the most traditional arguments for new towns is that, being small, they would give residents ready access to open land. By contrast, a resident of a large metropolitan area may have a long ride to get out of the urbanized area if he has a car, and he may find it hard to do that if he is poor and without a car. Yet this distance from open land can also be psychological rather than geographical. A small square within the city can be as powerful an antidote to claustrophobia as farmland on the city's edge. Although the restoring powers of contact with nature are an important motif in our culture, a question must be raised of the meaning and functions of different types of open land. An urban park, a regional park, agricultural fields, and untrammeled nature may all be colored green on a land-use map, but they are quite different from one another as potential places for recreation and contact with nature. One would have to attach an extraordinary importance to immediate access to *agricultural* land to advocate a new towns policy on this basis, which seems to point instead toward expanding urban parks and facilitating access to them.

CONCLUSION

On the whole, a national policy of settling millions of people in new towns is not likely to succeed and would not significantly advance the national welfare if it could be done. The principal flaw in new town proposals is their underestimation of the integration of modern society, which is expressed in the complex reticulation of functional areas and the counterpoint of centers and subcenters which constitute a metropolis. This complexity allows specialization and complementarity; its fluidity makes it capable of producing innovations and accepting change; and its ambiguities permit it to encompass the strains and inconsistencies which inevitably accompany change. We may be vexed at our slow response to problems like pollution, segregation, and ugliness; but new towns, with their stress on diverse "balances," seem to fall into a deterministic fallacy which, under the guise of increasing choice, would actually reduce it in nearly closed subsystems of too small a scale. It is curious that an idea rooted in humanism should assume such materialistic and deterministic dimensions, and end up slighting the importance of freedom, communication, and interaction.

One notable kind of myopia in new town proposals is to regard the system of existing metropolises as one that grows only by proportional expansion while ignoring the continuous processes which create urban novae. Washington, Dallas, Los Angeles, Chicago, and others have risen in the last century to join the constellation of large urban areas, absorbing in their growth larger shares of our population than those proposed for new towns and cities. This crucial aspect of national urbanization differs from the new towns proposals in that *the growth occurred because it wanted to be there and not because it wanted to get away from something.*

A new towns policy that aims at housing a substantial portion of the population makes little sense. But there is much to be said for a new towns policy that would create new towns to test or exhibit innovations which might be adaptable by existing cities. Such experiments in new towns, should, of course, be carefully designed to fulfill certain requirements. The first is that the findings be transferable to other areas. The second is that the experiment must be a reliable indicator of the probable success or failure of further applications of the innovation. The third is that the findings be available fairly promptly. The value of the expected findings must be discounted with respect to the time of their availability. In addition, there must be provision for objective reportage and evaluation, and only those experiments should be undertaken where there is the political will and means to learn from the findings. Most of the value of today's experiments is vitiated by the hyperbole and puffery of most new town advocacy, which effectively conceals what we might learn from our experience thus far.

There is much to be done to improve our cities, and perhaps some experiments with new towns would help. I say only that, even if new towns turned out to be wonderful places, they would still be almost powerless to affect our present urban problems; and I fear that, as sirens of utopia, they might distract us from our proper work.

FURTHER READINGS

de Leeuw, Frank. "Demand for Housing: A Review of Cross Section Evidence," *Review of Economics and Statistics* 53:1 (February 1971).

Grieson, Ronald E. "Notes on Effects of the Property Tax on Operating and Investment Decisions of Rental Property Owners," *National Tax Journal*, forthcoming.

Grieson, Ronald E. "The Economics of Property Taxes and Land Values." Economics working paper no. 72. Cambridge, Mass.: Massachusetts Institute of Technology, June 1971.

Grieson, Ronald E. "The Supply of Rental Housing: Comment," *American Economic Review*, forthcoming.

Grigby, William G. *Housing Markets and Public Policy.* Philadelphia: University of Pennsylvania Press, 1963.

Muth, Richard. *Cities and Housing*. Chicago: University of Chicago Press, 1969.

Muth, Richard. "The Demand for Nonfarm Housing," in Arnold Harberger, ed., *The Demand for Durable Goods* (Chicago: University of Chicago Press, 1960).

Netzer, Dick. *Economics of the Property Tax*. Washington, D.C.: The Brookings Institution, 1966.

Rothenberg, Jerome. *Economic Evaluation of Urban Renewal*. Washington, D.C.: The Brookings Institution, 1967.

Wilson, James Q., ed. *Urban Renewal: The Record and the Controversy*. Cambridge, Mass.: M.I.T. Press, 1966.

Chapter 6

POLLUTION

Experts and laymen alike see that pollution is excessive and undesirable. Why, then, has it been allowed to go unabated, reaching near-crisis proportions in some cities? One reason is that clean air and water were regarded as free goods by society — that is, goods whose supply always exceeded demand. Only within the last few years has society come to realize that the supply of clean air and water, particularly in urban areas, is limited, and that the air and water will become increasingly dirty and harmful as the concentration of pollutants rises. Air and water can absorb but limited amounts of pollutants before becoming soiled. Giving away our limited supplies of clean air and water has created the pollution problem.

Now that the harmful effects of pollutions are realized, we still cannot expect polluters voluntarily to limit their emissions. They have little or no incentive to do so. When an automobile exhaust or public-utility smokestack emits pollution, it harms many others around it. The damage done to the polluter as an individual from his own exhaust or smoke is almost immeasurably small, and he has little incentive to count harm done by his polluting activities to others if he does not have to compensate them for the full amount of the damage. Furthermore, a firm might be compelled to pollute by the pressures of a competitive market, even if it desired to act altruistically. Investment in antipollution devices would raise the costs of the altruistic firm. To cover costs, this firm would have to charge a higher price than its polluting competitors and, as a consequence, lose business. Society needs to step in and ration the amount of pollution firms and individuals can generate.

Once we decide to ration pollution, we must still estimate its costs and benefits and determine its optimal level. Estimates of the cost of pollution can be obtained from studies of its effect on the value of land (as done by Ronald Ridker and John Henning for air pollution). Land-value studies measure the full losses from pollution only if everyone is fully aware of its harmful effects and if all the losses from pollution are fully capitalized in land values. Even though these and other technical conditions are not likely to be realized, land-value studies can give a rough, but probably slightly low, estimate of pollution losses. The costs of air and water pollution include decreased recreational and aesthetic amenities, deterioration of physical structures (paint, buildings, and clothing), and loss of health and decreased longevity. Ezra Mishan's essay graphically depicts these losses.

Land-value studies of the costs of air pollution could be used to estimate the incremental or social costs of small changes in the level of pollution, thus obtaining a marginal social-cost schedule of pollution or a marginal social-benefit schedule of depollution. The schedule would indicate that the more we reduce pollution, the smaller are the marginal benefits from further reductions. At very low levels, the marginal benefits of additional reductions of some pollutants might be zero. In the same vein, the cost of reducing the level of pollution by one more unit, in terms of more expensive production technology, reduced output, or increased treatment facilities is called the marginal social cost of pollution. The more we reduce pollution, the higher the marginal cost of reduction becomes. Wherefore, since progressive reductions in the level of pollution bring fewer benefits and greater costs, the optimal amount of pollution for a city, at which the marginal social costs and benefits of pollution abatement are equal, is almost certainly some level greater than zero.

How do we ration the right to pollute to achieve optimality? As Edwin Mills explains, we can use taxes or charges on pollution emissions. Polluters thereby are given incentive to abate pollution to the point where the cost of depollution is equal to the tax. Pollution taxes are the most efficient way of reducing pollution to any desired level. They make the marginal cost of depolluting the same by all processes. This causes a given amount of pollution abatement to occur with minimum cost or sacrifice of other goods, or reduces the maximum amount of pollution for any given level of cost. Fixed-percentage or absolute-standard schemes could result in some firms depolluting at high cost to meet their quota while others could be reducing pollution beyond their quotas at much lower costs. If the tax is set at the marginal social cost of pollution, an optimal amount of pollution (rarely zero) is achieved. Pollution above the optimal level involves pollution costs for society greater than depollution costs to the firm. Similarly, pollution below the optimal level involves pollution abatement costs greater than the benefits.

Optimal depollution is desirable since it will always increase the community's well-being, even if it involves costs or a sacrifice of other goods. Decreased pollution will not necessarily involve a decrease in other goods available to society, since the first reductions in pollutions may actually increase availability of some goods. Paint, buildings, and clothing will not be deteriorated and soiled as rapidly when pollution is reduced.

User charges have additional advantages over fixed or absolute standards. They do not involve government in specifying the anti-pollution technology to be used by each firm. The government does not need to know what each firm's costs are in order to induce efficient pollution control. There are no complicated negotiations during which firms have every incentive to claim higher reduction costs and levels than exist in order to raise their pollution quotas. Instead, firms are motivated to develop the best abatement technology. Pollution taxes can be varied easily if the optimal or desirable level of pollution changes. Pollution charges involve fewer policing and measurement problems than other control methods, yet are more flexible and efficient.

All firms do not abate pollution by the same percentage, nor to the same absolute level. They will reduce pollution until the marginal cost of so doing is equal to the tax. Furthermore, each firm has the incentive to reduce its pollution in the least-cost way because as long as a firm can reduce pollution at a cost lower than the tax, it gains. The lower that cost, the larger the gains. Firms pay both the cost of pollution reduction and the tax on pollution generated. These costs and taxes raise the price a firm must charge to break even or earn a normal profit. Through increased prices, the consumer of the polluting goods or service indirectly pays part of, if not all, the social cost of pollution and its reduction.

These taxes should not be the same for all firms in all areas. Similar firms located in different cities or areas around a city would not necessarily pay the same tax rate per unit of pollution or pollute the same absolute amount. Pollution is measured by the concentration of pollutants in the air or water, not the absolute amount released by one polluter in isolation. Hence, if there are ten factories emitting a pollutant, each one will pay the same tax, but it will be higher than if there was only one polluting factory. Similarly, the harm done by a particular level of pollution depends upon the number of people and property affected by the pollution in a crowded city. Pollution charges will therefore be higher the greater the concentration of pollutants and the more dense the population. The density of people, automobiles, and commerce in central cities produces much higher pollution levels and affects more people and property than the generally lower levels of pollution found in suburban and rural areas. Thus, pollution charge rates and enforcement will need to be greater in cities.

Many believe subsidies for pollution abatement to be inequitable since they require those affected by pollution to pay the perpetrators to desist; granting a subsidy implies that polluters have the right to pollute. Subsidies are also difficult to administer since they require that we determine how much pollution would have been emitted in the absence of the subsidy. A firm would have a strong incentive to submit plans for the dirtiest possible production process, even if it were not the least-cost process in order to maximize its subsidy. With taxes, there is no such problem. The government only needs to know the actual amount of pollution emitted and its social cost in order to assess the tax and bring about optimal pollution. Furthermore, subsidies would increase expenses for cities while taxes would help alleviate the financial crisis.

The argument has been advanced that the imposition of pollution taxes is really a sale of the right to pollute. It would be neither desirable nor feasible to attempt to end all pollution. Going to the zero level of pollution would involve large costs, may even be impossible, and would yield little in the way of benefits. Consequently, under any set of regulations some pollution will exist. Selling permission to pollute is the most efficient way to allocate the limited pollution rights. Pollution charges make both the polluter and the consumer of goods produced by polluting processes pay for the right to pollute and hence appear equitable. They are no worse than selling other goods. Furthermore, pollution taxes make those polluted upon better off, since the tax paid by the polluter is above the average level of loss to those polluted upon.

Our general discussion has been within the framework of air pollution. As Allen Kneese explains, however, efficient water pollution abatement is achieved in the same manner. Benefit-cost studies are needed to determine the desired amount of water pollution abatement facilities; then taxes are needed to achieve optimal reduction. Solid waste pollution (for example, discarded containers of junked automobiles) can be handled in a like manner. A charge could be levied on disposable containers or new automobiles equal to the expected social cost of the object being junked on our landscape. The tax would be levied at the time of purchase of the container or auto and remitted when proof of acceptable disposal is presented. A bounty would be set equal to the social cost of having the object remain on the landscape.

There are justifiable exceptions to our user charge method. Automobile pollution, which many experts believe is responsible for more than half of all urban pollution, does not lend itself easily to pollution charges on individual drivers. Perhaps a tax equal to the cost of its expected lifetime pollution could be assessed on each type of automobile at the time of purchase. This would give auto purchasers a reason to demand less-polluting automobiles. Another solution would be to set a national standard for vehicle pollution with maintenance enforcement controls varying as the density of automobile use varies. Stricter enforcement standards could be required in areas of dense use and population. In cities, as we stated previously, air pollution is a function of concentration, which will be greater the more densely autos are used. The damage will also be greater the higher the population density.

Again the suburban automobile is largely responsible for one of the city's woes. It has created externalities that excessively damage the city's environment (and its air, buildings, residents, recreation, and other amenities), but does not pay or otherwise compensate the city for them. The second most important source of pollution in cities is often the sulphur dioxide emitted by public utilities, which produce electricity. They have also not been subject to emission charges. Instead the sulphur content of the oil burned in power plants has been restricted from .5 to 1 per cent. This practice may be reasonable in the short run since it is slightly easier to enforce such a rule than it is to levy charges on the sulphur dioxide content of smoke. But the policy has restricted the development of technologies to remove sulphur dioxide from smoke before its release, which might prove less expensive. Of course there are other, more important, exceptions to user charges, including outright bans on the dumping of extremely dangerous toxins such as mercury and nuclear wastes.

Unfortunately, cities are generally too small to regulate pollution effectively, since air and water pollution usually involve the entire air shed or water basin around the city. Responsibility therefore needs to be assumed by metropolitan areas, states, or regions.

Although we have devoted this section to the more measurable and well-known forms of pollution—air, water, and solid waste—it is important to remember other externalities that may be classed as pollution. These include noise, ugliness, and cultural destruction. Airplane noise, auto and motor bike noise, billboards, neon signs, unaesthetic and dehumanized architecture or design are striking examples. All of these reduce the welfare of individuals and communities. User charges or taxes often cannot as easily be levied upon such externalities because of problems in measurement, administration, and enforcement. But they may be handled by means of zoning restriction or by community participation in the design of facilities.

THE NATURE OF EXTERNAL DISECONOMIES

Ezra J. Mishan

In this [chapter] we shall concern ourselves closely with the implications for social welfare of those "neighbourhood effects" generated by a wide range of economic activities. The operations of firms, or the doings of ordinary people, frequently have significant effects on others of which no account need be taken by the firms, or the individuals, responsible for them. Moreover, inasmuch as the benefits conferred and the damages inflicted — or "external economies" and "external diseconomies" respectively — on other members of society in the process of producing, or using, certain goods do not enter the calculation of the market price, one can no longer take it for granted that the market price of a good is an index of its marginal value to society.[1]

If there are external diseconomies being generated either in the process

Ezra J. Mishan is Reader in Economics, London School of Economics.

From Ezra J. Mishan, *The Costs of Economic Growth* (New York: Praeger, 1967), pp. 53–56, 70–78. Reprinted with permission of Frederick A. Praeger, Inc., and Granada Publishing Limited.

[1] In the absence of all neighbourhood effects the changes of tastes and of techniques of production would cause changes in product and factor prices over time, and therefore changes in the distribution of income. Nobody engaged in private industry is concerned with the ultimate effects of his activity on the distribution of income, although of course each person is subject to some risk that the market will go against him. Yet even if we supposed everyone to be indifferent to the resulting pattern of distribution, a concern with allocative efficiency implies a concern with neighbourhood effects. Uncorrected external diseconomies in certain sectors of the economy, for instance, would indicate that a position in which everywhere price was equal to marginal cost was not in fact optimal. By correcting these external diseconomies an optimal position, one in which everyone could be made better off, is attainable.

of production of certain goods, or in their final use by the public, damages are being inflicted on other people to which some value may be attached. It follows that the *social* value of a good — the value remaining after subtracting from its market price the estimated value of the damage inflicted on others by producing and/or using the good — may not only be well below its market price, it may even be negative. In such cases we are required to reduce outputs until this social value of the good is raised sufficiently to become equal to its marginal cost of production. Alternatively, we may leave the market price uncorrected and instead transform the *private* marginal cost, calculable by the producer on strict commercial principles, into *social* marginal cost by adding to the private marginal cost the value of any incidental damage inflicted on the rest of society in the production, or final use, of the good in question.[2] When this correction is applied to each unit of any relevant output, the universal *private* marginal-cost pricing rule becomes amended to the more general *social* marginal-cost pricing rule. It follows that an apparently efficiently working competitive economy, one in which outputs are quickly adjusted so that prices everywhere tend to equal *private* marginal cost, may lead the economy very far indeed from an optimal position as defined. Such an optimal position in fact requires that in all sectors production be such that prices are equal to social marginal cost.

Although the principle is straightforward enough such estimates of damages (and benefits) can pose considerable practical difficulties. One reason for this, as we shall see, is that some sorts of external diseconomies, manifestly important ones at that, do not lend themselves easily to measurement — no small defect in a society so prone as ours is to equate relevance with quantification. Another reason is that, even though measurable, their incidence may be so widely dispersed that adequate data are difficult to procure. Furthermore, there may be difficulties both of concept and measurement in attributing to any single sector of the economy a variety of external diseconomies which depend for their effect upon complementary economic activities. The smoky factory chimney is a favourite example simply because it appears to limit itself so conveniently to spreading dirt within a locality; the additional costs of keeping one's person and one's clothes clean in the polluted areas can easily be estimated and added to the private costs in order to yield an estimate of the social costs of production. The costs of water pollution by one or more factories is also amenable to calculation of this sort since the authorities usually have estimates of the damages being caused and of the higher costs of alternative sources of pure water. Some of the simpler nuisances, on the other hand, such as excessive engine noise

---

[2] It should be obvious that the value of any benefit conferred on society by the good in question is to be subtracted from its private marginal cost.

and emission of noxious fumes, may be tackled most economically by enacting compulsory noise-muffling measures and compulsory installation of anti-fume devices, as in several states of the US. However, more general social afflictions such as industrial noise, dirt, stench, ugliness, urban sprawl, and other features that jar the nerves and impair the health of many are difficult both to measure and to impute to any single source — which is, of course, no reason for treating them with resignation.

One must insert a caveat at this juncture, however. The detection of some uncorrected external effect does not of itself warrant government intervention. First the external diseconomy that acts to reduce the social marginal cost and suggests a reduction of output may be generated by a highly monopolistic industry which, in the absence of the external diseconomy, would require expansion of output. In general it is the balance of these two features that determines the change of output. In fact we are concerned only with those external diseconomies so large as to be obviously in need of remedial correction. Secondly, it is possible that the affected groups will come to agreement by themselves, or with a little official encouragement, an event that is more likely to take place if the parties that suffer the damage are well organized, as are firms and industries, than if they comprise a host of individuals with no mutual connections, or interests in common, other than this. Thirdly, and if they do not reach any voluntary agreement, the cost of intervening and administering a satisfactory scheme may exceed the apparent social gain. Nevertheless, by concentrating in the following chapters on the more blatant examples of external diseconomies imposed on the public at large by modern industries we shall not need to invoke this caveat.

The growing incidence of the external diseconomies generated by certain sectors of the economy and suffered by the public at large, regarded as the most salient factor responsible for the misallocation of our national resources, is one of the chief themes of this essay and the motif of this second part of the volume. All professional economists are, of course, aware of the role played by external diseconomies[3] in the system; though alas, all too many of them tend to look at such effects merely as one of the chief obstacles to facile theorizing — as the sort of possibility that detracts from the optimal properties of the popular theoretical construct, a perfectly competitive economy — rather than as an existing social menace. Familiarity with so simple a concept, the ritual footnote references to it, seem to have imparted a feeling that the matter is well under control. Too many economists have, therefore, continued to ignore the events taking shape around

---

[3] As indicated in the last footnote to the preceding digression, the implications of external diseconomies may, under the conditions stated, be treated separately from those of external economies.

them and to immerse themselves instead in the intellectual fascination of quasi-mathematical models of growth, and the theoretical problems involved in general solutions of optimal systems.

Not that the damage wrought by external diseconomies is entirely ignored by the public at large. Apart from letters of protest and occasional newspaper comment, magazines such as *Punch* and *The New Yorker* which specialize in social satire frequently depict with biting humour the dilemmas of automobilization, and the frustration of the millions all trying simultaneously to get away to a quiet place. But this does not meet the problem since, if anything, this laughing at the follies of mankind serves to release social tension and makes bearable what in fact ought not to be borne with. If the problem is to be tackled by society, the economist must persist in revealing the nature of the beast, and must suggest the circumstances under which meaningful magnitudes may be attributed to external effects. Nor should he shirk detailed description of cases wherever the social consequences that escape the pricing system appear to be so involved that a comprehensive criterion for evaluating them cannot, as yet, be satisfactorily evolved. . . .

In so far as the activities of private or public industry are in question, the alteration required of the existing law is clear. For private industry, when it bothers at all to jutsify its existence to society, is prone to do so just on the grounds that the value of what it produces exceeds the cost it incurs — gains exceed losses, in other words. But what are costs under the existing law and what ought to count as costs is just what is in issue. A great impetus would doubtless take place in the expansion of certain industries if they were allowed freely to appropriate or trespass on the land or properties of others. Even where they were effectively bought off by the victims, the owners of such favoured industries would thereby become the richer. And one could be sure that if, after the elapse of some years, the Government sought to revoke this licence there would be an outcry that such arbitrary infringement of liberties would inevitably "stifle progress," "jeopardize employment" and, of course, "lose us valuable export markets." Such an example though admittedly farfetched is distinctly relevant. For private property in this country has been regarded as inviolate for centuries. Even if the Government during a national emergency or in pursuit of national policy takes over the ownership or management of private property it is obliged to compensate owners. It may well be alleged that in any instance the Government paid too little or too much, but it would not occur to a British Government merely to confiscate private property.

In extending this principle of compensation, largely on the grounds of equity, the law should explicitly recognize also the facts of allocation. Privacy and quiet and clean air are scarce goods — far scarcer than they were before the war — and sure to become scarcer still in the foreseeable future.

They are becoming more highly valued by millions of people, most of them anxious to find a quiet place to live not too far from their work. There is no warrant, therefore, for allowing them to be treated as though they were free goods, as though they were so abundant that a bit more or less made not the slightest difference to anyone. Clearly if the world were so fashioned that clean air and quiet took on a physically identifiable form, and one that allowed it to be transferred as between people, we should be able to observe whether a man's quantum of the stuff had been appropriated, or damaged, and institute legal proceedings accordingly. The fact that the universe has not been so accommodating in this respect does not in the least detract from the principle of justice involved, or from the principle of economy regarding the allocation of scarce resources. One has but to imagine a country in which men were invested by law with property rights in privacy, quiet, and in clean air — simple things, but for many indispensable to the enjoyment of life — to recognize that the extent of the compensatory payments that would perforce accompany the operation of industries, motorized traffic, and airlines, would constrain many of them to close down or to operate at levels far below those which would prevail in the absence of such a law, at least until industry and transport discovered economical ways of controlling their own noxious by-products.

The consequence of recognizing such rights in one form or another, let us call them *amenity rights,* would be far-reaching. Such innovations as the invisible electronic bugging devices currently popular in the US among people eager to "peep in" on other people's conversations could be legally prohibited in recognition of such rights.[4] The case against their use would rest simply on the fact that the users of such devices would be unable to compensate the victims, including all the potential victims, to continue living in a state of unease or anxiety. So humble an invention as the petrol-powered lawn-mower, and other petrol-driven garden implements would come also into conflict with such rights. The din produced by any one man is invariably heard by dozens of families who, of course, may be enthusiastic gardeners also. If they are all satisfied with the current situation or could come to agreement with one another, well and good. But once amenity

---

[4] According to *Life International* (June 13, 1966): "As manufacturers leap-frog each other turning out ingenious new refinements, the components they sell have been getting smaller and more efficient. . . . So rapidly is the field developing that today's devices may be soon outmoded by systems using microcircuits so tiny that a transmitter made of them would be thinner and smaller than a postage stamp, and could be slipped undetected virtually anywhere. . . . How to safeguard individual rights in a world suddenly turned into a peep-hole and listening-post has become the toughest legal problem facing the US today."

Whether the law could be made effective is, of course, a problem. To the extent it could not, one would have to recognize a loss of welfare arising directly from technological progress.

rights were enacted, at least no man could be forced against his will to absorb these noxious by-products of the activity of others. Of course, compensation that would satisfy the victim (always assuming he tells the truth) may exceed what the offender could pay. In the circumstances, the enthusiast would have to make do with a hand lawn-mower until the manufacturer discovered means of effectively silencing the din. The manufacturer would, of course, have every incentive to do so, for under such legislation the degree of noise-elimination would be regarded as a factor in the measurement of technical efficiency. The commercial prospects of the product would then vary with the degree of noise-elimination achieved.

Admittedly there are difficulties whenever actual compensation payments have to be made, say, to thousands of families disturbed by aircraft noise. Yet once the principle of amenity rights is recognized in law, a rough estimate of the magnitude of compensation payments necessary to maintain the welfare of the number of families affected would be entered as a matter of course into the social cost calculus. And unless these compensatory payments could also be somehow covered by the proceeds of the air service there would be no *prima facie* case for maintaining the air service.[5] If, on the other hand, compensatory payments could be paid (and their payment costs the company less than any technical device that would effectively eliminate the noise) some method of compensation must be devised. It is true that the courts, from time to time, have enunciated the doctrine that in the ordinary pursuit of industry a reasonable amount of inconvenience must be borne with. The recognition of amenity rights, however, does no more than impose an economic interpretation on the word "reasonable," and therefore also on the word "unreasonable," by transferring the cost of the inconvenience on to the shoulders of those who cause it. If by actually compensating the victims — or by paying to eliminate the disamenity by the cheapest technical method available — an existing service cannot be continued (the market being unwilling to pay the increased cost) the inconvenience that is currently being borne with is to be deemed unreasonable. And since those who cause the inconvenience are now compelled to shoulder the increased costs there should be no trouble in convincing them that the inconvenience is unreasonable and, therefore, in withdrawing the service in question.

A law recognizing this principle would have drastic effects on private enterprise which, for too long, has neglected the damage inflicted on society

---

[5] It is always open to the Government to claim that a certain air service should be maintained even though it cannot cover its social costs for reasons connected with the defence of the realm. However, it would now have to think twice about using such phrases, since it would have to vindicate its claims about the high value to the nation of this particular air service by a willingness to pay a direct subsidy to the company, from the taxpayers' money, in order to cover the costs of compensating the victims.

at large in producing its wares. For many decades now private firms have, without giving it a thought, polluted the air we breathe, poisoned lakes and rivers with their effluence, and produced gadgets that have destroyed the quiet of millions of families, gadgets that range from motorized lawn-mowers and motor-cycles to transistors and private planes. What is being proposed therefore may be regarded as an alteration of the legal frame-work within which private firms operate in order to direct their enterprise towards ends that accord more closely with the interests of society. More specifically, it would provide industry with the incentive necessary to under-take prolonged research into methods of removing the potential amenity-destroying features of so many of today's existing products and services.

The social advantage of enacting legislation embodying amenity rights is further reinforced by a consideration of the regressive nature of many existing external diseconomies. The rich have legal protection of their prop-erty and have less need, at present, of protection from the disamenity created by others. The richer a man is the wider is his choice of neighbour-hood. If the area he happened to choose appears to be sinking in the scale of amenity he can move, if at some inconvenience, to a quieter area. He can select a suitable town house, secluded perhaps, or made soundproof through-out, and spend his leisure in the country or abroad at times of his own choosing. *Per contra,* the poorer the family the less opportunity there is for moving from its present locality. To all intents it is stuck in the area and must put up with whatever disamenity is inflicted upon it. And, generalizing from the experience of the last ten years or so, one may depend upon it that it will be the neighbourhoods of the working and lower middle classes that will suffer most from the increased construction of fly-overs and fly-unders and road-widening schemes intended to speed up the accumulating road traffic that all but poison the air. Thus the recognition of amenity rights has favourable distributive effects also. It would promote not only a rise in the standards of environment generally, it would raise them most for the lower income groups that have suffered more than any other group from unchecked "development" and the growth of motorized traffic since the war.

*   *   *

The advantages of the city are too obvious to dwell upon. Regarded as a commercial centre it may attract buyers and sellers from all over the coun-try by offering a wide range of specialized services. In the past the city was the centre also of intellectual, artistic and scientific achievement. And today only the city, the big city or metropolis, can provide a sophisticated public large enough to form daily audiences for symphony orchestras, operas, ballets and theatres. Returning to more mundane matters, the scale of operation of such public services as water, gas, electricity, and even administration, may show appreciable economies. There are, however, technological limits to the economies of size, and if such economies were the sole consideration, we might want to promote the expansion of the city until they were all fully exploited — until, that is, it was no longer possible to lower the marginal cost of any good or service by increasing the size of the city, measured either by area, population density, or wealth.

But even assuming these economies of size to be large, there are countervailing diseconomies of size. The larger the city the more time and resources have to be spent within the city on the movement of people and goods. Even telephone communication can become wasteful as the numbers in commerce and the professions increase. Any growth of building densities in city centres adds further to the difficulties of traffic that has passed the point of mutual frustration.

It might be thought that in some providential manner all this "comes out in the wash," the right size being determined by a balance of forces in which the increasing economies are offset by increasing diseconomies. But whatever the equilibrium of forces, it is hardly one that providentially issues in a city of optimal size. There is, in fact, an asymmetry in the forces at work which tends to make the city too large. The economies of large-scale productions are apparent and there is every incentive for their exploitation by private and public companies.[6] Indeed, the more obvious external economies of a metropolitan area such as London — local availability of skilled labour and specialized personnel, accessibility to market and technical information, the provision of finance and other facilities — are so widely recognized as in fact to be overrated.[7] Even if we assumed a complete absence of countervailing forces, the scope for further exploitation of the economies of scale is likely to be negligible.[8] On the other hand, the effects of any additional population, in adding to the traffic, and ultimately in time spent commuting, in adding to the noise and grime, and the impact of this increased pressure on people's health and disposition are not taken into account by commerce and industry. Important though they are, they

[6] An 'optimal exploitation' takes place, however, only if the companies act as discriminating monopolists, or are guided by marginal-cost pricing.

[7] Despite the assumption of *laissez-faire* economists that businessmen know their own interests best, there is ample evidence to show that many private firms have an *irrational* (non-commercial) preference for expanding within the metropolis rather than for setting up branches in other regions of the country. In particular, see the evidence put forward in a paper by Dr Needleman, 'What are we to do about the Regional Problem?' *Lloyds Bank Review*, January 1965.

[8] Bear in mind also that the larger the economies of scale realized the more widespread are the effects of any accidental breakdown of public utilities, in the public transport system, the electricity supply, the telephone service or water supply. How vulnerable a large metropolis can be to a withdrawal of essential services for even a short period of time has recently been exemplified by the electricity failure (1965) and transport strike (1966) in the New York area.

are difficult to measure. In the absence of pertinent legislation the incentive for expanding firms to bring them into the cost calculus is virtually non-existent.

The extent of the social damage inflicted by traffic congestion, even on itself alone, tends to be underrated by a public which habitually thinks in terms of an average figure rather than in terms of the appropriate marginal concept. A homely example illustrates the point. Three men can sit comfortably on one side of the seats of a corridor train operated by British rail. The addition of one man will generally result in all four sitting a little too close for comfort. The additional man, in reaching a decision, need only weigh the advantage to himself of standing as against the alternative of sitting wedged between the others. He need take no account of the increased discomfort of the other three if he decides to sit down. The same principle is at work on the roads. Suppose that, over a certain period, just about a hundred cars can use a given stretch of road comfortably. Ten more cars contemplating the use of the road need reckon only the congestion to themselves. Ignoring all other social costs and assuming, for argument's sake, that the costs of congestion are the same to each motorist, the increment of cost caused by these ten is eleven times as high as the costs actually experienced by them, and on the basis of which experienced costs the ten make their decision. An unregulated traffic flow thus tends to be too large and, by one means or another, should be reduced to an "optimal" traffic flow — one at which the marginal, or incremental, cost of congestion is equal to (or no greater than) the value placed on driving in that stream of traffic, bearing in mind the costs of all the alternative modes of travel available.

The same principle applies to the additional firm that settles in a crowded city, so adding personnel and traffic that further impede the movement of others in the city. The firm, however, need take account only of its relatively negligible share of the additional inconvenience it inflicts on everyone. Analogous remarks apply to constructing additional floor space, and to demolishing an old building in order to build a taller one with a more "economical" use of floor space. They need take no account of the spill-over effects on the city's traffic.

Of no less topical interest is the growth of the city's population. Each person who chooses to live in the metropolis has no thought of the additional costs he necessarily imposes on others, and especially over the short period during which it is not possible to add to the existing accommodation,[9] road space or public transport facilities. In the more crowded parts of the

---

[9] In the absence of a rise in economic rents (which would distribute the limited accommodation so as to realize an optimal situation) the additional newcomer imposes inconveniences on others in excess of his payments to the landlord.

metropolitan area it requires no more than a few thousand immigrants to reduce in remarkable degree the standard of comfort of all the previous inhabitants of the area. If the immigrants into the city happen to arrive from other parts of the country, or from other parts of the world enjoying comparable standards, the degree of discomfort suffered by the existing inhabitants, though incompatible with any optimal situation, will remain within limits. For such immigration will not continue if living conditions in such areas fall too far below the standards generally expected. If, on the other hand, immigrants come from countries with standards of living, of hygiene and comfort, well below those prevalent in the host country, the standards of the neighbourhood within which the immigrants elect to settle may have to decline drastically before the standards themselves begin to act as a disincentive to further immigration. Indeed, the immigrants may be willing to tolerate worse conditions than in the homeland since (i) those who pioneer the immigration will be prepared to endure hardship for a year or two in the hope of bettering their lot later, and (ii) some are resigned to dwell in squalid conditions for several years with the aim, initially at least, of amassing a sum of money in order either to return or to bring over their families. Moreover, there is always a time-lag, measured perhaps in years, between the worsening of conditions in immigrant areas of the city and the general appreciation of this fact in the immigrants' homelands.

The phenomenon of external economies and diseconomies has relevance also to the physical layout of the city. A building in the city is today seldom regarded by the owners as more than a financial asset. But it may, in addition, be an asset or liability to the city. A stately building is a source of pride and pleasure to citizens while a shoddy one, of which there has been a proliferation since the war, is a source of continual annoyance and disgust. If the builder of these "functional" modern blocks were compelled to compensate citizens for "uglifying" their city, we might yet have hope for the future. When one considers that the architecture of the city influences the mood, the humour, even the character of its citizens; when one considers the civic pride, pleasure and sense of community that may be inspired by the architecture of a city, it is a strange reflection on our kind of civilization that we leave the initiative in designing our cities, piecemeal, largely to commercial interests, and their approval to penny-wise councillors, and we do so at a time when, more than ever before in history, pecuniary considerations are dominant.

Imagine an alternative dispensation in which some sort of ideal city is established having wide boulevards, majestic buildings, and spacious parks. The site of the city, we suppose, is owned entirely by an enlightened municipality which, as a matter of course, sets up a select committee of citizens, each of which is renowned for his taste and judgement, charged with promoting the beauty and dignity of the city.[10] If the committee become convinced of the virtues of the price mechanism to the point of willingness to sell land for development by private companies it could none the less ensure the working of "the invisible hand," provided it sold only on condition that purchasers defrayed all relevant social costs. These would be defined to include sums of money fixed by the committee as adequate compensation to citizens who continually would have to bear unsightly or incongruent edifices plus sums to compensate for additional disamenities such as increased traffic and air pollution. Extending the market under these conditions may be expected to provide incentives to preserve and promote the beauty of the city — at least, if it did not do so, the fault could be laid squarely on the shoulders of the citizenry. Whatever the outcome one must admit the possibility of problems arising in estimating adequate compensation. But the problems arise as an inevitable result of facing the issue squarely, of attempting to bring into the calculus those social costs that are, under existing institutions, systematically ignored to the undeniable detriment of our towns and cities.[11]

In view of the rampant post-war development not only in London and other cities but also in innumerable seaside resorts and small towns of Britain which before the war had still some remnants of local character, there is a particular urgency in recognizing these social costs. Intimate local architecture is everywhere being swamped by anonymous concrete egg-crates and the "new" slab architecture equally suitable and equally monotonous in London, Berlin, Buenos Aires and Singapore.[12]

[10] The principles by which local authorities and, ultimately, the central government, exercise limited control on building do not correspond with those proposed here. Local officers see themselves primarily as watchdogs of the "public interest" guided by an ad hoc set of criteria. They are peculiarly vulnerable to accusations of "holding up" progress, or discouraging growth and employment, and they can seldom resist the argument that "development" will bring in increased revenues.

[11] A more conservative version of this scheme, and one that does not require any institutional alteration, would seem to be to arrange for a committee of citizens to bid against the private builder in an open market. However, as we have seen, the results would not in general be the same. The maximum amount that the citizens would be willing to pay for land in order to bid it away from private use would be less than the minimum the citizens would be prepared to accept if they already owned the land. One would want to favour the method proposed in the text, however, not only for distributional reasons but also in support of the principle of vesting amenity rights in the citizens.

[12] I am far from suggesting that the architect be given a free hand, though his opinions are worth hearing and would become more so were he under less pressure to seek new forms and new methods of using materials, just because they are not traditional. For a great number of people traditional materials and older styles afford far more pleasure than the modern buildings that accord with a trend towards unadorned functionalism. We still find delight in many examples of Georgian or Regency architecture. The Crescent at Regents Park, St Paul's Cathedral, Somerset House, are justly prized not only because of their historic associations but for their inherent beauty and humanity. Much of this eighteenth and early nineteenth century architecture is

ECONOMIC INCENTIVES IN AIR-POLLUTION CONTROL

Edwin S. Mills

Smoke is one of the classic examples of external diseconomies mentioned in the writings of Alfred Marshall and his followers. Generations of college instructors have used this form of air pollution as an illustration to help their students to understand conditions under which competitive markets will or will not allocate resources efficiently. By now, the theoretical problems have been explored with the sharpest tools available to economists. The consensus among economists on the basic issue is overwhelming, and I suspect one would be hard-pressed to find a proposition that commands more widespread agreement among economists than the following: The discharge of pollutants into the atmosphere imposes on some members of society costs which are inadequately imputed to the sources of the pollution by free markets, resulting in more pollution than would be desirable from the point of view of society as a whole.

In spite of the widespread agreement on the fundamental issues regarding externalities such as air pollution, there have been remarkably few attempts in the scholarly literature to carry the analysis beyond this point. Most writers have been content to point out that the free market will misallocate resources in this respect, and to conclude that this justifies intervention. But what sort of intervention? There are many kinds, and some are clearly preferable to others.

Too often we use the imperfect working of a free market to justify *any* kind of intervention. This is really an anomalous situation. After all, markets are man-made institutions, and they can be designed in many ways. When an economist concludes that a free market is working badly — giving

---

suggestive of the better features of those times, of spaciousness, proportion, leisure and splendour. It is with a sense of relief that the eye picks them out from the dreary uniformity of most modern city blocks. Certainly if we cannot do better than the present assortment of engineering monstrosities — from which, for monumental folly, the palm must be handed to the architects of the Elephant and Castle centre — we had best call a halt to further building. Indeed, if we were emancipated enough to ignore strong religious feelings about "progress," and to recognize that the new was the enemy of the excellent, a good case could be made for a programme of removing the post-war crop of eye-sores, and replacing them by an older and more intimate style of architecture.

Edwin S. Mills is Professor of Economics, Princeton University.

Reprinted from *The Economics of Air Pollution*, A Symposium, edited by Harold Wolozin. By permission of W. W. Norton & Company, Inc. Copyright © 1966 by W. W. Norton & Company, Inc.

the wrong signals, so to speak — he should also ask how the market may be restructured so that it will give the right signals.

Thus, in the case of air pollution, acceptance of the proposition stated above leads most people to think entirely in terms of direct regulation — permits, registration, licenses, enforcement of standards and so on. I submit that this is rather like abandoning a car because it has a flat tire. Of course, in some cases the car may be working so badly that the presence of a flat tire makes it rational to abandon it, and correspondingly the inadequacies of some market mechanisms may make abandonment desirable. Nevertheless, I submit that the more logical procedure is to ask how a badly functioning market may be restructured to preserve the clear advantages of free and decentralized decision-making, but to remedy its defects. Only when there appears to be no feasible way of structuring a market so that it will give participants the right signals, should it be given up in favor of direct regulation.

It is easy to state the principle by which the socially desirable amount of pollution abatement should be determined: *Any given pollution level should be reached by the least costly combination of means available; the level of pollution should be achieved at which the cost of a further reduction would exceed the benefits.*

To clothe the bare bones of this principle with the flesh of substance is a very tall order indeed. In principle, if every relevant number were known, an edict could be issued to each polluter specifying the amount by which he was to reduce his discharge of pollutants and the means by which he was to do so. In fact, we are even farther from having the right numbers for air pollution than we are from having those for water pollution.

In this situation, I suggest that any scheme for abatement should be consistent with the following principles:

1. It should permit decision-making to be as decentralized as possible. Other things being equal, a rule that discharges must be reduced by a certain amount is preferable to a rule that particular devices be installed, since the former permits alternatives to be considered that may be cheaper than the devices specified in the latter.

2. It should be experimental and flexible. As experience with abatement schemes accumulates, we will gain information about benefits and costs of abatement. We will then revise our ideas about the desirable amount and methods of abatement. Control schemes will have to be revised accordingly.

3. It should be coupled with careful economic research on benefits and costs of air-pollution abatement. Without benefit-cost calculations, we cannot determine the desirable amount of abatement. We can, however, conjecture with confidence that more abatement is desirable than is provided by existing controls. Therefore, our present ignorance of benefits and costs

should not be used as an excuse for doing nothing. I would place great emphasis on doing the appropriate research as part of any control scheme. A well-designed scheme will provide information (*e.g.*, on the costs of a variety of control devices) that is relevant to the benefit-cost calculations.

MEANS OF CONTROL

We are not in a position to evaluate a variety of schemes that are in use or have been proposed to control or abate air pollution. It will be useful to classify methods of control according to the categories employed by Kneese in his discussion of water pollution:

1. *Direct Regulation.* In this category, I include licenses, permits, compulsory standards, zoning, registration, and equity litigation.

2. *Payments.* In this category I include not only direct payments or subsidies, but also reductions in collections that would otherwise be made. Examples are subsidization of particular control devices, forgiveness of local property taxes on pollution-control equipment, accelerated depreciation on control equipment, payments for decreases in the discharge of pollutants, and tax credits for investment in control equipment.

3. *Charges.* This category includes schedules of charges or fees for the discharge of different amounts of specified pollutants and excise or other taxes on specific sources of pollution (such as coal).

My objection to direct regulation should be clear by now. It is too rigid and inflexible, and loses the advantages of decentralized decision-making. For example, a rule that factories limit their discharges of pollutants to certain levels would be less desirable than a system of effluent fees that achieved the same overall reduction in pollution, in that the latter would permit each firm to make the adjustment to the extent and in the manner that best suited its own situation. Direct restrictions are usually cumbersome to administer, and rarely achieve more than the grossest form of control. In spite of the fact that almost all of our present control programs fall into this category, they should be tried only after all others have been found unworkable.

Thus, first consideration ought to be given to control schemes under the second and third categories.

Many of the specific schemes under these two categories are undesirable in that they involve charges or payments for the wrong thing. If it is desired to reduce air pollution, then the charge or payment should depend on the amount of pollutants discharged and not on an activity that is directly or indirectly related to the discharge of pollutants. For example, an excise tax on coal is less desirable than a tax on the discharge of pollutants resulting from burning coal because the former distorts resource use in favor of other fuels and against devices to remove pollutants from stack gases after burning coal. As a second example, a payment to firms for decreasing the discharge of pollutants is better than a tax credit for investment in pollution-control devices because the latter introduces a bias against other means of reducing the discharge of pollutants, such as the burning of nonpolluting fuels. Thus, many control schemes can be eliminated on the principle that more efficient control can normally be obtained by incentives that depend on the variable it is desired to influence rather than by incentives that depend on a related variable.

Many of the specific schemes under *Payments* can be eliminated on the grounds that they propose to subsidize the purchase of devices that neither add to revenues nor reduce costs. Thus, if a pollution-control device neither helps to produce salable products nor reduces production costs, a firm really receives very little incentive to buy the device even if the government offers to pay half the cost. All that such subsidy schemes accomplish is to reduce somewhat the resistance to direct controls. Of course, some control devices may help to recover wastes that can be made into salable products. Although there are isolated examples of the recovery of valuable wastes in the process of air-pollution control, it is hard to know whether such possibilities are extensive. A careful survey of this subject would be interesting. However, the key point is that, to the extent that waste recovery is desirable, firms receive the appropriate incentive to recover wastes by the use of fees or payments that are related to the discharge of effluents. Therefore, even the possibility of waste recovery does not justify subsidization of devices to recover wastes.

The foregoing analysis creates a presumption in favor of schemes under which either payments are made for reducing the discharge of pollutants or charges are made for the amount of pollutants discharged. The basic condition for optimum resource allocation can in principle be satisfied by either scheme, since under either scheme just enough incentive can be provided so that the marginal cost of further abatement approximates the marginal benefits of further abatement. There are, however, three reasons for believing that charges are preferable to subsidies:

1. There is no natural "origin" for payments. In principle, the payment should be for a reduction in the discharge of pollutants below what it would have been without the payment. Estimation of this magnitude would be difficult and the recipient of the subsidy would have an obvious incentive to exaggerate the amount of pollutants he would have discharged without the subsidy. The establishment of a new factory would raise a particularly difficult problem. The trouble is precisely that which agricultural policy meets when it tries to pay farmers to reduce their crops. Jokes about farm-

ers deciding to double the amount of corn not produced this year capture the essence of the problem.

2. Payments violate feelings of equity which many people have on this subject. People feel that if polluting the air is a cost of producing certain products, then the consumers who benefit ought to pay this cost just as they ought to pay the costs of labor and other inputs needed in production.

3. If the tax system is used to make the payments, *e.g.,* by permitting a credit against tax liability for reduced discharge of pollutants, a "gimmick" is introduced into the tax system which, other things being equal, it is better to avoid. Whether or not the tax system is used to make the payments, the money must be raised at least partly by higher taxes than otherwise for some taxpayers. Since most of our taxes are not neutral, resource misallocation may result.

I feel that the above analysis creates at least a strong presumption for the use of discharge or effluent fees as a means of air-pollution abatement.

Briefly, the proposal is that air pollution control authorities be created with responsibility to evaluate a variety of abatement schemes, to estimate benefits and costs, to render technical assistance, to levy charges for the discharge of effluents, and to adopt other means of abatement.

Serious problems of air pollution are found mostly in urban areas of substantial size. Within an urban area, air pollution is no respecter of political boundaries, and an authority's jurisdiction should be defined by the boundaries of a metropolitan air shed. Although difficult to identify precisely, such air sheds would roughly coincide with Standard Metropolitan Statistical Areas. Except in a few cases, such as the Chicago-Gary and the New York-northern New Jersey areas, jurisdiction could be confined to a single metropolitan area. In a number of instances, the authority would have to be interstate. In many large metropolitan areas, the authority would have to be the joint creation of several local governments. There would presumably be participation by state governments and by the federal government at least to the extent of encouragement and financial support.

Each authority would have broad responsibility for dealing with air pollution in its metropolitan air shed. It would institute discharge fees and would be mainly financed by such fees. It would have the responsibility of estimating benefits and costs of air-pollution abatement, and of setting fees accordingly. It would have to identify major pollutants in its area and set fees appropriate to each significant pollutant. The authority could also provide technical advice and help concerning methods of abatement.

Although there would be great uncertainty as to the appropriate level of fees at first, this should not prevent their use. They should be set conservatively while study was in progress, and data on the responses of firms to modest fees would be valuable in making benefit-cost calculations. Given present uncertainties, a certain amount of flexible experimentation with fees would be desirable.

Questions will necessarily arise as to just what kinds and sources of pollutants would come under the jurisdiction of the proposed authority. I do not pretend to have answers to all such questions. Presumably, standard charges could be set for all major pollutants, with provision for variation in each metropolitan air shed to meet local conditions. It is clear that provision should be made for the possibility of varying the charge for a particular pollutant from air shed to air shed. The harm done by the discharge of a ton of sulfur dioxide will vary from place to place, depending on meteorological and other factors. It is probably less harmful in Omaha than in Los Angeles. It is important that charges reflect these differences, so that locational decisions will be appropriately affected.

Consideration would also have to be given to the appropriate temporal pattern of charges. In most cities, pollution is much more serious in summer than at other times. Charges that were in effect only during summer months might induce a quite different set of adjustments than charges that were in effect at all times.

No one should pretend that the administration of an effective air-pollution control scheme will be simple or cheap. Measurement and monitoring of discharges are necessary under any control scheme and can be expensive and technically difficult. Likewise, whatever the control scheme, finding the optimum degree of abatement requires the calculation of benefits and costs; these calculations are conceptually difficult and demanding.

The point that needs to be emphasized strongly is that the cost of administering a control scheme based on effluent fees will be less than the cost of administering any other scheme of equal effectiveness. An effluent-fee system, like ordinary price systems, is largely self-administering.

This point is important and is worth stating in detail. First, consider an effluent-fee system. Suppose a schedule of fees has been set. Then firms will gradually learn the rate of effluent discharge that is most profitable. Meanwhile, the enforcement agency will need to sample the firm's effluent to ensure that the firm is paying the fee for the amount actually discharged. However, once the firm has found the most profitable rate of effluent discharge, and this is known to the enforcing agency, the firm will have no incentive to discharge any amount of effluent other than the one for which it is paying. At this point the system becomes self-administering and the enforcement agency need only collect bills. Second, consider a regulatory scheme under which the permissible discharge is set at the level that actually resulted under the effluent-fee scheme. Then the firm has a continuing incentive because of its advantage on the costside to exceed the permissible discharge rate so as to increase production. Monitoring by the enforcement agency therefore continues to be necessary.

Of course, under either a regulatory or an effluent-fee scheme, a change in conditions will require the search for a new "equilibrium." Neither system can be self-enforcing until the new equilibrium has been found. The point is that the effluent-fee system becomes self-enforcing at that point, whereas the regulatory system does not.

WATER QUALITY MANAGEMENT BY REGIONAL AUTHORITIES IN THE RUHR AREA WITH SPECIAL EMPHASIS ON THE ROLE OF COST ASSESSMENT

Allen V. Kneese

PART I — BACKGROUND AND CONCEPTS

Water quality management is coming to dominate the problem of planning for development and use of water resources in many parts of the United States. Moreover, it has become widely recognized that water quality is a problem which, in most respects, can be best analyzed and dealt with on a regional basis.[1] This is seen in the creation of the Delaware River Basin Commission, one major function of which will be the management of water quality, the United States Public Health Service Comprehensive Planning Studies for the various river basins, and the establishment of numerous watershed and metropolitan authorities.

The recent report of the Senate Select Committee on National Water Resources helps give perspective to the possible magnitude of the water quality management task in the various water resources regions. Indeed it replaces the prevalent image of quantitative shortage on a nationwide scale with the

Allen V. Kneese is Director of the Quality of the Environment Program, Resources for the Future, Inc.

Reprinted with permission from Allen V. Kneese, "Water Quality Management by Regional Authorities in the Ruhr Area." *Papers and Proceedings of the Regional Science Association* 11 (1963), pp. 229–250. Footnotes selectively omitted.

[1] This generalization does not hold completely, of course. An interesting exception is illustrated by the recent German detergents legislation. Regional methods of handling the problem were explicitly analyzed and weighed against the cost of a national measure to outlaw the sale of hard detergents. The latter was judged the superior alternative.

conclusion that in most areas water supply is more than sufficient to meet the various projected uses which man will make of concentrated supplies. But it also concludes that presently dependable supplies are generally far from adequate to provide dilutions of projected future municipal and industrial waste discharge. Based on its analysis, the Committee concluded that maintaining comparatively clean streams in the various regions might require a national investment of an additional $100 billion by the year 2000. This is indeed a huge sum. By contrast the cost of completing the Bureau of Reclamation program of multipurpose western water resources development is estimated at a mere $4 billion after 1954.

The estimates of the Committee cannot be viewed as more than broad indicators of the potential magnitude of various aspects of water supply problems. *They do suggest, however, that achieving fairly clean streams throughout the U.S., in view of expected future economic-demographic development, will involve public investment far higher than in any other field of resources development or conservation.*

Despite the fact that some institutions have been created a major or primary function of which is to plan for optimum water quality management on a regional basis, there is as yet little institutional, economic, or engineering-scientific analysis aimed explicitly at the problems of regional water quality management in the watersheds and river basins of the United States.

For example, questions concerning the appropriate spatial jurisdiction and appropriate powers of an authority responsible for water quality in a region have hardly been addressed. There are many such questions. For example, should a single authority be made responsible for the water resources of a small watershed, a river basin, or a whole system of river basins? If there are different authorities, what coordinating devices are available? Should authorities only make general framework plans or should they be directly responsible for their execution by (say) constructing and operating facilities (dams, treatment plants, etc.)? How should the obvious interdependencies between land use patterns (especially industrial and municipal location decisions) and water quality problems be handled? Where land use planning is undertaken should it be under the same authority as water resources? If not, what functional division of powers is appropriate? What information should the authorities provide each other? What incentive or disincentive devices should they have available to see to it that social costs which occur in their area of responsibility are reflected in decisions of fiscally independent decision makers?

In light of increasingly pressing questions of this kind, it is useful to examine the experience of an area where these problems have long been confronted and regional institutions have been developed for dealing with them. The area in question is the Ruhr industrial area of West Germany. Indeed, the Ruhr with its extremely concentrated economic and demographic development and with the extraordinarily heavy burden which its urban-industrial-area society puts on water resources, reflects the type of situation numerous areas in the U.S. are just beginning to face.

The aim of this paper is to provide a brief review and assessment of the regional quality management activities of the water authorities in the Ruhr area. Special emphasis is placed upon the methods used to articulate the system planning and operation activities directly under their control, with often equally important decisions impinging upon water quality but under the control of other private and public or semi-public decision makers. It will be seen that the cost assessment and distribution methods used have played a prominent role in this regard.

Before undertaking a discussion of water quality planning in the Ruhr area, I would like to make a few generalizations concerning the economics of resource allocation especially pertinent to water quality management. This will provide a setting for the subsequent discussion. Economists will readily understand that unrestricted waste disposal into "common" water courses produces technological external diseconomies. Since putting wastes into water courses gives rise to costs which occur primarily "offsite," the cost and production structure tends to be distorted. There is no inducement to undertake waste water treatment, and other abatement measures, materials recovery, process adjustments, and other measures to reduce waste loads generated are not implemented to an optimum degree. The effectiveness of process engineering and materials recovery processes in reducing waste loads has been richly demonstrated by various instances in this country and perhaps even more strikingly in the Ruhr area. Moreover, industry accounts for over two-thirds of the organic waste load in the U.S. and a far higher proportion of most other pollutants. This emphasizes the importance of regional water resources authorities providing the appropriate incentives for reduction of industrial waste loads by in some fashion causing offsite costs to be reflected in waste generation and disposal decisions.

Indeed the traditional tax subsidy solution of welfare economics to externality problems of this kind lays exclusive emphasis upon the incentives provided by means of a redistribution of opportunity costs. I have elsewhere [2] reviewed the circumstances under which this suggested solution might work in practice and some approaches to the complex measurement and conputational problems that are encountered, including such matters as difficult to value as damages, interrelationships between wastes, hydrological variability, etc. The general principle is, however, that an effluent charge equal to downstream damages (resulting from increased water supply treatment and value of physical damages) would be imposed on the

---

[2] Allen V. Kneese, "The Economics of Regional Water Quality Management," Mimeo, Resources for the Future, Inc.

decision unit responsible for the outfall. The decision unit would then take measures to reduce its waste discharge by an optimum combination of measures — process and product adjustments, waste treatment and perhaps others, until the marginal cost of an additional unit of abatement equals the marginal cost of damages imposed in the affected region. At this point the cost associated with the disposal of wastes in the region would be minimized. Several things may be noted (without elaboration here) about this solution with a view to the literature on external diseconomies: (1) Since "water floweth whither it listeth," the reciprocal effects which have recently come under discussion and which may destroy the possibility of achieving approximately optimum results via the charges or taxes route are not involved, at least in the case of streams. Pollution damage is essentially a serial phenomenon.[3] (2) In order to obtain an efficient (cost minimizing) solution the damaged parties need not be compensated. If the charge levied upon the waste discharger produces optimal water quality in the stream, the water users will be induced to adapt optimally to it. (This result may not be considered equitable but this paper offers no criteria of equity.) (3) Solely from the viewpoint of efficiency, the desired (cost minimizing) result can be achieved with a subsidy (for reducing effluent) based on damages. The subsidy must be paid to the waste dischargers since, for the reason indicated in (1), only they control the water quality available to downstream users. The significant thing is that the upstream waste discharger must view downstream costs as opportunity costs. The present discussion will, however, proceed in terms of effluent charges. (4) Effluent charges have not been used on a regional basis in this country. In some instances effluent "standards" have been proposed and used. Charges appear to have certain advantages over standards which cannot be examined here. Both, however, can be viewed as devices for redistributing opportunity costs with attendant effects on treatment, process and product adjustments, and industrial location decisions. (5) If there are economies of scale in abatement measures, which cannot be realized by individual waste dischargers, the "classical" tax approach (or analogous procedures) cannot achieve an optimal solution.

The last point requires some additional comment since it is basic to further discussion of the work of the German water authorities. When economies of scale exist in abatement measures "system design" arises as a problem confronting a regional authority, in addition to seeing to it that opportunity costs are distributed in such a way as to induce efficient behavior. This is true, for example, when economies of large scale exist in waste treatment which permit wastes from diverse sources to be brought together for collective treatment, or where measures such as augmentation of low streamflows

---

[3] Otto A. Davis and Andrew Whinston, "Externalities, Welfare, and the Theory of Games," *Journal of Political Economy*, June, 1962.

by reservoir releases or artificial reaeration of streams are efficient alternatives or supplements to treatment over certain ranges, or where the entire flow of a stream can be advantageously treated. In other words, the problem of system design presents itself when economical abatement measures exist which cannot be undertaken by individual polluters.

In virtually all highly developed regions efficient ways of controlling pollution will be available, the use of which cannot be induced by levying the net offsite costs of their waste disposal on the waste disposers. It is to such regions that the present paper is especially relevant.

In these areas a social cost-minimizing solution will demand planning of the system by an organization which can comprehend the significant large-scale alternatives and supervise their operation. Such an organization is thus confronted with a set of problems. These include designing the system, operating some elements of it, and making charges (or using other devices) to induce efficient use of alternatives, the construction and operation of which it does not control directly. The latter would ordinarily, and probably should, include *at least* process and production adjustments by manufacturers' pre-treatment of wastes, and decisions with respect to specific locations of industries.

If the objective of the regional authority is to minimize the sum of the costs associated with waste disposal in the region, the economic design criterion would be to equalize the costs of all alternatives *including the costs of pollution damages* at the margin. This would be accomplished by a combination of direct construction and operation of abatement measures and by effluent standards or charges. The latter can be shown to lead to more efficient industry responses than arbitrarily selected standards, and are especially advantageous in inducing adjustment to short-run changes in social cost. The abatement facilities actually constructed and operated by the authority must take into account the response of the waste load generated to the system of charges. The optimal mix between measures planned and executed by the regional authority and those induced on the part of other decision makers will of course depend upon the degree to which economies of collective measures can be realized. This in turn will largely depend upon the extent of development of the basin.

One of a number of difficulties in actually designing and operating a system which minimizes costs is that certain values diminished or destroyed by water pollution are exceedingly difficult to measure. Prominent among these are the value of aesthetic and recreational amenities. Where these values are not actually quantified, specific judgments concerning their physical requirements or standards can be made. In a formal sense they can be considered constraints on the objective (which we have taken to be the minimization of costs associated with waste disposal). For example, costs may be minimized provided that dissolved oxygen does not fall below 4 parts per million (ppm) in the stream (a generally accepted minimum level for fish life). There are various formal methods by which such constrained optimum problems can be solved. In general, the economic criteria for an optimum with such constraints are analogous to those indicated earlier (i.e. the equalization of marginal costs in all directions). In other words, the optimum system is not attained until a situation is reached in which it is impossible to make marginal "tradeoffs" (say, between waste treatment and pollution damages) which lower costs without violating the constraints. The marginal costs affected by the constraint (say, waste dilution) now, however, have a shadow price which derives from the limited supply of the constrained input (say, dissolved oxygen).

These general points have been made not to imply that *precisely* optimum (given the objective) regional water quality management systems are possible or even desirable goals but to provide a conceptual framework for discussion of the German experience.

The following discussion of the Ruhr-area authorities falls into essentially four topics: (1) a brief discussion of the institutional character of the planning authorities, (2) a brief description of the systems they have designed, (3) some discussion of the methods used to articulate decisions with respect to land use and industrial process and product adjustments with the design and operation of system features over which the water resources organization have direct authority, and (4) a brief critique based on economic criteria of the cost assessment procedures.

One warning is in order. Emphasis in the following discussion is necessarily on principles and broad generalizations. This may well leave the impression of greater system and precision than is true in actuality. In a way what is described comes to be rather a prototype based to a far-reaching extent on the conceptualizations and actions of the actual organizations.

PART II — THE GENOSSENSCHAFTEN

There are seven large water resources Cooperative Associations called Genossenschaften in the highly industrialized and heavily populated area generally known as the Ruhr.[4] . . . These organizations were created by special legislation in the period from 1904 to 1958.[5] There are thousands

[4] The only general description of these organizations in English known to the author is Gordon M. Fair, "Pollution Abatement in the Ruhr District," in Henry Jarrett, *et al.*, *Comparisons in Resource Management* (Baltimore: Johns Hopkins Press, 1961). . . .

[5] All of the Genossenschaften with one exception were established before 1930. The Erftverband (Verband and Genossenschaft are used interchangeably in this context) was created in 1958 primarily to deal with problems resulting from a massive pumping down of ground water tables by the coal industry in the area of Erft river, west of the Rhine.

of water Genossenschaften in Germany, most of them created for special purposes such as the drainage or flood protection of specific plots of land. The large Genossenschaften in the Ruhr region were given almost complete multipurpose authority over water quantity and quality in entire watersheds by their special laws. These organizations are henceforth referred to simply as *the Genossenschaften*. They have for up to 50 years made comprehensive plans for waste disposal, water supply, flood control, and land drainage (a problem of great significance in the coal mining areas). The Genossenschaften are comparable to cooperatives (in the Anglo-American sense) but with voting power distributed in accordance with the size of the contribution made to the associations' expenditures and with compulsory membership. Members of the associations are principally the municipal and rural administrative districts, coal mines and industrial enterprises.

General public supervision over the Genossenschaften is in the hands of the Ministry of Food, Agriculture and Forestry, of the State of Northrhine-Westphalia. The Ministry's supervision is, however, almost completely limited to seeing that the associations comply with the provisions of their constitutions.

The Genossenschaften have the authority to plan and construct facilities for water resources management and to assess their members with the cost of constructing and operating such facilities. A process of appeal (internal appeal to special boards and final appeal to the Federal administrative courts) is available to the individual members.

Statutes creating the Genossenschaften are limited to a few brief pages. Accordingly, the goals and responsibilities of these organizations are set forth in highly general terms. This has left the staffs and the members free to adapt to changing conditions and to develop procedures and concepts in line with experience. Perhaps one general provision of the statutes, the meaning of which has developed greater and greater specificity in the course of time, has proved most central to successful and efficient operation. This provision specifies that the costs of constructing and operating the system are to be paid for by those members whose activities make it necessary and by those who benefit from it. Comparatively elaborate procedures for fulfilling this directive have been developed in regard to the costs of land drainage, waste disposal and water supply. In the course of time these procedures have come to be accepted not only as rational and equitable but have played an important role in the efficient operation of the system.

The area of the Genossenschaften contains notable cities such as Essen, Bochum, Muelheim, Dortmund, Duisburg and Gelsenkirchen and is one of the most concentrated industrial areas in the entire world — containing some 40 per cent of German industrial capacity. The industrial complex consists heavily of coal mining, iron and steel, steel fabrication, and heavy chemicals. By far the dominant industries are coal, coke, iron and steel. Between 80 and 90 per cent of total German production in these industries is in the Ruhr area. There are some eight million residents in the region, which contains about 4,300 square miles of land area — roughly one-half the size of the Potomac River watershed in the U.S.

Water resources are extremely limited if one excludes the Rhine River (to which the Ruhr area streams are tributaries). The Rhine has a mean flow roughly comparable to that of the Ohio but is drawn upon to supply water to the Ruhr area only during periods of extreme low flow. There are two reasons for this. First, the Rhine itself is of very poor quality where the Ruhr enters it, and secondly, the water from the Rhine must be *lifted* into the industrial area. With present installations, it is possible to "back-pump" the Ruhr as far up as Essen by means of pump stations installed in dams creating a series of shallow reservoirs in the Ruhr. Back pumping was carried on during the extreme drought of 1959. A large new reservoir for the augmentation of low flows which is nearing completion on a tributary of the Ruhr will even further reduce the already modest dependence of the area on the use of Rhine water.

The Ruhr area has been dependent upon the waste-carriage capacity of the Rhine to a much more far-reaching extent than for water supply. A large proportion of the wastes discharged from the industrial region into the Rhine receives comparatively little treatment. However, the construction of a large new biological treatment plant on the Emscher (a highly specialized stream described in more detail subsequently), will mean that virtually all effluents reaching the Rhine are given far-reaching treatment and the contribution of this area to the pollution of the Rhine will be comparatively modest.[6]

Five small rivers constitute the water supply and water-borne waste carriage and assimilative capacity of the industrial area proper. In descending order of size, these are the Ruhr, Lippe, Wupper, Emscher and the Niers. The *annual* average low flow of all these rivers combined is less than one third of the *low flow of record* on the Delaware River near Trenton, New Jersey, or one half of the *low flow of record* on the Potomac River near Washington, D.C.

The three rivers serving the main industrial area — the Ruhr, the Lippe and the Emscher — run roughly parallel. The Ruhr and the Wupper Rivers are mountain streams suitable for damsites and both have some developed storage with more under development and/or planned. An indication of the amazing load which these rivers carry is the fact that in the Ruhr, which is heavily used for household and industrial water supply and which in general

---

[6] Except for saline pollution from the coal mines in the area. The Lippe carries considerable natural salinity and additional saline water is pumped up from the mines. Another major source of salinity in the Rhine is the potash industry, particularly in France. Effective arrangements for reducing salinity have not yet been made.

serves these uses well, at annual low water flow, the volume of river flow is only about .8 as large as the volume of wastes discharged into the river. A frequently used rule of thumb is that in order for a river to be generally suitable for reuse, each unit of waste discharge must be diluted by at least eight parts of river water.[7]

How was such an extensive industrial complex successfully built upon a comparatively minute water supply base with considerable attention to the recreational and aesthetic amenity of water resources and at relatively modest cost? [8] Broadly the answer lies in the design and operation *of a generally efficient system*, which because of the regional purview of the Genossenschaften, and the dense development of the area, *can make far-reaching use of collective abatement measures and stream specialization.* Moreover, so-called indirect measures (waste reclamation, process engineering and influence on the selection of industrial sites) play a large role in controlling the generation of industrial wastes and the expense of dealing with them.

In the present discussion references to the Genossenschaften may be taken to mean either the Ruhrverband-Ruhrtalsperrenverein (RV-RTV) or the Emschergenossenschaft-Lippeverband (EG-LV) unless a specific organization is indicated. While the EG-LV and the RV-RTV are nominally four organizations, the two linked pairs are each under a single management. These are by far the largest Genossenschaften with both the most complex physical water resource systems and the most sophisticated methods of assessing costs.

The regional system of waste disposal which these organizations have established is very interesting. However, time permits only a few general comments to be made about it here. While the process of design was done with little or no explicit attention for formal optimizing procedures, the systems are designed and operated with the explicit objective of minimizing the costs of attaining certain standards in the rivers.[9] Moreover, there is explicit recognition of the equi-marginal principle in the planning procedures. Perhaps most important, the Genossenschaften provide an institution which permits a wide range of relevant alternatives to be examined systematically within a functionally meaningful planning area. However, it is also

---

[7] This was originally proposed by the Royal Commission on Sewage Effluents in England. See Louis Klein, *Aspects of River Pollution, op. cit.,* p. 551.

[8] Despite rather impressive attention to amenities and recreation, the combined expenditure of the Genossenschaften (which build and operate all water treatment plants, dams, pump stations, etc.) amounts to about $60 million a year (exclusive of capital investments), somewhat over half of which is for land drainage. The largest water works in the area (which is a profit-making enterprise and which contributes heavily to the costs of the facilities on the Ruhr) delivers water for household and industrial use at 30 cents per thousand gallons (official exchange rates used in making conversions).

[9] The theoretical features of these aspects are discussed earlier in this paper.

recognized that in some instances efficient solutions require a super-regional view. This is illustrated by the recent German law forbidding the sale of "hard" detergents after October 1964. Scientific investigation and cost assessment of alternatives leading to this legislation were primarily carried out in the laboratories of the Genossenschaften.[10]

In the Ruhr itself the objective of the system generally is to maintain water quality suitable for recreation [11] and municipal-industrial water supply. In the Lippe the objective is much the same.[12] The Emscher, by far the smallest of the three streams, is used exclusively for waste dilution, degradation, and transport.

The Emscher has thus been converted to a single-purpose stream, and is sometimes referred to as the *cloaca maxima* of the Ruhr area. It is fully lined with concrete, and the only quality objective with respect to it is the avoidance of aesthetic nuisance. This is sufficiently accomplished by primary or, as the Germans say, mechanical treatment of effluents which largely removes materials in suspension. Since the Emscher cannot be used for purposes other than effluent discharge,[13] the area is dependent upon adjoining watersheds for water supply and waterbased recreation opportunities. The feasibility of this system is enhanced by the small size of the area and the fact that the streams are parallel and close together. Actually, as an aid to protecting the quality of the Ruhr, some of the wastes generated in the Ruhr basin are pumped over into the watershed of the Emscher. By the use of plantings, gentle curves of the canalized stream, attractive design of bridges, etc., care is taken to give the Emscher a pleasing appearance and to blend it gracefully into the surrounding countryside.

[10] See Ciriacy-Wantrup, "Water Quality — A Problem for the Economist," *Journal of Farm Economics,* December 1961, and Allen V. and Georgia Kneese, "The Recent German Detergents Legislation — Nature and Rationale," mimeo.

[11] However, the quality of the Ruhr varies considerably along the course of its flow. At the head of the Hengsteysee (a shallow reservoir in the Ruhr built essentially as an instream treatment plant) the quality of the water is very poor. Neutralization, precipitation and oxidation occur in the Hengsteysee, and further stabilization takes place in the Harkortsee, a similar instream oxidation lake. By the time the water reaches the Baldeneysee (a third such lake) the quality has improved to such an extent that the water is suitable for general recreational use. This is true despite the fact that there are further heavy discharges of treated wastes between the Hengsteysee and the Baldeneysee. These waste discharges are generally given far-reaching treatment, frequently by means of treatment plants with double biological stages (activated sludge and trickling filters).

[12] Complicated by the fact that the waters of the lower Lippe are *highly* saline both from natural causes and because saline water is pumped into it from coal mines.

[13] One reason why such stream specialization may be advantageous is that the rate at which oxygen passes into the stream through the air-water interface is directly proportional to the size of the oxygen deficit (i.e. the amount by which actual dissolved oxygen [D.O.] falls below saturation level). Thus a stream in which dissolved oxygen is heavily drawn on has a much larger capacity to degrade organic wastes than a stream with sufficient dissolved oxygen to support fish life or provide drinking water.

Near its mouth the entire dry weather flow of the Emscher up to about 1,000 cfs is given primary treatment thus realizing scale economies in treatment to a very far-reaching extent. The heavy burden put on the Rhine both from upstream sources and from the Ruhr industrial area (largely via the Emscher) has caused great downstream costs.[14] Consequently the Emschergenossenschaft is now laying detailed plans for biological treatment of the Emscher. An experimental plant indicates that this treatment will be highly successful.[15] When the new plant is built, the contribution to Rhine river pollution on the part of the Ruhr industrial area will be substantially mitigated [16] and the area will come quite near to being a closed water supply–waste water system.

While formal optimization procedures have not been utilized by the Genossenschaften, they probably have realized the major gains from viewing the waste disposal-water supply problem as one of a system character rather than solely as a matter of treating wastes at individual outfalls. They have made extensive use of scale economies in treatment by linking several towns and cities to a single treatment plant when the costs of transporting effluents to the plants were less than the saving due to additional scale economies that could be realized — in the case of the Emscher they have, in fact, linked an entire watershed to a single treatment plant. They have utilized opportunities for more effective treatment of wastes which accrue through combining industrial and household wastes. They have made use of stream specialization for recreational and water supply purposes, and artificial ground water recharge for quality improvement purposes. They have at various times and places used flow augmentation, and direct aeration of streams. They have explicitly considered the differential ability of streams to degrade wastes at various locations (resulting from the opposing effects on oxygen balance of waste degradation and natural reaeration) both in determining location of treatment plants and in influencing the selection of industrial plant sites. Where scale economies, or special technical competence of Genossenschaft staff,[17] merited it, they have established their own waste recovery plants (phenols). They have, in other instances, induced waste recovery or process changes by levying charges for effluent discharge based

[14] Especially in Holland where even recently introduced large-scale ground water recharge projects are failing to supply suitable quality water.

[15] Based on conversation with Dr. Ing. Knop, Baudirektor Emschergenossenschaft.

[16] With the above noted exception of saline waters pumped from coal mines.

[17] Administrators of the Genossenschaften place great emphasis on the economies which result from a single staff planning, building, operating, and supervising the water resources facilities of an entire basin. The Ruhrverband operates 84 effluent treatment plants (to which, on the average, four new ones are added each year), four large detention lakes, 27 pumpworks, 300 km of trunk-sewer, run-of-the-river power plants, six dams (one in addition is under construction), power plants associated with the dams, and their own electricity distribution systems with a total staff (including laborers, apprentices and janitorial help) of 780 persons. . . .

on quantity and quality of waste water and by acting as a cooperative marketing agency for recovered waste products. While not always in a comprehensive manner, decisions between different alternative ways of achieving objectives have, at least in a rough and ready fashion, been based upon consideration of cost "tradeoffs" between them. Finally, and of considerable importance, they have provided for monitoring of the streams (especially those used for water supply) and operation of facilities to take account of changing conditions in a more or less continuous fashion.

Whether, in view of the value of recreation use, the conversion of the Emscher into an open sewer,[18] or the very heavy use of waste degradation capacity on certain stretches of the Ruhr is optimal, cannot be determined because explicit valuations of recreation use have not been made. Actually, outdoor recreation is quite impressively catered to in the Ruhr area. This is probably due to the considerable power which the communities and counties exercise in both the water Genossenschaften and the Siedlungsverband (the latter is the agency responsible for land use planning in the Ruhr area and eighteen major cities are in its planning jurisdiction).[19] Coordination of the work of the Siedlundgsverband and the Genossenschaften is significant not only in producing an explicit weighing of recreational and aesthetic values against others in the development and use of water resources, but also in providing explicit consideration of industrial location (especially with respect to areas of compact industrial development) as a variable in water use and waste disposal planning. In other words, planning procedures which provide for cooperation between the staffs of the water and land use authorities make sure that a variety of costs and benefits involved in patterns of land use and water quality alteration are reflected in the planning process, even though neither takes a comprehensive view in all its details. Moreover, once a general pattern of development is laid out, the water authorities continue to influence more specific industrial location decisions as well as process engineering and waste recovery through their systems of charges.

PART III — COST ASSESSMENT PROCEDURES

It is of course clear that solely from the point of view of resource allocation, the method of pricing adopted, or indeed whether effluent charges are made at all, would be relatively unimportant if waste loads delivered to the system

[18] Actually it was an out-of-control and extremely offensive open sewer when the Emschergenossenschaft came into existence.

[19] A virtually certain source of non-optimality is the fact that the design flow for all facilities is arbitrarily chosen (annual mean low flow). There is interest in considering this as a variable in the system but so far technical complexities have prevented experimentation with design flows.

were unresponsive to the charges imposed on them. This would appear in general to be the case with respect to household effluents, since there is comparatively little households can do to diminish their waste loads.[20] However, through product and process adjustments, through waste recovery, through separation of wastes and various forms of pretreatment, industrial waste loads can be altered over very wide ranges.[21]

Numerous adjustments, especially in process design, are being made by the industrial plants in the Ruhr area as a consequence of the Genossenschaften's methods which force industry to bear at least a significant portion of the social costs of waste disposal. In general indirect methods of reducing wastes such as recovery and process changes are considered on a par with treatment in the work of the Genossenschaften. This is one of the reasons why the giant Northrhine-Westphalian industrial complex can operate on a water base which is tiny by U.S. standards.[22]

[20] Such matters as the use of garbage grinders and detergents could presumably be affected. However, checking effluent quality from individual households would appear to be unjustifiably expensive and consequently some other method of distributing municipal sewage handling costs is universally adopted.

[21] Bucksteeg has reported some of the existing differences in the BOD of industries with organic waste loads. His own study of 14 paper mills indicated a population equivalent BOD per ton of paper ranging from 51 to 1,254, a multiple of almost 25. He also reported ranges per ton of output for other industries, in part based on the work of others. Multiples computed from the ranges reported in these industries are 2.5 in malt factories, 6 in starch factories, 4 and 50 respectively for beef and pork slaughter houses, about 10 in tanneries and about 20 in textile factories. . . .

As might be expected in the presence of such a range of possibilities, waste loads delivered to the Genossenschaften's quality control system have responded to effluent charges and other measures used to diminish them. The phenol recovery plants operated by the Emschergenossenschaft have already been described. They have in the past been virtually self-sufficient. Even a modest effluent charge could have caused a profit-maximizing (cost-minimizing) firm to operate such a plant, although economies of marketing, staff, research, etc., are thought to have been achieved by centralized operation. These plants recover about 65 per cent of the waste phenols occurring in the Emscher area. . . .

Another example of intensive waste recovery is provided by the capture of iron sulfate and sulfuric acid from the waste water of the Ruhr's iron and steel working industry. The basic reasons for this recovery of these particularly destructive wastes are the incentive provided by the combined effect of effluent charges and technical marketing assistance offered by the Ruhrverband. As a result over thirty per cent of total industrial acid use in the Ruhr area is recovered. Recovery even though usually carried on at a loss is often considerably cheaper than treatment by neutralization. . . .

The author also saw a steel plant (Hoesch-Westfalenhuette in Dortmund) where a series of recirculation and treatment systems virtually eliminated effluent from the plant. This is attributed to a combination of water costs and effluent charges. All other iron and steel plants in the area are gradually adopting similar measures to economize water use and waste water generation. Based on a conversation with Maximilian Zur who is in charge of water economy at the Hoesch-Westfalenhuette.

[22] There have been a number of examples where waste recovery has proven profitable in the U.S. even without considering the external costs avoided. In the manufacture of synthetic phenol by the sulfonation process, liquid wastes have been

The vast variety and potentially large effect which recovery processes and process design can have on waste loads point to the important role which a correctly planned system for the assessment and distribution of costs may play in restricting to an optimum degree the amount of waste products which industrial society produces. This being the case, a closer look at the methods of cost assessment used by the Genossenschaften is in order.

PART IV — COST ASSESSMENT AND EFFLUENT CHARGES

DESCRIPTION

The formulas used for cost assessment are decribed in some detail elsewhere.[23] Here only the main features of those used by the Emschergenossenschaft and Ruhrverband are briefly sketched.

The question confronting both these organizations is how the diverse wastes produced by industrial enterprises can be assessed with an appropriate portion of costs.

Very briefly put, the Emschergenossenschaft procedure is roughly as follows: (1) There is estimated first an amount of water necessary to dilute a given amount of waste materials subject to sedimentation (no distinction is made between organic and inorganic material) in order that they not be destructive to fish life under the conditions of the area. An amount of dilution water required by such materials in a given effluent is then computed

---

essentially eliminated by process engineering. The value of recovered materials is reported to exceed recovery costs. See A. N. Helles and M. E. Wenger, "Process Engineering in Stream Pollution Abatement," *Sewage and Industrial Wastes,* February, 1954, Vol. 26, No. 2.

A few sulfite pulp mills in North America have constructed full-scale ethyl alcohol plants to convert the wood sugars in their waste liquors (the wood sugars constitute about 50 per cent of the BOD in sulfite waste liquor). These plants have been reported to be "profitable." Actual or expected competition from other alcohol processes is reported to have retarded other plants from establishing similar mills. The same study reports that another and perhaps more promising possibility for waste recovery from the sulfite process is the torula fodder yeast method. See Harold R. Murdock, "Water and Waste in the Wood Pulp Industry," *Sewage and Industrial Wastes,* January 1954, Vol. 26.

In the sugar beet industry recovery of monosodium glutamate and potash from the notorious "Steffens" process wastes have proven to be profitable. Conversation with Lloyd T. Jensen, Vice-President of Great Western Sugar and head of the National Technical Task Committee on Industrial Wastes.

A charge fully reflecting marginal damages, or operation costs of an optimal regional waste disposal system would change the way in which profits are calculated. The gross private (and social) return from the recovery operation would be the sales price of the recovered materials plus avoided effluent charges. Obviously the way in which the "costs" of materials saving or waste load reducing process changes are calculated would be similarly affected.

[23] Kneese, "Economics of Regional Water Quality Management," *op. cit.*

on that basis. (2) An analogous calculation made for materials subject to biochemical degradation (and which therefore exert an oxygen demand) but which are not subject to sedimentation. (3) The amount of dilution required under specified conditions in order that the toxic material in the effluent not kill fish is computed by direct experimentation. (4) Certain side calculations having to do with water depletion, heat in effluent, etc., are made. The derived dilution requirements are added together for the effluent and form a basis for comparison with all other effluents. In principle, costs are distributed in accordance with the proportion of aggregate dilution requirements accounted for by the specific effluent. One might say that this procedure is based on a particular physical objective, i.e. not to "kill fish." However, the result of the method is used as an "index" of pollution even when effluents are discharged to streams in which lower or higher standards prevail than needed to preserve fish life.

The Ruhrverband method is also based on a physical objective but on a different one. Again, the details are described elsewhere.[24] In essence, however, the method is founded on the concept that toxic wastes by killing bacteria and slowing down the rate at which wastes are degraded have somewhat the same effect on treatment plant effluents and the level of BOD in streams as an *increase* in the amount of degradable material. On the basis of laboratory tests, an equivalence is formed so that toxic as well as degradable wastes are converted into a standard unit — a "population equivalent BOD."

These procedures can be criticized on technical as well as economic grounds. They are indeed recognized as less than ideal by the Genossenschaften but are generally defended as being readily understandable and relatively inexpensive to administer. Further development of cost assessment procedures along even more meaningful lines appears possible, however, especially in light of new technology which has recently become available or is now under development and which points to an easing of certain measurement problems.

Three areas will be briefly commented upon: (1) a formula for the assessment of costs based upon a physical objective will tend to lead to some misallocation of costs. (2) The procedure distributes average costs rather than assessing marginal costs. (3) Important economies might be achieved by an application of peak load pricing.

COMMENTS

Deficiencies in the Use of Physical Objectives in Cost Distribution. The minimization of costs either in the limited sense of minimizing costs for given objectives or in the broader sense of minimizing the social costs as-

[24] *Ibid.*

sociated with waste disposal, has been taken to be the general objective of a regional water quality control system. This objective logically implies that both the system design criteria and the cost distribution criteria must be based on *costs* not directly upon *physical effects*. Thus in the matter of system design it is *costs* which must be balanced at the margin.

Similarly, in the matter of cost distribution, a procedure based upon physical results alone (as are the Emschergenossenschaft and the Ruhrverband procedures) will, in principle, not allocate costs properly. For example, a substance may be very destructive to fish (and thus merit a high weight in the Emschergenossenschaft's method) but be relatively inexpensive to treat or to deal with by other means. In this instance a disproportion between the costs of dealing with waste substances and costs allocated to those producing them will arise. This would be true even if the sole objective of the system were to avoid killing fish.

In the broader context of multipurpose water use a practical illustration of substances which are not handled at all adequately by either method is the phenols. Phenols are produced in the distillation of petroleum and coal products. In low concentrations (a few parts per million) they do not exert much oxygen demand nor are they very toxic to fish. But even in the smallest concentrations they pose the most serious problems in the preparation of drinking water. When water containing minute amounts of phenols is chlorinated in order to kill bacteria, extremely evil tasting chlorophenols are formed.

Phenolic substances present a problem in all the world's great industrial complexes. The recommended limit for phenols in the latest revisions of the U.S. Public Health Service recommended drinking water standards is an infinitesimal 0.001 mg/1. Unless water supplies drawn from surface sources are to be very unpalatable, phenols must be kept out of waste water or else removed at great expense by the application of activated carbon at the water plant. Moreover, very small amounts of phenols in streams can impart an unpleasant "carbolic" taste to fish which may as effectively destroy their value as though they were actually killed. If a stream standard is imposed (say, instead of attempting to balance the cost of damages and abatement at the margin), this may mean far-reaching treatment or recovery processes are necessary for the phenol containing effluents. Clearly the cost of those procedures and/or damages is not reflected in the allocation procedures used by the Genossenschaften. This follows because in one instance the implied objective of the cost allocation procedure is not to kill fish and in the other not to kill bacteria.

Where substances do involve a large disproportion between the costs they impose on the system and the costs allocated to them by the methods, side calculations are generally made to take this aspect into account. The basic point, however, is that the cost assessment procedure is not fully consistent with the design objective.

The Appropriate Concept of Costs.   As earlier indicated, in principle, charges made for effluent discharge should equal full opportunity costs including increased water supply costs and foregone productive opportunities downstream. If there is no separate system design problem, imposition of these costs on waste discharges would tend to produce an allocation of resources which maximizes social product.

If scale economies introduce a separate problem of system design, levying only the (appropriately defined) costs of a correctly designed system would tend to accomplish the resource allocation objective. The appropriate process, product and location adjustments would be induced even though the costs of residual damages (which most probably would exist in an optimum system) are not specifically imposed on the waste discharger. This remains true even if the objective is to accomplish minimum cost of achieving certain standards. Consequently, basing the charges on costs actually incurred by the system as the Genossenschaften do, is not *per se* incorrect.[25]

A number of different possibilities exist with respect to the elements of a system which are directly constructed and operated by a regional authority and those left in the hands of fiscally independent decision-makers. However, in general a charge set equal to marginal cost, at their optimum level of utilization, of those abatement measures directly undertaken by the authority will be appropriate.[26] (In essence each discharger is subjected to a "last added" test). This is because the marginal costs of induced measures will tend to be equated with the charge per unit of waste discharge and consequently with the marginal cost of other alternatives.

It is clear, however, that the Genossenschaften distribute average costs to the dischargers, not marginal costs. Thus, if the system displays declining costs the charges as levied will generally be too high, whereas if increasing costs are incurred, the opposite will generally be the case. The efficiency argument against average cost pricing in this context is that it will not induce appropriate use of measures controlled by fiscally independent decision makers.

Cost Variation over Time.   For purposes of planning, costs properly include all capital costs of new facilities. The system of abatement (ideally) should be expanded to the point where an additional unit of abatement (op-

25 For a fuller explanation of the principles involved, see Kneese, *Economics of Regional Water Quality Management, op. cit.*

26 If some action is taken by the authority for each pollutant.

timal combination of measures) for any given pollutant, or combination of pollutants, raises the expected present value of total abatement costs as much as it diminishes the expected present value of pollution damages. Or if there is a constraint, or a standard, until the constraint is met and the expected present value of marginal total cost of all alternative measures for achieving the constraint are equalized.

However, at any given time with an established abatement system, only current operating costs and opportunity costs internal to a multipurpose system are relevant. These systems costs tend to vary strongly over time due to hydrological variability. This is true whether the objective is to equate marginal abatement costs and marginal damage costs or to minimize the costs of meeting a standard. This suggests the possible desirability of attempting to base prices on a rather short-run variation in costs.

The cost distribution methods of the Genossenschaften fail to take account of the fact that waste disposal costs (in the broad sense) are highly variable through time. As already mentioned, this variability results from the fact that the dilution and degradation capacities of streams show strong variation over time. For example, the long-term average discharge of the Delaware River at Trenton, New Jersey, is about 12,000 cfs, the mean annual flow is roughly 1/4 that and the low flow of record about 1/10 of the average flow. The average flow of the Ruhr is about 2,600 cfs and the average annual low water flow is only about 140 cfs.[27] If the costs of waste discharge to the polluter do not vary in accordance with flow, there is no incentive to reduce discharges during low flow periods, even through the concentration of pollutants, attendant damages and the costs of optimally operating abatement works tend to rise sharply during low stream stages.[28]

---

[27] Delaware figure from *Surface Water Supply of the United States, 1956, Part 1-B, North Atlantic Slope Basins, New York to York River,* Geological Survey Water Supply Paper 1432, U.S. Government Printing Office, Washington, 1959. The Ruhr flow figures are from Helmut Moehle, "Wasserwirtschaftliche Probleme an Industriefluessen" (Problems of Water Economics on the Industrial Streams), *Die Wasserwirtschaft,* 45, 1954.

[28] Oxygen conditions are especially likely to deteriorate radically during such periods because high temperatures (which cause bacteriological activity to increase and the oxygen saturation level of water to decline) ordinarily correspond with low flows. The combination of high concentrations of toxins and low oxygen levels can easily be fatal to fish. If oxygen levels are below several parts per million, oxygen deficiency itself will kill fish and if oxygen becomes exhausted extreme nuisance conditions accompany the development of anaerobic processes in a stream.

The concentrations of substances which alter Ph value of water, affect its hardness, create tastes and odors, cause dissolved solids content to rise — all tend to be higher during periods of low flow. This leads to rising municipal and industrial water supply treatment costs and a variety of pollution-caused damages to facilities and equipment. The point is that the social costs of pollution rise strongly during periods of low flow.

An authority controlling a going waste disposal system and attempting to operate it in such a way as to equate the relevant marginal costs would necessarily incur much greater costs of operation during low flow periods than during higher flows.

If it were clearly uneconomical to change the amount and/or quality of waste discharge over short periods of time, it might not be a matter of great concern whether or not costs levied upon polluters varied correspondingly over time. However, it appears probable that measures to change the pattern of discharge would enter economically into a quality control system designed to minimize costs. For example, depending upon the location of a manufacturing concern and upon attendant land values, it may be less expensive for the company to withhold its waste discharge temporarily in a lagoon rather than bear its share of the costs of storing and, at long intervals, releasing a much larger volume of river water. In some instances, especially where the product is storable, it may be more economical to reduce or halt production during low flow periods rather than to provide additional treatment or dilution capacity for an unchanged effluent. In other instances it may pay the manufacturer to provide temporary treatment (like chemical neutralization of acids) rather than meet the full costs of putting his effluents into the receiving water during low flow periods. In the light of such possibilities, incentives should be provided to use them to an optimal degree.

The method of peak pricing has been extensively carried out by electrical utilities, hotels, resorts, and theatres, among others. It regards the service performed (in this case pollution abatement) as different according to the heaviness of the load on the system. In the case of electrical utilities, this necessitates a price varying by time of day and the season.[29] In the case of pollution probably no more than seasonal variations could be justified.

During the critical periods such measures as increased aeration in activated sludge plants and the addition of chemicals aid precipitation in all types of treatment plants might be undertaken, leading to an increase in operating costs. During such periods artificial reaeration of streams may be done directly in the stream or through the turbines of hydro plants which in the first instance involves direct costs, and in the second, indirect costs because power plant efficiency is cut down. During low stream stages the augmentation of flow from reservoir storage offers the opportunity to increase waste dilution and if there are alternative uses for the stored water (say, peak power generators, or for recreation), an opportunity cost (internal to the water resources system) is incurred.

It is thus quite clear that costs are strongly related to time of discharge. In fact the social costs of a given quantity of a pollutant discharged at one time may easily be a multiple of those at another. Indeed, during periods of high stream flow waste disposal into the stream is likely to be virtually without downstream damages. During such periods the only justification for operating treatment plants at all may be to avoid the aesthetic nuisance of floating materials in the water.

[29] See Thomas Marschak, "Capital Budgeting and Pricing in the French Nationalized Industries," *The Journal of Business,* April, 1960, p. 133. Jack Hirschleifer, James C. De Haven and Jerome W. Milliman, *Water Supply-Economics, Technology and Policy* (Chicago: University of Chicago Press, 1960), Chapter V. For recent theoretical discussion of peak load pricing with special reference to investment decisions, see M. Boiteux, "Peakload Pricing." *The Journal of Business,* April, 1960, p. 157 and P. O. Steiner, "Peak Loads and Efficient Pricing," *Quarterly Journal of Economics,* November 1957, 585; and Jack Hirschleifer, "Peak Loads and Efficient Pricing: Comment," *Quarterly Journal of Economics,* 1958, p. 460.

In assessing the merits of applying "peak load" pricing principles to effluent discharges, the costs of determining variation in the quality and quantity of effluent over the relevant period must of course be considered. Presently, the Genossenschaften generally establish by sampling an effluent quality which is taken to be typical for the year. The quantity of effluent discharged during the year is ordinarily based upon measurements reported by the plant.

The costs of operating analysis sampling programs along present lines would mount sharply if an effort were made to determine quality and quantity variation with sufficient continuity to permit peak load pricing.[30] Fortunately in recent years progress has been made in the development of automatic monitoring devices. Such variables of river quality as dissolved oxygen, acidity-alkalinity, salinity, specific conductance (dissolved solids), temperature and turbidity can be continuously measured with fairly simple devices.[31] Some measurements are already successfully carried out on effluents and there is considerable promise that others can be developed. Optimism appears justified that accurate and comparatively simple devices for continuous measurement of a wide variety of water quality characteristics can be worked out.

In some instances an occasional rather thorough laboratory test may have to be done in order to establish relations which will permit the use of certain continuously measurable characteristics as surrogates for those which can only be measured with difficulty. For example, if fish toxicity is an important variable (as it is for example in the Emschergenossenschaft cost allocation method), a relation may be established between certain measurable substances in the effluent and fish kills; thus over specified periods of time this would permit the surrogate measurement to substitute for a direct toxicity test.

It is probably not excessively visionary to foresee a time when a number of important quality characteristics can be continuously recorded, at a central point, for every major outfall in an entire basin at comparatively modest cost.

---

[30] The Ruhrverband has 718 directly assessed industrial numbers and 264 communities. There would seem to be little to be accomplished by attempting to estimate charges in effluent quantity and quality from the communities themselves since they have little opportunity to adapt discharges to variable streamflow quantity and quality. Moreover, existing procedures for appeal of the cost assessments would have to be revised.

[31] Some of the most advanced work on automatic monitoring systems has been done by the Ohio River Sanitation Commission (Cincinnati, Ohio). See the ORSANCO annual reports. For a description of some of the automatic monitoring activities in the Delaware Basin (including the estuary) see *The Interstate Commission on the Delaware River Basin Proceedings,* Pocono Manor, Pennsylvania, October 15–16, 1962, especially the papers delivered Monday forenoon, October 15.

PART IV — CONCLUDING COMMENT

The criticisms which have been made of specific features of the Genossenschaft procedures should not be permitted to obscure the achievements of these organizations. The design and operation of a regional system for waste disposal and water supply management taking extensive advantage of economies realizable through integrated design, explicitly taking into account efficiencies achievable through the reflection of regional waste disposal costs in industrial location and process design decisions, and incorporating cost assessment systems based upon concepts of pollution damages and independent of specific system elements, are a pioneering achievement of the first order. The work of these organizations merits the closest attention of all those concerned with the peculiar set of problems presented by water resources management in basins containing urban-industrial complexes.

FURTHER READINGS

Ayres, Robert U., and Kneese, Allen V. "Pollution and Environmental Quality," in *The Quality of the Urban Environment,* edited by Harvey S. Perloff. Baltimore: Johns Hopkins Press, for Resources for the Future, Inc. (1969), pp. 35–74.

Ridker, Ronald G., and Henning, John A. "The Determinants of Residential Property Values with Special Reference to Air Pollution." *Review of Economics and Statistics* (May 1967).

Turvey, Ralph. "On Divergence Between Social Cost and Private Cost." *Economica* (August 1963), pp. 594–613.

Wolozin, Harold, ed. *The Economics of Air Pollution.* New York: W. W. Norton, 1966.

Chapter 7

POVERTY

A disproportionate and growing number of the metropolitan area's and the nation's poor and disadvantaged are concentrated in the central cities. As Anthony Downs shows, using the Social Security definition of poverty, nearly two-thirds of the metropolitan poor are located in the central city. They comprise nearly 14 percent of the city's population as compared to 10 percent for metropolitan areas, 7 percent for suburbs, and under 13 percent for the nation as a whole. The percentage rate of decrease in the number of poor persons has been greatest among the poor who reside in rural areas and are white.

There are also strong racial imbalances in poverty. The rate of poverty is approximately three times higher among black Americans than among white: about 30 percent for blacks, 10 percent for whites. Over 60 percent of the national and metropolitan poor are white, however, except in central cities, where the number of black and white poor are approaching equality, and in suburbs, where four-fifths of the poor are white. We can expect poverty and discrimination to be increasingly concentrated in the central city as long as members of our population who are poor and prone to discrimination continue migrating to cities in search of employment and a better life.

Whatever the cause and irrespective of race, one who is poor has low-quality health care, housing, food, clothing, recreation, education, entertainment, furniture, transportation, political representation, and justice. There is virtually no good or service missing from this list. Poverty therefore means general deprivation relative to the standards of the nation and is not confined to the lack of any one particular good.

The income definition of poverty calculated by Mollie Orshansky for the Social Security Administration, which in 1972 would be a little over $4,000 for an urban family of four (Massachusetts currently provides this level of welfare) has been widely adopted. This level can be expected to grow at the rate of inflation in the future. Orshansky's definition was based on the average amount of food expenditures that a family of four would have to make to obtain adequate nutrition, given society's generally poor eating habits. She then multiplied that food budget by a fixed constant to get the well-known $3,000 poverty line for 1960. Rose Friedman and others have computed absolute standards for poverty using different criteria and arrived at a much lower level of income for the poverty line. Their poverty line was $1,800 in 1968, which is below the level of the 1972 negative income tax proposal of $2,400 for a family of four. In 1962, the Social Security definition put 20 percent of our population in poverty, while Friedman and others put the percentage living below poverty at about 10 percent. The definition of poverty adopted by the U.S. Government in 1969 was approximately 10 percent below that calculated by Orshansky. Absolute poverty lines, then, are somewhat arbitrary, making poverty at least in part a relative phenomenon. Even the absolute-poverty lines society has established over the last thirty years have increased in real terms with the growth of national income.

Victor Fuchs believes that poverty should be defined by a relative standard. He suggests it be defined by the level of the family's income relative to the average income of families of the same size and perhaps in the same locality. He similarly suggests that we aim at providing families with a certain proportion, say one-third, of the median family income. As the median family income for a family of four is nearly $10,000, such a definition of poverty would put the line at approximately $3,400 per year. The number of families with incomes below one-third of the median could theoretically be 5 percent, or 30 percent of the total number of families. (The actual proportion in the United States is approaching 5 percent.)

Having an income one-third below the median does not mean being in the lowest one-third of all family incomes. We will always have individuals whose income is in the lowest tenth of incomes of our population, but we can make sure that the income of the lowest tenth is not less than two-, three-, or four-tenths of the median. Our present poverty level would undoubtedly be considered a high standard of living in some countries, just as the national poverty level of income would be considered a moderate level in rural Mississippi. Neither relative nor absolute standards tell the entire poverty story.

Now that we have briefly explored some descriptive aspects of poverty, we come to the important questions involved in alleviating poverty. The first issue is whether we shall attempt to eradicate poverty by giving the poor income and letting the recipients decide how to spend it or by giving specific goods to the poor which society feels they need or ought spend more on than they normally would. Most people seem to think that, with the possible exception of medical care, housing, and food, the poor ought to be given income with which to purchase goods of their choosing. We will return to the subsidy and provision of these particular goods later, but let us now concentrate our attention on finding the most efficient fair way of supplementing the income of the poor.

Robert Lampman's essay suggests several alternatives for combating poverty. We will consider the present state and local welfare system, guaranteed jobs, guaranteed incomes, and negative income taxes.

The present welfare system places financial responsibility in the hands of government at the level of the city, town, county, and sometimes state. The levels of these payments are determined either by the government responsible for funding or another, usually higher, level of government. The federal government shares the costs of most categories of welfare with the localities and states. There are four major problems with the present system. First, there are inequitably large differences in the amount of welfare paid to similar families living in different states. Second, a tremendous burden is put upon localities with small taxing ability and large numbers of poor. Third, federal sharing has often been designed in an unreasonable way and has permitted too much leeway in local eligibility standards. Finally, it ignores welfare as a national problem and simply shifts more of the burden onto particular states. This would alleviate the pressure on some poor communities but would have little effect on the other inequities of the system.

Numerous instances of programs involving counterproductive funding can be found. A striking example is provided by Aid to Families with Dependent Children. In 1969, twenty-eight states required that fathers be mentally or physically incapacitated for children to be eligible. In other states, the fathers had to be unemployed. Employed fathers whose earnings were below the welfare level were completely bypassed by the programs, though some localities used their own funds to aid such families. There some situations include divorce, desertion, or migration among the prerequisites for receiving AFDC funds. This not only encourages welfare parents to break up their marriages, but also subjects them to snooping aimed at discovering whether the husband has actually left. This partly explains why one-half of AFDC families consist of deserted or divorced mothers. Only 8 percent of the women are widows, compared to 90 percent at the program's inception. Blacks, who represent one-half of the AFDC recipients and two-thirds of the recent increase in recipients, have borne the brunt of these inequities. AFDC rolls have grown dramatically in recent years and will probably continue to do so as awareness of eligibility continues to increase, but we should still eliminate harmful restrictions on eligibility that foster undesirable family breakups and human suffering, even if these eliminations mean a larger number of recipients.

Many proposals have been made for a guaranteed minimium income. For example, the federal government could specify a minimum equal to the average level of welfare payments in the United States. If local governments decided to provide for payments above that level, the federal government could share part of the extra cost. Some object that guaranteed annual incomes would weaken people's incentives to work, if the guaranteed level were reduced by one dollar for every dollar the individual earned. An alternative would be to give the guaranteed income to everyone regardless of incomes. Financing this plan, however, would probably require more than doubling the present income tax rates, which would probably have an undesirably large negative effect on work effort of higher-income individuals.

One proposal that has gained wide support among economists is the negative income tax. The government would give cash payments equal to some percentage of the amount by which an individual's income was below a fixed standard. If the standard were $6,000 for a family of four and the rate of negative income tax were 50 percent, a family earning zero would receive a $3,000 annual subsidy, whereas a family earning $2,000 per year would receive $2,000 in payments $(2,000 = .50 \times [6,000 - 2,000])$. Each dollar an individual earned would reduce his subsidy (or welfare or negative tax payment) by fifty cents. This would preserve greater work incentives and leave individuals with the same after-subsidy income ranking as before, preserving the notion that more work leads to more income. To make the work incentive even greater, the first $600 an individual earns could be exempt, bringing about no reduction in subsidy payments. Thus, a family with an income up to $600 would receive $3,000 in payments; a family with one member earning $2,000 would receive $2,300, or ½ [6,000 − (2,000–600)], from the government for a total income of $4,300. Of course, the rate of reduction need not be 50 percent; it could be 40 percent or 60 percent. The standard could also be set at a proportion of the median family income, say one-half or two-thirds, rather than at an absolute standard. With the federal minimum-income level set at a floor of one-quarter to one-third of median income, wealthier states and localities could make additional payments of their own irrespective of further federal participation.

Another advantage of the negative income tax is that all who are poor would qualify. Those who were previously too proud to take advantage of or unaware of their rights would automatically receive the benefits of this plan, eliminating the many inequities of the present system. Being realistic, we must acknowledge that this will increase the number of families receiving aid by more than 25 percent and will increase the cost of welfare by 5 and perhaps more than 10 billion dollars annually, depending upon what level of subsidy is chosen. Five to 10 billion dollars represents between ½ and 1 percent of the gross national product and could easily be financed by a 5 to 10 percent surcharge on personal income taxes. Negative income taxes were given wide exposure in Milton Friedman's *Capitalism and Freedom* and then gained support from James Tobin, though Mary Jean Bowman reports that Albert Hart, Walter Heller, and William Vickrey, who were Friedman's colleagues at the U.S. treasury in the 1940's, had also been discussing allowances for individuals whose income is so low that they pay too little tax to benefit from individual and special tax exemptions. If a family of five earns $2,400, its tax is not reduced by the $600 exemption they are allowed for the fifth person. Duncan Foley lucidly explains the proposal in our readings.

Many of the economists who advocate the negative income tax do so with the idea that it is both more equitable and more efficient than the present welfare system. They feel that the current system destroyed all work incentives by reducing an individual's welfare payments dollar for dollar of earned income, imposing a 100 percent tax on earnings. But, as Nicholas Barr and Robert Hall have found econometrically, welfare payments are in fact not reduced dollar for dollar with increased earnings as prescribed by law. Although income grants are decreased by the amount of income, special benefits given for travel, lunches, and clothing are increased by one-half to four-fifths of the reduction. This means an effective tax rate of one-fifth to one-half on welfare recipients' earnings. Barr and Hall found total welfare payments to be reduced by only 25 percent of the value of earnings in the San Francisco Bay area. This information was based on data collected by social workers, which if anything would underestimate recipients' earnings and thereby overestimate the rate of reduction of welfare as a consequence of family earnings. Nationally they discovered that total welfare payments were reduced by approximately 35 percent of earned income. Their discovery points out that individuals who would be ineligible to receive welfare with a current income of $4,000 per year might be able to receive $2,000 from welfare while earning $4,000 if they had gone on welfare when their income was lower. Equals are not being treated equally. Therefore, although the negative income tax may still be desirable because it federalizes welfare and reduces differences between locations and inequities between individuals, careful empirical work should precede a specific and perhaps costly adoption of the plan.

The federal negative income tax should probably not be adjusted for the cost of living, since this would inefficiently push recipients toward living in high cost areas where they might be no better off at a greater expense. Many feel it not only inefficient but unfair that citizens be aided differently who are living in different areas. For similar reasons we are not permitted to use differences in cost of living as an adjustment for federal personal income tax purposes even though adjustments would allow more efficient allocation of resources in this case. The first problem with guaranteed jobs, our last income-supplementary proposal, is that not more than one-half of the poor could ever be raised out of poverty through employment. The other half are either over sixty-five, disabled, mothers, or children of such families. Of the persons not falling into this category many may presently lack the education or discipline necessary for productive employment. So we are left with perhaps one-third of the poor who could, with training and motivation, undertake occupations. The public sector may well not have positions for even that many. Furthermore, the interests and abilities of many of these people would not best qualify them for public-sector occupations. There would also be huge costs of administration and inefficiency in attempting to place more than a modest number of the unemployed in so narrow a line of work and in having so many government employees in high-poverty areas. Again, it is probably best to keep resource allocation or efficiency somewhat separate from employment and income distribution.

Considering education as a possible method of combating poverty, the suggested readings by Burton Weisbrod, Eugene Smolensky, and Thomas Ribich indicates that supplemental educational counseling for dropouts and special educational programs for the hard-core unemployed have not been successful in alleviating poverty. The programs have often cost far more than they have increased the earnings of the poor, who might well be better off if the funds were instead used to increase income grants. This is not difficult to understand since those who drop out and become members of the hard-core unemployed probably often do so because they know that added education would not offset discrimination or other factors limiting job potential. Eliminating discrimination and creating a demand for their labor would provide both employment and incentives to obtain the needed education. Another reason educational programs are unsuccessful may lie in the home lives of the poor. Poverty at home may generally not provide the environment in which individuals can effectively study and learn. The demands of daily existence are so pressing that it may appear foolish to strive for an education whose benefits are dubious and far off. Greater income and improved home surroundings might do more for the education of the poor than increased school expenditures. This does not mean that educational opportunity should not be made equal. Central financing of higher-quality education would open the door wider for those whose potential gains from education were increasing because of greater opportunity and reduced deprivation at home. Other studies of education cited in Ribich's book have shown that training the working poor and structurally unemployed poor does have a large payoff and would be the natural starting point for developing and testing such programs.

Another program aimed at improving the employability of the poor is free day care for children. Unfortunately, the program seems to be of limited potential for women who are heads of large families, since the cost of labor-intensive day care facilities would often be much in excess of their earning potential. Deductibility of day care costs from income tax calculations is probably desirable, however, because the cost of day care is incurred for the purpose of employment.

John Meyer and John Kain explore the relationship between transportation and poverty. We have greatly encouraged the use of the suburban automobile by providing heavily subsidized highways and parking facilities. These highways, built through and at the expense of cities and communities have caused potential employers of the poor and black to move to suburban locations inaccessible to those too poor to afford automobiles. Highways have also stimulated the middle class to move to the suburbs from which they commute to urban employment, reducing the tax base and the demand for mass transit. Subsequently, public transit is allowed to deteriorate, reducing ridership and creating demand for even more urban highways, further inhibiting the mobility of the poor.

Special transportation services for the poor are not the answer, for although automobile-oriented transportation has hurt the poor excessively, it has also hurt other groups. An efficient transportation system would generally help society and especially the poor. To reiterate, what is needed is much higher urban-auto-user charges especially at rush hour, combined with more trains, buses, and freer licensing of taxis and jitneys. In most cities taxis and jitneys are used more by the poor than other groups so that the poor would gain most by the freer licensing. Once suburban jobs for the poor and black community are created, taxis, jitneys, and bus lines to those jobs would probably come naturally, aided by the operation of an efficient, equitable transportation policy. If sufficient transportation for the disadvantaged did not materialize, government subsidies could be appropriately used. Conversely, special buses only for the poor would often be used below their capacity and hence be expensive and inefficient. Buses are needed that serve the poor while at the same time transporting the general population and lowering travel costs for all.

Turning to the question of housing, the poor live in low-quality, usually inexpensive, housing. Poor blacks often live in low-quality housing at higher average cost than do poor whites. The housing occupied by the poor in cities is sometimes more expensive per square foot than higher-quality suburban housing. But smaller units and inexpensive mass transit are available in cities and not usually available in suburbs.

Is there some special externality to housing which says that among all the goods used by the poor it should be singled out for extra attention? As we discussed in the housing section, low quality housing does impose negative externalities on the immediate neighborhood, causing it to be downgraded. The neighborhood externalities could be taken care of by maintenance and upgrading requirements, perhaps enforced through user charges or taxes for improper maintenance, etc. However, this would be no different for poor than for middle-class housing. A special problem in the housing market is discrimination against blacks and minorities. The suburbs have excluded blacks and poor, bringing about an overutilized central city housing stock. We deal with this problem in our sections on zoning and discrimination.

The excessively high property taxes also seriously reduce the quantity and quality of all rental housing in cities. (This argument is presented in detail under housing.) The tax affects all renter groups directly by raising the price and lowering the quantity of housing available to them. It also affects all groups indirectly, because if there is insufficient middle-class housing available in cities, the middle class will do two things: they will move to the suburbs, reducing the city's tax base, and they will outbid the poor for central city housing, which the poor could otherwise occupy cheaply. Property taxes don't have the same effect on owner-occupied, usually suburban, housing because the taxes and interest paid on owner-occupied housing are deductible from the occupant's income for tax purposes. This exemption does not apply to rental housing or commercial structures.

Urban property taxes sometimes reach 5 percent of the value of housing and thereby constitute 30 to 40 percent of the housing rent. That is the equivalent of sales taxes on rental housing of 50 percent or more. Is it any wonder that there is too little central city housing? Rental housing has been taxed as though it were harmful and undesirable in the same way that gasoline and tobacco are taxed. In effect, we have greatly subsidized socially costly commuter highways at the expense of urban housing, especially urban rental housing. This policy seems not only to be inefficient but also reflects a lack of perspective. All urban residents are hurt by these policies, but especially the poor who are always the least mobile and most vulnerable.

As Welfeld's article, Grigsby's book of readings, and others have shown, public housing is all too often dehumanized, unaesthetic housing that concentrates the poor in ghettos at a building cost often double that for similar private housing. Public housing usually helps few poor and is sometimes so undesirable that many units go vacant and are even abandoned. Urban renewal has, if anything, reduced housing for the poor, while new towns are really planned suburbs for the upper-middle class with token units for the poor. As we have previously explained, rent control does nothing to increase the housing stock and is likely to bring about its depreciation, diminishing the amount of housing available to the poor in the long run.

Are subsidized and leased housing programs beneficial to the poor? Subsidized private housing or private homes leased by the state and then rented to the poor at 30 to 40 percent below cost is really a scheme to eliminate the distorting property tax for the poor. But the program only affects limited numbers of the poor and ignores the relationships between housing markets. Middle-class housing can easily be turned into housing for the poor and housing for the poor can be upgraded into housing for the middle class. Thus if action is restricted to the low-income housing market, there will be only limited effect on the total housing supply. Providing low-income housing would only reduce the price of low-income housing relative to that of middle-income housing and would cause the middle class to retain or acquire some of the housing that would otherwise have been available to the poor.

A better solution to the housing crisis may well lie in three areas: increased income for the poor; a general decrease in effective property taxes on rental property, either by letting renters deduct property taxes and interest paid by the landlords from their income for federal income tax purposes or through a general reduction of pro forma property tax rates; and increased maintenance, upgrading, and sanitation requirements backed up by taxes and charges on the owners who fail to comply. All groups would still not occupy equal housing but the poor would have more money and get more for their money in more efficient, properly functioning housing markets, as would everyone else.

It has also been suggested that the purchase of food ought to be subsidized for the poor through the use of vehicles like food stamps. I think not. The poor seem to allocate their budgets as well as any other group. Why use food stamps? One reason may be that anything is desirable that raises the unreasonably low levels of welfare in many areas. Another justification could be that we realize food prices are too high, particularly when surpluses are going to waste because of our farm-price-support programs. These supports operate to the detriment of consumers, especially those who are poor, and to the benefit of large efficient farmers, rather than the small farmers, who only gain indirectly and need aid to leave their small inefficient farms and retrain for other careers. Food stamps are desirable if the farm program cannot be phased out, but they help only the very poorest. Moderate-income groups are still faced with high food prices.

The last specific good we will examine is medical care. The United States usually provides either ultrahigh- or low-quality medical care. The marginal benefit of ultrahigh-quality medical care for middle- and upper-income groups is probably lower than the benefits the poor would gain from an increase in the quality of medical services. Suggested by many, socialized medicine would probably not achieve reallocation, because the free provision of medical services would cause the demand for medical care to far exceed capacity, fostering the concomitant inefficiencies and inequities of queuing and rationing. It would also cause people to use these valuable resources when they gained little from them. Again, raising the income of the poor would be a partial solution. Another would be to increase the supply of trained physicians, which many feel has been kept artificially low.

Others suggest a sort of negative income tax for medical care in which the government would pay a certain percentage (based on income) of an individual's medical bills. The subsidy of an urban family of four receiving $3,400 per year could be increased to $3,650 and the family left to pay medical bills of up to $250 per year. The government could thereafter pay 50 percent of the next $500 in medical expenses incurred, 60 percent of the next $500, and so on. Loans could be arranged to help families spread their share of medical expenses over three or four years. If the family's medical expenses were less than $250 in any year, they could either spend the saving or retain it to cover future medical expenses. This system would preserve efficiency in allocating medical services while providing needed insurance against medical catastrophes on an equal basis for all groups. It would not encourage excessive hospital use since the subsidy would be paid whether the service was in- or outpatient and would include pharmaceutical and other expenses. This subsidy could also be combined with an incentive to use group medical care. Many health care experts feel that group care is more efficient than the conventional health care systems because it avoids the unnecessary use of hospitals induced by insurance that only covers hospitalization and by physicians who are uncognizant of hospital costs. This scheme is similar to one suggested by Professor Martin Feldstein.

Have minimum wage laws, unions, and fair employment laws raised the income of the poor and black communities? Many economists including Friedman and Bowman feel that minimum-wage laws may have increased the unemployment of low-skilled individuals. Because minimum wages increase the price of labor, consumers and producers demand less of it, perhaps substituting capital for labor in production and consumption. This phenomena has probably not been very large except for low-skilled teenagers. Blacks who have low skills and face discrimination may also suffer unemployment because of minimum-wage laws. Areas in which these restrictions may have created substantial unemployment are the shoe industry, rural agriculture, and handicraft industries. It is also reported that minimum-wage laws have inhibited the development of handicraft and other industries among the immobile poor of the West Virginia and East Kentucky mountains. The negative income tax could replace much of the need and reason for minimum-wage laws and permit them to be pushed much less aggressively in the future.

Fair employment laws seem to have increased both wages and unemployment among blacks — a mixed blessing. Unions have at times set unduly high wages, long apprenticeships, and restrictive entry standards that work to the disadvantage of the poor and black who are kept out of these trades and suffer high unemployment and low incomes as a result. In the past, unions have probably been influential in reducing poverty, but they have recently ignored the poor, black, and Spanish-speaking worker in favor of achieving higher wages for the craft unions.

The last question which we will want to take up is the effect of full employment on poverty. Though continuous full employment and growth may only be able to reduce the present level of poverty by one-third to one-half, it has certainly had a major impact on the amount of poverty in the past. The number living below the poverty line has gone from one-fourth of our population in the late 1950's to below one-eighth of our population in the early 1970's, again by the social-security definition, moving approximately 15 million persons out of poverty. The reduction in the level of poverty was similarly large by other absolute standards but much less by relative standards — an outcome of an approximately constant relative-income distribution in which the income of all groups has risen about an equal percentage, the income of the poor rising slightly faster than others. The percentage decline was greatest for rural and white Americans and least for black urban Americans, though significant for all groups. Continuous full employment will be a necessary ingredient for further improvement, especially for blacks, who have historically had double the unemployment rate of whites.

We have discussed the problem of poor people and now we must take up the question of poor city governments. Even in the unlikely case that all local welfare were financed by the federal government, cities would still collect little revenue and need to make large public-service expenditures for the poor, leaving them in a near-bankrupt financial position. What is the answer — greater federal financing of education and health services which involve large components of income redistribution? It may be that even more is needed, such as greater federal and state aid to mass transit and to law enforcement, both of which often involve many nonresidents. Another part of the answer would be the previously discussed use of prices and charges to ration costly public services. All of this would come close to solving the city's financial crisis though there would still be a gap between the tax-paying ability of the poor and the costs of other government services.

The answer here might be lump-sum grants or revenue sharing with the city. Revenue sharing involves unassigned funds given to cities, with the amounts positively related to size of population, percentage of poor, and the median income of the city. This would permit cities to reduce their burdensome property taxes and to provide equal services for the same effort — tax rates — as the wealthier suburbs.

Another solution is to transfer the funding of all income redistributive services (health, education, welfare) and a significant part of most other services (policing, recreation, roads and parks, etc.) to metropolitan and state governments. The cities would provide the bulk of their share of financing through efficient pricing of (or benefit taxes for) the goods they provide. Such an arrangement would relieve them of the unfair burden of providing for their disproportionate share of the poor, reduce the incentive of wealthy communities to exclude poor and minority groups, and increase the efficient use of existing public facilities and the efficient long-run allocation of resources in these areas. The advantage of this plan over federal financing of most goods is the preservation of local initiative and community control and a reduction of the sense of alienation sometimes felt when dealing with the federal government. More vigorous action on the part of states and cities is long overdue and is needed in the face of the inertia and excessive dependence upon the federal government often exhibited by state and local officials.

WHO ARE THE URBAN POOR?

Anthony Downs

SUMMARY OF FACTUAL FINDINGS

The following significant findings and conclusions can be drawn from the extensive data and analysis presented in the body of [*Who Are the Urban Poor?*].

1. *Poverty in the United States is officially measured by a fixed standard of real income based upon the cost of a minimal human diet. But the concept of poverty is actually quite complex and controversial; so all statistics concerning it must be used and interpreted with caution.*

Anthony Downs is Senior Vice President, Real Estate Research Corporation.

Reprinted with permission from Anthony Downs, *Who Are the Urban Poor?* Revised Edition; New York: Committee for Economic Development, 1970), pp. 1–5.

Any household is officially defined as "poor" by the Social Security Administration if its annual money income is less than three times the cost (in current prices) of a minimal diet for the persons in that household. In 1968 the "poverty level" income for a four-person (nonfarm) household was $3,553.

In comparison with the incomes of much of the world's population, many Americans considered poor by this definition are actually quite well-off. On the other hand, official "poverty level" incomes are very low in comparison with either the nation's median family income (of $8,362 in 1968) or the income considered necessary for a "moderate" standard of living by the Bureau of Labor Statistics (over $9,600 in 1968 dollars for a four-person household).

Since the official definition of poverty is based upon an absolutely fixed level of income, continued national prosperity that raises all incomes in society inevitably causes the number of poor people to decline steadily. But if poverty is considered a *relative* matter, its disadvantages will continue to affect all people in the lowest income groups, unless there is a significant change in the *distribution* of income (which has not occurred in recent years).

All statistics concerning poverty in this paper are based upon the official Social Security Administration definition.

2. *In 1968 about 10.0 per cent of the total metropolitan-area population of the United States — or 12.9 million persons — lived in poverty.*

This was somewhat lower than the percentage of all U.S. citizens in poverty (12.8 per cent), and much lower than comparable figures for any nonmetropolitan areas.

Nevertheless, slightly over half of all poor persons in the United States lived in metropolitan areas in 1968.

3. *Within metropolitan areas, the proportion of poor people in 1968 was almost twice as high in central cities (13.4 per cent) as in suburbs (7.3 per cent).* Although more people lived in suburbs, the number of poor persons in central cities (7.8 million) was significantly larger than in suburbs (5.1 million).

4. *About two-thirds of all the poor persons in metropolitan areas in 1968 were white, and one-third nonwhite. However, the proportion of all metropolitan-area whites who were poor (7.6 per cent) was less than one-third the proportion of such nonwhites who were poor (25.7 per cent).*

About 76 per cent of the poor nonwhites and 52 per cent of the poor whites in metropolitan areas lived in central cities.

Within central cities, 57 per cent of all poor persons were white, and 43 per cent nonwhite. But 80 per cent of all poor suburbanites were white.

5. *From 1959 to 1968, the total number of poor persons in the United States declined by 14.1 million (or by 36 per cent) from 39.5 million to 25.4 million. In the same period, the number of poor living in metropolitan areas decreased by 4.1 million (or by 24 per cent) from 17.0 million to*

12.9 million. Because of the migration of rural poor to the nation's urban centers and a faster population increase there, the percentage decline of poor persons was less in metropolitan areas than in nonmetropolitan areas. Among the metropolitan poor, whites decreased more rapidly than non-whites. Furthermore, most of this decrease in the metropolitan poor took place among households headed by men. Poor persons living in male-headed households decreased nearly half between 1959 and 1968. But those in households headed by women actually increased (by 22 per cent) in this period. These trends were also evident for the nation as a whole.

6. *About 47 per cent of all poor in metropolitan areas are in households that cannot be expected to become economically self-sustaining at any time in the future.*

These households include:

Type of Household Head	Per Cent of All Poor Persons in Metropolitan Areas
Elderly	18.3%
Disabled males under sixty-five	4.5
Females under sixty-five with children	23.7
TOTAL	46.5

7. *Nearly one-fourth of all poor persons in metropolitan areas (24.5 per cent) are in households headed by regularly employed men under sixty-five whose poverty results from low earnings rather than unemployment, disability, or old age.*

8. *About one-eighth of all metropolitan-area poor are in households headed by non-disabled men under sixty-five who are either unemployed or underemployed.*

9. *About 5.4 million poor people in metropolitan areas — or 42.2 per cent of all such people in 1968 — were children under eighteen. The poverty in which they lived is likely to afflict them in such a way as to reduce their future income-earning capabilities.*

Almost two-thirds of these poor children lived in central cities, and over half the poor children in those cities were nonwhite.

From 43 to 56 per cent of all poor children in metropolitan areas lived in households unlikely to become economically self-sustaining.

Poor children are heavily concentrated in large families. In the United States as a whole, 44 per cent of all poor children in 1968 were in families with five or more children.

10. *Although poverty is technically defined as having a very low annual income, for many people it is also a chronic state of failure, disability, dependency, defeat, and inability to share in most of American society's major material and spiritual benefits. Their continuance in this deprived state is*

reinforced by many institutional arrangements in our society, including those supposedly designed to aid them.

11. *Future population changes in metropolitan areas are likely to cause certain groups with a high incidence of poverty, particularly within central cities, to expand greatly. Whether this will result in any increase in the number of poor persons depends upon future public policies and prosperity levels.*

The greatest *absolute* growth from 1960 to 1985 will occur in the following "poverty-prone" population groups: suburban, white elderly; central-city, nonwhite children under eighteen; central-city, nonwhite households with female heads under sixty-five; and white and nonwhite households headed by unemployed males under sixty-five in both central cities and suburbs.

Large absolute growth will also occur among suburban white children under eighteen — probably adding as many as one million of these children to urban poverty by 1985.

The nonwhite population of all U.S. central cities is expected to rise by 9.8 million — or 94.5 per cent — from 1960 to 1985. Since this population contains many highly "poverty-prone" groups, such rapid growth could cause sharp increases in nonwhite poverty within central cities — especially in the largest cities where, in many cases, nonwhites will form a majority of the population by 1985. But major rises in nonwhite poverty will probably not occur unless there are significant and substantial lapses from high-level prosperity — thus causing higher unemployment and lower incomes for many partly employed workers — or unless there is an acceleration of the recent trend toward a rise in the number of families headed by women with young children.

APPROACHES TO THE REDUCTION OF POVERTY [1]

Robert J. Lampman

The greatest accomplishment of modern economies has been the raising of living standards of the common man and the reduction of the share of the population in poverty. Contrary to the gloomy predictions of Malthus, pro-

Robert J. Lampman is Professor of Economics, University of Wisconsin.

Reprinted with permission from Robert J. Lampman, "Approaches to the Reduction of Poverty," *American Economic Review* 55:2 (May 1965), pp. 521–529.

[1] My colleagues Martin H. David, Harold M. Groves, and Burton A. Weisbrod have been helpful to me in criticizing an earlier version of this paper.

duction has increased faster than population and, unlike the expectations of Marx, inequality of income has not steadily increased. The growth in value of product per person is generally understood to arise out of more capital, economies of scale and specialization, better management and organization, innovation with regard both to end products and techniques of production, greater mobility of factors, and improved quality of labor. All of these in turn yield additional income which, in a benign spiral, makes possible more and higher quality inputs for further growth.

The process of growth has not meant simply higher property incomes. As a matter of fact, income from property has fallen as a share of national income.[2] Neither has growth meant a widening of differential for skill in labor incomes. Rates of pay for the most menial of tasks have tended to rise with average productivity. Social policies in fields such as labor and education aimed at assuring opportunities for all have narrowed initial advantages of the more fortunate. Such policies, along with taxation, social insurance, and public assistance measures which redistribute income toward the poor have tended to stabilize if not reduce the degree of income inequality.

A growth in productivity of 2 percent per person per year and a relatively fixed pattern of income inequality probably have combined to yield a net reduction in poverty in most decades of American history. However, the rate of reduction has undoubtedly varied with changes in the growth rate, shifts from prosperity to depression, changes in immigration, in age composition, and in differential family size by income level.

THE POVERTY RATE AND THE POVERTY INCOME GAP

Using a present-day standard for poverty and even without recognizing the relativity of poverty over long periods, we would estimate that poverty had become a condition that afflicted only a minority of Americans by the second decade of this century. This situation was upset by the Great Depression of the 1930's but later restored by the booming economy of World War II. The postwar period has yielded a somewhat above average rate of growth in productivity and a reduction in poverty which probably is at least average for recent decades. The number of families in poverty (as marked off from nonpoverty by a $3,000 income at 1962 prices) fell from 12 million in 1947 to 9 million in 1963. This was a drop from 32 percent to 19 percent of families.

The rate of reduction one records or predicts will vary somewhat with the definition of poverty which he adopts. The Council of Economic Ad-

[2] Irving Kravis, *The Structure of Income* (1962), pp. 127–42.

visers adopted an income cut-off of $3,000 of total money income for families and $1,500 for unrelated individuals.[3] It is not inconsistent with those guidelines to make further modification for family size, using $3,000 as the mark for an urban family of four persons with variations of $500 per person and to set a lower mark for rural families. Such a procedure yields a slightly lower rate of reduction in the percentage of all persons in poverty than is suggested by the 32 to 19 drop shown above.[4] This discrepancy is due to a shift in family size and the rural to urban migration during the postwar years.

It is possible that consideration of personal income as opposed to total money income, of average rather than one year's income, of assets and extraordinary needs as well as income, and of related matters would alter our understanding of how poverty has been reduced. It is clear that some of these considerations affect the number and the composition of the population counted as poor; and it is obvious that the rate of reduction would vary if we varied the poverty line over time.

These matters of definition are important to a refinement of the generalized goal of elimination of poverty to which President Johnson has called us. Economists can assist in reaching a national consensus on the specific nature of the goal, of ways to measure the distance from and rate of movement toward the goal. Currently we are in the stage of goal-setting with poverty that occurred in 1946 with unemployment and that we have experienced with respect to other national goals such as price stability and economic growth. Hopefully, out of current controversy there will emerge a refined and only infrequently changed measurement of poverty reduction which will take its place along with the unemployment rate and the growth rate and the consumer price index as guides to appraisal of the performance of the economy. In the meantime, we can carry on our discussion of ways and means to achieve the general goal with the rough and ready measures that are at hand.

At this point in time, poverty is clearly a condition which afflicts only a minority — a dwindling minority — of Americans. The recent average rate of change, namely, a fall in the percentage of families in poverty by one percentage point per year, suggests that the poverty problem is about twenty years from solution. This rate of reduction may be difficult to maintain as we get down to a hard core of poverty and a situation in which further growth will not contribute to the reduction of the poverty rate. My own view is that this rate is still highly responsive to changes in the growth rate and that it will continue to be so for some time ahead. The relationship be-

---

[3] *Annual Report* (1964), Chap. 2.

[4] This is roughly the procedure followed by my *Low Income Population and Economic Growth,* Study Paper No. 12, Joint Economic Committee, 86th Cong., 1st Sess., 1959.

tween the two rates is a complex one and is influenced by such things as demographic change, changes in labor force participation, occupational shifts in demands for labor, and derived changes in property incomes and social security benefits. Some groups — notably the aged, the disabled, and the broken families — have poverty rates that appear to be relatively immune to growth in average income. One powerful drag on the responsiveness of the poverty rate to growth, which has now about run its course and will shortly reverse, is the aging and reduction in labor force participation of family heads.[5]

While the size of the poverty population is dwindling, the size of what can be called the "poverty income gap" is diminishing. This gap — the aggregate amount by which the present poor population's income falls short of $3,000 per family or $1,500 per unrelated individual — is now about $12 billion, or 2 percent of GNP. As time goes on this gap will assuredly be less, both because of economic growth and because of scheduled increases in social insurance benefits. (Transfers now make up about $10 billion of the $25 billion income of the poor.) Projecting recent rates of change suggests that by 1975 the poor will be no more than 12 percent of the population and the poverty income gap will be as little as 1 percent of that year's GNP.

As I see it, the goal of eliminating poverty needs to have a time dimension and intermediate targets. I assume we want a rate of progress at least as fast as that of recent years. Further, it helps to think of the goal in two parts: the reduction of the poverty rate and the reduction of the poverty income gap. This means we want to work from the top down and from the bottom up, so to speak. The aim of policy should be to do each type of reduction without slowing the other and to do both with the least possible sacrifice of and the greatest possible contribution to other important goals.

WHY POVERTY PERSISTS

As background to such strategic decisions, it is useful to categorize the causes of poverty in today's economy. But perhaps it is necessary first to brush aside the idea that there has to be some given amount of poverty. Most economists have long since given up the idea that a progressive society needs the threat of poverty to induce work and sobriety in the lower classes. Similarly, one can consign to folklore the ideas that some are rich only be-

[5] These questions are pursued in the form of an exchange with John K. Galbraith in *ibid.*, pp. 13–28. For a different approach and different conclusions, see W. H. Locke Anderson, "Trickling Down: The Relationship Between Economic Growth and the Extent of Poverty Among American Families," *Q.J.E.*, Nov., 1964, pp. 511–24.

cause others are poor and exploited, that if none was poor then necessary but unpleasant jobs would go undone, that the middle class has a psychological need to exclude a minority from above-poverty living standards, and that poverty is a necessary concomitant of the unemployment which necessarily accompanies economic growth.

Why, then, is it that there remains a minority of persons who are involuntarily poor in this affluent society? How does our system select the particular members for this minority? To the latter question we offer a three-part answer: (1) Events external to individuals select a number to be poor. (2) Social barriers of caste, class, and custom denominate persons with certain characteristics to run a high risk of being poor. (3) The market assigns a high risk of being poor to those with limited ability or motivations.

One cannot look at the data on who are the poor without sensing that many are poor because of events beyond their control. Over a third of the 35 million poor are children whose misfortune arises out of the chance assignment to poor parents. In some cases this poverty comes out of being members of unusually large families. Among the poor adults, about a third have either suffered a disability, premature death of the family breadwinner, or family dissolution. A considerable number have confronted a declining demand for services in their chosen occupation, industry, or place of residence. Some have outlived their savings or have lost them due to inflation or bank failure. For many persons who are otherwise "normal" poverty may be said to arise out of one or a combination of such happenings.

A second factor that operates in the selection of persons to be poor is the maintenance of social barriers in the form of caste, class, and custom. The clearest example of this, of course, is racial discrimination with regard to opportunities to qualify for and to obtain work. (It is perhaps worth emphasizing here that only a fifth of the present poor are nonwhite, and that only a minority of the nonwhites are presently poor.) Similar types of arbitrary barriers or market imperfections are observable in the case of sex, age, residence, religion, education, and seniority. They are formalized in employer hiring procedures, in the rules of unions and professional and trade associations, in governmental regulations concerning housing and welfare and other programs, and are informally expressed in customer preferences. Barriers, once established, tend to be reinforced from the poverty side by the alienated themselves. The poor tend to be cut off from not only opportunity but even from information about opportunity. A poverty subculture develops which sustains attitudes and values that are hostile to escape from poverty. These barriers combine to make events nonrandom; e.g., unemployment is slanted away from those inside the feudalistic walls of collective bargaining, disability more commonly occurs in jobs reserved for those outside the barriers, the subculture of poverty invites or is prone to self-realizing forecasts of disaster.

The third factor involved in selecting persons out of the affluent society to be poor is limited ability or motivation of persons to earn and to protect themselves against events and to fight their way over the barriers.[6] To the extent that the market is perfect one can rationalize the selection for poverty (insofar as earnings alone are considered) on the basis of the abilities and skills needed by the market and the distribution of those abilities and skills in the population. But we note that ability is to some extent acquired or environmentally determined and that poverty tends to create personalities who will be de-selected by the market as inadequate on the basis of ability or motivation.

COUNTERING "EVENTS"

Approaches to the reduction of poverty can be seen as parallel to the causes or bases for selection recounted above. The first approach, then, is to prevent or counter the events or happenings which select some persons for poverty status. The poverty rate could be lessened by any reduction in early death, disability, family desertion, what Galbraith referred to as excessive procreation by the poor, or by containment of inflation and other hazards to financial security. Among the important events in this context the one most relevant to public policy consideration at this time is excessive unemployment. It would appear that if the recent level of over 5 percent unemployment could be reduced to 4 percent, the poverty rate would drop by about one percentage point.[7] Further fall in the poverty rate would follow if — by retraining and relocation of some workers — long-term unemployment could be cut or if unemployment could be more widely shared with the nonpoor.

To the extent that events are beyond prevention, some, e.g., disability, can be countered by remedial measures. Where neither the preventive nor the remedial approach is suitable, only the alleviative measures of social in-

[6] For an insight into the relative importance of this factor see James M. Morgan, Martin H. David, Wilbur J. Cohen, and Harvey E. Brazer, *Income and Welfare in the U.S.* (1962), pp. 196–98.

[7] Unemployment is not strikingly different among the poor than the nonpoor. Nonparticipation in the labor force is more markedly associated with poverty than is unemployment. However, it seems that about 1 million poor family heads experience unemployment during the year. (*Census Population Reports,* P-60, No. 39, Feb. 28, 1963, Tables 15 and 16.) If half of this group were moved out of poverty by more nearly full employment, then the poverty rate would be one percentage point lower. Another way to estimate this is as follows: The national income would be $30 billion higher than it is if we had full employment. And a $30 billion increase in recent years has generally meant a full percentage point drop in the percent of families in poverty.

surance and public assistance remain. And the sufficiency of these measures will help determine the poverty rate and the size of the poverty income gap. It is interesting to note that our system of public income maintenance, which now pays out $35 billion in benefits per year, is aimed more at the problem of income insecurity of the middle class and at blocking returns to poverty than in facilitating exits from poverty for those who have never been out of poverty. The nonpoor have the major claim to social insurance benefits, the levels of which in most cases are not adequate in themselves to keep a family out of poverty. Assistance payments of $4 billion now go to 8 million persons, all of whom are in the ranks of the poor, but about half of the 35 million poor receive neither assistance nor social insurance payments. One important step in the campaign against poverty would be to reexamine our insurance and assistance programs to discover ways in which they could be more effective in helping people to get out of poverty. Among the ideas to be considered along this line are easier eligibility for benefits, higher minimum benefits, incentives to earn while receiving benefits, ways to combine work-relief, retraining, rehabilitation, and relocation with receipt of benefits.

Among the several events that select people for poverty, the ones about which we have done the least by social policy are family breakup by other than death and the event of being born poor. Both of these could be alleviated by a family allowance system, which the U.S., almost alone among Western nations, lacks. We do, of course, have arrangements in the federal individual income tax for personal deductions and exemptions whereby families of different size and composition are ranked for the imposition of progressive rates. However, it is a major irony of this system that it does not extend the full force of its allowances for children to the really poor. In order to do so, the tax system could be converted to have negative as well as positive rates, paying out grants as well as forgiving taxes on the basis of already adopted exemptions and rates. At present there are almost $20 billion of unused exemptions and deductions, most of which relate to families with children. Restricting the plan to such families and applying a negative tax rate of, say, 20 percent, to this amount would "yield" an allowance total of almost $4 billion. This would not in itself take many people out of poverty, but it would go a considerable distance toward closing the poverty income gap, which now aggregates about $12 billion.

It would, of course, be possible to go considerably further by this device without significantly impairing incentive to work and save. First, however, let me reject as unworkable any simple plan to assure a minimum income of $3,000. To make such an assurance would induce many now earning less than and even some earning slightly more than $3,000 to forego earnings opportunities and to accept the grant. Hence the poverty income gap of

$12 billion would far understate the cost of such a minimum income plan. However, it would be practicable to enact a system of progressive rates articulated with the present income tax schedule.[8] The present rates fall from 70 percent at the top to 14 percent at income just above $3,700 for a family of five, to zero percent for income below $3,700. The average negative tax rates could move, then, from zero percent to minus 14 percent for, say, the unused exemptions that total $500, to 20 percent for those that total $1,000 and 40 percent for those that total $3,700. This would amount to a minimum income of $1,480 for a family of five; it would retain positive incentives through a set of grants that would gradually diminish as earned income rose.

The total amount to be paid out (interestingly, this would be shown in the federal budget as a net reduction in tax collections) under such a program would obviously depend upon the particular rates selected, the definition of income used, the types of income-receiving units declared eligible, and the offsets made in public assistance payments. But it clearly could be more than the $4 billion mentioned in connection with the more limited plan of a standard 20 percent negative tax rate. At the outset it might involve half the poverty income gap and total about $6 billion. This amount is approximately equal to the total federal, state, and local taxes now paid by the poor. Hence it would amount to a remission of taxes paid. As the number in poverty fell, the amount paid out under this plan would in turn diminish.

BREAKING DOWN BARRIERS

The approaches discussed thus far are consistent with the view that poverty is the result of events which happen to people. But there are other approaches, including those aimed at removing barriers which keep people in poverty. Legislation and private, volunteer efforts to assure equal educational and employment opportunities can make a contribution in this direction. Efforts to randomize unemployment by area redevelopment and relocation can in some cases work to break down "islands of poverty." Public policy can prevent or modify the forming of a poverty subculture by city zoning laws, by public housing and by regulations of private housing, by school redistricting, by recreational, cultural, and public health programs. It is curious that medieval cities built walls to keep poverty outside. Present arrangements often work to bottle it up inside cities or parts of cities and thereby encourage poverty to function as its own cause.

[8] Cf. Milton Friedman, *Capitalism and Freedom* (1962), pp. 192–93.

IMPROVING ABILITIES AND MOTIVATIONS

The third broad approach to accelerated reduction of poverty relates to the basis for selection referred to above as limited ability or motivation. The process of economic growth works the poverty line progressively deeper into the ranks of people who are below average in ability or motivation, but meantime it should be possible to raise the ability and motivation levels of the lowest. It is interesting that few children, even those of below average ability, who are not born and raised in poverty, actually end up in poverty as adults. This suggests that poverty is to some extent an inherited disease. But it also suggests that if poor children had the same opportunities, including preschool training and remedial health care, as the nonpoor (even assuming no great breakthroughs of scientific understanding), the rate of escape from poverty would be higher. Even more fundamentally, we know that mental retardation as well as infant mortality and morbidity have an important causal connection with inadequate prenatal care, which in turn relates to low income of parents.

A belief in the economic responsiveness of poor youngsters to improved educational opportunities underlies policies advocated by many educational theorists from Bentham to Conant. And this widely shared belief no doubt explains the emphasis which the Economic Opportunity Act places upon education and training. The appropriation under that Act, while it seems small relative to the poverty income gap, is large relative to present outlays for education of the poor. I would estimate that the half-billion dollars or so thereby added increases the national expenditure for this purpose by about one-seventh. To raise the level of educational expenditure for poor children — who are one-fifth of the nation's children but who consume about a tenth of educational outlay — to equal that of the average would cost in the neighborhood of $3 billion. Such an emphasis upon education and training is justified by the fact that families headed by young adults will tend, in a few years, to be the most rapidly increasing group of poor families.

SUMMARY

Past experience provides a basis for the belief that poverty can be eliminated in the U.S. in this generation. The poverty rate has been reduced at the rate of one percentage point a year; the poverty income gap is now down to 2 percent of GNP.

Preventing and countering the "events" which select people for poverty can help to maintain or accelerate the rate at which we have been making progress against poverty. For example, by returning to the 4 percent "full employment" rate of unemployment, we would instantaneously reduce the poverty rate by one percentage point. For another example, we could make a great stride toward early closing of the poverty income gap by modifying the income tax to pay out family allowances.

Another broad approach to the elimination of poverty is to break down the social barriers which restrict opportunities for the poor. Examples of this are legislating against practices of discrimination and making plans to bring the poor into the mainstream of community life.

The third approach is to make progressively greater investment in improving the abilities and motivations of the poor. Substantial increase in outlays for education and training is a promising example of this approach.

Reduction of poverty hinges on the attainment of other goals such as economic growth, full employment, income security, and equal opportunity. But it also turns upon the reduction of poverty itself since poverty to an important degree causes itself. Hence, any favorable break in the circle makes the next step easier. More nearly full employment makes barriers less meaningful; lower barriers shrink differences in motivation. Similarly, higher incomes for the poor work to reduce both acquired and at-birth limitations of ability.

But any one of the approaches will involve costs, and it would be valuable to know their comparative cost-benefit ratios. It is on this that, by theoretical and empirical research, including intercountry study, social scientists can make a distinctive contribution to the long-dreamed-of, but now explicitly stated, goal of eliminating poverty.

A PRIMER ON NEGATIVE TAXATION

Duncan K. Foley

WHAT IS THE "NEGATIVE INCOME TAX"?

The Negative Income Tax is a proposal for a universal system of income supplements based on family size and earned income which retains incentives to work. The government undertakes to pay a family some fraction

Duncan K. Foley is Associate Professor of Economics, Massachusetts Institute of Technology.

Reprinted with permission from Duncan K. Foley, "A Primer on Negative Taxation," *The Bond Buyer MFOA* (June 9, 1969).

(called the "tax rate") of the amount by which its earned income falls short of a specified target. As the family earns more income the supplement declines, but not by as much as earned income rises, so that the family's total income always rises if it earns more.

Perhaps the easiest way to see the idea is through an example. In Table 1 the target income for a family is $1,500 per person; for a family of four this comes to $6,000. The "tax rate" in this example is 50%. If the family earns nothing it gets an income supplement of $3,000, since its earned income falls short of the target by $6,000 and 50% of $6,000 is $3,000. If the family earns $4,000 a year the supplement falls to $1,000, but the family's total income has risen to $5,000. The family keeps 50% of any increase in its earnings, and the rest goes to reducing the income supplement. If the family earns $6,000, the supplement is zero. But at present a family of four with a $6,000 income pays an ordinary income tax of $230 (based on the standard $1,000 deduction and 4 exemptions). The family must continue to pay a 50% tax on its income above $6,000 until it earns $7,150, where the 50% tax on income above $6,000 just equals the ordinary income tax $575.

There are two ways of looking at the negative tax scheme. From the government's point of view the scheme pays a supplement equal to the tax rate times the family's deficiency from the target income. From the family's point of view the government pays it a minimum income and then taxes its earnings at the tax rate. In the example the minimum income is $3,000 = 50% × $6,000.

A negative tax scheme can be described by giving its tax rate and either

TABLE 1

Target income: $1,500 per person
Tax rate: 50%
Minimum income: $750 per person

	4-person family Target income $6,000		6-person family Target income $9,000	
Earned income	Income supplement (+) or tax (−)	Total income	Income supplement (+) or tax (−)	Total income
$ 0	$3,000	$3,000	$4,500	$ 4,500
2,000	2,000	4,000	3,500	5,500
4,000	1,000	5,000	2,500	6,500
6,000	0	6,000	1,500	7,500
7,150	− 575 [a]	6,575	925	8,075
9,000	− 894 [b]	8,106	0	9,000
11,245	−1,350 [b]	9,895	−1,122 [a]	10,123

[a] Income at which negative tax payment equals current ordinary income tax payment.
[b] Current ordinary income tax (1968 income taxes calculated without surcharge).

its target income, or its minimum income. The product of the tax rate and target income is the minimum income; the target income is equal to the minimum income divided by the tax rate. A plan with a higher target or minimum income represents a larger drain on the Treasury because it makes bigger payments and includes more families.

If two plans have the same *minimum* income the one with the *lower* tax rate will have the higher target income and will involve the larger drain on the Treasury because it will include more families, and make bigger payments to these families that earn some income. For example, if the tax rate in our first example were 33% and the minimum income for a family of four remained $3,000, the target income would be $9,000 instead of $6,000. For a family earning $6,000 the supplement would be $1,000 = 33% × ($9,000 − $6,000) instead of zero. Of course, of two plans with the same target income the one with the lower tax rate represents the smaller drain on the Treasury because it makes smaller payments for any earned income.

Negative tax schemes vary greatly in the drain they put on the Treasury. In Table II I present some estimates of this drain. These estimates are based on the incomes of families in 1966. I have assumed no change in earnings as a result of introducing the various systems, a doubtful assumption which I will comment on later. The incomes include current welfare payments. If welfare were eliminated the Negative Tax system would have to substitute dollar for dollar for families whose total income would be higher under the negative tax than it is under welfare. Therefore no savings on welfare can be anticipated if the Negative Tax System substitutes for welfare.

In Table 2 Plan A is the scheme I used in the example previously. Plan B is a negative tax with the same tax rate and a minimum income half as large as in Plan A. The revenue loss is about one-seventh as large because so many fewer families would get any payment at all. (In Plan B the cut-off income for four person families is $3,000 as opposed to $6,000 in Plan A.)

For comparison I exhibit two other income supplement plans which are frequently mentioned as alternatives to welfare. The first is a Guaranteed Minimum Income plan in which the government pays a supplement equal to the difference between a family's earned income and the minimum. The second is a Family Allowance plan under which the government pays families a set amount each year for each child regardless of family income.

I hope it is clear that the examples I have used in this section are only examples. Negative tax schemes can be designed in many ways. The minimum income need not be a flat amount per person, but can depend on the number of adults and children in the family in various ways. The system can be designed to give a bonus or a penalty for marrying or for having few or many children.

The Internal Revenue Service would administer a Negative Income Tax

TABLE 2

			Estimated Revenue Loss
Negative Tax			
Plan A	$750	per person (6 person limit) minimum income	
	50%	tax rate	$22 billion
Plan B	$375	per person (6 person limit) minimum income	
	50%	tax rate	$ 3 billion
Guaranteed Minimum Income			
	$750	per person minimum income	
	100%	tax rate	$ 7 billion
Family Allowances		(70 million children)	Direct Payments
		$100 per child per year	$ 7 billion
		$1,000 per child per year	$70 billion

(These estimates are based on the 1966 distribution of income as reported in U.S. Bureau of the Census, *Current Population Reports,* Series P-60, No. 53, "Income in 1966 of Families and Persons in the United States," U.S. Government Printing Office, Washington, D.C., 1967. Current welfare programs in the U.S. make payments of about $9 billion. These payments must be added to the Revenue Loss figures for the Negative Tax and Guaranteed Income schemes to the extent that the programs displace welfare. In other words if Plan A were enacted and welfare stopped entirely the Negative Tax System would have to pay out $31 billion a year.)

just as it does the ordinary income tax. Families would file estimated income statements and receive monthly payments based on the estimates. At the end of the year each family would file a regular tax return and any over- or under-payment of supplements would be corrected. Perhaps a negative withholding arrangement could be worked out so that the supplement would be added directly to paychecks for employed recipients.

There would be a substantial incentive to file fraudulent returns under a negative tax scheme. It will be difficult to control fraud because of the small amounts of money involved, the informality of low-income labor markets, the mobility of the poor, and the lack of any effective sanctions when violators are caught. It is self-defeating to try to fine violators heavily or make them pay the government back, since the point of the program is to raise income. It seems equally pointless to jail offenders. I think that enforcement will depend very much on the moral authority or image of the negative tax system itself. If violators are caught out speedily and regularly by using computers to make audits and to pick out statistically unusual returns, and if the system has a reputation for fairness, the motives for fraud will be weakened. We must expect that a certain amount of fraud will accompany a negative tax system and be prepared to live with it or reject the idea of the negative tax altogether.

PROS AND CONS OF INCOME MAINTENANCE SCHEMES

I would like to discuss alternative income maintenance schemes in relation to four important questions:

1) Does the proposed system concentrate payments where they are most needed or does it involve making large payments to those who are not poor? Does the proposed system meet the minimal needs of the poor without putting an unreasonable burden on the Treasury?

2) Does the proposed system operate universally, putting everyone on the same basis or does it define categories differently? How much humiliation and stigma are attached to recipients by categorization?

3) Does the proposed system overturn income rankings determined by earned income? Is it possible for one family to earn more than another similar family, yet end up with lower total income?

4) What effect does the proposed system have on economic incentives, especially the incentives to find work, to educate oneself and one's children, to form or break up families, and to move geographically in response to labor market opportunities?

The ideal system would be adequate but not very much of a burden, would be universal and operate without the humiliation of categories, would retain earned income rankings, and would not affect the incentives given by the economy or would increase the incentives for education and family stability. Unfortunately these different goals come into conflict with each other. For example, categorization is the best way to channel help to those who need it. Programs which retain desirable incentives involve a larger drain on the Treasury than those which do not. To illustrate these conflicts I would like to rate four programs on each of these four tests. The four programs are current welfare, the guaranteed minimum income, the negative income tax, and child or family allowances.

ADEQUACY AND EXPENSE

Of the four programs the present welfare system is the most selective. It is designed to channel aid to families in need defined by certain categories and to no one else. Further the system pays only as much as is required to lift family income to the standard level. These features, which cost a lot to administer keep the total drain on revenue fairly low while providing payments to some families in some states comparable to the $750 per person minimum income used in the examples.

The next most selective of the plans is the guaranteed minimum income. This plan includes everyone whose income falls below the minimum, but pays only what is needed to bring family income up to the minimum. The result is a plan which involves $7 billion more drain on the Treasury than current welfare to give current welfare recipients and many others a $750 per person income.

The Negative Tax plan is much larger because it makes payments to people who are not poor by any definition. In fact at the $750 per person minimum and the 50% tax rate the plan involves over 30% of all families including families earning as much as $6,000 for a family of four. The result is another jump in expense to $22 billion more than present welfare to achieve the same minimum income as the guaranteed minimum income plan.

Family or child allowances go to every family with children regardless of income. The only requirement is to have children. There are about 70 million children in the United States, so to make payments of $1,000 per year per child, which would provide a mother living with three children the same $3,000 minimum income as under the negative tax and guaranteed income plans, would involve a total expense of $70 billion dollars, or about $60 billion more than current welfare programs. This plan is the least selective of the three, since it makes payments to all families, and is accordingly the most expensive for a similar minimum income.

UNIVERSALITY VERSUS CATEGORIES

Present welfare programs are available only to families which meet certain criteria. They separate the population into earners and non-earners and treat the two groups very differently. The result is that a stigma is attached to those who receive welfare, even among other poor people, and the recipient himself becomes humiliated, self-contemptuous and angry at the rest of society. The fact that in most large cities many welfare recipients are black aggravates this situation. The existence of the welfare system defines a class, a class interest, and promotes class conflict. The categorization also comes to be reflected in the recipient's attitude toward himself or herself: if the society sees her as a non-earner she will come to think of herself as a non-earner. Whenever there are categories there are ambiguous cases which give rise to arbitrary decisions and lead people to feel that the system is irrational or unfair. Prime examples in the present situation are the residence requirements set up by many states and the tendency of families to become or remain fatherless because fatherless families are one category favored by welfare programs.

The guaranteed minimum income and the negative tax systems eliminate all categorical criteria but two: family size and earned income. Payments would be automatically available to every family whose income fell below the target. The line between recipients and the rest of society would be blurred because so many families would be getting some payment and because the system would work like the regular income tax which everyone is subject to. There would be no predetermined categories of earners and non-earners and the economic environment of recipients and non-recipients would be very similar. Now welfare recipients get their income in a very different way from the way the affluent majority get theirs. The remaining categories will still give rise to some difficulties.

Family allowances eliminate all categories except family size because they are paid to everyone, rich and poor alike.

RETENTION OF EARNED INCOME RANKINGS

Current welfare programs have a curious and disturbing consequence. It is possible in some states for a man to work full time at the minimum wage to support his family and earn less than another family, which has no bread-winner, gets from welfare. Because of the categories and because different states set widely different standards for payments there is not much connection between family work effort and total income under welfare. I think this is a very pernicious feature for an income supplement system to have in a society supposedly based on rewarding people according to the value of their effort. It is a matter of constant outrage for a working man to see another family fatherless and yet better off than his own. Again existing hatred against black people is inflamed by this situation. It is particularly serious because over 70% of all poor families have at least one earner. The welfare system rewards the non-working poor more than the working poor.

The guaranteed minimum income would obliterate distinctions between workers and non-workers below the minimum income set, but retain them above the minimum. This is not so bad as the current welfare system which overturns the earned income ranking in many cases. But the guaranteed minimum income still goes against the principle that people are rewarded in proportion to the value of their effort.

One of the great advantages of a negative tax system is that it retains earned income rankings between families of similar size. Families which earn more have a higher total income. It is easy to see this by looking back at Table I, which shows that higher earned incomes are always associated with higher total income. The negative tax does overturn rankings between families of different size as the regular income tax does. The exemption feature of the present tax system leads to situations where a man with few children may have a lower after-tax income than another man with many children who earns less. I think most people feel that it is fair to give larger families more.

The family allowance scheme is similar in this respect to a negative tax. It retains earned income rankings between families of the same size since all families with the same number of children get the same payment.

INCENTIVES

"Incentives" loom large in discussions of income maintenance schemes. The general idea is that choices in average are very much influenced by economic consequences. Take the simple case of incentives to find and keep jobs. An individual who chooses to work steadily at the highest paying job he can get finds his earned income higher than it would be if he worked only occasionally or not at all. But even if his earned income increases his total income may not increase by as much (or at all) under some income maintenance programs. The incentive for the individual to find work will be reduced if the income maintenance program has this effect.

It is not necessary for individuals to react consciously to incentives for the incentives to have effect. Take the example of present welfare programs which pay large amounts to fatherless families. Some men may calculate rationally that their families will be better off on welfare than depending on the man's earnings and abandon their families for this reason, but I think this is rare. What is not rare among poor families is temporary abandonment. Without the welfare program the wife and children have a strong interest in recovering the husband after a temporary desertion and he has a strong moral obligation to them. The existence of welfare weakens these forces. Dependency on welfare can be a habit developed because welfare is available in certain situations, rather than a conscious choice.

When we talk of economic incentives it is important to distinguish how many people are subject to them. In many cases people point out that a program improves incentives in some respects for some group and ignores its effect on incentives for other groups. We have to distinguish what the incentive effects of a program are, and how many people will be subject to its incentives.

The clearest case of incentive effects of income maintenance programs is their effect of incentives to work. Under present welfare arrangements a family's ability to increase its total income by working is limited. It used to be the case that every dollar earned meant a dollar deducted from the welfare payment so that total income remained unchanged. There has been an improvement in that now some retention of earned income is allowed under welfare. This effect of welfare in eliminating the connection between earned income and total income is referred to frequently as the "100% tax rate."

The phrase should be "100% tax rate on extra income" or "100% marginal tax rate," since the point is that earning more income has no effect on total income. This incentive effect, however, is limited to the 8 million or so who fall into the welfare categories. Those who receive no welfare have their incentive to work unimpaired.

The guaranteed minimum income would extend the welfare "100% marginal tax rate" to everyone whose income fell below the set minimum. I suspect that most economists oppose guaranteed minimum income programs because they believe that eliminating incentive to work for so many people is bound to reduce their work effort and the total output of the economy. This throws some doubt on the estimate in Table II of the revenue loss associated with the guaranteed minimum income, since in making that calculation I assumed no change in the earnings of recipients. If I had assumed that everyone who presently earned less than $750 per person per year stopped working entirely (since under the guaranteed minimum income stopping work would have no effect on their total income) the expense would rise to $16 billion, though this is not strictly comparable to the other figures since I have also assumed that welfare also stopped all payments less than $750 per person per year.

One of the strong selling points of the negative tax scheme is that it increases incentives to work compared to present welfare. Under the negative tax proposal a family always keeps some fraction [equal to (1-tax rate)] of extra earned income. Under the plan I have been using as an example families would retain 50% of extra earned income. The other effect of the negative tax is to extend a high marginal tax rate to many people who presently have a low marginal tax rate. Under Plan A of the example a family of four would be paying a 50% marginal rate up to $7,150 earned income. At present the family faces a zero rate up to $3,400 earned income and then a mild progression of rates below 20%.

The effect of a 50% tax rate on work effort remains an unknown at the present state of economic knowledge. It seems reasonable that very high marginal tax rates have a strong effect on work effort, and especially that at a 100% marginal tax rate many people will simply stop working. It seems equally reasonable that low marginal rates have very little effect on work effort because many people are limited in working by the availability of work and the fact that there are only 24 hours in a day. This is probably not true for people who have part-time second jobs, since they have opportunity to adjust their work effort very precisely to the extra income an extra hour's work gives them. To try to find out what effects a negative tax would have on work effort an experiment is being carried out in New Jersey at the present time on a random sample of low income working families. The results of the experiment seem to show only small incentive effects. My personal guess is that a 50% marginal tax rate would sharply decrease the number of people who work at two or three jobs and might reduce the number of families in which two people work. I think that its effect on primary employment of the main earner in a family would be small. I also feel personally that the reduction in second jobs and second earners would not on balance be a loss to the health of the society. This is a topic on which anyone can have an opinion. Think about people you know who earn less than $7,000 a year and imagine what effect a tax cut plus a 50% marginal tax rate would have on their working habits.

The family allowance plan has no direct effect on incentives to work, but its large size would require an increase in all tax rates for all brackets of substantial size. The $70 billion program I used as an example would lead to direct increase in tax collections of about $17 billion since the payments for affluent families would be taxed like other income. This leaves about $53 billion to be raised by increasing tax rates. This would mean almost doubling personal tax collections or almost doubling rates in most brackets. Whether this would have a significant effect on work effort is also a moot question at the present time. It would affect a very large number of people, including the most productive members of society, in contrast to the negative tax plan which concentrates its incentive effects on those who earn little.

There is another side to the work incentive question which is the incentive for people to undertake training and schooling. There are two costs to education: one is the direct cost of tuition and books, the other is the loss of earnings involved when an individual goes to school rather than working. Any plan which raises income will tend to make people more willing to accept the costs of additional education for themselves and especially their children. But to the extent that a plan reduces the marginal income from working it also directly reduces the opportunity costs of further education. This is particularly relevant to the case of adolescents deciding whether to drop out of school to find a job. Under the negative tax family income would rise by only half of what the teenager could earn, and the pressure to leave school for work would be much less.

We come now to a painful and sensitive area which is at the same time of fundamental social importance. Welfare competes directly with men as a source of family support. In states where welfare standards are high, like New York and Massachusetts, a man must earn more than $2 an hour working full time to give his family as high a standard of living as they can have on welfare. This is a tremendous burden to put on a man's pride, because the fact is that because of poor training, closed unions, discrimination, and casual work habits many men in our society cannot earn $4,000 a year steadily. There is not much hope, in my opinion, that any training or employment program can change this fact rapidly, or even in the long run raise the productivity of every single person to the level mentioned. What is worse is that our standards rise constantly as the average income of the society increases, so that what is "adequate" support today for a family will become "inadequate" as time goes on and welfare payments will rise even higher.

The incentive involved is the incentive for a family to become fatherless, which puts it in the non-earning, welfare-receiving category. Again I emphasize that in general this is not a matter of conscious individual choice, but of the system reinforcing certain patterns and penalizing others so that people get certain habits and attitudes more frequently.

All three of the alternative programs, because they do not distinguish fatherless families as a special favored category, eliminate this incentive.

Finally there is the problem of incentives for geographical movement. A very important feature of the economic system we have is that it generally encourages people to move in response to job opportunities and to seek out areas where wages are high and rents low. The present welfare system interferes with these incentives in several ways. First, the residency requirement (which has recently been found unconstitutional) greatly increased the riskiness of moving at all. A poor family takes many more risks in moving than an affluent family, anyway. The poor have much worse information about job availability and the labor markets they depend on are often fickle, changing rapidly from one season to the next, or one phase of the business cycle to the next. Welfare has another, probably more serious effect on mobility. Suppose a man decides that there is a 75% chance of his finding a better job in some distant city, and suppose he is right. Then it may be entirely rational for him to move, but 25% of the time men in this situation will not find jobs, and their families will wind up on welfare. But now the situation has changed, because welfare payments in different parts of the country are so different. The family cannot move again without losing the high welfare in the city, even if the man could earn more somewhere else. I think this story is much more frequent than families moving in the first place to take advantage of high welfare standards.

Once again all three alternative plans, because they set national standards eliminate the irrational consequences of the present welfare system and are neutral in regard to geography.

Of the four plans welfare scores highest on only one criteria. It makes payments very selectively so that a very large part of the money involved goes to people in need. The other plans do not do so well in this regard and the worst is the family allowance. On all the other tests welfare is the worst system. It involves the humiliation and red tape of categories, while the other plans are universal. It upsets the earned income ranking while the negative tax and family allowance plans preserve earned income relations. Finally it interferes greatly in incentives for family stability and geographic allocation, which the other plans do not affect, and produces very weak incentives for work for its recipients. The other plans also affect incentives for larger groups of people. Of the four plans family allowances score the highest in all respects except expense.

In this perspective the negative tax proposal appears to be a middle position. It is less expensive than family allowances and more expensive than welfare; while it improves on welfare in many respects it has worse effects on incentives and involves more red tape and temptation to fraud than the family allowance scheme.

NEGATIVE TAXES AND LOCAL GOVERNMENTS

In the United States our cities are running out of money. Labor costs are rising rapidly, which is part of the difficulty, but in many cities expenditures on welfare are rising even faster. This rapid rise in welfare payments is attributable, I think, to inherent difficulties in administering welfare programs and to growing militancy of recipients.

The administrative costs of categorical welfare are large. Administrators have essentially two choices. The first is to spend a lot of money policing welfare recipients. This has some effect because it increases the humiliation connected with welfare. The categories set up, however, especially under the Aid to Families of Dependent Children program, are so elastic that there are no legal grounds for greatly reducing the rolls. The other option is to streamline enforcement, reduce humiliation, and watch the program grow. Neither of these choices can much affect the size of the programs given the practice of setting welfare budgets according to "need." "Need" is a very humane, attractive idea but it has no definite meaning. Welfare budget setters seem to believe implicitly that categorization works and that welfare recipients through no fault of their own are incapable of earning. Given this cast of mind there is no reason why welfare families should get less than any middle-class family. While welfare budgets are not yet high in relation to the costs of a middle-class life they have come to be high in relation to the earning power of many men in our society. There appears to be no reason why welfare standards will not continue to rise faster than earning power and when this happens welfare rolls and expense will grow very rapidly.

Another development which is important in understanding the recent growth of welfare even in very prosperous periods is the growing militancy of poor people demanding their legal due under the system. All along there was a kind of hypocrisy built into the welfare system. The law as written contained many provisions which were never intended to be enforced. Militant groups have educated recipients in the details of the law which leads in turn to higher payments. The existence of militant poor who claim income maintenance as a right has weakened people's inhibitions against seeking welfare. These inhibitions were in the past very important in keeping the size of welfare expenditures under control. Even today there are probably many people who are eligible for welfare but are too proud to go on the rolls. As time passes, militancy and the standards will rise and many of these people will become willing to take welfare.

Obviously any scheme which nationalizes income maintenance will help the fiscal situation in the cities. I think the negative tax proposal which eliminates much of the administrative burden and shifts the remainder to the Federal government will be particularly helpful to the cities. There is another consequence of negative taxes which is sometimes overlooked. The negative tax system shifts purchasing power into the hands of the poor and relatively poor who will spend the money, mostly on housing, food and clothing. This will involve a rise in the general prosperity of city areas which are at present mostly a drain on city resources. This prosperity will be in turn reflected in higher rents, higher property values and larger tax collections. The desperate need of the cities to retain middle-income families would be reduced since the poor would have more money.

To sum up, there seem to me to be two great advantages to city finances from a Federal Negative Income Tax. The first and most important is the direct effect of reducing the welfare burden on city treasuries. The second is to shift income to the center city from the suburbs and some of this shifted income will find its way to city treasuries through existing city taxes.

THE POLITICS OF INCOME MAINTENANCE

What response will the United States make to the welfare crisis? I think that the negative tax which I have described is fundamentally a conservative idea. It meshes with the economic system we have, based on private property and strong material incentives, and retains the principle that people should be rewarded according to their productivity. However, the negative tax changes in a mild way the current distribution of income and wealth and has other features which make it subversive of the current distribution of political power in our society.

There are some places in this country where certain groups retain a monopoly of political power through coercion based on absolute economic need. One example is that white people in some parts of the South own all local productive resources and thereby control the livelihood of the black population. Another is the situation in some Appalachian counties where mine owners gain effective control of politics through controlling all sources of income. The present welfare system, because it is locally administered, reinforces the power of the dominant group to starve out dissenters and activists. Even where political control is not so blatantly monopolized the profits of some activities depend on a supply of extremely cheap labor which is offered at low wages only because the alternative for the workers is starvation. The use of migrant farm labor falls into this category. These profits would be severely threatened by a Negative Tax that partially removed the coercive element from bargaining between employers and laborers. Even in the big cities where welfare payments are high and labor markets are more competitive local control over welfare can be put to political uses. It represents patronage for political machines, and puts legal control over substantial resources in the hands of the relatively affluent. The negative tax would shift those resources directly to the poor, and remove one bargaining level in local politics from white middle-class hands.

These effects may seem to involve either small numbers of people or a small amount of influence. But in the United States today a coalition of big-city politicians with rural and Southern white interests wields a disproportionately large amount of power. If, as Norman Mailer says, "Politics is property," these people own almost all the secure political property in the country. Added to this is the fact that the suburban middle-class will be the ones from whom the tax money will ultimately come to be paid to the poor and the lower middle-class. Even if we manage not to raise taxes if we institute a negative tax system similar to Plan A, it will mean foregoing a substantial tax cut for middle-income families or it will mean paring the military budget by about one-quarter.

In reciting these facts I am only repeating what ought to be familiar, that the lower third of the people by incomes have almost no power compared to the rest of the society.

Against this unfavorable constellation of forces there is one strong point of the negative tax. Most programs designed to raise poor people's or black income do so at the expense of the white lower middle-class. Job training and special promotion programs which favor low income blacks essentially displace whites who earn only slightly more. Locally financed welfare makes homeowners who earn $5,000-$9,000 a year pay huge taxes to support the poor. The result of only a modest effort on programs like these has been to intensify tremendously the social conflicts between lower income whites and low income blacks. The negative tax, on the other hand, raises incomes of both blacks and whites who are below the $7,000 level at the expense of the truly affluent. There seems to be some possibility here of an alliance in political terms between the poor and the working class on this issue, which might offset the tremendous odds against the program.

But here we run into another fundamental problem, the attachment of most lower middle-class people to the idea that no one should get income who does not work. This notion is much less strong among the upper-middle class who are used to, or look forward to, living partly on income from property in the form of rents, dividends, and capital gains. The negative tax idea seems to be contrary to the Puritan ethic, which is still a powerful force.

But there is strong pressure to do something about welfare which the government must respond to in one way or another. I suppose the result will be as small an increase in the size of the transfers as possible, as little change in the political impact of income maintenance as possible, and a shift of financing to the Federal level; in other words, a nationalization of welfare with minimum standards. My guess is that this will be only a very temporary settlement of the welfare issue. Unless the categorical basis of welfare is changed the same problems I have already described concerning family formation and work incentives will haunt the Federal system. If the categories are eliminated and work incentives retained we will have adopted the main features of the negative tax along with its expense and its political consequences.

Another consideration is, I think, very important. As you undoubtedly are aware there is a tremendous conflict among young people going on. The moderate students are not so moderate as you may think. Most of them have rejected the Puritan ethic and are fiercely determined to improve the income distribution. They believe that this can and will be done by our present political system. The radical students are trying to persuade them that things are quite different. First, the radicals say that the constellation of political forces I have described will never permit any substantial change in the income distribution, or any substantial improvement in the life of the poor. The radicals would go on to reject the negative tax precisely because it is conservative in the sense I have mentioned. They say that the only way to end the political dominance of the rural and Southern oligarchs, the big city machines and the military-industrial complex is to change the basis of our economic system altogether, to eliminate private property and the principle of reward in proportion to effort. It is obvious that the negative tax has at best a limited relevance in such a perspective.

I am afraid I find the radical analysis, or at least part of it, more plausible. The negative tax is the kind of bold conservative stroke which simultaneously deals a tactical blow to the left and restores the faith of wavering moderates in the essential humanity and imagination of the system. But I see no signs of imagination or humanity in the people who have the power. If nothing happens the young moderates will continue to drift to the left and will make a revolution in earnest.

POSTSCRIPT

Soon after I had prepared this primer the Nixon Administration submitted sweeping proposals for welfare reform to the Congress. The Administration asked for a negative income tax with a $1,600 minimum income for a family of four and a 50% tax rate. The main differences between this proposal (Family Allowance Plan) and Plan B described above are a) that FAP, while it extends benefits to families with children headed by working men, does not include single individuals or childless couples; b) the plan would not be administered by the Internal Revenue Service, but in the Department of Health, Education and Welfare, although administrative procedures would be similar to those described above; c) those states which presently have higher welfare levels for some categories of recipients must maintain these levels; d) unemployed male recipients are required by vague and flexible provisions to be seeking work or undergoing training as a condition of receiving benefits.

As originally drafted the Family Allowance Program came into conflict with other programs that subsidize poor people, especially public housing and food stamps. These subsidies are available to families whose income is below a certain absolute level, and are cut off abruptly when the family's income rises above this level. This produces a very strong disincentive to earnings that raise income above the critical levels because the family that earns more finds its total income reduced through withdrawal of the subsidies. The Family Allowance Program aggravates this problem because it permits recipient families to retain half their earnings. Of course, the disincentive built into these earlier subsidy programs exists whether or not the FAP is enacted. The Administration has committed itself to propose further reforms to eliminate these disincentives in existing programs. This is an example of the dynamic effect of reform: the negative tax reform draws attention to other serious problems and leads to reform in other areas.

The FAP proposal is important because it could change the pattern of evolution of our welfare programs. The natural operation of politics will probably raise the levels of the program until it replaces other forms of public assistance entirely. Administration has chosen a modest version of the hold step I described above. Whether it ultimately will strengthen the capitalist system and foil the revolution remains to be seen.

INVESTMENT IN THE EDUCATION OF THE POOR: A PESSIMISTIC REPORT[1]

Eugene Smolensky

First I will propose a new approach to the measurement of poverty. This approach focuses attention upon the necessary conditions for declining income inequality, some of which will be discussed, therefore, in sections two and three. Finally, the analysis will be extended to evaluate the prospects for reducing the incidence of poverty by adding further financial incentives for completing high school.

As I view the problem, poverty is not likely to decline as a serious social issue in the foreseeable future,[2] even though the real income of the poor is likely to be rising all the while.

THE POVERTY LINE AS A SIGNAL

Twice during the past thirty years, a poverty line has been drawn to guide federal policy. In constant prices, the recent poverty line is about 53 percent above the earlier one [16]. Since this percentage increase is similar to the independently estimated rise, over the same period, in the cost of a varying minimum-decency market basket,[3] the rise has a substantial rationale: It reflects technical revisions in minimal nutritional requirements and other needs as seen by experts, taste changes, and product substitutions due

Eugene Smolensky is Professor of Economics, University of Wisconsin.

Reprinted with permission from Eugene Smolensky, "Investment in Education for the Poor: A Pessimistic Report," *American Economic Review* 56:2 (May 1966), pp. 370–378.

[1] I am greatly indebted to Millard F. Long. If he believed the results, he would properly be the coauthor. Paul Davidson, James Kindahl, Albert Rees, and Joel Segall contributed significantly to reducing the number of errors embodied herein. Jude Laspa was my very capable research assistant. Some of these views, which are strictly my own, were developed while working on quite a different problem, under contract with the Office of Economic Opportunity, and I am indebted to that Office.

[2] A few comments on what I am not saying seems appropriate. I am not saying that it is an unwise policy to promote investment in human capital. Nor am I asserting that alternative goals are less important than poverty reduction. Therefore I am not asserting that current policy is unwise. I cannot even assert that current policy will positively fail to reduce poverty. I am merely pessimistic and my pessimism extends only to a policy which calls for extending years of school by adding financial incentives to reduce the proportion of families in poverty.

[3] The market basket was for New York City.

to relative price changes and the introduction of new products. These market baskets, however, embody a rise in real income, too, and since no criteria for admitting a rise in real income into the definition of poverty has been agreed upon, the resulting change in the line over time poses problems of interpretation. I would like to suggest an alternative approach to setting the poverty line which would be free of this ambiguity, and which would also, I feel, better serve policy. More precisely, I will propose a rational basis for changing the real content of the poverty line over time in a growing economy.

The disutility that arises from the persistence of poverty is not confined to the poor, and the effective demand for federal antipoverty programs does not emanate solely, nor perhaps even primarily, from a concern for equity. The primary objective may very well be efficiency in the Pareto sense. If this be so, a poverty line which considers only the needs of the poor may not be the most pertinent guide to federal policy. Perhaps the most relevant requirement of a poverty line is that it serve as an index of the disutility to the community of the persistence of poverty.

Take as an example the externality in consumption due to slums. Satisfactions flow from two separate aspects of a house. One is the quality of service the house itself provides to its occupants. The other aspect is that the quality of the neighborhood in which the house stands may affect the satisfactions the dwelling unit provides to its occupants. The existence of substandard housing can, therefore, reduce the satisfactions of some who do not live in them. It follows, therefore, that since poverty is generally a precondition for slums, the elimination of poverty, and with it slums, will raise the real incomes of some who are not poor. These externality considerations suggest an approach quite different from the "needs" approach to the measurement of poverty. They suggest that the poverty line take into consideration the external benefits of raising families above the poverty line.

Imagine a community in which none may change address, but in which the quality of each house can be improved (at constant cost), including raising substandard housing to standard quality. As incomes rise, all individuals will want both the quality of their own housing to be improved and the proportion of substandard dwellings occupied by others in the community to decline. Only the former, however, can be directly affected through the market by each family, for the latter depends upon the actions of others. The change in the quantity of substandard housing will therefore depend in large part upon the income elasticity of those who live in substandard housing and upon the change in their income. The welfare of the whole community is, therefore, tied to the ratio of the growth of income of the poor to the growth in median income of the community and to the desires of the community for raising the quality of its neighborhoods relative to the desires of the poor to raise the quality of their own housing. These considerations taken together suggest the alternative approach to measurement. The rise in the poverty line over time should be such that were the incomes of the poor to rise at the same rate, the poor would, by voluntary market actions, satisfy the evolving desires of the community due to changes in its income level for those things in which there are externalities in consumption; e.g., housing.

It is feasible to implement this alternative ("consensus") approach,[4] but there are many problems of concept and of estimation.[5] Were these issues resolved and a new poverty line drawn, it would, I suspect, rationalize the recent increase in public concern over poverty.

The needs approach is something of an anachronism, for surely the material needs of the poor are being more adequately met than before. For public concern to increase at a time when a social problem is decreasing in significance appears to be irrational [14]. If poverty is not a declining social problem, then, of course, the increased public concern is understandable. Although the needs poverty line has fallen relative to per capita income over the past three decades [16], it is my hunch that if the consensus poverty line had been estimated, it would have risen relative to average income over the same period, and that consequently, there would not, in recent years, have been a decline in the incidence of poverty.

Let me return to my housing example. There is some evidence to suggest that the income elasticity of demand for better neighborhoods at the median of the personal income distribution is greater than the elasticity of demand for standard housing among the poor.[6] Differences in the relevant income elasticities can be offset by compensating differences in the income change which they modify, however. In my example, therefore, the preferences of the majority for better neighborhoods could be satisfied by voluntary action

---

[4] In one instance, for example, Muth [10] obtained the following estimate:

$$y(10^{-3}) = -.25 \ln s + \ldots$$

where: $y =$ the median income of a census tract in South Chicago in 1950
          $s =$ the percent of substandard houses in the tract.

Suppose, to take some arbitrary numbers, the median income of the poor to be $2,725 and the median income of the sample to be $3,870. If all incomes rose by 10 percent, the desired decline in substandard housing would be 15.4 percent. For the poor to voluntarily reduce the proportion of substandard houses by 15.4 percent, however, the median income of the poor would have to have advanced by 14 percent. That would imply that the poverty line, whatever its initial and perhaps arbitrary value, be advanced 14 percent.

[5] For example, should the line be based on a single class of goods or on many? If many, what should delimit the set and how are the various groups of commodities to be combined? The current needs line was derived from essentially one class of commodities—a food basket. At this juncture shelter may be a considerably more meaningful commodity on which to base a poverty measure than food, even on the needs criteria.

[6] See footnote 4 above.

if the incomes of the poor were to rise more rapidly (by the ratio of the elasticities) than median income.

One caveat: Even if the elasticities are as I suspect, it does not follow that the most efficient solution to the poverty problem is for income inequality to decline over time, simply because the poverty line rises relative to median income. The policy-makers would have a meaningful signal, however, for, given a consensus definition of poverty, a rise in the proportion of families in poverty would imply that with the same rise in income differently distributed, everyone could have been made better off, without anyone being made worse off and it would then be appropriate to consider community action.[7]

What are the circumstances under which the market economy will generate a fall in the proportion of families in poverty, if the consensus approach were accepted? More specifically, when is a general rise in income distributed in a way that avoids the threat to Pareto optimality at issue here? If my hunch about the magnitudes of the relevant elasticities is correct, a necessary, but not necessarily sufficient, condition is for income inequality to decline. In the next section I turn to a major aspect of declining income inequality: the circumstances in which the wages of the poor rise relative to the average wage.

THE HISTORICAL RECORD POINTS
TOWARD FULL EMPLOYMENT

We know from many sources (e.g., Kuznets [9], Goldsmith [7], and Kravis [8]) that most measures of income inequality in the United States exhibit long and short swings around a trend toward convergence during this century. The trend, in turn, is mainly attributable to a sharp decline in income inequality during the second World War which has survived subsequent cycles. Between 1935 and 1962, to report a somewhat more pertinent fact, the proportion of families in poverty (using the needs definition) fell by 43 percent with two-thirds of that decline occurring between 1935 and 1947. Over the same period, however, the needs poverty line fell relative to per capita income. If the poverty line had risen proportionately with per capita income, only the decline from 1935 to 1947 would have been observed [16], [6].

A large part of the convergence during the second World War is proximately attributable to convergence within wage income [15]. At the same time, occupational wage differentials narrowed relatively, and the theory

[7] Since the consensus poverty line has no direct implication for policy, it would probably be best to confine its use to policy discussion within the government.

most often invoked to explain that fact, suitably amended, explains, to a considerable extent, the significant interrelationships between a wartime economy and declining wage differentials. That analysis emphasizes only one aspect of a wartime economy — the historically low levels of unemployment which are achieved — but an important policy role for wage and interest rate controls is also implicit in the explanation.

FULL EMPLOYMENT AND DECLINING WAGE DIFFERENTIALS: THE TRICKLE-DOWN MECHANISM [8]

In a series of articles, Reder has developed a model to explain relative convergence in occupational wage differentials [11], [12], [13]. In the following paragraphs his argument is restated and, I believe, strengthened.

Normally employers believe that they can hire all the workers (of each grade) that they wish at prevailing wage rates, although they recognize that to do so will be to raise other costs (e.g., search costs). For each skill level above the unskilled, the labor supply is perceived to be infinitely elastic at the prevailing wage rate (but not prevailing unit labor costs), because increased demand can be responded to most profitably by drawing from among the disguised unemployed, or by upgrading less skilled workers through training, or by the dilution of job specifications, or by extending the time during which job vacancies go unfilled.[9] An increased demand for unskilled workers can normally be met, the real wage unchanged, by drawing upon the involuntarily unemployed and domestic workers. The money-wage rate for unskilled labor does not fall and involuntary unemployment persists because there exists a wage floor below which corporations and governments will not pay. Reder calls this wage floor "the social minimum." [10]

During periods of prolonged expansions of aggregate demand (e.g., the two world wars), involuntary and disguised unemployment among the unskilled is eliminated, despite a substantial rise in the labor force participation rate. Once full employment is reached, further increases in labor demand can be satisfied only if the real wage of the unskilled is raised. Since the real wage of skilled workers will not rise, the rise in the real wage of the un-

---

[8] Locke Anderson first used this term to describe "the relationship between economic growth and the extent of poverty among . . . families" [1].

[9] Allowing job vacancies to go unfilled is an aspect of allowing orders to go unfilled. Zarnowitz has shown that choosing to backlog orders rather than raising product prices is consistent with pure competition [18].

[10] This floor may be viewed as a perfectly elastic segment of the supply function of unskilled labor due to either unions or minimum wage legislation. Alternatively the effective demand curve for labor may be viewed as terminating at the social minimum wage, so that the marginal worker receives a wage above his supply price, and yet, involuntary unemployment persists.

skilled will reduce relative wage skill differentials.[11] This narrowing of wage differentials among skill groups is not reversed when unemployment increases (as will be explained below). With the narrowing of wage differentials, income inequality will also decline, *ceteris paribus.*

Some discussion of the role of inflation in the model must be added to this brief summary of Reder's arguments.[12] An analysis of the incidence of training costs must also be undertaken. First, note that raising the real wage rate of the unskilled above the initial social minimum requires moving from one full employment level to a higher full employment level. That is, the demand curve for unskilled labor must slide up the supply curve of unskilled labor, and the latter schedule is an increasing function of the real wage. The rise in the real wage requires income redistribution via inflation, with the rising consumer price level acting to transfer real income from rentiers and skilled workers to unskilled labor [5]. As the incomes of the unskilled rise, the money equivalent of the higher real wage rate becomes the new social minimum, and since it is rigid downward, the old skill differential cannot be reestablished even in periods of less than full employment. The level of employment must be the variable which brings the real wage and marginal value products into equality.[13]

Since the wage differential begins to narrow after full employment, the incentive to undertake training declines.[14] If the number of trainees declined with the fall in skill differentials, the real wage of the skilled would have to be raised to maintain the increased flow of skilled workers which would, in

[11] The model has been stated quite rigidly for heuristic reasons, but some cyclical and random fluctuations in the wage structure can and have been admitted into the argument by Reder without damaging the thrust of his argument, which is oriented toward explaining the trend, or more accurately, the once-over structural changes in skill differentials. A drift toward the old skill differentials over the long haul is likely, however, as gains in marginal physical product due to technological advance lead to a sharing between increases in wages and increases in employment. The greater unemployment among the unskilled suggests that they will take a greater proportion of the productivity gains in increased employment than will the skilled. On the other hand, the skilled face greater pressure from the adoption of laborsaving innovations. Finally, it may be noted that convergence in the face of inflation involves rising money wages of both skill groups, but rising real wages only among the unskilled; technology held constant.

[12] Reder dismissed the role of inflation, believing its effects were confined to money illusion [12]. There is no money illusion in what follows.

[13] If with the new higher wage floors, there are higher levels of unemployment than before, then there may be more poverty than before. Hopefully, this result is ruled out by the political pressures to sustain aggregate demand. Also, the inflation requires raising money transfers to forestall a rise in poverty among those outside the labor force as the proportions in poverty within the labor force fall.

[14] A general price increase widens absolute skill differentials (the marginal physical products serve as weights), but the relative skill differential is not changed. Since the price level change raises the differential and the foregone income proportionately, the return to training is virtually unaffected.

turn, tend to reestablish the original wage differentials. I do not believe that this, in fact, occurs.

The wage differential between skilled and unskilled workers reflects the return to investment in training [2]. In a purely competitive market, workers would shift from unskilled to trainee occupations, lowering the marginal value product and hence the wage rate of trainees. Eventually, equilibrium would be reached. The wage differential between skilled and trainees would yield a return on the investment in training (foregone income in the form of the differential between the wage of the unskilled and trainee wages plus any direct training costs) just equal to the interest rate. The wage of trainees and apprentices would be below the wage rate of the unskilled, and the employer would train anyone who chose to be trained since the employee would pay the full cost of his training.

Apprentice and other trainee wages are not lower than the real wage rate of the unskilled, however. They are set, to a very large extent, by unions as part of the effort to restrict entry into the skilled occupations.[15] The wage rates of trainees, like the wage rates of the skilled, are fixed and inflexible downward, so that the adjusting mechanism, here, as in the rest of the system, is from wages to employment and marginal products. With the trainee wage rate fixed at a level higher than the wage of the unskilled and inflexible downward, employers must now restrict the number of trainees (the return to training is virtually infinite) to equilibrate the marginal products of trainees and the trainee wage rate. With a sustained outward shift in aggregate demand, employers can now increase the number of trainees, just as they increase the number of skilled (with unions tolerating the increase) and they choose to do so as a part of the process of lifting the unskilled up the occupational ladder to maintain the skilled wage rate.[16] There is, therefore, considerable scope for the real wage of the unskilled to rise before the flow into training is curtailed.

Embracing trickling-down from growth to poverty reduction as an avowed public policy implies a most unappetizing program politically. Either it must be accompanied by a vigorous "incomes policy" or there will be substantial inflation. Since there is reason to believe that the rate of reduction in poverty for a 1 percent increase in prices will be smaller now than in the past [1], either the inflation will have to be severe or the incomes

[15] Trainees have more formal education than unskilled workers, and, therefore, part of their higher wages is attributable to returns to education. This is not necessarily in conflict with the hypothesis that unions are restricting entry into training, thereby creating a wage differential, since some rationing device into training is required.

[16] This is something of an overstatement. However, only 41 percent of 1964 high school drop-outs were employed in October, 1964. Of those employed in nonagricultural activities, 25 percent were employed only part time [3].

policy will have to be much more than a melt-the-metals policy for it to have an effect other than moving the unemployed and domestics to the unskilled category. With a consensus definition of poverty, there is likely to be no decline in poverty up to the point where the unskilled wage rises relative to the skilled wage.

Since a vigorous full employment policy has been ruled out because of its inflationary side effects, emphasis has been put on less aggregative policies. The hope is to make use of a detailed description of those socioeconomic characteristics which distinguish the poor from the rest of the population. Programs to encourage students to complete high school are a prominent feature of this "detailing" approach. What are the prospects for success?

INCREASED SCHOOLING AS AN ANTIPOVERTY POLICY

In the past, the proportion of families in poverty has declined when the incentive to invest in education has been the weakest; i.e., when the opportunity cost of education was high and rising while skill differentials and therefore returns to education were declining. In general, if the prior section is correct, full employment encourages the substitution of on-the-job training and work for formal education. Can a federal program of financial incentives invert the relationship between poverty reduction and years of schooling that is generated by individual profit maximizing behavior? The possibility certainly exists, for the probability of being impoverished is above the national rate at each education level below high school graduation. As years of schooling rise, the proportion of urban male white workers in the prime working years earning less than $3,000 falls toward 20 percent, finally reaching it at high school graduation [17]. While the possibility exists, it has a low probability.

Since the Korean war, unemployment levels have been high, especially for young people, so that the opportunity cost of education for a very large proportion of high school drop-outs has been close to zero.[17] Yet the unemployment rate has not been so high that large numbers of skilled workers

[17] Several additional points could be made here. First, in trying to maximize a joint product (skilled and apprenticed), the employer could, as part of profit maximizing, choose to run a loss on the training function. Second, it is clear that once full employment is reached, the government must tolerate some further inflation (it already must have faced inflation from diminishing returns) if it is to get increased output, but a severe wage price spiral must be prevented. That is, the unions must be banned, as they were with wage controls, from attempting to raise the real wage of the skilled and the trainees, but the government cannot prevent a rise in the money wage of the skilled and maintain the participation rate. The fall in the real rate of interest (money rates pegged) may also play a small part in contributing to the demand for training.

are being forced into disguised unemployment. The economic incentive to stay in school is very great, therefore; yet the drop-out rate is high. And if anything, the proportion of impoverished young people has risen and the penalty for failing to complete high school has been increasing even for those who find employment [4].

The two most basic reasons for a federal policy to add financial incentives to education are made largely irrelevant by these considerations. One justification for an education policy could be that the marginal social benefit of schooling exceeds the marginal private benefit. This argument would be pertinent, however, only if the marginal private benefit equaled marginal private cost at present. Yet the large number of drop-outs at this time suggests that the drop-outs are not now staying in school long enough for marginal private benefits to drop to marginal private costs. Staying in school even longer, so that the marginal social benefit falls to the marginal social cost, is not now an issue, therefore.

A second justification for a federal education policy could be that an imperfect capital market or a credit market lacking the necessary credit instruments exists which leads to underinvestment in education. When alternative earnings are close to zero, however, students cannot be dropping out of school in large numbers because they cannot borrow against the future returns to their training to forestall foregoing current consumption unnecessarily. Nor can it be important that the drop-outs may have a higher propensity to consume present as opposed to future commodities than the marginal borrower.

Assuming the government will use financial incentives (and not coercion) to gain its objectives, what scope is there for actions that have not already been undertaken? Where is the operative market failure in the present situation? Having undertaken to insure that poor children cannot get work and income, what more can be done to keep them in school? What can be achieved through economic incentives, since to be effective they require rational economic responses: but all we think we know suggests that drop-outs are behaving irrationally, at least as economists use that silly word. Under the circumstances, pessimism is the most optimistic position on an education policy for an economist with any compassion for the poor.

REFERENCES

1. W. H. Locke Anderson. "Trickling Down: The Relationship Between Economic Growth and the Extent of Poverty Among American Families," *Q.J.E.*, Nov. 1964.

2. G. S. Becker. *Human Capital* (N.B.E.R., 1964).
3. F. A. Bogan. *Employment of High School Graduates and Dropouts in 1964* (Special Labor Force Report No. 54, Bureau of Labor Statistics, June, 1965).
4. D. S. Brady. *Age and Income Distribution* (Research Report No. 8, Washington, D.C.: Government Printing Office, 1965).
5. P. Davidson and E. Smolensky. "Modigliani on the Interaction of Monetary and Real Phenomena," *Rev. of Econ. and Statis.*, Nov., 1964.
6. V. Fuchs. "Toward a Theory of Poverty," *The Concept of Poverty* (Chamber of Commerce of the U.S., 1965).
7. S. Goldsmith, *et al.* "Size Distribution of Income Since the Mid-Thirties," *Rev. of Econ. and Statis.*, Feb., 1954.
8. I. B. Kravis. *The Structure of Income* (Univ. of Pennsylvania, 1962).
9. S. Kuznets. *Shares of Upper Income Groups in Income and Savings* (N.B.E.R., 1953).
10. R. F. Muth. "The Spatial Pattern of Residential Land Use in Cities" (mimeographed).
11. M. W. Reder. "The Theory of Occupational Wage Differentials," *A.E.R.*, Dec., 1955.
12. ———. "Wage Differentials: Theory and Measurement," *Aspects of Labor Economics*, ed. H. G. Lewis (Princeton: N.B.E.R., 1963).
13. ———. "Wage Structure and Structural Unemployment," *Rev. of Econ. Studies*, Oct., 1964.
14. M. Reid. "Testimony," Hearings Before the Subcommittee on the War on Poverty Program, 88th Cong., 2nd sess., Part 3.
15. E. Smolensky. "An Interrelationship Among Income Distributions," *Rev. of Econ. and Statis.*, May, 1963.
16. ———. "The Past and Present Poor," *The Concept of Poverty* (Chamber of Commerce of the U.S., 1965).
17. U.S. Bureau of the Census. Subject Reports, AC (2)-5B, 1960, 884.
18. V. Zarnowitz. *Unfilled Orders, Price Changes, and Business Fluctuations*, Occasional Paper 84 (N.B.E.R., 1962).

TRANSPORTATION AND POVERTY [1]

John R. Meyer
John F. Kain

Widespread concern about the problems of poverty and race has led to a proliferation of schemes for reducing the unemployment, increasing the incomes, and generally improving the well-being of disadvantaged groups in our society. Prominent among these are several that would use transportation to increase the employment opportunities of the poor. The concept that inadequate transportation must be numbered among the disadvantages of the poor and that improved mobility, particularly as it improves access to jobs, could increase their self-sufficiency was publicized widely in the aftermath of the Watts riots in 1965. The McCone Commission report on the causes of the riots concluded that "the most serious immediate problem [facing] the Negro in our community is employment. . . ." The commission suggested that, although a serious lack of skill and overt discrimination are major causes of high Negro unemployment, inadequate and costly public transportation also limits Negro employment opportunities:

> Our investigation has brought into clear focus the fact that the inadequate and costly public transportation currently existing throughout the Los Angeles area seriously restricts the residents of the disadvantaged areas such as south central Los Angeles. This lack of adequate transportation handicaps them in seeking and holding jobs, attending schools, shopping and fulfilling other needs.[2]

The McCone Commission, therefore, recommended that public transit services in Los Angeles be expanded and subsidized. (Its report was strangely silent about the possibility of improving access to jobs by reducing segregation in the housing market.) This recommendation attracted

John R. Meyer is Professor of Economics, Yale University; John F. Kain is Professor of Political Economy, Harvard University.

Reprinted with permission from John R. Meyer and John F. Kain, "Transportation and Poverty," *The Public Interest* (Winter 1970). Copyright National Affairs, Inc., 1970.

[1] This article summarizes a Conference on Transportation and Poverty, held June 7, 1968, which was organized and chaired by the authors. The conference was sponsored by the American Academy of Arts and Sciences, and financed by the Department of Housing and Urban Development and by the Bureau of Public Roads of the Department of Transportation.

[2] California Governor's Commission on the Los Angeles Riots, *Violence in the City—An End or a Beginning?* (Los Angeles, 1965), p. 65.

considerable public attention, and the federal government, through the Department of Housing and Urban Development, has sponsored some demonstration projects designed to ascertain if better and more extensive transit services between ghettos and employment centers would yield additional jobs for ghetto residents. The entire subject is very fashionable. But it is astonishing how little knowledge lies behind the popular political opinions it provokes.

A NEW PROBLEM?

In light of the new public awareness of the relation between poverty and transportation, it is appropriate to ask whether the problem itself is new. Obviously, poverty is no new problem; nor is it a growing problem. But when the relation between transportation and poverty is examined, it becomes apparent that something *is* new. Post-war changes in urban ecology and transportation systems, while conferring significant improvements on the majority, have almost certainly caused a *relative* deterioration in the access to job opportunities enjoyed by a significant fraction of the poor.

To be sure, many, if not most, poor continue to live in centrally located residential areas; and these are reasonably well served by public transit to the central business district, where one usually finds the highest density of job opportunities. But in the past two decades, new job opportunities have grown more swiftly *outside* this central business district. It is estimated that there may be 100,000 fewer low-income jobs in New York City than there are low-income workers. A similar pattern has apparently emerged in several other American cities. Living in a neighborhood well served by public transit to the central business district is therefore less of an advantage for lower-income groups today than it once was.

THE AUTOMOBILE AND THE POOR

Reflecting these and other changes in the post-war pattern of American urban living, the total number of passenger trips by mass transit has declined in every year since World War II. Much of the early post-war decline must be viewed against the abnormal conditions of wartime, when transit use was artificially swollen by restrictions on automobile use; transit patronage in 1953 was almost the same as in 1940 or 1941. But the decline in transit use has continued well past 1953, and today transit patronage is about two-thirds of what it was in 1940 or 1953, in spite of a considerable growth in urban population during the past decade.

This can be explained by the fact that a growing proportion of the urban population chooses to travel by automobile. To a considerable extent this results from steadily expanding auto ownership. In 1950, 6 out of every 10 United States households owned one or more private automobiles. By 1967, the figure was nearly 8 out of every 10. But of family units with incomes between $2,000 and $2,999 before taxes, only 53 per cent owned an automobile in 1967. The percentage of those with autos in the below-$2,000 bracket is, of course, much lower still.

The low levels of auto ownership among the poor reflect the fact that the automobile, though a near necessity in much of urban America, is a very expensive one. The high initial capital outlay and operating costs of a private automobile are a heavy strain on the budgets of low-income households. In general, then, when adequate transit services are available, low-income households can and do obtain substantial savings by foregoing auto ownership.

The acquisition of an efficient private automobile (one without exorbitant maintenance costs) requires considerable financing, a chronic difficulty for the poor. Poor people, therefore, even when they own cars, generally own poor cars. Many of these are inadequate for long-distance commutation and expressway operation. Often they are also uninsured. Thus, statistics on car ownership among the poor, as adverse as they are, may paint a more favorable picture than is actually justified.

The dependence on public transit by the urban poor therefore continues to be very great. In the New York region, for example, less than 25 per cent of the households earning under $1,000 per year in 1963 used private automobiles to reach work; over 75 per cent used some form of transit. The proportions using automobiles were 57 per cent for those with incomes between $4,000 and $10,000, and 62 per cent for those with incomes over $10,000 per year.

Transit managements have made some effort to offset the steady decline in transit use by developing new markets. They have done this mainly by expanding route miles or services offered. The route miles of rapid and grade-separated rail transit service have increased about 2 per cent since 1945 and soon will increase further as new rail rapid transit systems under construction are completed. Route miles of all kinds of transit service, bus and rail, have risen nearly 20 per cent since 1955. In the same period, however, transit operators have curtailed the vehicle (revenue) miles of services offered by 20 per cent in response to decreases in ridership. To some extent this decline in vehicle miles of service has been offset by the use of larger vehicles with more seats. Nevertheless, the overall effect has been a reduction in the frequency and, therefore, the basic quality of the service rendered. In general, reductions in service offerings have been most severe on weekends and other off-peak periods (particularly evenings) and for commuter trains.

TRANSIT TO SUBURBAN JOBS

The effectiveness of the additional route miles, moreover, has been less than it might have been because modern bus transit tends to follow the same routes as the old streetcar lines. This means that a high percentage of services in most cities converge on the central business district. For an individual to make a trip from one point at the periphery of a city to another point at the periphery usually requires taking one radial line into the central business district and then transferring to another line to make the trip out to his destination. This arrangement tends to be costly for both operators and users. Bus lines operating through a central business district encounter congestion, with all that entails for increasing operating costs. For the user wanting to make a trip from one peripheral urban location to another, the radial trip to and from the CBD means a much longer and more time-consuming journey than is geographically necessary. Commuters at all income levels, therefore, tend to use automobiles for such trips. Even the poor tend to do so whenever they can make the necessary arrangements, either by owning an inexpensive car or by joining a carpool.

In general, conventional transit is at a performance disadvantage compared to driving or carpooling when serving thinly traveled, long-distance routes between central city residences and suburban workplaces. Even when available, the transit service is often too little and too slow to compete with the automobile. Moreover, such transit service can impose dollars-and-cents handicaps that go beyond the direct costs in money and time of the commuter's trip itself. For example, conventional transit often adapts to limited demand by providing only peak-hour service between the suburban work places and centrally located residential areas. The worker must either catch the bus when it leaves exactly at closing time, or find some other mode of transportation, often at considerable additional expense. This means that the worker who depends on public transit cannot easily accept overtime employment. The unavailability of a worker for overtime work not only denies him a lucrative opportunity, but can involve costs to his employer as well. Limited public transit scheduling, for example, can make it difficult for the employer to stagger shifts or closing hours. (And staggered closing hours can be helpful in solving such other transportation problems as traffic congestion at peak commuter hours.)

It is therefore not surprising that transit operators serving suburban plants report that low-income workers frequently use transit only when obtaining their jobs and for the first few days or weeks of employment. Once the workers manage to save enough for the down payment on a car, or become acquainted with some fellow workers living near them, they drive to work or join a carpool. *If this is a common pattern, existing transit*

*services may indeed be serving a critical function for low-income house-
holds, but one whose value is badly gauged by the fare box or by aggregate
statistics on transit use.*

The basic problem, however, remains: efficient transit requires that large
numbers of persons travel between the same two points at approximately
the same time. The growing dispersal of workplaces and residences means
that this condition is satisfied less frequently than before. As jobs, and particularly blue-collar jobs, have shifted from areas that are relatively well
served by public transit to areas that are poorly served, employment opportunities for low-income households dependent on public transit service have
been reduced. Increasingly, low-income workers are forced to choose between a higher-paying job that is inaccessible by public transit, and thereby
pay more for transportation (e.g., by buying and operating an automobile),
or a lower-paying job that is served by transit. To put it in somewhat different terms, low-income households now have at their disposal at most only
a bit more, and oftentimes less, transit service than they once did for reaching what is, in effect, a much larger metropolitan region.

THE PROBLEM OF RACE

The dispersal of the job market and the decline of transit systems have created particular difficulties for low-income Negroes. If the job of a low-
income white worker shifts to the suburbs, he is usually able to follow it by
moving to a new residence. If not, he may be able to relocate his residence
to be near a transit line serving his new suburban workplace reasonably
well. The low-income Negro worker, however, may not be so fortunate.
Regardless of his income or family situation, if his job moves to the suburbs, he may find it difficult to move out of the ghetto. That is, his residence
may not easily follow his job to the suburbs. For him, the service characteristics, coverage, and cost of the transportation system can therefore be
especially critical.

Unfortunately, conventional transit systems usually do not provide adequate services between the ghetto and suburban workplaces. The black
worker, confined to ghetto housing near but not directly at the urban core,
cannot readily reach many new suburban job locations by simple reverse
commuting on existing transit systems. Existing public transit tends to con-
nect suburban *residential* locations with the very core of the central business district; it may not pass through, or even near, new suburban industrial
or office parks, just as it may also fail to pass through the ghetto.

If the ghetto resident is able to reach a suburban workplace at all by public transit, the trip may be expensive. If he is lucky, he may be able to join
a carpool with a fellow worker and share the considerable expense of a

long-distance auto trip from the ghetto. Here, too, the limitations on his residential options and the remoteness of most suburban workplaces from the ghetto reduce the possibilities of him making an advantageous arrangement.

THE POLICY QUESTIONS

Despite the public discussion and federally financed experiments that followed publication of the McCone Commission report, virtually nothing has been done so far to establish a factual basis for evaluating the utility of improved transportation in reducing urban poverty and unemployment. In particular, answers must be found to a number of questions. What effects do existing transportation policies have on income distribution? Are they the ones that were anticipated? Can transportation policy be an effective tool for expanding the opportunities and increasing the welfare of the disadvantaged? Should transportation be used this way? If so, what specific policies and programs should be adopted for achieving these purposes?

JOBS AND TRANSPORTATION

Inferior access to new jobs is by no means the only disadvantage of the ghetto resident. Indeed, in terms of his participation in the labor market, it may be much less important than other factors. Thomas Floyd, who was deeply involved in the administration of demonstration projects in Watts and elsewhere, notes: "There is . . . reason to believe that some employers were using the transportation barrier as a convenient excuse for not hiring for other reasons. In addition to racial bias, there may be presumed or actual inadequate job skills or work habits." When the improved transportation services were provided, he observed, the jobs did not always materialize.

If transportation is but one of many factors influencing job opportunities, provision of more or cheaper transportation *by itself* is probably an inefficient method of reducing unemployment or increasing incomes. Effective measures to increase the opportunities, employment, and incomes of the long-term unemployed or underemployed must operate simultaneously on several fronts. Training, education, counseling, placement, and transportation programs complement one another. Most or all of these programs should have a role in any well designed assault on employment problems, and any one of these programs in isolation could well fail because it lacked other essential services. On the other hand, simply putting all these programs into effect simultaneously would not guarantee results either. The different programs must be properly articulated and synthesized.

INCOME REDISTRIBUTION AND TRANSPORTATION

Subsidies for urban transportation have long enjoyed wide support on the ground that such subsidies help the poor. In spite of the fact that the poor generally are more reliant on transit than the rich, the truth of this proposition is less than self-evident.

Advocates of public transit subsidies need to be discriminating if the subsidies they support are actually to aid the poor. Many proposed new systems, such as the BART system in San Francisco and the transit extensions in Boston, will provide only nominal benefits for the poor. In fact, it is probable that both systems will have a highly regressive impact. They are to be subsidized out of the property tax, which is heavily regressive; and virtually all of the benefits will accrue to high-income, long-distance commuters traveling between high-income suburbs and central employment centers. They will do practically nothing to improve accessibility between centrally located ghettos and suburban employment centers.

In general, users of high-speed, long-distance rail commuter systems are among the wealthier classes of society. Local bus systems by contrast, frequently serve large numbers of low-income users. Paradoxically, these local bus services rarely require large public subsidies. In fact, the available evidence suggests that local bus systems serving low-income and dense central city neighborhoods often make a profit, and often subsidize unprofitable long-distance commuter systems serving low-density, high-income neighborhoods.

Another anomalous fact is that a disproportionate number of taxi trips are made by poor persons. The explanation apparently is that many locations are simply inaccessible to carless households except by taxi. For many of the poor, occasional use of taxicabs as a supplement to transit and to walking is relatively economical compared with automobile ownership.

New York provides contrasting figures that illustrate this point. In New York, poor households do *not* make proportionately more taxi trips than middle-income families. The reason is that a smaller proportion of middle- and upper-income families own automobiles in New York than elsewhere. Moreover, the public transit system is much more extensive in New York than in most other cities and is thus a better substitute for taxicabs. In small cities and towns, however, taxicabs are sometimes the only form of public transit available to the poor. In these instances the poor and infirm may be almost the only users of taxicabs — because everyone else drives.

Thus, the apparently simple question of which income groups use which modes of transportation is a good deal more complex than is commonly imagined. Such hasty generalizations as "taxicabs are a luxury used only by the very rich"; "automobile ownership is limited to the well-to-do"; and "transit is used only by the poor" fail to hold up under scrutiny.

The mobility and transport choices of different income groups could be discussed more cogently if we had better measures of urban mobility. Unfortunately, the usual measure of "tripmaking" used in metropolitan transportation studies is poorly suited for defining mobility differences between different income classes. By definition, only vehicle trips (transit, truck, taxi, or automobile) and walk-to-work trips are counted as trips; walking trips other than those made to and from work are omitted. On average, such non-commuter walking trips are probably of far greater importance in low-income than in high-income neighborhoods. Poor people more often than higher-income people live in high-density neighborhoods where shopping, recreation, and employment are located close to home. Many trips that must be made by auto or transit in low density areas can conveniently be made by foot in high-density neighborhoods. Whether this means, as some believe, that the poor should be considered less mobile is not entirely clear.

In general, almost no data exist that describe how persons of different life styles, living at different urban densities and income levels, solve their personal transportation problems. Moreover, there is no hard information to demonstrate the existence of large and unfulfilled latent demands for alternative forms of transportation. Information on such matters is crucial for designing programs to improve the mobility of the poor and for evaluating the benefits of such programs as against their costs. Yet, to date, the information simply has not been gathered.

INDIRECT COSTS

Most observers agree that the indirect and secondary costs of major transportation investment, such as urban expressways and rapid transit, have not been given adequate consideration when choosing locations and alignment, designing facilities, and deciding whether construction is justified at all. At least two major kinds of such costs can be identified.

First, there are uncompensated costs imposed on individuals — residents, property owners, and businessmen — who are forced to move. These uncompensated costs commonly include not only the direct money outlays for moving but also losses engendered by destruction of cherished friendships, familiar environments, business relationships, and other intangibles.

Second, there are collective costs. These consist of adverse changes in the neighborhood or environment and largely affect those who are *not* required to move. It is sometimes remarked that the owners whose property is taken by eminent domain are often the lucky ones. Those located nearby, but not within, the right-of-way frequently suffer disruption and loss of value for which they receive no compensation. There can be no doubt that the building of a major highway or transit line through a residential area causes fundamental changes to the neighborhood. These changes may be either beneficial or harmful — quite often, they are both.

There is some evidence that the disruption may be greater if the highway or transit line is put through a tightly knit working-class community as opposed to a middle-class area. Some observers have argued that the working-class family is more immobile than the middle-class family, and more tightly linked to an extended family that typically lives within walking distance. If true, when a decision is made to carry out construction in a working-class neighborhood, greater aid may be needed to compensate displaced residents and to assist the reconstruction of their environment.

Unfortunately, few operational tools are available for improving route selection decisions by taking such broader social considerations into account. To do so, several hard questions must be faced. How much community-wide benefit from construction of a road should be sacrificed for these neighborhood and individual values? Can cash payments of whatever amount compensate residents for the real character of their loss? If they cannot reconstruct their present environment, would adequate resources allow the displaced to construct a different but equally satisfactory or better environment? Is the problem in question essentially unique, or is it typical of all or most low-income communities? If it is typical, the road builders' options are, of course, limited. Almost any alignment would impose comparable costs on the affected communities. The range of choice is then narrowed to whether the road should be built, which remedial actions should be taken to limit the displacement or damage, and how generously the damaged population should be compensated.

Existing compensation formulas and mechanisms, unfortunately, fail to compensate many losers altogether and provide many others with grossly inadequate compensation. These inadequacies are responsible for much of the current resistance to urban transportation construction. A few individuals are often required to bear a disproportionately large share of the costs of urban transportation improvements in order to provide benefits for all. In these circumstances, spontaneous community action to oppose the new construction is hardly surprising.

PROPOSED SOLUTIONS

Perhaps the most ambitious proposal for improving urban transportation services for the poor is to make public transit free, thereby eliminating income as a determinant of transit use. Clearly, though, this is inefficient. A large proportion of transit users are not poor, and free transit would subsidize the affluent as well as the poor. Moreover, the major difficulty facing the poor, and particularly the ghetto poor, is not that transit is too expensive, but that it is all too frequently unavailable in forms and services that are needed. In general, transit use seems far more sensitive to service improvements than to fare reductions, even for the poor. Nor is "free" transit particularly cheap. It has been estimated that, nationwide, the costs of free transit would be approximately $2 billion a year, assuming no increase in service.

Boston can be used to illustrate the comparative costs of free transit and service improvements for the poor. Until very recently, access between Boston's Roxbury ghetto and rapidly expanding suburban employment centers has been nonexistent for all practical purposes. The costs of providing transit services between all Boston's poverty areas (i.e., census tracts with median family incomes below $5,500 per year) and low-skill employment centers have been estimated at about $4.3 million annually. This is to be compared with an estimate of $75 million a year for free transit in Boston. The $4.3 million figure is, moreover, a total or gross cost; it would be less if any fare box revenues were realized. Furthermore, the $75 million subsidy for free transit would not provide any significant improvement in transit service between central city poverty areas and suburban employment centers.

An increasingly popular view is that public transit systems, as currently constituted, are incapable of increasing the mobility of the poor. The argument is that the transportation demands involved in serving outlying workplaces from central city residences are too complex to be met adequately by any kind of public transit services at costs that are competitive with private automobiles. At two persons per car, for example, the cost of private automobile operation often is comparable to or lower than bus transportation in serving dispersed workplaces.

If so, it may be cheaper and more effective to provide some form of personal transportation for the poor. One such proposal, which its originator terms "new Volks for poor folks," is to rent, lease, or otherwise finance new or relatively new cars for low-income households. Cheap used cars are seldom low-cost cars. If the cost of automobile use is to be reduced for low-income groups, their cars must be relatively new; if they are to have such new cars, the cost of credit must be lowered. A related proposal is to assist those workers who live in central ghettos and work in the suburbs to sell transportation services to fellow workers. Such sales would help pay the purchase and operating costs of an automobile. In many cities, however, this proposal would encounter a number of institutional and legal barriers.

Of course, new cars for poor people will not help nondrivers, who are now estimated to make up 20 per cent of the population over 17 years of age. In fact, any extension of automobile ownership among the able-bodied poor may only serve to further degrade public transit services for nondrivers. To provide mobility for nondrivers, some have advocated the development of so-called demand actuated systems. Different versions of this concept come under a variety of names or acronyms, including Taxi-bus, Dial-a-bus, DART, GENIE, and CARS. In all cases, however, the idea is to provide something approximating the point-to-point service of taxis, while achieving better utilization levels and load factors than transit vehicles can now achieve on fixed routes and schedules.

In these systems, vehicles intermediate in size between a taxicab and a conventional bus would be used to pick up and deliver passengers at specific origins and destinations. By use of electronic control and scheduling, it is claimed, loads could be assembled with a minimum of delay. Proponents believe these systems usually would have cost characteristics intermediate between the conventional bus and the taxicab. By providing more individualistic door-to-door service than public transit, these systems might be of particular use for the elderly and the infirm. Furthermore, if such systems have the advantages suggested, they might be a better and more politically acceptable solution to the problems of ghetto access than subsidies to extend ownership of private automobiles, particularly in older cities with high density central residential neighborhoods.

Indeed, were it not for franchise restrictions and prohibitions on group fares, taxicabs could improve their operating efficiency considerably without any technological improvements. Demand-activated systems are functionally identical with taxis, but have more sophisticated scheduling, control devices, and operating policies.

Indeed, many benefits would accrue to the poor if there were fewer restrictions on the provision of taxi and jitney services. A deregulated taxi industry would provide a considerable number of additional jobs for low-income workers. It has been calculated that removing entry barriers and other controls might expand the number of taxis by as much as two and a half times in most American cities. In Philadelphia, for example, deregulation could create an additional 7,400 jobs for drivers alone; if these jobs went to the poorest 20 per cent of the population, unemployment among these poor would fall by about 3.2 percentage points.

Taxi operation can also be an important income supplement for low-income households even where it is not a full-time job. A significant number of Washington's taxi drivers own and operate their own cabs on a part-time basis as a supplement to a regular job. The off-duty cab often doubles as the family car, thus substantially reducing the cost of auto ownership and increasing the mobility of residents of low-income neighborhoods.

A much expanded taxi and jitney industry could also provide an appreciable increase in urban mobility, particularly for the poor. Except for restrictive legislation, jitneys and taxicabs might now be providing a significant fraction of passenger service in urban areas. The greater number of taxis per hundred persons in Washington, D.C., an essentially unregulated city, and the sizable capital value of medallions (franchises to operate a cab) in New York, Boston, and several other cities, attest to a substantial latent demand for these services.

In short, simply providing larger subsidies to transit systems is unlikely to be an effective way of increasing the mobility of the poor. New systems seem needed, and there is some agreement on their characteristics. Such systems would normally use a smaller vehicle than conventional transit, would be demand-activated rather than on fixed routes and schedules, and would provide point-to-point service or some close approximation of it. Such systems would most likely have somewhat lower passenger mile costs than do taxicabs (even those operating in unrestricted markets like Washington), but unit costs probably would be somewhat above those of current transit systems. In some instances, such services might merely supplement the more heavily used transit services; in others, they might replace such services altogether.

Ownership of these more ubiquitous systems might vary from place to place and from time to time. Where elaborate control and scheduling are required, a fleet might be necessary. In other instances, the services could be provided by large numbers of owner-operators working either independently or in a cooperative. Another possibility is nothing more complicated than organized carpooling, compensated or uncompensated.

Most such systems require very little long-lived investment. The most extensive capital requirements, of course, would be for the more elaborate, electronically controlled, demand activated systems. All would require major changes in institutions and regulatory frameworks. Fortunately, however, most also lend themselves to experimentation on a modest scale. Such experimentation could do much to improve our fund of information, which at this point is simply inadequate to support bolder policy initiatives.

FURTHER READINGS

Anderson, W. H. Locke. "Trickling Down: The Relationship Between Economic Growth and the Extent of Poverty Among American Families." *Quarterly Journal of Economics* 78 (1964), pp. 511–524.

Barr, Nicholas, and Hall, Robert. "The Taxation of Earnings Under Public Assistance." M.I.T. working paper (April 1972).

Bowman, Mary Jean. "Poverty in an Affluent Society." In *Contemporary Economic Issues,* edited by Neil W. Chamberlain. Homewood, Ill.: Richard D. Irwin, 1968.

Duncan, Beverly. "Dropouts and the Unemployed." *Journal of Political Economy* 61 (1953), pp. 277–299.

Faltermayer, Edmund K. "A Way Out of the Welfare Mess." *Fortune* (July 1969).

Feldstein, Martin S. "A New Approach to National Health Insurance." *The Public Interest* (Spring 1971), pp. 93–105.

Friedman, Milton. *Capitalism and Freedom.* Chicago: The University of Chicago Press, 1962.

Friedman, Rose D. *Poverty, Definition and Perspective.* Washington, D.C.: American Enterprise Institute for Policy Research, 1965.

Fuchs, Victor R. "Toward a Theory of Poverty." In *The Concept of Poverty.* A report of the Task Force on Economic Growth and Opportunity. Washington, D.C.: Chamber of Commerce of the United States, 1965.

Green, Christopher. *Negative Taxes and the Poverty Problem.* Washington, D.C.: The Brookings Institution, 1967.

Grieson, Ronald E. *The Determinants of Juvenile Arrests,* MIT Working Paper, 87 (July 1972).

Johnson, Harry G. "The Economics of Poverty." *American Economic Review* 55 (May 1965), pp. 543–545.

Kosters, Marvin and Welch, Finis. "The Effects of Minimum Wages on the Distribution of Changes in Aggregate Employment." *American Economic Review* 62 (June 1972), pp. 323–332.

Maass, Arthur. "Benefit-Cost Analysis: Its Relevance to Public Investment Decisions." *Quarterly Journal of Economics* 80 (May 1966), pp. 208–226.

Newhouse, Joseph P., and Taylor, Vincent. "How Shall We Pay for Hospital Care?" *The Public Interest* (Spring 1971), pp. 78–92.

Orshansky, Mollie. "Counting the Poor: Another Look at the Poverty Profile." *Social Security Bulletin* 28 (January 1965).

Ribich, Thomas I. *Education and Poverty.* Washington, D.C.: The Brookings Institution, 1968.

Schultz, Theodore W. "Investing in Poor People: An Economist's View." *American Economic Review* 55 (1965), pp. 510–520.

Smolensky, Eugene. "Investment in Education of the Poor: A Pessimistic Report." *American Economic Review* 56 (May 1966), pp. 370–378.

Tobin, James; Pechman, Joseph A.; and Mieszkowski, Peter M. "Is the Negative Income Tax Practical?" *Yale Law Journal* (November 1967).

Watts, Harold W. "Graduated Work Incentives: An Experiment in Negative Taxation." *American Economic Review* 59 (May 1969), pp. 463–472.

Weisbrod, Burton A. "Income Redistribution Effects and Benefit-Cost Analysis." In *Problems in Public Expenditures Analysis,* edited by Samuel B. Chase, Jr. Washington, D.C.: The Brookings Institution, 1968.

Weisbrod, Burton A. "Preventing High School Dropouts," in Dorfman, Robert, ed. *Measuring the Benefits of Government Investment* (Washington, D.C.: The Brookings Institution, 1965).

Chapter 8

DISCRIMINATION

Black people constitute approximately one-third of the total urban population and one-half of the urban poor in our medium and large cities. By contrast, the black population is only one-eighth of the total U.S. population and a much smaller percentage of our suburban population. Those few suburbs in which blacks live usually have a black majority, but the typical suburb has only a small number. The expected continuation of black migration to cities in search of employment is likely to intensify this general concentration. Hence, discrimination is and will continue to be a serious concern of cities.

Discrimination is an extremely serious handicap for the black community in America. Blacks receive inferior education, are often paid less for equal work effort, pay more for food, housing, and clothing, and receive lower-quality public services and political representation than whites. The rate of poverty among blacks is triple that of whites. Everything we stated in our discussion of poverty is in a sense triply true for blacks. In addition to poverty, there is the suffering and anguish of knowing the root of your deprivation is discrimination and the experience of insulting innuendo at every step. Barbara Bergmann documents the loss in human capital due to inferior education and lack of equal opportunity for blacks. To know how to remedy the situation we must first have an accurate picture of discrimination and the economic mechanisms through which it operates.

Blacks pay more than whites for equivalent housing; yet studies of housing prices or rents have shown that after econometrically adjusting for density of occupation (by density we mean number of persons per room or per 100 square feet) as a determinant of rents blacks pay no more for housing than whites. Martin Bailey's econometric study of housing shows that if whites were to live at the same density as blacks they would pay as high a rent, which means that blacks are paying more per square foot for a given quality of housing and consume less housing per capita than whites. In other words, if whites had to house an equal number of persons in so small a quantity of residence they would bid up the rent and occupy housing at the same density at which blacks are forced to occupy housing. Whites generally utilize similar types of housing at much lower density than blacks, however.

As Professors Haugen and Heins explain in their article of market separation, blacks live at greater densities than whites because they have a restricted number of housing choices open to them due to discrimination, and therefore a smaller housing stock per capita than whites. Blacks thereby bid up the price of the limited housing available. The landlord rents to the individual or family offering the highest rent who is almost always black since a white person can go to another neighborhood and pay less. We can thus see that the higher rents are not primarily due to landlord's initiative, although they certainly do take advantage of and support (for financial and perhaps racial reasons) a system that does, but are due instead to the exclusion of blacks from the white community, most especially the suburbs. Because equivalent housing rents for higher prices in black neighborhoods than in white ones, it would seem quite likely that property values are also higher. Hence the argument that blacks lower property values does not fare well in our analysis. Studies by Luigi Laurenti, Anthony Downs, and Anthony Pascal point to these general conclusions. Our analysis does not imply that every white discriminates, but it does imply that enough whites have discriminatory feelings against blacks so as to impose effective discrimination. If all communities were racially open, rents to blacks would fall to the same levels as rents to whites even in what was formerly the ghetto.

Blacks also pay more for food, because food stores in black neighborhoods are small, and they are unable to take advantage of the economies of scale. In other words, small stores cannot take advantage of the reductions in costs brought about by the greater utilization of capital equipment that is possible with a large volume of sales. These economies enable the food to be merchandised at low prices. In addition, ghetto stores bear the cost of extending credit to customers and experience higher risk of fire and theft. Stores located in ghetto neighborhoods are small because black communities usually form too small a dollar-value market to support a large capital intensive store and need costly personal credit because of their low and unstable incomes. Blacks also cannot afford autos, which would permit stores to serve a larger community.

The increased risk of fire and theft in ghettos is probably brought about by inadequate police and fire protection and by the high cost of capital to finance secure, fireproof buildings. The small ghetto store is left with the alternative of paying high insurance premiums (if insurance is even available) or bearing the risk itself. Thus the cause of high prices is not necessarily the prejudice of the store owner (although there certainly are merchants who exploit the situation), but rather a result of low incomes.

Low income, discrimination, poor living conditions, and lack of sympathetic police may also contribute to a higher crime rate in ghettos. I have recently completed a study of the factors that correlate with and plausibly contribute to juvenile arrests and the effectiveness of programs aimed at limiting such arrests. The study, using data for the city of Rochester, suggests that poverty, low income, lack of home ownership (which perhaps indicates a lack of wealth), and segregation of minority groups may help cause juvenile arrests. Police patrolling, settlement houses, and recreation all seem to be of minor influence in preventing arrests.

Is the solution to discrimination black capitalism, special transportation programs, Job Corps, dropout prevention? Black capitalism may be important, though it would probably be of limited value to the black community with little capital and an educational disadvantage in management. It makes little sense to put the black community at a severe disadvantage by cutting them off from the large, white-owned supply of funds. It is desirable to encourage and aid black businessmen in a number of ways, but they alone cannot be expected to supply all the jobs and housing needed by the community. Any notion that black labor should work exclusively with black capital smacks of racism and continued inequality of opportunity.

Special transportation programs are also of little use if job opportunities do not exist. Again, transportation is only one of a list of goods and services unavailable to blacks because of discrimination and low income. Increased performance and fairness in transportation facilities would, with only moderate additional subsidy, meet the special needs of the ghetto.

As was demonstrated by the readings in our section on poverty, special education and dropout prevention programs are futile and hypocritical when job opportunities do not exist. In addition, minimum-wage and fair-employment legislation seem to be mixed blessings; they increase the salaries of those employed, but increase unemployment. William Landes's study of fair-employment legislation testifies to this.

Perhaps further analysis of the economics of discrimination will yield a solution. Lester Thurow, following lines originally developed by Gary S. Becker, suggests that in pure competition the level of discrimination is determined by the average (actually marginal) level of willingness to make or accept sacrifices in order to discriminate or allow others to do so that exists among the majority-group (white) employees, employers, or consumers (given the percentage of blacks in the community). Not all whites pay for the right to discriminate, however; some white labor gains financially from discrimination because of reduced competition from black labor, while white employers (or capital) and consumers lose by having to pay for discrimination. The diminished supply of labor causes higher prices.

Whether the white community as a whole profits or pays for discrimination is uncertain, but there can be no doubt that the black community sustains great losses. Becker originally stated that the white community would lose financially, as would any group restricting its trade with another group, but Anne Krueger has shown that the white community may profit, because such trade restrictions sometimes sufficiently improve the terms of trade of the group imposing them to increase the group's income. This analysis is theoretically difficult and will certainly require a careful reading of Thurow's work and perhaps some of the suggested material.

The rectification of discrimination may lie in tacit collusion agreement on the part of our industries, retailers, and educational institutions to employ and serve blacks on an equal, and perhaps a favored, footing with whites. Customers and employees who desire to discriminate cannot boycott a nondiscriminatory enterprise when all enterprises have forsaken discrimination.

Many educational institutions have recently undertaken the policy of admitting all qualified blacks and many who are unqualified by the usual standards, often by the use of quotas. This may be a step in the right direction, although the success of provisions for special tutoring programs to aid students who are unqualified by usual standards is still to be proven effective. In addition, not many institutions have sufficient funds to support large-scale efforts in this direction. Turning to the labor market we might inquire how effective black unions have been compared to white unions. Alan Batchelder describes the reduction in the relative income of black men during the recessions of the late 1950's. Black income has traditionally varied between 50 and 60 percent of white, the higher percentage occurring during periods of full employment. Detailed studies of black and white employment patterns also indicate that black men work fewer hours than white men, but black women work more than white women. Black women may have had to try to supplement family incomes because of the lack of employment opportunities available to black men. This lack of opportunity is likely to have been instrumental in increasing the number of black families headed by a woman.

Although conclusive proof is not yet in, there is reason to believe that the ratio of black-to-white earnings is exhibiting a slow rise above the 60 percent level. If this is the case, we can look to the rest of the 1970's with cautious optimism. There is also reason to believe that the enduring black-white unemployment ratio of two to one (that is unemployment rates for blacks run twice as high as those for whites), which has persisted for a generation, is improving as black and white employment rates approach each other. Full employment is and will remain one of the paramount factors in raising the absolute and relative incomes of blacks.

DISCRIMINATION

Lester C. Thurow

In the . . . [C]onditions facing Negroes have been shown to be fundamentally different from those facing whites. Negro income distribution lags approximately thirty years behind. The sheer fact of being black explains 38 percent of the difference in the incidence of poverty for whites and Negroes. Better utilization of economic resources improves job and income opportunities of Negroes, but after adjustment for cyclical effects there have been no favorable (or unfavorable) trends in those opportunities in the postwar period. Even at very high utilization levels, median Negro family incomes remain at only 60 percent of white family incomes.[1] Smaller amounts of

---

Lester C. Thurow is Professor of Economics, Massachusetts Institute of Technology.

Reprinted with permission from Lester C. Thurow, *Poverty and Discrimination*, pp. 111–137. © 1969 by The Brookings Institution.

[1] U.S. Bureau of the Census, *Current Population Reports,* Series P-23, No. 26, BLS Report 347, "Recent Trends in Social and Economic Conditions of Negroes in the United States" (1968), p. 6.

human capital prove to have a marked impact on the incomes of Negroes, who not only receive less education and training than whites but also obtain lower returns from them. Moreover, Negroes work in industries and occupations with significantly less physical capital and technical progress. All of these items reflect discrimination, but these factors alone do not account for Negro income levels. Something further remains to be explained.

Discrimination is important not only because it produces low incomes: it also diminishes the effectiveness of many of the instruments used in fighting poverty. If discrimination reduces Negro returns to education, for instance, education may be a poor weapon to reduce Negro poverty although excellent for reducing white poverty.

To understand how discrimination causes low Negro incomes, it is necessary to understand how it operates. How were the effects outlined above produced? What actions do whites take when they discriminate? What are the economic costs of discrimination? What must the government do to eliminate it?

These questions cannot be answered theoretically. To design a strategy for eliminating discrimination, the magnitudes of different types of discrimination must be known. To provide empirical estimates, the theory of discrimination is applied to actual data in order to calculate Negro losses and white gains from different types of discrimination, and the social costs. Analysis in previous chapters has centered on Negro economic losses. To emphasize the reverse side of the discrimination problem, this chapter focuses on white gains; but it should be remembered in either case that a white gain corresponds to a Negro loss and vice versa.

THE EXISTING THEORY

Current knowledge about the theory of discrimination rests almost entirely on the work of Gary Becker.[2] In his analysis, discrimination is a restrictive practice that interrupts free trade between two independent societies, white and Negro. If free trade existed, the Negro society would export labor (its relatively abundant factor of production) and the white society would export capital (its relatively abundant factor) until the marginal products of labor and capital were equal in both societies. This would come about because each individual is maximizing a utility function which has income as its single argument.

[2] Gary S. Becker, *The Economics of Discrimination* (University of Chicago Press, 1957).

However, when there is discrimination, individuals in the white society maximize a utility function which has both income and physical distance from Negroes as arguments. Whites are willing to pay a premium not to associate with Negroes; as a result they import less Negro labor and export less white capital. Since discrimination holds trade below free trade levels, not only does total output fall, but the output of both communities falls because of the inefficient distribution of economic resources. The returns to white labor and Negro capital rise, but these are more than offset by declining returns to white capital and Negro labor.

The central proposition following from this theory is that "when actual discrimination occurs, he [the discriminator] must, in fact, either pay or forfeit income for this privilege." [3] In other words, the discriminator must lose income if he wishes to discriminate. If this deduction is correct, empirical impressions are amazingly false. Do the whites of South Africa or the United States really have lower standards of living as a result of their discrimination? If they do, increases in those standards can be used as an inducement to persuade them to give up their prejudices against Negroes. Eliminating discrimination in this case is certainly easier than in the case where it results in reductions in white standards of living.

Becker's "discrimination coefficient" (DC) corresponds to a tariff in international trade. "Suppose an *employer* were faced with the money wage rate π of a particular factor; he is assumed to act as if $\pi (1 + d_i)$ were the *net* wage rate, with d_i as his DC against this factor." [4] The discrimination coefficient is a method of representing a downward shift in the white demand curve for Negro labor. The vertical shift represents the size of the coefficient, on which depends the effect that the downward shift will have on Negro and white incomes, but that effect also depends on the supply elasticity of Negro labor and the white demand elasticity for Negro labor, as shown in Figure 1.

If the elasticity of supply (S) is zero (first panel), Negro wages (W) decline with a downward shift in demand from D_1 to D_2, but the quantity of Negro labor (Q) is constant. The return to the white community must rise since Negro wages are now less than their marginal product. In this panel white gains are equal to the rectangle $ABCD$. If the elasticity of supply is infinite (second panel), wages are constant and all of the adjustment occurs in the quantity of labor supplied. The white community loses the intermarginal product (producer's surplus) $EFG;$ no gains are possible, since Negroes cannot be paid less than their marginal product. If the elasticity of supply is greater than zero but less than infinite (third panel), both gains

3 *Ibid.*, p. 6.
4 *Ibid.*

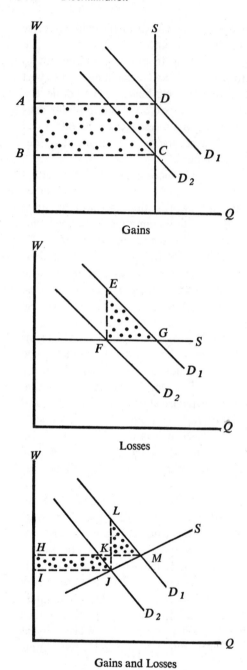

Gains

Losses

Gains and Losses
FIGURE 1.   *White Gains and Losses from Discrimination.*

and losses occur. The net gain or loss depends on the relative size of *HIJK* and *LKM*.[5]

Not only can whites gain from discrimination, but previous work has shown how to determine optimum tariffs (discrimination coefficients).[6] These studies have much stronger implications for discrimination than simply pointing out that the discriminator may benefit. The discriminator may gain in the face of retaliation or the retaliator may be able to improve on his free trade position in the face of discrimination.[7]

For Becker, the possibility of white monetary gains merely represents payment for the nonmonetary costs of production [8] (disutility) of having to associate with Negroes. The extra white incomes represent real psychological costs of production and not net returns. Three points should be established: (1) The additional output accrues to the white community and expands its consumption possibility schedule. (2) Using net utility rather

[5] More precisely:

(A) $$\Delta P(N_0 - \Delta N) \gtrless \tfrac{1}{2}N(DP_0 - \Delta P)$$

where

ΔP = change in the price of Negro labor
N_0 = initial quantity of Negro labor exported
ΔN = change in the quantity of Negro labor exported
N = Negro labor
D = discrimination coefficient
P_0 = initial price of Negro labor.

Substituting the relevant demand and supply elasticities into (A) yields

(B) $$\frac{De_0 P_0}{e_s + e_d}\left[N_0 - \frac{N_0 De_s e_d}{e_s + e_d}\right] \gtrless \frac{1}{2}\frac{N_0 e_s e_d D}{e_s + e_d}\left[DP_0 - \frac{De_0 P_0}{e_s + e_d}\right]$$

or

(C) $$1 - \frac{De_s e_d}{2e_s + e_d} \gtrless \frac{e_s D}{2}$$

where

e_d = white elasticity of demand for Negro labor
e_s = supply elasticity for Negro labor.

When $e_s = 0$, white losses are zero and when $e_s = \infty$, white gains are zero. Generally white losses do not exceed white gains unless both e_s and e_d are large.

[6] Harry G. Johnson, "Optimum Tariffs and Retaliation," *International Trade and Economic Growth* (George Allen & Unwin, Ltd., 1958), p. 31.

[7] *Ibid.*, p. 35 ff., for a proof of this proposition. Johnson finds that the discriminator (retaliator) benefits even in the face of retaliation (discrimination) when his elasticity of demand for imports is roughly more than two and one-half times as large as the elasticity of demand of the retaliator (discriminator). When the elasticities of demand are approximately equal, both countries lose, and between there is a range of indeterminacy.

For a formal application of these principles to Becker's model, see Anne O. Krueger, "The Economics of Discrimination," *Journal of Political Economy*, Vol. 71 (October 1963), pp. 481–86.

[8] Becker, *Economics of Discrimination*, p. 7.

than gross income is acceptable as long as everyone understands the unit of measurement. If net gains and losses are being examined, all other disutilities of production must also be subtracted from gross monetary incomes. Since labor is supplied to the point where the marginal disutility of giving up leisure and the disutilities of production (such as physical discomfort and monotony) are equal to the wage rate, the marginal return to labor or any other factor of production must be zero. If the marginal return were greater than zero, more labor would be supplied until wage rate reductions brought the marginal return back to zero. Introducing discrimination coefficients into a system of production means simply that the marginal disutility of supplying factors of production increases and that the supplies of these factors of production will be correspondingly reduced. (3) If racial prejudice already exists among whites but they have not been able to act upon it, introducing discrimination can give them a clear gain in net utilities. Real incomes can increase in the manner outlined above, and reducing the number of Negroes with whom whites are forced to associate results in higher utility from the physical distance argument of the utility function. Fewer Negroes means less disutility from associating with them. The result is a clear white gain in net utility.

Only if white economic incomes do not increase and if racial prejudices suddenly emerge at the instant discrimination is put into practice must whites' net utility fall. If only one of these conditions exists, empirical information is necessary to determine whether whites gain or lose.

AN ALTERNATIVE THEORY

Applying the theory of tariffs to a world of perfect competition has serious limitations in a world where much of the impact of discrimination comes from the monopoly powers of the discriminator rather than from his inability to distort perfect competition with trade barriers. Some types of discrimination seem to fit Becker's model but many do not. Discrimination cannot be represented adequately by a model of two independent societies freely trading with each other over the barriers created by economic discrimination. Racial discrimination occurs in one society, not two. The dominant group controls much more than its willingness to trade or not to trade with the minority group. Physical, social, or economic pressures may enable the dominant group to trade with the subservient group as a discriminating monopolist or monopsonist. The minority group may have few options and certainly not the option of refusing to trade. Subsistence (social or physical) may require trade. Negroes live in a white supremacist society, not just a segregated society.

Discrimination is not simply demanding a premium to associate with Negroes, as described by Becker.[9] The discriminator may want to work with, buy from, or hire Negroes, but he insists on specifying the relationships under which the two parties will meet and how the Negro will respond. Perhaps it is more accurate to say that whites maximize a utility function with social distance rather than physical distance as one of its arguments. A desire for social distance can lead to a very different set of actions. The discriminator may prefer to hire Negro maids, Negro garbage collectors, or to work with Negroes if he can be in a position of authority. He may also prefer to hire Negro labor if it can be exploited to increase his own profits.

VARIETIES OF DISCRIMINATION

A long list of types of discrimination could be compiled, but most can be subsumed under seven general categories: (1) employment (unemployment, both full-time and part-time, is concentrated among Negroes); (2) wages (Negroes are simply paid less for the same work); (3) occupation (quantitative controls limit or prevent Negro entry into some occupations, and supplies of Negro labor to the unrestricted occupations are correspondingly enlarged); (4) human capital (less is invested in human capital for Negroes than for whites); (5) capital (price discrimination and/or quantitative controls limit Negroes' ability to borrow from the capital markets, or the rate of return on Negro capital can be lowered by a variety of techniques); (6) monopoly power (Negro factors of production are not permitted to enter those areas where monopolies result in factor returns above those prevailing in a competitive economy); (7) price (Negro buyers are required to pay above market prices and Negro sellers must sell at below market prices).

These seven types are discussed in this section under the assumption that a rational discriminator (for example, a monopolist named "whites") is trying to maximize his gains from discrimination, including economic gains and increases in social distance. This procedure does not imply that the assumption is correct; it simply permits us to determine whether white gains are possible and to view the causes of the gains or losses. Additionally it focuses attention on the clashes between different types of discrimination. Maximizing the gains from one type of discrimination may clash with maximizing the gains from another type. Conflicts between different discriminators represent one of the major problems faced by them as a group. To solve these conflicts, anomalies often seem to appear in the observed pattern of discrimination.

[9] *Ibid.*

EMPLOYMENT

This type of discrimination results in gains for whites without any offsetting losses.[10] If Negroes suffer more than their proportionate share of unemployment, the number of employed whites increases and their incomes are larger than they would be otherwise.

To maximize white gains from employment discrimination, Negroes should be distributed across occupations, industries, and geographic areas in such a way that their employment is equal to the maximum expected unemployment in each category and they can be forced to bear the entire burden of unemployment in each. If the total Negro labor force is not as large as the maximum expected unemployment, efficient employment discrimination will dictate that Negro employment should be concentrated in high-wage areas since the greatest gains can be made by substituting whites for Negroes there. White unemployment would be allowed only in the lowest paying occupations. The employment distribution which attempts to maximize white gains from employment discrimination will obviously conflict with attempts to maximize gains from occupational discrimination. Employment discrimination may call for employment of Negroes in high-wage occupations, while occupational discrimination calls for employment of Negroes in low-wage occupations.

WAGES

If wage discrimination and quantitative controls over Negro employment are possible, white incomes can be enlarged by distributing Negro employment optimally (from the standpoint of resource allocation) throughout the occupational structure and thereupon appropriating part of each Negro's marginal product by paying him less than his product. If the distribution of white employment and capital is independent of the distribution of Negro employment, the discriminator will want to maximize the difference between Negro marginal products and Negro wages.[11] If the marginal products of Negro laborers are not affected by incentives, white incomes would be max-

---

[10] This refers simply to private monetary gains and does not include social costs such as the slums produced by Negro poverty.

[11] The discriminator would want to maximize the following expression:

$$\sum_{i=1}^{n} [(MP_{Li}{}^{N} - W_i{}^{N})(E_i{}^{N})]$$

where

$MP_{Li}{}^{N}$ = marginal product of Negro labor in occupation i
$W_i{}^{N}$ = wages of Negro labor in occupation i
$E_i{}^{N}$ = supply of Negro labor in occupation i.

imized by paying subsistence wages to Negroes and using quantitative controls to distribute their employment in such a way as to equalize the difference between marginal products and wages in each occupation. If Negro marginal products depend on incentives, wages should be set in each occupation to maximize the difference between the marginal product and the wage rate; quantitative employment controls could then equalize the differences across occupations. In either case white incomes are clearly larger as a result of discrimination. Whites have been able to appropriate part of the marginal product of Negro labor and there have been no losses from an inefficient distribution of economic resources.

If the distribution of white employment and capital is not independent of the distribution of Negro employment, the net gains or losses will depend on whether the gains from appropriating part of the Negro marginal product are greater than the losses from the inefficient distribution of white labor and capital.[12] Whether gains or losses occur depends on the supply price elasticities for white labor and capital and the elasticities of the marginal products of capital and labor with respect to changes in the quantities of each employed. If white labor and capital supply curves are inelastic, if the marginal product curves are inelastic, and if wage discrimination is extensive, whites probably gain. With these conditions, there is little distortion in the distribution of capital and labor, and the gains from discrimination are large.

In a different case, with wage discrimination but no quantitative controls over Negro employment, the analysis is very similar. Instead of considering only the effects of wages on work incentives within an occupation, the effect of wages on supplies of Negro labor to an occupation must also be taken into account. The lower the elasticity of the Negro labor supply curve, the larger are white gains from discrimination. With inelastic Negro labor supply curves, wage discrimination can be undertaken without causing large distortions in the supplies of Negro labor.

[12] Analytically, are the gains on the left side of the following expression greater or less than the losses on the right side?

$$\sum_{i=1}^{n} (MP_{L_i}{}^N - W_i{}^N) \, E_i{}^N \gtrless \sum_{i=1}^{n} (K_i{}^w)(\Delta MP_{K_i}{}^w) + \sum_{i=1}^{n} (E_i{}^w)(\Delta MP_{L_i}{}^w)$$

where
$MP_{L_i}{}^N$ = marginal product of Negro labor in occupation i
$W_i{}^N$ = wages of Negro labor in occupation i
$E_i{}^N$ = supply of Negro labor in occupation i
$K_i{}^w$ = supply of white capital in occupation i
$\Delta MP_{K_i}{}^w$ = change in the marginal product of white capital in occupation i
$E_i{}^w$ = supply of white labor in occupation i
$\Delta MP_{L_i}{}^w$ = change in the marginal product of white labor in occupation i

OCCUPATION

Here white income gains result from creating a white occupational distribution weighted toward high-wage occupations. Incomes are higher than they would be if whites were efficiently (on the basis of resource allocation) distributed across occupations. White costs are those of the extra investment necessary to train less talented whites for skilled occupations, or the losses to white capital or labor from having less qualified individuals in the occupations.[13]

The white community may lose from wage and occupational discrimination, but this is not to say that the actual discriminator within the white community also loses by practicing discrimination. Discrimination may produce inefficiency losses which are larger than the gains from appropriated marginal products or a favorable occupational distribution, but particular subgroups (the actual discriminator) may gain. The discriminator suffers a small fraction of the total inefficiency losses of the white community, but he is in a position to appropriate a major fraction of the gain from practicing discrimination. Thus the actual discriminator may gain although the white community as a whole losses. The opposite case is also possible. An individual discriminator may lose income by refusing to sell his home to Negroes while his neighbors gain. Thus to isolate economic gains or losses for whites as a group does not provide much information about those of specific whites.

HUMAN CAPITAL

Limiting investment in Negro human capital can increase white incomes in several ways. In the short run white consumption possibilities may be expanded, since fewer resources are devoted to education, on-the-job training, and other types of human investment.[14] The return to white human

---

[13] With occupation discrimination, the left side of the expression in note 12 becomes:

$$\left[\sum_{i=1}^{n} \frac{E_i^w}{E^w} MP_{Li} - \sum_{i=1}^{n} \frac{E_i}{E} MP_{Li} \times \right] E^w$$

where

$E^w =$ supply of white labor
$MP_{Li} =$ marginal product of labor in occupation i
$E_i =$ supply of labor (white plus Negro) in occupation i
$E =$ supply of labor

With both wage and occupation discrimination, the above expression is added to the left side of the expression in note 12.

[14] The actual effect will depend on the system used to finance human investment. If investment is publicly financed by a proportional or progressive tax system, whites gain when investment expenditures are cut. If a regressive tax system whereby Negroes finance all of their own human investment is in effect, there would be no short-run gains in white consumption.

capital also increases when the supplies of Negro human capital are reduced, but part of the gain may be offset by smaller returns to white labor or capital if their distribution depends on the quantity of Negro human capital. The net gains or losses depend on the elasticity of demand for human capital and the exact interdependence between Negro human capital and the productivity of white labor and capital.[15]

In addition to direct gains (or losses) from restricting investment in Negro human capital, restricting capital investment may be one of the best methods of enforcing effective employment, occupation, or wage discrimination. Lack of formal education or on-the-job training may be an effective method to limit the number of Negroes in certain occupations; lack of human investment removes business incentives to cut costs with Negro employees; it confines Negroes to those industries and jobs most subject to cyclical or secular unemployment; it makes wage discrimination more effective by making Negro labor a complement to white labor rather than a substitute for it; and by denying Negroes managerial experience it may be a means to discriminate against Negro capital (see the following section).

Initially human capital discrimination may arise from a distaste for educating Negro and white children together (though this does not explain lower expenditures on Negro schools), but the result is creation of a monopoly power that can be used to practice other types of economic discrimination. Just as maximizing white gains from employment and occupational discrimination can conflict, human capital discriminaton can conflict with occupation and wage discrimination. If wage discrimination were most effective in the skilled occupations (the largest difference between marginal products and wages), maximizing white incomes might call for a heavy investment in Negro human capital.

CAPITAL

This kind of discrimination generally takes one of two forms. Negroes can be prevented from having equal access to the capital markets, or they can be prevented from making efficient use of the capital generated within their own community. By making it difficult for Negroes to use capital, economic discrimination not only prevents them from importing capital, but

---

[15] Analytically, are the gains on the left side of the following expression greater or less than the losses on the right side?

$$(\Delta P)(H^w) \gtrless \sum_{i=1}^{n} (\Delta MP_{L_i}{}^w)(E_i{}^w) + \sum_{i=1}^{n} (\Delta MP_{K_i}{}^w)(K_i{}^w)$$

where

ΔP = change in the price of human capital
H^w = quantity of white human capital.

it also forces the export of their capital. In this case the Negro community exports all production factors and imports consumption goods.

Capital discrimination may be implemented by many techniques. Occupational discrimination and human capital discrimination may deny Negro capital the complementary factor of managerial experience and knowledge; rates of return on capital can be lowered by lack of cooperation from government or legal institutions; discrimination may reduce the real purchasing power of Negro capital; or the threat of white retaliation may make it impossible for Negro-managed capital to enter many areas. Direct price discrimination in the white capital markets may make Negroes pay a premium to borrow or may result in quantitative controls on the amounts or purposes of loans.

White capital loses from discrimination if the rates of return on capital are higher in the Negro community and white capital refuses to enter. Under Becker's physical distance interpretation of discrimination there should be little loss of this kind. Whites do not need to accompany their capital in most cases. However, under the social distance interpretation the losses may be much greater. There may be a reluctance to lend money to Negroes since Negro control over economic resources reduces social distance. The net gains or losses depend on whether the gains from being able to pay Negro capital less than its marginal product are greater than the losses from an inefficient distribution of white capital.[16]

MONOPOLY POWER

This type of discrimination [17] occurs when Negroes are not permitted to enter areas where monopolies result in factor returns above those prevailing in the competitive areas of the economy. For instance, if the total number of plumbers is restricted by union entry terms, their wages may be above competitive levels. If Negroes are not admitted to the plumbers' union, whites occupy more than their proportionate share of the fixed number of plumbing positions and collect all of the monopoly gains without having to share them with Negroes. This discrimination differs from occupation dis-

---

[16] Analytically, are the gains on the left side of the following expression greater or less than the losses on the right side?

$$\sum_{i=1}^{n} (MP_{Ki}{}^{N} - R_{Ki}{}^{N}) K_i{}^{Nw} \gtrless \sum_{i=1}^{n} (\Delta MP_{Ki}{}^{w})(K_i{}^{w})$$

where

$MP_{Ki}{}^{N}$ = marginal product of Negro capital in occupation i
$R_{Ki}{}^{N}$ = actual return to Negro capital in occupation i
$K_i{}^{Nw}$ = supply of Negro capital in occupation i under white control

[17] R. A. Musgrave first pointed out to me the existence of this variety.

crimination in that the wages in the areas with monopoly powers are not related to the skills needed. Thus white losses from the extra training that must be given to less qualified whites are presumably less.[18] The same gains from monopoly privileges can occur in the capital markets.

PRICE

Discrimination in selling prices results in gains for the white community if the Negro price elasticity of demand is less than one. In this situation, higher prices produce higher returns for white sellers. If the white community can practice price discrimination in a selective way, discrimination should be applied to those commodities where the elasticity of demand is less than one but not where it is greater than one.

Discrimination in buying prices is similar to wage discrimination (see Becker's theory of discrimination above); the gains depend on the Negro elasticity of supply to the white commodity markets. If supplies are inelastic whites gain, and if they are elastic whites lose. The losses that occur in the process are the inefficiencies that result from a disequilibrium price system.

The housing market is probably the clearest example of price discrimination. By refusing to sell homes in the suburbs to Negroes, whites suffer economic losses, but they also make gains from the higher prices that can then be charged in the central city ghettos. The net gains or losses depend on the relative elasticities of supply and demand inside and outside the ghetto. Since the supply and demand curves for housing are certainly more inelastic in the ghettos, whites as a group gain by housing discrimination, but the whites in the suburbs lose while the slumlords gain. On the other hand, white suburbanites may not perceive this loss if banking institutions refuse to lend money to Negroes (see following section on enforcing discrimination).

---

[18] The size of the gains from monopoly power discrimination is given in the following expression, which indicates the gains from having a more than proportionate share of the monopoly privileges of the economy:

$$\left[\sum_{i=1}^{n} \frac{E_i^w}{E^w} (MP_{Li}^M - MP_{Li}^C) - \sum_{i=1}^{n} \frac{E_i}{E} (MP_{Li}^M - MP_{Li}^C) \right] E^w$$

$$+ \left[\sum_{i=1}^{n} \frac{K_i^w}{K^w} (MP_{Ki}^M - MP_{Ki}^C) - \sum_{i=1}^{n} \frac{K_i}{K} (MP_{Ki}^M - MP_{Ki}^C) \right] K^w$$

where
MP_{Li}^M = marginal product of labor in occupation i under conditions of monopoly
MP_{Li}^C = marginal product of labor in occupation i under competitive conditions
(The capital variables are defined in the same way as those for labor.)

RELATIVE INCOME DISCRIMINATION

Several methods for maximizing absolute white income levels by discrimination have been explored, but the actual white goal may be to maximize relative rather than absolute incomes.[19] Social distance may be maximized in either case. Maximizing absolute incomes is achieved by making any change which will result in higher white incomes, maximizing relative incomes by any change which results in a larger decline in Negro incomes than in those of whites. The conditions for improving relative incomes are even less rigorous than those for improving absolute incomes. For example, wage discrimination can be more vigorously used if it can be carried to the point where the white and Negro losses are equal rather than to the point where white losses first occur.

ENFORCEMENT OF DISCRIMINATION

Both within and between the various types of discrimination there are conflicts among whites. Maximizing the gains for each type of discrimination independently or for any one individual will not result in maximum gains for whites as a group. To maximize the total gains, discrimination must be carried out to the point where the gains from one type are zero or where they are equal to the reductions in gains that it causes to other types, whichever comes first.

Since some whites suffer losses from discrimination — the suburban resident who could sell his home to a Negro for a higher price, the employer who could hire cheaper Negro labor — what mechanism is used to enforce losses on them?

When governments play an active role in discrimination, as in South Africa and in many American communities, the powers of government pro-

---

[19] In this case whites will want to maximize the following expression:

$$\frac{\sum\limits_{i=1}^{n} W_i^w E_i^w / \sum\limits_{i=1}^{n} E_i^w}{\sum\limits_{i=1}^{n} W_i^N E_i^N / \sum\limits_{i=1}^{n} E^N}$$

where

$W_i^w = $ white wage in occupation i
$W_i^N = $ Negro wage in occupation i

vide the enforcing mechanism.[20] Such powers are the chief means for building and enforcing white monopsony and monopoly powers and preventing countervailing powers from emerging in the Negro community. When a government wishes to practice discrimination, it is the major vehicle for restricting investment in Negro education; it enforces the community desire for discrimination on individual whites who might prefer less of it; it encourages the export of Negro capital by refusing the essential governmental cooperation necessary to run a Negro business; its housing codes prevent whites from selling to Negroes in the wrong locations; and its police powers can be used to discourage Negro retaliation. With central control over the practice of discrimination, compensation can be arranged for whites who lose by it. Thus in South Africa the occupational distribution of Negroes is a subject for negotiation when the wages of white miners are being determined. White wages go up if blacks are allowed into more skilled occupations.

When government does not actively practice discrimination and does not permit explicit legal practices which facilitate it, such as restrictive housing codes or union-management agreements to practice discrimination, enforcement is more difficult. Community or social pressure is one means of forcing whites to accept the concomitant losses. The main mechanism, however, comes from the interlocking nature of the different types of discrimination.

If the various types are viewed separately, there seem to be powerful economic pressures leading to their elimination. Suburban homeowners could gain by selling to Negroes. White employers could increase profits by hiring Negroes. When the several types of discrimination are viewed together, however, the economic pressures are either not present or present in a much more attenuated form.

In the abstract, the white suburban homeowner should be willing to sell to Negroes. Physical distance theories cannot explain his actions. Since he is moving, proximity to Negroes should not bother him. The social opinions of his ex-neighbors should be irrelevant. Perhaps his utility function includes the opinions of *former* neighbors, and social pressures prevent him from selling to Negroes. Or perhaps the desire for social distance is the explanation. If Negroes move into neighborhoods where whites formerly lived and into their old homes, the social distance between blacks and whites has been reduced. Negroes are only one jump behind.

More likely, other types of discrimination prevent all but a very few white homeowners from ever having to face this situation. Other types of economic discrimination result in low Negro incomes. Consequently, Ne-

---

[20] In Becker's analysis, government discrimination is treated as merely another discrimination coefficient to be added to the demand curve.

groes are seldom in an economic position to bid for the housing of whites. Even if an individual Negro has sufficient income, he still may be prevented from bidding for a white home if there is discrimination in lending institutions. Equal incomes do not lead to the same control over economic resources: a white can buy a more expensive house than a Negro who has a similar income.

Banks, like individuals, may have very little to lose by discrimination. Since most Negroes have low incomes, the profits from lending them money are small and may be outweighed by the losses from white retaliation. If many whites were confronted by Negro buyers willing and able to pay high prices for housing, or if banks were faced by the loss of large profits if they did not lend to Negroes, the strength of residential segregation patterns would be much less than it actually is.

A similar situation is visible in the lack of job opportunities for Negroes. Employers should be willing to hire them at lower wages than are now being paid. Profits would be larger and the employer need not personally work with them. Social pressures and the individual retaliatory power of white laborers may provide some of the answers. More likely, employers are seldom confronted by such a case. In most instances Negroes cannot be hired at lower wages. Human capital discrimination, in both school and on-the-job training, controls entry into skilled jobs. Thus the employer may seldom see an objectively qualified Negro. Historical practices may have persuaded Negroes not to apply. The Negroes who do apply simply lack the skills he needs. Monopoly powers of white labor as a group may effectively prevent him from paying lower wages to Negroes or from hiring them. In any case, his losses from not hiring them are obviously minimal, if he seldom or never sees a qualified Negro. Since potential losses are small, less monopoly power is necessary to prevent the employment of the few Negroes who are qualified.

In most cases, plants and firms are willing to hire Negroes for some jobs and not for others: they are not lily-white. Negroes may be hired as sweepers, janitors, and garbage men. There is a social gap between these jobs, which are not within the traditional lines of promotion, and the rest of the jobs in the organization. Negroes are not hired for other jobs since such hiring would reduce social distance between whites and blacks.

Thus it is clear that each type of discrimination makes it easier to enforce other types. Less schooling leads to fewer job skills, easing the problems of occupational, employment, and monopoly power discrimination. Together all of these lead to low incomes, which make price and human capital discrimination easier. Together they reduce Negro political power and make schooling discrimination possible. No matter what type of discrimination is examined, it is reinforced by other types. They exist in a system of mutual support. When all are viewed together, no white perceives great economic losses from discrimination, and consequently there are only minor economic pressures to put an end to it.

ENDING DISCRIMINATION

Under the Becker theory, there is very little that either governments or Negroes can do to end discrimination.[21] It arises in a free trade environment as a result of the desire of millions of white individuals not to associate with Negroes. Government and Negroes can only attempt to change these attitudes. Antidiscrimination laws merely allow the dispersion of discrimination coefficients to have some effect on the amount of discrimination in society. Negroes may find a white who is willing to sell a home to them if he is not prevented from doing so by law. If governments are enforcing discrimination, the median discrimination coefficient governs the amount of discrimination in society, but without government enforcement the marginal discrimination coefficient governs the amount.

Under the theory of discrimination presented in this chapter, there are many actions which governments and Negroes can take to end discrimination. Many of the effects of discrimination rest on monopoly or monopsony powers of whites. Governments and Negroes can attempt to break down these powers in government, labor, and business institutions.

WHITE GAINS

Since economic theory does not provide definitive conclusions about the white gains or losses from discrimination, empirical evidence must be examined. Even if it can be demonstrated that whites can gain from discrimination, this does not prove that they do. They may simply be inefficient practitioners of discrimination.

Data from the United States census of population for 1960 are used as the source of the estimates presented;[22] but data limitations mean that the formulae developed earlier cannot be applied directly. Rough approximations must be made to the desired equations, but these can be illustrative even if not definitive.

[21] According to Becker, the government could demonstrate to whites that they suffer economic losses from discrimination, but this is not correct. Becker also states that Negroes cannot gain by retaliation. When terms of trade effects are introduced into his model, this conclusion is also false.

[22] U.S. Bureau of the Census, *U.S. Census of Population: 1960*, Vol. 1, *Characteristics of the Population*, Pt. 1, *United States Summary* (1964), and *Occupation by Earnings and Education*, Final Report PC(2)-7B (1963).

White *employment* would have fallen if white and nonwhite employment rates had been equalized in 1960. To evaluate the gain from a favorable employment picture, the extra white employment must be multiplied by some income figure. Assuming that white employment was enlarged by squeezing the nonwhite community out of its average job, the white employment gain should be multiplied by the average nonwhite income. By this calculation, whites gained $0.8 billion in 1960 by having a lower unemployment rate than nonwhites.[23] If whites replaced nonwhites with above-average jobs, the white gain would be even larger.

However, if nonwhites are paid less than their marginal products due to wage discrimination, and if white incomes represent actual marginal products, the white employment gain should be multiplied by average white incomes, yielding a gain to white labor of $1.6 billion. But this is not a net gain to the entire white community. Higher wages for white labor reduce the income to white capital, which loses $0.8 billion because of fewer opportunities for practicing wage discrimination. Thus on the basis of both assumptions, there is a net gain of $0.8 billion to the white community.

White gains from *wage discrimination* can be calculated on the assumption that wage differences within sex, educational, and occupational categories are due to wage discrimination rather than to real differences in productivity. Generally, the more detailed the categories the more accurate the assumption, but more detailed categories may not make it possible to eliminate all the real differences in productivity if the classifications themselves are inaccurate. If seven years of Negro education is not equivalent to seven years of white education, the two groups should not be classified together. Unfortunately, there is little that can be done about this problem. The estimates presented here are based on two sexes, twelve occupations, and six educational categories — or one hundred forty-four individual cells. If white incomes in each of these cells reflect real marginal products, the gain to the white community from wage discrimination is merely the summation of the difference in white and Negro earnings in each category mul-

---

[23] This was calculated according to the following formula:

$$[(U \times LF^w) - (U^w \times LF^w)]I^N$$

where

U = national unemployment rate
LF^w = white labor force
U^w = white unemployment rate
I^N = nonwhite income for employed workers

Unemployment rates are from U.S. Bureau of Labor Statistics, *Employment and Earnings and Monthly Report on the Labor Force* (February 1966), pp. 20, 21. Labor force and income statistics are from U.S. Bureau of the Census, *U.S. Census of Population: 1960*, Vol. 1, *Characteristics of the Population*, Pt. 1, *United States Summary* (1964), pp. 488, 580.

tiplied by the number of Negroes in the cell. On these assumptions, wage discrimination raised white incomes by \$4.6 billion in 1960.[24]

If whites received the benefits of wage discrimination, white incomes would not represent real marginal products, because of the additional income from discrimination. The observed differential between white and nonwhite incomes would be twice as large as the real productivity differential. Thus the net gain would be \$2.3 billion rather than \$4.6 billion; however, to the extent that the benefits from wage discrimination were kept as retained earnings by white capital, the gains would be greater than \$2.3 billion.

White gains from *human capital discrimination* can be calculated on the assumption that whites are distributed across the educational spectrum in the same manner as the population as a whole rather than according to their more favorable actual distribution. With sixteen educational categories and with white income in each cell assumed to represent marginal productivity, a favorable distribution resulted in a white gain of \$7.9 billion in 1960.[25]

The gains from *occupational discrimination* cannot be calculated by simply distributing whites across occupations in the same manner as the population as a whole, since the occupational distribution partially reflects the educational distribution. To calculate the gains from occupational discrimination without allowing for this interaction would be to double-count some

[24] The formula used was:

$$\sum_{j=1}^{2} \sum_{i=1}^{12} \sum_{k=1}^{6} \left[(I_{ijk}{}^{w} - I_{ijk}{}^{N}) E_{ijk}{}^{N} \right]$$

where

$I_{ijk}{}^{w}$ = white income in sex j, occupation i, and educational category k

$I_{ijk}{}^{N}$ = nonwhite income in sex j, occupation i, and educational category k

$E_{ijk}{}^{N}$ = nonwhite employment in sex j, occupation i, and educational category k

Since the full breakdown of earnings by sex, occupation, and education is available only for males aged eighteen to sixty-four, while the breakdown for sex and occupation is available for males and females of all ages, data for males eighteen to sixty-four were used to calculate a percentage correction factor that was applied to data for all males and females.

[25] This was calculated by the following formula:

$$\left[\sum_{j=1}^{2} \sum_{k=1}^{8} \frac{P_{jk}{}^{w}}{P^{w}} I_{jk}{}^{w} - \sum_{j=1}^{2} \sum_{k=1}^{8} \frac{P_{jk}}{P} I_{jk}{}^{w} \right] P^{w}$$

where

$P_{ijk}{}^{w}$ = white persons in educational category k and of sex j

P^{w} = white persons in experienced labor force

$I_{jk}{}^{w}$ = white income in educational category k and of sex j

P_{jk} = total persons in educational category k and of sex j

P = total persons

of the gains from educational discrimination. A favorable white distribution across sex, occupational, and educational categories (144 cells) yields a gross gain of $12.4 billion,[26] but the educational gains of $7.9 billion must be subtracted in order to calculate the effects of occupational discrimination alone. Actually, this net gain of $4.5 billion also includes gains from monopoly power discrimination in the labor market, since the white income level in each cell may partially result from monopoly powers.

The total gain from employment, wage, human capital, occupational, and labor monopoly discrimination was $15.5 billion, or $248 per member of the white labor force in 1960 (the corresponding nonwhite loss was $2,100 per member of the labor force), but what about the white labor losses? Losses occur principally if the supply of nonwhite labor to the white community is reduced. With both an income and a substitution effect from discrimination, it is impossible to specify the results a priori. The nonwhite community has two methods for reducing its supplies of labor. Nonwhites can withdraw from the labor force or they can work for themselves or other nonwhites. Since nonwhite labor participation rates are higher than those for whites (56.3 versus 55.2 percent), they probably have not withdrawn from the labor force in the aggregate, though this total figure is composed of lower participation rates for men (72.1 versus 78.0 percent) and higher rates for women (41.8 versus 33.6 percent).[27] Since the null hypothesis is unknown, it is impossible to say that the nonwhite labor force is not affected by discrimination, but the probable effects are not large. Similarly, very few nonwhites have been able to use their labor within the nonwhite community rather than sell it to the white community, judging by the number of nonwhites who are self-employed farmers (2.2 percent for nonwhites and 4.0 percent for whites), the number of nonwhites who are self-employed managers (1.4 percent for nonwhites versus 3.9 percent of whites), and the small number and size of nonwhite corporations. Although there is little evidence that the supply of Negro labor to the white community has been reduced quantitatively, qualitative factors must be considered. These may

[26] Here the formula was:

$$\left[\sum_{j=1}^{2} \sum_{i=1}^{12} \sum_{k=1}^{6} \frac{P_{ijk}{}^{w}}{P^{w}} I_{ijk}{}^{w} - \sum_{j=1}^{2} \sum_{i=1}^{12} \sum_{k=1}^{6} \frac{P_{ijk}}{P} I_{ijk}{}^{w} \right] P^{w}$$

where

$P_{ijk}{}^{w}$ = white persons in occupational category i, educational category k, and sex j
P^{w} = white persons in experienced labor force
$I_{ijk}{}^{w}$ = white income in occupation i, educational category k, and sex j
P_{ijk} = total persons in occupation i, educational category k, and sex j
P = total persons

[27] U.S. Bureau of the Census, *U.S. Census of Population: 1960*, Vol. 1, *Characteristics of the Population*, Pt. 1, *United States Summary* (1964), pp. 213–14.

have caused a larger reduction in nonwhite labor than would appear from the raw data. With underinvestment in Negro human capital, the supply of Negro labor measured in efficiency units (units adjusted for quality) is certainly less. Working to offset the inefficiency losses from less Negro labor are the white gains from capital discrimination, monopoly power discrimination against nonwhite capital, and price discrimination. White economic gains from these three sources have not been considered.

Probably an estimate of $15 billion plus or minus $5 billion would be a good range for the annual white gains (or Negro losses) from discrimination in the United States. The $15 billion, however, is not an estimate of the maximum gain that would be achieved by discrimination. Considering the inefficiencies with which the system is actually run, an efficient system would probably yield a much larger gain.

Since discrimination produces large economic gains, there are important vested interests in its continuation. Programs to eliminate discrimination must take these interests into account; economic self-interest cannot be counted on to aid in eliminating discrimination. The magnitude of the gains also indicates that elimination would have a powerful impact on the distribution of income for nonwhites.

IMPACT ON POTENTIAL OUTPUT

Whites (individually or collectively) may or may not be able to gain from discrimination, but the total potential output of the country is always less, since productive resources are inefficiently allocated. Although some of the reduction is caused by using members of the preferred group in jobs where their individual productivities are below those of members of the disadvantaged groups, the main reduction in potential output is probably caused by discrimination in education and underutilization of the nonwhite labor force.

To the extent that there is a surplus of labor of all types and skills, eliminating discrimination and reshuffling the labor force would result in a redistribution of income but in no real gains in actual output. To keep general gains from a higher utilization of white capacity distinct from the gains from eliminating discrimination, aggregate economic policies are assumed to be specific enough to provide markets for the extra output gained by ending inefficiencies but not to have any impact on white utilization levels.

The production function approach outlined in Chapter 3 provides a convenient method for estimating the impact of discrimination on potential output. Four effects can be isolated. (1) Eliminating discrimination would reduce nonwhite unemployment and thus raise the stock of labor used in production. (2) The improvements in capacity utilization resulting from the increase in nonwhite employment would cause a small increase in productivity levels. (3) Raising nonwhite educational levels to those of whites would increase the amount of human capital contained in the labor force, with a consequent increase in output. (4) Equipping the larger labor force (measured in efficiency units) with the average amount of capital would cause a further increase in output. Neither increasing human capital nor providing physical capital is costless. Real resources must be devoted to raising educational levels and increasing investment. To determine net gains, these costs must be deducted from the increases in potential output.

Equalizing white-nonwhite unemployment rates in 1966 would have raised nonwhite employment by 356,000, by decreasing nonwhite unemployment from 7.5 percent to 3.4 percent (see Table 1). In addition to excessive unemployment, nonwhites suffered from underemployment relative to whites; they worked only 37.6 hours per week while whites worked 40.7 hours.[28] The elimination of this difference as well as the unemployment difference would have increased total labor supplies by 1.5 percent.

Before the output effects of this increase can be estimated, adjustments must be made for the different amounts of human capital embodied in white and nonwhite workers. Assuming that the quality of labor is proportional to the number of years of schooling completed, the human capital of a nonwhite worker represents 85 percent of that of a white worker, since the figure for his median years of schooling completed is 10.5 compared with 12.3 years for whites.[29] If total employment in 1966 were adjusted to a "white equivalent" basis, 72.9 million people were employed. Adjusting the raw increase in nonwhite labor supplies to the same basis yields an increase in the white equivalent labor force of 1.1 percent. Using the elasticity of output with respect to labor (λ) from the production function, output would rise by 0.9 percent. Improvements in utilization resulting from the

TABLE 1.   LABOR SUPPLY, BY COLOR, UNITED STATES, 1966 (IN THOUSANDS)

Item [a]	White	Nonwhite	Total
Labor force	68,424	8,617	77,041
Employment	66,096	7,968	74,064
Unemployment	2,328	649	2,977
Unemployment rate (percentage)	3.40	7.53	3.86

Source: Manpower Report of the President, April 1968, pp. 224, 230–231.
[a] Data are for persons fourteen years of age and over in the civilian labor force.

[28] U.S. Bureau of Labor Statistics, *Employment and Earnings* (January 1967), p. 103.
[29] *Manpower Report of the President, April 1968*, p. 259.

lower unemployment level would raise output by another 0.1 percent. If the larger labor stock were equipped according to the 1966 average capital-labor ratio, output would rise by 0.2 percent, using the production function elasticity of output with respect to capital. But investment would have to increase by $7.3 billion to accomplish this goal.

Programs to equalize white and nonwhite education levels in the labor force would increase the white equivalent labor force by another 1.6 percent. As a result, output would expand by 1.3 percent, and maintaining the effective capital-labor ratio would cause a further increase of 0.3 percent. The cost of the additional plant and equipment would be $10.2 billion and there would also be costs in increasing education levels of nonwhites. To equalize education levels would require 15 million man-years of education. At the average 1964 costs of $559 per man-year of education in public elementary and secondary schools,[30] educational expenditures would have to rise by $8.4 billion.

If all of the outlined changes were made, private output would rise by 2.83 percent or $18.8 billion per year, at the cost of an investment of $25.9 billion. Although additional costs would be incurred over time to cover the depreciation of both human and capital equipment, the annual increase in output of $18.8 billion compares very favorably with an initial investment of $25.9 billion. Assuming a twenty-year rate of depreciation on the extra human and physical capital, the investment produces a net return of 65 percent per year.

Since most of those in the labor force with a low level of education are above the normal school-leaving age, the costs of a man-year of schooling might be much higher than the national average for younger people. On the other hand, concentrating on on-the-job training, where productivity effects are probably larger than those for general education, might reduce the calculated costs. Additional benefits would also accrue from the elimination of the constraints on the efficient use of existing men and machines. Although there are enough unknowns to challenge any specific dollar estimate, rough calculations would certainly indicate that eliminating discrimination is a profitable social investment even when regarded strictly from an economic point of view.

[30] U.S. Bureau of the Census, *Statistical Abstract of the United States: 1967* (1967), p. 120.

A MARKET SEPARATION THEORY OF
RENT DIFFERENTIALS IN METROPOLITAN AREAS

Robert A. Haugen
A. James Heins

The character of our metropolitan areas is suggestive of a theory of market separation to explain economic differentials that obtain in the various geographic and racial sections of cities. Social and cultural characteristics that limit the free mobility of people, goods, and information create conditions under which economic variables may take on different values in two markets that are close in a geographic sense and nominally integrated.

The purpose of this paper is to generate a model designed to explain rent differentials between white and nonwhite sections of cities based upon rather simple notions of market separation. We then test these notions using a cross-section regression analysis on 1960 census data for U.S. metropolitan areas.

THE GENERAL MODEL

Figure 1 generally depicts the population forces at work in metropolitan areas of both the North and the South in the twentieth century. The influx of Negroes into the center city has created expanding ghettos that have pushed wealthier whites out to the suburbs. The underlying economic, social, and cultural differences have created rather well-defined borders between the races across which information flows, trade, and migration are not free. The rate at which Negroes have migrated to metropolitan ghettos has put severe pressure on the borders between the races, pushing them back and driving whites farther from the ghetto centers.

The racial borders act effectively as trade barriers that can make price differentials possible between the black and white market areas. And the more rapid the migration of Negroes into the ghetto area or the more re-

Robert A. Haugen is Assistant Professor of Finance, University of Wisconsin; A. James Heins is Professor of Economics, University of Illinois. The work for this article was partly done at the University of Wisconsin under the auspices of the Institute of Research on Poverty.

Reprinted with permission from Robert A. Haugen and A. James Heins, "A Market Separation Theory of Rent Differentials in Metropolitan Areas," *The Quarterly Journal of Economics* (1969), pp. 660–672.

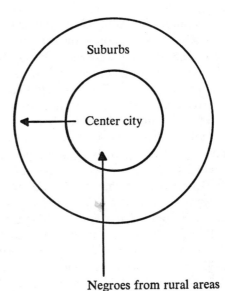

Whites moving to suburbs

Negroes from rural areas

FIGURE 1

sistant the white wall that surrounds the ghetto, the more evidence we should find of price differentials accompanying racial congregation. These price differentials may show up in many commodities, but the primary evidence should be in the most immobile commodity of all, land. Thus our study focuses on rents, the price of location.

The extent of observed rent differentials between white and black areas should generally be dependent on three basic characteristics of the metropolitan area: (1) the rate of influx of Negroes, (2) the rate at which whites pull back from the ghetto borders, and (3) the existence of spillover possibilities for Negroes to jump white areas altogether or to move into relatively unpopulated areas of the city.

The hypothesized relationship between rent differentials and growth in the Negro population is a straightforward derivation of a market separation model. Negroes have migrated from rural to metropolitan areas because of better economic opportunities. They bid up the prices of location in those areas of the city that are open to them; and, assuming a given propensity for new locations to be made available, greater growth in the Negro population will result in increasing rent differentials between Negro ghettos and other areas of the city.

The wall of whites around ghetto areas will resist the outflow of Negroes into surrounding areas. In the face of increasing rent differentials or simple threat of integration, whites in surrounding areas will be induced to move to the suburbs or other parts of the central city. But the speed of white evacuation is dependent on other variables, such as age, education, and income. Studies have shown that mobility is related inversely to age, and directly to education and income.[1] To the extent that ghetto areas are surrounded by a white community with adverse mobility characteristics, the outward movement of the ghetto will be resisted, and rent differentials between white and Negro areas will be greater.

The impact of Negro population growth and white evacuation on rent differentials has been previously described in the literature. For example, Gary Becker suggests that these forces explain the phenomenon that northern Negroes apparently paid relatively higher rents in 1957 than southern Negroes, even though white "discrimination" against Negroes was supposedly more severe in the South.[2] The Negro population was expanding more rapidly in the northern cities. Citing a 1935 census study that indicated Negroes paid higher rent than whites for equivalent housing, Robert Weaver suggested that this was inevitable *as long as there were appreciable numbers of colored people coming into the cities of the North.*[3] In neither case, however, were rent differentials systematically related to differential rates of growth in Negro communities.

A third, and we believe very important, characteristic that influences Negro-white rent differentials within metropolitan areas is the geographic nature of the wall surrounding the ghetto. Consider Figure 2, diagrams (a), (b), and (c). The situation in (a) is one in which the Negro community is completely contained by the surrounding white community. Compare this with (c), where the Negro community borders on the open regions surrounding the metropolitan area. In this case, rising rent levels will induce the Negro community to spill over into the surrounding countryside, thereby easing the upward pressure on rents. This notion can be derived from Turner's "safety-valve" theorem of frontier development.[4] Similarly, in (b), the existence of Negro communities in outlying areas of the metropolis may enable ghetto dwellers to urbanize the relatively cheap land of the countryside by leaping over the surrounding white community, thereby easing pressure on rents in central areas.[5]

[1] See, for example, U.S. Department of Commerce, Area Redevelopment Administration, *The Propensity to Move* (Washington, 1964).

[2] Gary S. Becker, *The Economics of Discrimination* (Chicago: University of Chicago Press, 1957), p. 61.

[3] Robert C. Weaver, *The Negro Ghetto* (New York: Russell Press, 1948), p. 36, his italics.

[4] See Frederick Jackson Turner, *The Frontier in American History* (New York: Holt, 1920). Also see Ray A. Billington, ed., *The Frontier Thesis* (New York: 1966).

[5] The adverse impact of centralization of ghetto areas on Negro employment has

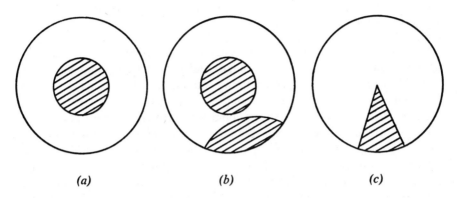

(a)   *(b)*   *(c)*

FIGURE 2

THE REGRESSION MODEL

To test the relationships hypothesized in the previous section, we have formulated a regression model using cross-section data for 82 metropolitan areas. The 82 areas selected were those standard metropolitan statistical areas (SMSA's) whose populations were in excess of 250,000 in 1960 and in which the nonwhite population was sufficiently large for the Census Bureau to provide the detailed data required in our analysis. (The list of 82 cities is shown in the Appendix.) Except where otherwise noted, data were taken from the various census publications for 1950 and 1960.[6]

Our dependent variable is an estimated ratio of median white rents to median Negro rents in the metropolitan areas. All rents are gross and unadjusted for size of dwelling unit or condition of repair. Because of the aggregate nature of our data, we judged that these factors would be more appropriately introduced via control variables, as indicated below.

The independent variables can be classified as either primary, those that test for one hypothesized effect, or control, those that account for other factors that influence the relationships to be tested.

---

been demonstrated in recent articles by John F. Kain, "Housing Segregation, Negro Employment, and Metropolitan Decentralization," *Quarterly Journal of Economics,* LXXXII (May 1968), 175–97, and by James O. Wheeler, "Work Trip Length and the Ghetto," *Land Economics,* XLIV (Feb. 1968), 107–12.

[6] Data were taken from U.S. Department of Commerce, Bureau of the Census, *Census of Housing: 1960,* "States and Small Areas" and *Census of Population: 1960,* "Characteristics of the Population" (Washington, 1963); *Census of Population: 1950,* "Characteristics of the Population," Series P (Washington, 1952).

PRIMARY VARIABLES

Our growth variable is measured by the log of the ten-year rate of increase in the nonwhite population in standard statistical metropolitan areas between 1950 and 1960. Adjustments were made for census changes in the geographic definition of metropolitan areas. Our use of the logged value of the growth rates derives from the notion that growth in the Negro population impinges directly on Negro rents, but not on white rents. The "safety valve," or ability of the white community to spill over into the countryside, would tap off pressure on white rents from population growth at the core. But the Negro community cannot freely spill over into other areas; it is contained. And since we assume a linear relationship between growth and Negro rents, the expected relationship between growth and the ratio of white to Negro rents is curvilinear. Thus the log of the growth variable was employed to linearize the growth and rent ratio relationships for purposes of our regression analysis. We hypothesize a negative relationship between growth and white rents relative to nonwhite rents.

To measure the rate at which the whites evacuate in the face of ghetto pressure, we have used an estimate of the ten-year rate of increase in the suburban population between 1950 and 1960.[7] The measure clearly does not allow for white mobility within the center city, and does not account for white influx to suburbs from other areas altogether; but the difficulty of obtaining data that would isolate such factors makes a more sophisticated measure impractical. The evacuation index was logged for reasons similar to those noted above for the growth variable. We hypothesize that the relationship between evacuation and the rent ratio will be positive.

To obtain a measure of the extent to which the black ghetto is centralized or well contained within the center city, we have constructed an index of centralization based upon a relationship between the percentage of nonwhites in the SMSA living within the center city and the size of the center city relative to the SMSA. Essentially, the index of centralization for any metropolitan area is the residual value of the percentage of nonwhites living in the center city from a regression line on the size of the center city relative to the total SMSA.[8] Again, logs were used for the index of cen-

---

[7] The Census Bureau's estimates reflect adjustments for annexations and changes in the size of the SMSA's.

[8] The value of the centralization variable for any metropolitan area i is u_i from the relationship

$$y_i = a + bx_i + u_i$$

where

$$y_i = \frac{\text{nonwhites in center city } (i)}{\text{nonwhites in total SMSA } (i)}$$

tralization. If our theory of containment measures up, we would expect the relationship between centralization and the rent ratio to be negative.

CONTROL VARIABLES

To control for the size and condition of housing in black and white areas of the metropolitan area, we have introduced as variable estimates of (1) the ratio of the percentage of white dwelling units judged to be dilapidated to the percentage of black units that are dilapidated, and (2) the ratio of median rooms in white dwelling units to median rooms in nonwhite units. The anticipated relationships with the dependent variable are negative in the case of (1) and positive in the case of (2).

Since income is an obvious determinant of housing expenditures, we have included the ratio of median white family income to median nonwhite family income as a third control variable. The expected relationship here with the dependent variable is obviously positive.

Another variable which we have used reflects the degree of physical segregation of the races, that is, the degree to which the white and nonwhite geographical areas are homogeneous in racial make-up. Physical segregation is, of course, only one attribute of social segregation, but it is an attribute in which we are particularly interested. There is no need for this characteristic to be systematically related to the centralization of the ghetto, and, indeed, our empirical evidence bears this out. In general, segregation evidences separation of housing markets; but it does not provide theoretical insight into which market, white or nonwhite, will have the relatively higher rents. Growth of the nonwhite community and white evacuation provide theoretically sound evidence of upward pressure on rents inside the ghetto, and centralization measures the ability of such pressure to find outlets through

$$x_i = \frac{\text{total population center city } (i)}{\text{total population SMSA } (i)}$$

This regression was run using data for the 82 cities. A value of u_i equal to zero means that the SMSA has an average concentration of Negroes in the center city. A positive or negative u_i implies greater or less than average concentration respectively.

This method of measuring concentration is preferred to the simple ratio y_i/x_i or differential $y_i - x_i$ since the density of Negroes relative to whites generally declines with distance from the core of the city. See Davis McEntire, *Residence and Race* (Berkeley: University of California Press, 1960), pp. 32–66. A decline in relative Negro density would lead to a decrease in both y_i/x_i and $y_i - x_i$ if the boundary of the center city expanded to encompass more of the metropolitan area *even though* the actual concentration of Negroes in the area remained the same. That is, y_i/x_i and $y_i - x_i$ are not independent of x_i. The residual in our regression takes account of declining relative Negro densities and may be taken to express the relative centralization of Negroes that cannot be explained by the relative centralization of the total population.

population spillovers from the ghetto to other areas. Segregation, however, does not identify pressure in either market, but merely the existence of different markets. Becker's growth explanation of higher Negro-white rent differentials in the North in the face of greater "discrimination" in the South reflects similar thinking, although he does not explicitly employ a segregation variable in a market separation model.[9] While we cannot, on an a priori basis, formulate a hypothesis to explain any relationship between segregation and rent differentials, policy concerns for this social situation and an intuitive feel for its significance lead us to include segregation as a variable in the regression analysis. Our measure of the degree of segregation was taken from the work of Taeuber and Taeuber; [10] essentially, it is an index of the percentage of nonwhite persons who would have to move to create a block-by-block perfectly integrated community. Consistent with the other nonratio variables, logs of the segregation variable were employed to linearize any expected relationship to the dependent variable.

The final variable considered was per capita welfare payments by states for family assistance. Some critics have asserted that increased welfare payments merely work to drive up rents paid by recipients. We wonder whether such an effect would show up in aggregate data, namely, whether relatively higher welfare payments would increase rent differentials between the white and nonwhite communities. Welfare data were taken from the *Compendium of State Government Finances for 1960*.[11]

SUMMARY OF THE VARIABLES

The following list summarizes and symbolizes the variables described above:

$Y =$ Ratio of median gross rents
$x_g =$ Rate of nonwhite population growth (logs)
$x_e =$ Rate of white evacuation (logs)
$x_c =$ Index of nonwhite centralization (logs)
$x_d =$ Ratio of dilapidated units
$x_r =$ Ratio of median rooms
$x_i =$ Ratio of median incomes
$x_s =$ Index of segregation (logs)
$x_w =$ Per capita welfare payments

[9] *Economics of Discrimination*, p. 62.

[10] Karl E. Taeuber and Alma F. Taueber, *Negroes in Cities* (Chicago: Aldine Publishing Co., 1965).

[11] U.S. Department of Commerce, Bureau of the Census, *Compendium of State Government Finances in 1960* (Washington, 1961).

CORRELATION AND REGRESSION RESULTS

The correlation matrix for the independent variables showed an absence of troublesome multicollinearity, save that between the room ratio and the income ratio variables. The simple correlation coefficient between those two variables was 0.65, but in all other cases the absolute value of the coefficient was less than 0.45. As between the primary independent variables, the highest correlation coefficient was 0.18. Accordingly we ran numerous variants of the basic regression and found that the T-ratios for the primary variables were insensitive to the combination of control variables included. In all variants, the growth (x_g) and centralization (x_c) variables were significant at the 5 per cent level; the evacuation (x_e) variable was significant at the 15 per cent level; and the segregation (x_s) variable, positive and insignificant.

The coefficients for the reference variant of the regression are as follows:

Variable	x_g	x_e	x_c	x_d	x_i	x_s
Coefficient	−0.074	0.023	−0.297	−0.065	0.210	0.228
T-ratio	−3.16	1.79	−2.92	−0.95	3.17	1.38

The coefficient of determination (R^2) was 0.566 with 74 degrees of freedom. Because of the high correlation between the ratio of rooms and ratio of incomes variables, the rooms variable was eliminated by the mean square error test significant at the 10 per cent level.[12]

EVALUATION

The results generally substantiate all of the hypotheses previously advanced. To the extent that aggregate data of this nature can reveal evidence of price differential phenomena, our theory of market separation indicates that rent differentials between the white and black communities depend upon the nature of the containment and growth of ghettos within the metropolitan area.

Location of the ghetto area inside the central city tends to increase rents that ghetto residents, primarily Negroes, pay. To indicate the magnitude of this relationship, *ceteris paribus*, when the ghetto is highly centralized — the value of our centralization index one standard deviation above the norm — Negroes paid rents approximately 8 per cent higher, relative to whites, than they paid when the ghetto was not centralized — one standard deviation below the norm. We are aware of an alternative hypothesis that would

[12] Carlos Toro-Viracarrondo and T. D. Wallace, "A Test of the Mean Square Error Criterion for Restrictions in Linear Regression." *Journal of the American Statistical Association*, Vol. 63 (June 1968), pp. 558–72.

explain this phenomenon through the proximity of ghettos to the high-value area at the core of the city. However, investigation of other studies on rents or land values in relationship to distance from the core of cities suggests that ours is the more viable hypothesis. Surveys performed at the Survey Research Center of the University of Michigan clearly indicate people's preference to live away from downtown areas.[13] Empirical evidence on location and rents or land values has shown that land values tend to decrease as one approaches the very business core of the city, where rents and values rise sharply.[14] If it is true that rents or land values are not generally subject to a decreasing gradient with increased distance from the city core, then our centralization hypothesis would seem to be the more reasonable explanation of the relatively higher rents paid by nonwhites when the ghetto is centralized.

Our finding that rapid growth of the nonwhite population tends to increase relative rents paid by nonwhites is less subject to question, and is evidence of the phenomenon that separation of the races in metropolitan areas creates price differentials that can only be explained by a market separation model. From our regression, when the Negro growth rate was 75 per cent over ten years — one standard deviation above the mean growth rate — Negro rents were approximately 9 per cent higher, relative to white rents, than they were with a growth rate of 23 per cent — one standard deviation below the mean. If the markets were not effectively separated by racial structure, we would expect that the influx of nonwhites to the cities would tend to increase rents across the board and not the relative rents paid by nonwhites.

Similarly, the findings show that a more rapid rate of suburbanization, largely by whites, tends to reduce relative rents paid by the nonwhite community. More particularly, a ten-year rate of suburbanization of only 14 per cent — one standard deviation below the mean — would find Negroes paying approximately 5 per cent higher rents, relative to whites, than they would pay with a ten-year rate of suburbanization of 111 per cent — one standard deviation above the mean. Again, we are aware that the simple rate of suburbanization is not a very precise measure of the force we wish to isolate, the rate at which the white barrier to black ghettos responds to social and economic pressure from ghetto expansion; however, its significance in our regression findings leads us to conclude that an evacuation

[13] John B. Lansing, *Residential Location and Urban Mobility* (Ann Arbor, Michigan: Survey Research Center, Institute for Social Research, University of Michigan, 1966).

[14] See Homer Hoyt, *One Hundred Years of Land Values in Chicago* (Chicago, 1933); Homer Hoyt, *Structure and Growth of Residential Neighborhoods in American Cities,* Federal Housing Administration (Washington, 1939); and Duane S. Knos, *Distribution of Land Values in Topeka, Kansas* (Lawrence, Kansas: University of Kansas, Center for Research in Business, 1962).

phenomenon operates in metropolitan areas to affect the rents paid by ghetto residents. And further studies at a less aggregate level to isolate more precisely the impact of mobility of whites in center cities, particularly in areas surrounding ghettos, would clearly be in order.

Parenthetically, we might note that our empirical model does not permit us to make inferences about any long-run equilibrium rent differential existent in the absence of Negro growth and white evacuation. Such inferences would require more exacting control for equivalency of housing units than is possible in our aggregate model, and specification of any taste differential between the racial communities. Theoretically, price differentials can exist as long as markets are indeed separate, even though demands may be stable in the various markets. However, our empirical model entitles us to say only that whatever differential may exist in a stable state, zero or otherwise, Negro growth will accentuate it and white evacuation attenuate it.[15]

Probably the most surprising result, and most pleasing in light of our hypothesis, is the insignificance of the segregation variable. Intuition and common concern might lead one to hypothesize that mere physical segregation could tend to increase Negro rents relative to whites. However, theoretical scrutiny should lead one to observe that segregation itself merely evidences market separation and not the economic pressures that dictate the nature of any price differentials which might arise. The insignificance of the physical segregation variable, and indeed its positive sign, tend to verify the theory, rather than the intuition and concern.[16]

Finally, we would note that welfare expenditures do not prove to be a significant determinant of rent differentials. Moreover, the positive relationship shown in all variants between welfare and the white-to-black rent ratio is counter to the sign expected under the notion that welfare payments merely lead to higher rents. The best one can conclude is that, if such an effect is present, it is not strong enough to show up systematically in aggregate data.

[15] Margaret Reid apparently holds that Negroes and whites pay the same rent for equivalent housing, attributing contrary observations to failure to account for permanent income. See her *Housing and Income* (Chicago: University of Chicago Press, 1962), pp. 106–107, 389–90. She explains exceptions to the zero differential by an information gap resulting from recent influx of Negroes to metropolitan areas and an overstatement of the housing-income relationship due to doubling-up. This is not necessarily variant from the central hypotheses of this paper; except that forces are couched in terms of an information theory rather than an explicit market separation theory, and that the Negro-white rent differential would be zero in a steady state, something which we are not prepared to say. For a further discussion of rent differentials, see Chester Rapkin, "Price Discrimination Against Negroes in the Rental Housing Market," *Essays in Urban Land Economics* (Los Angeles: University of California at Los Angeles, Real Estate Research Program, 1966), pp. 333–45.

[16] Because these results were surprising, we ran the same regressions using the unlogged index of segregation. In each case, the coefficient was positive and the T-ratio insignificant.

SOME CONCLUSIONS

Perhaps the most interesting observation that might be drawn from our analysis is that policies designed to reduce the rate of white migration out of center cities to suburbs may have adverse effects. White migration is alleged to increase problems with the declining tax base in center cities, the outward flow of industry, and their cumulative effect on urban blight, slum conditions, and violence.[17] In the absence of policies that would provide substantial outlets for population migration from ghettos, policies of encouraging whites to remain in the center city may tend to increase economic differentials between the white and Negro areas of the city. Market separation of the type with which we are concerned results from deep-seated social and cultural differences between the races and from the historical background of subjugation of one race by another. Policies that cannot break down these barriers, that only serve to increase the pressure which the white community places against expansion by the Negro community, can only result in increased economic differentials, particularly in rents, between the communities, and ultimately in greater conflict.

Our findings also imply that the observed relocation pattern of ghetto residents displaced under urban renewal programs may have been less than optimal. Ghetto dwellers tend to relocate no farther than to areas adjoining their old communities.[18] Here their containment by the surrounding white community continues unabated. The interests of those displaced might be better served if they were encouraged to migrate to outlying sections of the metropolitan area, to locations providing access to land which may ease the pressure of their rapidly expanding numbers.

Together with the Kain [19] and Wheeler [20] articles, we offer further evidence that centralization of ghettos tends to create adverse living and working conditions for Negroes. And, while integration might be an admirable goal of public policy, the goal of decentralization of the Negro community and provision of room for expansion, *regardless of the impact on integration*, may have higher priority.

Our findings, moreover, offer a potential explanation of the motives of the black separatist movement. Since the bulk of the resources, even in the ghetto areas, are controlled by whites, price and rent differentials tend to retard the rate of development of the black community. Simple segregation

[17] For example, see William J. Baumol, "Macroeconomics of Unbalanced Growth: The Anatomy of Urban Crises," *The American Economic Review*, LVII (June 1967), 415–26.

[18] Nathaniel Lichfield, "Relocation: The Impact of Housing Welfare," *The Journal of the American Institute of Planners*, Vol. 27 (Aug. 1961), 199–203.

[19] Kain, *op. cit.*

[20] Wheeler, *op. cit.*

of the races does not necessarily lead to economic differentials, but containment and pressure do. What separatists are asking for is not integration, but expansion. Our findings suggest that in the interest of their own development they may be looking in the right direction.

APPENDIX

Below is the list of 82 SMSA's for which data were included in the regression analysis:

1. Birmingham, Alabama
2. Mobile, Alabama
3. Fresno, California
4. Los Angeles, California
5. Sacramento, California
6. San Diego, California
7. San Francisco, California
8. San Jose, California
9. Denver, Colorado
10. Bridgeport, Connecticut
11. Hartford, Connecticut
12. New Haven, Connecticut
13. Wilmington, Delaware
14. Washington, D.C.
15. Jacksonville, Florida
16. Miami, Florida
17. Orlando, Florida
18. Tampa–St. Petersburg, Florida
19. Atlanta, Georgia
20. Chicago, Illinois
21. Peoria, Illinois
22. Gary, Indiana
23. Indianapolis, Indiana
24. Des Moines, Iowa
25. Wichita, Kansas
26. Louisville, Kentucky
27. New Orleans, Louisiana
28. Shreveport, Louisiana
29. Baltimore, Maryland
30. Boston, Massachusetts
31. Detroit, Michigan
32. Flint, Michigan
33. Grand Rapids, Michigan
34. Lansing, Michigan
35. Minneapolis–St. Paul, Minnesota
36. Kansas City, Missouri–Kansas
37. St. Louis, Missouri
38. Omaha, Nebraska
39. Jersey City, New Jersey
40. Newark, New Jersey
41. Paterson, New Jersey
42. Trenton, New Jersey
43. Albuquerque, New Mexico
44. Albany, New York
45. Buffalo, New York
46. New York, New York
47. Rochester, New York
48. Syracuse, New York
49. Charlotte, North Carolina
50. Akron, Ohio
51. Canton, Ohio
52. Cincinnati, Ohio
53. Cleveland, Ohio
54. Columbus, Ohio
55. Dayton, Ohio
56. Toledo, Ohio
57. Youngstown, Ohio
58. Oklahoma City, Oklahoma
59. Tulsa, Oklahoma
60. Portland, Oregon
61. Harrisburg, Pennsylvania
62. Philadelphia, Pennsylvania
63. Pittsburgh, Pennsylvania
64. Providence, Rhode Island
65. Columbia, South Carolina
66. Chattanooga, Tennessee
67. Knoxville, Tennessee
68. Memphis, Tennessee
69. Nashville, Tennessee
70. Beaumont–Port Arthur, Texas
71. Dallas, Texas
72. El Paso, Texas

73. Fort Worth, Texas
74. Houston, Texas
75. San Antonio, Texas
76. Norfolk, Virginia
77. Richmond, Virginia

78. Seattle, Washingon
79. Tacoma, Washington
80. Charleston, West Virginia
81. Huntington, West Virginia
82. Milwaukee, Wisconsin

FURTHER READINGS

Bailey, Martin J. "Effects of Race and of Other Demographic Factors on the Values of Single-Family Homes." *Land Economics* 42 (May 1966).

Batchelder, Alan. "Decline in the Relative Income of Negro Men." *The Quarterly Journal of Economics* 78 (1964), pp. 525–548.

Batchelder, Alan. "Poverty: The Special Case of the Negro." *American Economic Review* 55 (1965), pp. 530–540.

Becker, Gary S. *The Economics of Discrimination.* Chicago: The University of Chicago Press, 1957.

Bergmann, Barbara R. "Investment in Human Resources of Negroes." Washington: U.S. Government Printing Office.

Downs, Anthony. "An Economic Analysis of Property Values and Race." *Land Economics* 36 (May 1960), p. 181.

Gilman, Harry J. "Economic Discrimination and Unemployment." *American Economic Review* 55 (December 1965), pp. 1077–1096.

Kain, John F., and Persky, Joseph J. "Alternatives to the Golded Ghetto." *The Public Interest* (Winter 1969), pp. 74–87.

Krueger, Anne O. "The Economics of Discrimination." *Journal of Political Economy* 71 (October 1963), pp. 481–486.

Landes, William M. "The Economics of Fair Employment Laws." *Journal of Political Economy* 76 (1968), pp. 507–552.

Laurenti, Luigi. "Property Values and Race." *Studies in Seven Cities.* Berkeley: University of California Press, 1960.

Pascal, Anthony H. *The Economics of Housing Segregation.* Santa Monica: Rand Corporation, 1967.

Taeuber, Karl E., and Taeuber, Alma F. *Negroes in Cities: Residential Segregation and Neighborhood Change.* Chicago: Aldine, 1965.

Tobin, James. "On Improving the Status of the Negro." *Daedalus* (Fall 1963).

Chapter 9

METROPOLITANISM

Today's city government is a compromise between a true metropolitan government, able to handle transportation, pollution, and redistribution efficiently, and a true local community government that can responsibly and efficiently administrate local educational, zoning, policing, and street-maintenance services. Most cities are neither, yet are forced to perform the functions of both. The essays by Julius Margolis and Harvey Brazer analyze the fiscal implications of metropolitan versus the urban-suburban government.

The city government's boundaries and finances are almost invariably too small to carry out properly the vital metropolitan functions it is now performing. These functions include areawide transportation, pollution control, housing, poverty programs, and antidiscrimination efforts. Action in any one of these areas by a subdivision of the metropolis has spillover effects — costs, benefits, externalities — for the city and vice versa. Moreover, the city often provides services whose benefits accrue to the entire metropolis, such as museums, libraries, orchestras, and public television. The costs and control of these services should be shared with the suburbs.

At the same time, city governments are too large and inflexible to be responsive to local needs and don't even have the required funds due in part to financing of metropolitanwide activities. The cost of administering many government services reaches its minimum for political units whose constituency is far smaller than our present cities. The cost of these services is, in fact, often higher for medium and large cities. If this is so, we may conclude that cities could and probably should be decentralized by division into the smaller political units. Local community control of activities may be preferable even at additional expense. Charles Tiebout has suggested that many small competing political jurisdictions are likely to lead to lower cost and diversity in the public goods that can be efficiently supplied by such units — those having no or small economics of scale. Werner Hirsch and others have estimated cost functions for various government services. The cost functions have demonstrated that garbage collection, the administration of elementary and secondary education, police, medical care, and local street maintenance seem to attain all major economies of scale with a community of about 50,000 or 60,000 inhabitants. High schools are likely to exhaust most economies of scale at an enrollment of 1,500 to 1,600, while showing diseconomies at enrollment over 2,000. From the point of view of cost and community control, all these functions ought to be turned over to smaller communities of perhaps 50,000 or 60,000 within the city. Some argue that such diverse endeavors as poverty and beautification programs would be best administered at the local level to achieve maximum community control, participation, and effectiveness.

Econometric studies indicate that fire protection achieves all important economies of scale at a population of 100,000, but it might be technically feasible to obtain further economies of scale to populations over 300,000. Many museum, library, recreational, entertainment, and cultural activities also reach most all significant economies of scale in this population range. The production of electricity and gas, however, along with mass transit and many higher educational (and cultural) activities show economies of scale well past populations in the millions. These studies clearly show that the best jurisdictional area or population for the administration of many government functions is not conterminous with present city government units.

British town planners first decided the ideal metropolis had 50,000 inhabitants, then revised their figure to 250,000 on the basis of such econometric studies. Fortunately, they are coming to realize that this kind of data might point out the size of the community, city, metropolis, or region best able to handle particular functions. It does not tell us the optimum size for any particular metropolis, however.

For the city's residents to enjoy a fair share of well-allocated resources, a significant number of the city's present functions must be financed and administered on a metropolitan-wide basis. Others need to be administered by smaller subdivisions, which will often need subsidies from higher levels of government. Poor communities have especially intense need for this kind of financing. Metropolitan-wide administration and finance would lead to the establishment of a three-tiered government. The city would eventually disappear; its varying functions would be taken over either by the metropolis or communities.

MUNICIPAL FISCAL STRUCTURE IN A
METROPOLITAN REGION[1]

Julius Margolis

The metropolitan region is a "natural" economic unit with a geographic differentiation of function and variable rates of growth and decay of activities and areas. Superimposed on the map of changing activities are fixed municipal governmental divisions. The growth of metropolitan regions, which has brought non-uniform shifts in land uses within cities, has dramatically altered the fiscal bases of city governments. This growth has created a demand for a different pattern of public services; it has forced the destruction of some governments, the expansion of others, the transfer of functions, and often the creation of new governments.

Governments have responded to actual or anticipated changes in land use with such devices as zoning, subdivision control, building codes, urban redevelopment, capital improvements, and shifts in their tax instruments. The goal which has frequently dominated planning decisions has been the minimization of the tax rate. Residential suburbs claim that industrial cities benefit from tax-rich industry, while the suburbs bear the expensive burden of servicing the population. Industrial core cities claim the contrary. They assert that they must service the transient daytime population which crowds and dirties their streets, drinks their water, and creates fire hazards but which maintains its taxable property in the suburbs. Since these claims are contradictory, what is the true relation between the economic activities within a city and the fiscal status of its government? A definitive answer is beyond the scope of any paper, but some insights can be gained by examin-

Julius Margolis is Professor of Economics and Public Policy Analysis and Director of the Fels Institute, University of Pennsylvania.

Reprinted with permission from Julius Margolis, "Municipal Fiscal Structure in a Metropolitan Region," *The Journal of Political Economy* (June 1957), pp. 225–236. © 1957 by The University of Chicago. All rights reserved.

[1] This paper was written with the assistance of the Real Estate Research Program of the Bureau of Business and Economic Research, University of California, Berkeley.

ing the relationships which hold in one metropolitan region, the San Francisco Bay Area.

The first section of this paper will very briefly discuss some of the arguments and policies of the different types of cities in a metropolitan region. The second section will present the municipal property tax rates that are to be analyzed. The remaining sections will then discuss each of the items entering into the determination of the tax rate and show how these elements are related to the dominant activities within the city.

I

The index of fiscal status most commonly used by cities is their property tax rate. Planning policies are often developed in terms of their effects on this rate. Two questions immediately come to mind. First, is the minimization of the tax rate a sensible goal for city planning? It should be clear that this goal is inadequate.[2] The tax rate can be considered as a price necessary to supply the product of local government. The minimization of this price is irrational on two grounds. The local government is only one productive agency in an area. Any effort to allocate resources so as to reduce the costs of one industry (in terms of a partial analysis) would result in over-all inefficiencies. Even if the public insisted on a policy of allocation that would minimize costs to one industry, it would be irrational to select such a relatively unimportant industry as the local government. For example, food production is certainly more important. A more persuasive argument could therefore be developed that land should be allocated so as to minimize the costs of the agricultural sector. This argument has been made, but fortunately it is usually rejected because of the awareness that, although a particular acre may have the highest agricultural yield in an area, its productivity in an alternative use may be much greater.

Second, are the analyses of the effects of public policies on the tax rate an adequate basis for programs of action? In the case of the residential suburb the usual analysis [3] is to estimate the city government's costs and revenues arising from each possible land use and then to use zoning ordinances and capital improvement programs to encourage the fiscally most

[2] One writer has adopted the extreme position of defining the optimum-sized city as one where a given bundle of public services can be produced at the lowest average costs (Charles M. Tiebout, "A Pure Theory of Local Expenditures," *Journal of Political Economy*, LXIV, No. 5 [1956], 419).

[3] For a sample of these studies see Homer Hoyt Associates, *Economic Survey of the Land Uses of Evanston, Illinois*, prepared for the Evanston Plan Commission, September, 1949; Planning and Zoning Commission, Greenwich, Connecticut, *Economic Study of the Cost of Government Compared with Property Tax Income in Relation to Classified Property Uses* ("Plan of Development Report," No. 3 [Greenwich, Conn., 1954]); The Planning Board, New Rochelle, New York, *Land Use, Zoning and Economic Analysis* (New Rochelle, N.Y., July, 1951).

"profitable" uses. Such studies usually find that industry, commerce, and high-income residences are "profitable," and therefore the city officials are urged to encourage their expansion while discouraging or excluding non-profitable uses. The central cities share this belief that business uses of land are valuable, and they are actively trying to retain their commercial and industrial advantages. At the same time they claim that the "commuters pay their property tax in the suburbs, while enjoying police and fire protection and other services provided them during the working day by the city." [4] Therefore, they seek to annex to the central city some of the suburban growth. This is frequently politically unfeasible, so that their more typical policy is to expand the number of tax instruments in order to assess their transient daytime working and shopping population. Economic activities are concentrated in different parts of a metropolitan region, and any given city in the region may be highly specialized. But both central cities and suburbs implicitly claim that they are exploited by the absence of the activities complementary to their land uses.

The arguments of both types of city share the defect of an exclusive reliance on partial analysis. Both arguments identify the fiscal contributions of a household with its place of residence. For the argument that central cities are fiscally impoverished, this narrowness is fatal, since wherever the suburbanites shop, work, or play they create real property values. A priori, there is no reason to believe that the increment in the tax receipts of the central city accompanying the commuter is less than it costs the city to attract and to service him.

The suburbanites who seek to attract high-valued industry and to exclude low-income residents ignore the other capacities in which land users can be taxed. Furthermore, the implied assumption that one land use, such as industry, can be encouraged while a complementary use, housing for workers, can be discouraged is highly dubious.

I do not seek to defend either of these arguments. This paper is an analytical description of the relationships among the property tax rates, fiscal structures, and economic activities of cities that comprise a metropolitan region. As a by-product of the analysis, insights are gained which have implications for policy.

II

Unfortunately for the analyst, the variation of municipal tax rates among communities can be due to many forces. The announced tax rate is a levy on property contained on the assessment rolls. This levy is based on the ex-

[4] Kenyon E. Poole, *Public Finance and Economic Welfare* (New York: Rinehart & Co., 1956), p. 299.

penditures that a city must finance after it has raised some of its funds by other means; for example, other taxes and subventions from central governments. Symbolically, the tax rate can be expressed as follows:

$$t_v = \frac{E - R}{a\,(V - X)}$$

where t_v is the announced tax rate, E is the sum of expenditures, R is the sum of all other revenues, a is the ratio of the assessed to the true value of property, V is the true value of property, and X is the value of exemptions. My analysis is not of the announced but of the true tax rates, so that I must introduce another symbol, t_v', which is the true tax rate where $t_v' = at_v$. The variations in t_v' by communities can be affected by movements in any of the variables that enter into the identity that defines t_v. The plan of the paper is to discuss each of the variables, V, X, E, and R, after a preliminary description of the variation in tax rates.

The area of analysis is the metropolitan region surrounding the central cities of San Francisco and Oakland. It contains 55 city governments ranging in size from Colma, with a population of 270, to San Francisco, with 801,000. In area, the cities range from less than 1 square mile to more than 44 square miles. The cities comprise the full complement of types normally found in a metropolitan area and are part of a complex of almost 600 local governments, including counties and school and special districts and an additional 17 cities that are excluded from this analysis because they lie outside the area of active participation in the economic life of the region. Among these governments the cities are fiscally important but do not dominate. The cities account for almost half of locally raised revenues and slightly more than one-third of property taxes. If only the property taxes levied in incorporated areas are considered, the cities account for 44 per cent of property taxes.[5]

Table 1 presents the basic data to be analyzed. It gives the distribution of municipal tax rates for different types of cities in the metropolitan area. The main index used to distinguish the balanced cities from the dormitory cities was the ratio of employment in the city to resident labor force. A city was considered balanced if its ratio was between .75 and 1.25. If its ratio was greater than 1.25, a city was classified as an industrial enclave. If its ratio was smaller than .75, a city was classified as a dormitory city. Since these data were at least four years old and were not available for every city, this index was supplemented by examination of land-use maps, interpretation of origin and destination traffic studies, and conversations with "experts." Judgment was exercised in classifying a few marginal cases as

[5] Data on expenditures and revenues of the various types of local governments are reported annually in the California State Controller, *Annual Reports of Financial Transactions*.

TABLE 1. DISTRIBUTION OF MUNICIPAL PROPERTY TAX RATES
IN THE SAN FRANCISCO BAY AREA BY TYPE OF CITY,
1953–54

Municipal property tax rate per $100 of true value [a]	Number of cities			
	Central [b]	Balanced	Dormitory	Industrial Enclave [c]
$0.00–$0.09	—	—	3	2
$0.10–$0.19	—	—	4	—
$0.20–$0.29	—	3	9	1
$0.30–$0.39	—	4	8	—
$0.40–$0.49	—	6	5	—
$0.50–$0.59	2	1	3	—
$0.60–$0.69	—	—	2	—
$0.70–$0.79	—	—	1	—

Sources: Property tax collections: State Controller, Annual Report of Financial Transactions Concerning Cities and Counties of California, 1953–54, Table 3.
    a True value of property: County assessors' rolls adjusted by the ratios of appraised to assessed values as estimated by the State Board of Equalization, "Intercounty Equalization in California, July 18, 1955" (mimeographed), and special tabulations provided by the Board.
    b San Francisco has a unified county and city government. In order to make its municipal fiscal structure comparable to that of other cities, expenditures and revenues were imputed to a fictitious city and county government. The division was made by using the ratio of urban Alameda County expenditures and revenues to the sum of Alameda County cities' expenditures and revenues. The Alameda County expenditures and revenues were divided into urban and rural in proportion to population. Alameda County is most comparable to San Francisco, since it contains such cities as Oakland and Berkeley.
    c The city of Colma did not levy a property tax.

balanced or dormitory cities. To determine the tax rate on true value, the assessed values were adjusted by the ratios of assessed to true value as estimated by a special study of the California State Board of Equalization.

The differences in municipal tax rates by type of city are very marked. The average tax rate per $100 of true value was $0.56 for the central cities, $0.40 for the balanced cities, $0.31 for the dormitory cities, and $0.17 for the industrial enclaves.[6] The low rates of the industrial enclaves are to be expected. The enclaves are fiscally extremely rich and have relatively few persons to be served. The lower rates of the dormitory cities are somewhat surprising when we consider the growing tendency of these cities to seek "industrialization" as a way to increase their tax base. For the San Francisco Bay Area cities the presence of industrial and commercial properties is associated with higher tax rates.

As significant as the differences between the groups is the great variation in rates among the cities in each group. The variation is far greater for dormitory cities than for balanced cities. This is probably due to the greater

6 The average is the sum of the taxes of all the cities in the group divided by the sum of the taxable property values. It is not the mean of the averages of the cities.

social differences among dormitory cities. Though dormitory cities are homogeneous in a superficial sense — they perform the same economic function of housing — the differences in household income and social structure among them are far greater than the differences among the balanced cities. The average household income of the "poorest" dormitory city was 31 per cent of that of the "richest" dormitory city, while the average household income of the "poorest" balanced city was 62 per cent of that of the "richest."

To explain the large variation in rates among the cities and the lower rates of the dormitory cities, we must examine the variations in taxable property, expenditures, and other revenue sources as they are related to economic activity within the city.

III

The property tax base of cities, as measured by taxable property values per capita, is highly variable. Table 2 shows the distribution of true values of per capita taxable property by type of city. (Taxable property is the assessment roll less exemptions.) The mean per capita value of property for the industrial enclaves was $43,079. This far exceeds the mean for any other group, which was to be expected. The other findings are more surprising. There are only small differences in the mean values among the other types of cities: central cities, $5,552; balanced cities, $5,274; and dormitory cities, $5,411. The most significant difference is the larger range in the per capita taxable values of dormitory cities, which is accounted for by the greater socioeconomic differences among these cities.

Taxable property is composed of real property (land and structures) plus

TABLE 2.   DISTRIBUTION OF THE TRUE VALUE OF TAXABLE PROPERTY PER CAPITA IN SAN FRANCISCO BAY AREA CITIES BY TYPE OF CITY, 1954–55

Per capita true value of taxable property	Number of cities			
	Central	Balanced	Dormitory	Industrial Enclaves
$1,000–$1,999	—	—	1	—
$2,000–$2,999	—	1	2	—
$3,000–$3,999	—	3	7	—
$4,000–$4,999	—	1	12	—
$5,000–$5,999	2	5	1	—
$6,000–$6,999	—	3	3	—
$7,000–$7,999	—	1	5	—
$8,000–$8,999	—	—	1	—
$9,000 and over	—	—	3	4

Source: See Table 1.

personal property less exemptions. The similarity of the means for the central, balanced, and dormitory cities is due primarily to the non-real property elements in the tax base. The balanced cities have much more personal property than the dormitories do, because of the inventories and equipment of businesses. In addition, since the major exemptions in California are the property of churches and part of the property of veterans, the dormitories' tax rolls suffer most from exemptions. The dominant element in property value and the one of greatest interest to analysts is real property. The mean values of real property per capita are: central cities, $4,802; balanced cities $4,688; and dormitories, $5,598.

To analyze further the real property data, real property values and land values were each correlated with population for both the dormitory and the balanced cities. The regressions for the two types of property for dormitory and balanced cities are plotted in Figure 1. These regressions show not only

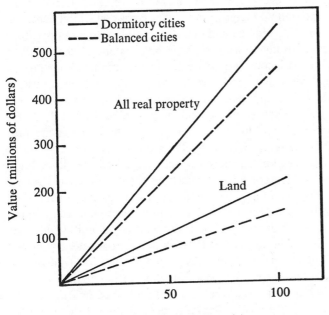

FIGURE 1. *Relationship between property values and population by type of city. Sources: For values, the assessed values of privately owned land, improvements, and utilities, which are included in real property, were taken from the assessment rolls of each of the counties in the area. These figures were adjusted by the ratio of assessed to appraised true value for each type of property as estimated by the California State Board of Equalization. For population, California State Controller,* Annual Report of Financial Transactions concerning Cities and Counties of California, 1953–54, *Table 1.*

that average values are higher for dormitory cities but also that the marginal relationships between values and population for dormitory cities are higher than for balanced cities. The higher slopes for the dormitory cities indicate that a given increment of population will result in more of an increase in values for dormitory cities than for balanced cities, assuming that the incremental population for each type of city has the same composition as the original.

The balanced and central cities have, in addition to their residences, a relatively large amount of commercial and industrial property. The values of real property shown in Figure 1 include this business property. If only residential property were considered, the differences would be far greater. The much-sought-for commercial and industrial property far from offsets the residential values advantage of the dormitory cities. Two factors, mean household income and gross residential densities (population per acre), seem to account for a large part of the differences among the types of cities and among the cities of each type. The balanced and central cities have both lower average household incomes and higher gross residential densities.

To analyze the variables income and density, the balanced and dormitory cities were ranked according to average household income and were then equally divided into two income groups. Each of the resulting four groups was equally divided into high- and low-density groups. For each city an estimate was made of the difference between the actual value of its real property and the value given by the equations plotted in Figure 1. These residuals were averaged for each of the eight groups; the averages are presented in Table 3. The results are striking. The value of real property varies for both types of cities by both density and income. Where density is high, per capita property values are lower in each of the four income groups. Where the average household income is high, per capita property values are higher in each density group. For land values the results are not so dramatic.

The effect of income on property value is to be expected, but the effect of density is less obvious. The density effect is, however, consistent with our knowledge of the building industry. For any given structure the average cost of a dwelling unit decreases for a range with the increasing number of units per structure. Similar economies are realized with attached housing, which is another form of denser settlement. It is also possible that the demand for housing in denser settlements is lower given equal population and income. The homes in denser areas are less desirable, and the families that live in them may allocate a smaller portion of their budget to housing.

The effects of gross residential density and household income on real property values are clear. That these relationships help explain the differences among types of cities can be seen from the gross residential density of each type. The population per acre of central cities is 18.9; of balanced cities, 8.9; and, of dormitory cities, 6.6. The average household income of

TABLE 3. EFFECTS OF HOUSEHOLD INCOME AND RESIDENTIAL DENSITY ON THE VALUE OF REAL PROPERTY AND LAND [a]

Type of city	Cities with	
	High density Per capita from real population	Low density residuals property–equation
A. Balanced		
High average household incomes [b]	$ 474	$1,260
Low average household incomes	— 739	214
B. Dormitory		
High average household incomes	756	2,883
Low average household incomes	—1,721	381
C. Central [c]	— 100	—
	Per Capita Residuals from Land–Population Equation	
A. Balanced		
High average household incomes [b]	$ 245	$ 175
Low average household incomes	— 242	56
B. Dormitory		
High average household incomes	327	1,178
Low average household incomes	— 863	— 57
C. Central [c]	147	—

[a] The residuals are the actual values less the values computed from the equations for each type of cities as shown in Figure 1. For each of the groups shown the residuals were summed and divided by the sum of the population for the group.

[b] The average household income for each city was estimated from the U.S. Bureau of Census. *U.S. Census of Population: 1950*, Vol. II: *Characteristics of the Population*. Part 5, *California* (Washington, D.C., 1952), Tables 37 and 39. Since the Census gives income by class intervals, in order to compute the mean for each city, I had to assign a mean value to each interval, including the open-ended interval "over $10,000." I assigned a mean of $20,000 to this interval. The value $20,000 is a conservative estimate of the mean income for the entire population whose income exceeds $10,000 (see H. P. Miller, *Income of the American People* [New York: John Wiley & Sons, 1955], p. 153). The use of the same mean for the open-ended interval for all the cities results in an underestimate of the differences among the cities. There is a great variation in the percentage of the city's households falling in the "over $10,000" group. It is reasonable to assume that the mean for the group varies with this percentage.

[c] The residual for central cities was estimated from the equation for balanced cities.

central cities is $3,709; of balanced cities, $3,890; and, of dormitory cities, $4,864, as shown in Table 4. It is probable that the lower household incomes and higher residential densities of balanced cities are not independent of their larger volume of industrial and commercial property. Proximity to jobs attracts workers, and the lowered amenities associated with factory sites repel the higher-income groups. Those who see the industrial development of residential suburbs as a way of reducing the property tax hope to

TABLE 4. GROSS RESIDENTIAL DENSITY, AVERAGE HOUSEHOLD INCOME, AND REAL PROPERTY VALUES BY TYPE OF CITY

Type of city	No. of cities	Popula-tion per acre (1954)	Average house-hold income (1950)	Real property values (1954–55)	
				Per capita	Per acre [a]
Central	2	18.9	$3,709	$ 4,802	$90,760
Balanced, all	14	8.9	3,890	4,688	41,566
Balanced, high income	7	7.5	4,495	5,156	38,481
Balanced, low income	7	9.6	3,647	4,502	43,152
Balanced, high income, high density	4	8.8	4,543	4,999	43,750
Balanced, high income, low density	3	5.4	4,370	5,562	30,073
Balanced, low income, high density	4	14.0	3,678	3,995	56,049
Balanced, low income, low density	3	7.3	3,618	4,997	36,543
Dormitory, all	25	6.6	4,864	5,598	36,793
Dormitory, high income	13	5.8	5,809	6,692	39,092
Dormitory, low income	12	7.5	3,930	4,517	33,876
Dormitory, high income, high density	7	8.4	5,697	6,331	53,381
Dormitory, high income, low density	6	2.6	6,253	8,082	21,369
Dormitory, low income, high density	6	12.2	4,016	3,846	46,867
Dormitory, low income, low density	6	4.4	3,769	5,764	25,213
Industrial enclave [b]	1	0.3	2,890	27,438	93,729

[a] Acreage was estimated from a map prepared by the San Francisco Bay Area Transit Commission.

[b] Only the city of Emeryville. The per acre and per capita values would have been greatly reduced if all the industrial enclaves had been included: per acre, $17,192, and per capita, $23,559. Emeryville is a typical industrial enclave. The two excluded enclaves are a city of cemeteries and a recently incorporated rural hamlet which contains farmland and a large, newly constructed automobile assembly plant. The ratios of all three cities would not be representative of industrial enclaves.

break this association. They seek to prevent the accompanying lower-income housing and increased residential density by zoning regulations. The correlations found in this study among income, density, and business suggest that the zoning regulations may prove ineffective. The administration of zoning regulations has been more marked by variances and other concessions to the more profitable use of land than by steadfast adherence to a "rational plan."

To summarize: The property tax base of cities, except for industrial enclaves, varies with household income and density. For dormitory cities household income is higher and density is lower, which explains the failure of balanced cities to derive fiscal advantage from their commercial and industrial properties. It is probable that the lower household incomes and higher residential densities of balanced cities are probably a necessary concomitant of industrial and commercial activity.

Before we can fully assess the fiscal advantages of the different types of land use we must examine the other elements of the property tax rate identity. Do lower levels of expenditure or higher revenues from other sources offset the property disadvantage of balanced and central cities?

IV

The major differences among the fiscal structures of the various types of cities are in their levels of expenditures. As can be seen in Table 5, column 1, the central and balanced cities clearly spend far more per capita than the dormitory cities. The per capita expenditures of dormitory cities are 58 per cent of those of central cities and 74 per cent of those of balanced cities. These data imply that the central and balanced cities have more difficult fiscal problems than the dormitory cities. Can we go beyond this statement and assert that the variation in per capita expenditures reflects differences in the real costs of providing public services and therefore assert that the cities with higher expenditures are "less efficient" or that they are being "exploited" by surrounding communities? [7] This latter interpretation of the expenditure differentials is sometimes made the basis of arguments for redistribution policies such as city payroll taxes and state grants to local governments. But before we can conclude that expenditure differentials represent inefficiency or exploitation we must be sure that the higher expenditures do not mean that more public services are provided because of differences in tastes. There is some evidence that the central and balanced cities do provide more real services relative to population.[8] Unfortunately, the methods of measuring the level of services that have been used are too complex to be considered in this article, and I can only introduce this consideration as a warning. Regardless of the level of services provided, the higher expenditures require higher taxes, which will result in higher rates unless offset by a larger fiscal capacity.

The first two columns of Table 5 relate municipal expenditures to taxable wealth. The types of cities have been broken into wealth groups. Per capita expenditures and the per capita value of taxable property are shown for each group. It is clear that, the higher taxable wealth is, the higher are municipal expenditures. The elasticity of the expenditure-wealth relationship can also

---

[7] Amos H. Hawley concludes that "the size of the metropolitan population not included in the corporate limits of the metropolitan center represents a cost factor to the residents of the center" on the basis of a finding that per capita central city expenditures are positively related to the percentage of the population of the metropolitan region residing outside the central city ("Metropolitan Population and Municipal Government Expenditures in Central Cities," *Journal of Social Issues,* VII [1951], 100–108).

[8] Herbert A. Simon, *Fiscal Aspects of Metropolitan Consolidation* (Berkeley: Bureau of Public Administration, University of California, 1943).

TABLE 5. Per Capita Municipal Expenditures and Municipal Tax
Rates as Related to Value of Taxable Property per
Capita and Type of City

Type of city	Average annual per capita municipal expenditures, 1952–55 [a]	Average true value of taxable property per capita, 1954	Average municipal property tax rate per $100 of true value, 1953–54
Central	69.0	$5,552	$0.562
Balanced	54.0	5,274	0.400
Cities with higher than mean property values per capita [b]	58.1	6,230	0.373
Cities with lower than mean property values per capita	49.0	4,240	0.435
Dormitory	40.0	5,411	0.310
Cities with higher than mean property values per capita	51.5	7,004	0.320
Cities with lower than mean property values per capita	28.2	3,517	0.300
Industrial enclave	126.0	43,079	0.170

Sources: For column 1 see California State Controller, *Annual Reports of Financial Transactions concerning Cities and Counties of California* for the respective years, Table 4; for column 2 see Table 2; for column 3 see Table 1.

[a] Expenditures do not include payments from debt obligations and for trust transactions or for public service enterprises which usually are financed by prices.

[b] Higher and lower than mean refer to a value of taxable property per capita for a city which is higher or lower than the mean for its group as reported in Table 2.

be computed from the data in the table. The wealth elasticity of expenditures is the ratio of the percentage change in municipal expenditures to the percentage change in taxable wealth. This elasticity suggests explanations of the differences in the levels of expenditures and the intensity of the fiscal problems of the different types of cities.

For balanced cities the wealth elasticity of expenditures is .40, while for dormitory cities it is .64. In both cases the "demand" for public services as a function of taxable wealth is inelastic. The greater inelasticity in the case of balanced cities makes it seem probable that the existence of extensive business activities in a city creates a need for public services which the residents feel must be met in spite of limited resources. For instance, the expenditures of the "poor" balanced cities are 95 per cent of those of the "rich" dormitories, though the value of taxable property of the "poor" balanced cities is only 59 per cent as great as that of the "rich" dormitories. There are no data that would enable us to discover whether the greater inelasticity and higher level of expenditures in balanced and central cities are due to the need for servicing business or to their different income levels and density patterns. Whatever the cause, the higher levels and greater inelasticity of expenditures create a more severe fiscal problem.

Several inferences about behavior can be drawn from an inelastic demand. If a specific income source declines, we expect that a larger share of the income will be spent on the commodity in question and, further, that a greater effort will be made to seek other income sources. Both courses of action are followed by the cities studied. The central cities with the highest expenditures have the highest tax rates. The second highest rates are found among the "poorer" balanced cities. Both groups also make the greatest efforts to find supplementary income sources. The third highest rates are not found among the "poorer" dormitory cities as we might expect. Instead, the "poorer" dormitory cities have the lowest rates. This surprising finding is a result of two forces: (1) the wealth elasticity of expenditures of dormitory cities is higher than that of balanced cities, and therefore a given decrease in taxable property means a larger decrease in municipal expenditures. (2) "Poorer" cities, including the "poorer" dormitory cities, seek other sources of revenues as substitutes for property taxes.

The next section will discuss the role of non-property taxes in altering the tax burden on property in the various types of cities.

V

The final element of the property tax rate identity to be discussed is non-property tax revenues. They are increasing in importance, and their use has clearly affected the property tax rate. Table 6 analyzes the major sources of the non-property tax revenues of the cities. In general, the non-property tax revenues are more important than property taxes as a source of revenues. For every type of city except the industrial enclaves, the collections of non-property tax revenues per capita or per hundred dollars of taxable value exceed those of the property tax. The major sources of municipal non-property tax revenues are state subventions and sales taxes. Almost all the subventions are shared revenues which are distributed primarily according to population. These two sources of non-property tax revenues account for almost half the non-property tax revenues of the cities.

The central and balanced cities benefit most from non-property tax revenues, measured either in per capita receipts or in terms of reductions in property taxes. This is to be expected, given the wider range of activities in these cities, which increases the number of revenue sources, and their greater need for funds, which encourages them to seek out other tax forms.

State subventions act as an equalizer of fiscal capacities among the cities. Subvention receipts per capita are roughly equal by type of city, but, since

TABLE 6. NON-PROPERTY TAX REVENUES OF CITIES, BY TYPE OF CITY, 1953–54

| Type of city | All non-property tax revenues | | Subventions | | Sales taxes | |
	Per capita	Per $100 of taxable property	Per capita	Per $100 of taxable property	Per capita	Per $100 of taxable property
Central [a]	$33.70	$0.616	$9.26	$0.116	$7.71	$0.139
Industrial enclave	36.88	0.086	8.99	0.020	—	—
Balanced	31.44	0.596	8.03	0.152	5.04	0.096
High [b] taxable property per capita	32.11	0.510	7.68	0.122	4.27	0.068
Low [b] taxable property per capita	30.77	0.726	8.39	0.198	5.82	0.137
Dormitory	22.59	0.423	7.93	0.149	1.20	0.022
High [b] taxable property per capita	27.69	0.396	7.99	0.114	0.61	0.008
Low [b] taxable property per capita	12.04	0.482	7.87	0.224	1.86	0.055

Source: See Table 1.
[a] See Table 1, n. [b].
[b] See Table 5, note [b], for definitions of high and low.

the value of taxable property per capita varies, the savings for property owners are greatest in the "poorer" cities.

The pattern of sales taxes is quite different. The central cities receive the greatest "benefits" from sales taxes both per capita and in terms of "property tax savings." Table 6 also indicates that the balanced cities benefit more than the dormitory cities and that, the "poorer" the city, the greater the benefits of sales taxes. Such a conclusion is oversimplified. Not all cities have sales taxes, and the findings of Table 6 are seriously affected by a pattern of selectivity in the adoption of sales taxes.

Table 7 analyzes some of the fiscal data for cities with and without sales taxes. The first inference that might be drawn from Table 7 is that, the lower its property tax capacity, the more likely it is that the city will adopt a sales tax. The greater frequency of sales taxes among "poorer" cities explains the higher yield of sales taxes for "poorer" cities indicated in Table 6. Second, the "richer" dormitory cities, followed by the central cities, benefit the most from the use of sales taxes. A third inference is that the sales tax may not provide substantial relief for property owners. For each group analyzed the average municipal property tax rate for cities with sales taxes was higher than that for cities without sales taxes. In general, the cities with sales taxes spend more per capita than the cities without sales taxes. The finding that sales-tax cities have higher municipal property tax rates and

TABLE 7.   SALES TAX REVENUES BY TYPE OF CITY, 1953–54

Type of city	No. of cities	Sales tax receipts		As percentage of total revenue	Municipal property tax receipts per $100 of taxable property	Municipal costs per capita
		Per capita	Per $100 of taxable property			
Central	2	$ 7.71 [a]	$0.139 [a]	11.9	$0.562	$ 69.0
Industrial enclave	4	5.04	0.096	a	0.170	126.0
Balanced	14		—	9.6	0.398	54.0
High taxable property per capita						
With sales tax	4	6.25	0.100	11.4	0.389	56.5
Without sales tax	3	—	—	—	0.339	61.8
Low taxable property per capita						
With sales tax	7	5.82	0.137	11.8	0.435	49.0
Without sales tax	0	—	—	—	b	40.0
Dormitory	35	1.20	0.022	3.04	0.314	40.0
High taxable property per capita						
With sales tax	2	13.50	0.164	13.4	0.535	72.8
Without sales tax	15	—	—	—	0.309	50.6
Low taxable property per capita						
With sales tax	10	3.60	0.128	10.7	0.418	32.2
Without sales tax	8	—	—	—	0.300	23.4

Source: See Table 1.
[a] No cities with a sales tax.
[b] All cities had a sales tax.

higher expenditures per capita implies that the addition of this revenue source reduced the budget restraint for the sales-tax cities and allowed them to spend more. The cities that adopted the tax are also taxing more of their property. It is therefore reasonable to speculate that the removal of this tax source is more likely to result in a reduction of expenditures than in an increase in property taxes.

The final implication to be drawn from Table 7 is that most of the larger "property tax savings" accruing to balanced cities because of their non-property tax revenues arises from their more frequent use of sales taxes. Receipts from non-property tax sources per $100 of taxable true values were $0.17 higher in balanced than in dormitory cities. If all the cities adopted sales taxes, and those without sales tax received the same receipts per $100 of value as comparable cities with sales taxes, the advantage of balanced cities would fall to $0.08.

VI

The conclusions of the analysis, in brief, are: The municipal property tax rate is higher for cities that have a high ratio of jobs to residents within their boundaries (Sec. II). The higher rates for the "business" cities are a function of their much higher public expenditures per capita, their lower real property values, and the insufficient fiscal advantages they receive from non-property tax revenues.

The public expenditures of "business" cities are both higher and more inelastic relative to wealth. Therefore, the lower the per capita wealth of "business" cities, the greater their tax burden (Sec. IV).

The per capita value of taxable property of "business" cities is lower than that of dormitory cities. This is due to the distinctly higher values of per capita real property in dormitory cities. The dormitory cities have this advantage in spite of the fact that the "business" cities have far more industrial and commercial land per capita. Clearly, the value of residential real property per capita is far greater for the dormitory cities. This higher value is due to the lower residential densities and higher household incomes in dormitory cities. These density and income differences are probably not independent of the pattern of economic activities within the city (Sec. III).

The findings of this study case doubt on the rationality of a program of encouraging industrial and commercial land use for suburbs. They suggest the hypothesis that accompanying the business use of land there will be a change in the nature of residential uses and an expansion of public services so that tax costs per dollar of property value will increase. The findings are consistent with a suburban-exploitation-of-central-cities hypothesis, but, before this hypothesis can be established, a more intensive examination of the public services is needed. Are the higher costs of "business" cities merely expenses of doing business and necessary to overcome the "disutilities" of higher densities, or do the expenditures reflect a higher level of amenities? If the former is the case, a redistributive argument can be justified, while, if the latter is true, the higher per capita expenditures reflect different tastes.

SOME FISCAL IMPLICATIONS
OF METROPOLITANISM

Harvey E. Brazer

This paper is concerned with some of the major problems that arise in connection with our efforts to provide and finance public services for nearly two thirds of the American population which currently lives in areas designated by the Census Bureau as "Standard Metropolitan Statistical Areas." Heterogeneity, in terms of economic function, income levels, social and political preferences, dominant ethnic origins, and so forth, typically characterizes the constituent parts of the metropolitan community, at least in the larger ones. And yet all residents, business units and families, as well as governing bodies, have a common stake in the performance of public services and the levying of taxes in all parts of the area. If a single central problem can be identified, therefore, it must be defined as *the problem of achieving efficiency in meeting common needs and reaching common goals within a framework of action that gives appropriate cognizance to the diversity in tastes and needs that exists.*

The general plan of this paper entails our taking up, in turn, the attempt to establish norms or "ideal" arrangements for supplying and financing public services in the metropolitan area, the obstacles in the way of achieving these norms, and the question of how we can most effectively live with or minimize these obstacles.

Harvey E. Brazer is Professor of Economics, University of Michigan.
Reprinted with permission from Harvey E. Brazer, "Some Fiscal Implications of Metropolitanism," in Guthrie S. Birkhead, ed., *Metropolitan Issues: Social, Governmental, Fiscal* (Syracuse, N.Y.: Maxwell Graduate School of Citizenship and Public Affairs, February 1962), pp. 61–82.

NORMATIVE GOALS FOR FISCAL ARRANGEMENTS

The establishment of norms of fiscal behavior for government requires that we define the roles we expect it to play. For government in general it is convenient to follow Musgrave's "multiple theory of the public household" which involves, for analytical purposes, separate treatment of public want satisfaction (his "allocation branch"), income redistribution through taxes and transfers (the "distribution branch"), and stabilization of the economy (the "stabilization branch").[1] Where government is expected to assume responsibility for all three, no one role or branch of the budget is, in practice, fully separable from the others; virtually all fiscal actions will have some repercussions of significance for allocation, distribution, and stabilization. And this remains true even if public want satisfaction is regarded as the sole overt objective of government, as, in my view, it must be in the case of local, as opposed to national, government. Nevertheless, we may, in this instance, regard effects on income distribution and stabilization as being incidental and unsought, to be avoided as much as possible. Thus the role assumed for local governments in the metropolitan community is that of providing public goods and services under circumstances in which the national government is presumed to have succeeded in achieving its goals with respect to income distribution and economic stability at high and rising levels of employment with stable prices.

Local neutrality with respect to income distribution is suggested because of the obvious impossibility of achieving any specified goal in this area if thousands of state and local units of government attempt either to offset or to supplement national action. Neutrality with respect to the stabilization function appears to be either desirable or unavoidable for a number of reasons. Local needs tend to be inflexible over short periods of time, being geared largely to changes in the size and character of the population or requiring continuity for their effective satisfaction. Stabilization measures pursued at the local level involve tremendous geographic leakages which give rise, among other things, to serious questions of interregional equity. The lack of monetary powers and existence of stringent debt limits, which frequently fluctuate countercyclically, impose major constraints upon policy. And, finally, mobility of resources in the national economy as a whole may be impaired through local efforts to increase employment by means of public action if such action is pursued at a time when unemployment is high locally but low nationally.

Most specifically relevant to our discussion of fiscal aspects of metro-

[1] Richard A. Musgrave, *The Theory of Public Finance* (New York: McGraw-Hill Book Company, 1959), Chap. 1.

politanism is the problem of allocating responsibility for public want satisfaction and its financing among the governmental units that operate within the metropolitan community. Our solution hinges primarily on externalities in consumption. At one extreme, if all of the benefits derived from consumption of a good are appropriable by a single individual, so that there are no external economies of consumption or spillover effects, there are no public aspects of consumption involved and neither must we face an allocation problem. But assuming that there are substantial external economies of consumption, and that we are therefore concerned with public want satisfaction, the interjurisdictional allocation problem involves the question of how far from the point of consumption, if one is identifiable, benefits extend. Conceptually, one may distinguish collective goods involving externalities that extend only to neighborhood or municipal boundaries, to county lines, to multi-country regions, to state lines, and finally those that extend to the nation as a whole or even to the community of nations.

The spelling out of a general rule that will provide the specific answer for each governmental function is obviously extremely difficult, if not impossible. However, we can obtain some guidelines for action within metropolitan areas with respect, at least, to some functions. Thus air and stream pollution control obviously involve important externalities that demand their being undertaken on an areawide basis, without regard to municipal boundary lines; the same may be said of arterial urban highways, mass transit, and water supply, with economies of scale adding weight to the argument for multiunit action. Not quite so clear is the position of recreational facilities, public libraries, museums, and police protection. In each of these cases benefits cannot be confined to the boundaries of individual municipal jurisdictions; nor, on the other hand, are they uniformly distributed within the metropolitan area. Complicating the problem is the fact that a function such as police protection encompasses many subfunctions, some of which are purely local, with no spillovers to neighboring communities, while others either involve substantial spillovers or indivisibilities and major economies of scale.[2]

The question of whether a given collective good should be provided by the submetropolitan jurisdiction or by some agency with broader geographical powers is further complicated by the fact that the issues involved

---

[2] The failure of statistical cross-section studies of city expenditures to reveal economies of scale is by no means evidence that they do not exist. Larger cities do not spend less, per capita, for police protection than smaller ones, but this is very likely a consequence of the fact that economies of scale may be offset by the performance of more subfunctions under the "police protection" heading. See my *City Expenditures in the United States* (New York: National Bureau of Economic Research, Inc., 1959), pp. 25–28.

cannot be regarded as being purely economic. We are necessarily concerned with something more than economic efficiency. The heterogeneity found among municipalities in a metropolitan area involves wide variations in tastes and preferences, the pursuit of which must be accorded a positive value. Thus the solution in terms of efficiency in an engineering sense—that is, the most product at the least cost—is inappropriate by itself. The problem may be fruitfully approached, perhaps, by drawing a distinction between those public services with respect to which taste differentials may be expected to be relatively unimportant, and for which narrowly construed economic efficiency criteria may be allowed to predominate, and those with respect to which purely local preferences will exhibit wide variations, with only minor spillover effects. What is wanted, of course, is a voluntary solution that can be achieved through voting or the political process. A solution that may be called for on grounds of economic efficiency may be rejected if members of local communities place a high value upon their ability to influence policy in the functional area involved. And, contrary to the views of those who are among the more extreme advocates of consolidation in metropolitan areas, there is no prima facie reason for insisting that the "efficient" solution be pursued.

In the attempt to define normative fiscal goals for the metropolitan area, attention must also be directed toward the revenue side of the budget. If redistribution of income through the operation of the local public fisc is to be avoided and an optimal allocation of resources achieved, public service benefits must be paid for by those who enjoy such benefits. The problem is extremely complex, even in a purely general setting, because collective consumption, by its very nature, involves benefits inappropriable by the individual, to which the private-market exclusion principle cannot be applied. A tax system under which liabilities are determined by the individual's preferences for public goods is inoperative, because failure or refusal to reveal one's preferences would reduce tax liability while not denying the opportunity to consume.[3]

Within the setting of metropolitan area finances the problem is even more intricate. Here we are concerned not only with the relationship between the individual and *the* government, but with the additional problems that arise because any one government may be expected to supply services the benefits from which accrue to its own residents *and* to residents of other jurisdictions. Thus even if it were possible for a municipality within the metropolitan area to finance its services by means of appropriate user

---

[3] See Musgrave's discussion of the problems involved, *op. cit.,* pp. 81–84, and Paul A. Samuelson, "The Pure Theory of Public Expenditure," *Review of Economics and Statistics,* 36 (November, 1954), pp. 387–89, and "Diagrammatic Exposition of a Theory of Public Expenditure," *Review of Economics and Statistics,* 37 (November, 1955), pp. 350–56.

charges and benefit levies upon its residents, spillover effects and consumption by nonresidents would ordinarily prevent an equation of benefits and charges at the margin. Ideally, benefits must be paid for by those who enjoy them, and all who enjoy public service benefits should participate in the decision-making process through which it is determined which goods and services are to be supplied and the quantities to be offered. Such an ideal solution is ruled out by spillover or neighborhood effects of local public services and nonresident collective consumption within the supplying jurisdiction, even if it were otherwise conceptually attainable. In setting out fiscal goals for metropolitan areas perhaps all that can be suggested is that the repercussions of these considerations should be minimized. This may be achieved through the appropriate allocation of functional responsibilities, coupled with the extension of taxing powers to overlapping jurisdictions and the employment, wherever feasible, of user charges.

OBSTACLES TO THE ACHIEVEMENT OF NORMATIVE GOALS

One of the more sanguine and interesting approaches to the theory of local finance in the metropolitan area is that of Professor Tiebout. In it, "The consumer-voter may be viewed as picking that community which best satisfies his preference pattern for public goods," having been offered a range of choices among jurisdictions, each of which has its "revenue and expenditure patterns more or less set."[4] Thus the problem of getting individuals to reveal their preferences is solved, much as it is in the private market sector, provided that there are enough communities from which to choose and the other assumptions of Tiebout's model hold. These other assumptions are: full mobility, including the absence of restraints associated with employment opportunities; full knowledge on the part of "consumer-voters"; no intercommunity external economies or diseconomies associated with local public services; some factor limiting the optimum size (the size at which its services can be provided at lowest average cost) of each community, given its set pattern of services; and communities constantly seeking to reach or maintain this optimum size.[5] If we add to this list of assumptions the insistence that residents of each community are not only not concerned with employment opportunities[6] but also refrain from venturing into other communities for shopping, recreation, or any other purpose, except when involved in a change in their places of residence, we may, indeed, have a "conceptual solution" to the problem of determining

[4] Charles M. Tiebout, "A Pure Theory of Local Expenditures," *The Journal of Political Economy*, 54 (October, 1956), p. 418.

[5] *Ibid.*, p. 419.

[6] In Tiebout's "model" everyone lives on his dividend checks.

optimal levels of consumption for a substantial portion of collective goods. And as an exercise in abstraction it may be a solution, as useful, perhaps, as many of the economist's abstractions.

Unfortunately, however, Tiebout's model cannot be said to be even a rough first approximation of the real world. The most pressing fiscal problems of metropolitanism arise precisely because of the very factors he denies in his assumptions. Even if individuals had full knowledge of differences among communities in revenue and service patterns and were willing to move in response to them and their own tastes, income, zoning, racial and religious discrimination, and other barriers to entry to various communities would restrict their mobility. (A low-income non-Caucasian family does not move from Detroit to Grosse Pointe because it prefers the latter's tax and expenditure pattern!) Families and individuals do extend their activities, in working, shopping, and playing, across community lines, so that there is no clear-cut coincidence between one's place of residence and the place in which services are consumed and taxes paid. Employment opportunities do condition the choice of community of residence, particularly for lower-income families, and for all families commuting costs, like all transport costs, restrict choices. And when the existence of external economies and diseconomies between communities associated with public services (or their nonperformance) is assumed away, we have not only thrown the baby out with the bath water, we have thrown away the bath.

DIFFERENCES IN COMMUNITY CHARACTERISTICS

A major source of fiscal difficulty in the metropolitan area arises as a consequence of differences among local communities in the characteristics of their populations. As the Advisory Commission on Intergovernmental Relations noted recently: "Population is tending to be increasingly distributed within metropolitan areas along economic and racial lines. Unless present trends are altered, the central cities may become increasingly the place of residence of new arrivals in the metropolitan areas, of nonwhites, lower-income workers, younger couples, and the elderly."[7] Thus although the total populations of five[8] of the six largest central cities declined between 1950 and 1960, this decline was the product of a reduction in the white population, ranging from 6.7 per cent in New York to 23.5 per cent in Detroit, and an increase in nonwhite population which ranged from 45.3 per cent in Baltimore to 64.4 per cent in Chicago.[9] Looking back over a

[7] *Governmental Structure, Organization, and Planning in Metropolitan Areas, A Report by the Advisory Commission on Intergovernmental Relations* (Washington, D.C.: U.S. Government Printing Office, 1961), p. 7.

[8] New York, Chicago, Philadelphia, Detroit, and Baltimore.

[9] Advisory Commission on Intergovernmental Relations, *op. cit.,* Table 1, p. 7.

longer period, 1930 to 1960, we find that for the twelve largest SMSA's combined the white population declined from 94 to 87 per cent of total population. But *all* of this decline took place in the central cities, where the white population declined from 92 to 79 per cent of the total.[10]

The Detroit Area Study's findings on the income experience of whites and nonwhites and residents of the suburbs and the central city, for the period 1951 to 1959, reveal some startling contrasts. Median family income rose from $4,400 to 4,800, by 9 per cent, in the central city (including Highland Park and Hamtramck, which are encircled by Detroit), and from $4,900 to $7,200, or by 47 per cent, in the suburbs. At the same time the median income of white families increased by 33 per cent, for the area as a whole, compared to only 8 per cent for nonwhites.[11] The movement of white, higher-income families to Detroit's suburbs, coupled with their replacement in the central city by low-income newcomers, has increased the median family income differential from 11 per cent in 1951 to 50 per cent in 1959.[12]

For Detroit and, one would expect, for other major central cities as well, developments of the kind described have had substantial fiscal repercussions. They have brought a high concentration to the central city of those who are most vulnerable to unemployment in recession and to loss of employment consequent upon technological change, and who tend to bring heavy demands upon welfare, health, and other public services. At the same time the value of residential property occupied per family declines, thus completing the fiscal squeeze.

None of this is new. It has been going on as long as newcomers of lower income and social or cultural values different from those predominating have concentrated in the central cities of our metropolitan communities. A growing difference between present and past experience arises, however, from the dispersion of industry to suburban locations. No longer is the core of the area necessarily the residential location that minimizes the costs of going to and from the job. Thus, strong pressures have developed which have resulted in the growth in suburban communities of conditions once confined to low-income central city residential sections. In some of these, fiscal problems that exist are even more intense than those experienced by the central city because the suburban community which houses the low-income worker is frequently not the location of the industrial plant employ-

---

[10] Harry Sharp, "Race as a Factor in Metropolitan Growth." A paper presented at the 1961 meetings of the Population Association of America, Table 2. Mimeographed.

[11] Harry Sharp, "Family Income in Greater Detroit: 1951–59," Project 870, No. 1681, Detroit Area Study (Ann Arbor: Survey Research Center, The University of Michigan, July, 1960), Table 2. Mimeographed.

[12] *Ibid.*, p. 8.

ing him. Lower-income families no longer necessarily occupy with increasing density the older residential sections of the central city. They are found concentrated as well in development tracts in suburban communities where the tax base represented by their houses is far too low to permit the financing of an accepable level of public services.[13]

On the other hand, the suburb may constitute either an industrial enclave, with a very large tax base and few people, or a tightly restricted area of high-value houses. In neither of these cases do fiscal problems of major magnitude arise.

The resulting contrasts in the size of tax bases relative to population may be dramatically illustrated with data from the Cleveland metropolitan area within Cuyahoga County. The range of assessed valuation per capita for 1956 extends from $122,237 in the Village of Cuyahoga Heights, an industrial enclave of less than three square miles with a population of 785, to $837 in the one half square mile area that remains of Riveredge Township. Among the larger communities the assessed value per capita ranges from $1,858 in Garfield Heights to $4,256 in Shaker Heights, with the City of Cleveland at $2,852.[14]

Similarly sharp contrasts, emphasizing the diversity among municipalities in structure rather than size of tax bases, may be seen in the Detroit area. In 1958 the assessed value of residential property in thirty-four cities, villages, and townships comprised 42 per cent of total assessed valuations in these communities. For the City of Detroit the ratio was 40 per cent, whereas for such industrial enclaves as River Rouge, Trenton, Hamtramck, Highland Park, and Warren, it was less than 20 per cent, while at the other end of the spectrum, in the Grosse Pointe communities, and Dearborn Township, the ratio was 85 per cent or higher.[15]

Such extreme inequalities as those in the distribution within metropolitan areas of socioeconomic groups of population and the property tax base give rise to wide differences in expenditures and tax rates. Tax rates and per capita expenditures both tend to be highest in central cities, but ranks with respect to tax rates and expenditures diverge for communities outside the central city. Margolis found that industrial enclaves spend most while levying the lowest tax rates; "balanced" cities rank next on both counts, fol-

---

[13] In the Detroit Area the proportions of families with money incomes in 1958 of less than $3,000 were 21 per cent for the central city, 15 per cent for low-income residential cities, 7 per cent for high-income residential cities, 8 per cent for balanced cities, and 11 per cent for industrial cities. See Table 1 for definitions of types of cities. Data from 1958–59 Detroit Area Study.

[14] Derived from Seymour Sacks, Leo M. Egand, and William F. Hellmuth, Jr., *The Cleveland Metropolitan Area—A Fiscal Profile* (Cleveland: Cleveland Metropolitan Services Commission, 1958), p. vii. Assessed values may be assumed to be "equalized" because the county is the sole assessing jurisdiction.

[15] Data were drawn from the records of local assessing officers.

lowed by "dormitory" cities. However, the omission from his data of school district taxes and expenditures results in a rather incomplete and, in substantial degree, misleading picture. It permits, among other things, the conclusion that balanced cities, relative to dormitory cities, fail "to derive fiscal advantage from their commercial and industrial properties."[16] This conclusion is not supported by data drawn from the Detroit area. Here we find (Table 1) that combined tax rates, including municipal, school, and county levies, are about the same for the central city and the residential cities, lower for the balanced cities, and, again, lowest for the industrial cities. The evidence suggests that residential or dormitory suburbs spend comparatively little for municipal functions, but bear a relatively heavy burden in school expenditures and taxes.

TABLE 1.   EFFECTIVE TAX RATES IN THE
DETROIT AREA, 1958, BY TYPE
OF CITY

Type of city [a]	Tax rate [b] (per cent)
Central	1.7
Low-income residential	1.6
High-income residential	1.6
Balanced	1.3
Industrial	1.0

[a] Detroit is the central city; residential cities are cities in which the assessed value of residential property exceeds 60 per cent of total assessed valuation in 1958; balanced cities are cities for which this ratio lies between 40 and 60 per cent; and industrial cities are those for which it is below 40 per cent.

[b] The effective tax rate is the mean of the ratios of property tax billed, according to local official records, to the owner's estimate of the value of his owner-occupied residential property, based on a total of 515 observations. Validity checks indicate a very close correspondence between owner's estimates and actual market values.

Source: Unpublished data compiled for the Detroit Area Study, 1958–59, Survey Research Center, The University of Michigan.

Thus, the Detroit Area data support the conclusion that addition to a community of industrial and commercial property does tend to reduce effective tax rates. But broad generalizations can easily be misleading. New industry entering a community may or may not relieve fiscal pressures. The

[16] See Brazer, *op. cit.*, p. 65, for per capita expenditures, by function and type of city, and Julius Margolis, "Municipal Fiscal Structure in a Metropolitan Region," *The Journal of Political Economy* 55 (June, 1957), p. 232, for per capita municipal expenditures and tax rates in cities within the San Francisco area. Both sources fail to take into account the expenditures and taxes levied by school districts, counties, and other local governments overlying the cities.

TABLE 2.   ESTIMATED PER CAPITA DIRECT GENERAL EXPENDITURES OF LOCAL GOVERNMENTS IN CENTRAL CITIES AND OUTSIDE OF CENTRAL CITIES, 12 LARGEST METROPOLITAN AREAS,[a] 1957 (DOLLARS)

Central city	Total direct general expenditure		Education		Highways		Welfare		Police and fire protection		All other	
	Central city	Outside c.c.	Central city	Outside c.c.	Central city	Outside c.c.	Central city	Outside c.c.	Central city	Outside c.c.	Central city	Outside c.c.
New York	257	212 [b]	63	106 [b]	18	16 [b]	28	9 [b]	28	19 [b]	120	62 [b]
Newark	242	212 [b]	74	106 [b]	7	16 [b]	12	9 [b]	38	19 [b]	111	62 [b]
Jersey City	235	212 [b]	49	106 [b]	7	16 [b]	11	9 [b]	35	19 [b]	133	62 [b]
Chicago	200	145 [c]	48	82 [c]	35	14 [c]	8	4 [c]	24	10 [c]	85	35 [c]
Los Angeles	261	202	95	93	16	11	29	26	30	14	91	58
Long Beach	325 [d]	202	115	93	25	11	32	26	29	14	124 [d]	58
Philadelphia	165	138	49	72	12	23	4	5	23	8	77	30
Detroit	201	200	62	114	16	19	9	3	25	12	89	52
San Francisco	220	230	62	112	11	15	33	23	35	15	79	65
Oakland	232	230	73	112	16	15	30	23	27	15	86	65
Baltimore	199	149	59	71	19	20	18	3	31	10	72	45
Cleveland	183	189	50	85	19	22	12	12	24	15	78	55
Minneapolis	182	194	59	97	16	17	22	15	16	6	69	59
St. Paul	189	194	51	97	19	17	22	15	19	6	78	59
St. Louis	147	125	45	71	10	15	1	3	23	10	68	26
Boston	272	182	48	70	12	17	41	22	37	21	134	52
Pittsburgh	188	132	41	66	13	13	5	3	24	8	105	42

[a] Metropolitan Areas are those defined as of the 1950 Census of Population, rather than Standard Metropolitan Statistical Areas.
[b] Includes Paterson-Clifton-Passaic.
[c] Includes Gary-Hammond-East Chicago.
[d] Excludes payment to the State of California for settlement of oil land litigation, a total of $138 million.

Source: Derived from U.S. Department of Commerce, Bureau of the Census, Local Government Finances in Standard Metropolitan Areas, 1957 Census of Governments, Vol. III, No. 6 (Washington: U.S. Government Printing Office, 1959), Tables 3 and 4: expenditures of counties containing the central city were apportioned according to the ratio of central city to county population, based on 1957 estimates of county population and 1950 to 1960 straight-line interpolation for the central cities; minor amounts of special district expenditures were not apportioned to the central cities.

answer in specific circumstances must depend on such things as the capital-labor ratio involved in production, the level of wage rates paid, the demand for the output of the community's economy that emanates from the plant's operation, the extent to which the labor force lives in or outside of the community in which the plant is located, and so on.

Data presented in Table 2 indicate that there are substantial differences between the central city and the rest of the metropolitan area in the amounts spent per capita in total and for the separate major functions. Part of such differences stems from the fact that the area outside the central city is less fully urbanized, but a large part is undoubtedly attributable to the differences in demographic and other characteristics outlined above. Highway expenditures tend to be inversely associated with population density, so that we should expect them to be higher outside the central city.[17] Rapid population growth requires large capital outlays for new schools, and thus accounts for the higher education expenditures in the suburbs. But with respect to police and fire protection and welfare, the higher population density, lower incomes, and concentration of newcomers and the aged in the central cities all point to the far higher level of per capita expenditure that we find. The last column of the table, which includes expenditures for such functions as health and hospitals, urban renewal, public housing, sanitation, and so forth, presents the most striking evidence of consistently higher expenditures being incurred in the central cities than in the satellite communities of metropolitan areas.

EQUITY AND EFFICIENCY

If there were no limitations upon the mobility of families and individuals between communities, one might contend that neither efficiency nor equity considerations need enter the discussion. If people chose their place of residence freely, it could then be argued that the price paid for living in one community rather than another, in terms of higher taxes paid for a given level of services or a given tax rate paid for a lower level of services, was voluntarily assumed. It might even be reflected in land values in such fashion as to be approximately offsetting in effect. But as long as barriers to mobility exist, through zoning regulations, racial discrimination, and so forth, such offsetting will not occur and neither equity nor efficiency can be achieved.

Equity, in the sense of equal treatment of equals vis-à-vis the local fisc, may not obtain as between equal individuals resident in different communities simply because of differences in the distribution of income and wealth between communities. Thus individual A, resident in wealthy community X, may be expected to enjoy a larger flow of public service benefits

[17] Brazer, op. cit., pp. 25, 36, 39, 42, and 56.

at a given tax cost to him than individual B, A's "equal," however defined, a resident of poor community Y.[18] In the absence of barriers to mobility between communities, we should expect B to remain in Y only if wage rates were higher and/or prices, including land values, were lower in Y than in X by amounts sufficient to offset the fiscal disadvantage. If wage rates were not higher or prices lower initially, the movement of people from Y to X should lead to their adjustment in equilibrium at levels that will just compensate for the fiscal disadvantage of living in Y. However, if B, for reason, say, of color, is barred from community X, the adjustment cannot take place.

The analysis is complicated, of course, by recognition of the fact that individuals may live in one community, work in another, and shop in a third. In this case wage rates and prices of goods and services in the place of residence may be unaffected (at the extreme the community may be a "pure" bedroom suburb) and the burden of adjustment would fall entirely on land values, directly or through land rents, and, at least in the short run, on housing values and rents.

Thus far we have ignored the influence on interpersonal equity of differences among communities in the value of commercial and industrial property. If the cost of providing services to such property is equal to its tax contribution, this influence is zero — but such cost-tax equality is extremely unlikely. If industry or commerce brings a net fiscal gain to the community, its residents can enjoy a higher public service to tax-cost ratio than can be enjoyed without it (all other things being equal). Again, with full mobility equity can be achieved, but not otherwise. The same conclusion holds, with opposite signs being attached to relative gains and losses, where the industrial or commercial property entails a net fiscal loss.

Efficiency in the allocation of resources, including those flowing through the public budget, requires a matching of benefits and costs at the margin, from the point of view of the consumer-voter, directly or on his behalf by "best-guessing" political representatives. On the assumption that the principal or only tax employed locally is the more or less uniformly applicable property tax, if the costs of providing public services to nonresidential property are regarded as given, a vote by individuals for a higher tax rate necessarily means that the increase in property tax receipts available for financing services for individuals will exceed the increment in taxes paid by them.[19] This should bring an excessive allocation of resources to the local public sector, since expenditure benefits will have been underpriced to the indi-

---

[18] See J. M. Buchanan, "Federalism and Fiscal Equity," *American Economic Review*, 40 (September, 1950), for his statement of equity in terms of fiscal residua.

[19] Assuming that they do not bear the property taxes paid by local industry or commerce through higher prices or lower wages, dividends, and rents, and that individuals are concerned with public services only in their capacities as consumers rather than as income earners.

vidual taxpayer. Inefficiency arises as well from the firm's point of view, because taxes paid under these circumstances exceed the cost of providing services to it.

All this suggests initially that the property tax as we know it is an inefficient tax instrument. Combined with differences among communities in the metropolitan area in relative size of industrial and commercial tax bases, it produces cost-benefit ratios for business and industry with respect to their inputs in the form of public services that may be expected to vary widely among communities. If individuals as voters act freely and fully in their own self-interest, we should expect the cost per unit of service received by industry to vary directly (if not proportionally) with the local ratio of non-residential to residential property.[20] To the extent that this expectation is fulfilled, its influence should lead to a spatial distribution of industry and trade that is different from that which we should expect in its absence. Within any region firms will be induced to locate at less economically attractive points than they would otherwise choose, because at more attractive points — where industry and commerce already exist — the cost of public service inputs will have been pushed to levels higher than those obtaining elsewhere.

This reasoning, plausible as it seems, is not consonant with the fact that industrial suburbs appear to levy lower tax rates than other satellite communities. It seems safe to hazard the guess that these lower tax rates are the product of political pressures brought to bear by industry and by the threat that industry will leave, or of efforts to attract new industry, coupled with imperfections in the political process which may be expected to dilute the effective expression of voter self-interest.

The fact that many people live in one community and work in another substantially complicates the decision-making process in the local public sector. It means that individuals live and pay taxes — property taxes and, in some jurisdictions, income taxes — in one municipality while consuming public services in at least two. What does this imply for fiscal policy and efficiency in the allocation of resources to the local public sector in the metropolitan area? Is the jurisdiction in which the individual works "subsidizing" the one in which he lives? This question has generally been asked in the context of central city versus suburb, but it seems equally applicable as between suburbs.

Since part of their consumption occurs in a jurisdiction other than their place of residence, some consumers of public services are not consumer-voters. This renders the decision-making process with respect to local budgets in the metropolitan area far more difficult to cope with, even in

---

[20] This neglects the very real prospect that local industry and commerce may succeed in exerting effective political influence.

conceptual terms. The usual benefit approach to budget theory requires that the consumer of public goods has either a direct or an indirect voice or vote in decisions as to what kinds and quantities of such goods are to be supplied and financed. But he is not permitted to vote when he is a commuter-consumer, unless the service is financed by means of user-charges, in which case there is no budget problem for either the resident or the commuter. Suppose we consider traffic control on arterial streets providing ingress to and egress from the central business district of the core city. Here, presumably, the commuter-consumer has no choice but to accept what he is offered, and he is offered such services as the resident-consumer voters determine shall be offered. From the point of view of all consumers of the specific service, we are bound to get underallocation of resources to its supply, because the resident-consumer-voter can be expected to be willing to pay only for the quantity and quality he wishes to purchase, the demand emanating from the commuter being ignored.[21] Alternatively, the commuter may be viewed as reducing, through his consumption, the product available to the resident per dollar's worth of input. This, again, would lead to less resources being allocated to traffic control than would be optimal were the demand of all consumers taken into account.

This line of argument offers one plausible explanation for the frequently stated observation that municipal services are undersupplied, in the sense, for example, that traffic control is inadequate to prevent heavy congestion in the metropolis. The illustration may readily be extended, with similar results, to a variety of other services, including recreation facilities, police protection, and so forth. The problem would not arise if Samuelson were correct in characterizing public goods as those the consumption of which by one person "leads to no subtraction from any other individual's consumption of that good. . . ."[22] Unfortunately, however, this characterization applies, if at all, only to a very small proportion of collective or public goods supplied by municipalities.[23]

The central cities of metropolitan areas and industrial suburbs have been shown to spend more per capita, in total and for major municipal functions (exclusive of education), than all local governments outside the central city in the metropolitan area, residential suburbs, and cities located outside the standard metropolitan areas.[24] Moreover, two studies of city expenditures

---

[21] Unless, of course, it is taken into account by resident individuals, not in their capacities as consumer voters, but in their capacities as income earners who may gain as bankers, realtors, storekeepers, and so forth, through attracting the commuter by offering better public services.

[22] "The Pure Theory of Public Expenditure," *loc. cit.*, p. 387.

[23] For a brief development of this point, see Julius Margolis, "A Comment on the Pure Theory of Public Expenditures," *Review of Economics and Statistics*, 37 (November, 1955), pp. 347–48.

[24] See Table 2 in the text, and Brazer, *op. cit.*, p. 65, Margolis' data "Municipal Fiscal Structure," *op. cit.*, p. 232) support this finding.

have found that the proportion of the metropolitan area's population that lies outside the central city is closely associated with the per capita expenditures of the central city.[25] Both sets of findings reflect the fact that the number of people for whom the city must provide services is the sum of its resident population and the nonresident or contact population which spends time in the city in the course of the working day, shopping, pursuing recreation, and so forth. Margolis' data on tax rates in the San Francisco-Oakland area add further evidence in support of the suburban-exploitation-of-the-metropolis hypothesis.[26]

Central cities may, in fact, provide more public services than surrounding communities, but it may be argued that this is a consequence not of differences in tastes, but of differences in needs, some of which are imposed on the central city by the behavior of suburban cities and socioeconomic forces beyond the control of municipal governments. Irrespective of whether or not the commuter "pays his way" through adding to property values in the central city, he cannot be said to share in the high costs of services engendered by the increasing concentration there of lower-income newcomers, including the nonwhite population. The latter, as we suggested earlier, tend to be less educated, more vulnerable to unemployment, and disorganized by moving from one cultural milieu to another that is totally unfamiliar and disruptive of traditional ties and mores. All these factors give rise to expenditure demands to which the suburban community is subject, typically, with far less intensity — expenditures in such fields as welfare, police protection, public health, public housing, and others. To the extent that suburban communities, through zoning regulations and discriminatory practices in rentals and real estate transactions, contribute directly to the concentration in the central city of socioeconomic groups which impose heavy demands upon local government services, they are, in fact, exploiting the central city.

One consequence of the multiplicity of governmental units within the metropolitan area is that the provision of public services (or failure to provide them) in one community has neighborhood or spillover effects associated with it for other communities in the area. A high quality of police protection in city A, for example, will be reflected in a lower incidence of crime in neighboring city B, or efficient sewage treatment by A will benefit its downriver neighbor B, and so forth. Obviously each jurisdiction will be both the source and beneficiary or victim of such spillovers. But even if all jurisdictions "come out even," getting as much as they give, the existence of

25 Amos H. Hawley, "Metropolitan Government and Municipal Government Expenditures in Central Cities," *Journal of Social Issues*, 7 (1951), pp. 100–108, reprinted, with supplementary tables, in Paul K. Hatt and Albert J. Reiss, Jr. (eds.), *Cities and Society*, rev. ed. (New York: The Free Press of Glencoe, Inc., 1957), and Brazer, *op. cit.*, pp. 54–59.

26 Municipal tax rates range downward from 56 mills for the central city to 17 mills for the industrial enclave. Margolis, "Municipal Fiscal Structure," *op. cit.*, p. 232.

these neighborhood effects will have important repercussions upon efficiency in the allocation of resources to the local public sector.

In arriving at their decision as to how much to spend for sewage treatment, for example, the resident-voters of a given community cannot be expected to take into account the repercussions of their decision on a neighboring community. To conclude otherwise is to assume that they are willing to engage in a form of public philanthropy. Nor can the fact that the first community enjoys some benefits emanating from the public services of another be expected to influence the voluntary decisions of its residents with respect to expenditures for collective consumption. The result, therefore, must be, again, an allocation of resources to collective consumption that is below the optimum level that would be indicated if all benefits of such consumption were appropriable in the spending community. At the extreme, public services that all residents of the congeries of jurisdictions want and are willing to pay for will not be supplied at all, because the proportion of the benefits appropriable by any one community's residents is so small as to make the expenditure less than worthwhile from their point of view.[27]

Finally, if we turn the coin of Tiebout's complex of municipalities from which individuals may choose places of residence, we find that business firms are offered a similar set of alternatives in the metropolitan area. And this side of the coin may and does display some very troublesome difficulties stemming from interlocal competition for industry. Efficiency in the allocation of resources requires that the costs of production of industrial firms reflect the costs of supplying them with inputs in the form of public services and the social costs they impose upon the community, such as through pollution of air and water. But if differences in local tax costs can be employed as an effective means of inducing firms to select one jurisdiction rather than another, competition for industry will force local industrial taxes below the level suggested by our criterion. Similarly, if the costs of adequate treatment of the plant's effluents into the air, streams, rivers, and lakes are substantial and can be avoided by location in one part of the metropolitan area rather than another, no one jurisdiction, acting alone, can be expected to be able to enforce adequate control. Thus it is hardly surprising that rivers become open sewers and air pollution occurs.

APPROACHES TO RATIONAL ACTION

The main burden of the foregoing discussion rests on the divisive, constraining, and conflicting interests and forces which emanate from the fact that our larger urban communities are served by aggregations of unco-

---

[27] This assumes that some indivisibilities exist, so that supply of the service below a given level is prohibitively expensive per unit produced.

ordinated governmental units. The inefficiencies, in terms of underallocation of resources to the public sector, and the accompanying inequities, go a long way toward providing some understanding, if not explanation, of the major problems confronting metropolitan America. Even if the forces discussed here could be eliminated others would remain. So-called land pollution, for example, may be simply an unavoidable consequence of our unwillingness to restrict private rights in property to the point necessary to eliminate it, and there is not in sight a means of relieving the choking congestion brought by the automobile, short of prohibiting its use in certain areas or drastically curtailing the freedom of the auto-owner to decide when and where he will drive. However, achieving a framework in which voter-choice is better enabled to satisfy the collective consumption wants of urban dwellers will provide a more efficient allocation of resources and reduce interpersonal inequities.

One approach is governmental consolidation. The further consolidation is carried, the greater is the extent to which spillover effects are reduced to appropriable benefits enjoyed by voter-consumers — that is, externalities are eliminated, as are interpersonal inequities. This can never be an entirely satisfactory solution, since border areas always remain. But more important is the fact that as the area covered by consolidation is extended the greater is the extent to which divergent interests and tastes are subordinated to the will of a more distant political majority. Thus efficiency, in an economic welfare sense, may or may not be improved, and the further dilution of the individual's ability to influence or participate directly in political decisions may be viewed as a major cost.

However, no one approach is likely to prove even conceptually satisfactory, whether or not it is politically feasible. Solutions to metropolitan area fiscal problems can, at best, only be compromises. The fact is that we cannot achieve desirable goals or objectives in a manner that permits the exercise of full freedom of individual choice. Rather, a modified objective appears necessary, one that will minimize the loss of consumer sovereignty in the local public sphere while avoiding a maximum of the inefficiencies and interpersonal inequities that arise under existing arrangements.

Perhaps a first requisite is the recognition and acceptance by the states, and to a lesser extent, the federal government, of their fiscal responsibilities in this area. The states can take several kinds of action. These might include establishment of minimum standards of performance with respect to those functions which involve strong neighborhood effects or which are subject to curtailment through interlocal competition. Such functions would certainly include areawide planning and air and water pollution control. In the case of these functions the neighborhood or spillover effects are of such overwhelming importance that their effective pursuit appears to be incompatible with freedom to establish purely local standards of performance and objectives. These appear to be cases which clearly justify the assertion that the primary obligation of people and individual municipal governments "is that of acceptance of some limitation of freedom of action in the interest of the greater good." [28]

A second role that may properly be assumed by the states is the reduction of local differences in fiscal capacity and interlocal competition based on tax inducements to industry and commerce. This objective may be achieved by expansion of state aid, essentially substituting state taxes for locally levied taxes. This approach need not impinge upon budgetary efficiency. If it is well designed, relationships at the margin, particularly in the choice among alternatives in the allocation of resources within the public sector, need not be disturbed.

State assumption of responsibility for certain functions, directly or through grants-in-aid, seems indicated as well, particularly in the fields of welfare, public health, public housing, and urban renewal — functions whose costs impinge with great unevenness among communities in the metropolitan area. Problems in urban transportation, including both mass transit and arterial streets and highways, may be met by the states through a combination of devices, including grants-in-aid, establishment of minimum standards of performance, and direct assumption of responsibility. Justification for such action by the states may be found in the fact that functions such as those mentioned must be performed because of socioeconomic forces that have their origin not in any one municipality but in the area, the state, or even the nation as a whole. They are a response to problems given by the social and technological environment in which we live. If that response is a purely local one, some members of society, those living in municipalities in which such problems may be avoided, are permitted to escape what may be regarded as a universal obligation.

Keeping in mind the fact that our primary objective is to achieve freedom of choice for individual consumer-voters while avoiding the costs emanating from uncoordinated local operations, what approaches seem indicated at the local level? If the states act in the manner suggested, some of the most pressing existing difficulties will have been eliminated or substantially reduced. One nonfiscal requirement would appear to be the elimination of barriers to mobility within the metropolitan community. Differences in zoning regulations will persist, and this may even be desirable, but other barriers are not tolerable, from the point of view of moral rectitude, efficiency, or equity. The more immediately fiscal issues involve traditionally local functions with substantial spillover effects or important economies of

---

[28] Hugh Pomeroy, "Local Responsibility." An address before the National Conference on Metropolitan Problems, East Lansing, Mich., April 29, 1956. Quoted in Advisory Commission on Intergovernmental Relations, *op. cit.*, p. 21.

scale. Proliferation of special-function agencies or districts which are not directly politically responsible has little to commend it, but some form of politically responsible federalism has much appeal. Alternatively, in some instances, the county government, with broadened powers, may be the appropriate instrument.

The function of either of these governmental forms can only be defined within the context of broader objectives sought in the metropolitan community. As was suggested above, economies of scale and spillover effects may be the forces upon which this definition may rest. Thus a federation of municipalities may assume responsibility for planning, water supply, sewage disposal, arterial highways, and mass transit, all of which involve economies of scale as well as spillover effects. Areawide recreation facilities may also be delegated to the federal body, while neighborhood parks and playgrounds remain purely local responsibilities; the federation may provide central police services in specialized fields of police work, while basic police protection remains a local function; the same approach may be taken with respect to fire protection, education, property assessment, and certain other functions. Financing may be accomplished by delegation of taxing powers, contractual arrangements, and, wherever appropriate, user charges.

The problems related to the fact that many people live in one jurisdiction and work in another would be much abated under the kind of programs envisaged here. They would be further reduced through the extension of user-charge financing and the use of nonproperty taxes. Particularly appealing among the latter is the income tax under which, as in the Toledo area, partial credit is provided for income taxes paid to the employee's place of residence.

More intensive employment of user charges and nonproperty taxes, coupled with the suggested expansion of state aid and/or state assumption of responsibility for some functions, should do much to alleviate existing local fiscal pressures. The deficiencies of the property tax, especially when it is levied at effective rates of 2 per cent or higher, are so manifest as to require that alternatives be sought. Very little is actually known about the effects of the property tax on land use in the metropolitan area, but as a tax that imposes substantial penalties upon improvement, rewards decay, and encourages land speculation that may have high social costs, it would appear to be a major contributor to the economic and fiscal ills of urban areas.

The very nature of collective consumption and the problems involved in attempting to achieve an approximation of maximum consumer-voter satisfaction in a local public sector operating within a predominantly free private economy are such as to defy conceptual, let alone actual, solution. But even conceptual models of the operation of the private-market economy are satisfactory only within the framework of first approximation assumptions that take us a long way from the real world — some would say too far away to be very useful. Perhaps the economist still knows too little about either the private or the public sector to permit him to do more than attempt to point up deficiencies relative to some commonly accepted criteria and, further, to indicate the kinds of actions that may minimize such deficiencies. With respect to one increasingly important part of the public sector, the urban complex known as the metropolitan area, a great deal more fruitful speculation and empirical investigation are needed before we can conclude that the economist can provide the needed guideposts to the policy-maker.

FURTHER READINGS

Grieson, Ronald E. "Decentralizing the City School, Community Control: Urban vs. Suburban." *Ripon Forum* 6 (June 1970).

Grieson, Ronald E. "The Allocation and Financing of Education," in Richard Lindholm, ed. *Property Taxes and Education*. Madison, Wis.: The Committee on Taxation, Resources and Economic Development, University of Wisconsin Press, January 1973.

Grieson, Ronald E. "The Tiebout Hypothesis, Revenue Sharing, Fiscal Equalization and Land Taxes." Mimeographed, Queens College and the Graduate Center of the City University of New York (January 1973).

Hirsch, Werner Z. "Cost Function of an Urban Government Service: Refuse Collection." *Review of Economics and Statistics* (February 1965).

———. *The Economics of State and Local Government*. New York: McGraw-Hill, 1970. See Chapter 8 especially.

Kiesling, Herbert J. "Measuring a Local Government Service: A Study of School Districts in New York State." *Review of Economics and Statistics* 49 (1967), pp. 356–367.

Riew, John. "Economies of Scale in High School Operation." *Review of Economics and Statistics* 48 (August 1966).

Tiebout, Charles M. "The Pure Theory of Local Expenditures." *Journal of Political Economy* 64 (1956), pp. 416–424.

Chapter 10

URBAN PUBLIC FINANCE

As I stated in the introduction to this volume, the same policies that have eroded the quality of city life have also created a financial crisis for the cities. This crisis can be attributed to the misallocation of resources and investments brought about by underpricing goods and services, to the provision of free public services to nonresidents, and to the financing of health, educational, and welfare services for a disproportionate number of society's poor, oppressed, and disabled (who have been systematically excluded from employment and housing in suburbs).

Cities have spent excessively for the construction, policing, and maintenance of roads and parking facilities, whose benefits often accrue to nonresidents. They have, moreover, failed to use rush hour congestion tolls to finance and allocate transportation facilities efficiently.

There has been too much investment in other public facilities as well. This has often been done to provide goods free or below their cost, which encourages waste. Dams, for instance, supply water at little or no cost to users. The Rand Corporation conducted a study of the benefits of metering water (charging a price for it) in New York City and compared them with the costs of building additional dam capacity to supply additional water that would be consumed at a price of zero. New York City's failure to meter water has encouraged people to use water to the point where they put little or no value on it. The Rand study suggested that the cost of metering plus the loss of benefit to the consumer from using less water would be approximately 15% of the cost of building a dam to supply the water demanded without metering. Metering would be preferable to building more dams, because it would be a means both of raising revenues and of achieving an efficient allocation of water resources.

Another and perhaps more widely recognized manifestation of this failure to charge a price corresponding to resource cost is excessive pollution and its resultant waste of clean air. Lyle Fitch's essay and William Vickrey's suggested article (footnote 10, Fitch essay) discuss the need for financing more of a city's services by means of user charges.

These examples may be representative of the quality of management of central city services. Reports indicate that such diverse services as garbage collection and mass transit could be provided at higher quality by the private economy for as little as one-half to one-third of the present public cost. Similar figures may apply to central city public education.

Another contribution to the city's fiscal crisis has been made by the reduction of the tax base that has occurred because of property tax exemption for religious, charitable, and educational institutions whose benefits accrue in large part to nonresidents. Concomitantly, property taxes on all other structures have been set at excessive levels. High property tax rates plus low assessments for housing units that are vulnerable to fire and deterioration have discouraged the construction of quality housing. A desirable remedy would be diminished reliance on property tax combined with higher taxes for defective structures than for quality structures.

The cities have come to house a disproportionate number of people who require large social service expenditures. This is partially due to cities' welfare policies and treatment of the poor and disadvantaged, which are relatively generous in comparison to the sometimes exclusionary attitudes of suburbs. As Dick Netzer's article points out, poverty and discrimination are metropolitan, state, and national problems requiring sharply increased action at these levels, by means of instruments like federalized welfare and revenue sharing.

Public education is another example of an income redistributing service — a service which most citizens feel ought to be provided equally regardless of family income. Since poor communities encounter some difficulty financing reasonable levels of education even with high regressive tax rates, the financing might better be handled at higher levels of government. Furthermore, the citizenship externalities and income benefits of public education are captured more by the state and nation than the particular locality (only 20 per cent of all students eventually reside where educated). Because income and citizenship benefits of education bear no relation to local property values, it would seem that fair, adequate, and efficient financing can be achieved by shifting the financing of education from local taxes on property to state and national taxes on income.

Many other local services (public health, for example) cannot be financed by poor localities and cause wealthy localities to exclude the poor in order to reduce local taxes. It has been suggested that the federal (and even state) governments give localities lump-sum grants from which they could finance these costs as they perceive their need. Specific federal direction may just duplicate local administration. Lump-sum grants or revenue sharing could be set at a per capita amount which is higher the lower the community's average income and the greater the number of poor people in the community. Revenue sharing could also be used to end snob zoning and discrimination: evidence of these practices could mean reduction of the grant.

The complex problems of the city will not yield quickly to any attempted remedies. However, economic theory and experience point clearly to several steps which, if taken, have a large probability of bringing about a marked improvement in those aspects of city living that we have discussed. Such improvement might well be sufficient to remove urban problems from the list of critical ills that plague societies today. First, user charges commensurate with social opportunity costs should be adopted to allocate scarce resources and to finance their use. In some cases, such as highway congestion tolls and polution taxes, this will involve raising prices that were previously too low or nonexistent. In other cases, such as property taxes and taxi licenses, this will require a reduction or elimination of prices previously too high.

The second step is to assign governmental authority and responsibility to whatever geographic jurisdiction corresponds to a reasonable economic boundary. A reasonable economic boundary includes the bulk of the externalities of the production, employment, housing, and transportation activities of a specific region. It is clear that the appropriate level of government would be different for the various sections of the nation. As our discussion in the previous chapter indicated, this may involve smaller or even a mixture of jurisdiction in some cases. It should also be clear that simply passing on the responsibility for a community's financial needs to a different level of government is futile if the new authority is not exercised according to the efficiency principle described as the first step.

Shifting the financing of health, education, and welfare to higher levels of government should not mean that our criteria of efficiency in allocation be forgotten, especially where research indicates that programs such as the Job Corps and day care have tended to have unfavorable benefit-cost ratios.

METROPOLITAN FINANCIAL PROBLEMS

Lyle C. Fitch

Abstract: Exuberant urbanism, advancing technology, and rising incomes and living standards, all are expanding demands for urban government services, some of which can be most efficiently supplied or financed by metropolitan jurisdictions. Since metropolitan areas are the focal points of income and wealth, the financial problem stems largely from the lack of machinery. Many of the most pressing metropolitan needs can be appropriately financed by user charges, but these need to be carefully designed to produce the most desirable over-all economic effects. Both property and nonproperty taxes should be administered by metropolitan-wide jurisdictions, leaving submetropolitan governments the power to set property tax rates for local needs.

Continued urban growth, economic development, and rise of living standards almost certainly will require maintaining, and probably increasing, the share of the national product taken in the form of urban government services. The evidence of current trends and existing unmet needs indicates the strength of the pressures for more and better services.

Expenditures of large cities rose by approximately 75 per cent between 1948 and 1956, and total local government expenditures in the corresponding metropolitan areas doubtless increased considerably more.[1]

Developed central cities and mushrooming suburbs have faced, and will continue to face, peculiar needs. The central cities have had to meet demands arising from population shifts within their own boundaries — shifts which are economic and social as well as geographic. The larger cities are tending to become concentration points of low-income groups and require disproportionately large outlays for welfare and social development. Many

Lyle C. Fitch is President of the Institute of Public Administration, New York City.
  Reprinted with permission from Lyle C. Fitch, "Metropolitan Financial Problems," in *Metropolis in Ferment* (Philadelphia: The American Academy of Political and Social Science, 1957), pp. 66–73.
  [1] Reference is to the forty-one cities with populations exceeding 250,000 in 1950.

cities are increasingly impressed with the necessity for large-scale physical rehabilitation and redevelopment if they are to compete with the suburbs as places to live and do business, and if they are to avoid untimely obsolescence of private and public investment in their central areas. In the suburbs, rapid expansion requires enormous amounts of new capital facilities in the form of streets, schools, recreational facilities, and the like.

The advent of the metropolitan age and the concomitant development of modern urban culture are creating new demands for many government services and increasing standards of other services. Many of the emergent needs can be supplied only by new governmental agencies designed to operate on a metropolitan scale.

This is the root of the metropolitan financial problem: how to divert a larger share of resources to government use, or, more simply, how to get more funds than existing revenue systems will produce, without unduly impinging on private production. (The last qualifying clause is added because one main objective of urban government should be to increase productivity of private firms by providing them with better-educated and healthier workers, better transportation facilities, and so on.) Solutions, even partial solutions, require better fiscal machinery and broader fiscal powers, as well as organizational innovations, at the local government level. Above all, they require public education and political leadership. Most of these requirements are outside the scope of this paper. Other articles [have considered] the task of organization of the metropolitan community for effective action; this discussion is concerned with equipping it with improved fiscal tools.

DEFICIENCIES OF METROPOLITAN FISCAL MACHINERY

Metropolitan financial problems arise primarily from the lack of adequate machinery rather than from any lack of capacity. Presumptively, today's large urban communities, being typically the focal points of wealth and income, have the resources to meet their urban needs.

The following deficiencies in the fiscal machinery characteristic of metropolitan areas seem to the writer to be the most important and the ones whose rectification will have greatest importance for the future:

1. Existing revenue-producing machinery is generally inadequate for the task of financing local government functions; this is true of functions appropriate for the conventional (submetropolitan) local government and functions which can best be handled by metropolitan jurisdictions.

2. The extension of activities across jurisdictional boundary lines makes it more and more difficult to relate benefits and taxes at the local government level. In the modern metropolitan community, a family may reside in

one jurisdiction, earn its living in one or more others, send the children to school in another, and shop and seek recreation in still others. But to a considerable extent, the American local financial system still reflects the presumption that these various activities are concentrated in one governmental jurisdiction.

3. In many areas there are great discrepancies in the capacities of local government jurisdictions to provide needed governmental services. At one extreme are the communities which have not sufficient taxable capacity for essential services. The most common case is the bedroom community of low- and middle-income workers which has little industry or commerce. At the other extreme are the wealthy tax colonies, zoned to keep out low-income residents.[2]

Three main types of decisions must be made in setting up and financing functions on an areawide scale. They concern:

The services and benefits which should be provided on an areawide basis.

The question of whether services should be financed by taxes or charges.

The type and rate of tax or charge which should be imposed.

Some services and benefits, like health protection and air pollution control, can be provided efficiently only if they extend over a wide area and their administration is integrated; some, like hospitals and tax administration, are more economical if handled on a large scale;[3] and some, like intrametropolitan transportation, can be controlled satisfactorily only by a central authority with powers to establish areawide standards and policies and to resolve intra-area conflicts.

TAXES AND CHARGES

This discussion distinguishes mainly between general taxes bearing no direct relation to benefits of expenditures, like sales and income taxes, and charges, or public prices, which vary directly with the amount of the service provided, like bridge tolls, subway fares, and metered charges for water.

General taxes and public prices are at the opposite ends of the revenue spectrum. In between are benefit taxes, which are imposed on beneficiaries of a related service, with the proceeds being devoted largely or entirely to

[2] See Julius Margolis, "Municipal Fiscal Structure in a Metropolitan Region," *Journal of Political Economy*, 55 (June, 1957).

[3] Results of two recent, as yet unpublished, studies indicate that the unit costs of government services may be less affected by the scale of operations than has been popularly supposed. Harvey Brazer's study (sponsored by the National Bureau of Economic Research) of general government expenditures in larger cities, the group exceeding 25,000 in 1950, finds little correlation between per capita costs of local government functions and city size. Werner Hirsch's study of municipal expenditures in St. Louis County, for the St. Louis Metropolitan Survey, shows similar results for some 80 municipalities, most of them under 25,000 population.

financing the service. Gasoline taxes used for financing highways are a familiar example; the real estate tax is at least in part a benefit tax where it pays for services which benefit the taxed properties.

LOCAL TAXES

Local governments, within the generally narrow confines of state-imposed restrictions, have shown considerable ingenuity in tapping pools of potential revenue, however small; few things on land, sea, or in the air, from pleasures and palaces to loaves and fishes, escape taxation somewhere. However, most of the principal local taxes used today are loosely enforced or expensive to administer and dubious in their economic effect. Even the property tax is not exempt from this indictment, although its praises have long been sung and its vices excused on the ground that it is the only tax which can be administered successfully even by the smallest local government. The fact is that it has generally not been successfully administered at all, according to most criteria of equity and efficiency. It is capricious and inequitable even in what it purports to do best.

Part of the typical difficulties of local taxation arise from smallness, both in size of jurisdiction and scale of administrative organization. These, of course, may be obviated by metropolitan areawide administration. Efficient collection of most types of revenues requires an organization large enough to afford trained personnel, costly equipment, and professional direction and research. Geographically, the taxing area must be large enough and isolated enough to discourage avoidance of taxes by persons who move their residences or business establishments over boundary lines or who go outside the jurisdiction to shop. When imposed by several neighboring local governments, many taxes involve issues of intergovernmental jurisdiction and allocation of tax bases.

Where taxes are imposed on an areawide basis, one issue of metropolitan area finance — allocation of government service costs among communities — is resolved; allocation is a function of the type of tax imposed. Areawide taxes also eliminate tax competition within the area; however this may not be an unmitigated blessing if competition by offering better services also is eliminated.

To date, the principal revenue sources of areawide public agencies have been property taxes and user charges, although some metropolitan counties in New York and California, for instance, impose sales taxes and occasionally other nonproperty taxes. The problems of granting taxing powers to metropolitan jurisdictions which extend over several counties remain largely unexplored. A bill introduced in the 1957 session of the California legislature to establish a multicounty San Francisco Bay area rapid transit district went further in this direction than most legislative proposals by giving the proposed district power to impose both a property and a sales tax. The sales tax authority was eliminated in the version of the bill finally adopted.[4]

The difficulties of working out harmonious tax arrangements between metropolitan jurisdictions and state and already existing local governments have been great enough when only one state was involved to block all but the feeblest beginnings beyond the one-county level. They have thus far been considered insuperable where interstate arrangements are involved. For some time to come, interstate functions probably will be financed by user charges, supplemented where necessary by contributions from the state or local governments involved.

In the almost perfect metropolitan area, we would expect to see metropolitan real estate taxes assessed by an areawide agency,[5] with metropolitan levies for such metropolitan services as were deemed to be of particular benefit to property and additional local levies for local government activities. Only metropolitan jurisdictions would be authorized to impose nonproperty taxes. In general, the permissible nonproperty taxes would include general sales and amusements taxes and a levy on personal income. Business firms might be taxed, if at all, by some simple form of value-added tax.

The following are among the taxes not used at the local level in the almost perfect metropolitan area: gross receipts taxes and taxes on utility services, because of their excessively deleterious economic effect; and corporate income taxes and such selective excises as gasoline, alcoholic beverages, and tobacco taxes, because they can be much better administered at the state level.

Along with several others, the revenue sources mentioned above are now being used by municipalities with two exceptions: The value-added tax and the general income tax. The so-called municipal income taxes now imposed in Pennsylvania, Ohio, and a few other states rest largely on wages and salaries. Considerations of equity manifestly require a broader tax base, and the need for administrative simplicity suggests a supplemental rate on an existing base where this is practicable.[6]

THE REAL ESTATE TAX

The principal justification for the real estate tax, aside from tradition, convenience, and expediency, is that by financing beneficial services, it benefits property. Another logical function, which it performs very inadequately, is to capture at least part of the unearned increments to land values accruing

---

[4] Tax revenues of the proposed district would be used mainly for service of debt incurred in building a rapid transit system and to meet expenses of the district board.

[5] Personal property, with the possible exception of depreciable business assets, would not be taxed in the almost perfect metropolitan area.

[6] See Harold M. Groves, "New Sources of Light on Intergovernmental Fiscal Relations," National Tax Journal, 5:3 (September, 1952).

by reason of urban developments. Special assessments have been widely used to recoup at least part of land values accruing from public improvements,[7] but no means has been devised, at least at the local level, of recapturing land values not attributable to specific public improvements.

The enormous increases of land values which typically occur as land is converted from rural to urban use and from less to more intensive urban use constitute a pool of resources which can be appropriately utilized to meet the social costs of urban development, if taxes can be devised to tap the pool. Such land value increases, however, seem characteristically to be concentrated in the expanding sections, mostly the suburbs. Available evidence suggests that land values in many core cities have lagged far behind general price levels and in some cities have not even regained levels reached in the 1920's.[8] In such cases, urban redevelopment, unlike the initial urban development, cannot count on pools of expanding land values; on the contrary, land costs often must be written down at government expense if redevelopment is to be economically feasible.[9]

Clearly the real estate tax must be adapted to the dynamic characteristics of the urban economy. The tax in its present form gives equal weight to the incremental values resulting from urban development, the values of land already developed, and the values of improvements. Several possible new features should be explored. Some of them are: a local capital gains tax on land value increments, special levies on property values accruing after the announcement of public improvements which benefit the whole community, and a differential tax on land values. Of these three possibilities, the last seems most promising, if only because the basic concept is familiar; it has been used in Australia, Canada, and elsewhere abroad, but by only a few cities in the United States.

THE ROLE OF USER CHARGES

There is a case for charging for a service instead of financing it by general taxation if the following conditions are met:

1. The charge must be administratively feasible. Among the other requirements, the service must be divisible into units whose use by the beneficiary can be measured, like kilowatts, gallons of water, trips across a bridge, or miles traveled on a turnpike.

[7] As an alternative to the special assessment device, developers in many instances are required to provide for streets, sewers, water mains, and similar improvements which otherwise would be provided by public funds.

[8] Such tendencies, however, do not necessarily reflect an absolute economic declining of the core.

[9] In the long run, of course, one test of urban redevelopment programs is whether they increase land and other property values, relative to the value that would otherwise have obtained.

2. The immediate benefits of the service should go mainly to the person paying for it. This condition, not always easy to apply, means that if a person refrains from using the service because of the charge, the rest of the community suffers relatively little loss. For example, the community is ordinarily not much damaged if a person uses less electricity or makes fewer long-distance telephone calls. In some cases, an additional use by a few individuals may greatly inconvenience many others; for example, a few additional vehicles on a roadway may produce traffic congestion.

3. The charge should encourage economical use of resources. Metered charges, for instance, encourage consumers to conserve water and electricity by turning off faucets and lights.

One of the most important functions of charges is to balance demand and supply in cases where excess demand produces undesirable results. If the number of curb parking spaces is less than the number of would-be parkers, the space will be allocated on a first-come first-served basis, in the absence of any better device, and there is no way of assuring that space will go to those who need it most. In such cases, a charge may be the most efficient way of rationing space. This is frequently attempted by use of parking meters, although nearly always in a crude fashion. Meter systems could be much improved if the elementary principles of charges were better understood.

Conversely, a charge — or the increase of an already existing charge — is not justified if it results in the underutilization or waste of resources. For example, as an immediate result of the increase of the New York subway fare from ten to fifteen cents in 1953, passenger traffic declined at least 120 million rides per year, the bulk of the drop being concentrated in nonrush hours and holidays when subways have excess capacity. Not only did the community lose 120 million rides per year, which could be provided at little additional cost, but traffic congestion increased because former subway riders switched to private passenger cars and taxis, and downtown shopping and amusement centers suffered to an undetermined extent.[10]

The peripatetic propensities of metropolitan man and the fact that he may consume services in several jurisdictions while voting in only one have disjointed local government fiscal structures in several places. First, the separation of workshops and bedrooms may create disparities between taxable capacities and service needs. Second, the separation of political jurisdictions in which individuals are taxed and in which they require services handicaps the budget-making process; it makes more difficult a rational determination

---

[10] For a general discussion see William Vickrey, *Revision of Rapid Transit Fares in the City of New York*, Mayor's Committee on Management Survey, Finance Project Publication, item No. 8, Technical Monograph No. 3 (New York, 1952); Lyle C. Fitch, "Pricing Transportation in a Metropolitan Area," *Proceedings of the National Tax Association* (New York: The Association, 1955).

of how much of the community's product should take the form of government services. Third, the necessity of providing services to outsiders, particularly commuters, creates pressure for taxation without representation.

MARKET FORCES

These considerations argue for a policy of structuring metropolitan governmental organizations in order to allow as much freedom as possible to the play of market forces in determining the kinds and quantities of government services to be supplied, subject to the general principles previously noted (section on the role of user charges).[11]

The market system can operate at two levels: that of the individual or firm purchasing services or goods from a government enterprise and that of the group — for example, the smaller governmental jurisdiction — purchasing goods or services from a larger jurisdiction. The second level is exemplified by the city of Lakewood, California, and several other cities which purchase their municipal services from Los Angeles County.[12]

One of the principal decisions respecting any government service is the quantity to be furnished. The important distinction between ordinary government services and services provided under enterprise principles lies in the nature of the decision-making process. Budgetary decisions affecting regular government services are political decisions, reflecting judgments of legislatures regarding how much of the services are needed by the community and how much the taxpayers are willing to pay. Not infrequently, decisions are referred directly to voters. The amount of service to be provided under enterprise principles is dictated by consumers, by the usual market test of how much individuals or firms in the aggregate will buy at cost-of-production prices.[13] In other words, the question of how much is decided by following the simple rule that where demand exceeds supply, the service should be expanded, and vice versa.

PRICE-MARKET TEST

The price-market test of resource allocation greatly simplifies the problem of citizen participation in the governmental process. Where services and goods are bought by individuals, each consumer takes part in the decision-making process by determining how much of the service he will buy.

[11] We can go this far without agreeing with Calvin Coolidge that legislatures should make it their business to discover natural economic laws and enact them into legislation.

[12] Another way of relating charges on particular areas to services rendered is the establishment of special service districts within a metropolitan jurisdiction which pay differential taxes for special services.

[13] The question of price cannot be disposed of by the simple qualification "cost-of-production," but that question need not be considered here.

Where purchases are by groups, decisions as to how much to spend must be political ones; but the issue of citizen participation can be simplified in several ways as compared with the situation where budgetary decisions are made by large political units. If the purchasing group is more homogeneous than the whole community, any decision is more wholly satisfactory to a larger percentage of the members. Even if the small group is no more homogeneous than the large, individuals may participate more effectively in small-group decisions.[14]

Although user charges and the demand-supply rule can simplify the budgetary problem, they do not divorce public enterprise operations from the political process; political participation in many decisions is essential, including the crucial decisions respecting organizational form, investment policies, and integrating the particular function with other community services. For instance, the quantity of services to be supplied by a basically enterprise type of operation may be extended by public decision and public subsidy beyond the amounts which could be made available at cost-of-production prices.[15] In some cases, public subsidies may be necessary to avoid waste of an already existing resource. Public prices too often are fixed to achieve narrow objectives, such as meeting debt service on construction bonds, without regard for their over-all economic effect.

Some of the most urgent areawide needs are appropriately financed partly or wholly by charges. They include the services which are frequently provided by private regulated utilities such as gas and electricity, water, and mass transportation and other transportation facilities, port development, waste disposal, many recreational services, and hospital services.[16]

BALANCING COSTS AND TAXABLE CAPACITY

There have been few studies of the over-all relationship of costs and taxable capacity in metropolitan areas — although endless attention has been lavished on particular functions, notably education — and the subject still abounds with unsettled questions. Brazer's analyses indicate that the relative

---

[14] This statement rests on the not uncomplicated assumption that the opportunity of participating in decisions of a smaller group is a positive value.

[15] Even more basic is the question, not considered here, of whether enterprises in particular instances should be private or public.

[16] A recent study of metropolitan government in the Sacramento area recommended that the capital and operating costs of water, sewage service, garbage pickup and disposal, and transit "be metered and charged to the new areas receiving them." Public Administration Service, *The Government of Metropolitan Sacramento* (Chicago: Public Administration Service, 1957), p. 144.

For discussions of transportation pricing see Vickrey and Fitch, *op. cit.;* also Fitch, "Financing Urban Roadways," in *Highway Financing,* Tax Institute Symposium (Princeton: 1957); and Wilfred Owen, *The Metropolitan Transportation Problem* (Washington, D.C.: Brookings Institution, 1956), Chap. 7.

size of the suburban population is an important determinant of local government expenditures in large cities, a finding consistent with the hypothesis that cities assume considerable expense in providing services to suburban residents. Both Brazer's and Hirsch's studies indicate, moreover, that per capita expenditures on some functions — police, for instance — typically increase with population density; this may in part result from the tendency of low-income groups to congregate in central cities. On the other hand, the worst cases of fiscal undernourishment appear to be in the suburbs.

This article has space only for several generalizations which may serve to indicate directions for further analysis:

1. Costs of essential services may be "equalized" over a metropolitan area, either by areawide administration and financing, or by grants to local jurisdictions financed at least in part by areawide taxes. Experience with state and federal subventions indicates that the subvention is a clumsy tool. On the other hand, putting services on an areawide basis may deprive local communities of the privilege of determining the amount of resources to be allocated to specific services.

2. In many cases, the remedy for fiscal undernourishment may lie in areawide planning and zoning; fiscal measures as such may strike only at symptoms rather than underlying difficulties.

3. Fiscal stress in the modern American community is often more psychological than economic. A common case is that of the former city apartment dweller who buys his own house in the suburbs and for the first time in his life is confronted with a property tax bill. It is not strange that he should resist taxes while demanding municipal services of a level to which he has been accustomed in the city, nor that he should seek outside assistance in meeting his unaccustomed burden.

4. The point has been made that intercommunity variations in the levels of services should allow metropolitan residents to satisfy their preferences as to levels of local government services and taxes and hence promote the general satisfactions of the entire community.[17] Although the argument may be valid within limits, the limits are narrow; they may extend, for instance, to the quality of refuse collection, but not air and water pollution control.

5. Services rendered to individuals in their capacity of workers, shoppers, and other economic functionaries may in some instances be properly treated as a charge upon the business firm involved rather than upon the individual. Suburbanites, like other persons, create real property values wherever they work, shop, or play.[18] This fact refutes the case for a general tax on com-

[17] See Charles Tiebout, "The Pure Theory of Local Government Expenditures," *Journal of Political Economy*, 64:5 (October, 1956).

[18] Margolis, *op. cit.:* "A priori, there is no reason to believe that the increment in the tax receipts of the central city accompanying the commuter is less than it costs the city to attract and service him."

muters, although it does not damage the case for user charges where these would improve the allocation of resources. On the other hand, the maintenance of minimal service levels in poor communities and care for the economically stranded, wherever located, are the responsibility of the entire community.

FINANCING URBAN GOVERNMENT

Dick Netzer

Few state or local governments are without fiscal problems. The rapid and virtually universal increase in public expenditures in the past two decades and the frequency and ubiquity of tax rate increases afford ample evidence of this. But the problems seem most severe for local governments serving the larger and older metropolitan areas of the country — say, the two dozen or so metropolitan areas with populations of more than one million and central city populations (usually) of more than 500,000, located mostly but not entirely in the Northeast and Midwest.

Their problems are more severe, despite the fact that much of the country's income and wealth is concentrated in such areas, in part because they operate with diverse and fragmented structures of local government. In part, their difficulties reflect the concentration of the urban poverty and race problems in the large old central cities. Also, the very fact of age creates problems associated with physical and functional obsolescence. In addition, there are difficulties stemming from extremely rapid growth rates on their urbanizing fringes.

The existence of these difficulties and the national interest in solving them have been recognized in various pieces of "Great Society" legislation enacted or proposed in the past few years. But these federal actions by no means solve all the local fiscal problems (nor should they be expected to). This paper is addressed to the fiscal problems of the larger older metropolitan areas, especially their central cities. It is not universal coverage, but it does encompass quite a large segment of our urban population and it does

Dick Netzer is Dean of the Graduate School of Public Administration, New York University.

Reprinted with permission from Dick Netzer, "Financing Urban Government," in James Q. Wilson, ed., *The Metropolitan Enigma* (Washington: Chamber of Commerce of the United States, 1967), pp. 58–75.

suggest something about the future prospects for some of the smaller and newer urban areas.

SOME RECENT TRENDS

In recent years, as throughout the twenty years following World War II, local (and state government) public expenditures have been increasing substantially more rapidly than has the nation's total output and income (see Table 1).[1] Public expenditures in urban areas have always been significantly higher, in relative terms, than those in nonurban areas, and recently have been increasing slightly faster, in dollar terms, within the urban areas. This is to be expected, since nearly all the nation's population growth has been occurring in urban areas. But urban population growth alone does not explain the rate of increase in public spending. Indeed, the increase in *per capita* local government expenditures in metropolitan areas has been more rapid than the increase in *aggregate* gross national product.

TABLE 1. PERCENTAGE INCREASES IN NONFEDERAL PUBLIC EXPENDITURES, 1957–1962 and 1957–1963/64

	Percentage Increase	
	1957–1962	1957–1963/64
Gross national product [a]	27	43
Total expenditures		
All state and local governments	48	70
All local governments	46	65
Local governments in metropolitan areas [b]	47	N.A.
Central city governments in large cities [c]	31	45
Per capita expenditures [d]		
All state and local governments	36	51
All local governments	34	47
Local governments in metropolitan areas	30	N.A.

Source: Adapted from various publications of the U.S. Bureau of the Census, Governments Division.
N.A. Not available.
[a] Includes only the municipal governments per se (i.e., excluding overlapping but separate county, school district, and special district governments); for the 42 cities with a 1960 population of more than 300,000, excluding Honolulu.
[b] For identical collections of metropolitan areas in 1957 and 1962.
[c] For calendar years 1957–1962 and 1957–1964.
[d] Based on estimated 1957, 1962, and 1964 populations.

Perhaps most striking, public expenditures in the larger central cities have been climbing steeply, despite their losses or slow growth in population. In

[1] The dates used here are related to data availability. A Census of Governments was conducted in 1962 and in 1957; the preceding Census of Governments occurred in 1942.

the most recent seven-year period for which data are available, expenditures of municipal governments in the larger cities rose by 45 per cent (see Table 1), about two-thirds as rapidly as expenditures of all other local governments combined. Consider the twelve largest metropolitan areas (1964 population over 1.8 million). In the eight-year period, 1957 to 1965, property tax revenues (used here as a partial proxy for local expenditures) rose by 86 per cent for these entire areas. In their central portions, property tax revenues rose by 69 per cent.[2] But there has been little population growth in the central portions — less than half the rate of the entire areas between 1960 and 1964.

To be sure, substantially more external aid to central cities in the provision of public services has been forthcoming in recent years. State and federal aid to central city governments has risen considerably more rapidly than have central city expenditures. Also, the *direct* role of state governments in the provision of public services in and for the central cities has expanded considerably. Since the passage of the Interstate Highway Act in 1956, the states have been far more active in the construction of central city highways than previously. In a growing number of states, the state government is directly involved in urban mass transportation, in park and open space activities, and in housing programs. In some states in the Northeast, expansion of state higher education programs has had an important effect on central city populations. But despite all this, the taxes imposed by central city governments, collected from static populations and slowly growing central city economies, continue to rise sharply.

THE PURPOSES OF URBAN GOVERNMENT

The explanation for rising public expenditures in urban areas is not hard to find. In the central cities, local-tax-financed outlays for services directly linked to poverty (in the health and welfare fields) have not been static; the central cities of the twelve largest metropolitan areas account for an eighth of the country's population, but nearly 40 per cent of health and welfare outlays financed from local taxes. For central city governments, the problems associated with poverty and race are by far the most urgent of public problems.

Neither poverty nor racial disabilities can be eliminated solely by governmental action, and still less by action by local or state and local governments combined (that is, governments other than the federal government). But local governments do have a major responsibility to grapple with these prob-

---

[2] "Central portions" are the counties which include the central cities. In five of the twelve areas, the "central portions" and central cities are substantially identical. In 1960, the central cities' population was 74 per cent of that of the "central portions."

lems and can make a major contribution toward their alleviation. In the American system of government, it is local governments which are responsible for providing educational services that over time will have a major bearing on the chances the poor and racially disadvantaged have to overcome their disadvantages. Local governments are also responsible for a wide range of health and welfare services, which are almost entirely oriented toward the poor in American cities. They have had, since the late forties, major responsibilities in connection with the housing of the poor. And, as far as the poor are concerned, local government recreational facilities are about the only recreational facilities available.

A second major set of problems confronting the older central cities lies in the fact that they have a huge legacy of obsolescence. Their stock of housing and other social capital — that is, public and quasi-public facilities of all kinds — is old, often physically deteriorated, and generally far from competitive with the newer parts of the same urban areas. It may be, as some have argued, that the best national policy would be to allow this obsolescence to continue, and allow further deterioration of the older parts of the older cities. In this case, population would decline in these sections and, presumably at some stage, values would be so low that private renewal of such areas would become possible. Or, if desirable, public renewal could be undertaken but on the basis of exceedingly low values.

Developments in recent years suggest that this is hardly a likely course of action. For one thing, there is the plight of those who, because they are poor, or Negro, or both, have little chance to escape the deteriorating areas. Amelioration, for these hundreds of thousands of people, is both politically and morally necessary. Quite apart from moral issues, most cities and the federal government appear to have decided that it is necessary to replace obsolete social capital and to compete for residents and businesses in an atmosphere of rising expectations. That is, the cities feel they must offer an environment of public facilities services which, together with other attractions that the central locations may have, offset the blandishments of the newer and presumably more modern sections of the metropolitan areas where standards of public services and amenity are high indeed.

In the newer sections of metropolitan areas — the new portions of central cities as well as the urbanizing fringes of the metropolitan area — the main governmental problem is the provision of the new social capital needed by a rising population, and a population which has peculiarly heavy demands for public services and facilities, notably schools.

In the aggregate, these urban problems have resulted in a diversion of resources from private to public uses, via tax increases. But this relative expansion of the public sector is costly in another way. If local governments are to command resources, they must pay prices for these resources which are competitive with those prevailing in the economy, notably salaries of public employees. If they are to expand *more rapidly* than the private sector, they must bid away resources by paying even more, which largely explains the rapid increase in urban government salary levels, especially for occupational groups whose talents are in heavy demand in the private sector.

IDEAL SOLUTIONS

This catalog of governmental problems suggests something about the nature of the solutions. Assume for the moment that we are free to devise a structure of local government which is ideal from both an administrative and a financial standpoint.

First, consider the governmental fiscal problems associated with poverty and race. It seems clear that, in an ideal world, the financial burden of public services which exist primarily to cope with these problems would not rest on particular local governments with small geographic coverage. Poor people tend to be concentrated in the central cities of metropolitan areas for good reasons. The supply of housing that they can afford is in such places, the kinds of jobs to which their skills give them access tend also to be located in these sections, and the variety of social services which they require tend to be available only in central cities. Indeed, it is probably in the national interest that the poor be concentrated in central cities, for it is rather unlikely that their needs would ever be sufficiently attended to were they not so conspicuous.

Another factor in the geographic location of the poor, and even more in the geographic location of those in racial minority groups, is national in character. This is a very mobile society which has over the years undergone rapid economic changes. There have been, in response to these economic changes, massive migrations of people from rural areas to urban areas, from central cities of urban areas to the suburbs, from the urban areas of the North and Midwest to the Southwest and West. No individual central city has been known to put up billboards advertising its attractions for the poor, trying to recruit them from other parts of the country. They have migrated to the cities in response to pressures in their older locations and attractions in the newer locations, but all these have been essentially national economic and social forces. This being the case, it seems appropriate that the costs of attending to the needs of such people should be spread over a fairly wide geographic area. And since it is the economies or, rather, the economic prosperity of the larger metropolitan areas which has been the attraction for the poor and the disadvantaged, it could be argued that the metropolitan areas as a whole ought to finance the poverty-linked social services.

There is a good case for this, for the great bulk of the wealth and income of the country is concentrated in metropolitan areas. But almost nowhere is there a governmental structure such that taxes can be levied throughout the metropolitan area on the economic base of the entire metropolitan area for the support of such services. In some places, in states which are overwhelmingly urban and metropolitan in character, the state government may be a reasonable substitute for metropolitan area government. But this is not true of all states, and, moreover, some metropolitan areas straddle state boundary lines. Also, the migration of the poor among the states has not been an even, proportional movement; some states, like New York, have been the recipients of very large numbers of poor in-migrants because of accidents of geography (access to Puerto Rico) rather than economic strength. All this suggests that the national government is the proper source of support for the bulk of poverty-linked services provided in urban areas.

In addition, it could be argued that some of the poverty-linked services actually provided by urban local governments should be directly *provided* as well as *financed* by governments covering a wider area. One example of this is the suggested negative income tax which would supplant state and local public assistance expenditures.

What about the rebuilding of the central cities and the provision of adequate amenities in the form of public services? In a broad sense, if a central city has sensible redevelopment policies and strategies, ones which actually provide a good pay-off in social terms relative to the funds invested, the cities themselves should be able to finance the costs fairly readily. That is, the additional public expenditures in time will improve the environment of the city sufficiently so that its tax base — broadly defined — will be enhanced considerably.

There are some exceptions to this. First, there is need for outside help to offset some biases and imperfections in present arrangements. For example, recent heavy investment in urban highway facilities, based on outside financial support, may make it rather difficult to finance, from local resources, investment in public transportation facilities. A second qualification is that the particular local tax devices used to finance these socially self-liquidating investments have side effects. High central city taxes on business activity may make the central cities much less attractive locations for businesses capable of operating elsewhere. Equally important, high taxes based on the value of real property can discourage private investment which raises real property values. In old cities which are full of obsolete private structures, an ideal fiscal solution would avoid taxes that defer private rebuilding. Instead, such a solution would involve taxes which either encourage the needed rebuilding or are neutral in their effect. And the most nearly neutral kind of tax that is widely used and produces much revenue at any level of government is that on individual income.

The newer parts of metropolitan areas in general are characterized by relatively high levels of personal income and wealth. This suggests that they should be able to finance themselves with a minimum of outside help, provided that they have boundaries which make some sense from the standpoint of the nature of the services provided and which do not fragment the potential tax base into wildly unequal portions. Also, since a good part of the problem in the newer areas is providing for new public investment, the outer areas would be able to finance themselves adequately only if they are free to meet the bunched-up (in time) needs they now face. That is, they should be able to borrow rather freely to meet current needs for capital outlays and repay this over the useful lives of the facilities. At a later stage, their capital needs will be much lower.

The poverty-linked services aside, many of the public services provided by local governments are in many ways like those provided by public utility companies. That is, they are not provided uniformly to the entire population, but rather in distinguishable quantities and qualities to individual families in the population, who consume them in accord with their personal preferences. For example, not all families use the same amount of water, not all use the same amount of highway transportation, and so on. There is a strong case for financing such services in the same way public utility services are financed — that is, via user charges which are like prices, rather than through general taxes.

If the purpose of providing the public service is to offer different consumers the services they want, and place some value on, then they ought to pay for such services in proportion to the costs. Otherwise, governments will be called upon to provide a great deal more of the service than people would be willing to consume if they did have to pay for it, which is a wasteful use of resources; or the service will be in such short supply that a form of non-price rationing will be employed to allocate the service among consumers. The outstanding example of this is street congestion in cities: users pay for highways in the aggregate but not for specific individual uses of the streets, and therefore, not surprisingly, treat highways as a free good. The only deterrent to use of the streets at the most crowded times and in the most crowded places is the value one places on time; the rationing in effect then results in those who place a low value on time pre-empting the street space from those who place a high value on time. Ordinarily, in our society, rationing is on the basis of price. Somebody who values a service highly bids it away from someone who places a lower value on that service and would rather use his income for alternative kinds of consumption.

This has relevance for public services in both the newly developing parts of urban areas and the older cities themselves. To the extent that price-like mechanisms are employed, there is likely to be a more sensible allocation of resources in urban areas. Moreover, prices are by definition neutral in their economic effects. People do not exchange money for services or goods unless they consider the value of the services or goods they receive at least equal to the money they surrender. Substituting neutral prices for unneutral taxes has much to commend it. Of course, there is a limit to the extent to which pricing devices can be used, but the general principle remains: where prices make sense at all, they should be utilized and not rejected simply because the services are organized under public rather than private auspices.

There is a further extension of the market analogy to urban government. People do differ in their preferences for various kinds of public and private goods and services. For some people, locally available recreational facilities — say, public parks and swimming pools — are exceedingly valuable services, while for others — those who prefer to travel long distances on vacation, for example — the value is much less. And such differences are not simply a matter of differences in income — people with similar incomes have different tastes.

Since tastes differ, it is entirely conceivable that one might find people of similar tastes — in this case similar preferences for public services — tending to move into particular sections of the metropolitan area. There are real advantages to such ordering of residential patterns based on differences in preferences for various kinds of public goods and services. Without this arrangement, some people would be taxed to provide services they do not desire, while others find that there are services they would desire and would be willing to pay more taxes for.

In an ideal urban governmental and fiscal structure, it would be desirable to try to provide some arrangements which foster this kind of expression of differences in tastes. One such arrangement would result in large numbers of small separate service areas for kinds of public services which are likely to have this character, such as recreational services.

Neither user charge financing (as a principal source of support) nor individual, preference-oriented service areas are appropriate for welfare and health services or any other poverty-linked services, and user charge financing is inappropriate for schools as well. All of these are services provided to the poorer members of the urban community despite their inability to pay for the services, indeed *because of* their inability to pay. The consensus is that the rest of the community is better off if the poor are not destitute (hence public assistance) and have some medical care (hence clinics and free hospital care), and if their children are educated. Indeed, we feel so strongly about education that we *require* people to send their children to schools and levy the taxes necessary to provide the school places. Such "meritorious wants" as minimal health and educational levels contrast sharply with society's indifference as to whether individual families own more or fewer water-using appliances or own one, two, or three cars.

This description of ideal solutions has not mentioned a frequent source of controversy: suburban exploitation of the central city or central city exploitation of commuters. The poverty-linked services, as noted, do present a problem. Putting them to one side, it is entirely possible to develop a system in which there is no significant degree of exploitation of either set of residents and to do this without setting up any sort of a massive metropolitan governmental structure.

The truly needed metropolitan-area wide governmental machinery is related to the nature of certain kinds of public services. Transportation, planning, water pollution, air pollution, and water supply are all services which, for the most part, cannot effectively be provided by small local governments and require fairly large geographic service areas. This is not just to save money, but to provide reasonably adequate standards of service. Where technology and geography dictate metropolitan governmental arrangements, they would exist in an ideal situation. Where technology does not dictate such arrangements, the real *metropolitan* governmental need is to ensure a wide area for financing the poverty-linked services.

THE REAL WORLD OF URBAN PUBLIC FINANCE

How do present arrangements for financing urban local governments compare with this ideal? First, there *is* a substantial local tax burden due to the financing of poverty-linked services, a burden which exists for many local governments but is especially important in the older central cities. Take public assistance, which is the most obvious poverty-linked public service. The federal government provides substantial amounts of funds for this, roughly 55 per cent of the total spent in 1964. In most states in the United States, the remaining funds are provided entirely from state government sources, and indeed the state government administers public assistance programs itself. However, there are urban states with large local public assistance expenditures. They include California, Ohio, Indiana, Minnesota, Wisconsin, New York, New Jersey, and Massachusetts. In fact, in all except six of the metropolitan areas with a population of over one million, there are significant locally financed outlays for public assistance. For the country as a whole, roughly one-sixth of the funds are provided from local financial resources.

Similarly, there are significant health expenditures (which in cities are primarily directed to the poor) and hospital expenditures financed from local tax funds. In 1964, the locally financed total of welfare expenditures, current expenditures for health purposes, and current expenditures for hospitals (net of charges received from hospital patients) was about $2 billion. Some idea of the relative importance of this amount can be seen by comparing it with the total of $20 billion which local governments received in that year from the local property tax. For the governments of the largest

American cities (those with populations over 300,000), the ratio is much higher. Locally financed services which are fairly directly linked to poverty absorbed nearly one-fourth of the big-city property tax revenues in 1964, or one-sixth of their collections of taxes of all types. In a number of the larger metropolitan areas, if the local tax drain due to central city financing of social services were equalized over the entire area, central city tax loads would be well below those elsewhere in the metropolitan areas, rather than well above, which is the more usual case.[3]

Another aspect of the poverty-linked services fiscal problem relates to the financing of schools in the older central cities. Most programs of state aid to the local school districts in a state appear to be fair; typically, state aid programs are based on the numbers of children and the local property tax base per pupil. Big cities tend to have fewer school children per family in public schools than in other parts of a given state and also tend to have relatively high business property values. As a result, they receive relatively small amounts of state school aid.

But this apparent equity is misleading, because the assumption underlying almost all state aid programs is that the cost of providing a given quality of education is uniform throughout a state. There is much evidence that it is not — to provide an equivalent-quality education to that received in the better suburban schools would cost enormously more in the slum schools in the big cities. One commentator, Christopher Jencks, recently estimated that this equivalent-quality education would cost approximately twice as much per pupil. The reason for this is obvious. The many disadvantages under which children in poverty and minority group families suffer at home and before they come to school mean that they require a great deal more in the way of special services, small classes, and the like to assure a performance in school equivalent to that of the suburban middle-class child. And state aid formulas generally do not recognize this.

The 1965 Federal Aid to Education Act is specifically addressed to the problem of children from poorer families. It thus provides a substantial aid for large central city schools, and partially makes up for the inadequacies of the state aid formulas. This is all to the good, but there are several hundreds of millions of dollars now spent by big city school systems which are poverty-related in character. The ideal solution would call for such expenditures to be *entirely* financed from external funds. Moreover, if the problems of poverty and race are really to be attacked, big city school ex-

---

[3] Per capita property tax revenues are significantly higher in most large central cities than in their surrounding areas; see Dick Netzer, *Economics of the Property Tax* (Brookings, 1966), p. 118. Where this is not the case, it is usually because the central city relies heavily on local *nonproperty* taxes (New York, St. Louis, cities in Ohio, for example).

penditures probably will need to be increased at a very rapid rate indeed. Under present arrangements, they will be increased at a much slower rate than they should be and, moreover, even that slower rate will be a severe economic burden on the big cities themselves.

There are serious problems with the existing arrangements for financing the rebuilding and improvement of central cities, aside from the poverty problem. The principal difficulty is the choice of tax instruments for local fiscal support. The main problem is the extremely heavy taxation of housing, which works at cross-purposes with the desire to rebuild and renew central cities. In the United States, local property taxes on housing equal roughly 20 per cent of the rental value of housing. That is, they are equivalent to a 25 per cent excise tax on housing expenditures. In the larger metropolitan areas, particularly in the northeastern part of the United States, the excise tax is more like 30 per cent, and for some of the central cities well over 30 per cent. There is no other type of consumer product aside from liquor, tobacco, and gasoline, which is as heavily taxed in the United States today. The effect of this very heavy taxation, other things being equal, is to deter people from spending their incomes for better housing.

Note the "other things being equal" clause. In suburban communities, particularly bedroom suburbs, the public services that a family receives or has access to are very closely tied to the local taxes that the same family pays. Therefore, in a sense, the property tax in many suburbs is analogous to a general charge for the use of public services, or perhaps even to a local income tax. It is unlikely to be a deterrent to consumption of housing, that is, to the expenditure of consumer income for housing. For the central cities, this is not the case. Central cities provide a wide variety of services and tax a wide variety of property types. Individuals cannot reasonably assume that the prices of housing confronting them include an identifiable tax component which is in effect a charge for a preferred package of public services. What they do observe is that housing is expensive in the central city. It may not be any more expensive in the central city than in the suburbs. But an effective city-rebuilding strategy requires that the central cities encourage more private expenditure for housing, and this may in turn require that housing be much cheaper in the central city than in the suburbs.

It may be argued that any tax paid by individuals and families in a central city will have some discouraging effect on their choice of the central city as a residence. This is true, as is the argument that any tax which reduces incomes will have some bearing on housing expenditure. However, a tax specifically related to housing expenditure is much more of a deterrent to the needed rebuilding of the central cities than a tax on income in general.

Another element in the choice of tax strategy for central city programs concerns the taxation of businesses by the central city. It is clear that many types of business activity have been decentralizing away from the central cities of the larger metropolitan areas. If, to all the other disadvantages of congestion and lack of adequate space and so on, the central city adds business taxes higher than those elsewhere in the area, it may very well spur the further migration of businesses. No doubt this has *not* been a serious problem in many areas, although in a few cases property taxes on business may have had a discouraging effect on economic activity. More often, the overall effect of taxation of business property in the cities at differentially heavier rates is to depress land values, which is not necessarily the worst thing in the world.

However, it is worth noting New York City's experience.[4] The city has had, for many years, exceptionally heavy taxes on business activity and real property, including a unique (and heavy) tax on gross receipts and a sales tax far higher than in surrounding areas. The gross receipts tax was exceptionally burdensome to manufacturing and wholesale trade activities, which would have been migrating away from the city in any case. But there is evidence that the tax accelerated the rate of decline in these economic sectors. Similarly, there is evidence that the decentralization of retail trade was substantially speeded by the sales tax differential. Fortunately, the city has now shifted to a less oppressive form of business taxation and the sales tax differential has also been reduced.

What about the newly developing parts of metropolitan areas? The major problem here is connected with boundary lines. The boundary lines of political subdivisions in the suburbs are those which have evolved over a long period. They have no necessary relationship to the natural areas for the performance of particular services or for grouping people of similar preferences, which is a less important consideration. Moreover, the tax base of the suburban areas tends to be so fragmented in some parts of the country that there are enormous disparities between needs and taxable resources, particularly in connection with financing the schools.

One consequence of this has been what has been referred to as "fiscal zoning": controlling land use in newly developing areas in such a way as to minimize tax costs (have as few school children as possible) and maximize tax base (have nonresidential or very high-value residential property rather than ordinary houses). It is easy to think of organizational arrangements which can offset this problem: governmental reorganization, additional state aid for particular functions such as schools, or some kind of second-tier local governmental structure — that is, some form of fiscal federation within metropolitan areas. The idea is to offer common access to the tax base of

[4] See Graduate School of Public Administration, New York University, *Financing Government in New York City,* Final Research Report to the Temporary Commission on City Finances (April 1966).

large parts of the metropolitan area and reduce the incentive to plan land use primarily from the standpoint of fiscal considerations, rather than from the standpoint of larger notions of the suitability of functional patterns in metropolitan areas.

Real world solutions also fall short of the ideal in connection with the application of user charges to finance particular public services. They are frequently not used at all in cases where they *can* be sensibly employed. They are also frequently used in a most inept fashion. Air and water pollution is an excellent example of failure to apply user charges where they clearly make sense. By and large, the construction and operation of sewerage systems and sewage treatment facilities are financed in the United States by local property taxes. Some places have sewer service charges of one kind or another, but they are by no means the majority. Yet here is a case where it is rather easy to identify the specific people who give rise to public costs. The benefits of water pollution control or air pollution control may be very broad, but the sources of the public costs are highly individual. Moreover, it is not impractical to apply charges that have some relationship to the costs occasioned. This has been done in the Ruhr basin in Germany for many years; there is an elaborate system of pollution charges designed to apportion the costs of treatment facilities among the industrial establishments which actually occasion those costs and also to deter firms from polluting.

As noted earlier, conventional highway financing illustrates the inept use of user charges. Gasoline taxes and licenses have some relationship to the amount of use of the highways by all users as a group and by individual users over long periods of time. But flat charges of this kind cannot possibly discourage people from freely using the very high-cost roads at the very high-cost periods. There is no discrimination among the parts of the road system depending on the cost to the public of those road systems, including the costs of congestion.

Another example of inept use of user charges is in connection with the common structure of transit fares in cities. The flat fare is a time-hollowed principle, although the structure of costs would dictate a substantially higher fare in the peak hours than in the off-peak hours, differentials between predominant and reverse direction riding and perhaps differentials based on distance in the larger cities. The use of parking meters as a user charge is also rather inept in most cases. Flat, low charges are the most commonly found kind of arrangement with relatively little discrimination among locations and times of day. As a result, in most places in central business districts metered curb space is cheaper but harder to find than less convenient off-street parking facilities. Moreover, since many cities use parking meter revenues to subsidize their own off-street parking facilities, they are to some extent competing with themselves by inept parking meter charge policies.

DIRECTIONS FOR REFORM

This comparison of prevailing practice with one man's notions of what is ideal is, of course, not a practical program of reform. It suggests, for example, abolition of the property tax on housing in central cities, which is hardly an immediate possibility. But it does indicate one set of views as to the proper *directions* for reform — more outside aid for poverty-linked services (although 100 per cent outside financing may be years off); refraining from increases in taxes on housing in the cities (although reduction may be even further off) and the substitution of other tax forms, preferably used on an area wide basis; governmental structural improvements such as many have urged for years; and wider and more sophisticated applications of the price mechanism in local government.

What are the policy alternatives? One is to call for substantially increased federal (and in some cases, state) aid for a long list of urban, especially central city, activities. Federal assistance in the provision of urban services, either via aid to local and state governments or via direct federal performance (e.g., expansion of social insurance, like Medicare), has increased sharply in the past few years. This can be viewed as a belated recognition of the national interest in the resolution of certain urban problems, notably those related to poverty and those which leap geographic boundaries (e.g., water pollution), with the increase in the federal role likely to level off at a new higher plateau, much as it did between the late 1930's and the late 1950's. Or it can be viewed as no more than the beginning of a continuously expanding federal role. The historical evidence suggests the former interpretation, but this is prophecy, not scholarship.

A second alternative is to reaffirm the received truth, discovered decades ago, that the property tax is inherently a good tax for local governments, which can be relied upon even more heavily, if only the abominations which characterize its administration are eliminated. This view has numerous proponents, but it is possible to entertain doubts as to whether a tax based on so ephemeral a standard as the "true value of property" can ever be equitably administered. Moreover, the persistence of bad administration over so many years makes one wonder whether good administration is publicly acceptable, even if attainable. It is worth noting that the advocates of a strengthened role for the property tax generally have little patience with those who propose to mitigate its effects on central city housing by special exemptions and abatements for administratively preferred types of housing investment.

The alternatives to the property tax are not easy ones. Proliferation of local nonproperty taxes imposed by existing local government units raises not only administrative problems, but, more important, economic ones for central cities. If central cities are where the fiscal difficulties bind, they will be the heavy users of nonproperty taxes; differentially heavy taxation by central cities can surely affect their economic future, at the margin. The prospect of nonproperty taxes imposed on a metropolitan-area wide basis, which would wash out competitive fears, is not promising, since there are few precedents in this country. But it remains an attractive concept. Finally, wider and more sophisticated applications of user charges demand local government imagination, administrative skill, and political courage. This course, more than any other, can run aground on the inherent conservatism of local government, a universal characteristic.

There is, perhaps, more knowledge concerning the mechanisms for financing urban public services than there is about the services themselves — consumer-voter preferences for public expenditures, cost functions for the major activities, alternative methods of achieving public *objectives* via differing public service *inputs,* and the like. The lack of knowledge on the expenditure side is considerable. There is, in addition, a special problem of uncertainty for central cities. We know very little indeed about the effects of differences in the supply of public services on locational choice within metropolitan areas — by businesses and households alike — and only slightly more about the effects of tax differentials on locational choice. But, in local finance as elsewhere, policy must be made daily, in the face of uncertainty. And the very fact that local finance has so many pressing problems has revived scholarly interest in the field, after a long lull, which ensures that the dimensions of uncertainty will be gradually narrowed in the years ahead.

FURTHER READINGS

Buchanan, James. "Federalism and Fiscal Equity." *American Economic Review* 40 (September 1950).

Grieson, Ronald E. *Land Taxes.* Mimeographed, 1971.

Grieson, Ronald E. *The Economics of Property Taxes and Land Values.* Economics working paper no. 72. Cambridge, Mass.: Massachusetts Institute of Technology, June 1971.

Heller, Walter W., et al. *Revenue Sharing and the City.* Baltimore: Johns Hopkins Press, for Resources for the Future, 1968.

Hirshleifer, J., and Milliman, J. "Urban Water Supply: A Second Look." *American Economic Review* (May 1967).

Hirshleifer, J.; Milliman, J.; and De Haven, J., *Water Supply.* Chicago: The University of Chicago Press, 1960.

Musgrave, Richard A. "An Economic Theory of Fiscal Decentralization." In *Public Finances: Needs, Sources, Utilization*. National Bureau of Economic Research, Princeton, N.J.: Princeton University Press, 1961.

Netzer, Dick. *Economics and Urban Problems*. New York: Basic Books, 1970.

Schaller, H. G., *Public Expenditure Decisions in the Urban Community*. Washington, D.C.: Resources for the Future, Inc., 1963. See especially Vickrey, William S., "General and Specific Financing of Urban Services."

Chapter 11

METHODOLOGICAL APPENDIX: MARGINAL ANALYSIS, BENEFIT-COST, AND THE SOCIAL RATE OF DISCOUNT

This appendix is designed to acquaint the reader with the analytic techniques economists use to analyze problems of resource allocation. These tools are essential to understanding urban economies, whose problems are frequently due to a misallocation of resources. An understanding of the nature of an *efficient* allocation of resources also sheds considerable light on the issue of an *equitable* one and on the connection between efficiency and equity. We need to consider the concepts of marginal social cost and marginal social benefit, and the method of benefit-cost analysis used to make decisions about long-time resource allocations and investments. A crucial concept for benefit-cost analysis is the social rate of discount used to place a present value on future benefits and costs of possible projects.

MARGINAL ANALYSIS

The marginal private cost of a good is equal to the value (or cost) of whatever additional labor, capital, and materials are needed to expand the production of the good by one extra unit. This cost includes normal returns to capital, and risk, and places a value upon all factors equal to their opportunity cost — the highest payment a factor would receive if employed in its next most useful way. Economic cost is therefore largely independent of how the money used to pay for the production is raised, except for the transaction cost of raising such funds. Whether one already owns a factor of production or has to purchase it from someone else, economic value is its opportunity cost. If the government owns land it is considering using as a repair yard for subway trains, it ought not value the land at zero but instead at the value it would have in the best alternative public or private use — the value if sold to a private developer minus the administrative cost of making a sale.

In the absence of imperfections — such as monopoly, legal restrictions on price and quality, or declining production cost — goods are priced by the market at their marginal private cost. (The marginal private cost is equal to the incremental cost of producing one more unit of the good.) Individuals, firms, and governments buy goods until the extra benefit they receive from the last unit they purchase is equal to the extra cost they have to pay to obtain it (the marginal private cost). In the absence of externalities (to be explained later) the competitive mechanism equates the marginal private cost and benefit of the last unit of each good consumed. The intersection of the demand curve (the marginal social-benefit schedule) and the supply curve (the marginal social-cost schedule) brings about this optimum allocation in the absence of externalities.

Why is it desirable that the marginal social benefit be equal to the marginal social cost of the last unit of a good produced? One's demand for (marginal utility of) a good falls as one has or consumes more of it. You become satiated with the good and come to prefer other goods more, according to your income. Someone is happy to have his first car but less happy to have a second car, and so forth.

The supply or marginal cost of producing goods usually rises. This analysis is not affected, however, if it falls instead. If the extra or marginal benefit of a good is above marginal cost, increasing consumption and production of the good would have benefits that exceed cost (or would add more to benefits than it adds to costs).

If the distribution of income is fair, according to some generally accepted standard, and if all markets are efficient and competitive, the value of society's output is optimized. If the income distribution is inequitable, individual and market demand curves will not reflect the true social benefit of each good, since market demands are summations of individual demand curves (individual priorities weighted by income). For the purposes of rectifying such an undesirable situation, economists tend to favor lump-sum income transfers, such as land taxes, rather than direct redistribution of goods and services. It seems more efficient to redistribute the wherewithal to make free choices than to decide for other people what those choices should be. Furthermore, it is generally thought a priori and found empirically to be more efficient for the private sector to produce the goods no matter who the customer is.

Marginal and benefit-cost analysis can help society to allocate efficiently even though the optimal or fairest distribution of income does not exist or is unknown. In this case economics can point out policies and projects that increase the total income of society. If a project increases the gainers' income more than it decreases the losers' income, those gaining could compensate or pay the losers and still be better off, subsequently making everyone better off. Actions that make some better off and no one worse off are efficient, or "Pareto-optimal," even if neither the initial nor final income distributions are perfect. The externalities we mentioned earlier are benefits and disbenefits that result from the production or consumption of a good and accrue to third parties other than the buyer and seller. That is, parties other than the producer or consumer of the good in question can be made better or worse off by either the consumption or the production of the good by someone else. An example of a positive externality would be the benefit received by citizen B when citizen A receives more education or becomes more interested and/or active in honest, efficient government and therefore makes citizen B better off. Citizen B receives a positive externality from citizen A's consumption of education, literature, or actions on public affairs. An example of a positive externality arising from the production of a good would be firm X's research on new production methods which will enable firm Y to produce at a lower cost. The disbenefit received by local residents from the smoke emitted by an automobile is an example of a negative externality.

If someone demands more of some good such as oriental rugs, and thereby raises its price to other consumers, it is not an example of an externality. In this case, the individual's increased demand raises the price and is thus included in his and others' decision whether or not to buy. The increase in price consequent to shifts in demand reflects the opportunity cost or marginal social cost of a rug. The oriental rug case may alter the income distribution but does not distort the allocation of resources, whereas, in the case of pollution, the cost or price of polluting is not brought directly into the polluter's calculation of his (society's) costs.

Marginal private and social costs differ by the value of externalities. The marginal social cost of producing a good is equal to the marginal private cost plus the value of the negative externalities and minus the value of the positive externalities involved in the good's production or consumption.

The free market cannot properly allocate a good that has externalities, because its cost or disbenefit cannot be included in the price of the good. In order to reduce excessive pollution caused by cost being ignored in private decision making, economists generally favor placing taxes on the emission of pollutants. The amount of the tax should be equal to the marginal social disbenefit of these emissions (the value of the negative externality produced by the last unit of the pollutant). Polluters would then have to pay the true marginal social cost of their activities and thus would cut back production, reducing pollution to its optimal level. Pollution taxes internalize the externality brought about by pollution. In the case of education for better citizenship, tuition may be subsidized by an amount equal to the positive externality to the rest of society in order to expand in such an activity to the optimal extent.

BENEFIT-COST

Another tool often used by economists is benefit-cost analysis. Benefit-cost analysis is a practical way of assessing the choosing between projects when that choice cannot be made by a market. It is primarily designed for and used in public-sector investment decisions. Here the market can not allocate investment efficiently, either because the good has zero marginal cost (e.g., public television) or declining marginal cost (as is often the case in public utilities), or the good is to be provided free because of social objectives (as in the case of job training for the poor). In these cases the price we would put on the good for efficiency is below the average cost of producing it. The good would not pay for itself at the efficient price (below average cost) and consequently, we would not know whether present or future investments in it were desirable. In the case of typical goods priced at their marginal cost, which is U-shaped or equal to average cost, greater or lesser than normal profits indicate the desirability of greater or lesser investment.

Given the inability to use profits as a guide to investment for some goods it is useful for us to know how great the benefits of the good are to its users, so that we might compare the average and marginal benefits with the average and marginal costs of the project. If the total (or average) benefits of the project, or of an addition to it (marginal), exceed the costs of same, the project should be undertaken and vice versa.

In practice, benefit-cost studies do not exactly fulfill the requirements of economic efficiency, as they do not usually adjust demand for the income effects of providing more of a particular good. Income effects are changes in demand brought about by changes in income (in this case occurring because the project might very significantly affect the income of some individuals, hence possibly changing demand for the good being provided by the project.[1] What we want to know are society's tradeoffs between this project and other goods (or income); substitution, not income effects.

The Marshallian (supply and demand) method of evaluating the benefits to society provided by an investment project involves calculating the value of the area under society's demand curve for the good, bordered by the amounts of the good available before and after the project is undertaken. Society's demand curve is thus interpreted as a marginal social-benefit

[1] Positive income effects can exaggerate the benefits of a project by adding the amount of increased demand for the project caused only by society's increased wealth brought about by a desirable project (the movement to a higher indifference curve); however, we want to determine what amount of other goods society would give up to have the project—the area under an income-adjusted demand curve (or the movement along an indifference curve).

schedule for the project, and each additional unit of it is being valued at a price equal to the marginal social benefit of the additional unit. We are thus adding together the values of each extra unit of the good provided.

Which benefits do we evaluate? We would like to take into account all of the benefits and costs (disbenefits) accruing to all members of society from the project. Both the costs and the benefits would be valued at market prices (which would be the same as economic or opportunity cost) except where there are significant market imperfections. Imperfections would include such things as monopoly pricing, prices fixed at levels different from marginal social cost by legal or institutional restrictions including taxes, or externalities in the production or consumption of relevant goods.

When such imperfections exist, considerations of efficiency suggest that we use the true economic cost of the resources rather than the existing price in evaluating the benefits and costs of a project (independently of whom they accrue to). But following efficiency in this case would lead to important political and distributional questions. Will the political unit accept the use of a price different from the accounting or nominal price of a good? Is it equitable to do so? For example, if a good is supplied by a monopoly, its true marginal cost will be below the monopoly price. If we consider the real cost of the good to be its marginal cost (below the monopoly price) we will use more of it than if we considered the monopoly price to be its cost. Hence, using true marginal cost will raise monopoly profits. Is it fair to undertake projects whose benefit will partially or significantly accrue to members of society already wealthy because of monopoly power?

Another consideration that we would want to include would be the effect of the project upon income distribution. What groups would pay the project's cost? What groups would receive the benefits and how would the project affect the relative and absolute distribution among these groups? We may want to have the society specify weighting factors for benefits accruing to American Indians be counted at more than one hundred per cent of market value. The alternative is to do the benefit-cost study without weights and specify the distributional impact of the program separately. Though weighted benefit-cost would be less efficient than lump-sum income transfers as a tool of income redistribution, they may be the only option available to society.

All costs and benefits are counted at their full employment opportunity cost. Full employment and stabilization are considered to be separate goals, accomplished by means of monetary and fiscal policy except in extreme circumstances (if you were the person unemployed). This would mean that the wages of labor, the cost of cement, and the construction company's profits associated with a mass transit project are all counted fully as costs. The increased value of nearby land due to a subway extension would be a benefit as would decongestion and depollution provided consequent to a subsequent lessening of auto use. However, increased profits made by real estate dealers would not be counted at all, since there ought to be long-run normal returns to capital in the area.

Furthermore, we would usually not use a multiplier on benefits except in the case of a project in an unusually high pocket of persistent unemployment untouched by monetary and fiscal policy. Even then, local multipliers are usually low (in the area of one to one-half times benefits). The reason multipliers are not used is twofold: first, the level of unemployment is a policy variable decided upon separately by the President and attained through fiscal and monetary policies by another branch of government; second, all private projects would also need to have the same multiplier attached to them and thus be subsidized equally by the government. The effect of this would be to lower taxes and cancel out the original multiplier on public projects.

We should consider all benefits and costs that occur in the future as well as at present. Future benefits and costs count for less than present ones because of the payment for waiting, the compound rate of interest called the social rate of discount or time preference. It is the interest rate individuals must be paid for postponing consumpion, or, in the case of perfect capital markets, the opportunity cost or marginal productivity of capital.

Total benefits are equal to the present (discounted) value of all future benefits:

$$B = B_o + \frac{B_1}{(1+r)} + \frac{B_2}{(1+r)^2} + \frac{B_3}{(1+r)^3} + \ldots + \frac{B_n}{(1+r)^n}$$

Cost is the present discounted value of all future costs.

$$C = C_o + \frac{C_1}{(1+r)} + \frac{C_2}{(1+r)^2} + \ldots + \frac{C_n}{(1+r)^n}$$

In this formulation B and C represent benefits and costs occurring within the time periods indicated by the subscripts, r is the discount rate, and n is the end of the project's life. In practice the life of a project is usually set at twenty to fifty years both because of the difficulty in predicting the future and because of the low weight that benefits accruing beyond twenty to fifty years will have.

In practice, we might expect urban areas to adopt societywide benefit-cost in the calculation of projects if the benefits and costs of the project accrue to the same political jurisdiction. If this is not the case, the political jurisdiction undertaking the project is likely to ignore benefits or costs accruing to other areas. Attempts at interjurisdiction compacts may fail because each jurisdiction will see itself gaining by not paying its share of the cost of a project from which it will benefit or by not paying other communities for the harmful spillover effects or externalities caused by its own projects.

THE SOCIAL RATE OF DISCOUNT

Going back to the rate of discount, we are faced with the question of what rate should be used. If there were perfect capital markets and no distortions in the economy we could simply use the rate of return accruing to similar private projects, but the personal and corporate income taxes and a possibly unfair income distribution preclude perfect capital markets. Corporate and personal income taxes cause the gross nominal return (before taxes and inflation), to corporate capital to be 10 to 12 percent, while the net (after taxes and inflation) real rate of return on riskless savings accounts is 1 to 3 per cent.

What rate should be used? One argument says we should use the rate of return that capital could earn in its best-possible, highest-return, use— the corporate sector. We would then evaluate all government projects at a 6 to 14 per cent rate of return. There are several objections to this method. For one thing, institutional restrictions may not permit the funds that we would otherwise use in the project to be used in the corporate sector. For another, restricting ourselves to high-return projects would cause too little aggregate capital formation, because the amount of investment would fall far short of the savings taking place.

The second argument says that we should use the low rate of 1 to 3 per cent because it is the rate at which individuals postpone consumption until the future—the consumption discount rate. The argument ignores the effect increased government borrowing and taxation to finance projects would have on reducing investments in the corporate sector where capital earns a far greater return.

A third synthesizing approach is the source-of-funds method. This says we should consider the source of government financing (the corporate sector, personal savings) and use a discount rate that is a weighted average of the rates of return (marginal) prevailing in the sectors from whence government revenues (taxes and borrowing) come. We ought to add that benefits would also be valued more highly when received by sectors having a high rate of return and vice versa.

A variant on this approach says that we should use the (low) consumption discount rate to discounting future benefits and put a shadow price on government capital approximately proportional to the corporate rate of return divided by the consumption discount rate. The method is theoretically correct but might prove quite difficult to administer.

If the corporate return on capital and the consumption discount rate are expected to decline over time, a declining rate of discount should be used in benefit-cost calculations independent of the method chosen.

A low discount rate will hurt the poor if it takes funds from the poor, who have a high-consumption discount rate, and returns the benefits to them in the future. Someone borrowing at eighteen per cent per annum to finance consumer purchases does not benefit from being taxed or given reduced subsidies so that a project can be financed which yields a two per cent rate of return to him.

FURTHER READINGS

Baumol, William J. "On the Social Rate of Discount." *American Economic Review* 57 (September 1968).

Chinitz, Benjamin, and Tiebout, Charles M. "The Role of Cost-Benefit Analysis of Metropolitan Areas." In *The Public Economy of Urban Communities,* edited by Julius Margolis. Baltimore: Johns Hopkins Press for Resource for the Future, Inc., 1965.

Diamond, Peter. "The Opportunity Cost of Public Investment, Comment." *The Quarterly Journal of Economics* (November 1968).

Dorfman, Robert, ed., *Measuring Benefits of Government Investments.* Washington, D.C.: The Brookings Institution, 1965.

Eckstein, Otto. "A Survey of the Theory of Public Expenditure Criteria." In *Public Finances: Needs, Sources and Utilization.* National Bureau of Economic Research, Princeton: Princeton University Press, 1961.

Feldstein, Martin S. "Net Social Benefit Calculation and the Public Investment Decision." *Oxford Economic Papers* (March 1964).

Harberger, Arnold. In "The Social Opportunity Cost of Capital: A New Approach." Mimeograph, to appear in *Journal of Political Economy.*

Maass, Arthur. "Benefit-Cost Analysis: Its Relevance to Public Investment Criteria." *The Quarterly Journal of Economics* 80 (May 1966).

Marglin, Steven A. "The Social Rate of Discount and Optimal Rate of Investment." *Quarterly Journal of Economics* (May 1963).

———. "The Social Rate of Discount and Optimal Rate of Investment." *The Quarterly Journal of Economics* (February 1963).

Margolis, Julius. "Secondary Benefits, External Economies, and the Justification of Public Investment." *Review of Economics and Statistics* 39 (August 1957).

McKean, Roland N. *Efficiency in Government Through Systems Analysis.* New York: John Wiley, 1959.

Samuelson, Paul A. "A Diagrammatic Exposition of a Pure Theory of Public Expenditure." *Review of Economics and Statistics* 37 (November 1956).

———. "Aspects of Public Expenditure Theories." *Review of Economics and Statistics* 40 (November 1958).

Schultz, Charles T. *The Politics and Economics of Public Spending.* Washington, D.C.: The Brookings Institution, 1968.

Turvey, Ralph, and Prest, A., "Cost-Benefit Analysis: A Survey." *Economics Journal* (December 1965).

Turvey, Ralph. "On Divergences Between Social Cost and Private Cost." *Economica* 30 (August 1963).